T0392813

INTERNATIONAL
LAW REPORTS

VOLUME 208

Volumes published under the title:

ANNUAL DIGEST AND REPORTS OF PUBLIC INTERNATIONAL LAW CASES

Vol. 1 (1919-22) ⎫ Edited by Sir John Fischer Williams, KC,
Vol. 2 (1923-24) ⎭   and H. Lauterpacht, LLD

Vol. 3 (1925-26) ⎫ Edited by Arnold D. McNair, CBE, LLD,
Vol. 4 (1927-28) ⎭   and H. Lauterpacht, LLD

Vol. 5 (1929-30) ⎫
Vol. 6 (1931-32)
Vol. 7 (1933-34)
Vol. 8 (1935-37)
Vol. 9 (1938-40)
Vol. 10 (1941-42)
Vol. 11 (1919-42) ⎬ Edited by H. Lauterpacht, QC, LLD, FBA
Vol. 12 (1943-45)
Vol. 13 (1946)
Vol. 14 (1947)
Vol. 15 (1948)
Vol. 16 (1949) ⎭

Volumes published under the title:

INTERNATIONAL LAW REPORTS

Vol. 17 (1950) ⎫
Vol. 18 (1951)
Vol. 19 (1952)
Vol. 20 (1953) ⎬ Edited by Sir Hersch Lauterpacht, QC, LLD, FBA
Vol. 21 (1954)
Vol. 22 (1955)
Vol. 23 (1956) ⎭

Vol. 24 (1957)   Edited by Sir Hersch Lauterpacht, QC, LLD,
               FBA, and E. Lauterpacht

Vol. 25 (1958-I) ⎫ Edited by E. Lauterpacht, QC
Vol. 26 (1958-II) ⎭

Vols. 27-68 *and* Consolidated Tables and Index to Vols. 1-35 *and* 36-45
Edited by E. Lauterpacht, QC
Vols. 69-123 *and* Consolidated Index and Consolidated Tables of Cases and
Treaties to Vols. 1-80, Vols. 81-100 *and* Vols. 1-125
Edited by Sir Elihu Lauterpacht, CBE, QC,
and Sir Christopher Greenwood, CMG, QC
Vols. 124-68 *and* Consolidated Index and Consolidated Table of Treaties to
Vols. 1-160
Edited by Sir Elihu Lauterpacht, CBE, QC, LLD,
Sir Christopher Greenwood, CMG, QC, and K. L. Lee
Vols. 169-208   Edited by Sir Christopher Greenwood, GBE, CMG, KC,
and K. L. Lee

Lauterpacht Centre for International Law
University of Cambridge

INTERNATIONAL
LAW REPORTS

VOLUME
208

Edited by

SIR CHRISTOPHER GREENWOOD, GBE, CMG, KC
Master of Magdalene College, Cambridge
Member of the Iran-United States Claims Tribunal
Bencher of Middle Temple
Formerly Judge of the International Court of Justice

and

KAREN LEE
Fellow of the Lauterpacht Centre for International Law, University of Cambridge
Fellow and former Vice-Mistress of Girton College, Cambridge

 CAMBRIDGE
UNIVERSITY PRESS

Shaftesbury Road, Cambridge CB2 8EA, United Kingdom

One Liberty Plaza, 20th Floor, New York, NY 10006, USA

477 Williamstown Road, Port Melbourne, VIC 3207, Australia

314–321, 3rd Floor, Plot 3, Splendor Forum, Jasola District Centre, New Delhi – 110025, India

103 Penang Road, #05–06/07, Visioncrest Commercial, Singapore 238467

Cambridge University Press is part of Cambridge University Press & Assessment, a department of the University of Cambridge.

We share the University's mission to contribute to society through the pursuit of education, learning and research at the highest international levels of excellence.

www.cambridge.org
Information on this title: www.cambridge.org/9781009473439

DOI: 10.1017/9781009473439

First published 2025

Printed in the United Kingdom by CPI Group Ltd, Croydon CR0 4YY

A catalogue record for this publication is available from the British Library

ISBN 978-1-009-47343-9 Hardback

CONTENTS

PREFACE

The present volume contains the 2021 judgment on preliminary objections of the International Tribunal for the Law of the Sea in *Dispute concerning Delimitation of the Maritime Boundary between Mauritius and Maldives in the Indian Ocean (Mauritius/Maldives)*. International jurisprudence is also reflected in decisions from the Court of Justice of the European Union (*Slovak Republic and Hungary v. EU Council* and *European Commission v. Hungary*) and the Inter-American Court of Human Rights (*Lhaka Honhat Association* (Interpretation)). National jurisprudence is reflected in decisions from the courts of Australia (*Spain v. Infrastructure Services*), England (*Webster, Infrastructure Services* and *Border Timbers*) and Germany (*Syrian Secret Agent* and *Energy Charter Treaty* cases).

The Editors wish to thank the many people whose work has made this volume possible. Mr Darren Peterson prepared the summaries of the cases from the Court of Justice of the European Union, Australia, and Germany as well as the decisions from England in *Webster* and *Infrastructure Services*. Ms Jessica Joly-Hébert prepared the summary of the case from the International Tribunal of the Law of the Sea and Ms Caroline Kimeu wrote the summary of the case from the Inter-American Court of Human Rights. Ms Karen Lee saw the volume through the press. Ms Nahide Basri, the ILR Editorial Assistant, prepared the Tables of Cases and the Digest. Mrs Rowena Gavars compiled the Table of Treaties and the Index. Mrs Alison Tickner checked the copy and Mrs Jenny Macgregor read the proofs.

The Editors are very grateful to the Court of Justice of the European Union (which owns the copyright in its material), the Inter-American Court of Human Rights and the High Court of Australia for kindly permitting these Reports to use the electronic files of the relevant judgments posted on their official websites. Thanks are also due to the International Tribunal for the Law of the Sea and to Brill publishers for their kind permission to publish the text of the judgment from the *ITLOS Reports* posted on the ITLOS website. The translation of the judgment of the *Syrian Secret Agent* case was provided by the German Federal Ministry of Justice; it was sent to us by Dr Michael Gressmann and is reproduced with thanks. The Editors are also grateful to the German Federal Court of Justice for permission to reproduce the translation of the judgment of the *Energy Charter Treaty* case, which was sent to us by Mr Tim Maxian Rusche. The judgments from England published in the volume carry Crown copyright and contain public sector information licensed under the Open Government Licence v3.0; the electronic files were sourced from the British and Irish Legal Information Institute and the United Kingdom Government Courts and Tribunals Service.

Finally, our thanks go to all the others who have worked to complete this volume, particularly our publishers, Cambridge University Press, and typesetters, Straive, and their staff.

C. J. GREENWOOD

Magdalene College
Cambridge

K. L. LEE

Lauterpacht Centre
    for International Law,
University of Cambridge

May 2024

EDITORIAL NOTE

The *International Law Reports* endeavour to provide within a single series of volumes comprehensive access in English to judicial materials bearing on public international law. On certain topics it is not always easy to draw a clear line between cases which are essentially ones of public international law interest and those which are primarily applications of special domestic rules. For example, in relation to extradition, the *Reports* will include cases which bear on the exception of "political offences" or the rule of double criminality, but will restrict the number of cases dealing with purely procedural aspects of extradition. Similarly, while the general rules relating to the admission and exclusion of aliens, especially of refugees, are of international legal interest, cases on the procedure of admission usually are not. In such borderline areas, and sometimes also where there is a series of domestic decisions all dealing with a single point in essentially the same manner, only one illustrative decision will be printed and references to the remainder will be given in an accompanying note.

DECISIONS OF INTERNATIONAL TRIBUNALS
The *Reports* seek to include so far as possible the available decisions of every international tribunal, e.g. the International Court of Justice, or ad hoc arbitrations between States. There are, however, some jurisdictions to which full coverage cannot be given, either because of the large number of decisions (e.g. the Administrative Tribunal of the United Nations) or because not all the decisions bear on questions of public international law (e.g. the Court of Justice of the European Union). In these instances, those decisions are selected which appear to have the greatest long-term value.

Human rights cases. The number of decisions on questions of international protection of human rights has increased considerably in recent years and it is now impossible for the *Reports* to cover them all. As far as decisions of international jurisdictions are concerned, the *Reports* will continue to publish decisions of the European Court of Human Rights and of the Inter-American Court of Human Rights, as well as "views" of the United Nations Human Rights Committee. Decisions of national courts on the application of conventions on human rights will not be published unless they deal with a major point of substantive human rights law or a matter of wider interest to public international lawyers such as the relationship of international law and national law, the extent of the right of derogation or the principles of the interpretation of treaties.

International arbitrations. The *Reports* of course include arbitral awards rendered in cases between States which involve an application of public international law. Beyond this, however, the selection of arbitral decisions is more open to debate. As these *Reports* are principally concerned with matters of public international law, they will not include purely private law commercial arbitrations even if they are international in the sense that they arise between parties of different nationality and even if one of them is a State. (For reports of a number of such awards, see *Yearbook Commercial Arbitration* (ed. Stephan W. Schill, under the auspices of the International Council for Commercial Arbitration).) But where there is a sufficient point of contact with public international law then the relevant parts of the award will be reported. Examples of such points of contact are cases in which the character of a State as a party has some relevance (e.g. State immunity, stabilization clauses, *force majeure*) or where there is a choice of law problem involving discussion of international law or general principles of law as possible applicable laws. The same criteria will determine the selection of decisions of national courts regarding the enforcement of arbitral awards.

DECISIONS OF NATIONAL TRIBUNALS
A systematic effort is made to collect from all national jurisdictions those judicial decisions which have some bearing on international law.

EDITORIAL TREATMENT OF MATERIALS
The basic policy of the Editors is, so far as possible, to present the material in its original form. It is no part of the editorial function to impose on the decisions printed in these volumes a uniformity of approach or style which they do not possess. Editorial intervention is limited to the introduction of the summary and of the bold-letter rubric at the head of each case. This is followed by the full text of the original decision or of its translation. Normally, the only passages which will be omitted are those which contain either statements of fact having no bearing on the points of international law involved in the case or discussion of matters of domestic law unrelated to the points of international legal interest. The omission of material is usually indicated either by a series of dots or by the insertion of a sentence in square brackets noting the passages which have been left out.

PRESENTATION OF MATERIALS
For reproduction of material in this volume, electronic files have been used wherever possible and their source acknowledged in the Preface. Citations of the reports in which the case may be found are listed in the "Report" section in square brackets at the end of the case; the language of the original decision is also mentioned there. The bold figures in square brackets in the body of the text indicate the pagination of the original report where included.

NOTES
Footnotes. Footnotes enclosed in square brackets are editorial insertions. All other footnotes are part of the original report.

Other notes. References to cases deemed not to be sufficiently substantial to warrant reporting will occasionally be found in editorial notes either at the end of a report of a case on a similar point or under an independent heading.

DIGEST OF CASES
With effect from Volume 75 the decisions contained in the *Reports* are no longer arranged according to the traditional classification scheme. Instead a Digest of Cases is published at the beginning of each volume. The main headings of the Digest are arranged alphabetically. Under each heading brief details are given of those cases reported in that volume which contain points covered by that heading. Each entry in the Digest gives the name of the case concerned and the page reference, the name of the tribunal which gave the decision and an indication of the main points raised in the case which relate to that particular heading of the Digest. Where a case raises points which concern several different areas of international law, entries relating to that case will appear under each of the relevant headings in the Digest. A list of the main headings used in the Digest is set out at p. xvii.

CONSOLIDATED INDEX AND TABLES
A Consolidated Index and a Consolidated Tables of Cases and Treaties for volumes 1-80 were published in two volumes in 1990 and 1991. A further volume containing the Consolidated Index and Consolidated Tables of Cases and Treaties for volumes 81-100 was published in 1996. A Consolidated Index, a Consolidated Tables of Cases and a Consolidated Table of Treaties for volumes 1-125 were published in 2004. A Consolidated Index and a Consolidated Table of Treaties for volumes 1-160 were published in 2017. Volume 205 contains Consolidated Tables of Cases for volumes 126-205.

TABLE OF CASES REPORTED
ALPHABETICAL

(Cases which are reported only in a note are distinguished from cases which are reported in full by the insertion of the word "note" in parentheses after the page number of the report.)

TABLE OF CASES REPORTED

ARRANGED ACCORDING TO COURTS AND TRIBUNALS
(INTERNATIONAL CASES) AND COUNTRIES (MUNICIPAL CASES)

(Cases which are reported only in a note are distinguished from cases which are reported in full by the insertion of the word "note" in parentheses after the page number of the report.)

I. DECISIONS OF INTERNATIONAL TRIBUNALS

II. DECISIONS OF MUNICIPAL COURTS

DIGEST OF CASES
List of Main Headings

(Those headings for which there are entries in the present volume are printed in italics. For a guide to the Digest, see the Editorial Note at p. xi.)

Air

Aliens

Arbitration

Canals

Claims

Comity

Conciliation

Consular Relations

Damages

Diplomatic Relations

Economics, Trade and Finance

Environment

Evidence before International Courts
    and Tribunals

Expropriation

Extradition

General Principles of International Law

Governments

Human Rights

International Court of Justice

International Criminal Law

International Organizations

International Tribunals

Jurisdiction

Lakes and Landlocked Seas

Nationality

Recognition

*Relationship of International Law and
    Municipal Law*

Reprisals and Countermeasures

Rivers

Sea

Sources of International Law

Space

State Immunity

State Responsibility

State Succession

States

Territory

Terrorism

Treaties

War and Armed Conflict

DIGEST OF CASES
REPORTED IN VOLUME 208

International Criminal Law

International Tribunals

Jurisdiction

Relationship of International Law and Municipal Law

State Immunity

State Immunity (*cont.*)

sovereign or governmental functions in context of employment — Whether Employment Tribunal applying correct test — England, Employment Appeal Tribunal

Foreign States Immunities Act 1985 (Cth) — Exceptions to immunity — Exception where foreign State agreeing by treaty to submit to jurisdiction — International Centre for Settlement of Investment Disputes — Spain acceding to international Convention on the Settlement of Investment Disputes between States and Nationals of Other States, 1965 ("ICSID Convention") — Whether constituting submission to jurisdiction of Federal Court of Australia — Whether Spain entitled to plead foreign State immunity — Whether ICSID Convention excluding any claim for foreign State immunity in proceedings for recognition and enforcement of an arbitral award — Australia, High Court

Jurisdictional immunity — Immunity from execution — Proceedings for recognition and enforcement of International Centre for Settlement of Investment Disputes arbitration award in national court — Whether engaging State immunity — United Kingdom State Immunity Act 1978, Sections 2 and 9 — England, High Court, King's Bench Division (Commercial Court)

State Immunity Act 1978 — Exceptions to immunity — Exception based on prior written agreement by State — Exception to immunity in matters of enforcement of arbitral awards — International Centre for Settlement of Investment Disputes — International Convention on the Settlement of Investment Disputes between States and Nationals of Other States, 1965 ("ICSID Convention") — Relationship between ICSID Convention and enforcement and recognition of arbitral awards by domestic courts — England, High Court, King's Bench Division (Commercial Court)

Treaties

War and Armed Conflict

TABLE OF TREATIES

This table contains a list, in chronological order according to the date of signature, of the treaties referred to in the decisions printed in the present volume. It has not been possible to draw a helpful distinction between treaties judicially considered and treaties which are merely cited.

In the case of bilateral treaties, the names of the parties are given in alphabetical order. Names of countries follow contemporaneous usage except in the case of small spelling changes (e.g. Roumania/Romania) where modern usage is adopted throughout. Where this seems helpful, the name of a treaty as it is commonly known is included.

Wherever possible, each treaty includes a reference to where an online English-language version of the treaty can be found. For treaties between 1648 and 1919, this is almost always the Consolidated Treaty Series (CTS), under Oxford Historical Treaties on the Oxford Public International Law website. Post-1919, references are most frequently to the League of Nations Treaty Series/United Nations Treaty Series (LNTS/UNTS). Here it should be noted that historically LNTS/UNTS references have taken the form "39 UNTS 55", 39 being the volume number, 55 the page number. With effect from UNTS volume 2301, UNTS no longer includes the volume and page number as part of the reference, using simply the registration number. UNTS references are now in the form UNTS 42146. For ILR purposes, because of its value as an identifier, the registration number is now being added parenthetically to pre-volume 2301 treaties in the form 213 UNTS 221 [UNTS 2889].

Reference is also made to other treaty databases such as the European Treaty Series (ETS), Organization of American States Treaty Series (OASTS) or to Official Journals, particularly where these are the only databases currently hosting a treaty. Where a treaty appears to be available only on the website of the parent international organization, usually without any citation identifier, users are referred to the relevant website. For bilateral treaties, often the only source it has been possible to find is a non-English-language version on one of the parties' official websites, such as the parliamentary proceedings approving the treaty. Users requiring a comprehensive list of written sources should refer to the CTS, or to the Flare Index to Treaties, available at IALS Digital.

For abbreviations used in the Table of Treaties reference should be made to the list of abbreviations attached to the index in individual volumes.

Aliens — Refugees — Asylum seekers — International protection — *Refoulement* — European Union — Council Decision 2015/1601 — Relocation mechanism — Relocation of migrants from Italy and Greece — Relocation of migrants to other EU Member States — Whether Council Decision relocating migrants followed appropriate procedure — Whether Council Decision relocating migrants disproportionate — Whether Council Decision relocating migrants placed a disproportionate burden on Hungary — Whether territory of all EU Member States to be taken as a single area for purposes of non-*refoulement*

Human rights — International protection — Migration — Whether there being right to choose host country — Convention Relating to the Status of Refugees, 1951 — Non-*refoulement* — Whether Council Decision 2015/1601 relocating migrants breached the principle of non-*refoulement*

Relationship of international law and municipal law — Treaty of the Functioning of the European Union, 2007 — Article 78(3) — Council Decision 2015/1601 — Convention Relating to the Status of Refugees, 1951 — Non-*refoulement* — Whether Council Decision relocating migrants breached the principle of non-*refoulement* — The law of the European Union

SLOVAK REPUBLIC AND HUNGARY *v.* COUNCIL OF THE EUROPEAN UNION[1]

(Joined Cases C-643/15 and C-647/15)

Court of Justice of the European Union (Grand Chamber).
6 September 2017

(Lenaerts, *President*; Tizzano, *Vice-President*; Silva de Lapuerta, Ilešič, Bay Larsen and Prechal (*Rapporteur*), *Presidents of Chambers*; Bonichot, Arabadjiev, Toader, Safjan, Jarašiūnas, Fernlund, Vajda, Rodin and Biltgen, *Judges*; Bot, *Advocate General*)

---

[1] The Slovak Republic was represented by Ministerstvo spravodilvosti Slovenskej republiky and Hungary was represented by M. Z. Fehér and G. Koós, acting as agents. The Council of the European Union was represented by M. Chavrier, K. Pleśniak, N. Pethő and Z. Kupčová, acting as agents.

SUMMARY:[2] *The facts*:—Over the course of 2014 and 2015, Italy and Greece saw significant inflows of migrants from Syria, Afghanistan, Iraq and Eritrea. In September 2015 the Council of the European Union ("the Council") adopted Council Decision 2015/1601 ("the Council Decision") establishing provisional measures in the area of international protection for the benefit of Italy and Greece. The decision was adopted pursuant to Article 78(3) of the Treaty on the Functioning of the European Union, 2007 ("TFEU") which provided the European Commission ("the Commission") with the power to adopt provisional measures where one or more Member States were being confronted by "an emergency situation characterised by a sudden inflow of nationals of third countries".

The Council Decision included a relocation mechanism in which EU Member States received binding allocations for the relocation of 120,000 migrants from Italy and Greece over a period of two years.[3] A previous proposal of the Council Decision included the relocation of 54,000 migrants from Hungary; however, prior to its adoption Hungary withdrew its participation as a beneficiary under the scheme.

The Slovak Republic and Hungary applied to the Court of Justice of the European Union ("the Court") seeking the annulment of the Council Decision. They argued, inter alia, that Article 78(3) of the TFEU could not constitute an adequate legal basis for the adoption of the impugned decision and that the manner in which the Council had reached its decision had breached the essential procedural requirements within relevant provisions of the TFEU. They further argued that the impugned decision breached the principle of proportionality, including on the grounds that the objective pursued by the Council Decision could have been achieved by measures that were less restrictive for Member States with respect to the impact on their sovereign right to decide freely on the admission of nationals of third countries to their territory. Finally, they argued that the Council Decision breached the Convention Relating to the Status of Refugees, 1951 ("the Geneva Convention"), particularly the principle of non-*refoulement*, by transferring applicants for international protection between EU Member States prior to their application for protection being decided.

Opinion of the Advocate General (26 July 2017)

Held:—The actions brought by the Slovak Republic and Hungary should be dismissed.

(1) The procedure that led to the adoption of the relevant Council Decision was lawful and the essential procedural requirements had not been infringed. Article 78(3) of the TFEU constituted an adequate legal basis for a

---

[2] Prepared by Mr D. Peterson.
[3] The content of the Council Decision appears at paras. 12-31 of the judgment.

non-legislative act that derogated, on a temporary basis, from certain provisions of legislative acts. This provision allowed the EU to react rapidly to an emergency by taking "provisional measures" which had to be interpreted broadly. To comply with Article 78(3) of the TFEU, measures must not be intended to eliminate, replace, or amend provisions in legislative acts. The impugned Council Decision did not have this intent, and merely provided for temporary derogation, within a strictly defined framework, from a number of provisions of legislative acts, and did not amend those acts in a lasting or general way (paras. 56–82).

(2) The temporal scope of the Council Decision was precisely defined, and the measures expired after a period of two years. The fact that the effects of a decision might be felt beyond the period referred to in the decision was irrelevant. Article 78(3) of the TFEU did not prescribe a specific period for which provisional measures might last, and a period of application of twenty-four months was justified in light of the foreseeable period necessary to prepare for the implementation of the relocation procedure in all Member States (paras. 99-107).

(3) The suddenness of the inflow of nationals of third countries was apparent from objective data, and whether or not the inflow of nationals of third countries was foreseeable was irrelevant. Article 78(3) conferred a wide discretion on the Council to take measures in order to respond adequately to an emergency situation (paras. 108-19 and 124-35).

(4) The European Parliament had been duly consulted on the amendments made by the Council to the Commission's initial proposal that led to the impugned decision as required by Article 78(3) of the TFEU. The amendments did not concern the very essence of the text considered as a whole and did not require a fresh consultation of the Parliament. As the amendments related to Hungary's withdrawal as a beneficiary from the temporary relocation mechanism, the Council had no choice other than to take note of Hungary's withdrawal and adjust its decision to circumstances that were beyond its control (paras. 152-83).

(5) The Council had not breached the essential procedural requirement within Article 293(1) of the TFEU by amending the Commission's proposal without complying with the requirement for unanimity. In adopting the contested decision, nothing was done to undermine the Commission's power of initiative preserved by Article 293 of the TFEU. There was a need to accept flexibility in decision-making processes to facilitate the search for political compromises (paras. 184-99).

(6) The temporary relocation mechanism could not be regarded as manifestly exceeding what was necessary in order to provide an effective response to the 2015 crisis. While some of the alternative solutions suggested by the Slovak Republic could have contributed to attaining the objective pursed by the relevant Council Decision, the Council had to be afforded a broad margin of discretion. At the time the Council adopted the decision, it was entitled to consider that there was no alternative measure that would enable the objective

pursued by the decision to be attained as effective, while restricting to a lesser degree the sovereignty of Member States or their financial interests (paras. 243-53, 256 and 265-71).

(7) Article 78(3) of the TFEU should be interpreted in light of the principle of solidarity and fair sharing of responsibility enshrined in Article 80 of the TFEU. Accordingly, it was consistent with this principle for a provisional measure to allocate binding burdens between the Member States (para. 254).

(8) The Council Decision was not rendered disproportionate by maintaining that 120,000 migrants were to be relocated from Greece and Italy after Hungary withdrew from being a beneficiary under the relocation mechanism, even though 54,000 individuals from within that number were initially to be relocated from Hungary. The Council had taken the need for adaptation into account having regard to the degree of uncertainty of the evolution of migration flows (paras. 279-83).

(9) The Council Decision had not violated the principle of proportionality. Hungary's argument that the Council Decision was disproportionate because it imposed an obligation on it under the relocation mechanism even though it was also a State facing a similar emergency to Greece and Italy was unfounded. A partial annulment of an EU act was possible only if the elements of the annulment sought could be severed from the remainder of the act. Hungary's argument would have required the recalculation of all other Member States' allocations under the relocation mechanism. It would also have affected an essential element of the decision which included mandatory allocations between Member States pursuant to the principle of solidarity and fair sharing of responsibility under Article 80 of the TFEU (paras. 273-97 and 299).

(10) The Council Decision had observed the principle of certainty and normative clarity. The decision was an emergency measure which formed part of the *acquis* of the common European asylum system. It was not necessary or desirable for the decision to mention all relevant rules governing the status, rights and obligations of persons relocated in their host Member State. In the recitals, the Council had sufficiently explained how the decision related to other provisions of legislative acts adopted by the EU (paras. 319-31).

(11) Neither the Geneva Convention nor European Union law guaranteed an applicant for international protection the right to freely choose their host country. The transfer of an applicant for international protection from one Member State to another did not constitute a breach of the principle of non-*refoulement*. For the purposes of the common European asylum system, the territory of all Member States had to be treated as a common area for the uniform application of EU law on asylum matters. The Council Decision further participated in the preservation of the fundamental rights of applicants, as guaranteed by the EU Charter of Fundamental Rights ("the Charter"), by transferring them to Member States that were in a better position to process their asylum applications (paras. 332-40).

Judgment of the Court of Justice (6 September 2017)

Held:—The action for annulment was dismissed.

(1) A Council Decision that was classified as a non-legislative act was not prevented from being adopted under Article 78(3) of the TFEU just because it included derogations from legislative acts. A restrictive interpretation of "provisional measures" within the meaning of Article 78(3) of the TFEU found no support in the wording of the Article and would significantly reduce its effectiveness. The provision had to be sufficiently broad in scope and allow derogation from provisions of legislative acts to enable the EU to adopt measures necessary to respond effectively and swiftly to an emergency characterized by a sudden inflow of nationals of third countries. However, provisional measures adopted under Article 78(3) of the TFEU must be circumscribed and limited to responding swiftly, effectively and temporarily, to a specific crisis. The derogations provided in the contested decision met these requirements as their material and temporal scope were sufficiently limited (paras. 57-84).

(2) For the purposes of Article 78(3) of the TFEU, the inflow of nationals of third countries on an unforeseeable scale could be classified as "sudden" even if it took place in the context of a migration crisis spanning a number of years. In the circumstances of a sharp increase in the inflow of third-country nationals into Greece and Italy over a short period of time the Council could, without manifest error of assessment, classify such an increase as "sudden". EU institutions must be allowed a broad discretion when adopting measures in areas which entailed choices, particularly of a political nature, and which required complex assessments (paras. 113-24 and 133).

(3) The finding of an emergency in Italy and Greece throughout 2015 was not undermined by the existence of other contributing factors, including alleged structural defects in their asylum reception and processing systems. Indeed, the Court held that the scale of the inflows that confronted Greece and Italy in 2015 would have disrupted any asylum system, even one without structural weaknesses (paras. 125-8).

(4) Article 78(3) of the TFEU allowed the Council to adopt measures by a qualified majority. The principle of institutional balance prevented the Council from altering the voting rules and requiring a unanimous vote. The rules regarding the manner in which EU institutions arrived at their decisions were laid down in the Treaties (the TFEU and the Treaty on European Union, 1992) and were not within the discretion of the Member States or the institutions themselves. The Treaties alone could empower an institution to amend a decision-making procedure established by the Treaties (paras. 143-50).

(5) The obligation to consult the European Parliament ("the Parliament") pursuant to Article 78(3) of the TFEU had been satisfied. The Court had consistently held that the obligation to consult the Parliament in the decision-making procedure meant that the Parliament must be consulted again

whenever the final text of a decision differed in essence from the text which the Parliament had already seen, except in cases in which the amendments substantially corresponded to the wishes of the Parliament itself. Amendments which went to the heart of established arrangements, or that affected the scheme of the proposal as a whole, were regarded as substantial amendments that required consultation. Hungary's refusal to be a beneficiary of the relocation mechanism amounted to an essential element of a measure adopted under Article 78(3) of the TFEU and therefore differed in essence from the Commission's initial proposal for which Parliament had been consulted. However, the Parliament had taken account of that fundamental change, and the Council's other amendments to the Commission's proposal did not affect its very essence (paras. 161-70).

(6) There were no grounds to object to the decision based on the procedure for which amendments had been adopted. Under Article 14 of the Council's rules of procedure, any member of the Council could oppose discussion of any proposed amendments that had not been provided in the languages specified in the rules in force governing languages. While the EU was committed to the preservation of multilingualism, a balanced and flexible approach that was conducive to efficacy was important in the particular context of urgency that was characterized by the adoption of provisional measures under Article 78(3) of the TFEU. In the present case, the Commission's initial proposal was made available to all Member States in all official languages of the EU. No Member State had raised any objection to subsequent discussions on the basis of documents drafted in English and the agreed amendments that were read by the President of the Council were simultaneously interpreted into all official languages of the EU (paras. 199-205).

(7) The measures adopted by the Council Decision were necessary and the submission that the objective of the decision could have been achieved by less restrictive measures was rejected. The Council Decision could only have been censured by the Court on this ground if it was found that, in adopting the relevant decision, the Council had made a manifest error of assessment based on the information and data that were available at the time. In view of the considerations and statistical data available to the Council at the time, there was no ground for maintaining that the Council made a manifest error of assessment by concluding that a temporary, binding, relocation measure for 120,000 migrants was required (paras. 206-8 and 235-61).

(8) The Council did not make a manifest error of assessment in maintaining the number of persons to be relocated at 120,000 even after Hungary had withdrawn from being a beneficiary under the relocation mechanism. Hungary had failed to establish that the statistical data relied on by the Council in setting the total number of persons to be relocated was not germane. Further, Articles 4(1)-(3) of the Council Decision enabled the Council to react, should the need arise, to future developments and made it possible for it to adapt the relocation mechanism to the needs of the emergency situation regarding migration flows (paras. 267-78).

(9) The imposition of binding quotas on Hungary under the relocation mechanism did not represent a disproportionate burden. When one or more Member States were faced with an emergency within the meaning of Article 78(3) of the TFEU, the principle of solidarity and fair sharing of responsibility under Article 80 of the TFEU required that the obligations within provisional measures adopted in response must, as a general rule, be divided between all other Member States. The Commission and the Council had therefore rightly considered, at the time the contested decision was adopted, that the distribution of relocated applicants among all Member States was a fundamental element of the decision. The Council Decision contained various adjustment mechanisms which demonstrated that the relocation mechanism enabled account to be taken, in a proportionate manner, of the particular situation of each Member State. Further, arguments that the ethnic origins of applicants for international protection should have been taken into account within the relocation mechanism were contrary to EU law, particularly Article 21 of the Charter (paras. 283-310).

(10) It could not be maintained that the contested decision, by providing for the transfer of an applicant for international protection before a decision on their application had been made, was contrary to the Geneva Convention. An applicant did not have the right, under EU law, to choose the Member State responsible for assessing their application. The transfer of an applicant for international protection from one Member State to another could not be regarded as *refoulement* to a third State (paras. 323-45).

The text of the judgment of the Court of Justice commences at p. 76. The following is the text of the Opinion of Advocate General Bot:

OPINION OF ADVOCATE GENERAL BOT[1]

1. By their applications, the Slovak Republic (C-643/15) and Hungary (C-647/15) seek annulment of Council Decision (EU) 2015/1601 of 22 September 2015 establishing provisional measures in the area of international protection for the benefit of Italy and Greece.[2]

2. That decision was adopted by the Council of the European Union on the basis of Article 78(3) TFEU, which provides that "in the event of one or more Member States being confronted by an emergency situation characterised by a sudden inflow of nationals of third countries, the Council, on a proposal from the [European] Commission, may adopt provisional measures for the benefit of the

---

[1] Original language: French.
[2] OJ 2015 L 248, p. 80, "the contested decision".

Member State(s) concerned. It shall act after consulting the European Parliament".

3. The decision was adopted in the context of the migration crisis that affected the European Union from 2014, then increased in 2015, in particular in July and August of that year, and of the catastrophic humanitarian situation to which that crisis gave rise, in particular in "front line" Member States such as the Italian Republic and the Hellenic Republic, which faced a massive inflow of migrants from third countries such as the Syrian Arab Republic, the Islamic Republic of Afghanistan, the Republic of Iraq and the State of Eritrea.

4. In order to deal with that migration crisis and the pressure which it placed on the asylum regimes in the Italian Republic and the Hellenic Republic, the contested decision provides for the relocation from those two Member States to the other Member States, over a period of two years, of 120 000 persons in clear need of international protection. The decision is accompanied by two annexes, which initially allocated 66 000 persons to be relocated from Italy (an allocation of 15 600) and Greece (an allocation of 50 400) on the basis of compulsory allocations fixed for each of the other Member States.[3]

5. Article 2(e) of the contested decision defines relocation as "the transfer of an applicant from the territory of the Member State which the criteria laid down in Chapter III of Regulation (EU) No 604/2013[4] indicate as responsible for examining his or her application for international protection to the territory of the Member State of relocation", which, according to Article 2(f) of the contested decision, is "the Member State which becomes responsible for examining the application for international protection pursuant to [the Dublin III] Regulation ... of an applicant following his or her relocation in the territory of that Member State".

<hr />

[3] The remaining allocation of 54 000 applicants referred to in Article 4(1)(c) of the contested decision (also known as "the reserve") to be relocated in a second phase, beginning on 26 September 2016, benefits either by default in the Italian Republic or the Hellenic Republic or in another Member State in an emergency situation within the meaning of Article 78(1) TFEU, and is to be allocated according to the mechanism provided for in Article 4(2) and (3) of the contested decision. Following the insertion of paragraph 3a into Article 4 of the contested decision by Council Decision (EU) 2016/1754 of 29 September 2016 amending Decision (EU) 2015/1601 (OJ 2016 L 268, p. 82), that reserve is to be allocated to the "one for one" mechanism established by the EU–Turkey Statement of 18 March 2016, in accordance with which voluntary admissions to the territory of the Member States of Syrian nationals from Turkey may be imputed to that Member State in the form of resettlements.

[4] Regulation of the European Parliament and of the Council of 26 June 2013 establishing the criteria and mechanisms for determining the Member State responsible for examining an application for international protection lodged in one of the Member States by a third-country national or a stateless person (OJ 2013 L 180, p. 31, "the Dublin III Regulation").

6. The temporary relocation mechanism provided for in the contested decision takes its place alongside other measures which had already been taken at Union level in order to deal with the migration crisis, including the European programme for the "resettlement"[5] of 22 504 persons in need of international protection, agreed upon on 20 July 2015 in the form of a "resolution" between the Member States and the States associated with the Dublin system, and Decision (EU) 2015/1523, adopted by the Council on 14 September 2015,[6] which provides for the relocation from Greece and Italy, over a period of two years, of 40 000 persons in clear need of international protection to the other Member States on the basis of distribution determined by consensus.[7]

7. It should also be pointed out that, on 9 September 2015, the Commission submitted not only the proposal for what would become the contested decision,[8] but also a proposal for a regulation amending the Dublin III Regulation.[9] That proposal provides for a "permanent" relocation mechanism, that is to say, a relocation mechanism which, unlike the mechanism provided for in Decision 2015/1523 and in the contested decision, is not limited in time. That proposal has thus far still not been adopted.

8. As regards the genesis of the contested decision, I shall mention the following elements.

9. The Commission's initial proposal provided for the relocation of 120 000 applicants for international protection, from Italy (15 600 persons), Greece (50 400 persons) and Hungary (54 000 persons), to

---

[5] Article 2(a) of Regulation No 516/2014 of the European Parliament and of the Council of 16 April 2014 establishing the Asylum, Migration and Integration Fund, amending Council Decision 2008/381/EC and repealing Decisions No 573/2007/EC and No 575/2007/EC of the European Parliament and of the Council and Council Decision 2007/435/EC (OJ 2014 L 150, p. 168), contains a definition of the concept of "resettlement", which is essentially the process whereby, on a request from the United Nations High Commissioner for Refugees (UNHCR) based on a person's need for international protection, third-country nationals are transferred from a third country and established in a Member State where they are permitted to reside with "refugee status", "subsidiary protection status" or any other status which offers similar rights and benefits.

[6] Council Decision of 14 September 2015 establishing provisional measures in the area of international protection for the benefit of Italy and of Greece (OJ 2015 L 239, p. 146).

[7] Initially, consensus on the allocation of those persons between Member States was reached only in respect of 32 256 persons, as certain Member States, like Hungary, refused to commit themselves and the Slovak Republic committed itself in respect of only 100 persons. See Resolution of 20 July 2015 of the Representatives of the Governments of the Member States meeting within the Council on relocating from Greece and Italy 40 000 persons in clear need of international protection; Annex B.2 to the Council's defence.

[8] Proposal for a Council Decision establishing provisional measures in the area of international protection for the benefit of Italy, Greece and Hungary (COM(2015) 451 final).

[9] Proposal for a Regulation of the European Parliament and of the Council establishing a crisis relocation mechanism and amending Regulation No 604/2013 (COM(2015) 450 final).

the other Member States. Annexes I to III to that proposal included three tables distributing those applicants from each of those Member States among the other Member States, with the exception of the United Kingdom of Great Britain and Northern Ireland, Ireland and the Kingdom of Denmark, in the form of allocations determined for each of those Member States.

10. On 13 September 2015, the Commission communicated that proposal to the national parliaments.

11. On 14 September 2015, the Council communicated the proposal to the Parliament for consultation.

12. On 17 September 2015, the Parliament adopted a legislative resolution approving the proposal, having regard, in particular, to the "exceptional situation of urgency and the need to address the situation with no further delay", while asking the Council to consult the Parliament again if it intended to substantially amend the Commission proposal.

13. During the various meetings held within the Council between 17 and 22 September 2015, the Commission's initial proposal was amended on certain points.

14. In particular, at those meetings, Hungary stated that it rejected the notion of being classified as a "frontline Member State" and that it did not wish to be among the Member States benefiting from relocation on the same basis as the Italian Republic and the Hellenic Republic. Accordingly, in the final version of the proposal, all reference to Hungary as a beneficiary Member State, including in the title of the proposal, was deleted. Also, Annex III to the initial proposal, concerning the distribution of 54 000 applicants who according to the initial version would be resettled from Hungary was deleted. On the other hand, Hungary was included in Annexes I and II as a Member State of relocation of applicants for international protection from Italy and Greece respectively and allocations were therefore attributed to it in those annexes.

15. On 22 September 2015, the Commission proposal as thus amended was adopted by the Council by a qualified majority. The Czech Republic, Hungary, Romania and the Slovak Republic voted against the adoption of that proposal and the Republic of Finland abstained.

16. The contested decision is an expression of the solidarity which the Treaty envisages between Member States.

17. The present actions provide me with the opportunity to recall that solidarity is among the cardinal values of the Union and is even among the foundations of the Union. How would it be possible to

deepen the solidarity between the peoples of Europe and to envisage ever-closer union between those peoples, as advocated in the Preamble to the EU Treaty, without solidarity between the Member States when one of them is faced with an emergency situation? I am referring here to the quintessence of what is both the *raison d'être* and the objective of the European project.

18. It is therefore appropriate to emphasise at the outset the importance of solidarity as a founding and existential value of the Union.

19. Already asserted in the Treaty of Rome,[10] the requirement of solidarity remains at the heart of the process of integration pursued by the Treaty of Lisbon. Although surprisingly absent from the list in the first sentence of Article 2 TEU of the values on which the Union is founded,[11] solidarity is, on the other hand, mentioned in the Preamble to the Charter of Fundamental Rights of the European Union[12] as forming part of the "indivisible, universal values" on which the Union is founded. Furthermore, Article 3(3) TEU states that the Union is to promote not only "solidarity between generations" but also "solidarity among Member States". Solidarity therefore continues to form part of a set of values and principles that constitutes "the bedrock of the European construction".[13]

20. More specifically, solidarity is both a pillar and at the same time a guiding principle of the European Union's policies on border checks, asylum and immigration, which form the subject matter of Chapter 2

---

[10] See Labayle, S., "Les valeurs de l'Union", doctoral thesis in public law submitted on 12 December 2016, which states that "the requirement of solidarity, referred to on many occasions throughout the Treaty of Rome, constitutes … a central characteristic of the Treaty. It is clear on reading the Treaty that solidarity is among the key guidelines of the project of European integration and in 1957 is already addressed to the Member States as well as to individuals" (point 282, pp. 117 and 118).

[11] *Ibid.*, point 431, p. 165.

[12] "The Charter".

[13] See Favreau, B., "La Charte des droits fondamentaux: Pourquoi et comment?", *La Charte des droits fondamentaux de l'Union européenne après le traité de Lisbonne*, Bruylant, Brussels, 2010, pp. 3 to 38, in particular p. 13. See also Bieber, R., and Maiani, F., "Sans solidarité point d'Union européenne, Regards croisés sur les crises de l'Union économique et monétaire et du Système européen commun d'asile", *Revue trimestrielle de droit européen*, Dalloz, Paris, 2012, p. 295. After pointing out that the concept of "solidarity" is not defined anywhere in the Treaties, those authors observe that "the Treaties confer on that concept a scope that varies according to the context—sometimes an objective or parameter for EU action, sometimes a basic value, sometimes a criterion of the obligations to which the Member States have subscribed by acceding to the European Union. The common denominator that links those various emanations of solidarity in the context of the European Union is the recognition of the existence of a 'common interest', separate from and separable from the sum of the individual interests". Last, for a collection of contributions relating to the principle of solidarity, see Boutayeb, C., *La solidarité dans l'Union européenne—Éléments constitutionnels et matériels*, Dalloz, Paris, 2011.

of Title V of the FEU Treaty, devoted to the area of freedom, security and justice.[14]

21. That may be seen from Article 67(2) TFEU, which states that the Union is to "frame a common policy on asylum, immigration and external border control, based on solidarity between Member States, which is fair towards nationals of third countries". In addition, Article 80 TFEU provides that "the policies of the Union set out in [that] Chapter and their implementation shall be governed by the principle of solidarity and fair sharing of responsibility, including its financial implications, between the Member States. Whenever necessary, the Union acts adopted pursuant to [that] Chapter shall contain appropriate measures to give effect to this principle".[15]

22. Given the de facto inequality between Member States because of their geographic situation and their vulnerability in the face of massive migration flows, the adoption of measures on the basis of Article 78(3) TFEU and their effective application is even more pressing. From that aspect, measures such as those provided for in the contested decision make it possible to confer a practical content on the principle of solidarity and fair sharing of responsibility between Member States laid down in Article 80 TFEU.

23. The particular feature of the contested decision is that it establishes a relocation mechanism on the basis of allocations assigned to the Member States which are binding in nature. With that decision, solidarity between Member States has a specific content and a binding nature. That essential and innovative characteristic of that decision explains the politically sensitive nature of the present cases, since it has crystallised the opposition on the part of Member States which advocate freely consented solidarity based solely on voluntary commitments.

---

[14] See, in particular, on this topic, "Searching for Solidarity in EU Asylum and Border Policies, a collection of short papers following the Odysseus Network's First Annual Policy Conference", 26-27 February 2016, Université libre de Bruxelles. See also Küçük, E., "The principle of solidarity and fairness in sharing responsibility: More than window dressing?", *European Law Journal*, Sweet and Maxwell, London, 2016, pp. 448 to 469, and Bast, J., "Deepening supranational integration: Interstate solidarity in EU migration law", *European Public Law*, No 22, Issue 2, Wolters Kluwer Law and Business, Alphen aan den Rijn, 2016, pp. 289 to 304.

[15] At the international level, solidarity is also a cardinal value of asylum policy. The fourth recital of the Preamble to the Convention of 1951 relating to the Status of Refugees, signed in Geneva on 28 July 1951, supplemented by the Protocol relating to the Status of Refugees of 31 January 1967 ("the Geneva Convention"), thus provides that "the grant of asylum may place unduly heavy burdens on certain countries, and . . . a satisfactory solution of a problem of which the United Nations has recognised the international scope and nature cannot therefore be obtained without international cooperation".

24. That opposition, together with the finding of a very incomplete application of the contested decision, to which I shall return below,[16] may give the impression that, behind what is by common consent called the "2015 migration crisis", another crisis is concealed, namely the crisis of the European integration project, which is to a large extent based on a requirement for solidarity between the Member States which have decided to take part in that project.[17]

25. From another side, it is just as possible to consider that, in adopting a firm response to that migration crisis, the Union has shown that it had the necessary tools and that it was prepared to use them. It remains to ascertain, as the present actions invite me to do, that, in taking measures such as those contained in the contested decision, the Union complied with the legal framework laid down in the Treaties.

I. PROCEDURE BEFORE THE COURT AND FORMS OF ORDER SOUGHT

26. In Case C-643/15, the Slovak Republic asks the Court to annul the contested decision and to order the Council to pay the costs.

27. In Case C-647/15, Hungary asks the Court to annul the contested decision or, in the alternative, in the event that its first head of claim is not upheld, to annul that decision insofar as it concerns Hungary, and to order the Council to pay the costs.

28. In Cases C-643/15 and C-647/15, the Council asks the Court to dismiss the actions as unfounded and to order the Slovak Republic and Hungary, respectively, to pay the costs in the cases concerning them.

---

[16] Suffice it to say at this point that, according to the information provided by the Council at the hearing before the Court on 10 May 2017, the number of relocations from Italy and Greece stood at 18 129 on 8 May 2017.

[17] See, in that regard, Labayle, S., op. cit., who observes, in regard to the discrepancies which have appeared between Member States in the management of that migration crisis, that while it is necessary to "be wary of any tendency to dramatise, . . . nonetheless the fear of the danger that the work patiently built up over more than half a century will disintegrate cannot be ignored. Such a gradual undermining of the foundations threatens the entire edifice and reinforces the need for absolute vigilance with respect to the matter. Failure by its own Member States to respect the founding principles of the Union introduces a potential factor of the disintegration of elements which are essential to its continuity and to the logic of its functioning" (point 1182, p. 477). See also Chassin, C.-A., "La crise des migrants: L'Europe à la croisée des chemins", *Revue Europe*, No 3, LexisNexis, 2016, pp. 15 to 21, in particular point 43, p. 21, which states that "the migrant crisis is . . . a human crisis, but also a moral crisis, for the European Union: beyond the short-term answers, it underlines the fragility of the European construction".

29. By decision of the President of the Court of 29 April 2016, the Kingdom of Belgium, the Federal Republic of Germany, the Hellenic Republic, the French Republic, the Italian Republic, the Grand Duchy of Luxembourg, the Kingdom of Sweden and the Commission were granted leave to intervene in support of the form of order sought by the Council in Cases C-643/15 and C-647/15.

30. By that decision of the President of the Court, the Republic of Poland was granted leave to intervene, in Case C-643/15, in support of the form of order sought by the Slovak Republic and, in Case C-647/15, in support of the form of order sought by Hungary.

II. THE ACTIONS

31. In support of the form of order which it seeks, the Slovak Republic relies on six pleas in law, alleging, respectively, (i) infringement of Article 68 TFEU and Article 13(2) TEU, and breach of the principle of institutional balance; (ii) infringement of Article 10(1) and (2) TEU, Article 13(2) TEU, Article 78(3) TFEU, Articles 3 and 4 of Protocol (No 1) on the role of the national parliaments in the European Union and Articles 6 and 7 of Protocol (No 2) on the application of the principles of subsidiarity and proportionality, annexed to the Treaties,[18] and breach of the principles of legal certainty, representative democracy and institutional balance; (iii) breach of essential procedural requirements governing the legislative process and infringement of Article 10(1) and (2) TEU, Article 13(2) TEU, and breach of the principles of representative democracy, institutional balance and sound administration (in the alternative); (iv) breach of essential procedural requirements laid down in Article 78(3) TFEU and Article 293 TFEU, and of Article 10(1) and (2) TEU, Article 13(2) TEU, and breach of the principles of representative democracy, institutional balance and sound administration (partly in the alternative); (v) infringement of Article 78(3) TFEU owing to non-fulfilment of the conditions of its applicability (in the alternative); and (vi) breach of the principle of proportionality.

32. In support of the form of order which it seeks, Hungary relies on 10 pleas in law.

33. The first two pleas allege infringement of Article 78(3) TFEU, in that that provision does not provide the Council with an adequate legal basis for the adoption of measures that entail a binding exception

---

[18] "Protocol (No 1)" and "Protocol (No 2)" respectively.

to the provisions of a legislative act, which are applicable for a period of 24 months, or indeed of 36 months in some cases, and the effects of which extend beyond that period, which is not compatible with the concept of "provisional measures".

34. The third to sixth pleas allege breach of essential procedural requirements, in that (i) when adopting the contested decision, the Council infringed Article 293(1) TFEU by departing from the Commission's proposal without a unanimous vote (third plea); (ii) the contested decision contains a derogation from the provisions of a legislative act and is itself a legislative act by virtue of its content, so that, even on the assumption that it would have been possible to adopt the contested decision on the basis of Article 78(3) TFEU, it would have been necessary, when adopting it, to respect the right of the national parliaments to issue an opinion on legislative acts, laid down in Protocol (No 1) and Protocol (No 2) (fourth plea); (iii) after consulting the Parliament, the Council substantially amended the text of the proposal without again consulting the Parliament on the matter (fifth plea); and (iv) when the Council adopted the contested decision, the proposal for a decision was not available in all the language versions corresponding to the official languages of the Union (sixth plea).

35. The seventh plea alleges infringement of Article 68 TFEU and of the European Council conclusions of 25 and 26 June 2015.[19]

36. The eighth plea alleges breach of the principles of legal certainty and legislative clarity, since on a number of points it is unclear how the provisions of the contested decision should be applied or how they interrelate with the provisions of the Dublin III Regulation.

37. The ninth plea alleges breach of the principles of necessity and proportionality, in that, as Hungary is no longer among the Member States that benefit from the temporary relocation mechanism, there is no reason why the contested decision should provide for the relocation of 120 000 seeking international protection.

38. The 10th plea, which is submitted in the alternative, alleges breach of the principle of proportionality and infringement of Article 78(3) TFEU in respect of Hungary, since the contested decision attributes a mandatory allocation to it, even though Hungary is recognised as a Member State whose territory has been entered by a large number of irregular migrants who have made applications for international protection there.

---

[19] EUCO 22/15.

III. MY ASSESSMENT

A. Preliminary observations

39. Since the legal basis of an act determines the procedure to be followed when that act is adopted,[20] it is appropriate to examine, in the first place, the pleas alleging that Article 78(3) TFEU was inadequate as a legal basis for the adoption of the contested decision. I shall examine, in the second place, the pleas alleging breach of essential procedural requirements purportedly committed when that decision was adopted and, in the third place, the substantive pleas.

40. In addition, under those three heads, I shall first of all examine the pleas of the Slovak Republic and Hungary which overlap in whole or in part and then, if necessary, the pleas specific to each of the applicants.

B. The pleas alleging that Article 78(3) TFEU is inadequate as a legal basis for the adoption of the contested decision

41. The Slovak Republic (second and fifth pleas) and Hungary (first and second pleas) contend that Article 78(3) TFEU cannot constitute an adequate legal basis for the adoption of the contested decision.

42. However, the positions argued by those two Member States differ: while Hungary acknowledges that the Italian Republic and the Hellenic Republic were in an "emergency situation characterised by a sudden inflow of nationals of third countries", within the meaning of Article 78(3) TFEU, at the time of the adoption of the contested decision, but at the same time denies that the contested decision was the appropriate measure in order to address that situation, the Slovak Republic maintains that such an emergency situation, within the meaning of that provision, did not exist (second part of the fifth plea).

43. In order to challenge the choice of the legal basis of the contested decision, those two Member States maintain, in the first place, that although the contested decision was adopted according to a non-legislative procedure and therefore constitutes a non-legislative act, it should nonetheless be classified as a legislative act because of its content, since it amends legislative acts. However, Article 78(3) TFEU does not permit the adoption of legislative acts.

44. In the second place, the Slovak Republic and Hungary dispute the provisional nature of the contested decision.

---

[20] See, to that effect, judgment of 10 September 2015, *Parliament* v. *Council* (C-363/14, EU: C:2015:579, paragraph 17).

45. In the third place, the Slovak Republic, unlike Hungary, maintains that Article 78(3) TFEU did not provide an adequate legal basis for the adoption of the contested decision, since the condition of the existence of an "emergency situation characterised by a sudden inflow of nationals of third countries" was not satisfied.

1. The Slovak Republic's second plea and Hungary's first plea, relating to the legislative nature of the contested decision

46. The Slovak Republic and Hungary claim that even though it was adopted according to the non-legislative procedure and is therefore formally a non-legislative act, the contested decision must nonetheless be classified as a legislative act because of its content and its effects, since it amends—and, moreover, does so fundamentally—a number of legislative acts of EU law. Article 78(3) TFEU provides no legal basis for the adoption of legislative acts, since it gives no indication that the measures adopted on the basis of that provision should be adopted in a legislative procedure.

47. As expressly confirmed in recital 23 of the contested decision, that decision derogates from a number of legislative acts of the Union. Although the contested decision classifies those amendments as mere derogations, the distinction between a derogation and an amendment is artificial, since in practice the effects of a derogation and those of an amendment are the same in that, in both cases, the application of a normative provision is excluded and, de facto, its effectiveness is therefore affected.

48. More specifically, the Slovak Republic contends that the Council has infringed Article 78(3) TFEU, on the ground that the contested decision derogates from provisions set out in legislative acts and such amendments can be made only by a legislative act. Article 78(3) TFEU, which mentions neither the ordinary legislative procedure nor the special legislative procedure, does not permit the adoption of legislative acts. It follows that the form of the contested decision does not correspond to its content.

49. In adopting the contested decision on the basis of Article 78(3) TFEU, the Council not only infringed that provision but also undermined the rights of the national parliaments and the Parliament. Both the former and the latter ought, under primary law, to have participated in the amendments of the legislative acts from which the Council derogated by the contested decision. Indeed, the Slovak Republic observes that those acts were adopted according to the ordinary legislative procedure.

50. The Slovak Republic therefore maintains that, in adopting the contested decision, the Council infringed not only Article 78(3) TFEU, but also Article 10(1) and (2) TEU, Article 13(2) TEU, Articles 3 and 4 of Protocol (No 1) and Articles 6 and 7 of Protocol (No 2), and breached the principles of legal certainty, representative democracy and institutional balance.

51. Hungary agrees with the Slovak Republic that a legal act adopted on the basis of Article 78(3) TFEU which, on the basis of a reading a contrario of Article 289(2) and (3) TFEU, does not constitute a legislative act, cannot amend in a binding manner, even on a provisional basis, legislative acts in force that were adopted in ordinary or special legislative procedures, such as the Dublin III Regulation. Because of its content, the contested decision is therefore without doubt a legislative act. Since that decision derogates from the provisions of the Dublin III Regulation, it could not be adopted on the basis of Article 78(3) TFEU, which, because it confers on the Council the power to adopt acts only in the framework of a non-legislative procedure, authorises it only to adopt non-legislative acts.

52. In Hungary's submission, Article 78(3) TFEU might at most serve as the legal basis for the adoption of measures supplementing legislative acts adopted on the basis of Article 78(2) TFEU, but consistent with those measures, or measures that facilitate their implementation in the light of the emergency situation.[21]

53. Hungary makes clear that, on the assumption that the Court should decide that it is possible to adopt, on the basis of Article 78(3) TFEU, an act that derogates from a legislative act adopted on the basis of Article 78(2) TFEU, such a derogation could not go so far as to affect the substance of such a legislative act or so far as to render its fundamental provisions devoid of meaning. However, that is the case of the contested decision, since it amends, in particular, the most essential element of that regulation, namely the designation of the Member State responsible for examining an application for international protection. Thus, the contested decision introduces a derogation from the provisions of that regulation to a degree that is unacceptable in the context of a non-legislative act. That constitutes an abuse of the ordinary legislative procedure provided for in Article 78(2) TFEU.

54. Last, in its reply and in its response to the statements in intervention, Hungary maintains, referring to points 151 to 161 of the Opinion of Advocate General Wathelet in the case of *Council*

---

[21] Hungary mentions, by way of examples, the grant of financial and technical assistance and the making available of professionals.

v. *Front Polisario*,[22] that the requirement to consult the Parliament, as provided for in Article 78(3) TFEU, may be regarded as "participation" by the Parliament, within the meaning of Article 289(2) TFEU, with the consequence that the special legislative procedure applies and that the contested decision should therefore be classified as a legislative act.

55. However, even if that were so, Article 78(3) TFEU would not authorise the Council to derogate from an essential provision of a legislative act adopted on the basis of Article 78(2) TFEU.

56. I find those various arguments unconvincing. I am of the view that Article 78(3) TFEU could serve as the legal basis for a non-legislative act, such as the contested decision, that derogates, on a temporary basis and within a well-defined framework, from certain provisions of legislative acts.

57. I shall begin by answering the argument put forward by Hungary in its reply,[23] namely that the contested decision might be regarded as a legislative act in spite of the fact that Article 78(3) TFEU does not mention that the measures adopted on that basis are to be adopted following a special legislative procedure. Hungary relies, in that regard, on the assertion that, in accordance with the requirement in Article 289(2) TFEU, the contested decision was indeed adopted by the Council "with the participation of the . . . Parliament".

58. It seems essential to answer that point of law unambiguously, insofar as the adoption of a legislative act has certain requirements that do not apply to the adoption of a non-legislative act. I am thinking, in particular, about the participation of the national parliaments provided for in Articles 3 and 4 of Protocol (No 1) and also in Articles 6 and 7 of Protocol (No 2), and also of the requirement that the Council is to sit in public when it deliberates and votes on a draft legislative act, which arises from Article 16(8) TEU and Article 15(2) TFEU.

59. The typology of the normative instruments of the Union resulting from the Treaty of Lisbon established, for the first time, a distinction between legislative acts and non-legislative acts, on the basis of what are above all institutional and procedural considerations.[24]

60. Article 289(3) TFEU defines the category of "legislative acts" as covering "legal acts adopted by legislative procedure". The "legislative procedure" consists either in the "ordinary legislative procedure" or in a

---

[22] C-104/16 P, EU:C:2016:677.

[23] Unlike Hungary, the Slovak Republic points out in its reply that the Council and the Slovak Republic are agreed that the contested decision is non-legislative in nature (paragraph 29).

[24] See Ritleng, D., "Les catégories des actes de l'Union—Réflexions à partir de la catégorie de l'acte législatif", *Les catégories juridiques du droit de l'Union européenne*, Bruylant, Brussels, 2016, pp. 155 to 174, in particular p. 159.

"special legislative procedure". As provided in Article 289(1) TFEU, it is the joint adoption of a legal act by the Parliament and the Council on a proposal from the Commission that characterises the ordinary legislative procedure.

61. In the words of Article 289(2) TFEU, a special legislative procedure is a procedure which, "in the specific cases provided for by the Treaties", consists in "the adoption of a regulation, directive or decision by the European Parliament with the participation of the Council, or by the latter with the participation of the European Parliament".[25] The special legislative procedure is therefore character-ised by the fact that it involves, in varying degrees, the Council and the Parliament in the adoption of an act of the Union.

62. In most cases in which a special legislative procedure is envis-aged, such an act must be adopted by the Council acting unanimously, after the European Parliament has given its consent,[26] or indeed, more usually, after the Parliament has been consulted.[27] In a few cases it is the Parliament that must adopt the act after the Council has given its consent.[28]

63. It follows from those provisions that the framers of the Treaty took a purely formal approach,[29] according to which legislative acts are to be classified as such if they are adopted according to the ordinary legislative procedure or according to a special legislative procedure.

64. It is therefore irrelevant to seek, as the applicants suggest, to classify the contested decision as a legislative act on the basis of its content.

65. The argument developed by Hungary raises the question whether it is necessary that a provision of the Treaty should indicate expressly that it permits the adoption of an act according to a special legislative procedure in order for such an act to be considered to constitute a legislative act.

66. To my mind, that question must be answered in the affirmative, in order to afford a sufficient degree of certainty and legal certainty to

---

[25] See Ritleng, D., op. cit., who observes that "the legislative act is the act the adoption of which involves the European Parliament and the Council, playing equal roles in the context of the ordinary legislative procedure or unequal roles in the context of a special legislative procedure. Thus an institutional criterion is established, marking the advent of a legislative power consisting of the Parliament and the Council" (p. 161).

[26] See, in particular, Article 86(1) TFEU.

[27] See, in particular, Article 77(3) TFEU.

[28] See, in particular, Article 223(2) TFEU.

[29] See Craig, P., and De Búrca, G., *EU Law—Text, Cases and Materials*, 6th Edition, Oxford University Press, Oxford, 2015, p. 114.

the classification of the acts of the Union that was established by the framers of the Treaty.

67. It must be stated, in that regard, that the Treaty contains numerous provisions relating to the adoption of Union acts that expressly state that a particular act is to be adopted following a "special legislative procedure", even though the details of that procedure may differ as regards the nature and the degree of involvement of the Council and the Parliament. The practical effect of such a reference is to make clear that, whatever the details may be, the procedure in question is indeed a "legislative procedure" and that it will therefore result in the adoption of a legislative act. The requirement for that reference also follows from the actual wording of Article 289(2) TFEU, according to which a special legislative procedure is to apply only "in the specific cases provided for by the Treaties".

68. Conversely, procedures which follow similar lines to those of special legislative procedures, but which are not expressly classified as such by the Treaty, must be considered to be non-legislative procedures, which therefore result in the adoption of non-legislative acts.[30]

69. Admittedly, it is possible to take the view that a distinction between legislative acts and non-legislative acts arising from such "legal nominalism"[31] will raise problems of consistency[32] and that the framers of the Treaty did not complete the task of classifying the legislative act of the Union.[33]

70. It is equally possible to consider—and this is my preferred solution—that, on the other hand, by opting for an exclusively formal approach to the legislative act, the framers of the Treaty made it possible to identify with certainty the legal bases that authorise the institutions of the Union to adopt legislative acts. The incompleteness, indeed, according to some, the evident inconsistency of the classification made by the framers of the Treaty must thus be seen as the consequence of their intention to afford certain acts the status of legislative act and to deny that status to other acts.

71. Such an examination of the wording of the provisions of the Treaty for the purposes of classifying an act of the Union as a legislative act or as a non-legislative act is, moreover, consistent with the finding of the Court that "it is not procedures that define the legal basis of a

---

[30] See, in particular, to that effect, Lenaerts, K., and Van Nuffel, P., *European Union Law*, 3rd Edition, Sweet and Maxwell, London, 2011, p. 677, paragraph 16-038.
[31] To employ the expression used by Ritleng, D., op. cit., p. 170.
[32] See Craig, P., and De Búrca, G., op. cit., p. 114.
[33] See Ritleng, D., op. cit., p. 174.

measure but the legal basis of a measure that determines the procedures to be followed in adopting that measure".[34]

72. Specifically, the interpretation which I advocate means that the contested decision does not have the status of a legislative act.

73. Indeed, it must be observed that although Article 78(3) TFEU provides for the adoption of measures by the Council acting after consulting the Parliament, it does not expressly state that such measures are to be taken in the framework of a special legislative procedure. Those measures, which are adopted in the framework of a non-legislative procedure, are, on the basis of a reading a contrario of Article 289(3) TFEU, non-legislative in nature. There is a clear contrast in that regard with Article 78(2) TFEU, which expressly states that the measures adopted on the basis of that article are to be adopted in accordance with a legislative procedure, in fact the ordinary legislative procedure.

74. Having made that clear, I must now address the concern at the heart of the arguments developed by the Slovak Republic and by Hungary, that is to say, whether and to what extent Article 78(3) TFEU authorises the Council to adopt a non-legislative act that derogates from provisions set out in legislative acts of the Union.

75. I consider, as do the Council and the interveners that support the form of order sought by it, that Article 78(3) TFEU permits the adoption of measures which, in order to address a clearly identified emergency situation, derogate temporarily and on specific points from legislative acts in asylum matters.

76. That provision of the Treaty has the specific objective of allowing the Union to react rapidly and effectively to an emergency situation characterised by a sudden inflow of nationals of third countries. Given that Article 78(2) TFEU covers the various aspects of the common European asylum system and that the measures adopted on the basis of that provision are legislative acts, it is inevitable that the provisional measures adopted, in connection with the same system, on the basis of Article 78(3) TFEU entail a temporary derogation from certain provisions of those legislative acts. The concept of "provisional measures", within the meaning of Article 78(3) TFEU, cannot therefore, contrary to what the applicants suggest, be understood as being limited to supplementary measures, of an operational or financial nature, without excessively restricting the scope of that legal basis and therefore its practical effect. The concept of "provisional measures"

---

[34] See, in particular, judgment of 19 July 2012, *Parliament* v. *Council* (C-130/10, EU: C:2012:472, paragraph 80).

must therefore, in my view, be interpreted broadly, as Article 78(3) TFEU authorises the Council to adopt all the measures which it deems necessary in order to deal with an emergency situation characterised by a sudden inflow of nationals of third countries.

77. In order to be considered to be properly based on Article 78(3) TFEU, measures must not be intended to definitively eliminate, replace or amend provisions in legislative acts adopted on the basis of Article 78(2) TFEU.

78. That certainly does not apply to the contested decision, which, in accordance with its nature as a provisional measure intended to respond to a very specific emergency situation, merely provides for temporary derogations, in a strictly defined framework, from a number of provisions of legislative acts of the Union. Contrary to the applicants' contention, such derogations cannot therefore be seen as amending those acts in a lasting and general fashion.

79. I must make clear, in that regard, that the derogations included in the contested decision apply only for a period of two years, that they concern only a limited number of 120 000 nationals of third countries who have submitted applications for international protection in Italy or in Greece, whose nationality is among those referred to in Article 3(2) of the contested decision, who will be relocated from one of those two Member States and who arrived or will arrive in those Member States between 24 March 2015 and 26 September 2017.

80. As the Council points out, after the final date of application of the contested decision, on 26 September 2017, the effects of the derogations will automatically expire and the general rules will begin to apply again, without the need for any intervention whatsoever on the part of the EU legislature.

81. As I have already stated, those ad hoc temporary derogations cannot be assimilated to a permanent amendment of the substantive rules contained in legislative acts of the Union in asylum matters, which could be adopted only on the basis of Article 78(2) TFEU.

82. To my mind, therefore, the adoption of the contested decision on the basis of Article 78(3) TFEU did not entail any abuse of the ordinary legislative procedure provided for in Article 78(2) TFEU.

83. It is appropriate, in that regard, to clarify the relationship between those two provisions of the Treaty.

84. When read in conjunction with Article 80 TFEU, Article 78(3) TFEU constitutes a specific legal basis for provisional measures which implement the principle of solidarity in emergency situations characterised by a sudden inflow of nationals of third countries.

85. The procedure provided for in Article 78(3) TFEU is characterised by the urgent need to act in a crisis situation. It is for that reason that it is not based on the ordinary legislative procedure.

86. As the Council points out, the measures provided for in Article 78(2) and (3) TFEU each have an autonomous legal basis in the Treaty and are applied in different situations with different objectives, without there being any need to define a hierarchy between them.

87. It is appropriate to emphasise the complementary nature of the legal bases consisting of Article 78(2)(e)[35] and Article 78(3) TFEU. The concurrent or successive use of those legal bases allows the Union, in particular, to take effective action in the event of migration crisis. Their complementary nature is illustrated by the Proposal of 9 September 2015 for a Regulation of the European Parliament and of the Council establishing a crisis relocation mechanism and amending the Dublin III Regulation.

88. In its proposal, the Commission clearly explains how the measures set out in that proposal and the emergency relocation programmes based on Article 78(3) TFEU interact.

89. As the Commission explains, "the proposal establishing a crisis relocation mechanism has to be distinguished from the proposals adopted by the Commission on the basis of Article 78(3) TFEU for the benefit of certain Member States confronted with a sudden inflow of nationals of third countries on their territories".[36] The Commission goes on to state that "while the measures proposed by the Commission on the basis of Article 78(3) TFEU are provisional, the proposal establishing a crisis relocation mechanism introduces a method for determining for a temporary period in crisis situations which Member State is responsible for examining applications for international protection made in a Member State confronted with a crisis situation, with a view to ensur[ing] a fairer distribution of applicants between Member States in such situations and thereby facilitate the functioning of the Dublin system even in times of crisis".[37]

90. It is therefore a matter, in the latter case, and unlike what is provided for in the contested decision, of a permanent mechanism establishing a method of determining which Member State is to be responsible for examining the applications for international protection submitted in a Member State in a crisis situation. That permanent

---

[35] This provision authorises the Parliament and the Council, acting in accordance with ordinary legislative procedure, to adopt "criteria and mechanisms for determining which Member State is responsible for considering an application for asylum or subsidiary protection".

[36] See the Proposal for a Regulation, p. 3.

[37] *Ibid.*

mechanism is of general application, in that its application is not targeted at certain Member States currently in a crisis situation, but may benefit any Member State confronted with such a situation.

91. The conditions for triggering the relocation mechanism are laid down in the proposal for a regulation. As the Commission states in that proposal, the beneficiary Member State must thus be "confronted with a crisis situation jeopardising the application of the Dublin Regulation due to extreme pressure characterised by a large and disproportionate inflow of third-country nationals or stateless persons, which places significant demands on its asylum system".[38]

92. The complementary nature of the measures adopted on the basis of Article 78(2)(e) TFEU and those adopted under Article 78(3) TFEU is further explained by the Commission as follows: "the establishment of a crisis relocation mechanism is without prejudice to the possibility for the Council to adopt, on a proposal from the Commission, provisional measures for the benefit of a Member State confronted by an emergency situation as characterised by Article 78(3) TFEU. The adoption of emergency measures on the basis of Article 78(3) TFEU will remain relevant in exceptional situations where an emergency response, possibly encompassing a wider migratory support, is needed, should the conditions for using the crisis relocation mechanism not be met".[39]

93. As regards the legal basis chosen, the Commission states in its proposal that that proposal "*amends* [the Dublin III] Regulation ... and should therefore be adopted on the same legal basis, namely Article [78(2)(e) TFEU], in accordance with the ordinary legislative procedure".[40] The Proposal for a Regulation amends the Dublin III Regulation by adding Section VII, entitled "Crisis relocation mechanism". Insofar as it amends that regulation, the proposal is therefore correctly based on Article 78(2)(e) TFEU and therefore subject to the ordinary legislative procedure.

94. In addition, the Commission states that "the crisis relocation mechanism contained in this proposal entails *permanent derogations*, to be activated in specific situations of crisis to the benefit of specific Member States, notably from the principle laid down in Article 3(1) of [the Dublin III] Regulation ... according to which an application for international protection shall be examined by the Member State which the criteria set out in Chapter III indicate as being responsible. In place

---

[38] See that proposal, p. 4.
[39] *Ibid.*
[40] *Ibid.*, emphasis added.

of this principle, the proposal establishes, for well prescribed crisis circumstances, a mandatory distribution key for determining the responsibility for examining applications".[41]

95. What the contested decision and the proposal for a regulation have in common is that they provide the Union with the tools to be able to respond to migrant crisis situations. However, whereas the former, as a measure adopted on the basis of Article 78(3) TFEU, is temporary and targeted at Member States confronted with an emergency situation characterised by a sudden inflow of nationals of third countries, the latter establishes a relocation mechanism of unlimited duration, which is not limited to a predetermined number of nationals of third countries and which does not identify one or more Member States in advance as being beneficiaries of that mechanism.

96. It follows from those factors that, whereas Article 78(3) TFEU is the legal basis that allows the Union to respond on a provisional basis and in an emergency to a sudden inflow of nationals of third countries, Article 78(2)(e) TFEU makes it possible to provide the Union with a framework designed to respond on a permanent basis and generally to a structural problem, namely the fact that Article 3(1) of the Dublin III Regulation is inadequate in the event of sudden migration pressure on the frontline Member States.

97. It follows from the foregoing that, to my mind, Article 78(3) TFEU may serve as the basis for provisional measures, such as those set out in the contested decision, which are intended to respond to an emergency situation even if they contain derogations from particular provisions of legislative acts of the Union, provided that those derogations are strictly defined in terms of their subject matter and the period during which they will apply.

98. The Slovak Republic's second plea and Hungary's first plea must therefore be rejected as unfounded.

2. The first part of the Slovak Republic's fifth plea and Hungary's second plea, alleging that the contested decision is not provisional

99. The Slovak Republic and Hungary maintain that Article 78(3) TFEU does not provide an adequate legal basis for the adoption of the contested decision, since that decision is not provisional, contrary to the requirements of that provision.

100. Under Article 13(1) and (2) of the contested decision, that decision is to apply from 25 September 2015 until 26 September 2017,

---

[41] *Ibid.*, emphasis added.

that is for a period of 24 months. Furthermore, Article 13(3) of that decision provides that it is to apply to persons arriving on the territory of the Italian Republic and the Hellenic Republic during that period, and also to applicants for international protection having arrived on the territory of those Member States from 24 March 2015 onwards.

101. It follows from those provisions that the temporal scope of the contested decision is precisely defined. It makes provision without possible ambiguity for an emergency mechanism of fixed duration, and its provisional nature cannot therefore in my view be disputed.

102. As Article 78(3) TFEU no longer refers to a maximum period of six months, as Article 64(2) of the EC Treaty did, it must be inferred that the provisional measures adopted on that basis may apply during a longer period.

103. Contrary to the Slovak Republic's and Hungary's contention, the fact that the effects of the contested decision may, owing to the lasting links between the applicants for international protection and the Member States of relocation, be felt beyond the period referred to in that decision is in my view irrelevant. Such more or less long term effects are inherent in the international protection that may be obtained in the Member State of relocation. If the argument put forward by the Slovak Republic and Hungary were to be followed, no relocation mechanism could be put in place on the basis of Article 78(3) TFEU.

104. Furthermore, as Article 78(3) TFEU does not prescribe a specific period, but provides only for the adoption of provisional measures, I consider that the Council was entitled, without infringing that provision and without exceeding the wide discretion which that provision confers on it, to establish a temporary relocation mechanism that would apply for 24 months. It is appropriate, in that regard, to note the desire expressed by the Commission in its proposal for a decision, that the duration of the provisional measures "should not be too short [so that they can] have a real impact in practice and provide genuine support for [the Italian Republic and the Hellenic Republic] . . . to cope with the influx of migrants".[42] Furthermore, the choice of a period of application of 24 months is also justified in the light of the foreseeable period necessary to prepare for the implementation of the relocation procedure in all Member States, a fortiori if, as the Hellenic Republic correctly emphasised at the hearing, the unprecedented nature of that procedure is taken into account.

105. In addition, the theory advanced by the Slovak Republic and by Hungary that the duration and the effects of a measure adopted on

---

[42] See that proposal, p. 4.

the basis of Article 78(3) TFEU could not exceed the period necessary for the adoption of a legislative act based on Article 78(2) TFEU finds no support in the wording of those two provisions. Furthermore, insofar as it is impossible to determine in advance the period that would be necessary for the adoption of a legislative act establishing a permanent relocation mechanism on the basis of Article 78(2) TFEU, the theory advanced by the Slovak Republic and by Hungary seems to me to be impossible to put into practice. That uncertainty may be illustrated by the fact that although the proposal for a regulation establishing a permanent relocation mechanism was submitted on 9 September 2015, or on the same day as the proposal that gave rise to the contested decision, it has still not been adopted, and that it is impossible to be certain that it will be adopted before 26 September 2017, the date of expiry of the contested decision, or indeed at a later date.

106. The other arguments put forward by the Slovak Republic and by Hungary are not such as to alter my assessment. Thus, the fact that the contested decision may be adjusted according to circumstances is not inconsistent with its provisional nature, nor is the possibility, provided for in Article 4(5), that the contested decision may be extended for a maximum period of 12 months.[43]

107. It follows from the foregoing that the first part of the Slovak Republic's fifth plea and Hungary's second plea must be rejected as unfounded.

3. *The second part of the Slovak Republic's fifth plea, alleging that the contested decision does not satisfy the conditions for the application of Article 78(3) TFEU*

108. The Slovak Republic contends in three aspects that the contested decision does not satisfy the condition for the application of Article 78(3) TFEU, namely that the Member State benefiting from the provisional measures must be confronted by "an emergency situation characterised by a sudden inflow of nationals of third countries".

109. In the first place, according to the Slovak Republic, the inflow of nationals of third countries into Italy and Greece at the time of the

---

[43] Article 4(5) of the contested decision envisages the possibility of an extension by up to 12 months in the specific context of the mechanism for the partial suspension of the resettlement obligations laid down in that provision. However, the mechanism can no longer be triggered and the extension is envisaged for the only Member State (the Republic of Austria) to have benefited from it only until 11 March 2017. The contested decision will therefore definitively expire on 26 September 2017.

adoption of the contested decision or immediately before its adoption was reasonably foreseeable and cannot therefore be described as "sudden". The statistics for 2013-14 and the first months of 2015 indicate that the number of nationals of third countries heading for Italy and Greece had increased continuously and that, from the period 2013-14, that increase was considerable. In addition, so far as Italy is concerned, current data for 2015 indicate rather a year-on-year drop in the number of migrants.

110. To my mind that argument cannot succeed.

111. I shall begin by pointing out, generally, and by reference to the "Annual Brief 2015" of Frontex, that in 2015 the number of irregular entries by nationals of third countries at the external borders of the Union reached more than 1.8 million, whereas that number was 285 532 in 2014, representing an increase of 546%. As the main points of entry of those nationals into the Union, Greece and Italy were exposed to a particularly intense migration pressure.

112. Article 78(3) TFEU provides a specific legal basis in order to respond to the emergency situations in migration matters with which one or more Member States are confronted, by providing for the adoption of provisional measures, which, as the Commission observed in its proposal for a decision, are "exceptional in nature", in that "they can only be triggered when a certain threshold of urgency and severity of the problems created in the Member States(s)' asylum system(s) by a sudden inflow of nationals of third countries is met".[44]

113. Like the Council and the interveners which have submitted observations in its support, I observe that the huge extent of the increase of the inflow of nationals of third countries in 2015 and, in particular, in July and August of that year, is an objective fact reflected by the Frontex data mentioned in recital 13 of the contested decision. Those data show, for Italy, that there were 42 356 irregular border crossings in July and August 2015, an increase of 20% over May and June 2015. As regards Greece, that figure reached 137 000 during July and August 2015, an increase of 250%.

114. As indicated in recital 13 of the contested decision, the Council took into account the fact that a large part of those migrants were, owing to their nationality, likely to be granted international protection.

115. Furthermore, it follows from recital 14 of the contested decision that, according to Eurostat and European Asylum Support Office (EASO) figures, between January and July 2015, a steep increase was

---

[44] See that proposal, p. 1.

observed in the number of persons who applied for international protection in Italy and Greece, which fully confirms the finding that there was an exponential increase in the pressure on the asylum systems of the Italian Republic and the Hellenic Republic.

116. I would add that it follows from recital 16 of the contested decision that the Council also took into account the fact that the emergency situation affecting the Italian Republic and the Hellenic Republic would in all likelihood continue owing to instability and conflicts in the immediate neighbourhood of those two Member States. Evidence of constant pressure on the asylum systems of the Italian Republic and the Hellenic Republic, contributing to the constant undermining of those systems, made it all the more necessary for the Union to adopt an immediate response, in the form of provisional measures adopted on the basis of Article 78(3) TFEU, to an emergency situation characterised by a sudden and massive inflow of nationals of third countries into the territory of those Member States.[45]

117. The suddenness of the inflow of nationals of third countries is thus apparent from objective data. Those data highlight a phenomenon of a rapid increase in the number of nationals of third countries arriving in Italy and Greece over a brief period. The inability of those two Member States to cope with that phenomenon characterises the existence of an emergency situation which the contested decision is intended to address.

118. Whether that inflow of nationals of third countries was or was not foreseeable, what matters in order to justify the use of Article 78(3) TFEU is that such an inflow, by its rapidity and degree, made an immediate reaction on the part of the Union, by the adoption of provisional measures to relieve the considerable pressure then being applied to the Italian and Greek asylum systems indispensable, as indicated in recital 26 of the contested decision.

119. The fact that the tendency for the number of nationals of third countries arriving irregularly in Italy and Greece to increase became apparent before 2015 is also immaterial. As I have already stated, what matters is the finding that there was a sudden increase in that number,

---

[45] See, along the same lines, the Proposal for a Decision, in which the Commission states that "Italy's and Greece's geographical situation, with the ongoing conflicts in the region of their immediate neighbourhood still makes them more vulnerable than the other Member States in the immediate future with unprecedented flows of migrants expected to continue to reach their territories. These external factors of increased migratory pressure add to the existing structural shortcomings in their asylum systems, putting further into question their ability to deal in an adequate manner with this situation of high pressure" (p. 3).

as shown by the objective data referred to above, the accuracy of which is not disputed by the applicants.

120. In the second place, the Slovak Republic maintains that Article 78(3) TFEU means that the Member State is confronted with an emergency situation which is specifically attributable to a sudden inflow of nationals of third countries, which is clear from the use of the word "characterised". However, the Slovak Republic observes that, at least in the case of the Hellenic Republic, that causal link does not seem to exist. In fact, it is established that the Greek (and also the Italian) asylum and migration system has long been confronted with significant problems without there being any direct causal link with the migration phenomenon characteristic of the period during which the contested decision was adopted.

121. To my mind, that argument must be rejected.

122. Admittedly, as the Council observes, there is a discrepancy between the language versions of Article 78(3) TFEU, in that, in 15 versions, the word "characterised" is used, while in nine versions the word "caused" appears. In both cases, however, the condition that there must be a close relationship between the emergency situation requiring the adoption of provisional measures and the sudden inflow of nationals of third countries is expressed. However, as is apparent from recitals 13 and 26 of the contested decision, it was indeed the sudden inflow of nationals of third countries during 2015, and in particular in July and August 2015, that contributed to unbearable pressure, characteristic of an emergency situation, being placed on the Italian and Greek asylum systems.

123. It is immaterial, in that regard, that the Italian and Greek asylum systems had already been weakened. As the Council correctly observes, it is likely that the strong pressure experienced by the Italian and Greek asylum systems would have seriously disrupted any asylum system, even one not suffering from structural weaknesses.

124. In the third place, according to the Slovak Republic, the contested decision could not be adopted on the basis of Article 78(3) TFEU, since it was intended to resolve not an existing or imminent emergency situation affecting the Italian Republic and the Hellenic Republic, but, at least in part, hypothetical future situations which, at the time of the adoption of the contested decision, could not have been claimed to be sufficiently likely to arise.

125. The Slovak Republic maintains that the period of application, of two, or indeed three years, of the contested decision is too long for it to be possible to assert that, throughout that period, the measures adopted would respond to the emergency situation, whether present

or imminent, affecting the Italian Republic and the Hellenic Republic. Thus, during that period, the emergency situation may no longer exist in those Member States. Furthermore, the relocation mechanism for the reserve of 54 000 additional persons provided for in Article 4(3) of the contested decision, read with Article 4(1)(c) of that decision, is intended to address wholly hypothetical situations in other Member States.

126. The Republic of Poland supports that point of view and maintains that Article 78(3) TFEU refers to a pre-existing and current crisis situation which requires the adoption of immediate corrective measures and not, as the contested decision does, to crisis situations that may arise in the future but the incidence, nature and degree of which are uncertain or difficult to foresee.

127. Unlike the Slovak Republic and the Republic of Poland, I consider that the fact that the contested decision refers to future events or situations does not mean that it is incompatible with Article 78(3) TFEU.

128. In fact, I would recall that it is apparent from recitals 13 and 26 of the contested decision that the adoption of that decision is primarily inspired by the need to respond to an emergency situation that manifested itself in particular in July and August 2015 in Italy and Greece. The fact that the contested decision contains a number of provisions that enable it to be adapted to developments in that situation must not conceal the fact that the decision is intended to resolve a problem that arose before it was adopted.

129. Be that as it may, I consider that Article 78(3) TFEU does not preclude the contested decision from containing several provisions that enable it to be adapted to developments in migration flows. That provision confers a wide discretion on the Council in the choice of the measures to be taken in order to provide an adequate response to an emergency situation characterised by the sudden inflow of nationals of third countries. As such an emergency situation is capable of continuing, developing and affecting other Member States, the Council was correct to envisage the possibility of adapting its action and, in particular, the characteristics and procedures of the application of the temporary relocation mechanism.

130. Thus, the need to respond to an emergency situation by means of provisional measures, expressed by the legal basis that is Article 78(3) TFEU, does not preclude either the adaptation of a measure such as the contested decision to the evolution of the situation or the adoption by the Council of implementing acts. Responding to the emergency does not exclude the developing and adapted nature of the response, provided that it retains its provisional nature.

131. From that aspect, provisions such as the second subparagraph of Article 1(2) and Article 4(3) of the contested decision, under which the Commission may submit proposals to the Council if it considers that an adaptation of the relocation mechanism is justified by the evolution of the situation on the ground or that a Member State is confronted with an emergency situation characterised by a sudden inflow of nationals of third countries due to a sharp shift of migration flows, are perfectly compatible with Article 78(3) TFEU.

132. The Council was also entitled, without thereby affecting the legality of the contested decision, to reproduce, in the first sentence of Article 9 of that decision, the circumstances in which provisional measures, distinct from the contested decision, may be taken on the basis of Article 78(3) TFEU and the consequences that may ensue as regards the application of the contested decision.

133. Last, as the Council correctly observes, the fact that provision is made in the contested decision for the adoption of implementing measures[46] and that the adoption of such measures is to depend on future events or situations cannot render the contested decision illegal. As is apparent from recital 28 of the contested decision, the exercise by the Council of such implementing powers is necessary in order to enable the temporary relocation mechanism to be adapted quickly to rapidly evolving situations.

134. The second part of the Slovak Republic's fifth plea is therefore unfounded.

135. It follows from the foregoing that the pleas put forward by the Slovak Republic and by Hungary, alleging that Article 78(3) TFEU is inadequate as a legal basis for the adoption of the contested decision, should all be rejected as unfounded.

C. *The pleas relating to the regularity of the procedure leading to the adoption of the contested decision and alleged breach of essential procedural requirements*

1. *The Slovak Republic's first plea and Hungary's seventh plea, alleging infringement of Article 68 TFEU*

136. The Slovak Republic and Hungary maintain that, since the contested decision exceeds the guidance defined by the European Council in its conclusions of 25 and 26 June 2015, according to

---

[46] See Article 4(2), (4) and (6), and Article 11(2) of the contested decision.

which the distribution of the persons relocated was to be decided "by consensus" in a manner "reflecting the specific situations of Member States",[47] the Council infringed Article 68 TFEU and breached the essential procedural requirements.

137. In the words of Article 15(1) TEU, "the European Council shall provide the Union with the necessary impetus for its development and shall define the general political directions and priorities thereof. It shall not exercise legislative functions".

138. Under Article 68 TFEU, "the European Council shall define the strategic guidelines for legislative and operational planning within the area of freedom, security and justice".

139. I observe that, although the conclusions of the European Council of 25 and 26 June 2015 do in fact contain a provision to the effect that the Member States should decide "by consensus" on the distribution of persons in clear need of international protection, and do so in a manner "reflecting the specific situations of Member States",[48] that provision relates to the temporary and exceptional relocation, over two years, from Italy and Greece, of 40 000 persons. In fact, that measure for the relocation of 40 000 persons was the subject matter of Decision 2015/1523, which therefore specifically responds to the guidance given by the European Council.

140. According to the Slovak Republic and Hungary, a new emergency relocation measure, such as that provided for in the contested decision, could not be proposed, and a fortiori could not be adopted, unless the European Council had first taken a position in that sense.

141. The Slovak Republic thus contends that, by adopting the contested decision without the mandate resulting from the conclusions of the European Council of 25 and 26 June 2015 being amended or extended, the Council encroached on the functions and powers of the European Council. It therefore infringed Article 68 TFEU and Article 13(2) TEU and breached the principle of institutional balance. In addition, in Hungary's submission, Article 15 TEU should be interpreted as meaning that the conclusions of the European Council are binding on the institutions of the Union.

142. Pursuant to Article 13(2) TEU, "each institution shall act within the limits of the powers conferred on it in the Treaties, and in conformity with the procedures, conditions and objectives set out in them". That provision reflects the principle of institutional balance,

---

[47] See point 4(b) of those conclusions.
[48] Ibid.

characteristic of the institutional structure of the Union, which requires that each of the institutions must exercise its powers with due regard for the powers of the other institutions.[49]

143. To my mind, neither the Commission nor the Council exceeded the powers conferred on them, respectively, by Article 78(3) TFEU by proposing and then adopting the contested decision.

144. In particular, the conclusions of the European Council of 25 and 26 June 2015 cannot have the effect of prohibiting the Commission from proposing, and then the Council from adopting, a provisional binding mechanism for the relocation of applicants for international protection that supplements Decision 2015/1523.

145. I would point out, in that regard, that the provisional measures that can be adopted by the Council on the basis of Article 78(3) TFEU are adopted on a proposal from the Commission. That power to initiate legislation, conferred on the Commission generally by Article 17(2) TEU, could be called in question if it were accepted that it depended on the prior adoption of conclusions by the European Council. That applies a fortiori when a provision of the Treaty, such as Article 78(3) TFEU, confers on the Commission the power to propose an immediate response by the Union to an emergency situation. In the exercise of its power of initiative, the Commission, which, in accordance with Article 17(1) TEU, "shall promote the general interest of the Union and take appropriate initiatives to that end", must be able to determine the subject matter, objective and content of its proposal.[50]

146. As the Italian Republic and Grand Duchy of Luxembourg submit, in essence, the contested decision addresses a new emergency situation that arose in July and August 2015. The adoption of a temporary mechanism for the relocation of 120 000 applicants for international protection, on the basis of Article 78(3) TFEU, did not need to be specifically referred to in advance in conclusions of the European Council. Apart from the fact that such a requirement is not apparent from the wording of that provision, it would have the effect of destroying the ability to respond that the institutions of the Union must demonstrate when Member States are faced with an emergency situation.

---

[49] See, in particular, judgment of 14 April 2015, *Council* v. *Commission* (C-409/13, EU: C:2015:217, paragraph 64 and the case law cited).

[50] See, to that effect, judgment of 14 April 2015, *Council* v. *Commission* (C-409/13, EU: C:2015:217, paragraph 70). In my view, that case law must also apply to non-legislative acts.

147. Nor must the conclusions of the European Council of 25 and 26 June 2015 be construed as having effects going beyond the adoption of the measure having the specific object of giving effect to those conclusions, namely Decision 2015/1523, which concerns the voluntary relocation of 40 000 persons.

148. In any event, even on the view that Decision 2015/1523 did not exhaust the recommendations made in the conclusions of the European Council of 25 and 26 June 2015, I do not detect in the steps taken by the Commission and the Council, on the basis of Article 78(3) TFEU, for the purpose of the adoption of the contested decision, any fundamental variation from the guidance defined by the European Council in its conclusions of 25 and 26 June 2015.

149. In fact, the European Council states, in point 2 of its conclusions, that work should be taken forward "further to the Commission's European Agenda on Migration". That agenda provides for the activation of the emergency mechanism provided for in Article 78(3) TFEU. In addition, the European Council calls, in point 3 of those conclusions, for "wider efforts" to be deployed "to better contain the growing flows of illegal migration", in particular by developing the aspect relating to relocation. The Commission and the Council therefore followed the line of action recommended by the European Council by proposing and then adopting the contested decision on the basis of Article 78(3) TFEU.

150. Last, insofar as the basis of the challenge mounted by the Slovak Republic and by Hungary is that the contested decision was adopted by a qualified majority, it should be observed that, since Article 78(3) TFEU allows the Council to adopt measures by a qualified majority, the European Council cannot, in the absence of a provision to the contrary in the Treaty, alter that voting rule by imposing on the Council a rule requiring a unanimous vote. It is clear from the Court's case law that, as the rules regarding the manner in which the EU institutions of the Union arrive at their decisions are laid down in the Treaties and are not within the discretion of the Member States or the institutions themselves, the Treaties alone may, in particular cases, empower an institution to amend a decision-making procedure established by the Treaties.[51]

151. It follows from the foregoing that the Slovak Republic's first plea and Hungary's seventh plea must be rejected as unfounded.

---

[51] See, in particular, judgment of 10 September 2015, *Parliament* v. *Council*, C-363/14, EU: C:2015:579, paragraph 43 and the case law cited.

2. The third part of the Slovak Republic's third plea and the first part of its fourth plea, and Hungary's fifth plea, alleging breach of essential procedural requirements in that the Council did not comply with the obligation to consult the Parliament laid down in Article 78(3) TFEU

152. The Slovak Republic and Hungary claim that, since the Council made substantial amendments to the Commission's initial proposal and adopted the contested decision without again consulting the Parliament, it breached the essential procedural requirements laid down in Article 78(3) TFEU, and that the contested decision should therefore be annulled. The Slovak Republic maintains that, in doing so, the Council also infringed Article 10(1) and (2) TEU and Article 13(2) TEU and breached the principles of representative democracy, institutional balance and sound administration.

153. In that regard, the Slovak Republic and Hungary mention the following substantial amendments.

154. Both Member States observe that, in the contested decision, Hungary is no longer among the Member States that benefit from the relocation mechanism, but is among the Member States of relocation, which entailed the deletion of Annex III to the initial proposal and Hungary's inclusion in Annexes I and II to the contested decision.

155. The fundamental amendment lies in the fact that, although the total number of 120 000 persons remained the same, the number of 54 000 persons included in that total number which, as initially envisaged, related to persons to be relocated from Hungary, was transformed into a "reserve" which had not been envisaged in the Commission's initial proposal. Consequently, the structure and a number of essential elements of that proposal were profoundly altered, such as the title and its scope *ratione personae*, the list of beneficiary Member States and Member States of relocation and the number of persons to be relocated in each of the Member States. That gave rise to amendments incorporated in Articles 1 and 3 and also in Article 4(1)(c) of the contested decision.

156. The Slovak Republic mentions other amendments to the Commission's initial proposal. It thus states that, contrary to the situation in that proposal, the contested decision provides, in Article 4(3), that other Member States may benefit from the relocation mechanism if they satisfy the conditions set out in that provision. Furthermore, Article 13(3) of the contested decision provides that that decision is to apply retroactively to applicants having arrived from

24 March 2015 onwards, or a period of six months preceding the adoption of the decision, whereas in its initial proposal the Commission had limited that retroactive effect to one month.

157. Likewise, Article 4(5) and (6) of the contested decision contains substantial amendments by comparison with the Commission's initial proposal as regards the arrangements for the temporary suspension of a Member State's participation in the relocation process. The Slovak Republic claims that the contested decision provides that the power to decide on such suspension is vested in the Council, whereas the Commission had proposed that that power be entrusted to it. The contested decision also limits the suspension to 30% of applicants allocated to the Member State concerned, whereas the Commission's initial proposal did not include such a restriction. In addition, whereas the Commission's initial proposal provided that a Member State whose participation was suspended would be required to pay financial compensation, such an obligation does not appear in the text of the contested decision.

158. Last, the Slovak Republic observes that, whereas recital 25 of the Commission's initial proposal indicated the distribution key on the basis of which the figures relating to the persons to be relocated to each Member State had been determined, the contested decision does not mention such a key and therefore does not disclose the criteria on which the allocations to each Member State were made.

159. The applicants take issue with the Council for having failed to consult the Parliament again after making those fundamental amendments, even though, in its resolution of 17 September 2015, the Parliament had requested the Council to consult it again if it intended to substantially amend the Commission's proposal.

160. Although the Presidency of the Union regularly informed the Parliament, in particular the Parliament's Civil Liberties, Justice and Home Affairs Committee ("the LIBE Committee"), of how the Council's dossier was progressing, that cannot replace a formal resolution of the Parliament adopted in plenary session.

161. Hungary refers to two letters sent by the President of the Parliament's Legal Affairs Committee to the President of the Parliament, in which it is stated, in particular, that that committee had also reached the conclusion that the Council had substantially amended the Commission's initial proposal by removing Hungary from the group of beneficiary Member States and that the Parliament should therefore have been consulted again. Nonetheless, for political reasons, that committee recommended that the Parliament should not intervene in the present cases before the Court.

162. The Council objected to those two letters being used in these proceedings and, in particular, requested the Court to adopt a measure of inquiry in order to verify their authenticity. In my view, those two letters should not be taken into account by the Court, which is ultimately responsible, independently of what is stated in those letters, to decide whether the Council fulfilled its obligation to consult the Parliament in accordance with the requirements of Article 78(3) TFEU.

163. The Court has held that "due consultation of the Parliament in the cases provided for by the Treaty constitutes an essential formal requirement breach of which renders the measure concerned void".[52] I would also point out that, according to the settled case law of the Court, "the requirement to consult the . . . Parliament . . . in the cases provided for by the Treaty, means that it must be freshly consulted whenever the text finally adopted, taken as a whole, differs in essence from the text on which the Parliament has already been consulted, except in cases in which the amendments substantially correspond to the wishes of the Parliament itself".[53]

164. It is therefore necessary to examine whether the amendments to which the applicants refer concern the very essence of the text considered as a whole.

165. In that regard, it must be stated that the Commission's initial proposal, like the amended proposal, provided, in order to cope with an emergency situation characterised by a sudden inflow of nationals of third countries, for a temporary mechanism for the relocation of 120 000 persons, providing, in a binding manner, for the distribution of those persons among the Member States over a specific period. Hungary's withdrawal from the Member States benefiting from that mechanism does indeed constitute a legal amendment, but does not affect the fundamental characteristics of that mechanism.

166. Following Hungary's withdrawal, the Commission's initial proposal necessarily received a number of amendments, in particular as regards the reserve of 54 000 persons. However, those adjustments do not affect the fundamental structure of the contested decision. Furthermore, the other amendments to which the Slovak Republic refers do not strike me as being of such a kind as to affect the hard core of the initial proposal, as I have previously emphasised.

---

[52] See, in particular, judgment of 10 June 1997, *Parliament* v. *Council* (C-392/95, EU: C:1997:289, paragraph 14 and the case law cited).
[53] See, in particular, judgment of 10 June 1997, *Parliament* v. *Council* (C-392/95, EU: C:1997:289, paragraph 15 and the case law cited).

167. All in all, the various amendments which the Commission made to its proposal did not therefore affect the very essence of the contested decision considered as a whole and therefore did not require a fresh consultation of the Parliament.

168. I would add that it may be asked why a fresh consultation of the Parliament should be necessary where the main amendment which the Council made to the Commission's initial proposal is not the result of a choice freely made by the Council but is limited to taking note of a new circumstance beyond its control which, moreover, it is required to take into account.

169. In this instance, it must be emphasised that the Council was not in a position to require Hungary to remain a beneficiary of the temporary relocation mechanism, as envisaged in the Commission's initial proposal. The Council could therefore only take note of Hungary's stated intention not to be included among the Member States for whose benefit that mechanism was to be applied.

170. Furthermore, unless consultation of the Parliament must be regarded as a purely formal step, the *raison d'être* of the consultation of the Parliament is to arrive, where appropriate, at amendments by the Council of the text submitted which will accord with the Parliament's intention. In the present case, however, the Council had no choice other than to take note of Hungary's withdrawal, by adjusting its decision to that circumstance beyond its control.

171. All in all, I consider that, in order to determine whether or not the Parliament should have been consulted again, a factor over which the Council has no control cannot be regarded as an essential element of legislation. What occurred in this instance is not the result of a political compromise, but the result of the refusal expressed by a Member State to benefit from a provisional measure adopted on the basis of Article 78(3) TFEU. While the Council may compel the Member States, on the basis of that provision, read in conjunction with Article 80 TFEU, to show solidarity and to accept their share of responsibility in order to cope with an emergency situation, it cannot in my view require a Member State to benefit from that solidarity.

172. In any event, even on the assumption that it might be considered that the text eventually adopted, considered as a whole, differs in essence from the text on the basis of which the Parliament adopted its legislative resolution of 17 September 2015, I consider that, having regard to the emergency circumstances in which a measure based on Article 78(3) TFEU, such as the contested decision, was adopted, the Parliament was duly consulted throughout the procedure,

concerning both the Commission's proposal and the amendments made thereto.

173. It is apparent from the observations submitted to the Court, in particular by the Council and the Grand Duchy of Luxembourg, that the Parliament, on the occasion of numerous formal and informal contacts, was informed by the Council of virtually all the amendments made to the initial text and that it had no objections to them.

174. More specifically, the Council states, without being contradicted, that on 14 September 2015 at 12 noon it decided to consult the Parliament concerning the Commission's proposal. On the same day the Secretary-General of the Council communicated, for the attention of the President of the Parliament, a formal consultation letter in which the Council undertook to keep the Parliament fully informed of developments in the case within the Council. On 16 September 2015, Mr Jean Asselborn, the Luxembourg Minister for Immigration and Asylum, President of the Council, attended the extraordinary plenary sitting of the Parliament. Addressing the Parliament, he presented the results of the meeting of the "Justice and Home Affairs" Council held on 14 September 2015. On that occasion, he announced that Hungary had stated that it refused to be regarded as a frontline Member State and to benefit from the solidarity mechanism, and also that, in spite of Hungary's withdrawal, the number of 120 000 persons to be relocated would be maintained.

175. As the Grand Duchy of Luxembourg correctly observes, the Parliament was therefore put in a position to take that circumstance into account when adopting its legislative resolution on 17 September 2015. It was therefore able to take note, at the stage of its formal consultation, of Hungary's withdrawal from the group of beneficiaries of the temporary mechanism for the relocation of 120 000 persons. If that new circumstance had seemed to the Parliament to stand in the way of the adoption of the contested decision, it would thus have been in a position to express its opinion in that regard.

176. The fact that the Parliament's legislative resolution of 17 September 2015 does not reflect Hungary's withdrawal and that no other resolution formalises the consultation of the Parliament on the amendments made to the Commission's proposal following that Member State's withdrawal is not in my view decisive.

177. I consider that the particular characteristics of the legal basis that is Article 78(3) TFEU argue in favour of relative flexibility when ascertaining whether the Parliament was duly consulted again following Hungary's withdrawal and the amendments of the initial text that are the consequence of that withdrawal.

178. I note, moreover, that the situation of urgency was fully taken into account by the Parliament in the context of its consultation. In fact, the Parliament's legislative resolution of 17 September 2015 was adopted according to the emergency procedure provided for in Article 154 of the Parliament's Rules of Procedure. It should also be observed that the Parliament highlighted, in that resolution, "the exceptional situation of urgency and the need to address the situation with no further delay".

179. Admittedly, in that resolution, the Parliament "asks the Council to consult the Parliament again if it intends to substantially amend the Commission proposal". However, I consider that, given the exceptional nature of the emergency situation and the requirement for rapidity in the adoption of a response to the migration crisis which was emphasised by the Parliament itself, there is no need to require that a new consultation was carried out in a strictly defined formal and procedural framework.

180. Furthermore, the Council provides information about the way in which the Parliament was duly informed between 17 September 2015, the date of its legislative resolution, and 22 September 2015, the date of the adoption of the contested decision.

181. Thus, within the framework of the informal contacts announced in the consultation letter, the Presidency of the Council prepared for the Parliament a consolidated version of the text of the proposal, containing all the changes made by the Council up to 21 September 2015 at 10 p.m. That text was communicated to the Parliament on 22 September 2015 at 9 a.m. On the same day, the LIBE Committee, which is undisputedly the Parliamentary Committee with competence in asylum matters, held a meeting during which the Presidency of the Council presented the text of the amended Commission proposal. In that regard, the Presidency of the Council was able to incorporate in its presentation the most recent amendments made to the text during the extraordinary meeting of the Committee of Permanent Representatives (Coreper) held on the same morning. The Parliament was also informed of the agenda of the meeting of the Council scheduled to take place at 2.30 p.m. on the same day, and also of the Presidency's intentions and the foreseeable development of the file during that meeting of the Council. Thereafter, the LIBE Committee discussed the text as thus amended, in preparation for the extraordinary meeting of the Council.

182. It follows from those elements that the Council closely involved the Parliament in the drafting of the contested decision. Given the situation of urgency, recognised and taken into account by

the Parliament itself, and the necessary flexibility that must guide the procedure in such a situation, it must be accepted that the Parliament was duly consulted, as required by Article 78(3) TFEU.

183. I therefore propose that the Court should reject the third part of the Slovak Republic's third plea and the first part of its fourth plea, and Hungary's fifth plea, as unfounded.

3. The second part of the Slovak Republic's fourth plea and Hungary's third plea, alleging breach of essential procedural requirements in that the Council did not act unanimously, contrary to Article 293(1) TFEU

184. The Slovak Republic and Hungary maintain that, in adopting the contested decision, the Council breached the essential procedural requirement prescribed in Article 293(1) TFEU, in that it amended the Commission's proposal without complying with the requirement for unanimity laid down in that provision. The Slovak Republic submits that, in so doing, the Council also infringed Article 13(2) TEU and breached the principles of institutional balance and sound administration.

185. According to the applicants, the requirement for unanimity laid down in Article 293(1) TFEU applies to any amendment of the Commission's proposal, including where there is a minor amendment, and independently of whether the Commission has explicitly or implicitly accepted the amendments made to its proposal during the discussions within the Council.

186. The applicants also claim that there is nothing to indicate that, during the procedure leading to the adoption of the contested decision, the Commission withdrew its proposal and submitted a new proposal drafted in identical terms to those of the text that subsequently became the contested decision. On the contrary, it follows from the minutes of the Council's sitting of 22 September 2015 that the Commission neither lodged a new proposal nor made a preliminary declaration concerning the amended proposal as finally adopted by the Council. Yet the Commission is required to adhere actively and explicitly to the amendments concerned before it can be considered to have altered its proposal within the meaning of Article 293(2) TFEU. Furthermore, the present case is different from that at issue in the judgment of 5 October 1994, *Germany* v. *Council.*[54]

---

[54] C-280/93, EU:C:1994:367.

187. Last, the applicants deny that the two Members of the Commission who were present at the various meetings held within the Council were duly authorised by the College of Commissioners to approve the text as finally adopted by the Council.

188. I do not share the position supported by the applicants.

189. As I have previously stated, the FEU Treaty confers on the Commission a power of legislative initiative. Article 293(1) TFEU allows that power to be guaranteed insofar as it provides that, except in the cases referred to in the provisions of the FEU Treaty mentioned by it, where, pursuant to the Treaties, the Council acts on a proposal from the Commission, it may amend that proposal only by acting unanimously.[55]

190. Furthermore, Article 293(2) TFEU states that "as long as the Council has not acted, the Commission may alter its proposal at any time during the procedures leading to the adoption of a Union act".

191. In the context of the procedure leading to the adoption of the contested decision, I consider that nothing was done to undermine the Commission's power of initiative, which Article 293 TFEU is intended to preserve. I observe, moreover, that the Commission itself has asserted, in the context of the present proceedings, that its institutional powers were respected.

192. It follows from the explanations provided to the Court by the Commission that the Commission set itself the priority objective, at its meeting of 16 September 2015, of having the Council adopt, during its sitting on 22 September 2015, a binding and immediately applicable decision concerning the relocation of 120 000 persons in clear need of international protection. In order to achieve that priority objective, Mr Frans Timmermans, First Vice-President of the Commission, and Mr Dimitris Avramopoulos, the Member of the Commission responsible for migration, home affairs and citizenship, were, according to the information supplied by the Commission, given the necessary margin of discretion in respect of the other aspects of the proposal.

193. As the Commission states, Article 13 of its Rules of Procedure permits it to "instruct one or more of its Members to adopt, with the agreement of the President, the definitive text of any instrument or of any proposal to be presented to the other institutions, the substance of which has already been determined in discussion". I observe that the applicants adduce no evidence to support their assertions that the two Members of the Commission were not duly authorised by the College

---

[55] See judgment of 14 April 2015, *Council* v. *Commission* (C-409/13, EU:C:2015:217, paragraphs 71 and 72).

of Commissioners to approve, on behalf of the Commission, the amendments to the initial proposal. In those circumstances, and having regard to the explanations provided by the Commission, it may in my view be presumed that the First Vice-President of the Commission and the Commissioner responsible for asylum and immigration were duly authorised by the College of Commissioners to take part in full, on behalf of the Commission, in the procedure that led to the adoption of the contested decision.

194. The Commission's power of initiative was preserved in the context of the procedure that led to the adoption of the contested decision, insofar as it must be considered that the Commission, in accordance with the possibility afforded by Article 293(2) TFEU, amended its proposal.

195. It should be emphasised, in that regard, that the Court attaches no importance to the form taken by the amended proposal. It has held that "such amended proposals are part of the [Union] legislative process, which is characterised by a certain flexibility, necessary for achieving a convergence of views between the institutions".[56]

196. The need to accept a certain flexibility in the decision-making process in order to facilitate the search for political compromises is all the more acute in a context of urgency such as that which characterises the implementation of Article 78(3) TFEU.

197. It follows that what matters, in order to ensure that the Commission's power of initiative has been respected, is to ascertain whether the Commission gave its consent to the amendments made to its proposal. As the Council correctly observes, it follows from a reading of the combined provisions of Article 293(1) and (2) TFEU that the requirement for a unanimous vote by the Council applies only in a situation where the Commission objects to an amendment of its proposal.

198. However, it is apparent from the file that the First Vice-President of the Commission and the Member of the Commission responsible for asylum and immigration actively and continuously participated in seeking a political compromise within the Council. To that end, those two Members of the Commission accepted the Council's amendments to the initial proposal. At the time of acting, the Council therefore had before it a Commission proposal amended in accordance with the political compromise accepted by two Members of

---

[56] See, in particular, judgment of 5 October 1994, *Germany* v. *Council* (C-280/93, EU: C:1994:367, paragraph 36 and the case law cited).

the Commission, duly authorised to that effect by the Commission, in accordance with the requirements of Article 293(2) TFEU.[57]

199. In the light of the foregoing, I propose that the Court should reject the second part of the Slovak Republic's fourth plea and Hungary's third plea as unfounded.

4. *The second part of the Slovak Republic's third plea and Hungary's fourth plea, alleging breach of essential procedural requirements, in that the right of the national parliaments to issue an opinion in accordance with Protocol (No 1) and Protocol (No 2) was not respected*

200. The Slovak Republic, by way of alternative plea, and Hungary claim that, at the time of the adoption of the contested decision, the right of the national parliaments to issue an opinion on any draft proposal for a legislative act, as provided for in Protocol (No 1) and Protocol (No 2), was not respected.

201. Since, in the applicants' submission, the contested decision constitutes, by its content, a legislative act, insofar as it amends legislative acts of the Union, that decision ought to have been adopted by the legislative procedure, so that the right of the national parliaments to issue an opinion on the proposal for that act had to be respected. Communication of the draft to the national parliaments for their information, as was done on 13 September 2015, was therefore not sufficient. In any event, as the draft was adopted by the Council, in its amended version, on 22 September 2015, the eight-week period within which the national parliaments are to issue an opinion under Article 4 of Protocol (No 1) and Article 6 of Protocol (No 2) was not observed.

202. In addition, the exception in urgent cases as provided for in Article 4 of Protocol (No 1), which enables the eight-week period to be shortened, is not applicable since no document issued by the Council refers to the need that, owing to the urgent nature of the case, the national parliaments must issue their opinions within a shorter period.

203. Like the Council, I consider that, since, as I have previously demonstrated, the contested decision is a non-legislative act, it was not subject to the requirements linked with the participation of the national parliaments which are attached to the adoption of a legislative act, as provided for in Protocol (No 1) and Protocol (No 2).

[57] See, along the same lines, judgment of 11 September 2003, *Austria* v. *Council* (C-445/00, EU:C:2003:445, paragraphs 16 and 17 and also paragraphs 44 to 47).

204. The second part of the Slovak Republic's third plea and Hungary's fourth plea must therefore be rejected as unfounded.

5. *The first part of the Slovak Republic's third plea, alleging breach of essential procedural requirements, in that the Council failed to fulfil the requirement that the deliberations and the vote within the Council be held in public*

205. The Slovak Republic maintains, in the alternative, that if the Court should find that the contested decision was adopted according to a legislative procedure and is therefore a legislative act, it follows that the Council breached an essential procedural requirement by adopting the contested decision in private in the exercise of its non-legislative activities, since Article 16(8) TEU and Article 15(2) TFEU provide that the meetings of the Council are to be held in public when it considers and votes on a draft legislative act.

206. I consider, as does the Council, that since, as I have already demonstrated, the contested decision is a non-legislative act, that decision is not subject to the conditions attached to the adoption of a legislative act, including the requirement that the Council deliberate and vote in public.

207. The first part of the Slovak Republic's third plea must therefore be rejected as unfounded.

6. *Hungary's sixth plea, alleging breach of essential procedural requirements in that, when adopting the contested decision, the Council did not comply with the language rules of Union law*

208. Hungary claims that the Council breached an essential procedural requirement in that it adopted the contested decision although the text of the decision put to the vote was not available in all the official languages of the Union.

209. More specifically, the Council did not comply with the language rules of Union law and, in particular, with Article 14(1) of its Rules of Procedure,[58] since the texts representing the successive amendments to the Commission's initial proposal, including the text of the contested decision as finally adopted by the Council, were distributed to the delegations of the Member States only in English.

---

[58] Council Decision 2009/937/EU of 1 December 2009 adopting the Council's Rules of Procedure (OJ 2009 L 325, p. 35).

210. The Slovak Republic raised the same plea in its reply. To my mind, in the context of the action brought by that Member State, that plea must be considered to be out of time and therefore inadmissible.

211. Article 14 of the Rules of Procedure of the Council, entitled "Deliberations and decisions on the basis of documents and drafts drawn up in the languages provided for by the language rules in force", provides:

1. Except as otherwise decided unanimously by the Council on grounds of urgency, the Council shall deliberate and take decisions only on the basis of documents and drafts drawn up in the languages specified in the rules in force governing languages.

2. Any member of the Council may oppose discussion if the texts of any proposed amendments are not drawn up in such of the languages referred to in paragraph 1 as he or she may specify.

212. The Council maintains that that provision of its Rules of Procedure must be understood as meaning that, although paragraph 1 requires that the documents and drafts that constitute the "basis" of the Council's deliberations, in this instance the Commission's initial proposal, be made available to the Member States in all the official languages of the Union, paragraph 2 of that provision lays down a simplified procedure for amendments, which do not necessarily have to be available in all the official languages of the Union. Only where a Member State objects does the language version indicated by that Member State also have to be submitted to the Council before it can continue to deliberate.

213. I consider that the explanation thus provided by the Council of the way in which Article 14 of its Rules of Procedure must be understood[59] is convincing, in that it constitutes a balanced and flexible approach that can ensure the effectiveness of the Council's works, especially in the context of the urgency that characterises the provisional measures adopted on the basis of Article 78(3) TFEU. Furthermore, that explanation coincides with the conduct of the procedure that led to the adoption of the contested decision.

214. In the present case, as the Council states, without being contradicted, the Commission made its proposal for a decision available to all the delegations of the Member States in all the official languages

---

[59] It should be emphasised that the explanation provided by the Council in the context of these proceedings is consistent with its comments on its Rules of Procedure: "Article 14(2) [of the Council's Rules of Procedure] enables any member of the Council to oppose discussion if the text of any proposed amendments is not drawn up in all the official languages" (see Comments on the Council's Rules of Procedure, pp. 48 and 49).

of the Union. Furthermore, the Council indicates, without being challenged by the applicants, that all the amendments requested orally by various Member States, set out in working documents drafted in English and distributed to the delegations, were read by the President of the Council and simultaneously interpreted into all the official languages of the Union. According to the Council, no Member State raised any objection under Article 14(2) of the Rules of Procedure of the Council.

215. Last, and in any event, as the Council correctly observes, it follows from the case law of the Court that, even on the assumption that, in adopting the contested decision, the Council infringed Article 14 of its Rules of Procedure, a procedural irregularity of that nature could entail annulment of the act ultimately adopted only if, were it not for that irregularity, the procedure could have led to a different result.[60] In fact, Hungary has put forward no material of such a kind as to show that, if the amendments to the Commission's initial proposal had been drawn up in all the official languages of the Union, the procedure could have led to a different result.

216. Consequently, Hungary's sixth plea must be rejected as unfounded.

217. It therefore follows from the examination of the pleas in law put forward by the Slovak Republic and by Hungary relating to the legality of the procedure leading to the adoption of the contested decision and alleging breach of essential procedural requirements that those pleas must all be rejected as unfounded.

D. The substantive pleas

1. The Slovak Republic's 6th plea and Hungary's 9th and 10th pleas, alleging breach of the principle of proportionality

218. Both the Slovak Republic and Hungary maintain, relying on arguments that differ on certain points, that the contested decision breaches the principle of proportionality.

219. According to settled case law, the principle of proportionality requires that acts of the EU institutions be appropriate for attaining the legitimate objectives pursued by the legislation at issue and do not exceed the limits of what is necessary in order to achieve those object-ives; when there is a choice between several appropriate measures,

---

[60] See, in particular, judgment of 25 October 2005, *Germany and Denmark* v. *Commission* (C-465/02 and C-466/02, EU:C:2005:636, paragraph 37).

recourse must be had to the least onerous, and the disadvantages caused must not be disproportionate to the aims pursued.[61]

220. With regard to judicial review of observance of that principle, it has consistently been held that the institutions of the Union must be allowed a broad discretion in the areas which entail political choices on their part and in which they are called upon to undertake complex assessments. In such situations, the legality of a measure adopted in one of those areas can be affected only if the measure is manifestly inappropriate having regard to the objective which the competent institutions are seeking to pursue.[62]

221. There is no doubt in my mind that that case law is applicable in the present case, insofar as the contested decision reflects the political choices made by the Council in order to address an emergency situation, and the response which it thus provided to the phenomenon of a sudden inflow of nationals of third countries to the territory of the Union is the result of complex assessments for which the Court cannot substitute itself.

222. I recall that the objective pursued by the contested decision is, in accordance with Article 1(1) of that decision, read with recitals 12 and 26, to support the Italian Republic and the Hellenic Republic in better coping with an emergency situation characterised by a sudden inflow of nationals of third countries to their territories, by adopting provisional measures in the area of international protection in order to relieve the considerable asylum pressure on those two Member States.

223. Only if the contested decision were found to be manifestly inappropriate for attaining the objective which it pursues, or to exceed the limits of what is necessary to attain that objective, could that decision be annulled.

224. It is now necessary to examine the content of the pleas whereby the Slovak Republic and Hungary seek to challenge the proportionality of the contested decision.

(a) The appropriateness of the contested decision for attaining the objective which it pursues

225. The Slovak Republic, supported by the Republic of Poland, claims that the contested decision is not appropriate for attaining the objective which it pursues, since the pressure on the Italian and Greek

---

[61] See, in particular, judgment of 4 May 2016, *Poland* v. *Parliament and Council* (C-358/14, EU:C:2016:323, paragraph 78 and the case law cited).

[62] See, in particular, to that effect, judgments of 4 May 2016, *Poland* v. *Parliament and Council* (C-358/14, EU:C:2016:323, paragraph 79 and the case law cited), and of 9 June 2016, *Pesce and Others* (C-78/16 and C-79/16, EU:C:2016:428, paragraph 49 and the case law cited).

asylum systems is the consequence of the serious structural weaknesses in those systems in terms of lack of reception capacity and of capacity to process applications for international protection. The temporary relocation mechanism provided for in the contested decision is not capable of redressing such structural defects.

226. I do not agree with that argument.

227. I consider that by removing the processing of numerous applications for international protection from the competence of the Italian Republic and the Hellenic Republic, the contested decision automatically helps to relieve the considerable pressure on the asylum systems of those two Member States following the migration crisis in the summer of 2015. The fact that the main objective of the contested decision is not to redress the structural defects in those asylum systems cannot obscure that finding.

228. Moreover, it should be emphasised that the contested decision most certainly does not ignore the problem of improving the functioning of the asylum systems of the Italian Republic and the Hellenic Republic.

229. In fact, the contested decision provides, in Article 8(1), that "[the Italian Republic and the Hellenic Republic] shall, bearing in mind the obligations set out in Article 8(1) of Decision . . . 2015/1523, and by 26 October 2015, notify to the Council and the Commission an updated roadmap taking into account the need to ensure appropriate implementation of this Decision". In accordance with Article 8(1) of Decision 2015/1523, that roadmap must provide "adequate measures in the area of asylum, first reception and return, enhancing the capacity, quality and efficiency of [the Italian Republic's] and [the Hellenic Republic's] systems in these areas". Recital 18 of the contested decision states, in that regard, that Decision 2015/1523 "sets out an obligation for [the Italian Republic] and [the Hellenic Republic] to provide structural solutions to address exceptional pressures on their asylum and migration systems, by establishing a solid and strategic framework for responding to the crisis situation and intensifying the ongoing reform process in these areas". By requiring the updating of the roadmaps drawn up by the Italian Republic and the Hellenic Republic in application of Decision 2015/1523, the contested decision represents the continuation of the latter decision. The aim pursued here is to require those two Member States to manage their asylum systems in order to enable them, after the period of application of the contested decision, to better cope with any increase in the inflow of migrants to their territories.

230. In application of the contested decision, the Italian Republic and the Hellenic Republic are therefore under an obligation, in parallel

with the relocations from their territories, to correct the structural weaknesses in their asylum systems. Failure by one of those two Member States to comply with that obligation may, in accordance with Article 8(3) of the contested decision, entail the suspension of the application of that decision with regard to that Member State for a period of up to three months, which may be extended once.

231. Furthermore, it must be borne in mind that the contested decision is not the only measure adopted by the Union in order to take pressure off the Italian and Greek asylum systems. As the Grand Duchy of Luxembourg has pointed out, that decision must be seen as forming part of a set of measures, one of the most important of which in operational terms is certainly the establishment of "hotspots".[63]

232. Last, as I have already indicated, I share the Council's view that it is likely that the great pressure experienced by the Italian and Greek asylum systems would have seriously disrupted any asylum system, even one with no structural weaknesses. It therefore seems to me to be wrong to maintain, as does the Slovak Republic, that the pressure on the asylum systems of Italy and Greece is solely the consequence of the structural weaknesses in those two systems.

233. In the light of those factors, I consider that it is not apparent, still less is it manifestly apparent, that the relocation of a significant number of persons in clear need of international protection, in such a way as to relieve the Italian and Greek asylum systems of the processing of the corresponding applications, is an inappropriate measure for contributing in a real and effective manner to the objective of relieving the considerable pressure on those two asylum systems.

234. According to the Slovak Republic and Hungary, the inappropriateness of the contested decision for attaining the objective which it pursues is also confirmed by the small number of relocations carried out pursuant to that decision.

235. As the Council correctly states, proportionality must be assessed in the light of the information available to it when it adopted the contested decision.

236. It is important, in that regard to bear in mind the case law of the Court, according to which, in the context of an action for annulment, the legality of a measure must be assessed on the basis of the facts and the law as they stood at the time when the measure was adopted

---

[63] The "hotspots" are intended, in particular, to assist the frontline Member States, such as the Italian Republic and the Hellenic Republic, to fulfil their obligations with respect to the checking, identification, registration of testimony and fingerprinting of arrivals.

and cannot depend on retrospective considerations of its efficacy.[64] The Court has also held that where the legislature of the Union is obliged to assess the future effects of rules to be adopted and those effects cannot be accurately foreseen, its assessment is open to criticism only if it appears to be manifestly incorrect in the light of the information available to the legislature at the time of the adoption of the rules in question.[65]

237. As is apparent from a number of recitals of the contested decision, the Council relied on a detailed analysis of the causes and effects of the crisis situation that arose in the summer of 2015, on the basis of the figures available to it at the time of the adoption of that decision.

238. As the Council observes, the low effectiveness of the measures provided for in the contested decision[66] may be explained by a set of factors which it could not foresee at the time of the adoption of that decision, in particular the "*laisser passer*" policy applied by a number of Member States, which led to the disorderly movement of a large number of migrants to other Member States; the slow pace of the relocation procedures; the uncertainty created by the numerous cases of refusal on public order grounds put forward by certain relocation Member States; and the insufficient cooperation of certain Member States in the implementation of the contested decision.

239. On the latter point, I would add that the applicants' argument amounts, all in all, to an attempt to take advantage of their failure to implement the contested decision. I would point out that, by failing to comply with their relocation obligations, the Slovak Republic and Hungary have contributed to the fact that the objective of 120 000 relocations laid down in the contested decision is to date still far from being attained.

240. It must be pointed out, in that regard, that, according to the updated figures of 10 April 2017,[67] Hungary has not relocated any person from Italy and Greece, while the Slovak Republic has relocated only 16 persons from Greece and none from Italy. Those figures correspond to 0% and 2%, respectively, of the relocation quotas

---

[64] See, in particular, judgment of 17 May 2001, *IECC* v. *Commission* (C-449/98 P, EU: C:2001:275, paragraph 87 and the case law cited).

[65] See, in particular, judgment of 9 June 2016, *Pesce and Others* (C-78/16 and C-79/16, EU: C:2016:428, paragraph 50 and the case law cited).

[66] As at 10 April 2017, the number of resettlements from Italy and Greece stood at 16 340. See the Commission's Eleventh report of 12 April 2017 on relocation and resettlement, COM(2017) 212 final, Annex 3. According to the information provided by the Council at the hearing before the Court on 10 May 2017, the number of relocations from Italy and Greece came to 18 129 as at 8 May 2017.

[67] See the Commission's Eleventh report on relocation and resettlement, Annex 3.

allocated to Hungary and the Slovak Republic by the contested decision. I would observe, moreover, that neither the Slovak Republic nor Hungary has requested that the mechanism for the temporary suspension of their obligations provided for in Article 4(5) of the contested decision be applied to it.

241. While it is clear to me that the appropriateness of the contested decision for attaining the objective which it pursues cannot be disputed by the applicants on the basis of the weakness of its application or of its ineffectiveness in practice, there is, on the other hand, one thing which to my mind is indisputable, namely that that decision can succeed in resolving the emergency situation that justified its adoption only on condition that all the Member States, in the same spirit of solidarity as that which constitutes its *raison d'être*, make an effort to implement it.

242. It should be borne in mind, in that regard, that the non-application of the contested decision also constitutes a breach of the obligation concerning solidarity and the fair sharing of burdens expressed in Article 80 TFEU. To my mind there is no doubt that, in an action for failure to fulfil obligations on this matter, the Court would be entitled to remind the offending Member States of their obligations, and to do so in no uncertain terms, as it has done in the past.[68]

(b) The necessity of the contested decision in the light of the objective which it seeks to attain

(1) The arguments put forward by the Slovak Republic

243. The Slovak Republic maintains that the objective pursued by means of the contested decision could be achieved just as effectively by measures that could have been taken in the context of existing instruments that were less restrictive for Member States as regards their impact on the sovereign right of each Member State to decide freely on the admission of nationals of third countries to their territory and also the right of Member States, proclaimed in Article 5 of Protocol

---

[68] See, in particular, judgment of 7 February 1973, *Commission* v. *Italy* (39/72, EU:C:1973:13), where the Court held that, "in permitting Member States to profit from the advantages of the Community, the Treaty imposes on them also the obligation to respect its rules. For a State unilaterally to break, according to its own conception of national interest, the equilibrium between advantages and obligations flowing from its adherence to the Community brings into question the equality of Member States before [Union] law and creates discriminations at the expense of their nationals ... This failure in the duty of solidarity accepted by Member States by the fact of their adherence to the Community strikes at the fundamental basis of the [Union] legal order" (paragraphs 24 and 25). See also judgment of 7 February 1979, *Commission* v. *United Kingdom* (128/78, EU:C:1979:32, paragraph 12).

(No 2), that the financial and administrative burden should be the lightest possible.

244. As regards, in the first place, less restrictive measures that might have been taken, the Slovak Republic first of all mentions Council Directive 2001/55/EC of 20 July 2001 on minimum standards for giving temporary protection in the event of a mass influx of displaced persons and on measures promoting a balance of efforts between Member States in receiving such persons and bearing the consequences thereof.[69] That directive was intended to respond to the same situations of massive inflows of migrants as the contested decision by providing temporary protection, as stated in recitals 8, 9 and 13 and Article 1 of that directive, while being less restrictive than the contested decision in a number of aspects. Furthermore, Article 26 of Directive 2001/55 expressly establishes a procedure for the relocation of persons benefiting from temporary protection.

245. That directive is less harmful to the interests of the Member States, since it provides for the return of the persons concerned when the temporary protection comes to an end. In addition, Article 25 of that directive provides, in a spirit of solidarity, that the Member States are to indicate, in figures or in general terms, their capacity to receive such persons, and that they are to determine the number of persons to be received, having due regard to their sovereignty.

246. The Republic of Poland, which supports the Slovak Republic in this argument, submits that Directive 2001/55 is based on the principle of voluntary agreement and that the transfer is carried out with the consent of the person being relocated and the Member State of relocation. In addition, the status of temporary protection provided for in that directive confers fewer rights than the status of international protection that the contested decision seeks to afford, in particular as regards the period of protection, thus imposing significantly fewer burdens on the Member State of relocation.

247. Next, the Slovak Republic maintains that the Italian Republic and the Hellenic Republic could have triggered what is known as the "EU civil protection" mechanism provided for in Article 8a of Council Regulation (EC) No 2007/2004 of 26 October 2004 establishing a European Agency for the Management of Operational Cooperation at the External Borders of the Member States of the European Union,[70] that could have provided them with the necessary material assistance. The Slovak Republic also claims that the Italian Republic and the

[69] OJ 2001 L 212, p. 12.
[70] OJ 2004 L 349, p. 1.

Hellenic Republic could have sought assistance from the Frontex Agency in the form of "rapid intervention". The Slovak Republic submits, in that regard, that the effectiveness of the borders of the frontline Member States whose borders are the external borders of the Union is directly linked to the state of the asylum and migration systems of the Member States concerned.

248. Likewise, in accordance with Article 2(1)(f) and Article 9(1) and (1b) [*sic*] of Regulation No 2007/2004, in order to relieve the burdens on their asylum systems, the Italian Republic and the Hellenic Republic could, in the Slovak Republic's submission, have asked the Frontex Agency to provide the necessary assistance to arrange the return operations.

249. Furthermore, the Slovak Republic claims that it was not necessary to adopt other measures on the basis of Article 78(3) TFEU, having regard to Decision 2015/1523, which leaves it to the Member States to decide, in a spirit of solidarity, the extent to which they will participate in the common commitment and which is therefore less harmful to their national sovereignty. In addition, since the contested decision was adopted only eight days after Decision 2015/1523, it was impossible to conclude in such a brief period that the latter decision was insufficient. At the time of the adoption of the contested decision, the Council had no reason to consider that the reception capacities provided for in Decision 2015/1523 would be quickly achieved and that it would therefore be necessary to provide additional capacity in the context of the contested decision.

250. Last, Article 78(3) TFEU also made it possible to adopt less restrictive measures in order to attain the objective pursued, for example by providing assistance to facilitate return and registration or financial, material, technical and personnel support to the Italian and Greek asylum systems. The Member States could also take bilateral initiatives, on a voluntary basis, in order to provide such support.

251. In the second place, the relocation of applicants as provided for in the contested decision inevitably entails a financial and administrative burden. Since it was not necessary to bear such a burden, that decision constitutes a superfluous and premature measure, contrary to the principle of proportionality and to Article 5 of Protocol (No 2).

252. In answer to those arguments, it is appropriate to underline the particularly delicate context in which the contested decision was adopted, namely the emergency situation characterised by a sudden inflow of nationals of third countries in July and August 2015. The institutions of the Union were required to react as quickly as possible

and effectively to the considerable pressure on the Italian and Greek asylum systems.

253. I consider, as does the Council, that although at least some of the alternative solutions suggested by the Slovak Republic could contribute to the attainment of the objective pursued by the contested decision, that finding, having regard to the broad margin of discretion that must be afforded to the Council, cannot suffice to establish that that decision is manifestly disproportionate and to call its legality into question. In my view, the Council, at the time of the adoption of the contested decision, was entitled to consider that there was no alternative measure that would enable the objective pursued by the contested decision to be attained as effectively, while restricting to a lesser degree the sovereignty of the Member States or their financial interests.

254. I am of the view, as is the Federal Republic of Germany, that the principle of solidarity and the fair sharing of responsibility between the Member States, expressly enshrined in Article 80 TFEU as regards the Union policies on border control, asylum and immigration, plays a major role in the interpretation of Article 78(3) TFEU. Accordingly, it seems to me to be consistent with the latter provision, read in the light of Article 80 TFEU, that a provisional measure such as the contested decision should allocate between the Member States, in a binding fashion, the burdens which it imposes.

255. The Hellenic Republic observes, moreover, that the need to adopt a programme for the mandatory relocation of applicants for international protection from Greece and Italy, on the basis of quotas per Member State, can be explained by the unprecedented migratory flows in those two Member States in 2015, especially in July and August 2015. The actions that were progressively decided upon up to the adoption of the contested decision proved insufficient to alleviate to a significant degree the burden resulting in Greece and Italy from the admission of such a large number of migrants and the processing of their applications for international protection. I do not have convincing material that would disprove the assertion thus made by the Hellenic Republic.

256. It follows that, having regard to the figures relating to the 2015 migration crisis mentioned in the recitals of the contested decision and to the panel of measures suggested by the Slovak Republic in order to respond to that crisis, I do not think that the temporary relocation mechanism put in place by that decision may be regarded as manifestly exceeding what is necessary in order to provide an effective response to that crisis.

257. As regards, first of all, the alternative measure consisting in the implementation of Directive 2001/55, that directive is, as the Court observed in its judgment of 21 December 2011, *N. S. and Others*,[71] an example of the solidarity between Member States provided for in Article 80 TFEU.[72] As is apparent from recital 20 of that directive, one of the objectives of that directive is to provide a solidarity mechanism intended to contribute to the attainment of a balance of effort between Member States in receiving and bearing the consequences of receiving displaced persons in the event of a mass influx.

258. Although it appears that the application of such a solidarity mechanism, like that provided for in the contested decision, is to be confined to wholly exceptional situations involving a mass influx of displaced persons,[73] I note that the two mechanisms differ on one essential point. In fact, unlike the mechanism provided for in Directive 2001/55, the temporary relocation mechanism put in place by the contested decision entails a mandatory allocation of a specific number of applicants for international protection among the Member States. Given the emergency context in which the contested decision was adopted and the fact that it was impossible to obtain commitments from the Member States to take specific numbers of the applicants for international protection, the Council in my view made the appropriate choice by opting for a rapid and binding response in order to deal with the migration crisis confronting the Union. In any event, such a choice cannot be described as manifestly inappropriate.

259. In that regard, the assertion, which to a large extent crystallises the opposition to the contested decision shown by certain Member States, that the objective pursued by that decision ought to have been achieved solely by means of voluntary commitments on the part of the Member States to receive a certain number of applicants does not bear scrutiny. The genesis of the contested decision shows that it was because consensus could not be reached between all Member States on a voluntary distribution among them of the applicants for international protection that it was decided to opt for a mandatory relocation mechanism, that is to say, one based on binding quantitative allocations. On that point, I am of the view that the institutions of the Union, which are often the targets of complaints of impotence and inactivity, cannot be criticised for having chosen to impose on the

---

[71] C-411/10 and C-493/10, EU:C:2011:865.
[72] Paragraph 93 of that judgment.
[73] See, to that effect, judgment of 21 December 2011, *N. S. and Others* (C-411/10 and C-493/10, EU:C:2011:865, paragraph 93).

Member States quotas of applicants to be relocated rather than simply abandoning the project for a relocation mechanism.

260. I conclude that the adoption of the contested decision, rather than the implementation of Directive 2001/55, is the result of a political choice by the three institutions that participated in the procedure leading to the adoption of the contested decision and that none of the arguments put forward by the Slovak Republic is in my view capable of demonstrating that that choice must be regarded as manifestly incorrect in the light of the principle of proportionality.

261. As regards, next, the argument that the adoption of the contested decision was not necessary given the previous adoption of Decision 2015/1523, I observe that the Commission clearly stated, in its proposal for a decision, that, since the point at which agreement had been reached within the Council on 20 July 2015 on the content of what would become Decision 2015/1523, concerning the relocation of 40 000 persons from Italy and Greece, "the migratory situation in the Central and Eastern Mediterranean ha[d] intensified. The flows of migrants and refugees ha[d] more than doubled over the summer months giving impetus to trigger a new emergency relocation mechanism to alleviate pressure faced by [the Italian Republic], [the Hellenic Republic] and also Hungary".[74]

262. That finding that the migratory situation had deteriorated, making the adoption of an additional relocation mechanism necessary, is expressed in recital 12 of the contested decision, which is worded as follows: "During recent months, the migratory pressure at the southern external land and sea borders has again sharply increased, and the shift of migration flows has continued from the central to the eastern Mediterranean and towards the Western Balkans route, as a result of the increasing number of migrants arriving in and from Greece. In view of the situation, further provisional measures to relieve the asylum pressure from [the Italian Republic and the Hellenic Republic] should be warranted". That finding is substantiated by figures which are set out in recital 13 of the contested decision.

263. Whereas the voluntary relocation mechanism for 40 000 persons put in place by Decision 2015/1523 is intended, as may be seen from recitals 10, 11 and 21 of that decision, to cope with the flow of migrants witnessed in 2014 and the first months of 2015, the mandatory relocation mechanism provided for in the contested decision is intended, as may be seen from the statistics provided in recitals 12,

---

[74] See that Proposal for a Decision, p. 2.

13 and 26 of that decision, to respond to the pressure resulting from
the flow of migrants in July and August 2015.

264. Those factors seem to me to demonstrate to the requisite
standard that the Commission did not make a manifest error of
assessment in considering that, following the sudden flow of nationals
of third countries to the territory of the Union in July and
August 2015, and having regard to the latest figures available to it, an
additional provisional measure for the relocation of 120 000 persons
was necessary.

265. As regards the Slovak Republic's argument that the
strengthening of the surveillance of the external borders of the Union
would constitute an alternative measure to the contested decision, it is
sufficient in my view to emphasise that such a measure, while indeed
useful, could not replace a relocation mechanism whose primary purpose is to cope with a flow of nationals of third countries which has
already happened. That measure intended to strengthen the surveillance of the external borders of the Union is in my view not appropriate, as such, for decreasing the pressure on the Italian and Greek asylum
systems following the sudden flow of nationals of third countries in the
summer of 2015. That measure must therefore be considered to be
complementary to and not capable of replacing that provided for in the
contested decision.

266. The same applies to the measure consisting in providing
financial, material, technical and personnel support to the Italian and
Greek asylum systems.

267. On that point, the Council states, without being contradicted,
that financial support was provided by the Union from the beginning
of the migratory crisis, in the form of a payment of EUR 9.2 billion in
2015 and 2016. Furthermore, the contested decision itself provides, in
Article 10, that financial support is to be provided for each person
relocated in accordance with that decision.

268. In addition, the different follow-up reports drawn up by the
Commission mention operational support measures involving agencies
such as EASO and the Member States.[75] The contested decision states,
moreover, in recital 15, that "many actions have been taken so far to
support [the Italian Republic and the Hellenic Republic] in the framework of the migration and asylum policy, including by providing them
with substantial emergency assistance and EASO operational support".

---

[75] See, in particular, the Commission's Eleventh report on relocation and resettlement, op. cit.,
which is the most recent one available at the time of writing this Opinion.

269. However useful those various support measures may be, the institutions of the Union were to my mind entitled to consider that, without their utility being called into question, they were not sufficient to respond to the emergency situation with which the Italian Republic and the Hellenic Republic had to cope from the summer of 2015.[76]

270. Last, as regards the argument relating to the excessive administrative and financial burdens which the contested decision imposed on the Member States, the Slovak Republic does not show that the alternative measures which it proposes would have been less costly than a temporary relocation mechanism.

271. In the light of the foregoing factors, I consider that the arguments whereby the Slovak Republic disputes the necessity of the contested decision must therefore all be rejected.

272. It is now necessary to examine the arguments put forward by Hungary in order to challenge the necessity of the contested decision.

(2) The arguments put forward by Hungary

273. Hungary, supported by the Republic of Poland in this argument, claims, in the first place, that since, contrary to the provisions made in the Commission's initial proposal, Hungary is no longer among the Member States benefiting from the relocation mechanism, it was not right that the contested decision should provide for the relocation of 120 000 applicants, and that for that reason the decision is contrary to the principle of proportionality. In effect, fixing that total number of 120 000 applicants exceeds what is necessary in order to attain the objective pursued by the contested decision, since it includes a number of 54 000 applicants who, according to the Commission's initial proposal, were to be relocated from Hungary. Thus, there is no explanation of why such a high total number of applicants, which had been determined on the basis of a mechanism benefiting three Member States, would still be necessary when the number of beneficiary Member States was reduced from three to two.

274. Hungary adds that the distribution of the 54 000 applicants initially envisaged as being relocated from Hungary became hypothetical and uncertain, since the contested decision provides that it will be

---

[76] In its Proposal for a Decision, the Commission proceeded from the finding that the different financial and operational measures which it had thus far taken to support the Italian, Greek and Hungarian asylum systems had not proved sufficient to address the current crisis situations in those three Member States. It therefore considered that, given the urgency and the severity of the situation created by the influx of third-country nationals into those Member States, opting for further EU action in reaction to that phenomenon did not go beyond what was necessary to achieve the objective of addressing the situation effectively (p. 8).

the subject of a final decision taken in the light of subsequent developments.

275. In answer to those arguments, it must be observed that, as is apparent from recital 26 of the contested decision, the Council considered, on the basis of the overall number of nationals of third countries who have entered Italy and Greece irregularly in 2015, and the number of those who are in clear need of international protection, that, in spite of Hungary's decision not to be part of the Member States benefiting from the temporary relocation mechanism, a total of 120 000 applicants in clear need of international protection should be relocated from Italy and Greece.

276. Recital 26 states that that number "corresponds to approximately 43% of the total number of third-country nationals in clear need of international protection who have entered Italy and Greece irregularly in July and August 2015". At the hearing, the Council explained that the reference to that percentage was the result of a technical error and that the figure of 78% should be substituted.

277. In arriving at such a number, the Council had to reconcile two requirements, namely the requirement that that number would be sufficiently high to actually reduce the pressure on the Italian and Greek asylum systems and the requirement that it would not be set at such a level that it would place too high a burden on the Member States of relocation.

278. I see nothing in Hungary's argument to show that in acting in that way the Council clearly exceeded its margin of discretion. On the contrary, I consider that, in the light of the data relating to the number of irregular entries available to the Council at the time of the adoption of the contested decision, and having regard to the fact that there were at the time sound reasons to think that the migration crisis would extend beyond the date of adoption of that decision, the Council set the number of applicants to be relocated at a reasonable level. As already stated, the fact that that number is far from being attained today cannot undermine that assessment.

279. As regards the number of 54 000 applicants who were initially to be relocated from Hungary, Article 4(1)(c) of the contested decision provides that they "shall be relocated to the territory of the other Member States, proportionally to the figures laid down in Annexes I and II, either in accordance with paragraph 2 of this Article or through an amendment of this Decision, as referred to in Article 1(2) and in paragraph 3 of this Article".

280. In that regard, the Commission explains in its written observations that, following Hungary's refusal to be among the Member

States benefiting from the relocation measure, it was decided to introduce, in Article 4(2) of the contested decision, what is known as a
"by default" rule, under which those 54 000 applicants were, as of
26 September 2016, to be relocated from Italy and Greece to the other
Member States and, in Article 4(3) of the contested decision, a flexible
rule enabling that mechanism for the relocation of those 54 000
persons to be adapted if justified by the evolution of the situation on
the ground or if a Member State were confronted with an emergency
situation characterised by a sudden inflow of nationals of third countries owing to a sharp shift of migration flows.

281. To my mind, in thus providing for a reserve corresponding to
the number of 54 000 applicants to be relocated in conditions precisely
defined in the contested decision, the Council not only did not act in a
disproportionate manner but also took fully into account the need to
adapt the temporary relocation mechanism to the evolution of the
situation.

282. In that regard, it should be recalled that the Court has already
emphasised the need for the institutions of the Union to ensure that the
rules are adapted to the new data.[77] That need to adapt its rules where
necessary was also provided for by the Council in the contested decision, in particular in Article 1(2) and Article 4(3).

283. In providing for a reserve of 54 000 applicants that could be
used in one way or another depending on circumstances, the Council
took that need for adaptation into account at the time of the adoption
of the contested decision, in a particularly relevant way having regard
to the degree of uncertainty as to the evolution of the migratory flows.
As the Council correctly states, such a flexible solution is justified
owing to the very dynamic nature of migratory flows and allows the
content of the contested decision to be adapted to circumstances, in
the desire for solidarity, effectiveness and proportionality. It cannot
therefore be considered that by acting in that way the Council went
beyond what is necessary in order to attain the objective pursued by
the contested decision.

284. I would observe, last, that, in accordance with that same
requirement for adaptation, the reserve of 54 000 applicants was eventually attributed to the resettlement programme negotiated between the
Union and the Republic of Turkey on 18 March 2016.[78]

---

[77] See, in particular, to that effect, judgment of 9 June 2016, *Pesce and Others* (C-78/16 and
C-79/16, EU:C:2016:428, paragraph 51 and the case law cited).
[78] See Decision 2016/1754, which inserted paragraph 3a in Article 4 of the contested decision.

285. In the second place, Hungary maintains, in the alternative, that if the Court were not to uphold any of its pleas for annulment, the contested decision would nonetheless be illegal so far as Hungary is specifically concerned, since it infringes Article 78(3) TFEU and breaches the principle of proportionality vis-à-vis that Member State.

286. It is apparent from the explanations provided by Hungary in support of its 10th plea that it takes issue with the Council for having included it among the Member States of relocation when in Hungary's submission it cannot be disputed that it was subject to particularly strong migratory pressure both during the period preceding the adoption of the contested decision and at the time of its adoption. In those circumstances, the contested decision places a disproportionate burden on Hungary by setting a mandatory relocation quota for it as for the other Member States.

287. Hungary maintains that, if the objective of Article 78(3) TFEU is to provide assistance to Member States in an emergency situation in the light of migratory pressure, it is then contrary to that objective to impose an additional burden on a Member State which is actually in such a situation.

288. In essence, Hungary criticises the fact that its refusal to be included among the Member States benefiting from the temporary relocation mechanism had the automatic consequence of placing it among the Member States contributing to that mechanism, that is to say, among the Member States of relocation.

289. Hungary explains its refusal to be included among the Member States benefiting from the temporary relocation mechanism put in place by the contested decision as follows. In the first place, it rejects the idea that it should be classified as a "frontline Member State". Hungary makes clear, in that regard, that the Italian Republic and the Hellenic Republic are Member States which, owing to their geographic situation, are the first point of entry for applicants for international protection in the Union, unlike Hungary, whose territory, having regard to the migration routes and to geographic reality, can be accessed by such applicants only when they necessarily pass through Greece. Classifying Hungary as a "frontline Member State" obscured that reality and suggested that Hungary could be considered to be the Member State responsible for examining the application for asylum, which in its view was unacceptable. In the second place, Hungary states that it expressed its disagreement with a relocation of applicants based on quotas, explaining that it considered that such a procedure was not an instrument that would permit an adequate response to the migration crisis, especially in the form of mandatory quotas per Member State,

which contradicts the conclusions of the European Council of 25 and 26 June 2015. Hungary states that it could not accept the idea that applicants should be relocated from its territory, because that ran counter to the position of principle which it had expressed. However, in Hungary's contention, none of that can be interpreted as meaning that it was not itself faced with the effects of the migration crisis and that it was not itself in an emergency situation.

290. Hungary claims that, by rejecting the arrangement whereby applicants for international protection would be relocated from its territory, it, to use its expression, accepted "its share of the common burden". Thus, Hungary does not breach the principle of solidarity. It continues to form part of the Member States that support the Italian Republic and the Hellenic Republic even though, owing to its own situation, namely that it was itself in an emergency situation, it does so in a different way from the other Member States.

291. It is apparent from Hungary's application, from its reply and from its response to the statements in intervention that this 10th plea, which it raises in the alternative, is meant to support the claim, which it also puts forward in the alternative, that the contested decision should be annulled "insofar as it concerns Hungary".

292. I understand that claim as seeking the annulment in part of the contested decision. Hungary thus seeks to remove itself from the group of Member States of relocation by seeking annulment of the provision of the contested decision that determines the number of migrants to be relocated to Hungary.

293. Such a claim is in my view inadmissible.

294. It is settled case law that the partial annulment of an act of the Union is possible only if the elements the annulment of which is sought may be severed from the remainder of the act.[79] The Court has repeatedly held that the requirement of severability is not satisfied in the case where the partial annulment of an act would have the effect of altering its substance.[80]

295. The claim for partial annulment of the contested decision submitted in the alternative by Hungary is in reality directed at two figures which specifically concern that Member State and are set out in the annexes to that decision. However, the deletion of those figures would entail the annulment of those annexes in their entirety, since the

---

[79] See, in particular, judgment of 30 March 2006, *Spain* v. *Council* (C-36/04, EU:C:2006:209, paragraph 9 and the case law cited, and also paragraph 12).

[80] See, in particular, judgment of 30 March 2006, *Spain* v. *Council* (C-36/04, EU:C:2006:209, paragraph 13 and the case law cited).

figures for the other Member States would have to be recalculated in order to keep the total number of 120 000 relocations. That would affect an essential element of the contested decision, namely the mandatory determination of the allocations per Member State which gives real scope to the principle of solidarity and fair sharing of responsibility between Member States laid down in Article 80 TFEU.

296. In addition, as is apparent, in particular, from recitals 2, 16, 26 and 30 of the contested decision, which refer to that principle, the idea of a distribution of the applicants for international protection who have arrived in Italy and Greece among all the other Member States is a fundamental element of the contested decision. The limitation of the scope *ratione territoriae* of the contested decision that would result from the partial annulment of that decision would thus strike at the very heart of the decision. I infer that the element which Hungary seeks to have annulled cannot be severed from the contested decision, insofar as its disappearance would objectively alter the very substance of the contested decision.

297. It follows from the foregoing that the contested provisions, which correspond to the quotas from Italy and from Greece allocated to Hungary which are set out in Annexes I and II to the contested decision, cannot be severed from the remainder of the contested decision. It follows that the claims for partial annulment of that decision submitted by Hungary, to which its 10th plea relates, must be rejected as inadmissible.

298. In any event, if Hungary's 10th plea were to be understood as seeking more generally the annulment of the contested decision in its entirety, on the ground that the failure to take its particular situation into account constituted as such a breach of the principle of proportionality affecting the entire decision, such a plea would in my view have to be rejected as unfounded.

299. More specifically, I consider that, even on the assumption that Hungary was, as it maintains, in an emergency situation characterised by constant migratory pressure at the time of the adoption of the contested decision,[81] it does not follow, in my view, that the

---

[81] The existence of an emergency situation in Hungary at the time of the adoption of the contested decision is disputed by the Council, which maintains that the situation changed during the summer of 2015 owing to the unilateral measures taken by Hungary, in particular the construction of a barrier along its border with the Republic of Serbia, which was completed on 14 September 2015, and the transit policy to other Member States, in particular to Germany, practised by Hungary. Those measures put an end to the arrival of migrants on the territory of Hungary, while those who had succeeded in entering Hungarian territory had to leave quickly. In order to illustrate the fact that it was in a situation of emergency, Hungary states, in particular, that between 15 September and 31 December 2015 the Hungarian police apprehended 190 461 illegal migrants, including 31 769

imposition on it of quotas of applicants for relocation from Italy and Greece is contrary to the principle of proportionality.

300. In effect, it should first of all be borne in mind that Hungary's withdrawal from the Member States benefiting from the temporary relocation mechanism originates solely in its refusal to benefit from that mechanism. Whatever the reasons that gave rise to that refusal, I must emphasise that the institutions of the Union could not but take note of such a refusal.

301. As the Grand Duchy of Luxembourg observes, in essence, since Hungary had expressly requested not to be included among the Member States benefiting from the temporary relocation mechanism, it had to be considered, in accordance with the principle of solidarity, that it was included among the Member States of relocation.

302. Next, it follows from the case law that the mere fact that an act of the Union is likely to affect one Member State more than others cannot be contrary to the principle of proportionality, as long as the conditions laid down by the Court in order to ensure compliance with that principle are met.[82]

303. I observe, in that regard, that the contested decision has an impact on all the Member States and assumes that a balance will be struck between the different interests involved, regard being had to the objective which it pursues. Therefore, the attempt to strike such a balance, taking into account not only the particular situation of a single Member State, but that of all the Member States of the Union, cannot be regarded as being contrary to the principle of proportionality.[83] That applies a fortiori when account is taken of the principle of solidarity and fair sharing of responsibility between the Member States laid down in Article 80 TFEU, from which it follows that the burdens constituted by the provisional measures adopted on the basis of Article 78(3) TFEU in favour of one or more Member States in an emergency migratory situation must be shared among all the other Member States.

---

between 15 and 22 September 2015. Hungary states that it was under "enormous migratory pressure" characterised by the following factors: up to 15 September 2015 there were 201 126 illegal breaches of the border. That figure was 391 384 as at 31 December 2015. In the second half of September, the number of illegal breaches of the Croatian-Hungarian border was as high as 10 000 on some days. Hungary adds that during 2015, 177 135 applications for international protection were lodged with the competent asylum authority of that Member State.

[82] See, to that effect, judgment of 4 May 2016, *Poland* v. *Parliament and Council* (C-358/14, EU: C:2016:323, paragraph 103).

[83] See, by analogy, judgment of 4 May 2016, *Poland* v. *Parliament and Council* (C-358/14, EU: C:2016:323, paragraph 103 and the case law cited).

304. Incidentally, it should be emphasised that the contested decision is more nuanced than the impression that Hungary seeks to give. That decision cannot be reduced to a binary arrangement, with the Member States benefiting from the temporary relocation on one side and the Member States which are allocated quotas of persons to be relocated on the other side.

305. In fact, the contested decision includes adjustment mechanisms which enable it to be adapted to the evolution of migratory flows and thereby to take account of the particular situation, characterised by variable migratory pressure, with which certain Member States might be confronted.

306. Thus, it should be recalled that the second subparagraph of Article 1(2) and the first subparagraph of Article 4(3) of the contested decision provide that the Commission may submit proposals to the Council if it considers that an adaptation of the relocation mechanism is justified by the evolution of the situation on the ground or that a Member State is confronted with an emergency situation characterised by a sudden inflow of nationals of third countries due to a sharp shift of migration flows. Under the second subparagraph of Article 4(3) of the contested decision, a Member State may, giving duly justified reasons, notify the Council and the Commission that it is confronted with a similar emergency situation. The Commission is then to assess the reasons given and submit, as appropriate, proposals to the Council, as indicated in Article 1(2) of the contested decision.

307. In addition, Article 4(5) of that decision provides that the relocation of applicants may be temporarily suspended for Member States which duly notify the Council and the Commission.

308. Furthermore, Article 9 of the contested decision refers to the possibility that the Council may adopt provisional measures pursuant to Article 78(3) TFEU if the conditions laid down in that provision are met, and states that such measures may include, where appropriate, a suspension of the participation of a Member State confronted with a sudden inflow of nationals of third countries in the relocation as provided for in the contested decision.

309. I would point out that the Republic of Austria and the Kingdom of Sweden have availed themselves of those adjustment mechanisms.[84]

---

[84] See, as concerns the Kingdom of Sweden, Council Decision (EU) 2016/946 of 9 June 2016 establishing provisional measures in the area of international protection for the benefit of Sweden in accordance with Article 9 of Decision (EU) 2015/1523 and Article 9 of Decision (EU) 2015/1601 establishing provisional measures in the area of international protection for the benefit of Italy and Greece (OJ 2016 L 157, p. 23). Article 2 of that decision provides that the obligations of the Kingdom

310. On the other hand, Hungary has not relied on any of those mechanisms, which seems to contradict the argument whereby it disputes its position as a full Member State of relocation.

311. The existence of adjustment mechanisms in the contested decision does indeed show that, contrary to the impression given by Hungary, the situation is not binary. In providing for such mechanisms, of which the Republic of Austria and the Kingdom of Sweden have taken advantage, the Council has succeeded in reconciling the principle of solidarity with the taking into account of the particular needs that some Member States may have owing to the evolution of migratory flows. Such a reconciliation seems to me, moreover, to be perfectly consistent with Article 80 TFEU, which, as will be seen on a careful reading, provides for the "*fair* sharing of responsibility ... between Member States".[85]

312. The existence of such adjustment mechanisms in the contested decision can thus only reinforce my finding that, by imposing on Hungary quotas of applicants for relocation from Italy and Greece, that decision did not breach the principle of proportionality.

313. In addition, I would point out that it is not disputed that the quotas mentioned in the annexes to the contested decision were determined on the basis of a distribution key which is explained in recital 25 of the Commission's proposal for a decision. In order to ensure the fairness of the sharing of responsibility, that distribution key takes into account the size of the population, total gross domestic product, the average number of asylum applications per one million inhabitants over the period 2010 to 2014 and the unemployment rate. On that basis, the distribution key therefore contributes to the proportionate nature of the contested decision.

314. Having regard to the foregoing factors, the arguments whereby Hungary disputes the necessity of the contested decision must therefore in my view all be rejected.

315. It is appropriate, finally, to answer the argument put forward by the Republic of Poland in support of the pleas alleging that the contested decision is disproportionate, according to which that decision

___

of Sweden as a Member State of relocation under Decision 2015/1523 and the contested decision are to be suspended until 16 June 2017. As concerns the Republic of Austria, see Council Implementing Decision (EU) 2016/408 of 10 March 2016 on the temporary suspension of the relocation of 30% of applicants allocated to Austria under Decision (EU) 2015/1601 establishing provisional measures in the area of international protection for the benefit of Italy and Greece (OJ 2016 L 74, p. 36). Article 1 of that decision provides that the relocation to Austria of 1 065 of the applicants allocated to that Member State under the contested decision is to be suspended until 11 March 2017.

[85] Emphasis added.

interferes with the exercise of the Member States' responsibility to maintain law and order and to safeguard internal security, contrary to Article 72 TFEU. The Republic of Poland recalls, in that regard, that the principle of proportionality requires that the disadvantages caused by the acts of the Union must not be disproportionate to the aims pursued by those acts.[86] In fact, the Commission does not make provision for mechanisms sufficient to enable the Member States to check that applicants will not represent a danger for security.

316. I consider, however, that in providing for an orderly and controlled mechanism for the relocation of applicants for international protection, the contested decision fully takes into consideration the requirement of protection of the national security and public order of the Member States. That requirement thus governs the "close administrative cooperation between Member States"[87] whereby the contested decision must be implemented. I observe, in that regard, that recital 32 of that decision states that "national security and public order should be taken into consideration throughout the relocation procedure, until the transfer of the applicant is implemented. In full respect of the fundamental rights of the applicant . . . where a Member State has reasonable grounds for regarding an applicant as a danger to its national security or public order, it should inform the other Member States thereof". Likewise, the description of the relocation procedure set out in Article 5 of the contested decision demonstrates the desire of the institutions of the Union to take into account the requirement to safeguard the national security and public order of the Member States. Thus, apart from the fact that that article expressly provides that applicants for international protection must be identified, registered and fingerprinted for the purposes of the relocation procedure, Article 5(7) of the contested decision provides that "Member States retain the right to refuse to relocate an applicant only where there are reasonable grounds for regarding him or her as a danger to their national security or public order or where there are serious reasons for applying the exclusion provisions set out in Articles 12 and 17 of Directive 2011/95/EU".[88]

---

[86] See, in particular, judgment of 4 May 2016, *Poland* v. *Parliament and Council* (C-358/14, EU: C:2016:323, paragraph 78 and the case law cited).

[87] See recital 31 of the contested decision.

[88] Directive of the European Parliament and of the Council of 13 December 2011 on standards for the qualification of third-country nationals or stateless persons as beneficiaries of international protection, for a uniform status for refugees or for persons eligible for subsidiary protection, and for the content of the protection granted (OJ 2011 L 337, p. 9). Among the grounds of exclusion from being a refugee or receiving subsidiary protection are the existence of serious reasons for considering that the applicant has committed a crime against peace, a war crime, or a crime against humanity, as defined in

317. In the light of those factors, that argument put forward by the Republic of Poland in support of the claim that the contested decision must be held to be disproportionate must in my view be rejected.

318. It follows from the foregoing that, insofar as neither Hungary nor the Slovak Republic, nor indeed the Republic of Poland, has succeeded in demonstrating that the contested decision is disproportionate in the light of the objectives which it pursues, the corresponding pleas raised by the applicants must be rejected as unfounded.

2. *Hungary's eighth plea, alleging breach of the principles of legal certainty and of normative clarity, and also of the Geneva Convention*

319. Hungary maintains, in the first place, that the contested decision fails to observe the principles of legal certainty and of normative clarity, since, on a number of points, it does not clearly indicate the way in which its provisions must be applied or how they relate to the provisions of the Dublin III Regulation.

320. Thus, although recital 35 of the contested decision addresses the issue of the legal and procedural safeguards applicable to the relocation decisions, none of its normative provisions regulates that matter or refers to the relevant provisions of the Dublin III Regulation. That raises a problem from the viewpoint, in particular, of the applicants' right to a remedy, in particular those who are not designated for relocation.

321. Nor does the contested decision clearly determine the criteria against which the applicants are chosen for relocation. The way in which the authorities of the Member States are called upon to decide on the transfer of applicants to a Member State of relocation makes it extremely difficult for applicants to know in advance whether they will be among the persons relocated and, if so, in which Member State they will be relocated. The absence of objective criteria for the designation of the applicants to be relocated amounts to a breach of the principle of legal certainty and renders the selection arbitrary, which constitutes a breach of the applicants' fundamental rights.

322. In addition, the contested decision does not define in an appropriate manner the applicants' status in the Member State of relocation and does not ensure that an applicant will actually remain

the international instruments drawn up to make provision in respect of such crimes, that he has committed a serious crime or that he constitutes a danger to the community or to the security of the Member State in which he is present.

in that Member State while a decision is taken on his application. As regards "secondary" movements, Article 6(5) of the contested decision does not in itself ensure that that decision will attain its objectives, namely the distribution of applicants between Member States, unless it is guaranteed that applicants will actually remain in the Member States of relocation.

323. In the second place, the fact that applicants may, where applicable, be relocated to a Member State with which they have no particular connection raises the question whether the contested decision is compatible in that respect with the Geneva Convention.

324. In fact, according to the interpretation adopted in the guide published by the HCR,[89] the applicant should be permitted to remain in the country in which he has lodged his request pending a decision on his request by the competent authority of that Member State.

325. That right to remain in that Member State is also recognised in Article 9 of Directive 2013/32/EU of the European Parliament and of the Council of 26 June 2013 on common procedures for granting and withdrawing international protection.[90]

326. Indeed, the contested decision deprives applicants of their right to remain on the territory of the Member State in which they lodged their application and allows them to be relocated to another Member State even though the existence of a significant link between the applicant and the Member State of relocation cannot be established.

327. Although the right that applicants thus enjoy seems to be undermined by the Dublin III Regulation, in that it provides for the transfer of applicants from the Member State in which they lodged their application to the Member State responsible for examining the application, that procedure takes the applicants' personal situation into account and ultimately serves their interests.

328. I shall examine, in the first place, the complaint alleging breach of the principles of legal certainty and normative clarity.

329. Like the Council, I observe that the contested decision is an emergency measure which forms part of the *acquis* related to the common European asylum system and which derogates from that *acquis* only on certain specific points and on a temporary basis. Consequently, that decision must be interpreted and applied in the light of all the provisions constituting that *acquis*, without its being necessary, or indeed desirable, to mention in that decision all the rules

---

[89] Handbook and guidelines on procedures and criteria for determining refugee status under the 1951 Convention and the 1967 Protocol relating to the status of refugees, Geneva, 1992, point 192(vii).
[90] OJ 2013 L 180, p. 60.

governing the status, rights and obligations of persons relocated in their host Member State. In that regard, the Council seems to me to have sufficiently explained, in particular in recitals 23, 24, 35, 36 and 40 of the contested decision, the way in which that decision must relate to the provisions of legislative acts adopted by the Union in that area.

330. As regards, in particular, the right to an effective remedy, it is clear from recitals 23 and 35 of the contested decision that, when that decision does not provide for a temporary derogation, the legal and procedural safeguards set out in the Dublin III Regulation continue to apply with respect to applicants coming within the scope of that decision. That is the case of the right of appeal provided for in Article 27(1) of that regulation. In any event, in the context of the implementation of the contested decision, Article 47 of the Charter must be observed.

331. As for the criticism, still made from the aspect of the principle of legal certainty, that the contested decision does not contain effective rules ensuring that an applicant for international protection will remain within the Member State of relocation while a decision is taken on his application, I would point out that the contested decision provides, in Article 6(5), that "an applicant or beneficiary of international protection who enters the territory of a Member State other than the Member State of relocation without fulfilling the conditions for stay in that other Member State shall be required to return immediately" to the Member State of relocation, which "shall take back the person without delay". Furthermore, recitals 38 to 41 of the contested decision set out in a sufficiently clear and precise manner the measures to be taken by the Member States in order to avoid secondary movements by the persons who have been relocated.

332. In the second place, I consider that Hungary has not demonstrated how the temporary relocation mechanism put in place by the contested decision, in that it provides for the transfer of an applicant for international protection before a decision on his application has been taken, is contrary to the Geneva Convention.

333. It should be emphasised, first of all, that, as the Council observes, neither the Geneva Convention nor Union law guarantees an applicant for international protection the right freely to choose his host country. In particular, the Dublin III Regulation establishes a system for the determination of the Member State responsible for processing applications for international protection which is based on a list of objective criteria, none of which is connected with the applicant's preference. From that aspect, the relocation provided for in the

contested decision does not differ substantially from the system established by that regulation.

334. Next, I consider, as does the Council, that the passage from the HCR guide, mentioned in footnote 89 of this Opinion, on which Hungary relies, must be understood as an expression of the principle of non-*refoulement*, which prohibits the expulsion of an applicant for international protection to a third country while a decision has not been taken on his application. In fact, the transfer, in the context of a relocation operation, of an applicant for international protection from one Member State to another Member State does not constitute a breach of that principle. It must be emphasised that the aim of relocation is to facilitate access to the asylum procedures and to the reception infrastructures, with a view to offering appropriate status to persons requiring international protection, as required by Article 78(1) TFEU. In fact, the Union decided to establish the temporary relocation mechanism provided for in the contested decision precisely because, at the time of the adoption of that decision, it was impossible to offer such status to those requesting it in Italy and Greece.

335. Thus, the contested decision does not merely respect the fundamental rights and observe the principles recognised by the Charter, as recital 45 of that decision states, in the traditional manner: it goes further, by playing an active role in that area. It participates in the preservation of the fundamental rights of applicants in clear need of international protection, as guaranteed by the Charter, and in particular by Article 18 thereof, by transferring them to Member States, other than the Italian Republic and the Hellenic Republic, which are in a better position to process their applications.

336. I would add, moreover, that, as the Council observes, for the purposes of the common European asylum system, the territory of all the Member States must be treated as a common area for the uniform application of the Union *acquis* in asylum matters. It follows that transfers between the territories of the Member States cannot be treated as *refoulement* outside the territory of the Union.

337. Last, it should be observed that, contrary to what appears to emerge from the line of argument developed by Hungary, and as the Council points out, the particular situation of the individuals affected by the relocation, including any family ties, is taken into account not only in the context of the application of the criteria of the Dublin III Regulation, but also in the context of Article 6(1) and (2) of the contested decision, read in conjunction with recital 34 of that decision.

338. Article 6(1) of the contested decision thus provides that "the best interests of the child shall be a primary consideration for Member

States when implementing this Decision". In addition, under Article 6(2) of that decision Member States are to ensure "that family members who fall within the scope of this Decision are relocated to the territory of the same Member State".

339. As for recital 34 of the contested decision, it states that "the integration of applicants in clear need of international protection into the host society is the cornerstone of a properly functioning Common European Asylum System". For that reason, that recital states that "in order to decide which specific Member State should be the Member State of relocation, specific account should be given to the specific qualifications and characteristics of the applicants concerned, such as their language skills and other individual indications based on demonstrated family, cultural or social ties which could facilitate their integration into the Member State of relocation".

340. It follows that the eighth plea raised by Hungary must be rejected as unfounded.

341. As none of the pleas raised by the Slovak Republic and by Hungary can in my view be upheld, I propose that the Court should dismiss the actions brought by those two Member States.

IV. COSTS

342. Under Article 138(1) of the Rules of Procedure of the Court of Justice, the unsuccessful party is to be ordered to pay the costs if they have been applied for in the successful party's pleadings. As the Council has claimed that the Slovak Republic and Hungary should be ordered to pay the costs, and as those two Member States have been unsuccessful, they must be ordered to pay the costs.

343. In addition, as interveners, the Kingdom of Belgium, the Federal Republic of Germany, the Hellenic Republic, the French Republic, the Italian Republic, the Grand Duchy of Luxembourg, the Republic of Poland, the Kingdom of Sweden and the European Commission must bear their own costs, in accordance with Article 140(1) of the Rules of Procedure of the Court of Justice.

V. CONCLUSION

344. In the light of all of the foregoing, I propose that the Court should:

(1) dismiss the actions brought by the Slovak Republic and by Hungary;

(2) order the Slovak Republic and Hungary to pay the costs;
(3) order the Kingdom of Belgium, the Federal Republic of Germany, the Hellenic Republic, the French Republic, the Italian Republic, the Grand Duchy of Luxembourg, the Republic of Poland, the Kingdom of Sweden and the European Commission to bear their own costs.

[Report: EU:C:2017:618]

JUDGMENT OF THE COURT*

TABLE OF CONTENTS

*   Languages of the case: Slovak and Hungarian.

1. By their applications, the Slovak Republic and Hungary seek annulment of Council Decision (EU) 2015/1601 of 22 September 2015 establishing provisional measures in the area of international protection for the benefit of Italy and Greece (OJ 2015 L 248, p. 80, "the contested decision").

I. THE CONTESTED DECISION: CONTEXT, HISTORY AND CONTENT

A. Context of the contested decision

2. The context in which the contested decision was adopted is described as follows in recitals 3 to 7 and 10 to 16 thereof:

(3) The recent crisis situation in the Mediterranean prompted the [European] Union institutions to immediately acknowledge the exceptional migratory flows in that region and call for concrete measures of solidarity towards the frontline Member States. In particular, at a joint meeting of Foreign and Interior Ministers on 20 April 2015, the [European] Commission presented a 10-point plan of immediate action to be taken in response to the crisis, including a commitment to consider options for an emergency relocation mechanism.

(4) At its meeting of 23 April 2015, the European Council decided, inter alia, to reinforce internal solidarity and responsibility and committed itself in particular to increasing emergency assistance to frontline Member States and to considering options for organising emergency relocation between Member States on a voluntary basis, as well as to deploying European Asylum Support Office (EASO) teams in frontline Member States for the joint processing of applications for international protection, including registration and fingerprinting.

(5) In its resolution of 28 April 2015, the European Parliament reiterated the need for the Union to base its response to the latest tragedies in the Mediterranean on solidarity and fair sharing of responsibility and to step up its efforts in this area towards those Member States which receive the highest number of refugees and applicants for international protection in either absolute or relative terms.

(6) Besides measures in the area of asylum, Member States at the frontline should increase their efforts to set up measures to cope with mixed migration flows at the external borders of the European Union. Such measures should safeguard the rights of those in need of international protection and prevent irregular migration.

(7) At its meeting of 25 and 26 June 2015, the European Council decided, inter alia, that three key dimensions should be advanced in parallel: relocation/resettlement, return/readmission/reintegration and cooperation with countries of origin and transit. The European Council agreed in particular, in the light of the current emergency situation and the commitment to reinforce solidarity and responsibility, on the temporary and exceptional relocation over 2 years, from Italy and from Greece to other Member States of 40 000 persons in clear need of international protection, in which all Member States would participate.

. . .

(10) Among the Member States witnessing situations of considerable pressure and in light of the recent tragic events in the Mediterranean, Italy and Greece in particular have experienced unprecedented flows of migrants, including applicants for international protection who are in clear need of international protection, arriving on their territories, generating significant pressure on their migration and asylum systems.

(11) On 20 July 2015, reflecting the specific situations of Member States, a Resolution of the representatives of the Governments of the Member States meeting within the [European] Council on relocating from Greece and Italy 40 000 persons in clear need of international protection was adopted by consensus. Over a period of 2 years, 24 000 persons will be relocated from Italy and 16 000 persons will be relocated from Greece. On 14 September 2015, the Council [of the European Union] adopted Decision (EU) 2015/1523 [establishing provisional measures in the area of international protection for the benefit of Italy and of Greece (OJ 2015 L 239, p. 146)], which provided for a temporary and exceptional relocation mechanism from Italy and Greece to other Member States of persons in clear need of international protection.

(12) During recent months, the migratory pressure at the southern external land and sea borders has again sharply increased, and the shift of migration flows has continued from the central to the eastern Mediterranean and towards the Western Balkans route, as a result of the increasing number of migrants arriving in and from Greece. In view of the situation, further provisional measures to relieve the asylum pressure from Italy and Greece should be warranted.

(13) According to data of the European Agency for the Management of Operational Cooperation at the External Borders (Frontex), the central and eastern Mediterranean routes were the main areas for irregular border crossing into the Union in the first eight months of 2015. Since the beginning of 2015, approximately 116 000 migrants arrived in Italy in an irregular manner . . . During May and June 2015, 34 691 irregular border crossings were detected by Frontex and during July and August 42 356, an increase of 20%. A strong increase was also witnessed by Greece in 2015, with more than 211 000 irregular migrants reaching the country . . . During May and June 2015, 53 624 irregular border crossings were detected by Frontex and during July

and August 137 000, an increase of 250%. A significant proportion of the total number of irregular migrants detected in those two regions included migrants of nationalities which, based on the . . . data [of the Statistical Office of the European Union (Eurostat)], meet a high Union-level recognition rate.

(14) According to Eurostat and EASO figures, 39 183 persons applied for international protection in Italy between January and July 2015, compared to 30 755 in the same period of 2014 (an increase of 27%). A similar increase in the number of applications was witnessed by Greece with 7 475 applicants (an increase of 30%).

(15) Many actions have been taken so far to support Italy and Greece in the framework of the migration and asylum policy, including by providing them with substantial emergency assistance and EASO operational support. . . .

(16) Due to the ongoing instability and conflicts in the immediate neighbourhood of Italy and Greece, and the repercussions in migratory flows on other Member States, it is very likely that a significant and increased pressure will continue to be put on their migration and asylum systems, with a significant proportion of the migrants who may be in need of international protection. This demonstrates the critical need to show solidarity towards Italy and Greece and to complement the actions taken so far to support them with provisional measures in the area of asylum and migration.

B. *History of the contested decision*

3. On 9 September 2015, the Commission submitted, on the basis of Article 78(3) TFEU, a Proposal for a Council Decision establishing provisional measures in the area of international protection for the benefit of Italy, Greece and Hungary (COM(2015) 451; "the Commission's initial proposal").

4. On the same day, the Commission also submitted, on the basis of Article 78(2)(e) TFEU, a Proposal for a Regulation of the European Parliament and of the Council establishing a crisis relocation mechanism and amending Regulation (EU) No 604/2013 of the Parliament and of the Council of 26 June 2013 establishing the criteria and mechanisms for determining the Member State responsible for examining an application for international protection lodged in one of the Member States by a third-country national or a stateless person (COM(2015) 450).

5. The Commission's initial proposal provided for the relocation of 120 000 applicants for international protection, from Italy (15 600 persons), Greece (50 400 persons) and Hungary (54 000 persons), to the other Member States. The Annexes accompanying that proposal contained three charts allocating those applicants from each of those three Member States among the other Member States, with the exception of the United Kingdom, Ireland and Denmark, in the form of quotas determined for each of those Member States.

6. On 13 September 2015, the Commission forwarded that proposal to national parliaments.

7. By a letter of 14 September 2015, the Council forwarded the proposal to the Parliament for consultation. In that letter the Council asked the Parliament to give its opinion as quickly as possible in view of the critical situation in the Mediterranean Sea and on the Western Balkans route and undertook to keep the Parliament informed, on an informal basis, about developments in the case within the Council.

8. On 17 September 2015, the Parliament adopted a legislative resolution approving the proposal, having regard, in particular, to the "exceptional situation of urgency and the need to address the situation with no further delay", while asking the Council to consult the Parliament again if it intended to substantially amend the Commission's initial proposal.

9. At the various meetings held within the Council between 17 and 22 September 2015, the Commission's initial proposal was amended on certain points.

10. In particular, Hungary stated at those meetings that it rejected the notion of being classified as a "frontline Member State" and that it did not wish to be among the Member States benefiting from relocation as were Italy and Greece. Accordingly, in the final version of the proposal, all reference to Hungary as a beneficiary Member State, including in the title of the proposal, was deleted. Likewise, Annex III to the Commission's initial proposal, concerning the distribution of 54 000 applicants for international protection whom it had initially been planned to relocate from Hungary, was deleted. On the other hand, Hungary was included in Annexes I and II as a Member State of relocation of applicants for international protection from Italy and Greece respectively and allocations were therefore attributed to it in those annexes.

11. On 22 September 2015, the Commission's initial proposal as thus amended was adopted by the Council by a qualified majority. The Czech Republic, Hungary, Romania and the Slovak Republic voted against the adoption of that proposal. The Republic of Finland abstained.

C. Content of the contested decision

12. Recitals 2, 22, 23, 26, 30, 32, 35 and 44 of the contested decision state:

(2) According to Article 80 TFEU, the policies of the Union in the area of border checks, asylum and immigration and their implementation are to be

governed by the principle of solidarity and fair sharing of responsibility between the Member States, and Union acts adopted in this area are to contain appropriate measures to give effect to this principle.

. . .

(22) In accordance with Article 78(3) TFEU, the measures envisaged for the benefit of Italy and of Greece should be of a provisional nature. A period of 24 months is reasonable in view of ensuring that the measures provided for in this Decision have a real impact in respect of supporting Italy and Greece in dealing with the significant migration flows on their territories.

(23) The measures to relocate from Italy and from Greece, provided for in this Decision, entail a temporary derogation from the rule set out in Article 13(1) of Regulation (EU) No 604/2013 of the European Parliament and of the Council [of 26 June 2013 establishing the criteria and mechanisms for determining the Member State responsible for examining an application for international protection lodged in one of the Member States by a third-country national or a stateless person (OJ 2013 L 180, p. 31, "the Dublin III Regulation")], according to which Italy and Greece would otherwise have been responsible for the examination of an application for international protection based on the criteria set out in Chapter III of that regulation, as well as a temporary derogation from the procedural steps, including the time limits, laid down in Articles 21, 22 and 29 of that regulation. The other provisions of [the Dublin III Regulation] ... remain applicable ... This Decision also entails a derogation from the consent of the applicant for international protection as referred to in Article 7(2) of Regulation (EU) No 516/2014 of the European Parliament and of the Council [of 16 April 2014 establishing the Asylum, Migration and Integration Fund, amending Council Decision 2008/381/EC and repealing Decisions No 573/2007/EC and No 575/2007/EC of the European Parliament and of the Council and Council Decision 2007/435/EC (OJ 2014 L 150, p. 168)].

. . .

(26) The provisional measures are intended to relieve the significant asylum pressure on Italy and on Greece, in particular by relocating a significant number of applicants in clear need of international protection who will have arrived in the territory of Italy or Greece following the date on which this Decision becomes applicable. Based on the overall number of third-country nationals who have entered Italy and Greece irregularly in 2015, and the number of those who are in clear need of international protection, a total of 120 000 applicants in clear need of international protection should be relocated from Italy and Greece. This number corresponds to approximately 43% of the total number of third-country nationals in clear need of international protection who have entered Italy and Greece irregularly in July and August 2015. The relocation measure foreseen in this Decision constitutes fair burden sharing between Italy and Greece on the one hand and the other Member States on the other, given the overall available figures on irregular

border crossings in 2015. Given the figures at stake, 13% of these applicants should be relocated from Italy, 42% from Greece and 45% should be relocated as provided for in this Decision.

. . .

(30) With a view to implementing the principle of solidarity and fair sharing of responsibility, and taking into account that this Decision constitutes a further policy development in this field, it is appropriate to ensure that the Member States that relocate, pursuant to this Decision, applicants from Italy and Greece who are in clear need of international protection, receive a lump sum for each relocated person which is identical to the lump sum provided for in Article 18 of Regulation ... No 516/2014, namely EUR 6 000, and is implemented by applying the same procedures. ...

. . .

(32) National security and public order should be taken into consideration throughout the relocation procedure, until the transfer of the applicant is implemented. In full respect of the fundamental rights of the applicant, including the relevant rules on data protection, where a Member State has reasonable grounds for regarding an applicant as a danger to its national security or public order, it should inform the other Member States thereof.

. . .

(35) The legal and procedural safeguards set out in [the Dublin III] Regulation remain applicable in respect of applicants covered by this Decision. In addition, applicants should be informed of the relocation procedure set out in this Decision and be notified with the relocation decision which constitutes a transfer decision within the meaning of Article 26 of [the Dublin III] Regulation. Considering that an applicant does not have the right under Union law to choose the Member State responsible for his or her application, the applicant should have the right to an effective remedy against the relocation decision in line with [the Dublin III Regulation], only in view of ensuring respect for his or her fundamental rights. In line with Article 27 of that Regulation, Member States may provide in their national law that the appeal against the transfer decision does not automatically suspend the transfer of the applicant but that the person concerned has the opportunity to request a suspension of the implementation of the transfer decision pending the outcome of his or her appeal.

. . .

(44) Since the objectives of this Decision cannot be sufficiently achieved by the Member States but can rather, by reason of the scale and effects of the action, be better achieved at Union level, the Union may adopt measures, in accordance with the principle of subsidiarity as set out in Article 5 [TEU]. In accordance with the principle of proportionality, as set out in that Article, this Decision does not go beyond what is necessary in order to achieve those objectives.

13. Under Article 1 of the contested decision, which is entitled "Subject matter":

1. This Decision establishes provisional measures in the area of international protection for the benefit of Italy and of Greece, in view of supporting them in better coping with an emergency situation characterised by a sudden inflow of nationals of third countries in those Member States.
2. The Commission shall keep under constant review the situation regarding massive inflows of third-country nationals into Member States.
The Commission will submit, as appropriate, proposals to amend this Decision in order to take into account the evolution of the situation on the ground and its impact upon the relocation mechanism, as well as the evolving pressure on Member States, in particular frontline Member States.

14. Article 2 of that decision, which is entitled "Definitions", provides:

For the purposes of this Decision, the following definitions apply:

. . .

(e) "relocation" means the transfer of an applicant from the territory of the Member State which the criteria laid down in Chapter III of [the Dublin III] Regulation . . . indicate as responsible for examining his or her application for international protection to the territory of the Member State of relocation;
(f) "Member State of relocation" means the Member State which becomes responsible for examining the application for international protection pursuant to [the Dublin III Regulation] of an applicant following his or her relocation in the territory of that Member State.

15. Article 3 of the contested decision, which is entitled "Scope", provides as follows:

1. Relocation pursuant to this Decision shall take place only in respect of an applicant who has lodged his or her application for international protection in Italy or in Greece and for whom those States would have otherwise been responsible pursuant to the criteria for determining the Member State responsible set out in Chapter III of [the Dublin III Regulation].
2. Relocation pursuant to this Decision shall be applied only in respect of an applicant belonging to a nationality for which the proportion of decisions granting international protection . . . is, according to the latest available updated quarterly Union-wide average Eurostat data, 75% or higher. . . .

16. Under the title "Relocation of 120 000 applicants to Member States", Article 4(1) to (3) of the contested decision provides:

1. 120 000 applicants shall be relocated to the other Member States as follows:

(a) 15 600 applicants shall be relocated from Italy to the territory of the other Member States in accordance with the table set out in Annex I;

(b) 50 400 applicants shall be relocated from Greece to the territory of the other Member States in accordance with the table set out in Annex II;

(c) 54 000 applicants shall be relocated to the territory of the other Member States, proportionally to the figures laid down in Annexes I and II, either in accordance with paragraph 2 of this Article or through an amendment of this Decision, as referred to in Article 1(2) and in paragraph 3 of this Article.

2. As of 26 September 2016, 54 000 applicants, referred to in point (c) of paragraph 1, shall be relocated from Italy and Greece, in proportion resulting from points (a) and (b) of paragraph 1, to the territory of other Member States and proportionally to the figures laid down in Annexes I and II. The Commission shall submit a proposal to the Council on the figures to be allocated accordingly per Member State.

3. If by 26 September 2016, the Commission considers that an adaptation of the relocation mechanism is justified by the evolution of the situation on the ground or that a Member State is confronted with an emergency situation characterised by a sudden inflow of nationals of third countries due to a sharp shift of migration flows and taking into account the views of the likely beneficiary Member State, it may submit, as appropriate, proposals to the Council, as referred to in Article 1(2).

Likewise, a Member State may, giving duly justified reasons, notify the Council and the Commission that it is confronted with a similar emergency situation. The Commission shall assess the reasons given and submit, as appropriate, proposals to the Council, as referred to in Article 1(2).

17. Article 1 of Council Decision (EU) 2016/1754 of 29 September 2016 (OJ 2016 L 268, p. 82) added the following paragraph to Article 4 of the contested decision:

3a. In relation to the relocation of applicants referred to in point (c) of paragraph 1, Member States may choose to meet their obligation by admitting to their territory Syrian nationals present in Turkey under national or multi-lateral legal admission schemes for persons in clear need of international protection, other than the resettlement scheme which was the subject of the Conclusions of the Representatives of the Governments of the Member States meeting within the Council [on] 20 July 2015. The number of persons so admitted by a Member State shall lead to a corresponding reduction of the obligation of the respective Member State.

. . .

18. It follows from Article 2 of Decision 2016/1754 that the latter entered into force on 2 October 2016 and is applicable until

26 September 2017 to all the persons who, for the purposes of Article 4(3a) of the contested decision, have been admitted from Turkey by the Member States as from 1 May 2016.

19. Article 4(4) of the contested decision provides for the possibility of Ireland and the United Kingdom taking part, on a voluntary basis, in executing the decision. Ireland's participation was subsequently confirmed by the Commission and the Council set a number of applicants who were to be relocated to that Member State and adapted the quotas of the other Member States accordingly.

20. Article 4(5) of the contested decision provides that in exceptional circumstances a Member State may, subject to the conditions laid down in that provision, request, by 26 December 2015, a temporary suspension of the relocation of up to 30% of the applicants allocated to it.

21. That provision was applied at the request of the Republic of Austria and the matter was dealt with by Council Implementing Decision (EU) 2016/408 of 10 March 2016 on the temporary suspension of the relocation of 30% of applicants allocated to Austria under [the contested decision] (OJ 2016 L 74, p. 36). Article 1 of Decision 2016/408 provides that the relocation to Austria of 1 065 of the applicants allocated to it under the contested decision was to be suspended until 11 March 2017.

22. Article 5 of the contested decision, which is entitled "Relocation procedure", provides:

. . .

2. Member States shall, at regular intervals, and at least every 3 months, indicate the number of applicants who can be relocated swiftly to their territory and any other relevant information.

3. Based on this information, Italy and Greece shall, with the assistance of EASO and, where applicable, of Member States' liaison officers referred to in paragraph 8, identify the individual applicants who could be relocated to the other Member States and, as soon as possible, submit all relevant information to the contact points of those Member States. Priority shall be given for that purpose to vulnerable applicants within the meaning of Articles 21 and 22 of Directive 2013/33/EU [of the European Parliament and of the Council of 26 June 2013 laying down standards for the reception of applicants for international protection (OJ 2013 L 180, p. 96)].

4. Following approval of the Member State of relocation, Italy and Greece shall, as soon as possible, take a decision to relocate each of the identified applicants to a specific Member State of relocation, in consultation with EASO, and shall notify the applicant in accordance with Article 6(4). The Member State of relocation may decide not to approve the relocation of an

applicant only if there are reasonable grounds as referred to in paragraph 7 of this Article.

...

6. The transfer of the applicant to the territory of the Member State of relocation shall take place as soon as possible following the date of the notification to the person concerned of the transfer decision referred to in Article 6(4) of this Decision. Italy and Greece shall transmit to the Member State of relocation the date and time of the transfer as well as any other relevant information.

7. Member States retain the right to refuse to relocate an applicant only where there are reasonable grounds for regarding him or her as a danger to their national security or public order ...

...

23. Article 6 of the contested decision, which is entitled "Rights and obligations of applicants for international protection covered by this Decision", provides:

1. The best interests of the child shall be a primary consideration for Member States when implementing this Decision.

2. Member States shall ensure that family members who fall within the scope of this Decision are relocated to the territory of the same Member State.

3. Prior to the decision to relocate an applicant, Italy and Greece shall inform the applicant in a language which the applicant understands or is reasonably supposed to understand of the relocation procedure as set out in this Decision.

4. When the decision to relocate an applicant has been taken and before the actual relocation, Italy and Greece shall notify the person concerned of the decision to relocate him in writing. That decision shall specify the Member State of relocation.

5. An applicant or beneficiary of international protection who enters the territory of a Member State other than the Member State of relocation without fulfilling the conditions for stay in that other Member State shall be required to return immediately. The Member State of relocation shall take back the person without delay.

24. Article 7 of the contested decision contains provisions concerning operational support to the Hellenic Republic and the Italian Republic.

25. Article 8 of that decision lays down further measures that are to be taken by those two Member States.

26. Article 9 of the decision empowers the Council to take provisional measures under Article 78(3) TFEU if the conditions laid down by that provision are met. It states that such measures may, where

appropriate, include a suspension of the participation of the Member State which is faced with a sudden inflow of nationals of third countries in the relocation provided for by the contested decision.

27. That provision was applied at the request of the Kingdom of Sweden and the matter was dealt with in Council Decision (EU) 2016/946 of 9 June 2016 establishing provisional measures in the area of international protection for the benefit of Sweden in accordance with Article 9 of Decision 2015/1523 and Article 9 of Decision 2015/1601 (OJ 2016 L 157, p. 23). Article 2 of Decision 2016/946 provides that the obligations of the Kingdom of Sweden as a Member State of relocation under Decision 2015/1523 and the contested decision are to be suspended until 16 June 2017.

28. Article 10 of the contested decision makes provision for financial support for each person relocated pursuant to that decision, such support being given to both the Member State of relocation and to either the Hellenic Republic or the Italian Republic.

29. Article 11 of the contested decision provides that, with the assistance of the Commission, bilateral arrangements may be made between those two Member States and the "associated" States, namely the Republic of Iceland, the Principality of Liechtenstein, the Kingdom of Norway and the Swiss Confederation and that, where such bilateral arrangements are made, the Council is accordingly to adapt, on a proposal from the Commission, the allocations of Member States by reducing them in due proportion. Such agreements have subsequently been concluded and the associated States are thus participating in the relocation for which the contested decision provides.

30. Article 12 of the contested decision provides, inter alia, that the Commission is to report to the Council every six months on the implementation of the decision. The Commission subsequently undertook to submit monthly reports on the implementation of the various measures adopted at EU level for the relocation and resettlement of applicants for international protection, including the contested decision.

31. Finally, under Article 13(1) and (2) of the contested decision, the latter entered into force on 25 September 2015 and is to apply until 26 September 2017. Article 13(3) provides that the decision is to apply to persons arriving on the territory of Italy and Greece from 25 September 2015 until 26 September 2017, as well as to applicants having arrived on the territory of those Member States from 24 March 2015 onwards.

II. PROCEDURE BEFORE THE COURT AND FORMS OF ORDER SOUGHT

32. In Case C-643/15 the Slovak Republic claims that the Court should annul the contested decision and order the Council to pay the costs.

33. In Case C-647/15 Hungary claims that the Court should:

– principally, annul the contested decision;
– in the alternative, annul that decision in so far as it concerns Hungary; and
– order the Council to pay the costs.

34. In Cases C-643/15 and C-647/15 the Council asks the Court to dismiss the actions as unfounded and to order the Slovak Republic and Hungary, respectively, to pay the costs.

35. By decision of the President of the Court of 29 April 2016, the Kingdom of Belgium, the Federal Republic of Germany, the Hellenic Republic, the French Republic, the Italian Republic, the Grand Duchy of Luxembourg, the Kingdom of Sweden and the Commission were granted leave to intervene in support of the form of order sought by the Council in Cases C-643/15 and C-647/15.

36. By the same decision, the Republic of Poland was granted leave to intervene, in Case C-643/15, in support of the form of order sought by the Slovak Republic and, in Case C-647/15, in support of the form of order sought by Hungary.

37. The parties and the Advocate General having been heard in this regard, it is appropriate, on account of the connection between the present cases, to join them for the purposes of the judgment, in accordance with Article 54 of the Rules of Procedure of the Court.

III. THE ACTIONS

A. Overview of the pleas in law

38. In support of its action in Case C-643/15, the Slovak Republic relies on six pleas in law, alleging (i) infringement of Article 68 TFEU and Article 13(2) TEU, and breach of the principle of institutional balance; (ii) infringement of Article 10(1) and (2) TEU, Article 13(2) TEU, Article 78(3) TFEU, Articles 3 and 4 of Protocol (No 1) on the role of the national parliaments in the European Union, annexed to the EU and FEU Treaties ("Protocol (No 1)"), and Articles 6 and 7 of Protocol (No 2) on the application of the principles of subsidiarity and

proportionality, annexed to the EU and FEU Treaties ("Protocol (No 2)"), and breach of the principles of legal certainty, representative democracy and institutional balance; (iii) breach of essential procedural requirements relating to the legislative process and infringement of Article 10(1) and (2) TEU and Article 13(2) TEU, and breach of the principles of representative democracy, institutional balance and sound administration (in the alternative); (iv) breach of essential procedural requirements and infringement of Article 10(1) and (2) TEU and Article 13(2) TEU, and breach of the principles of representative democracy, institutional balance and sound administration (partly in the alternative); (v) failure to meet the conditions under which Article 78(3) TFEU is applicable (in the alternative); and (vi) breach of the principle of proportionality.

39. In support of its action in Case C-647/15, Hungary relies on 10 pleas in law.

40. The first and second pleas allege infringement of Article 78(3) TFEU, since, in Hungary's submission, that provision does not afford the Council an appropriate legal basis for the adoption of measures which, in the present case, entail a binding exception to the provisions of a legislative act, which are applicable for a period of 24 months, or indeed of 36 months in some cases, and the effects of which extend beyond that period, something which, in its view, is incompatible with the concept of "provisional measures".

41. The third to sixth pleas allege breach of essential procedural requirements, in that (i) when adopting the contested decision, the Council infringed Article 293(1) TFEU by departing from the Commission's initial proposal without a unanimous vote (third plea); (ii) the contested decision contains a derogation from the provisions of a legislative act and is itself a legislative act by virtue of its content, so that, even if it were decided that the contested decision could properly have been adopted on the basis of Article 78(3) TFEU, it would have nonetheless been necessary, at the time of its adoption, to respect the right of the national parliaments to issue an opinion on legislative acts, laid down in Protocol (No 1) and Protocol (No 2) (fourth plea); (iii) after consulting the Parliament, the Council substantially amended the text of the proposal without consulting the Parliament again on the matter (fifth plea); and (iv) when the Council adopted the contested decision, the proposal for a decision was not available in all the language versions corresponding to the official languages of the European Union (sixth plea).

42. The seventh plea alleges infringement of Article 68 TFEU and of the conclusions of the European Council of 25 and 26 June 2015.

43. The eighth plea alleges breach of the principles of legal certainty and normative clarity, since on a number of points it is, in Hungary's view, unclear how the contested decision should be applied or how its provisions interrelate with those of the Dublin III Regulation.

44. The ninth plea alleges breach of the principles of necessity and proportionality, in that, as Hungary is no longer among the beneficiary Member States, there is no reason why the contested decision should provide for the relocation of 120 000 persons seeking international protection.

45. The 10th plea, which is submitted in the alternative, alleges breach of the principle of proportionality and infringement of Article 78(3) TFEU so far as Hungary is concerned, since the contested decision attributes a mandatory quota to it as a host Member State, even though it is recognised that a large number of migrants have entered Hungary irregularly and have made applications for international protection there.

B. Preliminary observation

46. Since it is the legal basis of a measure that determines the procedure to be followed in adopting that measure (see, to that effect, judgment of 10 September 2015, *Parliament* v. *Council*, C-363/14, EU:C:2015:579, paragraph 17), it is appropriate to examine, first, the pleas alleging that Article 78(3) TFEU does not provide a proper legal basis for the contested decision, secondly, the pleas alleging that procedural errors were made when the decision was adopted and that such errors amounted to breaches of essential procedural requirements and, thirdly, the substantive pleas.

C. The pleas alleging that Article 78(3) TFEU is not a proper legal basis for the contested decision

1. The Slovak Republic's second plea and Hungary's first plea, relating to the legislative nature of the contested decision

(a) Arguments of the parties

47. The Slovak Republic and Hungary maintain that even though the contested decision was adopted in accordance with the non-legislative procedure and is therefore formally a non-legislative act, it must nevertheless be classified as a legislative act because of its content and its effects, since—as is expressly confirmed in recital 23 of the decision—it amends a number of legislative acts of EU law and, moreover, does so fundamentally.

48. They argue that that is particularly true of Article 13(1) of the Dublin III Regulation, under which the Hellenic Republic or the Italian Republic, as the case may be, are in principle responsible for examining the application for international protection, a rule from which Article 3(1) of the contested decision derogates.

49. Although the contested decision classifies these amendments as mere "derogations", the distinction between a derogation and an amendment is, in the applicants' view, artificial, since, in both cases, the effect is to exclude the application of a normative provision and, by the same token, to undermine its effectiveness.

50. However, it follows, so they argue, from the provisional and urgent nature of the measures referred to in Article 78(3) TFEU that that provision is intended to provide a legal basis for support measures capable of accompanying legislative acts adopted on the basis of Article 78(2) TFEU. The measures concerned are, in particular, rapid-response measures to manage or alleviate a crisis, including financial or technical assistance or the provision of qualified personnel.

51. Thus, they argue, Article 78(3) TFEU does not provide a legal basis for the adoption of legislative measures, since that provision gives no indication that the measures adopted on the basis of it must be adopted in accordance with a legislative procedure.

52. The Slovak Republic maintains in particular that a non-legislative act based on Article 78(3) TFEU, such as the contested decision, can under no circumstances derogate from a legislative act. It submits that the extent of the derogation and the question whether or not the provision derogated from is essential are irrelevant. Any derogation, however limited its scope, by a non-legislative act from a legislative act is prohibited given that it amounts to a circumvention of the legislative procedure, in the present case the procedure provided for in Article 78(2) TFEU.

53. Hungary argues that, in any event, even though the derogations from legislative acts for which the contested decision provides are limited in time, they interfere with the fundamental provisions of existing legislative acts relating to the fundamental rights and obligations of the individuals concerned.

54. Finally, Hungary maintains that Article 78(3) TFEU can be interpreted as meaning that the requirement to consult the Parliament, laid down in that provision, should be regarded as "participation" of the Parliament within the meaning of Article 289(2) TFEU, with the consequence that the special legislative procedure applies. In that case, Article 78(3) TFEU could in fact constitute a valid legal basis for the contested decision, as a legislative act.

55. However, if that interpretation of Article 78(3) TFEU were accepted, the procedural requirements associated with the adoption of a legislative act would have to be observed, in particular the participation of the Parliament and of national parliaments in the legislative process: that clearly did not occur in the present case.

56. The Council contends that it follows from Article 289(3) TFEU that the test for determining whether or not an act is a legislative act is exclusively procedural in the sense that, whenever a legal basis in the Treaty expressly provides that an act is to be adopted "in accordance with the ordinary legislative procedure" or "in accordance with a special legislative procedure", the act in question is a legislative act. It disputes the allegation that the contested decision amended a number of legislative acts of EU law and should thus be classified as a legislative act on account of its content. Nor is there any ground for maintaining that the derogations introduced by the contested decision are means of circumventing the ordinary legislative procedure, as provided for in Article 78(2) TFEU.

(b) Findings of the Court

57. Consideration must be given, first, to whether, as Hungary maintains, Article 78(3) TFEU is to be interpreted to the effect that acts adopted under it must be classified as "legislative acts" on the ground that the requirement for consultation of the Parliament which that provision imposes constitutes a form of participation of that institution within the meaning of Article 289(2) TFEU, with the consequence that such acts must follow the special legislative procedure. That did not occur in the case of the contested decision.

58. In the words of Article 289(3) TFEU, legal acts adopted by legislative procedure are to constitute legislative acts. Accordingly, non-legislative acts are those that are adopted by a procedure other than a legislative procedure.

59. The distinction between legislative and non-legislative acts is undoubtedly significant, since it is only on the adoption of legislative acts that certain obligations must be complied with, relating, inter alia, to the participation of national parliaments in accordance with Articles 3 and 4 of Protocol (No 1) and Articles 6 and 7 of Protocol (No 2) and also to the requirement that the Council is to meet in public when considering and voting on a draft legislative act, which arises from Article 16(8) TEU and Article 15(2) TFEU.

60. In addition, it is clear, on reading Article 289(1) TFEU in conjunction with Article 294(1) TFEU, that the ordinary legislative procedure, which is characterised by the joint adoption of an act of EU

law by the Parliament and the Council on a proposal from the Commission, applies only where the provision of the Treaties forming the legal basis for the act in question "[makes] reference" to that legislative procedure.

61. As regards the special legislative procedure, which is characterised by the fact that it envisages the adoption of an EU act either by the Parliament with the participation of the Council or by the Council with the participation of the Parliament, Article 289(2) TFEU provides that it is to apply "in the specific cases provided for by the Treaties".

62. It follows that a legal act can be classified as a legislative act of the European Union only if it has been adopted on the basis of a provision of the Treaties which expressly refers either to the ordinary legislative procedure or to the special legislative procedure.

63. A systemic approach of that kind provides the requisite legal certainty in procedures for adopting EU acts, in that it makes it possible to identify with certainty the legal bases empowering the institutions of the European Union to adopt legislative acts and to distinguish those bases from bases which can serve only as a foundation for the adoption of non-legislative acts.

64. Accordingly, contrary to what is argued by Hungary, it cannot be inferred from the reference—made in the provision of the Treaties that forms the legal basis for the act at issue—to the requirement for consultation of the Parliament that the special legislative procedure applies to the adoption of that act.

65. In the present case, whilst Article 78(3) TFEU provides that the Council is to adopt the provisional measures referred to therein on a proposal from the Commission and after consulting the Parliament, it does not contain an express reference to either the ordinary legislative procedure or the special legislative procedure. By contrast, Article 78(2) TFEU expressly provides that the measures listed in points (a) to (g) of that provision are to be adopted "in accordance with the ordinary legislative procedure".

66. In view of the foregoing, it must be held that measures which are capable of being adopted on the basis of Article 78(3) TFEU must be classified as "non-legislative acts" because they are not adopted at the end of a legislative procedure.

67. The Council, when it adopted the contested decision, was therefore fully entitled to take the view that it had to be adopted following a non-legislative procedure and was accordingly a non-legislative EU act.

68. As a consequence, there arises, secondly, the question whether, as the Slovak Republic and Hungary maintain, Article 78(3) TFEU was

not a proper legal basis for the contested decision because the decision is a non-legislative act which derogates from a number of legislative acts, whereas only a legislative act can derogate from another legislative act.

69. In that regard, recital 23 of the contested decision states that the relocation from Italy and Greece provided for in the decision entails a "temporary derogation" from certain provisions of legislative acts of EU law, including (i) Article 13(1) of the Dublin III Regulation, under which the Hellenic Republic or the Italian Republic would in principle have been responsible for examining an application for international protection on the basis of the criteria set out in Chapter III of that regulation, and (ii) Article 7(2) of Regulation No 516/2014, which requires the consent of an applicant for international protection.

70. Article 78(3) TFEU does not define the nature of the "provisional measures" that may be adopted pursuant to it.

71. Therefore, contrary to what is maintained by the Slovak Republic and Hungary, the wording of Article 78(3) TFEU does not in itself support a restrictive interpretation of the concept of "provisional measures" to the effect that the concept covers only accompanying measures which support a legislative act adopted on the basis of Article 78(2) TFEU and deal, in particular, with financial, technical or operational support to Member States confronted with an emergency situation characterised by a sudden inflow of nationals of third countries.

72. That finding is borne out by the overall scheme and objectives of paragraphs 2 and 3 of Article 78 TFEU.

73. They are in fact two distinct provisions of primary EU law pursuing different objectives and each having its own conditions for application, which provide a legal basis for the adoption, in the case of Article 78(3) TFEU, of provisional, non-legislative, measures intended to respond swiftly to a particular emergency situation facing Member States and, in the case of Article 78(2) TFEU, legislative acts whose purpose is to regulate, generally and for an indefinite period, a structural problem arising in the context of the European Union's common policy on asylum.

74. Accordingly, those provisions are complementary, permitting the European Union to adopt, in the context of the common policy on asylum, a wide range of measures in order to ensure that it has the necessary tools to respond effectively, both in the short term and in the long term, to migration crises.

75. In that regard, a restrictive interpretation of the concept of "provisional measures" in Article 78(3) TFEU to the effect that it

permits only the adoption of accompanying measures which supplement the legislative acts adopted on the basis of Article 78(2) TFEU, but not the adoption of measures derogating from such acts, would, apart from the fact that such an interpretation finds no support in the wording of Article 78(3) TFEU, also significantly reduce its effectiveness, given that those acts have covered, or may cover, the various aspects of the common European asylum system listed in points (a) to (g) of Article 78(2) TFEU.

76. That is specifically the case of the area mentioned in point (e) of Article 78(2) TFEU, concerning criteria and mechanisms for determining which Member State is responsible for examining an application for asylum or subsidiary protection, which is covered by a full set of rules, at the forefront of which are the rules laid down by the Dublin III Regulation.

77. In the light of the foregoing, the concept of "provisional measures" within the meaning of Article 78(3) TFEU must be sufficiently broad in scope to enable the EU institutions to adopt all the provisional measures necessary to respond effectively and swiftly to an emergency situation characterised by a sudden inflow of nationals of third countries.

78. Although, with that end in mind, it has to be accepted that the provisional measures adopted on the basis of Article 78(3) TFEU may in principle also derogate from provisions of legislative acts, both the material and temporal scope of such derogations must nonetheless be circumscribed, so that the latter are limited to responding swiftly and effectively, by means of a temporary arrangement, to a specific crisis: that precludes such measures from having either the object or effect of replacing legislative acts or amending them permanently and generally, thereby circumventing the ordinary legislative procedure provided for in Article 78(2) TFEU.

79. In the present case, the Court finds that the derogations provided for in the contested decision meet the requirement that their material and temporal scope be circumscribed and have neither the object nor the effect of replacing or permanently amending provisions of legislative acts.

80. Indeed, the derogations from particular provisions of legislative acts for which the contested decision provides apply for a two-year period only, subject to the possibility of extending that period under Article 4(5) of the decision, and will, in the event, cease to apply on 26 September 2017. Moreover, they concern a limited number of 120 000 nationals of certain third countries who have made an application for international protection in either Greece or Italy, who have

one of the nationalities referred to in Article 3(2) of the contested decision, who will be relocated from either Greece or Italy and who arrive in those Member States between 24 March 2015 and 26 September 2017.

81. In those circumstances, there is no ground for maintaining that the ordinary legislative procedure provided for in Article 78(2) TFEU was circumvented by the adoption of the contested decision on the basis of Article 78(3) TFEU.

82. In view of the foregoing, the fact that the contested decision, whose classification as a non-legislative act cannot be called in question, entails derogations from particular provisions of legislative acts did not prevent its adoption on the basis of Article 78(3) TFEU.

83. The Court also rejects, on the same grounds, the Slovak Republic's arguments alleging infringement of Article 10(1) and (2) TEU and Article 13(2) TEU and breach of the principles of legal certainty, representative democracy and institutional balance.

84. The Slovak Republic's second plea and Hungary's first plea must therefore be rejected as unfounded.

2. The first part of the Slovak Republic's fifth plea and Hungary's second plea, alleging that the contested decision is not provisional and that its period of application is excessive

(a) Arguments of the parties
85. The Slovak Republic and Hungary maintain that Article 78(3) TFEU does not provide a proper legal basis for the adoption of the contested decision, since the decision is not provisional, contrary to the requirements of that provision.

86. They submit that, since the contested decision applies, pursuant to Article 13(2) thereof, until 26 September 2017, that is, for a period of two years which may, moreover, be extended by one year under Article 4(5) and (6) of the decision, it cannot be classified as a "provisional measure" within the meaning of Article 78(3) TFEU.

87. That is a fortiori the case, according to the Slovak Republic and Hungary, given that the temporal effects of the contested decision vis-à-vis the applicants for international protection concerned will far exceed that period of two or even three years. In their view, the decision will, in all likelihood, result in lasting ties being created between the applicants for international protection and the Member States of relocation.

88. The Council explains that the contested decision, in accordance with Article 13(2) thereof, will apply for 24 months, that is, until

26 September 2017. An extension by up to 12 months in the specific context of the suspension mechanism provided for in Article 4(5) of the contested decision is no longer possible. It submits that the duration of the effects which the contested decision may have with regard to persons who have been relocated is irrelevant for the purpose of determining whether the decision is provisional. The question of the provisional nature of the contested decision must be assessed by reference to the temporal application of the relocation mechanism for which it provides, namely a period of 24 months.

(b) Findings of the Court
89. Under Article 78(3) TFEU, only "provisional measures" may be adopted.
90. A measure may be classified as "provisional" in the usual sense of that word only if it is not intended to regulate an area on a permanent basis and only if it applies for a limited period.
91. Nevertheless, by contrast with Article 64(2) EC, under which the period of application of measures adopted on the basis of that provision could not exceed six months, Article 78(3) TFEU, which is the successor to that provision, no longer provides for such temporal limitation.
92. Accordingly, Article 78(3) TFEU, whilst requiring that the measures referred to therein be temporary, affords the Council discretion to determine their period of application on an individual basis, in the light of the circumstances of the case and, in particular, of the specific features of the emergency situation justifying those measures.
93. It is clear from Article 13 of the contested decision that the decision is to apply from 25 September 2015 to 26 September 2017, that is, for a period of 24 months, to persons arriving in Greece and Italy during that period and to applicants for international protection having arrived on the territory of those Member States from 24 March 2015 onwards.
94. As for Article 4(5) of the contested decision, it provides that, "in exceptional circumstances" and where a Member State has given notification by 26 December 2015, the 24-month period referred to in Article 13(2) of the decision may be extended by up to 12 months in the context of the mechanism for the temporary and partial suspension of the obligation of the Member State concerned with regard to the relocation of applicants for international protection. It thus confirms the temporary nature of the various measures in the contested decision. Moreover, since that mechanism could no longer be triggered after

26 December 2015, the contested decision will definitively expire on 26 September 2017.

95. Accordingly, the contested decision must be found to apply for a limited period.

96. Moreover, the Council did not manifestly exceed the bounds of its discretion when it set the period of application of the measures provided for in the contested decision, given that it took the view, in recital 22 of the decision, that "a period of 24 months is reasonable in view of ensuring that the measures provided for in this Decision have a real impact in respect of supporting Italy and Greece in dealing with the significant migration flows on their territories".

97. That choice of a period of application of 24 months is justified in view of the fact that the relocation of a large number of persons, such as that provided for in the contested decision, is an unprecedented and complex operation which requires a certain amount of preparation and implementation time, in particular as regards coordination between the authorities of the Member States, before it has any tangible effects.

98. The Court also rejects the argument put forward by the Slovak Republic and Hungary that the contested decision is not provisional since it will have long-term effects because many applicants for international protection will remain in the Member State of relocation well beyond the 24-month period of application of the contested decision.

99. If, in assessing whether a relocation measure is provisional within the meaning of Article 78(3) TFEU, it were necessary to take into account the duration of the effects of that measure on the persons relocated, no measures for the relocation of persons in clear need of international protection could be taken under that provision, since such more or less long-term effects are inherent in such relocation.

100. Nor can the Court accept the argument of the Slovak Republic and of Hungary that, for a measure to be considered provisional within the meaning of Article 78(3) TFEU, the period of application of the measure in question must not exceed the minimum period necessary for the adoption of a legislative act based on Article 78(2) TFEU.

101. Quite apart from the fact that such an interpretation of Article 78(2) and (3) TFEU is not supported by any argument based on the wording of the provisions and disregards the complementary nature of the measures referred to in paragraphs 2 and 3 of that article respectively, it is very difficult, or even impossible, to determine in advance the minimum period that would be necessary for the adoption of a legislative act on the basis of Article 78(2) TFEU, with the consequence that that criterion appears impossible to put into practice.

102. That is also illustrated by the fact that, in the present case, although the proposal for a regulation including a permanent relocation mechanism was submitted on 9 September 2015—namely on the same day as the Commission submitted its initial proposal which would later become the contested decision—it has not been adopted as at the date of delivery of the present judgment.

103. In view of the foregoing, the first part of the Slovak Republic's fifth plea and Hungary's second plea must be rejected as unfounded.

3. *The second part of the Slovak Republic's fifth plea, alleging that the contested decision does not satisfy the conditions for the application of Article 78(3) TFEU*

(a) *Arguments of the parties*

104. The Slovak Republic contends that, in three respects, the contested decision does not satisfy the condition for the application of Article 78(3) TFEU, namely that the Member State benefiting from the provisional measures must be confronted by "an emergency situation characterised by a sudden inflow of nationals of third countries".

105. First, according to the Slovak Republic, the inflow of nationals of third countries into Italy and Greece at the time of the adoption of the contested decision or immediately before its adoption was reasonably foreseeable and therefore cannot be described as "sudden".

106. It submits in that regard that the statistics for 2013 and 2014 and the early part of 2015 indicate that the number of nationals of third countries heading for Greece and Italy had been steadily increasing and that, from late 2013 until early 2014, that increase was considerable. In addition, so far as Italy is concerned, the data for 2015 instead suggested a year-on-year fall in the number of migrants.

107. Secondly, the Slovak Republic submits that, at least as regards the situation in Greece, there is no causal link between the emergency situation and the inflow of third-country nationals into that Member State, although such a link is required as a result of the emergency situation referred to in Article 78(3) TFEU being qualified by the word "characterised". It is not disputed that there have long been serious shortcomings in the way the Hellenic Republic's asylum policy is implemented, which have no direct causal link with the migration phenomenon characteristic of the period in which the contested decision was adopted.

108. Thirdly, the Slovak Republic maintains that, whilst the purpose of Article 78(3) TFEU is to resolve existing or imminent

emergency situations, the contested decision addresses, at least in part, hypothetical future situations.

109. In its view, the period of application, of two, or even three years, of the contested decision is too long for it to be possible to assert that, throughout that period, the measures adopted will respond to the emergency situation, whether present or imminent, affecting the Hellenic Republic and the Italian Republic. Thus, during that period, the emergency situation may cease to exist in those Member States. Furthermore, the mechanism for relocating 54 000 persons provided for in Article 4(3) of the contested decision is intended to address wholly hypothetical situations in other Member States.

110. The Republic of Poland supports that point of view and maintains that Article 78(3) TFEU is directed at a pre-existing and current crisis situation which requires the adoption of immediate corrective measures and not, as the contested decision is, at crisis situations that may arise in the future but whose incidence, nature and degree are uncertain or difficult to foresee.

111. The Council and the Member States supporting it contend that the unprecedented emergency situation that gave rise to the contested decision, which is illustrated by the statistical data mentioned in recitals 13 and 26 of the decision, was both characterised and principally caused by a sudden and massive inflow of nationals of third countries, in particular in July and August 2015.

112. The Council further submits that the fact that the contested decision refers to future events or situations does not mean that it is incompatible with Article 78(3) TFEU.

(b) Findings of the Court

113. It is appropriate, first, to consider the Slovak Republic's argument that the inflow of nationals of third countries to Greece and Italy in 2015 cannot be classified as "sudden" for the purposes of Article 78(3) TFEU, since it represented the continuation of what was already a large inflow of such nationals in 2014 and was therefore foreseeable.

114. In that regard, an inflow of nationals of third countries on such a scale as to be unforeseeable may be classified as "sudden" for the purposes of Article 78(3) TFEU, even though it takes place in the context of a migration crisis spanning a number of years, inasmuch as it makes the normal functioning of the EU common asylum system impossible.

115. In the present case, as the Advocate General has noted in point 3 of his Opinion, the contested decision was adopted in the context of the migration crisis, alluded to in recital 3 of the decision, which

affected the European Union from 2014, then became more acute in 2015, in particular in July and August of that year, and of the catastrophic humanitarian situation to which that crisis gave rise in the Member States, in particular in frontline Member States such as the Hellenic Republic and the Italian Republic, which faced a massive inflow of migrants, most of whom came from third countries such as Syria, Afghanistan, Iraq and Eritrea.

116. According to statistics from the Frontex Agency, provided in an annex to the statement in intervention of the Grand Duchy of Luxembourg, in 2015, for the European Union as a whole, 1.83 million irregular border crossings were detected at the Union's external borders as against 283 500 in 2014. Moreover, according to statistical data from Eurostat, in 2015, almost 1.3 million migrants applied for international protection in the Union as against 627 000 in the previous year.

117. In addition, the statistical data included in recital 13 of the contested decision, which were provided by the Frontex Agency, specifically show that the Hellenic Republic and the Italian Republic were confronted, in the first eight months of 2015—and, in particular, in July and August of that year—with a massive inflow of third-country nationals into their territory, in particular of persons whose nationality was among those referred to in Article 3(2) of the decision, with the consequence that the migratory pressure on the Italian and Greek asylum systems increased sharply in that period.

118. Thus, according to those data, 116 000 irregular crossings of the Italian Republic's external borders were detected in the first eight months of 2015. In July and August 2015, 34 691 migrants arrived in Italy irregularly, representing an increase of 20% as compared with May and June 2015.

119. The statistical data for the Hellenic Republic, which are mentioned in recital 13 of the contested decision, give an even clearer indication in that sharp increase in the number of migrants arriving. In the first eight months of 2015, more than 211 000 irregular migrants arrived in Greece. During July and August 2015 alone, the Frontex Agency counted 137 000 irregular border crossings, an increase of 250% as compared with May and June 2015.

120. Moreover, recital 14 of the contested decision states that, according to Eurostat and EASO figures, 39 183 persons applied for international protection in Italy between January and July 2015, as against 30 755 in the same period of 2014 (an increase of 27%), while a similar increase was witnessed in Greece, where there were 7 475 applicants (a 30% increase).

121. It is also stated in recital 26 of the contested decision that the Council specifically set the total of 120 000 persons to be relocated on the basis of the overall number of third-country nationals who entered Greece and Italy irregularly in July and August 2015 and were in clear need of international protection.

122. It follows that the Council thus identified—on the basis of statistical data that have not been challenged by the Slovak Republic—a sharp increase in the inflow of third-country nationals into Greece and Italy over a short period of time, in particular during July and August 2015.

123. It must be held that in such circumstances the Council could, without making a manifest error of assessment, classify such an increase as "sudden" for the purposes of Article 78(3) TFEU even though that increase represented the continuation of a period in which extremely high numbers of migrants had already arrived.

124. It should be recalled in that regard that the EU institutions must be allowed broad discretion when they adopt measures in areas which entail choices, in particular of a political nature, on their part and complex assessments (see, to that effect, judgment of 4 May 2016, *Poland* v. *Parliament and Council*, C-358/14, EU:C:2016:323, paragraph 79 and the case law cited).

125. With regard, secondly, to the argument, raised by the Slovak Republic, concerning the strict interpretation of the word "characterised" qualifying the "emergency situation" referred to in Article 78(3) TFEU, the Court observes that, although a minority of the language versions of Article 78(3) TFEU do not use the word "characterised" but rather the word "caused", in the context of that provision and in view of its objective of enabling the swift adoption of provisional measures in order to provide an effective response to a migration crisis, those two words must be understood in the same way, namely as requiring there to be a sufficiently close link between the emergency situation in question and the sudden inflow of nationals of third countries.

126. It is apparent from recitals 12, 13 and 26 of the contested decision and from the statistical data mentioned in those recitals that a sufficiently close link has been established between the emergency situation in Greece and Italy, namely the significant pressure on the asylum systems of those Member States, and the inflow of migrants throughout 2015, in particular in July and August of that year.

127. That finding of fact is not undermined by the existence of other factors that may also have contributed to that emergency situation, including structural defects in those systems in terms of lack of reception capacity and of capacity to process applications.

128. Moreover, the inflow of migrants with which the Greek and Italian asylum systems were confronted in 2015 was on such a scale that it would have disrupted any asylum system, even one without structural weaknesses.

129. Thirdly, the Court must reject the Slovak Republic's argument, which is supported by the Republic of Poland, that the contested decision could not properly be adopted on the basis of Article 78(3) TFEU because, instead of an existing or imminent emergency situation affecting the Hellenic Republic and the Italian Republic, it sought to resolve, at least in part, hypothetical future situations, that is to say, situations which, at the time of the adoption of the contested decision, could not have been claimed to be sufficiently likely to arise.

130. In fact, recitals 13 and 26 of the contested decision make clear that the decision was adopted on account of an emergency situation with which the Hellenic Republic and the Italian Republic were confronted in 2015, more specifically in July and August 2015. Accordingly, that situation had patently arisen before the date on which the contested decision was adopted even though it is apparent from recital 16 of the decision that the Council also took account of the fact that the emergency situation would very probably continue owing to the ongoing instability and conflicts in the immediate vicinity of Italy and Greece.

131. In addition, in view of the fact that migration flows are inherently likely to evolve rapidly, notably by shifting towards other Member States, the contested decision contains various mechanisms, in particular in Article 1(2), Article 4(2) and (3) and Article 11(2), to adapt its arrangements in the light of any change in the initial emergency situation, in particular in the event of such a situation arising in other Member States.

132. Article 78(3) TFEU does not preclude the provisional measures taken under it being supplemented by such adjustment mechanisms.

133. That provision confers a broad discretion on the Council in the choice of the measures that may be taken in order to respond rapidly and efficiently to a particular emergency as well as to any possible developments in the situation.

134. As the Advocate General has observed in point 130 of his Opinion, responding to the emergency does not mean that the response cannot evolve and adapt, provided that it retains its provisional nature.

135. The second part of the Slovak Republic's fifth plea must therefore be rejected.

*D. The pleas relating to the lawfulness of the procedure leading to the
adoption of the contested decision and alleging breach of essential
procedural requirements*

   *1. The Slovak Republic's first plea and Hungary's seventh plea,
alleging infringement of Article 68 TFEU*

   (a) Arguments of the parties

   136. The Slovak Republic and Hungary maintain that, since the
contested decision was adopted by qualified majority although it
followed from the European Council's conclusions of 25 and
26 June 2015 that the decision had to be adopted "by consensus"
in a manner "reflecting the specific situations of Member States", the
Council infringed Article 68 TFEU and breached essential
procedural requirements.

   137. The Slovak Republic and Hungary submit that the Council
should, at the time of the adoption of the contested decision, have
followed the guidelines deriving from those conclusions, in particular
the requirement that a distribution of applicants in clear need of
international protection between the Member States should be by a
decision adopted unanimously or in the form of voluntary allocations
agreed by the Member States.

   138. They submit that it was particularly important that the
Council abide by the conclusions of the European Council since
the Council should have taken account of the fact that the relocation
of applicants for international protection is a politically sensitive
question for several Member States given that such a relocation
measure significantly undermines the present system under the
Dublin III Regulation.

   139. Hungary submits in particular that, since the conclusions of
the European Council of 25 and 26 June 2015 expressly provided for
the Council to take a decision only in respect of the relocation of
40 000 applicants for international protection, the Council was not
entitled to decide on the relocation of 120 000 additional applicants
without having obtained the European Council's agreement in
principle in that regard. Consequently, both the Commission's presentation of a proposal for a decision entailing such additional relocation
and the Council's adoption of that proposal constitute, in its view, an
infringement of Article 68 TFEU and a breach of essential procedural
requirements.

   140. The Council contends that there is no contradiction between
the contested decision and the European Council's conclusions of
25 and 26 June 2015.

141. The Council further submits that the conclusions whereby the European Council defines "directions" do not provide the action taken by the other institutions either with a legal basis or with rules and principles by reference to which the Court reviews the legality of the acts of the other EU institutions, even though such directions are binding on the European Union under Article 15 TEU and are therefore not purely political in nature.

142. The Commission argues that, as the conclusions of the European Council are not binding but merely have effects at a political level, such conclusions cannot determine or limit, from the legal standpoint, the Commission's right of initiative to propose measures on the basis of Article 78(3) TFEU or the Council's power to adopt a decision under that provision after consulting the Parliament.

(b) Findings of the Court

143. The conclusions of the European Council of 25 and 26 June 2015 state that the Member States should agree "by consensus" on a distribution "reflecting the specific situations of Member States". On that point, those conclusions expressly refer to "the temporary and exceptional relocation over two years from Italy and Greece ... to other Member States of 40 000 persons in clear need of international protection" by means of "the rapid adoption by the Council of a decision to this effect".

144. That mechanism for the relocation of 40 000 persons formed the subject matter of Decision 2015/1523, which was adopted on 14 September 2015 by consensus. Thus, on that point Decision 2015/1523 implemented those conclusions in full.

145. As regards the alleged effect of the "political" nature of the conclusions of the European Council of 25 and 26 June 2015 on both the Commission's power of legislative initiative and the voting rules within the Council, as provided for in Article 78(3) TFEU, such an effect—assuming it to be established and discussed within the European Council—cannot be a ground on which the Court may annul the contested decision.

146. First, the power of legislative initiative accorded to the Commission by Article 17(2) TEU and Article 289 TFEU—which reflects the principle of conferred powers, enshrined in Article 13(2) TEU, and, more broadly, the principle of institutional balance, characteristic of the institutional structure of the European Union—means that it is for the Commission to decide whether to bring forward a proposal for a legislative act. In that connection, it is also for the Commission, which, in accordance with Article 17(1) TEU, is to

promote the general interest of the European Union and take appropriate initiatives to that end, to determine the subject matter, objective and content of the proposal (see, to that effect, judgment of 14 April 2015, *Council* v. *Commission*, C-409/13, EU:C:2015:217, paragraphs 64 and 70).

147. Those principles also apply to the Commission's power of initiative in the context of the adoption, on the basis of Article 78(3) TFEU, of non-legislative acts, such as the contested decision. In that regard, as the Advocate General has also observed in point 145 of his Opinion, Article 78(3) TFEU does not make the Commission's power of initiative conditional upon the European Council's having previously defined guidelines under Article 68 TFEU.

148. Secondly, Article 78(3) TFEU allows the Council to adopt measures by a qualified majority, as it did when it adopted the contested decision. The principle of institutional balance prevents the European Council from altering that voting rule by imposing on the Council, by means of conclusions adopted pursuant to Article 68 TFEU, a rule requiring a unanimous vote.

149. Indeed, as the Court has already held, as the rules regarding the manner in which the EU institutions arrive at their decisions are laid down in the Treaties and are not within the discretion of the Member States or of the institutions themselves, the Treaties alone may, in particular cases, empower an institution to amend a decision-making procedure established by the Treaties (judgment of 10 September 2015, *Parliament* v. *Council*, C-363/14, EU:C:2015:579, paragraph 43).

150. The Slovak Republic's first plea and Hungary's seventh plea must therefore be rejected as unfounded.

2. The third part of the Slovak Republic's third plea and the first part of its fourth plea, and Hungary's fifth plea, alleging breach of essential procedural requirements in that the Council did not comply with the obligation to consult the Parliament laid down in Article 78(3) TFEU

(a) Arguments of the parties

151. The Slovak Republic and Hungary claim that, since the Council made substantial amendments to the Commission's initial proposal and adopted the contested decision without consulting the Parliament afresh, it breached the essential procedural requirements laid down in Article 78(3) TFEU, with the consequence that the contested decision must be annulled. The Slovak Republic maintains that, in proceeding in that way, the Council also infringed Article 10(1)

and (2) and Article 13(2) TEU and breached the principles of representative democracy, institutional balance and sound administration.

152. It is argued that the most significant amendments to the Commission's initial proposal concern the fact that, in the contested decision, Hungary is no longer among the Member States that benefit from relocation as do the Hellenic Republic and the Italian Republic, but is instead among the Member States of relocation. That entailed, in particular, the deletion of Annex III to the Commission's initial proposal, which concerned relocation quotas from Hungary, and the inclusion of Hungary in Annexes I and II to the contested decision.

153. The Slovak Republic mentions other amendments which were made to the Commission's initial proposal and are included in the contested decision, including the fact that that decision does not lay down an exhaustive list of the Member States that may benefit from the system of relocation which it establishes but provides, in Article 4(3), that other Member States may benefit from it if they satisfy the conditions set out in that provision.

154. The applicants take issue with the Council for having failed to consult the Parliament again after making those amendments to the Commission's initial proposal, even though, in its resolution of 17 September 2015, the Parliament had asked the Council to consult it again if it intended to substantially amend the Commission's proposal.

155. Although the Presidency of the European Union regularly informed the Parliament, in particular the Parliament's Civil Liberties, Justice and Home Affairs Committee, of how the Council's dossier was progressing, that cannot, in the applicants' submission, replace a formal resolution of the Parliament adopted in plenary session.

156. Hungary refers in that regard to two letters sent by the President of the Parliament's Legal Affairs Committee to the President of the Parliament, in which it is stated that that committee had reached the conclusion that the Council had substantially amended the Commission's initial proposal by removing Hungary from the group of beneficiary Member States and that the Parliament should therefore have been consulted again.

157. The Council's primary contention is that, in view of the urgent nature of the case, its consultation of the Parliament was sufficient, enabling the latter to familiarise itself, in good time, with the substance of the final text of the contested decision and to express a view on the matter. In any event, the text of the contested decision, as finally adopted and taken as a whole, did not substantially depart

from the text on which the Parliament had been consulted on 14 September 2015.

(b) Findings of the Court

158. It should be noted as a preliminary point that the Council contends that the letters from the Parliament's Legal Affairs Committee, which were produced by Hungary in an annex to its reply and are mentioned in paragraph 156 of the present judgment, are inadmissible as evidence since they were improperly obtained. It requests that the Court, as a precautionary step, remove those letters from the file in the present cases. Like Hungary, it asks the Court to adopt a measure of inquiry inviting the Parliament to confirm whether the letters are authentic and, if they are, to clarify their legal status and to let the Court know whether it would agree to Hungary using the letters as evidence.

159. In that regard, the Court considers that, since it has been sufficiently informed of the facts relating to the question whether, in the present case, the Council complied with its obligation to consult the Parliament, as provided for in Article 78(3) TFEU, it is in a position to decide that question of law without it being necessary to address the requested measure of inquiry to the Parliament.

160. As for the substance, it must be recalled that due consultation of the Parliament in the cases provided for by the Treaty constitutes an essential procedural requirement disregard of which renders the measure concerned void. Effective participation of the Parliament in the decision-making process, in accordance with the procedures laid down by the Treaty, represents an essential element of the institutional balance intended by the Treaty. This function reflects the fundamental demo-cratic principle that the people should take part in the exercise of power through the intermediary of a representative assembly (see, to that effect, inter alia, judgments of 11 November 1997, *Eurotunnel and Others*, C-408/95, EU:C:1997:532, paragraph 45, and of 7 March 2017, *RPO*, C-390/15, EU:C:2017:174, paragraphs 24 and 25).

161. The Court has consistently held that the obligation to consult the Parliament in the decision-making procedure in the cases provided for by the Treaty means that the Parliament must be consulted again whenever the text finally adopted, taken as a whole, differs in essence from the text on which the Parliament has already been consulted, except in cases in which the amendments substantially correspond to the wishes of the Parliament itself (see judgments of 11 November 1997, *Eurotunnel and Others*, C-408/95, EU:C:1997:532, paragraph 46, and of 7 March 2017, *RPO*, C-390/15, EU:C:2017:174, paragraph 26).

162. Amendments which go to the heart of the arrangements established or affect the scheme of the proposal as a whole are to be regarded as substantial amendments (see, to that effect, judgment of 1 June 1994, *Parliament* v. *Council*, C-388/92, EU:C:1994:213, paragraphs 13 and 18).

163. In this regard, the various amendments to the Commission's initial proposal which related to the change of Hungary's status were made by the Council after Hungary had refused to be a beneficiary of the relocation mechanism provided for by the proposal. Nevertheless, taking account in particular of the fact that Article 78(3) TFEU concerns the adoption of provisional measures for the benefit of one or more Member States confronted with an emergency situation within the meaning of that provision, the determination of the Member States benefiting from those provisional measures is an essential element of any measure adopted on the basis of Article 78(3) TFEU.

164. It must therefore be held that the text of the contested decision as finally adopted, taken as a whole, differs in essence from the Commission's initial proposal.

165. It must, however, be noted that on 16 September 2015 the President of the Council stated at an extraordinary plenary sitting of the Parliament:

Given the urgency of the situation and as mentioned in the letter consulting the Parliament, I am taking the opportunity to inform you that there will be a significant departure from the [Commission's] initial proposal.

Hungary does not consider itself to be a frontline country and has told us that it does not wish to be a beneficiary of relocation.

The Parliament will be able to take this information into account in its opinion.

166. Accordingly, in its legislative resolution of 17 September 2015 expressing its support for the Commission's initial proposal, the Parliament must necessarily have taken account of that fundamental change in Hungary's status, which the Council was bound to respect.

167. Furthermore, although the Council made other amendments to the Commission's initial proposal following the Parliament's adoption of that legislative resolution, those amendments did not affect the very essence of the proposal.

168. Moreover, the Council Presidency, within the framework of the informal contacts mentioned in the consultation letter, kept the Parliament fully informed of those amendments.

169. The obligation to consult the Parliament laid down in Article 78(3) TFEU was therefore complied with.

170. In view of the foregoing, the Court rejects as unfounded the third part of the Slovak Republic's third plea and the first part of its fourth plea and Hungary's fifth plea.

3. *The second part of the Slovak Republic's fourth plea and Hungary's third plea, alleging breach of essential procedural requirements in that the Council did not act unanimously, contrary to Article 293(1) TFEU*

(a) Arguments of the parties

171. The Slovak Republic and Hungary maintain that, in adopting the contested decision, the Council breached the essential procedural requirement imposed in Article 293(1) TFEU, in that it amended the Commission's proposal without complying with the requirement for unanimity laid down in that provision. The Slovak Republic submits that, in so doing, the Council also infringed Article 13(2) TEU and breached the principles of institutional balance and sound administration.

172. The applicants argue that the requirement for unanimity laid down in Article 293(1) TFEU applies to any amendment of the Commission's proposal, including where the amendment is minor and regardless of whether the Commission has explicitly or implicitly accepted the amendments made to its proposal during the discussions within the Council.

173. They also claim that there is nothing to indicate that, during the procedure leading to the adoption of the contested decision, the Commission withdrew its proposal and submitted a new proposal drafted in identical terms to those of the text that was finally adopted. On the contrary, it follows from the minutes of the Council's sitting of 22 September 2015 that the Commission neither lodged a new proposal nor made a preliminary declaration concerning the amended proposal as finally adopted by the Council.

174. However, the Commission is required to endorse actively and explicitly the amendments concerned before it can be considered to have altered its proposal within the meaning of Article 293(2) TFEU. The present case is, they submit, different in this respect from that at issue in the judgment of 5 October 1994, *Germany* v. *Council* (C-280/93, EU:C:1994:367).

175. The Council replies that, on 22 September 2015, during the Council meeting at which the contested decision was adopted, the

Commission, represented by its First Vice-President and by the Commissioner responsible for asylum and immigration, agreed to all the Council's amendments to the Commission's initial proposal. That agreement—even if it were considered to be implicit—would amount to an alteration of the proposal on the part of the Commission.

176. The Commission similarly submits that it amended its proposal in accordance with the amendments adopted by the responsible Commissioners on its behalf in order to facilitate the proposal's adoption.

(b) Findings of the Court

177. Article 293 TFEU attaches to the Commission's power of initiative—in this case the power conferred by Article 78(3) TFEU in the framework of a non-legislative procedure—a twofold safeguard. On the one hand, Article 293(1) TFEU provides that where, pursuant to the Treaties, the Council acts on a proposal from the Commission, it may amend that proposal only by acting unanimously, except in the cases referred to in the provisions of the FEU Treaty which are mentioned in Article 293(1) and which are of no relevance in the present case. On the other hand, Article 293(2) TFEU states that, as long as the Council has not acted, the Commission may alter its proposal at any time during the procedures leading to the adoption of an EU act (see, to that effect, judgment of 14 April 2015, *Council* v. *Commission*, C-409/13, EU:C:2015:217, paragraphs 71 to 73).

178. It follows that if, under Article 293(2) TFEU, the Commission amends its proposal during the procedure for adoption of an EU act, the Council is not subject to the requirement for unanimity laid down in Article 293(1) TFEU.

179. So far as Article 293(2) TFEU is concerned, the Court has already held that the amended proposals that the Commission adopts do not have to be in writing as they are part of the process for adopting EU acts, a characteristic of which is a degree of flexibility, necessary for achieving a convergence of views between the institutions (see, to that effect, judgment of 5 October 1994, *Germany* v. *Council*, C-280/93, EU:C:1994:367, paragraph 36).

180. Such considerations as to flexibility must, a fortiori, prevail in the case of the procedure for adopting an act on the basis of Article 78(3) TFEU, since the purpose of that provision is to make it possible for provisional measures to be adopted quickly so as to provide a rapid and effective response to an "emergency situation" within the meaning of that provision.

181. It follows that, in the particular context of Article 78(3) TFEU, the Commission may be considered to have exercised its power of amendment under Article 293(2) TFEU when its participation in the process for adopting the measure concerned clearly shows that it has approved the amended proposal. Such an interpretation is consistent with the objective of Article 293(2) TFEU, which seeks to protect the Commission's power of initiative.

182. In the present case the Commission does not consider its power of initiative under Article 78(3) TFEU to have been undermined.

183. It submits in that regard that it amended its initial proposal since it approved the amendments made to that document at the various meetings held within the Council.

184. It states that it was represented at those meetings by two of its Members, namely its First Vice-President and the Commissioner responsible, inter alia, for immigration. They were duly empowered by the College of Commissioners, pursuant to Article 13 of the Commission's Rules of Procedure, to approve amendments to its initial proposal in keeping with the priority objective, set by the College of Commissioners at its meeting of 16 September 2015, which was that the Council should adopt a binding and immediately applicable decision concerning the relocation of 120 000 persons in clear need of international protection.

185. In this connection, it follows from Article 13 of the Commission's Rules of Procedure, interpreted in the light of the objective of Article 293(2) TFEU of protecting the Commission's power of initiative, that the College of Commissioners may authorise one or more of its Members to amend, in the course of the procedure, the Commission's proposal within the limits that the College has previously defined.

186. Although the Slovak Republic and Hungary dispute the fact that the two Members of the Commission in question had been duly empowered by the College of Commissioners, as required by Article 13 of the Commission's Rules of Procedure, to approve the amendments to the initial proposal, those Member States have adduced no evidence which casts doubt on the veracity of the Commission's remarks or the reliability of the evidence that it has put before the Court.

187. In view of those matters, it must be held that in the present case the Commission exercised its power under Article 293(2) TFEU to amend a proposal, since its participation in the process for adopting the contested decision clearly shows that the amended proposal was

approved on behalf of the Commission by two of its Members, who were authorised by the College of Commissioners to adopt the amendments concerned.

188. Accordingly, the Council was not subject to the requirement for unanimity laid down in Article 293(1) TFEU.

189. In the light of the foregoing, the Court rejects as unfounded the second part of the Slovak Republic's fourth plea and Hungary's third plea.

4. *The first and second parts of the Slovak Republic's third plea and Hungary's fourth plea, alleging breach of essential procedural requirements, in that the right of the national parliaments to issue an opinion in accordance with Protocol (No 1) and Protocol (No 2) was not respected and that the Council failed to fulfil the requirement that the deliberations and the vote within the Council be held in public*

(a) Arguments of the parties

190. The Slovak Republic, by way of alternative plea, and Hungary claim that, at the time of the adoption of the contested decision, the right of the national parliaments to issue an opinion on any draft proposal for a legislative act, as provided for in Protocols (No 1) and (No 2) was not respected.

191. The Slovak Republic further maintains, in the alternative, that if the Court were to hold that the contested decision had to be adopted by means of a legislative procedure, the Council breached an essential procedural requirement by adopting the contested decision in camera, following the rule applicable when it carries out its non-legislative activities, whilst Article 16(8) TEU and Article 15(2) TFEU provide that the meetings of the Council are to be held in public when it considers and votes on a draft legislative act.

192. The Council contends that since the contested decision is a non-legislative act, the decision is not subject to the conditions attached to the adoption of a legislative act.

(b) Findings of the Court

193. Since, as is apparent from paragraph 67 of the present judgment, the contested decision must be classified as a non-legislative act, it follows that the adoption of that act in a non-legislative procedure was not subject to the requirements relating to the participation of the national parliaments provided for by Protocols (No 1) and (No 2) or the requirements relating to the public nature of the deliberations and

the vote within the Council, which apply only when draft legislative acts are adopted.

194. Accordingly, the first and second parts of the Slovak Republic's third plea and Hungary's fourth plea must be rejected as unfounded.

5. *Hungary's sixth plea, alleging breach of essential procedural requirements in that, when adopting the contested decision, the Council did not comply with the rules of EU law on the use of languages*

(a) Arguments of the parties

195. Hungary maintains that the contested decision is vitiated by a fundamental procedural error inasmuch as the Council failed to comply with the rules of EU law on the use of languages.

196. It claims, in particular, that the Council infringed Article 14(1) of its Rules of Procedure since the texts setting forth the successive amendments to the Commission's initial proposal, including, ultimately, the text of the contested decision as adopted by the Council, were provided to the Member States only in English.

197. In its reply, the Slovak Republic raises a similar plea, which it considers to involve a question of public policy, alleging breach of essential formal requirements, in that the Council failed to comply with the language rules, in particular Article 14(1) of its Rules of Procedure, in the adoption of the contested decision.

198. The Council submits that the Council's deliberations were conducted in accordance with EU law on the use of languages and, in particular, with the simplified language rules that apply in the case of amendments, as provided for by Article 14(2) of the Council's Rules of Procedure.

(b) Findings of the Court

199. As a preliminary point, the Court notes, without there being any need to rule on the admissibility of the plea raised by the Slovak Republic alleging an infringement of the rules of EU law on the use of languages, that that plea overlaps with Hungary's sixth plea, which must be examined as to its substance.

200. Hungary's sixth plea alleges infringement of Article 14 of the Council's Rules of Procedure, which is headed "Deliberations and decisions on the basis of documents and drafts drawn up in the languages provided for by the language rules in force" and in particular of Article 14(1) of those rules, which provides that except as otherwise decided unanimously by the Council on grounds of urgency, the Council is to

deliberate and take decisions only on the basis of documents and drafts drawn up in the languages specified in the rules in force governing languages. Under Article 14(2) of those rules, any member of the Council may oppose discussion if any proposed amendments are not drawn up in such of the languages referred to in paragraph 1 of that article.

201. The Council submits that Article 14 must be interpreted—and is applied in practice by the institution—to the effect that, whilst paragraph 1 of that article requires that the drafts that constitute the "basis" of the Council's deliberations, in this instance the Commission's initial proposal, must as a rule be drawn up in all the official languages of the European Union, paragraph 2 lays down a simplified procedure for amendments, which do not necessarily have to be available in all the official languages of the European Union. Only where a Member State objects do the language versions indicated by that Member State also have to be submitted to the Council before it can continue to deliberate.

202. The Council's Comments on its Rules of Procedure explain, in the same vein, that Article 14(2) of those rules enables any member of the Council to oppose discussion if any proposed amendments are not drawn up in all the official languages of the European Union.

203. Even though, as the Court has already stated, the European Union is committed to the preservation of multilingualism, the importance of which is stated in the fourth subparagraph of Article 3(3) TEU (see, to that effect, judgment of 5 May 2015, *Spain* v. *Council*, C-147/13, EU:C:2015:299, paragraph 42), the Council's interpretation of its Rules of Procedure must be accepted. That interpretation in fact reflects a balanced and flexible approach conducive to efficacy and speed in the Council's work, which are especially important in the particular context of urgency characterising the procedure for adopting provisional measures on the basis of Article 78(3) TFEU.

204. It is common ground that in the present case the Commission's initial proposal was made available to all the delegations of the Member States in all the official languages of the European Union. Furthermore, Hungary has not disputed the fact that no Member State raised any objection to discussions being on the basis of documents drafted in English and setting out the agreed amendments and that, moreover, all the amendments were read by the President of the Council and simultaneously interpreted into all the official languages of the European Union.

205. Having regard to all the foregoing, the Court rejects as unfounded the plea raised by the Slovak Republic and Hungary's sixth plea, which concern an alleged infringement of the European Union's language rules.

E. The substantive pleas in law

1. The Slovak Republic's 6th plea and Hungary's 9th and 10th pleas, alleging breach of the principle of proportionality

(a) *Preliminary observations*

206. As a preliminary point, it must be recalled that, according to settled case law of the Court, the principle of proportionality requires that acts of the EU institutions be appropriate for attaining the legitimate objectives pursued by the legislation at issue and do not go beyond what is necessary in order to achieve those objectives; when there is a choice between several appropriate measures, recourse must be had to the least onerous, and the disadvantages caused must not be disproportionate to the aims pursued (see, inter alia, judgment of 4 May 2016, *Poland* v. *Parliament and Council,* C-358/14, EU: C:2016:323, paragraph 78 and the case law cited).

207. With regard to judicial review of compliance with that principle, it should also be borne in mind, as has already been stated in paragraph 124 of the present judgment, that the EU institutions must be allowed broad discretion when they adopt measures in areas which entail choices on their part, including of a political nature, and in which they are called upon to undertake complex assessments. Consequently, the legality of a measure adopted in one of those areas can be affected only if the measure is manifestly inappropriate having regard to the objective which those institutions are seeking to pursue (see, to that effect, judgment of 4 May 2016, *Poland* v. *Parliament and Council,* C-358/14, EU:C:2016:323, paragraph 79 and the case law cited).

208. The principles thus affirmed by the Court's case law are fully applicable to the measures adopted in the area of the European Union's common policy on asylum and, in particular, to provisional measures adopted on the basis of Article 78(3) TFEU, such as those provided for in the contested decision. Those measures entail essentially political choices and complex assessments that must, in addition, be made within a short time in order to provide a swift and tangible response to an "emergency situation" within the meaning of that provision.

(b) *The Slovak Republic's sixth plea, in so far as it alleges that the contested decision is not appropriate for attaining the objective which it pursues*

(1) Arguments of the parties

209. The Slovak Republic, supported by the Republic of Poland, claims that the contested decision is not appropriate for attaining the objective which it pursues and that the decision is therefore contrary to

the principle of proportionality, laid down in Article 5(4) TEU and Articles 1 and 5 of Protocol (No 2).

210. In its view, the contested decision is not appropriate for attaining that objective because the relocation mechanism for which it provides is not capable of redressing the structural defects in the Greek and Italian asylum systems. Those shortcomings, which relate to lack of reception capacity and of capacity to process applications for international protection, need to be remedied before the relocation can actually be implemented. Moreover, the small number of relocations that have so far been carried out shows that, ever since its adoption, the relocation mechanism set up by the contested decision has been inappropriate for attaining the intended objective.

211. The Council and the Member States supporting it contend that, although there are structural defects in the Greek and Italian asylum systems, the relocation mechanism set up by the contested decision is appropriate for attaining its objective, in that it relieves the unsustainable pressure to which the asylum systems of the Hellenic Republic and the Italian Republic were subject after the unprecedented influx of migrants to their respective territories in 2015. They submit that any Member State whatsoever would have found that pressure unsustainable, including those whose asylum systems do not suffer from structural weaknesses. Moreover, the relocation mechanism is one of a broad range of financial and operational measures to support the asylum systems of the Hellenic Republic and the Italian Republic. The contested decision also imposes obligations on those two Member States, the aim of which is to enhance the efficiency of their respective asylum systems.

(2) Findings of the Court

212. The objective of the relocation mechanism provided for in the contested decision, in the light of which the proportionality of that mechanism must be considered, is, according to Article 1(1) of the decision, read in conjunction with recital 26 thereof, to help the Hellenic Republic and the Italian Republic cope with an emergency situation characterised by a sudden inflow, in their respective territories, of third-country nationals in clear need of international protection, by relieving the significant pressure on the Greek and Italian asylum systems.

213. The mechanism for relocating a significant number of applicants in clear need of international protection for which the contested decision provides cannot be considered a measure that is manifestly inappropriate for working towards that objective.

214. It is equally hard to deny that any asylum system, even one without structural weaknesses in terms of reception capacity and capacity to process applications for international protection, would have been seriously disrupted by the unprecedented influx of migrants that occurred in Greece and Italy in 2015.

215. In addition, the relocation mechanism provided for in the contested decision forms part of a set of measures intended to relieve the pressure on Greece and Italy. The specific purpose of a number of those measures is to improve the functioning of their respective asylum systems. Consequently, the appropriateness of the relocation mechanism for attaining its objectives cannot be assessed in isolation but must be viewed within the framework of the set of measures of which it forms part.

216. Thus, Article 8 of the contested decision provides for complementary measures, in particular to enhance the capacity, quality and efficiency of the asylum systems, which must be taken by the Hellenic Republic and the Italian Republic. Those measures supplement the measures already prescribed by Article 8 of Decision 2015/1523 and their aim is, according to recital 18 of the contested decision, to oblige those Member States "to provide structural solutions to address exceptional pressures on their asylum and migration systems, by establishing a solid and strategic framework for responding to the crisis situation and intensifying the ongoing reform process in these areas".

217. Furthermore, Article 7 of the contested decision allows for the provision of operational support for the Hellenic Republic and the Italian Republic and Article 10 provides for them to receive financial support for each person relocated.

218. The relocation mechanism provided for in the contested decision also supplements other measures intended to take pressure off the Greek and Italian asylum systems, which have been severely disrupted by the successive surges in migratory flows since 2014. That is the case of (i) the European programme for the resettlement of 22 504 persons in need of international protection agreed upon on 20 July 2015 by the Member States and the States associated with the system deriving from the Dublin III Regulation, (ii) Decision 2015/1523 concerning the relocation of 40 000 persons in clear need of international protection, and (iii) the establishment of "hotspots" in Italy and Greece, where all the EU agencies responsible for asylum-related matters and experts from the Member States work specifically with local and national authorities to help the Member States concerned meet their obligations under EU law with regard to such persons, in terms of checking, identification, registration of testimony and fingerprinting.

219. Moreover, as is stated in recital 15 of the contested decision, the Hellenic Republic and the Italian Republic have received substantial operational and financial support from the European Union in the framework of the migration and asylum policy.

220. Lastly, it cannot be concluded, a posteriori, from the small number of relocations so far carried out pursuant to the contested decision that the latter was, from the outset, inappropriate for attaining the objective pursued, as is argued by the Slovak Republic and by Hungary in the context of its ninth plea.

221. In fact, the Court has consistently held that the legality of an EU act cannot depend on retrospective assessments of its efficacy. Where the EU legislature is obliged to assess the future effects of rules to be adopted and those effects cannot be accurately foreseen, its assessment is open to criticism only if it appears manifestly incorrect in the light of the information available to it at the time of the adoption of the rules in question (see, inter alia, judgments of 12 July 2001, *Jippes and Others*, C-189/01, EU:C:2001:420, paragraph 84, and of 9 June 2016, *Pesce and Others*, C-78/16 and C-79/16, EU: C:2016:428, paragraph 50).

222. In the present case, as can be seen from, inter alia, recitals 13, 14 and 26 of the contested decision, when the Council adopted the mechanism for the relocation of a large number of applicants for international protection, it carried out, on the basis of a detailed examination of the statistical data available at the time, a prospective analysis of the effects of the measure on the emergency situation in question. In the light of those data, that analysis does not appear manifestly incorrect.

223. Moreover, it is apparent that the small number of relocations so far carried out pursuant to the contested decision can be explained by a series of factors that the Council could not foresee at the time when the decision was adopted, including, in particular, the lack of cooperation on the part of certain Member States.

224. Having regard to the foregoing, the Court rejects as unfounded the Slovak Republic's sixth plea, in so far as it alleges that the contested decision is not appropriate for attaining the objective which it pursues.

(c) The Slovak Republic's sixth plea, in so far as it alleges that the contested decision is not necessary in the light of the objective which it seeks to attain

(1) Arguments of the parties

225. The Slovak Republic, supported by the Republic of Poland, maintains, first of all, that the objective pursued by means of the

contested decision could be achieved just as effectively by other measures which could have been taken in the context of existing instruments
and would have been less restrictive for Member States and impinged
less on the "sovereign" right of each Member State to decide freely
upon the admission of nationals of third countries to its territory and
on the right of Member States, set out in Article 5 of Protocol (No 2),
that the financial and administrative burden should be minimised.

226. First, the Slovak Republic submits that recourse could have
been had to the mechanism provided for by Council Directive 2001/
55/EC of 20 July 2001 on minimum standards for giving temporary
protection in the event of a mass influx of displaced persons and on
measures promoting a balance of efforts between Member States in
receiving such persons and bearing the consequences thereof (OJ 2001
L 212, p. 12).

227. It argues that the purpose of Directive 2001/55 is in essence to
respond to the same situations of massive inflows of migrants as the
contested decision by laying down a procedure for relocating persons
qualifying for temporary protection. However, that directive is less
harmful to the sovereign right of each Member State to decide freely
on the admission of nationals of third countries to its territory, above
all because it permits the Member States to decide themselves, in view
of their reception capacity, how many persons are to be relocated to
their territory. In addition, the status of temporary protection confers
fewer rights than the status of international protection that the contested decision seeks to afford, in particular as regards the period of
protection, and thus imposes significantly fewer burdens on the
Member State of relocation.

228. Secondly, the Slovak Republic submits that the Hellenic
Republic and the Italian Republic could have triggered what is known
as the "EU civil protection" mechanism provided for in Article 8a of
Council Regulation (EC) No 2007/2004 of 26 October 2004 estab-
lishing a European Agency for the Management of Operational
Cooperation at the External Borders of the Member States of the
European Union (OJ 2004 L 349, p. 1). That mechanism could have
provided them with the necessary material assistance.

229. The Slovak Republic claims, thirdly, that the Hellenic
Republic and the Italian Republic could also have sought assistance
from the Frontex Agency in the form of "rapid intervention". Likewise,
in accordance with Article 2(1)(f) and Article 9(1) and (1b) of
Regulation No 2007/2004, those two Member States could, in its
submission, have asked the Frontex Agency to procure for them the
necessary assistance to arrange return operations.

230. Such assistance from the Frontex Agency would have been capable of providing direct relief for the asylum and migration systems of those two Member States, since it would have allowed them to concentrate their resource on migrants who were applying for international protection.

231. Next, the Slovak Republic claims that it was not necessary to adopt other measures on the basis of Article 78(3) TFEU, as Decision 2015/1523 leaves it to the Member States to decide, in a spirit of solidarity, upon the extent to which they will participate in the common commitment. That decision is therefore less prejudicial to their sovereignty. Since the contested decision was adopted only eight days after Decision 2015/1523 providing for the relocation of 40 000 persons, it was impossible to conclude in such a brief period that Decision 2015/1523 was not appropriate for the purpose of responding to the situation obtaining at that time. Indeed, at the time of the adoption of the contested decision, nothing gave the Council grounds for considering that the reception measures provided for in Decision 2015/1523 would quickly become insufficient and that additional measures would be necessary.

232. The Slovak Republic further argues that Article 78(3) TFEU also made it possible to adopt measures which, whilst less restrictive for the Member States, would be suitable for attaining the objective pursued, such as the provision of assistance to facilitate return and registration or the provision of financial, material, technical and personnel support to the Italian and Greek asylum systems. The Member States could also take bilateral initiatives, on a voluntary basis, in order to provide such support and such initiatives have in fact been taken.

233. The Slovak Republic submits, finally, that the relocation of applicants provided for in the contested decision inevitably entails a financial and administrative burden for the Member States. The imposition of such a burden was not necessary since other, less restrictive measures were feasible. Consequently, the decision constitutes a superfluous and premature measure, contrary to the principle of proportionality and to Article 5 of Protocol (No 2).

234. The Council contends that, at the time of the adoption of the contested decision, it made sure, in accordance with the principle of proportionality, that there was no alternative measure that would enable the objective pursued by that decision to be attained as effectively, while impinging as little as possible on the sovereignty of the Member States or their financial interests. The alternative measures listed by the Slovak Republic do not, however, work to that effect.

(2) Findings of the Court

235. The Slovak Republic has put forward various arguments to demonstrate that the contested decision was unnecessary because the Council could have achieved the objective pursued by the decision by means of less restrictive measures that impinged less on the right of the Member States to decide, in compliance with the rules adopted by the European Union in the area of the common asylum policy, on the access to their territories of third-country nationals. Before examining those arguments, it is necessary to recall the particularly sensitive context in which the contested decision was adopted, namely the acute emergency in Greece and Italy at that time, which was characterised by a sudden massive inflow of nationals of third countries in July and August 2015.

236. In such a particular context and in view of the principles already outlined in paragraphs 206 to 208 of the present judgment, it must be accepted that the decision to adopt a compulsory mechanism for relocating 120 000 persons under Article 78(3) TFEU, whilst it must be founded on objective criteria, may be censured by the Court only if it is found that, when the Council adopted the contested decision, it made, in the light of the information and data available at that time, a manifest error of assessment in the sense that another measure that was less restrictive, but equally effective, could have been adopted within the same period.

237. In that regard, it should be noted, first, that, whilst it is true that Decision 2015/1523 was adopted on 14 September 2015—in other words eight days before the contested decision—there is a connection between those measures.

238. Decision 2015/1523 was intended to put into effect the conclusions of the European Council of 25 and 26 June 2015 as well as the agreement between the Member States in the form of a resolution dated 20 July 2015. As can be seen from the statistical data mentioned in recitals 10 and 11 of Decision 2015/1523, the purpose of the latter was to respond to an emergency situation that had arisen in the first six months of 2015.

239. It is also clear from recital 21 of that decision that the total of 40 000 applicants was set on the basis of (i) the overall number of third-country nationals who entered Italy or Greece irregularly in 2014 and (ii) the number of those persons who were in clear need of international protection, who represented around 40% of the overall number of third-country nationals. It was decided on the basis of those 2014 figures that, of those 40 000 persons, 60% should be relocated from Italy and 40% from Greece.

240. On the other hand, it is apparent from the considerations and statistical data which the Council took as its basis when it adopted the contested decision and which are mentioned in particular in recitals 12, 13 and 26 thereof that the Council considered that a relocation mechanism for 120 000 persons, in addition to the mechanism provided for by Decision 2015/1523, had to be established in order to relieve the pressure on the Italian Republic and, above all, on the Hellenic Republic in the light of the new emergency arising from the fact that a huge number of migrants had entered those Member States irregularly in the first eight months of 2015, in particular in July and August of that year.

241. That further inflow of migrants, which was on an unprecedented scale, was also characterised by the fact that it came about, as is stated in recital 12 of the contested decision, because migration flows had shifted from the central to the eastern Mediterranean and towards the Western Balkans route. That partial shift of the crisis from Italy to Greece also explains why it was decided that 13% of the total of 120 000 applicants for international protection should be relocated from Italy and 42% from Greece.

242. In those circumstances, the Council cannot be held to have made a manifest error of assessment in considering, in view of the most recent data available to it, that the emergency situation as at 22 September 2015 justified relocating 120 000 persons and that the relocation of 40 000 persons already provided for in Decision 2015/1523 would not be sufficient.

243. Secondly, as regards the impact of the contested decision on the legal framework governing the admission of third-country nationals, the Court notes that the relocation mechanism provided for in the decision, whilst mandatory, applies for a two-year period only and concerns a limited number of migrants in clear need of international protection.

244. The binding effect of the contested decision is also limited because the decision makes it a condition of a relocation that Member States indicate, at regular intervals, and at least every three months, the number of applicants who can be relocated swiftly to their territory (Article 5(2) of the contested decision) and that they approve the relocation of the person concerned (Article 5(4) of the decision), with the proviso that, under Article 5(7) of the decision, a Member State may refuse to relocate an applicant only where there are reasonable grounds for doing so, related to public order or national security.

245. Thirdly, as regards the Slovak Republic's argument that the contested decision is disproportionate because it needlessly imposes a

binding mechanism entailing the compulsory distribution between the Member States, in the form of quotas, of specific numbers of relocated persons, the Council does not appear to have made a manifest error of assessment in having chosen to introduce a binding relocation mechanism of that kind.

246. In fact, the Council was fully entitled to take the view, in the exercise of the broad discretion which it must be allowed in this regard, that the distribution of the persons to be relocated had to be mandatory, given the particular urgency of the situation in which the contested decision was to be adopted.

247. The Council has stated moreover, without being challenged on this point, that it had had to accept that the distribution by consensus between the Member States of the 40 000 persons concerned by Decision 2015/1523 had, even after long negotiations, ended in failure: consequently, when that decision was finally adopted, it did not include a table setting out the commitments of the Member States of relocation.

248. Nor is it disputed that, in the discussions on the contested decision within the Council, it quickly became clear that a decision by consensus, in particular on the distribution of the persons relocated, would prove to be impossible in the short term.

249. The Council was, however, bound, in view of the critical situation of the Hellenic Republic and the Italian Republic following the unprecedented inflow of migrants in July and August 2015, to take measures which could be swiftly put in place and actually have an effect in helping those Member States to control the large migration flows on their territory.

250. In addition, in view of the considerations and statistical data referred to, inter alia, in recitals 12 to 16 of the contested decision, there is no ground for maintaining that the Council made a manifest error of assessment in concluding that the situation called for the adoption of a temporary relocation measure that was binding in nature.

251. It is thus apparent (i) from recital 15 of the contested decision that the Council found that many actions had already been taken to support the Hellenic Republic and the Italian Republic in the framework of the migration and asylum policy and (ii) from recital 16 of the decision that, since it was likely that significant and growing pressure would continue to be put on the Greek and Italian asylum systems, the Council considered it vital to show solidarity towards those two Member States and to complement the actions already taken with the provisional measures provided for in the contested decision.

252. In that regard, the Council, when adopting the contested decision, was in fact required, as is stated in recital 2 of the decision, to give effect to the principle of solidarity and fair sharing of responsibility, including its financial implications, between the Member States, which applies, under Article 80 TFEU, when the EU common policy on asylum is implemented.

253. Thus, in the circumstances of this case, there is no ground for complaining that the Council made a manifest error of assessment when it considered, in view of the particular urgency of the situation, that it had to take—on the basis of Article 78(3) TFEU, read in the light of Article 80 TFEU and the principle of solidarity between the Member States laid down therein—provisional measures imposing a binding relocation mechanism, such as that provided for in the contested decision.

254. Fourthly, contrary to what is maintained by the Slovak Republic and Hungary, the choice of a binding relocation mechanism cannot be criticised on the ground that Article 78(3) TFEU only permits the adoption of provisional measures that can be swiftly put into effect, whereas the preparation and implementation of a binding relocation mechanism requires a certain amount of time before relocations can proceed at a steady pace.

255. Article 78(3) TFEU seeks to ensure that effective action is taken and does not prescribe for that purpose any period within which provisional measures must be implemented. The Council thus did not go beyond the bounds of its broad discretion when it considered that the situation obtaining in July and August 2015 justified the adoption of a binding relocation mechanism to address that situation and that the mechanism should be established as soon as possible in order to produce tangible results equally soon, following any period necessary for preparation and implementation.

256. As regards Directive 2001/55 in particular, the Council has also maintained, without being contradicted on this point, that the system of temporary protection under that directive did not actually provide a solution to the problem in the present case—namely the complete saturation of reception facilities in Greece and Italy and the need to relieve those Member States as quickly as possible of a large number of migrants who had already arrived in their territory—since that system of temporary protection provides that persons eligible under it are entitled to protection in the Member State where they are located.

257. Fifthly, the choice made in the contested decision to grant international protection rather than a status conferring more limited

rights, such as the status of temporary protection for which Directive 2001/55 provides, is an essentially political choice, the appropriateness of which cannot be examined by the Court.

258. So far as concerns, sixthly, the other measures mentioned by the Slovak Republic which it claims would be less restrictive than the contested decision, the Court observes that, unlike the relocation mechanism for which the contested decision provides, measures to strengthen the external borders or measures giving financial or operational support to the Greek and Italian asylum systems, do not provide an adequate response to the need to relieve the pressure on those systems caused by an influx of migrants that had already taken place.

259. They are in fact complementary measures which may contribute to the better control of future inflows of migrants but which, in themselves, cannot solve the existing problem, namely the saturation of the Greek and Italian asylum systems by persons who are already in those Member States.

260. Finally, seventhly, with regard to the argument that establishment of the relocation mechanism provided for in the contested decision will entail disproportionate costs for the Member States, the Slovak Republic has produced nothing concrete to show that the alternative measures that it proposes—such as increasing the resources, in particular of a technical and financial nature, made available to the Hellenic Republic and the Italian Republic—would clearly involve lower costs than a temporary relocation mechanism.

261. Accordingly, the Court must reject as unfounded the Slovak Republic's arguments whereby it disputes the necessity of the contested decision. Thus, the Slovak Republic's sixth plea must therefore be rejected in its entirety.

(d) *Hungary's ninth plea, alleging that the contested decision is not necessary in the light of the objective which it seeks to attain*

(1) Arguments of the parties

262. Hungary, supported by the Republic of Poland, argues that, since the final text of the contested decision, in contrast to the Commission's initial proposal, no longer included Hungary among the beneficiary Member States, there was no reason why the decision should provide for the relocation of 120 000 applicants and that, on that account, the decision is contrary to the principle of proportionality.

263. It is argued that setting that total number of 120 000 persons to be relocated under the contested decision exceeds what is necessary

in order to achieve the objective of the decision, since that number includes 54 000 persons who, under the Commission's initial proposal, were to be relocated from Hungary. The failure to reduce the total number of applicants to be relocated is unjustified, given that that number had initially been set on the basis of three, rather than two, beneficiary Member States.

264. It is further submitted that the distribution of the 54 000 applicants whom it was initially envisaged would be relocated from Hungary became hypothetical and uncertain, since the contested decision provides that that distribution is to be the subject of a final decision taken in the light of subsequent developments.

265. Hungary submits that, whilst the purpose of Article 78(3) TFEU is to ensure a rapid response to a situation that is not hypothetical but real, it was not clearly established, when the contested decision was adopted, that the relocation of those 54 000 applicants was necessary and, if that were the case, from which beneficiary Member States the applicants should come.

266. The Council disputes Hungary's arguments, contending, in particular, that—on the basis of all the statistics available when the contested decision was adopted—it could properly take the view that, even after Hungary had given up the status of beneficiary Member State, it was necessary to retain the total of 120 000 persons to be relocated.

(2) Findings of the Court

267. It is apparent, first of all, from recital 26 of the contested decision that the Council considered it necessary to relocate "a significant number of applicants in clear need of international protection" and that the figure of 120 000 applicants was set "on the [basis of] the overall number of third-country nationals who have entered Italy and Greece irregularly in 2015, and the number of those who are in clear need of international protection".

268. In recital 13 of the contested decision, the Council set out inter alia the statistical data relating to the number of irregular entries into Greece and Italy in 2015, and more specifically in July and August 2015, which it accordingly took into account in setting that figure of 120 000 applicants.

269. That information shows that, even after Hungary had given up the status of beneficiary Member State, the Council chose, in view of the gravity of the situation in Greece and Italy in 2015, particularly in July and August of that year, to keep to the total number of 120 000 persons to be relocated.

270. It can also be inferred from recital 26 of the contested decision that the Council retained that total of 120 000 persons because it believed that only the relocation of a "significant" number of applicants in clear need of international protection could actually reduce the pressure to which the Greek and Italian asylum systems were subject at that time.

271. The fact that it was necessary to retain the 54 000 applicants who had initially been assigned for relocation from Hungary is also supported by recital 16 of the contested decision. That recital states that, because of the ongoing instability and conflicts in the immediate vicinity of Greece and Italy, it was very likely that significant and increased pressure would continue to be put on the Greek and Italian asylum systems after the adoption of the contested decision.

272. Hungary has failed to establish, on the basis of specific information, that the statistical data relied on by the Council in setting at 120 000 the total number of persons to be relocated were not germane. It must thus be found that the Council did not make a manifest error of assessment in retaining that number on the basis of the aforementioned considerations and data, even after Hungary had given up the status of beneficiary Member State.

273. Next, Hungary maintains that the rules governing the 54 000 applicants whom it was initially envisaged would be relocated from Hungary are hypothetical and uncertain because the contested decision provides that those relocations will be the subject of a final decision taken in the light of subsequent developments.

274. However, it is clear from Article 4(1)(c), (2) and (3) of the contested decision that the allocation of those 54 000 applicants is governed by a mechanism which includes a primary rule, set out in Article 4(2) of the decision, whereby, as of 26 September 2016, those applicants will be relocated from Greece and Italy to the territory of other Member States in proportions resulting from the numbers of applicants referred to in Article 4(1)(a) and (b) of the decision.

275. That primary rule is a default rule in the sense that it is accompanied by a flexible rule, set out in Article 4(3) of the contested decision, which enables the primary rule to be adapted or varied if that is justified by the way the situation has evolved or by the fact that a Member State is confronted with an emergency situation characterised by a sudden inflow of nationals of third countries owing to a sharp shift of migration flows.

276. Such a default rule makes it possible to react, should the need arise, to future developments and thereby makes it possible to better adapt relocations to the most urgent needs.

277. If a mechanism that is implemented in two stages over a two-year period for the relocation of a large number of applicants, such as that established by the contested decision, is to be effective, it must be possible, under certain conditions, to adapt that mechanism during its period of application.

278. Consequently, Hungary's ninth plea must be rejected as unfounded.

(e) Hungary's 10th plea, alleging breach of the principle of proportionality because of the particular effects of the contested decision on Hungary

(1) Arguments of the parties

279. Hungary maintains, in the alternative, that if the Court were not to uphold any of its pleas for annulment, the contested decision would in any event be unlawful, since it infringes Article 78(3) TFEU and the principle of proportionality so far as Hungary is concerned.

280. Hungary takes issue with the Council for having included it among the Member States of relocation after it had given up the status of beneficiary Member State assigned to it in the Commission's initial proposal. In Hungary's submission it cannot be disputed that it was subject to particularly strong migratory pressure both during the period preceding the adoption of the contested decision and at the time of its adoption. In those circumstances, the contested decision places a disproportionate burden on Hungary by setting mandatory relocation quotas for it as it does for the other Member States.

281. The imposition of such quotas on Hungary when it had need itself of support in order to manage the large numbers of migrants is, in its view, contrary to Article 78(3) TFEU, since that provision envisages the adoption of provisional measures for the benefit of Member States confronted with a sudden inflow of nationals of third countries and therefore precludes the imposition of an additional burden on a Member State experiencing an emergency situation characterised by an inflow of that kind.

282. The Council submits that this plea is inadmissible since it seeks partial annulment of the contested decision in so far as the latter concerns Hungary, even though the decision forms an indivisible whole. On the substance of the plea, the Council contends inter alia that, at the time of the adoption of the contested decision, Hungary was no longer in an "emergency situation" within the meaning of Article 78(3) TFEU, which would have justified its being included among the beneficiary Member States under the contested decision. In addition, the relocation mechanism provided for in the contested

decision is accompanied by adjustment mechanisms enabling a Member State to request that its relocation obligations be suspended in the event of a sharp shift of migration flows.

(2) Findings of the Court

283. As a preliminary point, the Court considers that the proper administration of justice justifies, in the present case, examining the substance of Hungary's 10th plea—which it raises in the alternative and which alleges breach of the principle of proportionality because of the particular effects of the contested decision on Hungary—without ruling on the objection of inadmissibility raised by the Council, since this plea must in any event be rejected on the substance (see, to that effect, judgment of 24 June 2015, *Fresh Del Monte Produce* v. *Commission* and *Commission* v. *Fresh Del Monte Produce*, C-293/13 P and C-294/13 P, EU:C:2015:416, paragraph 193 and the case law cited).

284. The examination of Hungary's 10th plea calls for an outline of the way the contested decision evolved.

285. In its proposal of 9 September 2015, the Commission had included Hungary among the Member States benefiting from relocation because the data for the first eight months of 2015, and in particular for July and August 2015, showed that migrants were arriving there in very large numbers, mostly from Greece, via the so-called "Western Balkans" route, thus putting significant pressure on the Hungarian asylum system, comparable to the pressure on the Greek and Italian asylum systems.

286. However, following the construction by Hungary of a fence along its border with Serbia and the large-scale westward transit of migrants in Hungary, mainly to Germany, that pressure reduced considerably towards mid-September 2015, as the number of migrants with irregular status in Hungary fell significantly.

287. Against the background of those events, which took place in September 2015, Hungary made a formal request to the Council, asking that it no longer be included among the Member States benefiting from relocation.

288. The Council took note of that request and made the statement cited in paragraph 165 of the present judgment at the plenary sitting of the Parliament on 16 September 2015.

289. According to Hungary, the imposition of binding quotas on it represents a disproportionate burden, taking account of the fact that it was, even after mid-September 2015, in an emergency situation because the migratory pressure on its borders had not diminished but had, at the most, shifted towards its border with Croatia where

significant numbers of irregular border crossings were taking place every day. Consequently, since, in its view, Hungary thus continued even after the contested decision was adopted to be confronted with an emergency situation, the decision to include it among the Member States of relocation and, for that purpose, to impose additional burdens on it in the form of relocation quotas was contrary to the objective of Article 78(3) TFEU of supporting Member States in such a situation.

290. In that regard, it cannot be denied that the contested decision, in so far as it includes provision for a compulsory distribution between all the Member States of migrants to be relocated from Greece and Italy (i) has an impact on all the Member States of relocation and (ii) requires that a balance be struck between the different interests involved, account being taken of the objectives which that decision pursues. Therefore, the attempt to strike such a balance, taking into account not the particular situation of a single Member State, but that of all Member States, cannot be regarded as being contrary to the principle of proportionality (see, by analogy, judgment of 18 June 2015, *Estonia* v. *Parliament and Council*, C-508/13, EU:C:2015:403, paragraph 39).

291. When one or more Member States are faced with an emergency situation within the meaning of Article 78(3) TFEU, the burdens entailed by the provisional measures adopted under that provision for the benefit of that or those Member States must, as a rule, be divided between all the other Member States, in accordance with the principle of solidarity and fair sharing of responsibility between the Member States, since, in accordance with Article 80 TFEU, that principle governs EU asylum policy.

292. Accordingly, in the present case the Commission and the Council rightly considered, at the time of adoption of the contested decision, that the distribution of the relocated applicants among all the Member States, in keeping with the principle laid down in Article 80 TFEU, was a fundamental element of the contested decision. That is clear from the many references which the contested decision makes to that principle, in particular in recitals 2, 16, 26 and 30.

293. Faced with Hungary's refusal to benefit from the relocation mechanism as the Commission had proposed, the Council cannot be criticised, from the point of view of the principle of proportionality, for having concluded on the basis of the principle of solidarity and fair sharing of responsibility laid down in Article 80 TFEU that Hungary had to be allocated relocation quotas in the same way as all the other Member States that were not beneficiaries of the relocation mechanism.

294. It should, moreover, be noted that Article 4(5) and Article 9 of the contested decision enable a Member State, under certain

conditions, to request that its obligations as a Member State of relocation under that decision be suspended.

295. Thus, by Decision 2016/408, adopted under Article 4(5) of the contested decision, the Council—acknowledging inter alia that the Republic of Austria was facing exceptional circumstances and an emergency situation characterised by a sudden inflow of nationals of third countries into its territory, and that it had the second highest number, after the Kingdom of Sweden, of applicants for international protection per capita in the European Union—decided that the Republic of Austria's obligations relating to the relocation quota allocated to it were to be suspended for one year in respect of 30% of that quota.

296. Similarly, by Decision 2016/946, the Council, considering inter alia that the Kingdom of Sweden was facing an emergency situation characterised by a sudden inflow of nationals of third countries into its territory because of a sharp shift in migration flows and that it had by far the highest number of applicants for international protection per capita in the European Union, decided that its obligations as a Member State of relocation under the contested decision were to be suspended for one year.

297. Above all, it follows from the adjustment mechanism provided for in Article 4(3) of the contested decision that a Member State which considers itself to be facing an emergency situation characterised by a sudden inflow of nationals of third countries into its territory owing to a sharp shift in migration flows may inform the Commission and the Council of that emergency situation, giving duly justified reasons. That may lead to an amendment of the contested decision, with the consequence that that Member State can benefit, as of 26 September 2016, from the relocation of the 54 000 applicants referred to in Article 4(1)(c) of the decision.

298. The existence of those various adjustment mechanisms shows that the relocation mechanism for which the contested decision provides, taken as a whole, enables account to be taken, in a proportionate manner, of the particular situation of each Member State in this regard.

299. The proportionate nature of the relocation mechanism provided for in the contested decision is also shown by the distribution key, on the basis of which the allocations were set, in Annex I and Annex II to the decision, for relocations from Greece and Italy.

300. Although the contested decision as finally worded merely states, in recital 26, that the relocation mechanism provided for in the decision "constitutes fair burden sharing between Italy and Greece on the one hand and the other Member States on the other, given the overall available figures on irregular border crossings in 2015", it is not

disputed that the quotas in the contested decision were set on the basis of a distribution key the calculation of which is explained in the following terms in recital 25 of the Commission's initial proposal:

... The proposed distribution key should be based on (a) the size of the population (40% weighting), (b) the total of the GDP (40% weighting), (c) the average number of asylum applications per one million inhabitants over the period 2010-14 (10% weighting, with a 30% cap of the population and GDP effect on the key, to avoid disproportionate effects of that criterion on the overall distribution) and (d) the unemployment rate (10% weighting, with a 30% cap of the population and GDP effect on the key, to avoid disproportionate effects of that criterion on the overall distribution). ...

301. That makes clear that the purpose of that key is to ensure that the distribution of the persons relocated between the Member States concerned is, in particular, proportionate to the economic weight of each of those States and to the migration pressure on their asylum systems.

302. In that regard, the Republic of Poland develops—on the basis of Hungary's 10th plea, alleging that the imposition of binding quotas on it has disproportionate effects in its regard—a more general argument criticising the allegedly disproportionate effects of those quotas on a number of host Member States which, in order to meet their relocation obligations, have to make far greater efforts and bear far heavier burdens than other host Member States. That is said to be the case of Member States which are "virtually ethnically homogeneous, like Poland" and whose populations are different, from a cultural and linguistic point of view, from the migrants to be relocated on their territory.

303. That argument, apart from the fact that it is inadmissible because it was put forward in a statement in intervention and goes far beyond the argument made by Hungary, which is strictly limited to Hungary's own situation (see, to that effect, judgment of 7 October 2014, *Germany v. Council*, C-399/12, EU:C:2014:2258, paragraph 27), must be rejected.

304. If relocation were to be strictly conditional upon the existence of cultural or linguistic ties between each applicant for international protection and the Member State of relocation, the distribution of those applicants between all the Member States in accordance with the principle of solidarity laid down by Article 80 TFEU and, consequently, the adoption of a binding relocation mechanism would be impossible.

305. It should be added that considerations relating to the ethnic origin of applicants for international protection cannot be taken into account since they are clearly contrary to EU law and, in particular, to Article 21 of the Charter of Fundamental Rights of the European Union ("the Charter").

306. Finally, the Court rejects the Republic of Poland's argument that the contested decision is contrary to the principle of proportionality since it does not allow the Member States to ensure the effective exercise of their responsibilities with regard to the maintenance of law and order and the safeguarding of internal security as required under Article 72 TFEU. The Republic of Poland submits that that is particularly serious given that the contested decision will give rise to significant "secondary" movements, caused by applicants leaving their host Member State before the latter has been able to rule definitively upon their application for international protection.

307. It must be noted in this regard that recital 32 of the contested decision states, inter alia, that national security and public order should be taken into consideration throughout the relocation procedure, until the transfer of the applicant is implemented and that, in that context, the applicant's fundamental rights, including the relevant rules on data protection, must be fully respected.

308. With that in mind, Article 5 of the contested decision, which is entitled "Relocation procedure", provides, in paragraph 7, that Member States retain the right to refuse to relocate an applicant only where there are reasonable grounds for regarding him or her as a danger to their national security or public order.

309. If, as the Republic of Poland maintains, the mechanism provided for in Article 5(7) of the contested decision were ineffective because it requires Member States to check large numbers of persons in a short time, such practical difficulties are not inherent in the mechanism and must, should they arise, be resolved in the spirit of cooperation and mutual trust between the authorities of the Member States that are beneficiaries of relocation and those of the Member States of relocation. That spirit of cooperation and mutual trust must prevail when the relocation procedure provided for in Article 5 of the contested decision is implemented.

310. In view of all the foregoing, Hungary's 10th plea must be rejected as unfounded.

*2. Hungary's eighth plea, alleging breach of the principles of legal
certainty and of normative clarity, and also of the
Geneva Convention*

(a) Arguments of the parties

311. Hungary, supported by the Republic of Poland, maintains, first, that the contested decision fails to observe the principles of legal certainty and normative clarity, since, on a number of points, it does

not clearly indicate the way in which its provisions must be applied or how they relate to the provisions of the Dublin III Regulation.

312. Thus, although recital 35 of the contested decision addressed the issue of the legal and procedural safeguards applicable to the relocation decisions, none of its normative provisions regulates that matter or refers to the relevant provisions of the Dublin III Regulation. That raises a problem from the viewpoint, in particular, of the right of applicants to a remedy, especially of those applicants who are not designated for relocation.

313. Nor does the contested decision clearly determine the criteria by reference to which applicants are chosen for relocation. The way in which the authorities of the Member States are called upon to decide on the transfer of applicants to a Member State of relocation makes it extremely difficult for applicants to know in advance whether they will be among the persons relocated and, if so, to which Member State they will be relocated.

314. Hungary further submits that the contested decision does not define in an appropriate manner the status of the applicants in the Member State of relocation and does not ensure that those applicants will actually remain in that Member State while a decision is taken on their application. As regards "secondary" movements, Article 6(5) of the contested decision does not in itself ensure that that decision will attain its objectives, namely the distribution of applicants between the Member States, if there is no guarantee that applicants will actually remain in the Member States of relocation.

315. Secondly, the fact that applicants may possibly be relocated to a Member State with which they have no particular connection raises the question whether the contested decision is compatible in that respect with the Convention relating to the Status of Refugees, signed in Geneva on 28 July 1951 (United Nations Treaty Series, Vol. 189, p. 150, No 2545 (1954)), supplemented by the Protocol relating to the Status of Refugees of 31 January 1967 ("the Geneva Convention").

316. Hungary argues that, according to the interpretation adopted in point 192 of the Handbook and guidelines on procedures and criteria for determining refugee status under the 1951 Convention and the 1967 Protocol relating to the status of refugees (United Nations High Commissioner for Refugees (HCR), May 1992), the applicant should be permitted to remain in the Member State in which he has lodged his request pending a decision on that request by the authorities of that country.

317. The right to remain in that Member State is also recognised in Article 9 of Directive 2013/32/EU of the European Parliament and of

the Council of 26 June 2013 on common procedures for granting and withdrawing international protection (OJ 2013 L 180, p. 60).

318. The contested decision deprives applicants for international protection of that right to remain and allows them to be relocated without their consent to another Member State with which they have no significant ties.

319. The Republic of Poland maintains that the contested decision falls short of the standards for human rights protection essentially because it takes the place of the system provided for by the Dublin III Regulation, whilst failing to lay down any clear criterion determining the Member State to which the applicant will be relocated and where his application for international protection will be examined.

320. It submits that persons applying for international protection could, under the contested decision, be resettled in distant regions of the European Union with which they have no cultural or social ties, which would make their integration in the society of the host Member State impossible.

321. The Council disputes, first, the allegation that the contested decision does not respect the principles of legal certainty and normative clarity. It is an emergency measure forming part, on the one hand, of the *acquis* relating to the common European asylum system which remains in principle fully applicable and, on the other, of the legal order created by the system of Treaties and by the Charter.

322. Secondly, as regards the alleged infringement of the right to remain in a Member State, which, it is argued, is safeguarded by the Geneva Convention, the Council contends that neither the Geneva Convention nor EU law gives an asylum seeker the right freely to choose his host country.

(b) Findings of the Court

323. As regards, first, the complaint alleging infringement of the principles of legal certainty and normative clarity, it must be borne in mind that the contested decision is composed of a series of provisional measures, including a temporary relocation mechanism which derogates from the *acquis* relating to the common asylum system only on certain specific points which are expressly listed. That mechanism is an integral part of that *acquis* and the latter therefore remains, in general terms, applicable.

324. In that regard, the Council observed the principles of legal certainty and normative clarity, explaining, in particular in recitals 23, 24, 35, 36 and 40 of the contested decision, the interaction between the provisions of that act and the provisions of legislative

acts adopted within the framework of the European Union's common asylum policy.

325. In addition, there must be a right to an effective remedy under national law, in accordance with Article 47 of the Charter, against any decision to be taken by a national authority in the course of the relocation procedure laid down in Article 5 of the contested decision.

326. Hungary has also criticised the contested decision for allegedly failing to include proper rules for ensuring that applicants for international protection will remain in the Member State of relocation while a decision is taken on their applications or, in other words, for ensuring that "secondary" movements are prevented.

327. It should be noted in that regard that recitals 38 to 41 of the contested decision refer, with sufficient detail and precision, to the measures that may be taken by the Member States, on the basis of a number of EU legislative acts forming part of the *acquis* relating to the common asylum policy, in order to avoid such "secondary" movements.

328. In addition, Article 6(5) of the contested decision provides, clearly and precisely, that an applicant for, or beneficiary of, international protection who enters the territory of a Member State other than the Member State of relocation without fulfilling the conditions for stay in that other Member State shall be required to return immediately to the Member State of relocation.

329. As regards Hungary's complaint that the contested decision does not include criteria for determining which is the Member State of relocation, it must be recalled that, as is made clear in recital 2 of the decision and as has been stated, inter alia, in paragraphs 253 and 291 to 293 of the present judgment, the decision took account of Article 80 TFEU, which applies when the European Union's asylum policy is implemented and, in particular, when provisional measures based on Article 78(3) TFEU are adopted and from which it follows that the determination of the Member State of relocation must be based on criteria related to solidarity and fair sharing of responsibility between the Member States.

330. It should be added that paragraphs 1 and 2 of Article 6 of the contested decision lay down certain specific criteria for determining the Member State of relocation, which relate to the best interests of the child and to family ties and which are, moreover, similar to the criteria laid down in the Dublin III Regulation.

331. Moreover, recital 34 of the contested decision lists a series of elements which seek to ensure, inter alia, that applicants are relocated to a Member State with which they have some family, cultural or social ties and of which particular account should be taken when the Member

State of relocation is selected, the aim being to facilitate the applicants' integration in that State.

332. The contested decision therefore cannot be regarded as comprising an arbitrary system which has taken the place of the objective system laid down by the Dublin III Regulation.

333. On the contrary, there is ultimately no substantial difference between those two systems in the sense that the system established by the contested decision is based—like the system established by the Dublin III Regulation—on objective criteria rather than on a preference expressed by an applicant for international protection.

334. In particular, the rule concerning the responsibility of the Member State of first entry, laid down in Article 13(1) of the Dublin III Regulation, which is the only rule for determining the responsible Member State laid down in that regulation from which the contested decision derogates, is not linked to the applicant's preference for a particular host Member State and does not specifically seek to ensure that there are linguistic, cultural or social ties between the applicant and the responsible Member State.

335. Furthermore, although no provision is made, in the context of the relocation procedure, for the applicant to consent to his relocation, Article 6(3) of the contested decision provides that, prior to the relocation decision, the applicant is to be informed that he is the subject of a relocation procedure and Article 6(4) of the decision requires the authorities of the beneficiary Member State to notify the applicant of the relocation decision before he is actually relocated and to specify in that decision the Member State of relocation.

336. Moreover, as is made clear by recital 35 of the contested decision, it is because applicants do not have the right to choose which Member State is to be responsible for examining their applications that they must have the right to an effective remedy against the relocation decision, so as to ensure respect for their fundamental rights.

337. Finally, if the authorities of the beneficiary Member States are afforded some latitude when they have to identify, under Article 5(3) of the contested decision, the individual applicants who can be relocated to a given Member State of relocation, such latitude is justified in the light of the objective of the decision, which is to take pressure off the Greek and Italian asylum systems by actually relocating, within a short time frame, a significant number of applicants to other Member States, in compliance with EU law and, in particular, with the fundamental rights guaranteed by the Charter.

338. Secondly, contrary to Hungary's contention, it cannot validly be maintained that the contested decision, in so far as it provides for the

transfer of an applicant for international protection before a decision on his application has been taken, is contrary to the Geneva Convention because that convention allegedly includes a right to remain in the State in which the application has been lodged while that application is pending.

339. In this regard, the Council, in recital 35 of the contested decision, rightly pointed out that an applicant does not have the right under EU law to choose the Member State responsible for examining his application. The criteria which the Dublin III Regulation lays down for determining which Member State is to be responsible for processing an application for international protection are not connected with the applicant's preference for a particular host Member State.

340. Nor can it be inferred from the passage in the Handbook and guidelines on procedures and criteria for determining refugee status under the 1951 Convention and the 1967 Protocol relating to the status of refugees to which Hungary refers that the Geneva Convention guarantees an applicant for international protection the right to remain in the State in which the application for protection was lodged while the application is pending.

341. That passage must be understood as a particular expression of the principle of non-*refoulement*, which prohibits the expulsion of an applicant for international protection to a third country as long as a decision has not been taken on his application.

342. The transfer, in the context of a relocation operation, of an applicant for international protection from one Member State to another for the purpose of ensuring that his application is examined within a reasonable time cannot be regarded as *refoulement* to a third State.

343. It is on the contrary a crisis-management measure, taken at EU level, whose purpose is to ensure that the fundamental right to asylum, laid down in Article 18 of the Charter, can be exercised properly, in accordance with the Geneva Convention.

344. Hungary's eighth plea must therefore be rejected as unfounded.

345. As none of the pleas in law put forward by the Slovak Republic or by Hungary can be accepted, the actions must be dismissed.

IV. COSTS

346. Under Article 138(1) of the Rules of Procedure, the unsuccessful party is to be ordered to pay the costs if they have been applied for in the successful party's pleadings. Since the Council has applied for costs and the Slovak Republic and Hungary have been unsuccessful in

their respective actions, they must be ordered to bear their own costs and to pay those incurred by the Council.

347. In accordance with Article 140(1) of the Rules of Procedure, the Kingdom of Belgium, the Federal Republic of Germany, the Hellenic Republic, the French Republic, the Italian Republic, the Grand Duchy of Luxembourg, the Republic of Poland, the Kingdom of Sweden and the European Commission are to bear their own costs.

On those grounds, the Court (Grand Chamber) hereby:

1. Dismisses the actions;
2. Orders the Slovak Republic and Hungary to bear their own costs and to pay those of the Council of the European Union;
3. Orders the Kingdom of Belgium, the Federal Republic of Germany, the Hellenic Republic, the French Republic, the Italian Republic, the Grand Duchy of Luxembourg, the Republic of Poland, the Kingdom of Sweden and the European Commission to bear their own costs.

[Report: EU:C:2017:631]

Economics, trade and finance — The law of the World Trade Organization — Trade in services — General Agreement on Trade in Services, 1995 — Article XVI — Article XVII — Higher education service providers — Whether measures adopted by Hungary contravened obligation on national treatment — Whether measures justified to prevent deceptive practices — Whether measures justified to maintain public order

Human rights — Charter of Fundamental Rights of the European Union, 2000 — Article 13 — Article 14 — Article 16 — Freedom to provide services — Freedom to found educational establishments — Freedom to conduct business — Academic freedom — European Convention on Human Rights, 1950 ("the Convention") — Article 10 — Freedom of expression — Relationship between the Charter of Fundamental Rights of the European Union and the Convention — Relationship between academic freedom and freedom of expression — Whether restrictions on providing higher education services a restriction of academic freedom — Whether measures adopted by Hungary contravened freedom to found educational establishments — Whether measures adopted by Hungary contravened freedom to conduct business

Treaties — European Union — Treaties binding European Union and Member States — General Agreement on Trade in Services, 1995 — Infringement proceedings — Whether infringement proceedings can be based on infringement of obligations under GATS — Jurisdiction of the Court of Justice of the European Union — Whether the Court having jurisdiction to determine matters based on breach of GATS

Relationship of international law and municipal law — Relationship between the law of World Trade Organization and the law of the European Union — Obligations of Member States of the EU — Competence of the EU — Whether WTO law forms part of EU law — Whether infringement proceedings under EU law can be based on contraventions of WTO law — The law of the European Union

EUROPEAN COMMISSION *v.* HUNGARY[1]

(Case C-66/18)

Court of Justice of the European Union (Grand Chamber).
6 *October* 2020

(Lenaerts, *President*; Silva de Lapuerta, *Vice-President*; Arabadjiev, Prechal, Vilaras, Safjan and Rodin, *Presidents of Chambers*; Juhász, Malenovský (*Rapporteur*), Bay Larsen, von Danwitz, Toader and Lycourgos, *Judges*; Kokott, *Advocate General*)

SUMMARY:[2] *The facts*:—In 2017, Hungary adopted two amendments to the Hungarian Law on higher education ("the impugned amendments"). These amendments conditioned the establishment or continuation of foreign higher education service providers on the conclusion of an international treaty between Hungary and their State of origin, as well as requiring that foreign higher education institutions operating within Hungary also provided education services within their State of origin. Six foreign higher education institutions carried on activities within Hungary at the time of the impugned amendments, with the Central European University ("the CEU") being the only institution that was unable to satisfy the new requirements. As a result of the impugned amendments the CEU ceased operations in Hungary and in November 2019 transferred its operations to Vienna.

In April 2017, the European Commission ("the Commission") informed Hungary that it considered that the impugned amendments contravened, inter alia, the freedom to provide services and academic freedom that were protected by Articles 13, 14(3) and 16 of the Charter of Fundamental Rights of the European Union, 2000 ("the Charter"). The Commission also argued that as the impugned amendments applied only to higher education institutions from States outside the European Economic Area ("EEA"), Hungary had infringed the law of the World Trade Organization ("WTO"), specifically Article XVII of the General Agreement on Trade in Services, 1995 ("GATS") which required Hungary to accord foreign service suppliers no less favourable treatment than it accorded its own service suppliers.[3] According to the Commission, the GATS formed part of European Union ("EU") law pursuant to Article 258 of the Treaty of the Functioning of the European Union, 2007 ("TFEU"). After a series of exchanges between April and November 2017

[1] The European Commission was represented by V. Di Bucci, L. Malferrari, B. De Meester and K. Talabér-Ritz, acting as agents. Hungary was represented by M. Z. Fehér and G. Koós, acting as agents.
[2] Prepared by Mr D. Peterson.
[3] The text of Article XVII of the GATS appears at para. 7 of the judgment.

between the Commission and Hungary, the Commission initiated, in February 2018, infringement proceedings before the Court of Justice of the European Union ("the Court").

In response to these proceedings, Hungary argued that the Court lacked jurisdiction to hear and determine the present action as it was based on its alleged failure to fulfil its obligations under Article XVII of the GATS which did not form part of its obligations under EU law. Hungary further alleged that the action was inadmissible as the Commission had breached its duty of independence and impartiality by initiating the procedure for purely political reasons and had failed to fulfil its obligations by only providing limited time for pre-litigation procedures, thus restricting its rights of defence.

Opinion of the Advocate General (5 March 2020)

Held:—The measures adopted by Hungary infringed provisions of the GATS, the TFEU and the Charter.

(1) While Member States retained an extensive internal competence over education, trade in services, including in health and education, fell within the external competence of the EU. Hungary's obligations under the GATS had been transferred to the EU by the Treaty of Lisbon, 2007 and constituted an obligation under EU law that could be the subject of infringement proceedings. This view was strengthened by the fact that the EU had undertaken to be fully bound by the GATS and the conduct of its Member States was attributable to the EU. As such, the EU had assumed responsibility for defending a national measure before the WTO dispute settlement procedure. While Hungary remained free to exercise its internal competence to regulate higher education, it could only do so in so far as its regulations did not infringe its obligations under the WTO agreements, as this would render the EU liable under international law and could expose other Member States to the risk of countermeasures (paras. 40-55).

(2) The specific character of the WTO dispute settlement procedure, and the special role of the WTO dispute settlement bodies, did not preclude infringement proceedings before EU courts based on contraventions of WTO law. A judgment delivered by the Court in infringement proceedings did not call into question the exclusive competence of the WTO dispute settlement bodies to find infringements of the GATS in proceedings between two WTO Member States (paras. 56-9).

(3) While WTO law could not, as a rule, serve as a standard of review for EU acts in proceedings before EU courts, the Court could review national measures in light of WTO law. If the EU was not able to bring infringement proceedings on the basis of WTO law, the internal implementation of the EU's international trade law obligations would be jeopardized. The capacity to review national measures in light of WTO law also increased the credibility of the EU during negotiations with third countries under the dispute settlement procedure of the WTO (paras. 60-8).

(4) Article XVII:1 of the GATS obliged WTO Member States to ensure that service suppliers of other Members received treatment no less favourable than its own service suppliers, subject to any conditions and qualifications set out in the Schedule of Commitments which formed an integral part of the agreement between Member States pursuant to Article XX:3 of the GATS. Hungary's Schedule of Commitments contained no limitations for service suppliers within the higher education sector. While it was perfectly possible for Hungary to have inscribed such limitations for national treatment, this option had not been taken (paras. 95-110).

(5) The requirement within the impugned amendments for the State of origin of a foreign higher education service provider to conclude an international treaty with Hungary could not be regarded as a permissible exception under Article XIV of the GATS as this appeared to be a means of arbitrary discrimination within the meaning of Article XVI. Further, this requirement was not an objective means for combating fraud as it was not evident how fraudulent activity could be countered by an agreement with the State of origin of a foreign higher education service provider (paras. 113-24 and 183-5).

(6) Pursuant to Article 51(1) of the Charter, Member States were only bound by the Charter when implementing EU law. Therefore, measures within the education sector of Member States were generally not assessed by reference to the fundamental rights of the EU. However, Article XVII of the GATS imposed a comprehensive duty of national treatment, and the application of the Charter was a consequence of the fact that the Hungarian legislation was incompatible with the duty of national treatment. Therefore, the impugned amendments could not be regarded as a lawful limitation on the freedom to found educational establishments under Article 14(3) of the Charter (paras. 127-9 and 134-40).

(7) The fundamental right to freedom of the arts and sciences under Article 13 of the Charter was independent of the general freedom to hold opinions and included substantively autonomous research and teaching that were free from State interference. A requirement that meant no teaching or research activities could take place at a university if it was not fulfilled fell within the scope of protection offered by Article 13 of the Charter. Although Article 13 did not guarantee the continued existence of each individual educational institution, any rule which resulted in the closure of a higher education institution was required to be proportionate. The impugned amendments implemented by Hungary did not satisfy this requirement and could therefore not justify a limitation on the freedoms protected by Article 13 of the Charter (paras. 141-51, 181 and 189).

(8) By adopting the impugned amendments, Hungary had infringed Article 49 of the TFEU. The impugned amendments by Hungary limited the freedom of establishment of foreign higher education institutions. Hungary's justification of public policy should have been rejected by the Court as no fundamental interests of society were affected (paras. 153-63 and 180).

Judgment of the Court of Justice (6 October 2020)

Held:—The infringement proceedings were admissible. In adopting the impugned measures Hungary had failed to fulfil its obligations under the GATS and the Charter.

(1) The present infringement action against Hungary was admissible. The fact that the Commission had made the pre-litigation procedure subject to a short time limit was reasonable and was not in itself capable of leading to the inadmissibility of the subsequent proceedings. Such a finding of inadmissibility was only to be made where the Commission's conduct prevented the Member State concerned from availing itself of its rights of defence (paras. 45-57).

(2) Hungary's argument that the Court lacked jurisdiction to hear an action regarding its failure to fulfil obligations under the GATS was rejected. Under Article 258 of the TFEU, an action for failure to fulfil obligations could only be based on a failure to comply with obligations under EU law. The Court had repeatedly held that an international agreement entered into by the EU, which included the GATS, formed an integral part of EU law (paras. 68-9 and 93).

(3) While Member States had broad competence in the area of education under the TFEU, the commitments entered into under the GATS fell within the exclusive competence of the EU. Therefore, the commitments of Member States entered into under the GATS, including those related to the liberalization of trade in private educational services, fell within the exclusive competence of the EU (paras. 70-6).

(4) Under the WTO agreements, which bound the EU, a review undertaken as part of the dispute settlement system could result in a legal finding that measures taken by a WTO Member did not conform with the WTO agreements. Such a finding could give rise to international liability on the part of the EU. In those circumstances, under Article 258 of the TFEU, the exercise of the jurisdiction conferred by the Court was entirely consistent with the obligation of each WTO Member to ensure the observance of its obligations under the law of the WTO. The EU was bound to observe international law in its entirety and, under Article 32 of the Articles on the Responsibility of States for Internationally Wrongful Acts, 2001, a State could not rely on the provisions of its internal law as a justification for its failure to comply with an obligation under international law. As such, neither the EU nor the Member State concerned could rely on EU law to refuse to comply with their legal obligations under the law of the WTO (paras. 80-91).

(5) The impugned amendments enacted by Hungary introduced formally different treatment to foreign education service providers within the meaning of Article XVII(3) of the GATS, resulting in a competitive disadvantage for service providers in Member States of the WTO that were not members of the EEA. The impugned measures therefore modified the conditions of

competition in favour of Hungarian providers contrary to Article XVII of the GATS (paras. 103-14, 118-21 and 207).

(6) In adopting the impugned amendments, Hungary had also failed to fulfil its obligations under Article XVII of the GATS. The requirement of concluding a prior international treaty could not be justified by Hungary's arguments based on the prevention of deceptive practices or the maintenance of public order under Article XIV of the GATS. Pursuant to footnote 5 of that provision, a restrictive measure would only be justified where there was a genuine and sufficiently serious threat posed to a fundamental interest of society. However, Hungary had failed to establish that the provision of higher education teaching activities within its territory constituted, in the absence of the impugned amendments, a genuine and sufficiently serious threat that affected a fundamental interest of society. Similarly, the prior conclusion of an international treaty was contrary to Article XIV of the GATS as it enabled Hungary to arbitrarily prevent an institution from entering or carrying on activities in its market and was not proportionate to the objective of preventing fraudulent or deceptive practices (paras. 126-39 and 152-6).

(7) By adopting the impugned amendments Hungary had failed to fulfil its obligations under Article 49 of the TFEU. Pursuant to the Court's case law, any measure which prohibited, impeded or rendered the exercise of the freedom of establishment less attractive had to be regarded as a restriction on Article 49. In justifying the measure, Hungary had failed to establish that the operation of foreign higher education institutions constituted a genuine, present and sufficiently serious threat affecting a fundamental interest of society (paras. 159-63, 167-70, 178-90 and 207).

(8) Hungary had failed to fulfil its obligations under Articles 13, 14(3) and 16 of the Charter. Pursuant to Article 52(3) of the Charter, the rights protected by the Charter must, so far as possible, be given the same meaning and scope as corresponding rights within the European Convention on Human Rights, 1950 ("the Convention") (paras. 222-3, 228 and 234).

(9) Although academic freedom was not expressly referred to in the Convention, it was apparent from the relevant case law that it was associated with the freedom of expression protected under Article 10. As such, academic freedom in research and teaching guaranteed the freedom of expression, the freedom to disseminate information, and the freedom to conduct research and distribute knowledge and truth without restriction. Therefore, the impugned measures, in endangering the academic activity of foreign education institutions located within Hungary, and depriving concerned universities of their autonomous organizational structure, limited academic freedom contrary to Article 13 of the Charter (paras. 224-8).

(10) The impugned amendments also limited the freedom to found educational establishments contrary to Article 14(3) of the Charter, as well as the freedom to conduct a business contrary to Article 16. The measures adopted by Hungary were not justified by any of the objectives of general interest recognized by the EU (paras. 229-34 and 239-42).

The text of the judgment of the Court of Justice commences at p. 188. The following is the text of the Opinion of Advocate General Kokott:

OPINION OF ADVOCATE GENERAL KOKOTT[1]

I. INTRODUCTION

1. These infringement proceedings concern two amendments to the Hungarian Law on higher education in 2017. Following those amendments, higher education institutions from States outside the European Economic Area (EEA) are required, in order to commence or continue their activities in Hungary, to prove the conclusion of an international treaty between Hungary and their State of origin, which, in the case of federal States, must be concluded by the central government. In addition, the activity of all foreign higher education institutions is conditional on higher education also being offered in their State of origin.

2. According to critics, by introducing this law the Hungarian Government has the sole aim of preventing the activity of the Central European University (CEU) in Hungary. It has therefore sometimes been referred to in the public debate as a "lex CEU".

3. The CEU was founded in 1991 through an initiative which, by its own account, sought to promote critical analysis in the education of new decision-makers in the Central and Eastern European States in which pluralism had previously been rejected. The CEU is a university founded under the law of New York State and holding an operating licence issued by that State ("the absolute charter"). The main funders are the Open Society Foundations established by the Hungarian-born US businessman George Soros, a controversial figure in some circles.[2] Because of its specific remit, the CEU has never undertaken any teaching or research activities in the United States.

4. Of the six foreign higher education institutions which carried on activities subject to a licence in Hungary at the time of the amendment of the Law on higher education, the CEU was, on account of its particular model, the only one that was unable to fulfil the new

---

[1] Original language: German.

[2] His foundations are affected by another piece of Hungarian legislation adopted alongside this, Law LXXVI of 2017 on the transparency of organisations receiving foreign support, which imposes certain enforceable obligations of registration, declaration and transparency on civil society organisations receiving foreign financial support. The law is the subject of infringement proceedings in Case C-78/18, *Commission* v. *Hungary* (Transparency of associations).

requirements. It therefore ceased operation in Hungary. In November 2019 a new campus opened in Vienna.

5. Against this background, the Commission considers the new rules to be not only a restriction of freedom to provide services, but in particular an infringement of academic freedom, as enshrined in the Charter of Fundamental Rights of the European Union.

6. Furthermore, as one of the two new requirements applies only to higher education institutions from States outside the EEA, the case takes on a further special dimension, as the Commission alleges that Hungary infringed the law of the World Trade Organization (WTO), specifically the GATS. In this case, the Court will therefore also have to decide to what extent infringement proceedings can serve as an instrument to enforce and increase the effectiveness of international trade law.

II. LEGAL FRAMEWORK

A. EU law

1. *Council Decision 94/800/EC concerning the conclusion of the agreements reached in the Uruguay Round multilateral negotiations*

7. By Decision 94/800/EC of 22 December 1994 concerning the conclusion on behalf of the European Community, as regards matters within its competence, of the agreements reached in the Uruguay Round multilateral negotiations (1986-1994),[3] the Council approved the Agreement establishing the WTO and the Agreements in Annexes 1, 2 and 3 to that Agreement, which include the General Agreement on Trade in Services ("GATS").

8. Article I of the GATS provides:

1. This Agreement applies to measures by Members affecting trade in services.

2. For the purposes of this Agreement, trade in services is defined as the supply of a service

   (a) from the territory of one Member into the territory of any other Member;

   (b) in the territory of one Member to the service consumer of any other Member;

   (c) by a service supplier of one Member, through commercial presence in the territory of any other Member;

   (d) by a service supplier of one Member, through presence of natural persons of a Member in the territory of any other Member.

---

[3] OJ 1994 L 336, p. 1.

9. Article XIV of the GATS, under the heading "General Exceptions", provides:

Subject to the requirement that such measures are not applied in a manner which would constitute a means of arbitrary or unjustifiable discrimination between countries where like conditions prevail, or a disguised restriction on trade in services, nothing in this Agreement shall be construed to prevent the adoption or enforcement by any Member of measures:

(a) necessary to protect public morals or to maintain public order;[4] ...
(c) necessary to secure compliance with laws or regulations which are not inconsistent with the provisions of this Agreement including those relating to:
  (i) the prevention of deceptive and fraudulent practices or to deal with the effects of a default on services contracts, ...
(iii) safety; ...

10. Article XVI of the GATS appears in Part III of the Agreement on "Specific Commitments". That provision, headed "Market Access", stipulates as follows:

1. With respect to market access ... each Member shall accord services and service suppliers of any other Member treatment no less favourable than that provided for under the terms, limitations and conditions agreed and specified in its Schedule. ...
2. In sectors where market-access commitments are undertaken, the measures which a Member shall not maintain or adopt ... are defined as:
  (a) limitations on the number of service suppliers whether in the form of numerical quotas, monopolies, exclusive service suppliers or the requirements of an economic needs test;
  (b) limitations on the total value of service transactions or assets in the form of numerical quotas or the requirement of an economic needs test;
  (c) limitations on the total number of service operations or on the total quantity of service output expressed in terms of designated numerical units in the form of quotas or the requirement of an economic needs test;
  (d) limitations on the total number of natural persons that may be employed in a particular service sector or that a service supplier may employ and who are necessary for, and directly related to, the supply of a specific service in the form of numerical quotas or the requirement of an economic needs test;
  (e) measures which restrict or require specific types of legal entity or joint venture through which a service supplier may supply a service; and

---

[4] "The public order exception may be invoked only where a genuine and sufficiently serious threat is posed to one of the fundamental interests of society" (footnote in the original).

(f) limitations on the participation of foreign capital in terms of maximum percentage limit on foreign shareholding or the total value of individual or aggregate foreign investment.

11. Article XVII of the GATS, headed "National Treatment", provides:

1. In the sectors inscribed in its Schedule, and subject to any conditions and qualifications set out therein, each Member shall accord to services and service suppliers of any other Member, in respect of all measures affecting the supply of services, treatment no less favourable than that it accords to its own like services and service suppliers.

. . .

3. Formally identical or formally different treatment shall be considered to be less favourable if it modifies the conditions of competition in favour of services or service suppliers of the Member compared to like services or service suppliers of any other Member.

12. Article XX of the GATS provides:

1. Each Member shall set out in a schedule the specific commitments it undertakes under Part III of this Agreement. With respect to sectors where such commitments are undertaken, each Schedule shall specify:
   (a) terms, limitations and conditions on market access;
   (b) conditions and qualifications on national treatment; . . .
2. Measures inconsistent with both Articles XVI and XVII shall be inscribed in the column relating to Article XVI. In this case the inscription will be considered to provide a condition or qualification to Article XVII as well.
3. Schedules of specific commitments shall be annexed to this Agreement and shall form an integral part thereof.

2. Council Decision (EU) 2019/485 on the conclusion of the relevant Agreements under Article XXI of the General Agreement on Trade in Services

13. By Council Decision (EU) 2019/485 of 5 March 2019 on the conclusion of the relevant Agreements under Article XXI of the General Agreement on Trade in Services with Argentina, Australia, Brazil, Canada, China, the Separate customs territory of Taiwan, Penghu, Kinmen and Matsu (Chinese Taipei), Colombia, Cuba, Ecuador, Hong Kong China, India, Japan, Korea, New Zealand, the Philippines, Switzerland and the United States, on the necessary compensatory adjustments resulting from the accession of Czechia, Estonia, Cyprus, Latvia, Lithuania, Hungary, Malta, Austria, Poland, Slovenia,

Slovakia, Finland and Sweden to the European Union,[5] the Council approved the Agreements described in the title, which was a condition for the entry into force of the "Consolidated Schedule" of EU-25 GATS commitments. The Consolidated Schedule entered into force on 15 March 2019. It adopts Hungary's commitments from its Schedule of Specific Commitments[6] without modification.[7]

14. The Schedule of Specific Commitments for Hungary consists of two parts, Part I concerning limitations relating to horizontal commitments and Part II concerning limitations on certain vertical (sector-specific) commitments.

15. Part II of the Schedule lists the sectors in which specific commitments under Article XVI (market access) or Article XVII (national treatment) of the GATS are made. For higher education services[8] it is stated, with regard to market access for the third mode of supply ("commercial presence"), which is relevant here: "Establishment of schools is subject to licence from the central authorities". In the national treatment column no limitations were inscribed ("None").

3. Charter of Fundamental Rights of the European Union

16. Article 13 of the Charter of Fundamental Rights of the European Union ("the Charter"),[9] which is headed "Freedom of the arts and sciences", provides:

The arts and scientific research shall be free of constraint. Academic freedom shall be respected.

17. Article 14(3) of the Charter reads as follows:

The freedom to found educational establishments with due respect for democratic principles and the right of parents to ensure the education and teaching of their children in conformity with their religious, philosophical and pedagogical convictions shall be respected, in accordance with the national laws governing the exercise of such freedom and right.

---

[5] OJ 2019 L 87, p. 1.
[6] Hungary Schedule of Specific Commitments, WTO Doc. GATS/SC/40 of 15 April 1994.
[7] WTO Doc. S/C/W/273, pp. 166 and 167. With regard to entry into force, see the Communication of 7 March 2019 from the European Union to the Members of the WTO.
[8] Hungary Schedule of Specific Commitments, WTO Doc. GATS/SC/40 of 15 April 1994, p. 19 (section 5.C.).
[9] OJ 2007 C 364, p. 1.

18. Article 16 of the Charter states:

The freedom to conduct a business in accordance with Union law and national laws and practices is recognised.

4. Directive 2006/123/EC

19. Under Article 2(1) thereof, Directive 2006/123/EC of the European Parliament and of the Council of 12 December 2006 on services in the internal market ("the Services Directive")[10] applies "to services supplied by providers established in a Member State".

20. Article 4(1) of that directive defines "service" as "any self-employed economic activity, normally provided for remuneration, as referred to in Article [57 TFEU]".

21. Article 16 of the Services Directive provides:

1. Member States shall respect the right of providers to provide services in a Member State other than that in which they are established.

The Member State in which the service is provided shall ensure free access to and free exercise of a service activity within its territory.

Member States shall not make access to or exercise of a service activity in their territory subject to compliance with any requirements which do not respect the following principles:

(a) non-discrimination: the requirement may be neither directly nor indirectly discriminatory with regard to nationality or, in the case of legal persons, with regard to the Member State in which they are established;

(b) necessity: the requirement must be justified for reasons of public policy, public security, public health or the protection of the environment;

(c) proportionality: the requirement must be suitable for attaining the objective pursued, and must not go beyond what is necessary to attain that objective.

. . .

3. The Member State to which the provider moves shall not be prevented from imposing requirements with regard to the provision of a service activity, where they are justified for reasons of public policy, public security, public health or the protection of the environment and in accordance with paragraph 1. . . .

---

[10]   OJ 2006 L 376, p. 36.

B. National law

22. Hungarian higher education law is regulated in Nemzeti felsőoktatásról szóló 2011. évi CCIV. törvény (Law CCIV of 2011 on national higher education). That law was revised in 2017 by Nemzeti felsőoktatásról szóló 2011. évi CCIV. törvény módosításáról szóló 2017. évi XXV. törvény (Law XXV of 2017 amending Law CCIV of 2011 on national higher education, "the Law on higher education").

23. Under Paragraph 76(1)(a) of the Law on higher education, a foreign higher education institution may carry on teaching activities leading to a qualification in the territory of Hungary only if "the binding application of an international treaty on fundamental support for the activities in Hungary, concluded between the Government of Hungary and the State responsible on the basis of the seat of the foreign higher education institution—in the case of a federal State in which the central government is not responsible for recognition of the binding effect of an international treaty, on the basis of a prior agreement with the central government—has been recognised by the parties".

24. Under Paragraph 77(2) of the Law on higher education, that requirement applies to foreign higher education institutions having their seat in a State outside the EEA.

25. Under Paragraph 76(1)(b) of the Law on higher education, a foreign higher education institution may carry on teaching activities leading to a qualification in the territory of Hungary only if "it is classified, in the State responsible on the basis of its seat, as a higher education institution recognised by the State and carrying on genuine higher education teaching activities there".

26. Under Paragraph 77(3), that requirement also applies to foreign higher education institutions having their seat in an EEA State.

27. Paragraph 115(7) of the Law on higher education, in the version applicable at the time of the Commission's reasoned opinion, provided that the requirement under Paragraph 76(1)(a) of the law had to be fulfilled by 1 January 2018. In the case of federal States, the agreement with the central government was to be concluded within six months following the promulgation of Law XXV of 2017. Paragraph 115(7) also makes clear that foreign higher education institutions which do not comply with the legal requirements when the period expires will forfeit their licence. In that case, they may not admit any new entrants to a course of study in Hungary after 1 January 2018, while courses already in progress on that date are to be concluded no later than the 2020/2021 academic year, with no change in conditions.

28. On 18 October 2017 Hungary informed the Commission that the Law on higher education had been amended again by Law CXXVII

of 2017. It extended the period prescribed for fulfilling the requirements under Paragraph 76(1) of the Law on higher education until
1 January 2019 and the other periods under Paragraph 115(7) and (8)
likewise by one year.

III. BACKGROUND TO THE DISPUTE AND
PRE-LITIGATION PROCEDURE

29. On 28 March 2017, the Hungarian Government introduced a
draft law revising Law CCIV of 2011 in the Hungarian National
Assembly. The draft was adopted a few days later, on 4 April 2017,
in an urgent legislative procedure as Law XXV of 2017.

30. By letter of 27 April 2017, the Commission informed Hungary
that it considered that, by adopting Law XXV of 2017, Hungary had
infringed Articles 9, 10 and 13, Article 14(3) and Article 16 of
Directive 2006/123, in the alternative Articles 49 and 56 TFEU,
Article XVII of the GATS and Article 13, Article 14(3) and Article
16 of the Charter, and invited Hungary to submit its observations.
Hungary replied by letter of 25 May 2017, in which it disputed the
abovementioned infringements.

31. On 14 July 2017 the Commission issued a reasoned opinion in
which it maintained its position. After the Commission had refused a
request made by Hungary for an extension of the period for replying,
Hungary replied by letters of 14 August 2017 and 11 September 2017
in which it stated that the alleged infringements did not exist.

32. On 5 October 2017 the Commission issued a supplementary
reasoned opinion. On 6 October 2017, Hungary submitted supplementary information to the letters of 14 August and 11 September 2017.

33. On 18 October 2017 Hungary replied to the supplementary
reasoned opinion and, by letter of 13 November 2017, submitted
further supplementary information.

IV. FORMS OF ORDER SOUGHT AND PROCEDURE
BEFORE THE COURT

34. By the present action for failure to fulfil obligations, which was
received by the Court on 1 February 2018, the Commission claims that
the Court should:

– declare that Hungary has failed to fulfil:
  – its obligations under Article XVII of the GATS by requiring, in
    Paragraph 76(1)(a) of Law CCIV of 2011, as amended, the conclusion

of an international agreement between Hungary and the State of origin for foreign higher education institutions outside the EEA as a condition for supplying education services;

- its obligations under Article 16 of Directive 2006/123 and, in any event, under Articles 49 and 56 TFEU and under Article XVII of the GATS by requiring foreign higher education institutions, in Paragraph 76(1)(b) of Law CCIV of 2011, as amended, to offer higher education in their countries of origin;
- its obligations under Article 13, Article 14(3) and Article 16 of the Charter of Fundamental Rights, in relation to the restrictions described above;
- order Hungary to pay the costs.

35. Hungary contends that the Court should:

- dismiss the action brought by the Commission as being inadmissible; in the alternative
- dismiss the action brought by the Commission as being unfounded;
- order the Commission to pay the costs.

36. The Commission and Hungary presented oral argument at the hearing on 24 June 2019.

V. LEGAL ASSESSMENT

37. In these infringement proceedings it must be considered whether two conditions to which the Hungarian Law on higher education, as amended, makes subject teaching activities by foreign higher education institutions in Hungary are compatible with EU law. These are, first, the requirement of the conclusion of an international treaty between Hungary and the State of origin of the higher education institution. Second, a foreign higher education institution must now also genuinely carry on teaching activities in its State of origin.

38. As the first of those rules applies only to higher education institutions having their seat in third countries outside the EEA, the Commission alleges in particular a breach of the principle of national treatment under Article XVII of the GATS. With regard to that allegation, it is necessary first to examine the Court's jurisdiction under Article 258 TFEU (see under A). Second, the admissibility (see under B) and the substance (see under C) of the action for failure to fulfil obligations in other respects must be assessed. In addition to infringements of the GATS, the Commission considers the conditions described above to constitute infringements of the Services Directive, the fundamental freedoms and the Charter.

A. The Court's jurisdiction in respect of the allegation of an infringement of the GATS

39. The Court's jurisdiction to hear an action is a matter of public policy, which may be considered of its own motion.[11]

1. The GATS as an integral part of EU law

40. An action for failure to fulfil obligations can have as its subject, according to the case law on the first paragraph of Article 258 TFEU, only infringements of obligations under EU law.[12] Hungary considers, however, that any obligation under Article XVII of the GATS in conjunction with the specific commitment for the education sector is not an obligation for Hungary under EU law, but its own obligation under international law.

41. Infringements by the Member States of certain obligations under international law have certainly already been the subject of infringement proceedings.[13] The Court has consistently held that international agreements concluded by the Union are, as from their entry into force, an integral part of the legal order of the European Union.[14] They are therefore binding upon the institutions of the Union and on its Member States pursuant to Article 216(2) TFEU.

42. According to case law, that binding force applies to mixed agreements at least in so far as the provisions of that agreement fall within the external competence of the Union.[15]

43. The Court has ruled, with regard to Article 133 EC, that trade in services, including in services relating to particularly sensitive sectors such as health and education, falls within the external competence of

---

[11] Judgment of 12 November 2015, *Elitaliana* v. *Eulex Kosovo* (C-439/13 P, EU:C:2015:753, paragraph 37).

[12] Judgment of 19 March 2002, *Commission* v. *Ireland* (C-13/00, EU:C:2002:184, paragraph 13).

[13] Judgments of 25 February 1988, *Commission* v. *Greece* (194/85 and 241/85, EU:C:1988:95); of 10 September 1996, *Commission* v. *Germany* (C-61/94, EU:C:1996:313); of 19 March 2002, *Commission* v. *Ireland* (C-13/00, EU:C:2002:184); of 7 October 2004, *Commission* v. *France* (C-239/03, EU:C:2004:598); and of 21 June 2007, *Commission* v. *Italy* (C-173/05, EU:C:2007:362).

[14] Judgments of 30 April 1974, *Haegeman* (181/73, EU:C:1974:41, paragraphs 2/6); of 30 September 1987, *Demirel* (12/86, EU:C:1987:400, paragraph 7); and of 8 March 2011, *Lesoochranárske zoskupenie* (C-240/09, EU:C:2011:125, paragraph 30).

[15] Judgments of 7 October 2004, *Commission* v. *France* (C-239/03, EU:C:2004:598, paragraph 25); of 16 November 2004, *Anheuser-Busch* (C-245/02, EU:C:2004:717, paragraph 41); of 11 September 2007, *Merck Genéricos—Produtos Farmacêuticos* (C-431/05, EU:C:2007:496, paragraph 33 et seq.); and of 8 March 2011, *Lesoochranárske zoskupenie* (C-240/09, EU:C:2011:125, paragraph 31 et seq.).

the Union.[16] By Article 207 TFEU, which replaced Article 133 EC under the Treaty of Lisbon, the external competence of the Union for trade in services was expanded even further and now forms part of its exclusive competence within the framework of the common commercial policy (CCP).

44. This holds even though the Member States retain an extensive internal competence in education, as Hungary mentions. This is taken into account by point (b) of the third subparagraph of Article 207(4) TFEU.[17] Under that provision, the Council may unanimously conclude international agreements on trade in education services only where these agreements risk seriously disturbing the national organisation of such services and prejudicing the responsibility of Member States to deliver them. Such unanimity is necessary because inevitably the Member States are internally responsible for implementing the obligations entered into. The Union has only a competence to coordinate in the area of education in accordance with Article 6(e) TFEU.

45. Furthermore, Article 207(6) TFEU provides that the exercise of the competences conferred by Article 207(1) TFEU does not lead to harmonisation of legislative or regulatory provisions of the Member States in so far as the Treaties exclude such harmonisation. As far as the education sector is concerned, Article 166(4) TFEU contains such a prohibition on harmonisation. However, this does not call into question at all the existence of an external competence of the Union per se.

46. Accordingly, the agreements with third countries necessary for the entry into force of the Consolidated Schedule of EU-25 GATS commitments were approved by the Union without participation by the Member States.[18] The Schedule adopts Hungary's commitments in respect of higher education without modification.

47. The obligation at issue under the GATS, which was originally entered into by Hungary, was therefore transferred to the European Union by the Treaty of Lisbon at the latest and thus constitutes an

---

[16] At that time, the European Union still shared that external competence with its Member States; see Opinion 1/08 (Agreements modifying the Schedules of Specific Commitments under the GATS) of 30 November 2009 (EU:C:2009:739, paragraph 135).

[17] See my Opinion in *Commission* v. *Council* (C-13/07, EU:C:2009:190, point 124).

[18] See Council Decision (EU) 2019/485 of 5 March 2019 (OJ 2019 L 87, p. 1). Prior to the entry into force of the Treaty of Lisbon, the Court had ruled in Opinion 1/08 (Agreements modifying the Schedules of Specific Commitments under the GATS) of 30 November 2009 (EU:C:2009:739) that that modification fell within the shared competence of the Union and its Member States and participation by the Member States was necessary.

obligation under EU law the infringement of which can be the subject of infringement proceedings.[19]

2. *Liability of the Union in international law for infringements of the GATS by Member States*

48. The Court's jurisdiction to find infringements of the GATS by the Member States in infringement proceedings is further suggested by the fact that the European Union may be held liable by a third country for such an infringement before the WTO dispute settlement bodies.[20]

49. This follows, first, from the fact that the GATS is fully binding upon the European Union externally. It is true that under Article 1(1) of Council Decision 94/800 the consent of the European Union is intended to relate only to the portion of the WTO Agreement and its Annexes which falls within its competence. However, the allocation of competences has not been disclosed, unlike in the case of other mixed agreements,[21] and does not therefore lead to any limitation of the binding force. Article 46(1) of the Vienna Convention on the Law of Treaties (VCLT) makes clear in this regard that "a State may not invoke the fact that its consent to be bound by a treaty has been expressed in violation of a provision of its internal law regarding competence to conclude treaties as invalidating its consent unless that violation was manifest and concerned a rule of its internal law of fundamental importance".[22]

50. In any case, the European Union has an extensive competence in the field of the CCP under the Treaty of Lisbon.

51. Second, the Member States' actions within the scope of the GATS can be attributed to the European Union. The European Union cannot directly influence the Member States' action in all the areas covered by the GATS because compliance with the Union's obligations under the WTO Agreement depends largely on how the Member

---

[19]   See Opinion 2/15 (Free Trade Agreement with Singapore) of 16 May 2017 (EU:C:2017:376, paragraph 248).

[20]   The WTO dispute settlement procedure is laid down in the Understanding on Rules and Procedures governing the Settlement of Disputes (DSU) in Annex 2 to the WTO Agreement. It provides for the establishment of panels to settle certain disputes, which report to the Dispute Settlement Body (DSB). On that basis, it produces a final report, which is binding on the parties unless an appeal is made to the Appellate Body (AB) within 60 days.

[21]   See, for example, Article 6(1) of Annex IX to the United Nations Convention on the Law of the Sea, signed on 10 December 1982 at Montego Bay (United Nations Treaty Series, Vol. 1833, 1834 and 1835, p. 3).

[22]   The same provision is made, *mutatis mutandis*, in Article 46(2) of the Vienna Convention on the Law of Treaties between States and International Organizations or between International Organizations (VCLTIO) with regard to an international organisation's internal distribution of competences.

States exercise their own regulatory competences. Nevertheless, the European Union has undertaken to be fully bound by that Agreement from an external point of view. The conduct of its Members must therefore be attributed to it.

52. Consequently, in practice the European Union assumes responsibility, even in respect of national measures, for negotiations with the other WTO Members and for defending a measure in the dispute settlement procedure.[23]

53. According to the Court's case law, in the internal implementation of an international agreement the Member States fulfil an obligation in relation to the European Union, which has assumed responsibility, externally, for the due performance of the agreement.[24]

54. This obligation is an expression of the duty of sincere cooperation under Article 4(3) TEU, which acts as a limit on the exercise of competence. Hungary thus remains free to exercise its internal competence to regulate higher education, but only in so far as the relevant rules do not infringe obligations under the WTO agreements. This would not only render the European Union liable in international law, but also expose the other Member States to the risk of countermeasures. This risk is clearly illustrated by recent developments in the dispute concerning subsidies granted to Airbus by France, Spain, Germany and the United Kingdom. The United States punitive tariffs approved by the WTO as a countermeasure relate to Parmesan cheese from Italy, among other things.

55. Compliance with this duty of sincere cooperation can also be enforced in infringement proceedings.

3. *Relationship between infringement proceedings and the WTO dispute settlement procedure*

56. This conclusion is also not called into question by the other objections raised by Hungary.

---

[23] Examples from the practice of the WTO dispute settlement organs: WTO Appellate Body Report of 5 June 1998, adopted by the DSB on 1 July 1998, WT/DS62/AB/R, WT/DS67/AB/R and WT/DS68/AB/R, European Communities—Computer Equipment, concerning certain Irish and British measures; WTO Appellate Body Report of 12 March 2001, adopted by the DSB on 5 April 2001, WT/DS135/AB/R, European Communities—Asbestos, concerning a French decree; most recently, WTO Appellate Body Report of 15 May 2018, WT/DS316/AB/RW, European Union—Large Civil Aircraft.

[24] Judgments of 26 October 1982, *Kupferberg* (104/81, EU:C:1982:362, paragraphs 11 and 13); of 30 September 1987, *Demirel* (12/86, EU:C:1987:400, paragraph 11); of 19 March 2002, *Commission* v. *Ireland* (C-13/00, EU:C:2002:184, paragraph 15); and of 7 October 2004, *Commission* v. *France* (C-239/03, EU:C:2004:598, paragraph 26).

57. In this regard, Hungary highlights above all the specific character of the WTO dispute settlement procedure and the special role played by the WTO dispute settlement bodies.

58. However, first, a judgment delivered by the Court in infringement proceedings does not in any way call into question the exclusive competence of the WTO dispute settlement bodies to find infringements of that agreement in proceedings between two Members,[25] as infringement proceedings are a purely internal regulatory instrument. The judgment is thus binding only as between the European Union and the Member State and does not prevent the WTO bodies from finding an infringement of the WTO Agreement upon application by a third country, even if the Court has previously rejected such an infringement.

59. In practice, conflicting decisions can be avoided by staying infringement proceedings and awaiting the decision of the WTO bodies if concurrent proceedings are in progress before the WTO. In addition, consideration can be given to restricting the intensity of review of the Court to manifest infringements to take account of the fact that the WTO dispute settlement bodies ultimately have jurisdiction on particularly contentious issues.[26]

60. Second, it is true that, relying on the particular importance of negotiations within the framework of the WTO, the Court has rejected the direct applicability of WTO law in settled case law.[27] This merely means, however, that Member States, in an action for annulment, or the parties in a reference for preliminary ruling on the validity of an EU act, may not rely on the incompatibility of an EU act with the WTO Agreement.[28]

61. These considerations follow from the specific features of the WTO dispute settlement mechanism. In such a procedure, it is conceivable that, in negotiations with third countries, the European Union declares its willingness to withdraw a certain measure or act if the third country makes other commitments to it in return. If a concurrent action for annulment brought by a Member State or a reference for preliminary ruling on the validity of an EU act could be based directly on an infringement of WTO law, the European Union's negotiating

---

[25] See Article 23(1) of the DSU [the WTO Dispute Settlement Understanding].

[26] See below, point 90 of this Opinion.

[27] Judgments of 12 December 1972, *International Fruit Company and Others* (21/72 to 24/72, EU:C:1972:115); of 23 November 1999, *Portugal* v. *Council* (C-149/96, EU:C:1999:574); and of 9 January 2003, *Petrotub and Republica* (C-76/00 P, EU:C:2003:4).

[28] Judgment of 5 October 1994, *Germany* v. *Council* (C-280/93, EU:C:1994:367, paragraph 109).

position would be weakened, as at the end of such proceedings the EU act in question could be declared to be void.[29] The European Union's action would thereby be unilaterally undermined by a Member State or even by a party in the preliminary ruling procedure.

62. However, this only means that WTO law cannot, as a rule, serve as the standard of review for *EU acts* in proceedings before the EU Courts. It is a different question whether the EU Courts may review *national measures* in the light of WTO law.

63. The Court has already answered that question in the affirmative in *Commission* v. *Germany*, where it reviewed a national measure in the light of an agreement concluded within the framework of the General Agreement on Tariffs and Trade (GATT).[30] In doing so, it did not follow the proposal made by Advocate General Tesauro, who had argued that no distinction should be made between national and EU measures as far as the standard of review is concerned.[31]

64. I consider that the Court was essentially correct in its view in that decision that the considerations on the basis of which a review of EU acts in the light of the WTO Agreement is precluded cannot be applied to infringements of WTO law by Member States. The possibility of bringing infringement proceedings against a Member State does not run counter to the aims and particular character of dispute settlement in the WTO.

65. First, the possibility of basing infringement proceedings on an infringement of WTO law can ensure the effective enforcement of any negative ruling by the WTO dispute settlement bodies. If the European Union was not able to bring infringement proceedings against Member States in such cases, the internal implementation of international trade law would even be seriously jeopardised. Yet this is particularly important against the background of threatened sanctions for uninvolved Member States and the European Union.

66. Second, infringement proceedings can take on a significance of their own within the framework of negotiations with third countries in the dispute settlement procedure. The European Union takes responsibility for negotiations with third countries, on the basis of its extensive competence, even for national measures, in the field of the CCP.[32] Where it defends a Member State's measure on account of legal, political or other considerations, it will not seek of its own motion to

---

[29]   See the first paragraph of Article 264 TFEU.
[30]   Judgment of 10 September 1996 (C-61/94, EU:C:1996:313, paragraph 16).
[31]   Opinion of Advocate General Tesauro in *Commission* v. *Germany* (C-61/94, EU:C:1996:194, points 23 and 24).
[32]   See points 49 to 52 of this Opinion.

bring infringement proceedings against the Member State in question.[33] However, infringement proceedings give it an instrument in relation to third countries which strengthens its negotiating position, as it thereby shows its negotiating partners that it can, if necessary, ensure internally that infringements of the WTO Agreement are effectively eliminated. Its credibility is therefore increased and account is taken of the need for prompt united external action.

67. Lastly, there may be cases like the present one where the European Union itself is convinced that a national measure is unlawful. By bringing infringement proceedings against the Member State concerned in such cases, it manifests its decision to be responsible for compliance with the WTO Agreement. Where, however, the European Union "has intended to implement a particular obligation assumed in the context of the WTO, or where the [Union] measure refers expressly to the precise provisions of the WTO agreements", according to settled case law, it is for the Court to review the legality even of EU acts in the light of the WTO rules.[34] This must apply a fortiori to the measures of a Member State.

68. Neither the specific character of the WTO dispute settlement procedure nor the special role played by the WTO dispute settlement bodies therefore precludes the present infringement proceedings.

4. Conclusion

69. The first ground of complaint thus falls within the Court's jurisdiction.

B. Admissibility of the action for failure to fulfil obligations

70. The objections raised by Hungary to the admissibility of the action should now be examined.

71. Hungary asserts in this regard, first, that the periods granted to it by the Commission in the pre-litigation procedure were too short and its rights of defence were thereby restricted. Second, Hungary alleges that the Commission breached its duty of independence and

---

[33] The Airbus dispute can be mentioned again as a prominent, current example.
[34] See judgments of 22 June 1989, *Fediol* v. *Commission* (70/87, EU:C:1989:254, paragraphs 19 to 22); of 7 May 1991, *Nakajima* v. *Council* (C-69/89, EU:C:1991:186, paragraph 31); of 30 September 2003, *Biret International* v. *Council* (C-93/02 P, EU:C:2003:517, paragraph 53); of 23 November 1999, *Portugal* v. *Council* (C-149/96, EU:C:1999:574, paragraph 49); and of 1 March 2005, *Van Parys* (C-377/02, EU:C:2005:121, paragraph 40).

impartiality and initiated the procedure for purely political reasons, taking into account individual interests on one side.

1. Setting of periods in the pre-litigation procedure

72. The objective of the pre-litigation procedure is to give the Member State concerned an opportunity to comply with its obligations under EU law or to avail itself of its right to defend itself against the complaints made by the Commission.[35] The Commission must therefore allow Member States a reasonable period to reply to the letter of formal notice and to comply with a reasoned opinion or, where appropriate, to prepare their defence. If the period was so short that the Member State's right to an effective defence is impaired without sufficient justification, the consequence is that the pre-litigation procedure was not validly carried out and the action brought by the Commission must be dismissed as being inadmissible.[36]

73. As master of the procedure, the Commission enjoys broad discretion in setting the periods.[37] In order to determine whether the period allowed is reasonable, furthermore, account must be taken of all the circumstances of the case. According to case law, very short periods may be justified especially where there is an urgent need to remedy a breach or where the Member State concerned is fully aware of the Commission's views long before the procedure starts.[38]

74. In the case at issue, the Commission set a period of one month in both the letter of formal notice and the reasoned opinion. It is true that the Commission generally sets two-month periods in the pre-litigation procedure. Nevertheless, a one-month period is not a "very short" period within the meaning of the case law cited in point 73.[39]

---

[35] Judgments of 5 November 2002, *Commission* v. *Austria* (C-475/98, EU:C:2002:630, paragraph 35), and of 18 July 2007, *Commission* v. *Germany* (C-490/04, EU:C:2007:430, paragraph 25).

[36] Judgment of 2 February 1988, *Commission* v. *Belgium* (293/85, EU:C:1988:40, paragraph 20).

[37] See Opinion of Advocate General Mischo in *Commission* v. *France* (C-1/00, EU:C:2001:467, point 57). See also, to that effect, judgment of 10 July 1985, *Commission* v. *Netherlands* (16/84, EU:C:1985:309, paragraph 10).

[38] Judgments of 2 February 1988, *Commission* v. *Belgium* (293/85, EU:C:1988:40, paragraphs 13 and 14); of 2 July 1996, *Commission* v. *Luxembourg* (C-473/93, EU:C:1996:263, paragraphs 19 and 20); of 28 October 1999, *Commission* v. *Austria* (C-328/96, EU:C:1999:526, paragraph 51); and of 13 December 2001, *Commission* v. *France* (C-1/00, EU:C:2001:687, paragraphs 64 and 65).

[39] In the case in which the judgment of 2 February 1988, *Commission* v. *Belgium* (293/85, EU:C:1988:40) was delivered, the periods were 8 and 14 days; in *Commission* v. *France* (C-1/00, EU:C:2001:687), the periods were 15 days and 5 days; in *Commission* v. *Austria* (C-328/96, EU:C:1999:526), the periods were one week and 15 days; in the case in which the judgment of 31 January 1984, *Commission* v. *Ireland* (74/82, EU:C:1984:34) was delivered, a period of five days was at issue.

It should also be stated that there were around three and a half months between the letter of formal notice of 27 April 2017 and the expiry of the second one-month period in mid-August of that year in which the Hungarian Government was aware of the Commission's views and, accordingly, had time to assess the possibilities of defending itself and preparing its letter in reply.

75. Furthermore, in this case the Commission rightly relies on the urgency of the matter. It has not expressly explained to Hungary the reasons for urgency. However, the reasons are immediately clear from the circumstances of the case, in particular from the fact that, according to the original version of Paragraph 115(7) of the Law on higher education, higher education institutions which did not fulfil the conditions under Paragraph 76(1) of that law were to have their licence withdrawn and were to be prohibited from admitting new students on 1 January 2018.

76. It was only on 18 October 2017 that Hungary gave notification that this period had been extended by one year, that is, after the relevant periods for the pre-litigation procedure had been set. Therefore, the fact that the Commission did not bring the action for failure to fulfil obligations until February 2018 also fails to rebut the presumption of urgency in setting the periods allowed, contrary to the view taken by the Hungarian Government.

77. Last, according to case law, consideration is to be given to whether the Member State's ability to defend itself against the Commission's complaints was essentially restricted.[40] Even a "too short" period does not result in the action being inadmissible if the Commission has taken into consideration a late defence submission and the Member State was therefore able to defend itself adequately against the Commission's complaints.[41]

78. In this case, in addition to its letters of 14 August 2017 and 18 October 2017, the Hungarian Government submitted three further letters by which it replied to the original and the supplementary reasoned opinion. The Commission closely examined all those letters and took them into account in its decision to bring an action.

79. For this latter reason, it is also irrelevant that the Commission also set one-month periods in two other sets of infringement proceedings initiated concurrently against Hungary. It is true that it is conceivable that, as a result of a cumulation of multiple proceedings with short

[40] Judgment of 10 July 1985, *Commission* v. *Netherlands* (16/84, EU:C:1985:309, paragraph 10).
[41] Judgment of 31 January 1984, *Commission* v. *Ireland* (74/82, EU:C:1984:34, paragraph 13).

time limits, such a burden is placed on a Member State that it can no longer effectively exercise its rights of defence. The Commission must also take that possibility into consideration when it sets the relevant periods. However, provided the necessary reasons for the correspondingly short periods apply and the rights of defence of the Member State are not eroded—for which Hungary does not submit any evidence in this case—this fact alone cannot mean that the setting of the relevant periods in an individual case is unlawful.

2. The allegation of political motivation

80. Hungary takes the view, furthermore, that the Commission brought infringement proceedings for purely political reasons, in breach of its duty of impartiality. The proceedings are, it is contended, solely in the interests of the CEU in Budapest.

81. As far as this allegation is concerned, it is questionable, first of all, whether it can be concluded from the fact that the CEU was mentioned once in the letter of formal notice that the proceedings are solely in the interests of that university. There is no doubt that the Commission must be able to single out and name specific affected institutions as examples.

82. In any case, the considerations which led the Commission to bring infringement proceedings cannot in themselves call into question the proper conduct of the pre-litigation procedure or therefore affect the admissibility of the action under Article 258 TFEU.[42] While the Commission must explain why it considers there to be an infringement of EU law, it does not have to state the reasons why it is bringing an action for failure to fulfil obligations.[43]

83. On these grounds, the objections of inadmissibility raised by the Hungarian Government should be rejected in their entirety.

C. Substance of the action for failure to fulfil obligations

84. I will now examine first the Commission's complaints concerning the requirement of the conclusion of an international treaty between Hungary and the State of origin of a foreign higher education institution (see under 1) and then the complaints concerning the requirement of genuine teaching activities in the State of origin (see under 2).

---

[42] Judgment of 3 March 2016, *Commission* v. *Malta* (C-12/14, EU:C:2016:135, paragraph 24).
[43] Judgment of 3 March 2016, *Commission* v. *Malta* (C-12/14, EU:C:2016:135, paragraph 26).

1. Requirement of the conclusion of an international treaty, Paragraph 76(1)(a) of the Law on higher education

85. With regard to the condition of an international agreement between Hungary and the State of origin of a foreign higher education institution on the provision of education services by higher education institutions having their seat outside the EEA, as laid down in Paragraph 76(1)(a) of the Law on higher education, the Commission alleges an infringement of Article XVII of the GATS in conjunction with the specific commitment for the higher education sector and under Article 13, Article 14(3) and Article 16 of the Charter.

(a) Infringement of Article XVII of the GATS in conjunction with Article 216(2) TFEU

86. An infringement of Article XVII:1 of the GATS in conjunction with Hungary's specific commitment for the higher education sector would also constitute an infringement of its obligation under Article 216(2) TFEU.[44]

(1) Intensity of review

87. As regards the examination of infringements of customary international law, the Court has acknowledged in the past that its review is limited to establishing manifest infringements.[45] It is true that it has rejected this, in principle, for the review of international agreements concluded by the European Union.[46]

88. In the present case, however, limiting the Court's intensity of review to manifest infringements of the GATS could be contemplated in view of two arguments which Hungary raised against the jurisdiction of the Court.

89. First, the specific implementation of the obligations under the GATS in this case is based on the Member States' own internal competence in the education sector. In such sensitive sectors, the Member States are intended to retain a degree of organisational freedom which can be taken into account by decreasing the intensity of review.

---

[44] In such a case, the Court finds an infringement not only of the international treaty in question, but also of Article 216(2) TFEU (formerly Article 300(7) EC); see judgments of 19 March 2002, *Commission* v. *Ireland* (C-13/00, EU:C:2002:184), and of 7 October 2004, *Commission* v. *France* (C-239/03, EU:C:2004:598).

[45] Judgments of 25 January 1979, *Racke* (98/78, EU:C:1979:14, paragraph 52), and of 21 December 2011, *Air Transport Association of America and Others* (C-366/10, EU:C:2011:864, paragraph 110).

[46] Judgment of 21 December 2011, *Air Transport Association of America and Others* (C-366/10, EU:C:2011:864, paragraph 110).

90. Second, the specific character of the WTO dispute settlement procedures and the fact that the WTO dispute settlement bodies ultimately have jurisdiction for the binding determination of infringements of the WTO Agreement are conducive to leaving the resolution of particularly contentious and difficult questions to those specialised bodies and limiting the review of the GATS for "internal purposes" to manifest infringements.[47]

91. As far as the present case is concerned, however, I take the view that there is a manifest infringement of the GATS, as I will explain below.

(2) Higher education activities as a service within the meaning of the GATS

92. Hungary asserts that the CEU, in the sole interest of which, in reality, the infringement proceedings were initiated, is a non-profit-making organisation and its activities are not therefore covered by the GATS. It is correct that, in Article I:3(b), the GATS excludes from its scope services which are supplied neither on a commercial basis nor in competition with other services.

93. The Commission does not, however, object to the specific treatment of the CEU, but to Paragraph 76(1)(a) of the Law on higher education.[48]

94. The Hungarian Government itself states in this regard that Paragraph 76(1)(a) of the Law on higher education is applicable to all higher education institutions, but does not deny that it also covers institutions which offer services for remuneration, and therefore undoubtedly carry on an economic activity.

(3) Substance of Hungary's specific commitments for the education sector

95. Because the condition in Paragraph 76(1)(a) of the Law on higher education applies only to foreign service suppliers, it might breach the principle of national treatment.

96. Under Article XVII:1 of the GATS, however, the obligation of each WTO Member to accord service suppliers of any other Member treatment no less favourable than that it accords to its own like service suppliers is subject to any conditions and qualifications set out for the sector concerned in the Schedule of Commitments.

97. In other words, the national treatment obligation under the GATS is a specific commitment which must have been assumed

---

[47] See point 59 of this Opinion.
[48] See, to that effect, judgment of 15 November 2016, *Ullens de Schooten* (C-268/15, EU:C:2016:874, paragraph 49).

definitely and in some measure by a Member, unlike under the GATT, for example, where it stems directly from Article III thereof. Under Article XX:3 of the GATS, the schedules of commitments of each Member are annexed to the Agreement and form an integral part thereof.

98. In Hungary's specific commitments[49] for higher education services, the condition "Establishment of schools is subject to licence from the central authorities" is inscribed in the third mode of supply ("commercial presence") in the market access column, whilst no limitations were stipulated for national treatment ("None").

99. The parties in this case disagree as to whether and, if appropriate, to what extent the prima facie unlimited obligation of Hungary to accord national treatment is restricted by the limitation on market access relating to licences.

100. It follows from Article XX:2 of the GATS that the inscription "None" in the national treatment column does not necessarily establish an obligation to accord comprehensive national treatment. Under that provision, "measures inconsistent with both Articles XVI [on market access] and XVII [on national treatment] shall be inscribed in the column relating to Article XVI. In this case the inscription will be considered to provide a condition or qualification to Article XVII as well".

101. According to the decision-making practice of the WTO dispute settlement bodies, Article XX:2 of the GATS is a simplification rule.[50] Thus, for measures inconsistent with *both* the market access obligation *and* the national treatment obligation, it is sufficient to inscribe the limitation for market access only. This then covers any difference in treatment between domestic and foreign service suppliers also caused by the measure.[51]

---

[49] Hungary Schedule of Specific Commitments, WTO Doc. GATS/SC/40 of 15 April 1994, p. 19 (section 5.C.). See now the Consolidated Schedule of Specific Commitments of the European Union and its Member States of 15 March 2019, WTO Doc. S/C/W/273, pp. 166 and 167 (section 5.C.).

[50] WTO Panel Report of 16 July 2012, adopted by the DSB on 31 August 2012, WT/DS413/R, China—Electronic Payment Services, section 7.658. ". . . [T]he special rule in Article XX:2 provides a simpler requirement: a Member need only make a single inscription of the measure under the market access column, which then provides an implicit limitation under national treatment."

[51] WTO Panel Report of 16 July 2012, adopted by the DSB on 31 August 2012, WT/DS413/R, China—Electronic Payment Services, section 7.661: ". . . Article XX:2 provides . . . that the measure inscribed in the market access column encompasses aspects inconsistent with both market access and national treatment obligations . . . [This thus permits] China to maintain measures that are inconsistent with both Articles XVI and XVII. With an inscription of 'Unbound' for subsector (d) in mode 1 under Article XVI, and a corresponding 'None' for Article XVII, China has indicated that it is free to maintain the full range of limitations expressed in the six categories of Article XVI:2, whether discriminatory or not."

102. It should be stated in this regard that Article XVI of the GATS does not prohibit all conceivable measures affecting market access. In fact, only six precisely defined categories of limitations are incompatible with Article XVI of the GATS. They are set out in Article XVI:2 of the GATS and are of a mainly quantitative nature.[52] Only if one of those categories is concerned does a condition inscribed in the "market access" column also characterise the national treatment obligation.

103. As for measures which are not incompatible with Article XVI:2 of the GATS, on the other hand, the inscription "None" in the national treatment column in this case means that the Member concerned is fully required to grant national treatment.[53]

104. There may certainly be licence-related limitations which are of a quantitative nature and thus fall within one of the categories referred to in Article XVI:2 of the GATS. For example, the grant of a licence may be made dependent on a needs test. On the basis of the inscribed limitation on market access, Hungary is permitted to maintain and introduce such measures. Furthermore, under Article XX:2 of the GATS such measures may also be discriminatory as, according to that provision, the limitation inscribed for market access also applies to the national treatment obligation.

105. A licence-related limitation can, however, also be of a qualitative nature, such as where the grant of the licence is subject to certain substantive criteria being met. Such a measure is not prohibited a priori by Article XVI of the GATS. Therefore, Article XX:2 is also not applicable to it. Qualitative licence-related limitations should therefore be (also) inscribed in the column on limitations on national treatment. Otherwise, the national treatment obligation would remain fully applicable to such measures, following from the inscription "None".[54]

106. As regards the measure at issue, it should be stated that the requirement of the conclusion of an international treaty, like the requirement of the existence of teaching activities in the State of origin, does not seek a quantitative restriction. Nor does it constitute a

---

[52] WTO Panel Report of 16 July 2012, adopted by the DSB on 31 August 2012, WT/DS413/R, China—Electronic Payment Services, section 7.652: "Unlike Article XVII, however, the scope of the market access obligation does not extend generally to 'all measures affecting the supply of services'. Instead, it applies to six carefully defined categories of measures of a mainly quantitative nature. The issue thus arises whether the scope of these measures, and thus the extent of China's absence of obligation with respect thereto, extends to discriminatory measures in the sense of Article XVII."

[53] WTO Panel Report of 16 July 2012, adopted by the DSB on 31 August 2012, WT/DS413/R, China—Electronic Payment Services, section 7.663: ". . . Due to the inscription of 'None', China *must grant national treatment with respect to any of the measures at issue that are not inconsistent with Article XVI:2*" (emphasis added).

[54] See, *mutatis mutandis*, footnote 53.

requirement as to legal form (see Article XVI:2(e) of the GATS). Consequently, the measures are not such as to fall under Article XVI:2 of the GATS. Thus, Article XX:2 of the GATS is also not applicable to them.

107. It follows that Hungary is free to introduce such requirements from the point of view of market access. Nevertheless, this holds only if they are applicable without distinction as, by the inscription "None", Hungary has committed itself fully to national treatment.

108. It would have been perfectly possible under the GATS opt-in system for Hungary to inscribe such a limitation for national treatment. That option was not taken, however.

109. It must therefore be stated that, with regard to the contested measures, Hungary is fully obliged to accord national treatment.

110. This conclusion is also to be regarded as manifest in accordance with the standard of review described above, in the light of the existing decision-making practice of the WTO dispute settlement organs.[55]

(4) Existence of a difference in treatment

111. The requirement of the conclusion of an international treaty for higher education institutions having their seat in third countries leads to a difference in treatment between institutions having their seat in Hungary and institutions having their seat in third countries. The same applies, moreover, to the requirement of offering teaching courses in the State of origin.

112. This conclusion is not called into question by the fact that domestic service suppliers naturally would not be able to fulfil the requirement in question. Under Article XVII:3 of the GATS, less favourable treatment requires only a modification of the conditions of competition on the domestic market in favour of domestic services or service suppliers. Through the introduction of additional requirements, however, competition is modified to the detriment of higher education institutions having their seat in third countries.

(5) Exception under Article XIV of the GATS?

113. Lastly, it must be examined whether an exception under Article XIV of the GATS applies to the requirement of the conclusion of an international treaty.

114. The Hungarian Government maintains in this regard that the measure is necessary to guarantee public policy and public security and

---

[55] See above, points 88 and 90 of this Opinion.

to prevent deceptive and fraudulent practices. Those aims are expressly mentioned in Article XIV(a) and (c)(i) of the GATS.

115. Under Paragraph 76(1)(a) of the Law on higher education, the treaty must be concluded with the State responsible, while in the case of a federal State in which the central government is not responsible for recognition of higher education institutions, a prior agreement must be concluded with the central government. Substantively, the treaty must relate to fundamental support for the activities of the institution concerned in Hungary from the government of the State of origin.

116. The conclusion of international treaties, in particular on recognition of qualifications, is a common instrument of international cooperation in higher education. With a view to preventing fraudulent practices, a treaty relating to the activities of a certain educational establishment in the host State, concluded with the government of the State of origin, performs a kind of guarantee function in principle. It makes it clear to the host State that the State of origin considers the establishment to be credible and supports its activities.

117. However, Article XIV of the GATS provides that exceptions are not to be "applied in a manner which would constitute a means of arbitrary or unjustifiable discrimination between countries where like conditions prevail, or a disguised restriction on trade in services".

118. Against this background, the requirement of the conclusion of an international treaty cannot, on closer examination, be regarded as a permissible exception as, in its specific form, it appears to be a means of arbitrary discrimination within the meaning of Article XVI of the GATS.

119. First, the Commission rightly asserts that the conclusion of an international treaty necessarily involves the exercise of political discretion, which is not fully amenable to judicial review. Paragraph 76(1)(a) of the Law on higher education thus makes the grant of an operating licence for higher education institutions having their seat in third countries subject to a condition the fulfilment of which is ultimately in the control of Hungary. In the final analysis, this amounts to a "subject to licence" condition. Hungary did not impose any such condition when it entered into its obligation to offer treatment equal to that afforded to nationals.[56] In any event, the Hungarian Government can arbitrarily delay the conclusion of the treaty, which can result in a higher education institution being refused an operating licence solely due to the short period under Paragraph 115(7) of the Law on higher education.

---

[56] See above, points 107 to 109 of this Opinion.

120. As, under Paragraph 76(1)(a) of the Law on higher education, the necessary treaty relates only to fundamental support for the activities of the higher education institution concerned in Hungary, it is also unclear why that requirement could not also be met by a unilateral declaration made by the government of the State of origin.

121. Second, Paragraph 76(1)(a) of the Law on higher education specifies the requirements for international treaties with federal States, providing that a prior agreement with the central government is necessary if it is not responsible for recognition of the binding effect of an international treaty. This particular requirement is a condition that possibly cannot be fulfilled and is thus ultimately arbitrary. It is at any rate uncertain whether the constitutional framework of the federal State in question actually permits the required agreement with the central government where higher education is the responsibility of the constituent States.[57]

122. Lastly, it is clear from the fact that the condition at issue is also imposed on higher education institutions already operating in Hungary that it is not an objective requirement for combating fraud. It is not evident how fraudulent activity by such an institution could be countered by an agreement with the central government of its State of origin.

123. Paragraph 76(1)(a) of the Law on higher education cannot therefore be justified as an exception under Article XIV of the GATS.

124. Given the arbitrary character of the measure, this conclusion is also to be regarded as manifest.

125. In the light of the foregoing, the requirement of the conclusion of an international treaty is not compatible with the obligations entered into by Hungary in the light of Article XVII:2 of the GATS and the specific commitment for the education sector. By adopting Paragraph 76(1)(a) of the Law on higher education, Hungary therefore infringed Article XVII of the GATS in conjunction with Article 216(2) TFEU.

(b) Infringement of Article 14(3) of the Charter

126. The Commission further asserts that the condition of the conclusion of an international treaty with the State of origin in order for higher education institutions having their seat in third countries to commence or continue their activities in Hungary constitutes an infringement of the freedom to found educational establishments

---

[57] This applies, for example, to the conclusion of an international treaty with US States, whose area of responsibility includes higher education.

enshrined in Article 14(3) of the Charter. It also infringes the freedom to conduct a business enshrined in Article 16 of the Charter.

(1) Applicability of the Charter

127. As has already been shown, the individual commitments under the GATS constitute obligations on the European Union under international law. Under Article 51(1) of the Charter, the EU institutions are bound by the Charter in implementing all their obligations.

128. The Member States, on the other hand, are bound by the Charter, under Article 51(1) of the Charter, only "when they are implementing Union law". There is precisely such implementation of Union law where the Member States internally put into effect the European Union's obligations under international law on the basis of their own regulatory competence. In doing so, they fulfil an obligation in relation to the European Union, which has assumed responsibility, externally, for the due performance of the agreement.[58] The applicability of the Charter ensures that the Member States do not infringe fundamental rights "as representatives" of the European Union.[59]

129. That naturally does not mean that measures within the education sector of the Member States are generally to be assessed by reference to the fundamental rights of the European Union. Only measures that are governed by EU law are subject to those fundamental rights.[60] That applies in particular to measures in relation to which EU law imposes particular obligations on the Member States. In the present case Article XVII GATS imposes on Hungary a comprehensive duty of national treatment. The application of the Charter is a consequence of the fact that the Hungarian legislation is not compatible with the duty of national treatment imposed by Article XVII of the GATS.

(2) Infringement of Article 14(3) of the Charter

130. Article 14(3) of the Charter establishes the freedom to found educational establishments. This must necessarily include the subsequent operation of the educational establishment, otherwise its foundation is pointless. It is clear from the Explanations relating to the Charter that Article 14(3) of the Charter represents a specific

---

[58]   See points 53 and 47 of this Opinion.

[59]   See also, in this respect, Opinion of Advocate General Saugmandsgaard Øe in *Commission v. Hungary (Usufruct over agricultural land)* (C-235/17, EU:C:2018:971, point 82).

[60]   To this effect, judgments of 6 March 2014, *Siragusa* (C-206/13, EU:C:2014:126, paragraph 25 et seq.), and of 10 July 2014, *Julián Hernández and Others* (C-198/13, EU:C:2014:2055, paragraph 36 et seq.).

expression of the freedom to conduct a business under Article 16 of the Charter in the field of privately financed education.[61]

131. This means, first, that Article 16 of the Charter, which is also relied on by the Commission, should not be examined separately in this case, as Article 14(3) of the Charter is more specific in this regard.

132. Second, it means that Article 14(3) of the Charter in any case protects the business side of the private higher education institution's activities, that is to say, the commercial aspects of establishing and operating a higher education institution.

133. A condition like the one laid down in Paragraph 76(1)(a), whereby, if it is not fulfilled, the foundation and operation of such a private institution are prohibited, therefore falls within the scope of protection offered by Article 14(3) of the Charter, especially since the creation of an autonomous fundamental right to found private educational establishments suggests that, over and above the economic aspect, it is intended to afford specific protection to the existence of private educational establishments as such. In my view, this indicates that Article 14(3) of the Charter is intended to guarantee the continued existence of private educational establishments alongside State colleges and universities, and ultimately a diversity of education opportunities.

(3) Possibility of limitation in the present case

134. As regards the possibility of limiting Article 14(3) of the Charter, it is clear from its wording that the freedom to found educational establishments is "in accordance with the national laws governing the exercise of such freedom and right". This means that the freedom to found educational establishments is guaranteed, in principle, only within the scope of the applicable legal requirements for their foundation. In other words, the legislature may, in principle, lay down the conditions for the foundation and operation of educational establishments by statute without infringing Article 14(3) of the Charter. However, as is clear from Article 52(1) of the Charter, it must in any case respect the principle of proportionality.[62]

135. The aims cited by Hungary as justification are, first, protection of public policy, in particular against deceptive and fraudulent practices, and, second, assurance of the quality of teaching courses.

136. As far as the first of these aims is concerned, it has already been explained that "fundamental support for the activities" of the higher

---

[61] OJ 2007 C 303, p. 22.

[62] See, with regard to the similarly worded Article 16 of the Charter, judgment of 22 January 2013, *Sky Österreich* (C-283/11, EU:C:2013:28, paragraph 47).

education institution concerned, as required under Paragraph 76(1)(a) of the Law on higher education, can also be expressed by a unilateral declaration made by the State[63] and the conclusion of an international treaty is therefore not necessary.

137. In addition, as has also already been discussed, in its specific form, the rule entails the risk of arbitrary treatment,[64] as the special requirement relating to the conclusion of a treaty by the central government does not ensure that it can actually be fulfilled. In addition, the conclusion of the treaty, and in particular the time when it is done, is entirely at the discretion of the Hungarian Government. This factor is even more significant since the operation of previously lawful educational establishments is also subject to supplementary conditions, the fulfilment of which is not in the control of the institutions concerned and which they could not have foreseen.[65]

138. As regards the second aim of quality assurance, Hungary has not explained how the mandatory conclusion of an international treaty with the central government of the State of origin of a foreign higher education institution might help to further that aim.

139. This holds all the more since that requirement is also imposed on existing institutions, without the need to demonstrate quality deficiencies or to provide evidence of how they might be eliminated through the conclusion of an international treaty with the institution's State of origin.

140. Paragraph 76(1)(a) of the Law on higher education cannot therefore be regarded as a lawful limitation of the freedom to found educational establishments. Accordingly, I conclude that the adoption of Paragraph 76(1)(a) of the Law on higher education also constitutes an infringement of Article 14(3) of the Charter.

(c) Infringement of the second sentence of Article 13 of the Charter
141. Because higher education institutions which do not fulfil the requirement laid down in Paragraph 76(1)(a) of the Law on higher education are, as a consequence, also not permitted to carry out any teaching or research activities in Hungary or must cease such activities, if appropriate after the expiry of a transitional period, the Commission also alleges an infringement of the second sentence of Article 13 of the Charter. Under that provision, academic freedom must be respected.

---

[63] See points 116 and 119 of this Opinion.
[64] See points 118 to 121 of this Opinion.
[65] See also point 122 of this Opinion.

142. As far as is apparent, the Court has not yet had an opportunity to take a view on the scope of protection offered by the second sentence of Article 13 of the Charter.

143. One possible point of reference is Article 52(3) of the Charter, under which the meaning and scope of the rights of the Charter which correspond to rights guaranteed by the Convention for the Protection of Human Rights and Fundamental Freedoms (ECHR) is the same as those laid down by the ECHR. In the case law of the European Court of Human Rights (ECtHR), academic freedom is treated as a manifestation of freedom of expression under Article 10 ECHR,[66] to which the Explanations on Article 13 of the Charter also refer.[67] This includes, according to the case law of the ECtHR, in particular the freedom to conduct academic research and to adopt and disseminate academic opinions.[68]

144. The legal rule regarding the conclusion of an international treaty in Paragraph 76(1)(a) of the Law on higher education does not limit that freedom directly. It is nevertheless likely to deprive academics working at the universities concerned of the infrastructure needed to exercise academic freedom.

145. From a schematic point of view, academic freedom can be found in Article 13 of the Charter together with the protection of freedom of the arts, which, according to the case law of the ECtHR, is also a manifestation of the freedom to hold opinions. It follows that academic freedom under the second sentence of Article 13 of the Charter can also be regarded as a fundamental right of communication. Academic freedom is not, however, restricted to mere communication.

146. Rather, the Charter, unlike the ECHR, contains a fundamental right to freedom of the arts and sciences which is autonomous of the general freedom to hold opinions. This includes not only substantively autonomous research and teaching that is free from State interference, but also its institutional and organisational framework. Affiliation with a State or private university is, in practice, an essential condition for academic research. The university serves as a platform for academic discourse and a network and infrastructure for teaching staff, students and donors. The freedom to found educational establishments enshrined in Article 14(3) of the Charter protects only part of that

---

[66] ECtHR, judgments of 23 June 2009, *Mustafa Erdoğan* v. *Turkey* (CE:ECHR:2009: 0623JUD001708903), and of 15 April 2014, *Hasan Yazıcı* v. *Turkey* (CE:ECHR:2014: 0527JUD000034604).

[67] OJ 2007 C 303, p. 22.

[68] ECtHR, judgment of 15 April 2014, *Hasan Yazıcı* v. *Turkey* (CE:ECHR:2014: 0527JUD000034604, § 40).

institutional framework, namely in so far as private educational establishments are concerned.

147. A requirement which, if not fulfilled, means that no teaching or research activities can take place at a university or must be ended thus also falls within the scope of protection offered by the second sentence of Article 13 of the Charter.

148. As regards the possibility of limiting the second sentence of Article 13 of the Charter, it is clear from the Explanations relating to the Charter that it is subject to the limitations authorised by Article 10 ECHR. These are limitations which are prescribed by law and are necessary in a democratic society in order to safeguard certain aims listed therein. They include, for example, the protection of public safety and the prevention of disorder and crime. These requirements are essentially the same as those in Article 52(1) of the Charter.

149. It should be noted that the second sentence of Article 13 of the Charter, in so far as it also protects the institutional and organisational framework for research and teaching, does not guarantee the continued existence of each individual educational institution. Nevertheless, a rule which results in the closure of a higher education institution must be proportionate, as is already evident from Article 52(1) of the Charter.

150. For the reasons already mentioned, the requirement in Paragraph 76(1)(a) of the Law on higher education is to be regarded as disproportionate and, consequently, also cannot justify a limitation of the second sentence of Article 13 of the Charter.[69]

(d) Conclusion

151. In summary, I therefore suggest that the Court find that, by adopting Paragraph 76(1)(a) of the Law on higher education, Hungary infringed its obligations under Article XVII of the GATS in conjunction with Article 216(2) TFEU and under the second sentence of Article 13 and Article 14(3) of the Charter.

2. Requirement of the existence of genuine teaching activities in the State of origin, Paragraph 76(1)(b) of the Law on higher education

152. With regard to Paragraph 76(1)(b) of the Law on higher education, which makes the establishment and continued operation of a foreign higher education institution in Hungary dependent on the existence of genuine teaching activities in the State of origin, the

---

[69]   See points 136 to 139 of this Opinion.

Commission alleges infringements of Article 16 of Directive 2006/123, Articles 49 and 56 TFEU, Article 13, Article 14(3) and Article 16 of the Charter and Article XVII of the GATS. Unlike the requirement of the conclusion of an international treaty that has just been examined, the condition now under review also applies to higher education institutions having their seat in another Member State of the European Union or the EEA.

(a) Infringement of Article 49 TFEU in conjunction with Article 54 TFEU
153. It is first necessary to consider the alleged infringement of freedom of establishment. It must be assumed that "teaching activities leading to a qualification", which are subject to special requirements under Paragraph 76(1) of the Law on higher education, are offered in the vast majority of cases by a permanent establishment in Hungary.

(1) Limitation of freedom of establishment
154. According to the Court's case law, the organisation of remuneration of university courses falls within the scope of freedom of establishment when that activity is carried on by a national of one Member State in another Member State on a stable and continuous basis from a principal or secondary establishment in the latter Member State.[70]
155. It is settled case law that Article 49 TFEU includes the right to take up and pursue activities as self-employed persons and to set up and manage undertakings under the same conditions as are laid down by the law of the Member State of establishment for its own nationals. On the other hand, all measures which prohibit, impede or render less attractive the exercise of freedom of establishment within the meaning of the first paragraph of Article 49 TFEU must be regarded as constituting restrictions on that freedom.[71]
156. By these standards, Paragraph 76(1)(b) of the Law on higher education limits the freedom of establishment of foreign higher education institutions in Hungary, as they are impeded in commencing higher education activities and are required to cease those activities after the expiry of the transitional period if they do not offer higher education in their State of origin.

---

[70] Judgment of 13 November 2003, *Neri* (C-153/02, EU:C:2003:614, paragraph 39).
[71] Judgments of 11 July 2002, *Gräbner* (C-294/00, EU:C:2002:442, paragraph 38), and of 13 November 2003, *Neri* (C-153/02, EU:C:2003:614, paragraph 41).

(2) Justification of the limitation

157. As regards the justification for this measure, Article 52(1) TFEU provides that special treatment for foreign nationals may be justified only on grounds of public policy, public security or public health.

158. There is a case of "special treatment for foreign nationals" here, as only foreign higher education institutions are required to prove the existence of an institution in their State of origin in order to commence or continue teaching activities in Hungary. Domestic higher education institutions are naturally unable to provide such proof because they do not have a seat in another Member State. This does not mean, however, that foreign higher education institutions would not be comparable in this respect with domestic higher education institutions.[72] Having a seat in another Member State cannot be a permissible criterion for differentiation in this connection. The discriminatory character of the rules resides precisely in the fact that the activities of foreign higher education institutions are subject to additional conditions because they have their seat in another Member State.

159. Hungary also relies on the protection of public policy and claims that the requirement at issue is necessary to prevent deceptive and fraudulent practices. In addition, it is contended, it is the only way to assure teaching quality.

160. The justification of public policy means protection against a genuine and sufficiently serious threat affecting one of the fundamental interests of society. Although the importance of the aims of preventing deceptive and fraudulent practices and assuring high teaching quality should not be dismissed, no fundamental interests of society are affected within the meaning of this definition.[73]

161. It should be pointed out in this regard that the Court has ruled that Article 49 TFEU prohibits Member States, in principle, from prohibiting the formation of a branch solely on the ground that the company concerned has not carried on business activities in the State in which it has its seat.[74] It is another matter whether the Member State may impose requirements for the activities of the branch and, if so, which.

---

[72] The fundamental freedoms are specific prohibitions of discrimination which thus prohibit only different treatment of comparable situations; see judgment of 14 February 1995, *Schumacker* (C-279/93, EU:C:1995:31, paragraph 30).

[73] The Court considered, for example, the prevention of serious offences as affecting one of the fundamental interests of society; see judgment of 13 July 2017, *E* (C-193/16, EU:C:2017:542, paragraph 20).

[74] Judgments of 9 March 1999, *Centros* (C-212/97, EU:C:1999:126, paragraph 38), and of 30 September 2003, *Inspire Art* (C-167/01, EU:C:2003:512, paragraph 97).

162. Moreover, a justification for other overriding reasons in the public interest can be taken into consideration only in the case of restrictions of freedom of establishment which are applied without discrimination on grounds of nationality.[75]

163. By adopting Paragraph 76(1)(b) of the Law on higher education, Hungary therefore infringed Article 49 TFEU.

(b) Infringement of Article 16 of the Services Directive

164. The Commission also considers that the condition in Paragraph 76(1)(b) of the Law on higher education constitutes an infringement of the Services Directive.

(1) Applicability

165. Under Article 2(1) of the Services Directive, the directive applies to services supplied by providers established in a Member State, "service" being defined in Article 4(1) of the directive as a "self-employed economic activity, normally provided for remuneration". According to case law, courses provided by educational establishments financed essentially by private funds that do not come from the provider itself constitute services, since the aim of such establishments is to offer a service for remuneration.[76]

166. Article 2(1) of the Services Directive does not explicitly lay down any other requirements governing applicability. In particular, it does not have regard to the temporary nature of the activities, which is used in connection with the fundamental freedoms in distinguishing between freedom of establishment and freedom to provide services,[77] as the Services Directive also contains rules on freedom of establishment for providers.[78] I consider this distinction to be relevant in this case, however, as the Commission specifically alleges an infringement of Article 16 of the Services Directive, which is in Chapter IV on free movement of services.

167. Paragraph 76(1)(b) of the Law on higher education falls within the scope of Article 16 of the Services Directive only in so far as it

---

[75] See, for example, judgments of 9 March 2017, *Piringer* (C-342/15, EU:C:2017:196, paragraph 53), and of 14 November 2018, *Memoria and Dall'Antonia* (C-342/17, EU:C:2018:906, paragraph 51).

[76] Judgments of 11 September 2007, *Commission* v. Germany (C-318/05, EU:C:2007:495, paragraph 69); of 11 September 2007, *Schwarz and Gootjes-Schwarz* (C-76/05, EU:C:2007:492, paragraph 48); and of 27 June 2017, *Congregación de Escuelas Pías Provincia Betania* (C-74/16, EU: C:2017:496, paragraph 48).

[77] Judgment of 11 December 2003, *Schnitzer* (C-215/01, EU:C:2003:662, paragraphs 27 and 28).

[78] See Chapter III of the Services Directive.

makes the temporary provision of teaching activities leading to a degree subject to special conditions. Such business models are perfectly feasible, although the vast majority of higher education institutions offering qualifications undoubtedly do so through a permanent establishment.

168. In any event, Paragraph 76(1)(b) of the Law on higher education does not distinguish between institutions which carry on teaching activities in Hungary permanently and those which do so only temporarily. Nor does the rule distinguish between suppliers of privately financed education services and those whose activities are not for profit.

169. The rule therefore falls at least partly within the scope of Article 16 of the Services Directive.

(2) Lawful requirement for the purposes of Article 16(1) and (3) of the Services Directive?

170. Under Article 16(1) and (3) of the Services Directive, Member States may make access to or exercise of a service activity in their territory only subject to compliance with requirements which are non-discriminatory, necessary and proportionate. The requirements set out must, in accordance with point (b) of the third subparagraph of Article 16(1) and Article 16(3) of the directive, serve to maintain public policy, public security, public health or the protection of the environment.

171. In the present case, the requirement in Paragraph 76(1)(b) of the Law on higher education is not lawful because of its discriminatory character.[79]

172. In any event, however, the measure cannot be justified on any of the grounds mentioned in point (b) of the third subparagraph of Article 16(1) or Article 16(3). It has already been shown that the rule at issue cannot be justified on grounds of protection of public policy.[80]

173. The EU legislature did not provide in Article 16 of the Services Directive—unlike in other provisions of the directive[81]—for a justification for other overriding reasons in the public interest, which, according to recital 40 of the directive, include a high level of education.

174. It is true that case law recognises a justification for overriding reasons in the public interest in the context of Article 56 TFEU. However, such a justification has not thus far been recognised in

---

[79] See, with regard to discriminatory character, point 158 of this Opinion.
[80] See, *mutatis mutandis*, point 160 of this Opinion.
[81] See, for example, Article 9(1) and (4), Article 10(2) and Article 11(1) of the Services Directive.

similar cases where there are discriminatory measures.[82] Consequently, there is no need to determine in the present case whether the possible justifications in the context of Article 16 of the Services Directive could be lawfully restricted by the EU legislature vis-à-vis the justifications recognised in primary law,[83] as the measure at issue likewise could not be considered to be justified under Article 56 TFEU.

175. It must therefore be stated that the requirement of the existence of genuine teaching activities in the State of origin does not satisfy the requirements of Article 16(1) and (3) of the Services Directive. By Paragraph 76(1)(b) of the Law on higher education, Hungary thus infringed Article 16 of the Services Directive.

176. The Services Directive contains more specific rules than Article 56 TFEU, which is relied on in the alternative, and there is thus no need to examine the latter provision in this case.[84]

(c) Infringement of the Charter

177. Finally, it must be examined whether by adopting Paragraph 76(1)(b) of the Law on higher education, Hungary breached the fundamental rights of the higher education institutions concerned, in particular those under Article 13 and Article 14(3) of the Charter.[85]

(1) Applicability of the Charter

178. Paragraph 76(1)(b) of the Law on higher education constitutes a deficient transposition of the Services Directive.[86] The Charter is therefore applicable under Article 51(1) thereof.[87]

179. The question whether a separate infringement of the Charter can be found if EU law is applicable merely by reason of a restriction of

---

[82] Judgments of 25 July 1991, *Collectieve Antennevoorziening Gouda* (C-288/89, EU:C:1991:323, paragraphs 11 to 13); of 19 July 2012, *Garkalns* (C-470/11, EU:C:2012:505, paragraph 37); and of 30 April 2014, *Pfleger and Others* (C-390/12, EU:C:2014:281, paragraph 43).

[83] With regard to the parallel problem in respect of Article 14 of the Services Directive, see judgment of 16 June 2015, *Rina Services and Others* (C-593/13, EU:C:2015:399, paragraph 40). For the arguments, see Opinion of Advocate General Szpunar in *X and Visser* (C-360/15 and C-31/16, EU:C:2017:397, point 99 et seq.).

[84] Judgment of 23 February 2016, *Commission* v. *Hungary* (C-179/14, EU:C:2016:108, paragraph 118). See, by analogy, on the relationship between Article 15 of the Services Directive and Article 49 TFEU, judgment of 7 November 2018, *Commission* v. *Hungary* (C-171/17, EU:C:2018:881, paragraph 87).

[85] In this case, Article 14(3) of the Charter takes precedence, as a *lex specialis*, over Article 16 of the Charter, which is also relied upon; see above, points 130 and 132 of this Opinion.

[86] See points 170 to 175 of this Opinion.

[87] See, to that effect, judgment of 1 December 2016, *Daouidi* (C-395/15, EU:C:2016:917, paragraph 64 et seq.). See also judgment of 13 September 2016, *Rendón Marín* (C-165/14, EU:C:2016:675, paragraph 66).

fundamental freedoms does not therefore arise in this case, contrary to the view taken by Hungary.[88]

180. However, the finding of a separate breach of a fundamental right has no particular repercussions in this case, as the action for failure to fulfil obligations is already well founded on account of the infringements of the Services Directive and Article 49 TFEU. The separate examination of fundamental rights nevertheless reflects the particular significance and nature of the infringement more clearly. This holds especially if, as in this case, the alleged breach of fundamental rights goes beyond the detrimental economic effects which are already covered by a finding of infringements of the internal market rules.

(2) Interference

181. As has already been explained, a condition which, if not fulfilled, means that a university's teaching and research activities may not be commenced or must be ended and the foundation and operation of such an institution on a profit-making basis are prohibited falls within the scope of protection offered by both the second sentence of Article 13 and Article 14(3) of the Charter.[89]

(3) Justification

182. It must therefore be examined whether interference with those fundamental rights caused by Paragraph 76(1)(b) of the Law on higher education can be justified. In particular, interference would have to be proportionate.[90] According to the wording of Article 52(1) of the Charter, limitations of fundamental rights may be made only if they are necessary and genuinely meet objectives of general interest recognised by the Union or the need to protect the rights and freedoms of others.

183. Hungary asserts, first, that only where teaching activities exist in the State of origin can its authorities be certain that the activities are lawful and that all the conditions for teaching activities in the State of origin are fulfilled. Fraudulent practices can thereby be prevented. Second, the authorities can verify, on the basis of the education offered in the State of origin, whether the institution has

---

[88] See, on this point, Opinions of Advocate General Saugmandsgaard Øe in Joined Cases *SEGRO and Horváth* (C-52/16 and C-113/16, EU:C:2017:410, points 121 to 142), and *Commission v. Hungary (Usufruct over agricultural land)* (C-235/17, EU:C:2018:971, points 64 to 112).

[89] See points 133 and 147 of this Opinion.

[90] See points 134 and 148 of this Opinion.

a sustainable strategy and qualified teaching staff, thereby assuring the quality of teaching.

184. It is true that the successful operation of a higher education institution in the State of origin indicates that it meets all the legal conditions for operation there. That condition is therefore appropriate for eliminating illegal and fraudulent institutions at any early stage.

185. The legality and integrity of a higher education programme certainly cannot, however, be verified solely on the basis of existing teaching activities in the State of origin. If there are no such activities in the State of origin, a Member State must therefore also accept other appropriate proof, particularly given the paramount importance of the right to free establishment in the European Union, which, according to case law, specifically includes the right of companies to carry on their activities principally or exclusively in a Member State other than the one in which they have their seat.[91] In order to avoid contradictory assessments, proof of activities in the State of origin cannot therefore be regarded as necessary.

186. As regards the aim of quality control, the Hungarian Government has not explained at all how the mere existence of higher education in the State of origin might assure the quality of education in the host State. It can hardly be presumed that the university employs the same teaching staff and teaches the same content in both States or that quality standards are the same in both States. The appropriateness of the measure is thus questionable.

187. As regards the necessity of the requirement, it should be noted that it would be impossible to carry out quality control upon the initial foundation of domestic higher education institutions if existing provision was the only means to verify quality. Consequently, recourse must inevitably be had to other quality control measures which could also be applied to foreign higher education institutions.

188. Therefore, the link to the existence of teaching activities in the State of origin is, in itself, not appropriate and generally not necessary in any case for ensuring the legality and quality of higher education.

(4) Conclusion

189. By adopting Paragraph 76(1)(b) of the Law on higher education, Hungary thus also infringed the second sentence of Article 13 and Article 14(3) of the Charter.

---

[91] See point 158 of this Opinion and judgment of 30 September 2003, *Inspire Art* (C-167/01, EU:C:2003:512, paragraph 97).

(d) Infringement of Article XVII of the GATS in conjunction with Article 216(2) TFEU

190. In so far as the Commission also alleges an infringement of Article XVII of the GATS in respect of the requirement in Paragraph 76(1)(b) of the Law on higher education, it is sufficient to note that the rules of primary and secondary EU law prevail over international trade law in relations between Member States.[92]

191. However, Paragraph 76(1)(b) of the Law on higher education also applies to universities from third countries. For the abovementioned reasons,[93] that rule thus infringes the national treatment obligation under Article XVII of the GATS and cannot be regarded as a permissible exception in accordance with Article XIV of the GATS. That provision permits measures necessary to protect public morals or to maintain public order[94] or to prevent deceptive and fraudulent practices. As has been explained, the requirement of teaching activities in the State of origin does not fulfil those requirements.[95]

192. An infringement of Article XVII of the GATS in conjunction with Article 216(2) TFEU should thus also be taken to exist with regard to the requirement in Paragraph 76(1)(b) of the Law on higher education.

VI. CONCLUSION

193. In the light of all the foregoing considerations, I propose that the Court should rule as follows:

(1) By adopting Paragraph 76(1)(a) of Nemzeti felsőoktatásról szóló 2011. évi CCIV. törvény (Law CCIV of 2011 on national higher education), as amended, Hungary infringed Article XVII of the General Agreement on Trade in Services in conjunction with Article 216(2) TFEU and the second sentence of Article 13 and Article 14(3) of the Charter of Fundamental Rights of the European Union.

(2) By adopting Paragraph 76(1)(b) of Law CCIV of 2011, as amended, Hungary infringed Article 16 of Directive 2006/123/EC of the European Parliament and of the Council of

---

[92] See, to that effect, judgment of 29 July 2019, *Inter-Environnement Wallonie and Bond Beter Leefmilieu Vlaanderen* (C-411/17, EU:C:2019:622, paragraph 161 et seq. and paragraph 165 et seq.).
[93] See points 106 and 111 of this Opinion.
[94] This is defined in the Agreement as a "genuine and sufficiently serious threat is posed to one of the fundamental interests of society".
[95] See, *mutatis mutandis*, point 160 and points 183 to 188 of this Opinion.

12 December 2006 on services in the internal market, Article 49 TFEU in conjunction with Article 54 TFEU, Article XVII of the General Agreement on Trade in Services in conjunction with Article 216(2) TFEU and the second sentence of Article 13 and Article 14(3) of the Charter of Fundamental Rights.

(3) Hungary shall bear the costs.

[Report: EU:C:2020:172]

JUGDMENT*

TABLE OF CONTENTS

---
* Language of the case: Hungarian.

1. By its application, the European Commission requests that the Court:

– declare that, by requiring foreign higher education institutions situated outside the European Economic Area (EEA) to conclude an international agreement as a prerequisite for providing education services, pursuant to Article 76(1)(a) of Nemzeti felsőoktatásról szóló 2011. évi CCIV. törvény (Law No CCIV of 2011 on national higher education) (*Magyar Közlöny* 2011/165), as amended by Nemzeti felsőoktatásról szóló 2011. évi CCIV. törvény módosításáról szóló 2017. évi XXV. törvény (Law No XXV of 2017 amending Law No CCIV of 2011 on national higher education), adopted by the Hungarian Parliament on 4 April 2017 (*Magyar Közlöny* 2017/53) ("the Law on higher education"), Hungary has failed to fulfil its obligations under Article XVII of the General Agreement on Trade in Services ("the GATS"), in Annex 1B to the Agreement establishing the World Trade Organization (WTO), signed in Marrakesh and approved by Council Decision 94/800/EC of 22 December 1994 concerning the conclusion on behalf of the European Community, as regards matters within its competence, of the agreements reached in the Uruguay Round multilateral negotiations (1986-94) (OJ 1994 L 336, p. 1) ("the Agreement establishing the WTO");
– declare that, by requiring foreign higher education institutions to offer higher education in their country of origin, pursuant to Article

76(1)(b) of the Law on higher education, Hungary has failed to fulfil its obligations under Article 16 of Directive 2006/123/EC of the European Parliament and of the Council of 12 December 2006 on services in the internal market (OJ 2006 L 376, p. 36), and, in any event, under Articles 49 and 56 TFEU and Article XVII of the GATS;
– declare that, by imposing the abovementioned measures, pursuant to Article 76(1)(a) and (b) of the Law on higher education ("the measures at issue"), Hungary has failed to fulfil its obligations under Article 13, Article 14(3) and Article 16 of the Charter of Fundamental Rights of the European Union ("the Charter"); and
– order Hungary to pay the costs.

I. LEGAL CONTEXT

A. WTO law

1. The Agreement establishing the WTO

2. Article XVI(4) of the Agreement establishing the WTO provides:

Each Member shall ensure the conformity of its laws, regulations and administrative procedures with its obligations as provided in the annexed Agreements.

2. The GATS

3. Article I(1) to (3) of the GATS states:

1. This Agreement applies to measures by Members affecting trade in services.
2. For the purposes of this Agreement, trade in services is defined as the supply of a service:
. . .
   (c) by a service supplier of one Member, through commercial presence in the territory of any other Member;
. . .
3. For the purposes of this Agreement:
   (a) "measures by Members" means measures taken by:
      (i) central, regional or local governments and authorities; and
      (ii) non-governmental bodies in the exercise of powers delegated by central, regional or local governments or authorities;
In fulfilling its obligations and commitments under the Agreement, each Member shall take such reasonable measures as may be available to it to

ensure their observance by regional and local governments and authorities and non-governmental bodies within its territory;

. . .

4. Article XIV of the GATS provides:

Subject to the requirement that such measures are not applied in a manner which would constitute a means of arbitrary or unjustifiable discrimination between countries where like conditions prevail, or a disguised restriction on trade in services, nothing in this Agreement shall be construed to prevent the adoption or enforcement by any Member of measures:

(a) necessary to protect public morals or to maintain public order;

. . .

(c) necessary to secure compliance with laws or regulations which are not inconsistent with the provisions of this Agreement including those relating to:
   (i) the prevention of deceptive and fraudulent practices or to deal with the effects of a default on services contracts;

. . .

5. Articles XVI to XVIII of the GATS fall within Part III of that agreement, entitled "Specific commitments".

6. Article XVI of the GATS, entitled "Market access", provides:

1. With respect to market access through the modes of supply identified in Article I, each Member shall accord services and service suppliers of any other Member treatment no less favourable than that provided for under the terms, limitations and conditions agreed and specified in its Schedule.

2. In sectors where market-access commitments are undertaken, the measures which a Member shall not maintain or adopt either on the basis of a regional subdivision or on the basis of its entire territory, unless otherwise specified in its Schedule, are defined as:
   (a) limitations on the number of service suppliers whether in the form of numerical quotas, monopolies, exclusive service suppliers or the requirements of an economic needs test;
   (b) limitations on the total value of service transactions or assets in the form of numerical quotas or the requirement of an economic needs test;
   (c) limitations on the total number of service operations or on the total quantity of service output expressed in terms of designated numerical units in the form of quotas or the requirement of an economic needs test;
   (d) limitations on the total number of natural persons that may be employed in a particular service sector or that a service supplier may employ and who are necessary for, and directly related to, the supply of

a specific service in the form of numerical quotas or the requirement of an economic needs test;

(e) measures which restrict or require specific types of legal entity or joint venture through which a service supplier may supply a service; and

(f) limitations on the participation of foreign capital in terms of maximum percentage limit on foreign shareholding or the total value of individual or aggregate foreign investment.

7. Article XVII of the GATS, entitled "National treatment", provides:

1. In the sectors inscribed in its Schedule, and subject to any conditions and qualifications set out therein, each Member shall accord to services and service suppliers of any other Member, in respect of all measures affecting the supply of services, treatment no less favourable than that it accords to its own like services and service suppliers.

2. A Member may meet the requirement of paragraph 1 by according to services and service suppliers of any other Member, either formally identical treatment or formally different treatment to that it accords to its own like services and service suppliers.

3. Formally identical or formally different treatment shall be considered to be less favourable if it modifies the conditions of competition in favour of services or service suppliers of the Member compared to like services or service suppliers of any other Member.

8. According to Article XX(1) and (2) of the GATS:

1. Each Member shall set out in a schedule the specific commitments it undertakes under Part III of this Agreement. With respect to sectors where such commitments are undertaken, each Schedule shall specify:
(a) terms, limitations and conditions on market access;
(b) conditions and qualifications on national treatment;
. . .

2. Measures inconsistent with both Articles XVI and XVII shall be inscribed in the column relating to Article XVI. In this case the inscription will be considered to provide a condition or qualification to Article XVII as well.

3. Understanding on the settlement of disputes

9. The Understanding on rules and procedures governing the settlement of disputes, in Annex 2 to the Agreement establishing the WTO ("the Understanding on the settlement of disputes"), provides, in Article 1(1), that the rules and procedures it contains are to apply to disputes brought pursuant to the consultation and dispute settlement provisions of the agreements listed in Annex 1 to the Agreement establishing the WTO, which include the GATS.

10. Article 3(2) of that understanding states:

The dispute settlement system of the WTO is a central element in providing security and predictability to the multilateral trading system. The Members recognise that it serves to preserve the rights and obligations of Members under the covered agreements, and to clarify the existing provisions of those agreements in accordance with customary rules of interpretation of public international law. Recommendations and rulings of the [Dispute Settlement Body] cannot add to or diminish the rights and obligations provided in the covered agreements.

11. According to Article 11 of that understanding:

The function of panels is to assist the [Dispute Settlement Body] in discharging its responsibilities under this Understanding and the covered agreements. Accordingly, a panel should make an objective assessment of the matter before it, including an objective assessment of the facts of the case and the applicability of and conformity with the relevant covered agreements, and make such other findings as will assist the [Dispute Settlement Body] in making the recommendations or in giving the rulings provided for in the covered agreements. Panels should consult regularly with the parties to the dispute and give them adequate opportunity to develop a mutually satisfactory solution.

12. Article 17 of that understanding, entitled "Appellate Review", provides in particular:

6. An appeal shall be limited to issues of law covered in the panel report and legal interpretations developed by the panel.

. . .

13. The Appellate Body may uphold, modify or reverse the legal findings and conclusions of the panel.

. . .

13. According to Article 19(1) of the Understanding on the settlement of disputes:

Where a panel or the Appellate Body concludes that a measure is inconsistent with a covered agreement, it shall recommend that the Member concerned bring the measure into conformity with that agreement. In addition to its recommendations, the panel or Appellate Body may suggest ways in which the Member concerned could implement the recommendations.

14. Article 21 of that understanding, entitled "Surveillance of Implementation of Recommendations and Rulings", provides:

1. Prompt compliance with recommendations or rulings of the [Dispute Settlement Body] is essential in order to ensure effective resolution of disputes to the benefit of all Members.

. . .

3. At a [Dispute Settlement Body] meeting held within 30 days after the date of adoption of the panel or Appellate Body report, the Member concerned shall inform the [Dispute Settlement Body] of its intentions in respect of implementation of the recommendations and rulings of the [Dispute Settlement Body]. If it is impracticable to comply immediately with the recommendations and rulings, the Member concerned shall have a reasonable period of time in which to do so. . . .

. . .

6. The [Dispute Settlement Body] shall keep under surveillance the implementation of adopted recommendations or rulings. . . .

. . .

15. Article 22(1) of that understanding states:

Compensation and the suspension of concessions or other obligations are temporary measures available in the event that the recommendations and rulings are not implemented within a reasonable period of time. . . .

16. According to Article 23(1) of that understanding:

When Members seek the redress of a violation of obligations or other nullification or impairment of benefits under the covered agreements or an impediment to the attainment of any objective of the covered agreements, they shall have recourse to, and abide by, the rules and procedures of this Understanding.

B. European Union law

17. Recital 41 of Directive 2006/123 states:

The concept of "public policy", as interpreted by the Court of Justice [of the European Union], covers the protection against a genuine and sufficiently serious threat affecting one of the fundamental interests of society and may include, in particular, issues relating to human dignity, the protection of minors and vulnerable adults and animal welfare. . . .

18. As provided in Article 2(1) of Directive 2006/123, the directive is to apply to services supplied by providers established in a Member State.

19. Article 4(1) of Directive 2006/123 defines "service" as "any self-employed economic activity, normally provided for remuneration, as referred to in Article [57 TFEU]".

20. Article 16 of that directive, entitled "Freedom to provide services", states, in paragraphs (1) and (3):

1. Member States shall respect the right of providers to provide services in a Member State other than that in which they are established.

The Member State in which the service is provided shall ensure free access to and free exercise of a service activity within its territory.

Member States shall not make access to or exercise of a service activity in their territory subject to compliance with any requirements which do not respect the following principles:

(a) non-discrimination: the requirement may be neither directly nor indirectly discriminatory with regard to nationality or, in the case of legal persons, with regard to the Member State in which they are established;

(b) necessity: the requirement must be justified for reasons of public policy, public security, public health or the protection of the environment;

(c) proportionality: the requirement must be suitable for attaining the objective pursued, and must not go beyond what is necessary to attain that objective.

...

3. The Member State to which the provider moves shall not be prevented from imposing requirements with regard to the provision of a service activity, where they are justified for reasons of public policy, public security, public health or the protection of the environment and in accordance with paragraph 1. ....

C. Hungarian law

21. Under Article 76(1)(a) of the Law on higher education, a foreign higher education institution may carry on teaching activities leading to a qualification in the territory of Hungary only if "the binding application of an international treaty on fundamental support for the activities in Hungary, concluded between the Government of Hungary and the government of the State in which the foreign higher education institution has its seat—in the case of a federal State in which the central government is not responsible for recognition of the binding effect of an international treaty, on the basis of a prior agreement with the central government—has been recognised by the parties" ("the requirement of a prior international treaty").

22. Under Article 77(2) of the Law on higher education, Article 76(1)(a) of that law is not to apply to foreign higher education institutions established in another Member State of the EEA.

23. Article 76(1)(b) of the Law on higher education provides that a foreign higher education institution carrying on activities in Hungary must not only be a State-recognised higher education institution in the country in which it has its seat, but must also "genuinely offer

higher education" in the country concerned ("the requirement that the institution concerned provide education in the State where it has its seat").

24. In accordance with Article 77(3) of the Law on higher education, the provisions of Article 76(1)(b) of that law are to apply also to higher education institutions having their seat in a Member State of the EEA.

25. Article 115(7) of the Law on higher education set 1 January 2018 as the date by which foreign higher education institutions were required to satisfy the conditions laid down in Article 76(1) of that law, with the exception of federal States, in which case a prior agreement was required to be concluded with the central government within the six-month period following the publication of Law No XXV of 2017, that is before 11 October 2017. Under that provision, moreover, foreign higher education institutions not satisfying the conditions laid down by that law would forfeit their licence and, with effect from 1 January 2018, no new first-year students could be admitted to a course of study provided in Hungary by a foreign higher education institution, while courses already in progress in Hungary on 1 January 2018 may be completed in the academic year 2020/2021 at the latest, under the same conditions as before, according to a scheme of progressive abandonment.

II. PRE-LITIGATION PROCEDURE

26. The Commission, having considered that, by adopting Law No XXV of 2017, Hungary had failed to fulfil its obligations under Articles 9, 10 and 13, Article 14(3) and Article 16 of Directive 2006/123, and, in the alternative, Articles 49 and 56 TFEU, Article XVII of the GATS, and Article 13, Article 14(3) and Article 16 of the Charter, sent a letter of formal notice to Hungary on 27 April 2017, setting a period of one month for the submission of observations. Hungary replied by a letter dated 25 May 2017 in which it disputed the infringements alleged against it.

27. On 14 July 2017, the Commission issued a reasoned opinion in which it concluded, in particular, that:

– by requiring foreign higher education institutions situated outside the EEA to conclude an international agreement as a prerequisite for providing education services, pursuant to Article 76(1)(a) of the Law on higher education, Hungary had failed to fulfil its obligations under Article XVII of the GATS;

– by requiring foreign higher education institutions to offer higher education in their country of origin, pursuant to Article 76(1)(b) of the Law on higher education, Hungary had failed to fulfil its obligations under Article 16 of Directive 2006/123 and, in any event, under Articles 49 and 56 TFEU; and

– by imposing the measures at issue, Hungary had failed to fulfil its obligations under Article 13, Article 14(3) and Article 16 of the Charter.

28. The Commission set Hungary a period of one month within which to take the necessary measures in order to comply with the reasoned opinion or to submit observations to the Commission.

29. By a letter dated 17 July 2017, Hungary requested an extension of that time limit, which the Commission refused.

30. Hungary replied to the reasoned opinion by a letter dated 14 August 2017, in which it contended that the alleged infringements did not exist.

31. By a letter dated 11 September 2017, Hungary sent further observations to the Commission seeking, in particular, to draw a comparison between its own situation and that of other Member States and to provide additional information concerning a number of Member States.

32. On 26 September 2017, a meeting of experts was held between the Commission's representatives and those of Hungary.

33. On 5 October 2017, the Commission sent a supplementary reasoned opinion to Hungary, in which it maintained that, by requiring foreign higher education institutions to offer higher education in their country of origin, pursuant to Article 76(1)(b) of the Law on higher education, Hungary had also failed to fulfil its obligations under Article XVII of the GATS.

34. By a letter dated 6 October 2017, Hungary provided the Commission with additional information, explaining that the United States of America was the only federal State not a member of the EEA with which a prior agreement, as provided for in Article 76(1)(a) of the Law on higher education, needed to be concluded. According to the information provided subsequently by the Hungarian authorities, such a prior agreement was concluded within the time limit originally laid down in Article 115(7) of that law, the deadline being 11 October 2017.

35. Hungary replied to the supplementary reasoned opinion by a letter dated 18 October 2017 in which it informed the Commission that the Hungarian Parliament had, on 17 October 2017, adopted a

draft law amending the Law on higher education, the effect of which, inter alia, was to postpone until 1 January 2019 the deadline laid down in Article 115(7) of that law for compliance with the conditions referred to in Article 76(1).

36. Hungary stated, moreover, in that letter that the law promulgating the agreement on cooperation in matters of higher education between the Government of Hungary and the State of Maryland (United States), concerning the activities undertaken by McDaniel College in Hungary, had been published in the *Magyar Közlöny* (Official Journal of Hungary).

37. Last, by a letter dated 13 November 2017, Hungary sent further supplementary information to the Commission, stating that the international agreement necessary for the continued operation in Hungary of the University of Medicine of Heilongjiang Daxue (China) had been signed on 30 October 2017.

38. It is in those circumstances that the Commission initiated the present infringement proceedings, on 1 February 2018, in respect of the measures at issue.

39. By decision of 25 July 2018, the President of the Court of Justice gave the case priority over others, pursuant to Article 53(3) of the Rules of Procedure of the Court of Justice.

III. THE ACTION

A. *Admissibility*

1. *Arguments of the parties*

40. In its statement in defence, Hungary contends that the action must be dismissed as inadmissible on account of the Commission's conduct during the pre-litigation procedure and the resulting illegalities. Hungary states first of all that the Commission required it, without providing any justification, to submit its observations on the letter of formal notice, and subsequently on the reasoned opinion, within one month, instead of the period of two months that is usually applied in pre-litigation procedures, and that it did so even though Hungary was required to deal with two other infringement procedures initiated in parallel and in which similar time limits were imposed. Next, Hungary submits that the Commission refused its requests for that time limit to be extended, without providing an appropriate statement of reasons.

41. According to Hungary, such conduct shows that the Commission did not seek to give it an adequate hearing, contrary to

the principle of sincere cooperation and the right to good administration. That conduct also constitutes an infringement of Hungary's
right to avail itself of its right to defend itself.

42. In its rejoinder, Hungary also states that the Commission seeks
to justify its conduct by invoking the fact that the Hungarian authorities were not prepared to repeal the disputed provisions of the Law on
higher education. It maintains, however, that that circumstance cannot
be relied upon to justify a reduction in the time limits applicable to the
pre-litigation procedure if the objectives of that procedure are not to
be disregarded.

43. Furthermore, Hungary contends that, by giving a clear indication that it had initiated the present infringement procedure solely in
the interest of the Central European University (CEU) and for purely
political considerations, the Commission seriously undermined the
right to good administration, provided for in Article 41(1) of the
Charter.

44. The Commission disputes the merits of those arguments.

2. Findings of the Court

45. As regards, in the first place, the arguments relating to the
allegedly excessively short time limits for reply which the
Commission imposed on Hungary, it must be borne in mind that
the purpose of the pre-litigation procedure is to give the Member State
concerned an opportunity to comply with its obligations under EU law
or to avail itself of its right to defend itself against the complaints made
by the Commission (judgment of 26 October 2006, *Commission
v. Italy*, C-371/04, EU:C:2006:668, paragraph 9). The proper conduct
of that procedure constitutes an essential guarantee required by the
FEU Treaty, not only in order to protect the rights of the Member
State concerned, but also so as to ensure that any contentious procedure will have a clearly defined dispute as its subject matter (judgment of
2 April 2020, *Commission v. Poland, Hungary and Czech Republic
(Temporary mechanism for the relocation of applicants for international
protection)*, C-715/17, C-718/17 and C-719/17, EU:C:2020:257,
paragraph 91 and the case law cited).

46. Those objectives require the Commission to grant the Member
States concerned a reasonable period to reply to letters of formal notice
and to comply with reasoned opinions, or, where appropriate, to
prepare their defence. In order to determine whether the period
allowed is reasonable, account must be taken of all the circumstances
of the case (see, to that effect, judgment of 2 April 2020, *Commission*

v. *Poland, Hungary and Czech Republic (Temporary mechanism for the relocation of applicants for international protection)*, C-715/17, C-718/ 17 and C-719/17, EU:C:2020:257, paragraph 92 and the case law cited).

47. The Court has thus held that a short period may be justified in particular circumstances, especially where there is an urgent need to remedy an infringement or where the Member State concerned is fully aware of the Commission's views long before the procedure starts (judgment of 2 April 2020, *Commission v. Poland, Hungary and Czech Republic (Temporary mechanism for the relocation of applicants for international protection)*, C-715/17, C-718/17 and C-719/17, EU: C:2020:257, paragraph 92).

48. In the present case, on 4 April 2017 the Hungarian Parliament adopted Law No XXV, under which higher education institutions not satisfying the conditions now set out in Article 76(1) of the Law on higher education would have their authorisation to carry out their activities withdrawn and would no longer be entitled to admit new first-year students from 1 January 2018, while courses already in progress must be completed at the latest during the 2020/2021 academic year.

49. On 27 April 2017, the Commission sent a letter of formal notice to Hungary and set a period of one month for Hungary to submit observations. On 14 July 2017, the Commission issued a reasoned opinion in which it set Hungary a period of one month within which to take the necessary measures to comply with the reasoned opinion or to submit observations.

50. In the light of the circumstances referred to above, from which it is apparent that the reason for the time limit imposed on Hungary was the urgency, according to the Commission, of the need to remedy the infringement alleged against Hungary, a period of one month does not appear to be unreasonable.

51. Moreover, contrary to the Hungarian Government's contention, that assessment is not called into question by the fact that the Commission did not initiate the present infringement proceedings until 1 February 2018. The Commission had previously been informed, by a letter of 18 October 2017, that the date from which higher education institutions not satisfying the requirements of Article 76(1) of the Law on higher education would cease to be entitled to admit new first-year students had been postponed until 1 January 2019.

52. In any event, as is apparent from the case law of the Court, the fact that the Commission makes the pre-litigation procedure subject to

short time limits is not in itself capable of leading to the inadmissibility of the subsequent action for failure to fulfil obligations. Such a finding of inadmissibility is only to be made where the Commission's conduct prevented the Member State concerned from availing itself of its right to defend itself against complaints made by the Commission and thus infringed the rights of the defence, which it is for that Member State to prove (see, to that effect, judgment of 18 June 2020, *Commission v. Hungary (Transparency of associations)*, C-78/18, EU:C:2020:476, paragraph 30 and the case law cited).

53. Such proof has not, however, been produced by Hungary in the present case.

54. On the contrary, examination of the conduct of the pre-litigation procedure, as recalled in paragraphs 26 to 37 of the present judgment, shows, first of all, that Hungary did submit detailed observations in relation to the letter of formal notice, and subsequently the reasoned opinion, within the period of one month allowed by the Commission. Hungary went on to submit further observations in that regard in three letters dated 11 September, 6 October and 13 November 2017, all of which were accepted by the Commission. Last, analysis of the documents exchanged in the pre-litigation procedure and of the application initiating proceedings shows that the Commission duly took into consideration all the comments made by Hungary at the various stages of that procedure, including those submitted after the deadlines imposed had expired.

55. In those circumstances, it is irrelevant that similar time limits were imposed on Hungary, during the same period, in two other infringement procedures.

56. As regards, in the second place, Hungary's assertion that the Commission allegedly initiated the present infringement procedure with the sole aim of protecting the interests of the CEU and that it did so for purely political purposes, it must be recalled that the objective of the procedure provided for in Article 258 TFEU is an objective finding that a Member State has failed to fulfil its obligations under EU law (see, to that effect, judgment of 27 March 2019, *Commission v. Germany*, C-620/16, EU:C:2019:256, paragraph 40 and the case law cited). According to settled case law, in the context of such proceedings, the Commission enjoys a discretion as to whether or not to commence such proceedings, which is not for review by the Court (see, to that effect, judgment of 16 July 2020, *Commission v. Romania (Anti-money laundering)*, C-549/18, EU:C:2020:563, paragraph 49 and the case law cited).

57. It follows from the foregoing considerations that the present action for failure to fulfil obligations is admissible.

B. *The jurisdiction of the Court*

1. *Arguments of the parties*

58. Hungary submits that the Court does not have jurisdiction to hear and determine the present action for failure to fulfil obligations with respect to the Commission's complaints concerning infringements of the GATS.

59. In the first place, Hungary claims that, in accordance with Article 6(e) TFEU, the area of higher education does not fall within the competence of the European Union and that it is therefore, in that area, the Member States concerned which answer individually for any failure to comply with their obligations under the GATS.

60. In the second place, in accordance with the general rules of international law, it is exclusively for the panels and the Appellate Body of the WTO ("the Appellate Body") established by the Dispute Settlement Body ("the DSB") to assess whether the Law on higher education is compatible with the commitments undertaken by Hungary under the GATS.

61. In Hungary's submission, it is apparent from the case law of the Court (judgment of 10 September 1996, *Commission* v. *Germany*, C-61/94, EU:C:1996:313, paragraphs 15 and 16) that the Commission is competent to examine the implementation of a WTO agreement which has become an integral part of EU law in the context of relations between Member States and the EU institutions, but not in the context of relations between a Member State and a third country.

62. Furthermore, should the Court grant the Commission's application in so far as it is based on an infringement of the GATS, it would, by its autonomous interpretation of the articles of the GATS and Hungary's schedule of specific commitments, be interfering with the exclusive competence of WTO members and of the bodies constituting the WTO's dispute settlement system to interpret WTO agreements, contrary to Article 216(2) TFEU, and would thereby risk undermining the uniform interpretation of the GATS.

63. Once a Member State's failure to fulfil its obligations under the GATS has been established by the Court, third countries would no longer have any reason to initiate a procedure within the framework of the WTO's dispute settlement system.

64. The Commission's reply is, in the first place, that, in accordance with Article 207(4) TFEU, trade in education services falls within the exclusive competence of the Union in so far as it is included within the scope of the common commercial policy. Consequently, by ensuring that commitments arising from the GATS are complied with, the Member States are fulfilling an obligation vis-à-vis the Union, which has assumed responsibility for the proper implementation of that agreement.

65. In the second place, in the Commission's submission, in accordance with Article 216(2) TFEU, international agreements concluded by the Union are binding on the Member States. Consequently, as is apparent from the case law of the Court (judgment of 10 September 1996, *Commission* v. *Germany*, C-61/94, EU: C:1996:313, paragraph 15), non-compliance with those agreements by the Member States falls within EU law and constitutes a failure to fulfil obligations that is capable of being the subject matter of an action under Article 258 TFEU.

66. In the present case, since the GATS is an international agreement concluded by the Union, it is for the Commission to ensure that the Member States comply with the international obligations that arise for the Union under that agreement, which, in particular, enables the Union to avoid incurring international liability in a situation in which there is a risk of a dispute being brought before the WTO.

67. The Commission submits that the existence of the WTO's dispute settlement system is of no relevance in that regard. The Union, as a member of the WTO, is required to ensure that its obligations under the WTO agreements are complied with in the territory of the Union. Moreover, third countries are bound neither by the settlement within the Union of disputes concerning international obligations that are binding on the Union and its Member States, nor by the Court's interpretation of those international obligations.

2. Findings of the Court

68. As a preliminary point, it must be borne in mind that, in accordance with Article 258 TFEU, an action for failure to fulfil obligations can have as its subject only the finding of a failure to comply with obligations under EU law (see, to that effect, judgment of 19 March 2002, *Commission* v. *Ireland*, C-13/00, EU:C:2002:184, paragraph 13).

69. The Court has repeatedly held that an international agreement entered into by the Union is, from its entry into force, an integral part

of EU law (see, in particular, judgments of 30 April 1974, *Haegeman*, 181/73, EU:C:1974:41, paragraphs 5 and 6; of 21 December 2011, *Air Transport Association of America and Others*, C-366/10, EU: C:2011:864, paragraph 73; and Opinion 1/17 (*EU–Canada CET Agreement*) of 30 April 2019, EU:C:2019:341, paragraph 117).

70. In the present case, the Agreement establishing the WTO, of which the GATS is part, was signed by the Union and then approved by it, on 22 December 1994, by Decision 94/800. It entered into force on 1 January 1995.

71. It follows that the GATS is part of EU law.

72. As regards, in the first place, the objection raised by Hungary and mentioned in paragraph 59 of the present judgment, it should be noted that, in accordance with Article 3(1)(e) TFEU, the Union is to have exclusive competence in the area of common commercial policy.

73. The Court has held that the commitments entered into under the GATS fall within the common commercial policy (see, to that effect, Opinion 2/15 (*Free Trade Agreement with Singapore*) of 16 May 2017, EU:C:2017:376, paragraphs 36 and 54).

74. It follows that, while it is apparent from Article 6(e) TFEU that the Member States are to have broad competence in the area of education, the Union having competence in that area only "to carry out actions to support, coordinate or supplement the actions of the Member States", the commitments entered into under the GATS, including those relating to the liberalisation of trade in private educational services, fall within the exclusive competence of the Union.

75. Accordingly, Hungary is wrong to maintain that it is, in the area of trade in educational services, the Member States concerned which answer individually for any failure to comply with their obligations under the GATS.

76. As regards, in the second place, the objection raised by Hungary and set out in paragraphs 60 to 63 of the present judgment, it must be pointed out that Hungary does not dispute, in general terms, the Court's jurisdiction to hear and determine, under Article 258 TFEU, an action seeking a declaration that a Member State has failed to fulfil its obligations under an international agreement that is binding on the Union. However, Hungary maintains that it is the particular context resulting from the existence of the WTO's dispute settlement system, which applies inter alia to the obligations of WTO members arising from the GATS, that precludes the Court from exercising that jurisdiction.

77. It must be observed that that issue has not been settled by the Court in the case law concerning the relationship of EU law with WTO law.

78. Until now, the Court has ruled either in the context of the assessment of the validity of an act of EU secondary law on grounds of the incompatibility of EU law with WTO law (see, in particular, judgment of 1 March 2005, *Van Parys*, C-377/02, EU:C:2005:121, paragraphs 1 and 39 and the case law cited), or in the context of the possible non-contractual liability of the Union and the exercise of the right to compensation for damage suffered (see, in particular, judgment of 9 September 2008, *FIAMM and Others* v. *Council and Commission*, C-120/06 P and C-121/06 P, EU:C:2008:476, paragraphs 1 and 107).

79. In particular, in the cases that gave rise to the judgments cited in the preceding paragraph of the present judgment, the Court had been presented with WTO rulings that were unfavourable to the Union and had had to adjudicate on various aspects of the implementation of those rulings, in particular as to whether the persons concerned could rely on WTO law.

80. In the present case, first, the Commission claims that certain legislative provisions adopted by a Member State are incompatible with the GATS, with the result that that Member State has failed to comply with EU law of which that international agreement is an integral part. Second, in the absence of a DSB ruling declaring conduct of the Union or of a Member State to be incompatible with WTO law, the question of the possible implementation of such a ruling does not arise.

81. That being the case, as is apparent from paragraph 66 of the present judgment, the Commission submits that the objective of the present infringement proceedings is to ensure that the Union does not incur any international liability in a situation in which there is a risk of a dispute being brought before the WTO.

82. In that respect, Article 3(2) of the Understanding on the settlement of disputes states that the dispute settlement system of the WTO is a central element in providing security and predictability to the multilateral trading system, serving to preserve the rights and obligations of WTO members and to clarify the provisions of the covered agreements in accordance with customary rules of interpretation of public international law.

83. More specifically, under Article 11 of the Understanding on the settlement of disputes, a panel is empowered to make an objective assessment of the matter before it, including an objective assessment of the facts of the case and the applicability of and conformity with the relevant covered agreements. Under Article 17(13) of that understanding, the Appellate Body may uphold, modify or reverse the legal findings and conclusions of that panel, its jurisdiction being limited, in accordance with Article 17(6) of that understanding, to issues of law covered in

the panel report and legal interpretations made by the panel. Members of the WTO are in principle required to comply immediately with the recommendations and rulings of the DSB, as is apparent from Article 21(1) and (3) of the Understanding on the settlement of disputes.

84. It follows from those considerations that, in certain circumstances, the review undertaken as part of the WTO's dispute settlement system may result in a legal finding that measures taken by a WTO member are not in conformity with the law of that organisation and can, ultimately, give rise to international liability on the part of the Union, a member of the WTO, because of a wrongful act.

85. It must also be recalled that, under Article XVI(4) of the Agreement establishing the WTO, each member of the WTO is obliged, within the framework of its internal legal order, to ensure compliance with its obligations under WTO law within the various parts of its territory. A similar obligation is, moreover, laid down in Article I(3)(a) of the GATS.

86. In those circumstances, not only does the particular context resulting from the existence of the WTO's dispute settlement system have no bearing on the jurisdiction conferred on the Court under Article 258 TFEU, but the exercise of that jurisdiction is entirely consistent with the obligation of each WTO member to ensure observance of its obligations under the law of that organisation.

87. It should also be recalled that, in accordance with settled case law, the Union is bound, when exercising its powers, to observe international law in its entirety, including not only the provisions of international conventions that are binding on it, but also the rules and principles of general customary international law (see, to that effect, judgment of 27 February 2018, *Western Sahara Campaign UK*, C-266/16, EU:C:2018:118, paragraph 47 and the case law cited).

88. First of all, as is apparent from Article 3 of the articles on the responsibility of States for internationally wrongful acts—drawn up by the International Law Commission of the United Nations Organisation and of which that organisation's General Assembly took note in its Resolution 56/83 of 12 December 2001—which codify customary international law and are applicable to the Union, the characterisation of an act of a State as being "internationally wrongful" is governed solely by international law. Consequently, that characterisation cannot be affected by any characterisation of the same act that might be made under EU law.

89. In that regard, while the Commission correctly notes that the assessment of the alleged conduct of the Member State concerned which it is for the Court to make under Article 258 TFEU is not

binding on the other members of the WTO, it should be observed that that assessment also does not affect any assessment that might be made by the DSB.

90. Next, it is clear from Article 32 of the articles on the responsibility of States for internationally wrongful acts that the responsible State may not rely on the provisions of its internal law as justification for failure to comply with its obligations under international law.

91. It follows, in particular, that neither the Union nor the Member State concerned can rely on the assessment, with regard to WTO law, of the conduct of that Member State by the Court, in the context of infringement proceedings under Article 258 TFEU, in order to refuse to comply with the legal consequences provided for by WTO law should the DSB find that conduct not to be in conformity with WTO law.

92. Last, without prejudice to the limits placed on the possibility of reliance upon WTO law in order to review the legality of acts of the EU institutions before the Courts of the European Union, recalled in the case law cited in paragraph 78 of the present judgment, it must be noted that the general international law principle of respect for contractual commitments (*pacta sunt servanda*), laid down in Article 26 of the Vienna Convention on the Law of Treaties of 23 May 1969 (*United Nations Treaty Series*, Vol. 1155, p. 331), means that the Court must, for the purposes of interpreting and applying the GATS, take account of the DSB's interpretation of the various provisions of that agreement. In addition, should the DSB not yet have interpreted the provisions concerned, it is for the Court to interpret those provisions in accordance with the customary rules of interpretation of international law that are binding on the Union, while observing the principle, set out in Article 26, that that international agreement should be implemented in good faith.

93. It follows from the foregoing considerations that the arguments relied on by Hungary as to the lack of jurisdiction of the Court to hear and determine the present action for failure to fulfil obligations with respect to the complaint of infringement of the GATS must be rejected in their entirety.

C. *Substance*

1. *The requirement of a prior international treaty*

94. In order to rule on the first complaint, it is necessary, first of all, to clarify the scope of Hungary's commitments in respect of higher

education services in the light of the rule on national treatment set out in Article XVII of the GATS; next, to examine the question whether the requirement of a prior international treaty modifies the conditions of competition to the benefit of national providers of such services or of the services which they supply, contrary to that provision; and, last, if so, to examine the arguments by which Hungary seeks to justify that modification on the basis of one of the exceptions provided for in Article XIV of the GATS.

(a) *The effects to be ascribed to Hungary's commitment in respect of higher education services, in the light of the rule on national treatment set out in Article XVII of the GATS*

(1) Arguments of the parties

95. The Commission maintains, in the first place, that the inscription of privately financed higher education services in Hungary's schedule of specific commitments and, as regards the establishment of a commercial presence, referred to in Article I(2)(c) of the GATS ("mode of supply 3"), the entry of the word "none" in the column relating to "limitations on national treatment" referred to in Article XVII of that agreement mean that there is no qualification in respect of that commitment and, therefore, that Hungary has undertaken a full commitment in that respect.

96. In the second place, the Commission submits that the condition mentioned by Hungary in the column relating to "limitations on market access" referred to in Article XVI of the GATS, according to which the "establishment of schools is subject to licence from the central authorities", cannot be considered to relate also to the rule on national treatment under Article XX(2) of the GATS.

97. In that regard, the Commission submits first of all that that condition is worded in such vague and general terms that it enables the obtaining of that licence to be made subject to any specific condition, contrary to the terms of Article XX(1)(a) and (b) of the GATS. Such a condition in relation to the obtaining of a prior licence is, moreover, capable of undermining the purpose of entering into commitments under Articles XVI and XVII of the GATS that is set out in the second paragraph of the preamble to the GATS and consists in the "expansion of [trade in services] under conditions of transparency and progressive liberalisation". In addition, even on the assumption that that condition, inscribed in the column relating to "limitations on market access", does indeed apply to national treatment, the condition as formulated cannot encompass the specific requirement under Article

76(1)(a) of the Law on higher education that the binding application of an international treaty on fundamental support for activities that may be undertaken by a foreign higher education institution in Hungary, concluded between the Government of Hungary and the government of the State in which that institution has its seat, must have been recognised by the parties.

98. Next, the Commission submits that, in accordance with the Guidelines for the Scheduling of Specific Commitments under the General Agreement on Trade in Services (GATS), adopted by the WTO's Council for Trade in Services on 23 March 2001 (S/L/92), the authorisation requirements cannot be regarded as limitations on market access under Article XVI of the GATS. Consequently, Hungary cannot shelter behind the requirement of a prior licence in order to rule out any breach of the principle of national treatment.

99. Last, the Commission submits that that requirement is not a measure that falls within the scope of Article XVI of the GATS. Article XVI(2) of that agreement contains an exhaustive list of the limitations falling within the scope of that article. That requirement does not, however, appear in that list, nor does it resemble any of the measures that are listed.

100. The Commission concludes from this that, in the case of mode of supply 3, Hungary has committed itself to applying to service providers from third country members of the WTO treatment no less favourable than that which Hungary accords to its domestic providers.

101. Hungary contends that, in accordance with Article XX(2) of the GATS, the condition which it inscribed in the column relating to "limitations on market access", mentioned in paragraph 96 of the present judgment, also has effect with respect to the national treatment obligation.

102. Hungary further submits that formulating that condition in general terms permits it to maintain a "discretionary licence system" the details of which it can freely adjust, if necessary by restricting the establishment of foreign providers, including by requiring the prior conclusion of an international treaty.

(2) Findings of the Court

103. First of all, according to Article XVII(1)of the GATS, each member of the WTO is required, in the sectors inscribed in its schedule of specific commitments and subject to any conditions and qualifications set out therein, to accord to services and service suppliers of any other member of the WTO treatment no less favourable than that it accords to its own like services and service suppliers.

104. Next, in accordance with Article XVI(1) of the GATS, with respect to market access through the modes of supply identified in Article I of the GATS, each member of the WTO is required to accord services and service suppliers of any other member of the WTO treatment no less favourable than that provided for under the terms, limitations and conditions agreed and specified in its schedule of specific commitments.

105. Last, Article XX(1) of the GATS states that each member of the WTO is required to set out in a schedule the specific commitments it undertakes under Part III of the GATS, which includes Articles XVI and XVII. With respect to sectors where such commitments are undertaken, each schedule must specify the terms, limitations and conditions on market access and the conditions and qualifications on national treatment. Those schedules of specific commitments are an integral part of the GATS.

106. It is apparent, therefore, from Articles XVI, XVII and XX of the GATS that a WTO member's own schedule of specific commitments specifies the commitments which that member has undertaken by sector and by mode of supply. Such a schedule specifies, in particular, the terms, limitations and conditions relating to "limitations on market access" and the conditions and qualifications relating to "limitations on national treatment". That information is set out in two separate columns.

107. Furthermore, in accordance with Article XX(2) of the GATS, measures that are inconsistent with both Articles XVI and XVII of the GATS must, in the interests of simplification, be inscribed only in the column relating to "limitations on market access" of the schedule of specific commitments of the member concerned, that single inscription being then regarded as providing an implicit condition or qualification in respect of national treatment (see the WTO panel report of 16 July 2012 entitled "China—Certain measures affecting electronic payment services" (WT/DS 413/R), adopted by the DSB on 31 August 2012, paragraph 7.658).

108. It follows that a condition that is formally inscribed only under Article XVI of the GATS allows for derogation from the national treatment obligation provided for in Article XVII only where the type of measures that it introduces is inconsistent with both the obligation provided for in Article XVI and that provided for in Article XVII of the GATS (see the WTO panel report of 16 July 2012 entitled "China—Certain measures affecting electronic payment services" (WT/DS 413/R), adopted by the DSB on 31 August 2012, paragraph 7.658).

109. In the present case, the schedule of specific commitments adopted by Hungary (GATS/SC/40 of 15 April 1994) includes, in the column relating to "limitations on market access", in respect of higher education services supplied by means of a commercial presence, the condition that the establishment of schools is subject to licence from the central authorities.

110. The column relating to "limitations on national treatment" contains the word "none" in respect of the subsector of higher education services.

111. In those circumstances, it is necessary to determine whether or not the condition relating to prior licence, referred to in paragraph 109 of the present judgment, inscribed in the column relating to "limitations on market access", is equally applicable to the national treatment obligation provided for in Article XVII of the GATS.

112. In that regard, it is apparent from the effect of the simplifying rule in Article XX(2) of the GATS, as explained in paragraph 108 of the present judgment, that a condition can be covered by that rule and, therefore, apply equally to Article XVII of the GATS only if it is discriminatory in nature.

113. It must be noted that, as is apparent from the actual wording of the condition relating to prior licence, the condition is intended to cover all educational institutions, regardless of their origin, and therefore does not have any discriminatory element. Consequently, the rule laid down in Article XX(2) of the GATS cannot be applied in the present case. It follows that that condition does not enable Hungary to claim a derogation from the national treatment obligation provided for in Article XVII of the GATS.

114. Having regard to the foregoing considerations, it must be concluded that the Commission is fully entitled to maintain that Hungary's inscription of privately financed higher education services in its schedule of specific commitments and, with respect to mode of supply 3, the entry of the word "none" in the column relating to "limitations on national treatment" mean that there is no qualification on Hungary's commitments under Article XVII of the GATS in respect of those services.

(b) Modification of the conditions of competition to the benefit of like national providers

(1) Arguments of the parties

115. The Commission submits that, in so far as higher education institutions that have their seat in a member country of the WTO other

than those of the EEA may supply higher education services in Hungary only if the State in which they have their seat has entered into an international treaty with the Government of Hungary beforehand, the Hungarian legislation accords those service providers less favourable treatment than that enjoyed by like Hungarian providers or those established in an EEA State, contrary to the national treatment obligation provided for in Article XVII of the GATS.

116. Referring to the wording of the Law on higher education, the Commission adds that the Government of Hungary has a discretion as regards the content of that treaty and the decision to enter into negotiations with a view to concluding it. Consequently, it would be open to that government to refuse, even on arbitrary grounds, to conclude such a treaty even though the State in which the service provider has its seat would be prepared to do so.

117. Hungary contends that the primary objective of the requirement of a prior international treaty is to intensify diplomatic efforts in relation to cultural policy. The Government of Hungary has, it maintains, repeatedly declared its readiness to enter into negotiations and makes every effort to ensure that they are brought to a conclusion. The fact that two treaties were signed—one with the State of Maryland (United States) and the other with the People's Republic of China—after the Law on higher education was amended is proof, in its submission, that the measure adopted is not a condition that is impossible to fulfil.

(2) Findings of the Court

118. As a preliminary point, it must be noted that the requirement of a prior international treaty, which calls for the conclusion of an agreement between Hungary and another State which is not a member of the EEA, can in any event affect only certain foreign providers. In so far as that requirement imposes on those foreign providers an additional condition for the supply of higher education services in Hungary compared to those applicable to providers of like services that are established in Hungary or in another Member State of the EEA, it introduces formally different treatment of those categories of providers, within the meaning of Article XVII(3) of the GATS.

119. In accordance with that provision, it is necessary therefore to determine whether, by introducing formally different treatment, the requirement of a prior international treaty modifies the conditions of competition in favour of providers of higher education services established in Hungary, or of the services that they supply.

120. In that regard, it must be noted that that requirement, as formulated in Article 76(1)(a) of the Law on higher education, means that Hungary has a discretion both as to whether it is appropriate to conclude such a treaty and as regards its content. In those circumstances, the opportunity for higher education institutions having their seat in a member country of the WTO other than those of the EEA to carry out their activities in Hungary is entirely in the discretion of the Hungarian authorities.

121. This results in competitive disadvantages for service suppliers having their seat in a Member State of the WTO that is not a member of the EEA, with the result that the requirement of a prior international treaty does modify the conditions of competition in favour of Hungarian providers, contrary to Article XVII of the GATS.

(c) Justification under Article XIV of the GATS

(1) Arguments of the parties

122. Hungary contends that the requirement of a prior international treaty is necessary for the purposes of maintaining public order and preventing deceptive practices. In its submission, that requirement serves to ensure that the State in which the seat of the institution concerned is situated considers that provider to be "reliable" and supports the institution's future activities in Hungary. The requirement also serves to ensure that the institution concerned complies with the legislation of the State in which it has its seat and which may in some circumstances require certain conditions to be met as a prerequisite to being able to carry on an activity in Hungary.

123. Hungary also contends that there is no alternative, compatible with WTO rules, that would enable the Hungarian legislature's objectives to be attained.

124. In particular, contrary to what is advocated by the Commission, it would be unrealistic to apply the relevant national legislation to the foreign higher education institutions concerned in the same way as to Hungarian institutions.

125. The Commission maintains that the requirement of a prior international treaty cannot be justified on the basis of any of the exceptions permitted by the GATS, in particular those provided for in Article XIV(a) and (c)(i) and (ii) thereof.

126. In that respect, according to the Commission, Hungary has, more specifically, failed to provide any evidence to support its assertion that that requirement contributes to the maintaining of public order, nor has it explained, in that context, the nature of the genuine and

sufficiently serious threat allegedly posed to one of the fundamental interests of Hungarian society, or, moreover, clarified how that requirement might be necessary for the purpose of attaining the objective of maintaining public order, assuming that objective to be established, and why there is, in that case, no alternative that would be less restrictive.

127. The Commission further maintains that, because of Hungary's discretion to enter into negotiations with the State in which a foreign higher education institution has its seat, the requirement does not in any event meet the condition laid down in Article XIV of the GATS, according to which measures that might be justifiable in the light of that article must not be "applied in a manner which would constitute a means of arbitrary or unjustifiable discrimination between countries where like conditions prevail, or a disguised restriction on trade in services".

(2) Findings of the Court

128. In the first place, it should be noted that Article XIV of the GATS provides in particular, in paragraph (a) and in paragraph (c)(i), that nothing in that agreement is to be construed to prevent the adoption or enforcement of measures necessary, on the one hand, to protect public morals or to maintain public order, and, on the other, to secure compliance with laws or regulations which are not inconsistent with the provisions of that agreement, including those relating to the prevention of deceptive and fraudulent practices or to deal with the effects of a default on services contracts.

129. In those circumstances, it must be noted that both of the objectives invoked by Hungary, namely, first, maintaining public order and, second, the prevention of deceptive practices, are indeed referred to in the GATS.

130. In the second place, as regards the examination as to whether the requirement of a prior international treaty is justified in the light of the objective of maintaining public order, it is clear from footnote 5, under Article XIV(a) of the GATS, that "the public order exception may be invoked only where a genuine and sufficiently serious threat is posed to one of the fundamental interests of society".

131. Hungary has not, however, put forward any arguments that might establish, in a specific and detailed manner, how the exercise, within its territory, of higher education teaching activities by institutions that have their seat in a State that is not a member of the EEA would constitute, in the absence of such a treaty, a genuine and sufficiently serious threat affecting a fundamental interest of Hungarian society.

132. Therefore, it must be concluded that the requirement of a prior international treaty cannot be justified by Hungary's arguments concerning the maintaining of public order.

133. In the third place, as regards the objective of preventing deceptive practices, it is apparent from Hungary's arguments on this point, summarised in paragraph 122 of the present judgment, that Hungary seems to consider the prior conclusion of an international treaty to be necessary for the purpose of obtaining a guarantee from the third country concerned that the foreign higher education institution concerned is reliable, and thereby preventing any risks from arising in that respect.

134. Those arguments cannot, however, justify the requirement of a prior international treaty.

135. Article XIV of the GATS provides that the exceptions listed cannot be applied in a manner which would constitute a means of arbitrary or unjustifiable discrimination between countries where like conditions prevail, or a disguised restriction on trade in services.

136. First, it should be noted that, as the Advocate General essentially stated in points 119 and 120 of her Opinion, the requirement of a prior international treaty enables Hungary arbitrarily to prevent an institution from entering its market or from carrying on its activities in that market, since the conclusion of such a treaty and, therefore, the fulfilment of that requirement ultimately depend solely on the political will of that Member State. The requirement is in that respect fundamentally distinguishable from a condition requiring the reliability of a foreign education institution to be evidenced by a unilateral declaration of the government of the third country in which that institution has its seat.

137. Second, in so far as it applies to foreign higher education institutions already present on the Hungarian market, the requirement of a prior international treaty is not, in any event, proportionate, since the objective of preventing deceptive practices could be more effectively met by monitoring the activities of such institutions in Hungary and, if necessary, prohibiting the continuation of only those activities in respect of which it could be established that they had adopted such practices.

138. In those circumstances, the requirement of a prior international treaty cannot be justified by Hungary's arguments based on the prevention of deceptive practices.

139. Having regard to the foregoing considerations, it must be held that, by adopting the measure provided for in Article 76(1)(a) of the Law on higher education, Hungary has failed to fulfil its obligations under Article XVII of the GATS.

2. The requirement that the institution concerned provide education in the State where it has its seat

(a) Article XVII of the GATS

140. As a preliminary point, it should be noted, first, that Article 76(1)(b) of the Law on higher education, to which the Commission's complaint relates, requires the foreign higher education institution wishing to carry on an activity in Hungary to offer education or training in the State in which it has its seat, regardless of whether that State is a Member State or a third country, and, second, that the arguments put forward by the Commission in support of that complaint cover the requirement that the institution concerned provide education in the State where it has its seat without any distinction as to whether the requirement applies to foreign higher education institutions having their seat in a Member State or in a third country. Given, however, that, as is apparent from paragraph 73 of the present judgment, Article XVII of the GATS falls within the common commercial policy, that provision is relevant to the examination of this complaint only in so far as that requirement applies to higher education institutions that have their seat in a third country member of the WTO.

141. The scope of Hungary's commitments under Article XVII of the GATS, as regards higher education services, having been clarified in paragraph 114 of the present judgment, it is necessary to examine whether the requirement that the institution concerned provide education in the State where it has its seat, in so far as that State is a third country member of the WTO, modifies the conditions of competition to the benefit of like national providers or the services which they supply, contrary to that provision, and, if so, to examine the arguments by which Hungary seeks to justify that modification on the basis of one of the exceptions provided for in Article XIV of the GATS.

(1) Modification of the conditions of competition to the benefit of like national providers

(i) Arguments of the parties

142. The Commission maintains that the requirement that the institution concerned provide education in the State where it has its seat modifies the conditions of competition to the benefit of national providers and, therefore, that it is contrary to the national treatment obligation with which Hungary is required to comply fully under Article XVII of the GATS.

143. More specifically, the Commission submits that the GATS does not require that, in order to be recognised as a provider enjoying

the rights guaranteed by that agreement, the provider must supply services in the country of origin. Therefore, in so far as that requirement would have the effect of preventing foreign service providers from initially establishing an institution in Hungary, it is discriminatory in relation to such providers.

144. Hungary refers, *mutatis mutandis*, to the arguments expounded in relation to the requirement of a prior international treaty.

(ii) Findings of the Court

145. As a preliminary point, it should be borne in mind that, as is apparent from paragraph 114 of the present judgment, Hungary is committed, under Article XVII of the GATS, to ensuring full national treatment as regards the commercial presence of providers of higher education services.

146. It must be noted that the requirement that the institution concerned provide education in the State where it has its seat specifically covers providers which have their seat abroad.

147. It is therefore necessary to determine whether, by introducing this formally different treatment, the requirement that the institution concerned provide education in the State where it has its seat modifies the conditions of competition to the benefit of Hungarian providers or the services that they supply, as compared to suppliers of like services that have their seat in any third country member of the WTO or to the services that they supply.

148. It should be noted in that regard that providers of higher education services that have their seat in a third country member of the WTO and wish to establish themselves in Hungary are required first to establish an institution in that third country and to genuinely offer higher education in that country.

149. This results in a competitive disadvantage for the foreign suppliers of services concerned, and therefore the requirement that the institution concerned provide education in the State where it has its seat modifies the conditions of competition to the benefit of like Hungarian providers.

(2) Whether there is justification

(i) Arguments of the parties

150. In order to justify such a modification of the conditions of competition, Hungary relies, first, on the objective of maintaining public order and, second, on that relating to the prevention of deceptive practices.

151. The Commission maintains that the requirement that the institution concerned provide education in the State where it has its seat cannot be justified on the basis of either of those objectives. It claims, more specifically, that Hungary has failed to provide any evidence to support its assertion that that requirement contributes to the maintaining of public order, nor has it explained the nature of the genuine and sufficiently serious threat posed to one of the fundamental interests of Hungarian society, or, moreover, clarified how that requirement might be necessary for the purpose of attaining the objective of maintaining public order, assuming that objective to be established, and why there is, in that case, no alternative that would be less restrictive.

(ii) Findings of the Court

152. As is apparent from paragraphs 128 and 129 of the present judgment, both of the objectives invoked by Hungary, namely, first, maintaining public order and, second, the prevention of deceptive practices, are referred to, respectively, in Article XIV(a) and in Article XIV(c)(i) of the GATS.

153. Hungary refers in that regard, without further substantiation, to its arguments in relation to the requirement of a prior international treaty.

154. It must be observed that, in so doing, Hungary has not put forward any arguments that might establish, in a specific and detailed manner, how the exercise, within its territory, of higher education teaching activities by institutions that have their seat in a State that is not a member of the EEA constitutes, in the event that those institutions do not offer education or training in the State in which they have their seat, a genuine and sufficiently serious threat affecting a fundamental interest of Hungarian society enabling Hungary to rely on the justification of maintaining public order.

155. Likewise, by thus confining itself to referring to its arguments in relation to the requirement of a prior international treaty, Hungary has not provided any specific evidence that might demonstrate why the requirement that the institution concerned provide education in the State where it has its seat is necessary in order to prevent deceptive practices.

156. Consequently, it must be concluded that, by adopting the measure provided for in Article 76(1)(b) of the Law on higher education, Hungary has, in so far as that provision applies to higher education institutions which have their seat in a third country member of the WTO, failed to fulfil its obligations under Article XVII of the GATS.

(b) Article 49 TFEU

(1) Applicability of Article 49 TFEU

(i) Arguments of the parties

157. Hungary contends, principally, that education and training offered by educational institutions financed largely by private funds cannot be characterised as an "economic activity" within the meaning of the FEU Treaty if, as in the case of the CEU, it is the service provider itself which finances the teaching activities. It follows, in its submission, that Article 49 TFEU is not applicable in the present case.

158. The Commission maintains, on the contrary, that higher education services supplied by private institutions for remuneration constitute "services" within the meaning of the FEU Treaty. Consequently, private institutions carrying out teaching and scientific research activities in Hungary on a stable and continuous basis are justified in relying on the right to the freedom of establishment, under Article 49 TFEU.

(ii) Findings of the Court

159. Article 49(1) TFEU provides that, within the framework of the provisions in Chapter 2 of Title IV in Part Three of the FEU Treaty, restrictions on the freedom of establishment of nationals of a Member State in the territory of another Member State are to be prohibited.

160. It must first of all be noted in that regard that the Court has ruled that the provision for remuneration of higher education courses is an economic activity falling within Chapter 2 when that activity is carried on by a national of one Member State in another Member State on a stable and continuous basis from a principal or secondary establishment in the latter Member State (judgment of 13 November 2003, *Neri*, C-153/02, EU:C:2003:614, paragraph 39).

161. In the present case, Article 76(1)(b) of the Law on higher education is applicable to higher education institutions, without any distinction being made as to whether the courses leading to a qualification that are offered by those institutions are offered for remuneration or not.

162. Next, the Court has ruled that freedom of establishment extends to a situation in which a company formed in accordance with the legislation of one Member State, where it has its registered office, wishes to set up a branch in another Member State, even where that company was formed, in the first Member State, solely for the purpose of establishing itself in the second, where its main, or indeed entire,

business is to be conducted (judgment of 25 October 2017, *Polbud—Wykonawstwo*, C-106/16, EU:C:2017:804, paragraph 38).

163. Consequently, Article 49 TFEU covers the requirement that the institution concerned provide education in the State where it has its seat in so far as that requirement applies to a higher education institution that has its seat in a Member State other than Hungary and offers education or training for remuneration in Hungary.

(2) Whether there is a restriction

(i) Arguments of the parties

164. According to the Commission, the requirement that the higher education institutions concerned must, under Article 76(1)(b) of the Law on higher education, satisfy specific conditions in the Member State in which they have their seat in order to be able to establish another institution in Hungary constitutes a restriction on the freedom of establishment within the meaning of Article 49 TFEU.

165. In particular, a Member State cannot deny the advantages of the freedom of establishment to a legal entity on the ground that that entity does not carry on any economic activity in the Member State in which it was formed.

166. Hungary contends, in the alternative, that the requirement that the institution concerned provide education in the State where it has its seat does not restrict the freedom of establishment. The requirement is linked to the exercise of an activity, and not to the formation of companies. In particular, it does not prevent a foreign higher education institution from setting up, for example, as a secondary establishment, a branch in Hungary. Nor does it limit the choice of legal form of the establishment; it merely lays down, in the case of service providers already established in Hungary through a secondary establishment, a condition relating to the exercise of higher education teaching activities.

(ii) Findings of the Court

167. In accordance with the case law of the Court, any measure which prohibits, impedes or renders less attractive the exercise of the freedom of establishment must be regarded as a restriction on that freedom (judgment of 6 September 2012, *Commission* v. *Portugal*, C-38/10, EU:C:2012:521, paragraph 26).

168. In the present case, Article 76(1)(b) of the Law on higher education requires that the suppliers of services concerned who wish to supply higher education services in Hungary through a stable

institution must genuinely offer higher education in the State in which they have their seat.

169. Such a requirement is liable to render less attractive the exercise of the freedom of establishment in Hungary for nationals of another Member State who wish to establish themselves in Hungary in order to supply higher education services in that country.

170. Consequently, the requirement that the institution concerned provide education in the State where it has its seat constitutes a restriction on the freedom of establishment, within the meaning of Article 49 TFEU.

(3) Whether there is justification

(i) *Arguments of the parties*

171. Hungary contends first of all that the requirement that the institution concerned provide education in the State where it has its seat is necessary for the purposes of maintaining public order and preventing deceptive practices. That requirement is, in its submission, also necessary in order to safeguard the quality of the education offered by the institutions concerned in Hungary, particularly as the qualifications which they issue are official documents producing legal effects.

172. Hungary goes on to claim that that requirement is a means of appropriately ensuring that those objectives are observed, in that the competent authority is thus able to satisfy itself that there is a genuine and lawful activity in the country in which the service provider has its seat, and does so with the aim of ensuring that university education in Hungary is of a high quality.

173. However, Hungary observes that, in practice, its authorities merely examine the higher education teaching activity, the qualifications already issued, the education or training attested by those qualifications, that is to say, the teaching conditions and programme, and the qualifications of the teaching staff delivering that education.

174. Last, there is no measure that is less restrictive, since the objective of ensuring high standards of higher education can only be met by examining the activity carried on in the State in which the institution has its seat. In any event, in so far as higher education has not been harmonised at EU level, the Member States have significant latitude in that regard.

175. The Commission maintains first of all that the requirement that the institution concerned provide education in the State where it has its seat is not capable of meeting any of the objectives invoked by Hungary. It submits that Hungary has not put forward any convincing

arguments as to why that requirement is justified and proportionate with regard to those objectives, nor has it indicated the nature of the abuses that that requirement would serve to prevent.

176. The Commission claims, in particular, that that requirement is inappropriate in that the quality of the education offered in the State in which the institution concerned has its seat does not provide any indication of the quality of the service supplied in Hungary. Furthermore, if its objective was really to prevent fraud and abuses, Hungary should have adopted specific rules in that respect.

177. Last, according to the Commission, the requirement that the institution concerned provide education in the State where it has its seat is disproportionate. The exchange of information with quality assurance agencies and/or accreditation agencies of the State in which the education institution concerned has its seat, as advocated in the Council's conclusions of 20 May 2014 on quality assurance supporting education and training (OJ 2014 C 183, p. 30), and enhanced cooperation within the EEA between higher education authorities are less restrictive alternatives.

(ii) Findings of the Court

178. As the Court has consistently held, a restriction on the freedom of establishment is permissible only if, in the first place, it is justified by an overriding reason in the public interest and, in the second place, it observes the principle of proportionality, which means that it is suitable for securing, in a consistent and systematic manner, the attainment of the objective pursued and does not go beyond what is necessary in order to attain it (judgment of 23 February 2016, *Commission v. Hungary*, C-179/14, EU:C:2016:108, paragraph 166).

179. Moreover, it is for the Member State concerned to demonstrate that those cumulative conditions are met (judgment of 18 June 2020, *Commission v. Hungary (Transparency of associations)*, C-78/18, EU:C:2020:476, paragraph 77).

180. In the present case, Hungary relies, in the first place, on the need to maintain public order.

181. It must be borne in mind first of all in that regard that, in the context of the fundamental freedoms guaranteed by the Treaties, reasons of public policy may be relied on only if there is a genuine, present and sufficiently serious threat to a fundamental interest of society (judgment of 19 June 2008, *Commission v. Luxembourg*, C-319/06, EU:C:2008:350, paragraph 50).

182. Hungary merely states that the requirement that the institution concerned provide education in the State where it has its seat

enables the competent authority to satisfy itself that there is a genuine and lawful activity in the country in which the service provider concerned has its seat. As has been noted in paragraph 154 of the present judgment, Hungary has not put forward any arguments that might establish, in a specific and detailed manner, how the exercise, within its territory, of higher education teaching activities by such institutions constitutes, should that requirement not be met, a genuine, present and sufficiently serious ' threat affecting a fundamental interest of Hungarian society.

183. Accordingly, it must be concluded that the existence of such a threat has not been established in the present case.

184. In the second place, Hungary invokes the objective of preventing deceptive practices. Without further substantiating its reasoning, Hungary seems to consider that access of foreign higher education institutions to the Hungarian market entails a risk of such practices developing.

185. In relying on a general presumption, Hungary fails to demonstrate, notwithstanding the burden of proof which it bears, as noted in paragraph 179 of the present judgment, what the precise nature of such a risk is, and how the requirement that the institution concerned provide education in the State where it has its seat would obviate that risk.

186. In any event, as the Advocate General essentially noted in point 185 of her Opinion, Hungary has not explained why the objective of preventing deceptive practices could not be attained if a supplier that was not already providing higher education in the Member State in which it had its seat were permitted to establish by any other means that it complies with the legislation of that State and that it is, moreover, reliable.

187. In the third place, the objective, invoked by Hungary, of ensuring high standards in the quality of higher education is indeed capable of justifying restrictions on the freedom of establishment (see, to that effect, judgment of 13 November 2003, *Neri*, C-153/02, EU:C:2003:614, paragraph 46).

188. It should, however, be noted that the requirement that the institution concerned provide education in the State where it has its seat does not include any details as to the standard required as regards the quality of the education offered by the foreign institution in the Member State in which it has its seat, nor does it prejudge, moreover, in any respect the quality of the education that will be provided in Hungary, with the result that it is not in any event capable of guaranteeing that that objective will be attained.

189. It follows from the foregoing considerations that the requirement that the institution concerned provide education in the State where it has its seat cannot be justified by Hungary's arguments based on maintaining public order, nor on those based on overriding reasons in the public interest relating to the prevention of deceptive practices and the need to ensure the good quality of higher education.

190. Consequently, it must be concluded that, by adopting the measure provided for in Article 76(1)(b) of the Law on higher education, Hungary has, in so far as that provision applies to higher education institutions which have their seat in another Member State, failed to fulfil its obligations under Article 49 TFEU.

(c) Article 16 of Directive 2006/123 and, in the alternative, Article 56 TFEU

(1) Applicability of Directive 2006/123

(i) Arguments of the parties

191. Hungary contends that education or training offered by educational institutions financed largely by private funds cannot be characterised as an "economic activity" within the meaning of Article 4(1) of Directive 2006/123 if, as in the case of the CEU, it is the service provider itself which finances the teaching activities. Consequently, that directive is not applicable in the present case.

192. The Commission maintains that, in accordance with Article 2 of Directive 2006/123, and also Article 4(1) thereof, which refers to the definition of services included in the FEU Treaty, the scope of that directive includes teaching activities and training courses that are financed essentially by private contributions. Consequently, private institutions carrying out teaching and scientific research activities in Hungary on a temporary basis are justified in relying on the right to the freedom to provide services under that directive.

(ii) Findings of the Court

193. In accordance with Article 2(1) of Directive 2006/123, the directive is to apply to services supplied by providers established in a Member State.

194. In accordance with Article 4(1) of that directive, "service" means any self-employed economic activity, normally provided for remuneration, as referred to in Article 57 TFEU.

195. In the present case, Article 76(1)(b) of the Law on higher education concerns in general terms education services that may be

provided by foreign higher education institutions in Hungary and, therefore, also the provision of education or training courses for remuneration. Such provision constitutes an "economic activity" within the meaning of Article 4(1) of Directive 2006/123. Accordingly, that directive is applicable in the present case.

(2) Whether there is a restriction

(i) Arguments of the parties
196. The Commission maintains that, in so far as the requirement that the institution concerned provide education in the State where it has its seat also covers higher education institutions which intend to supply cross-border services in Hungary, the requirement constitutes a restriction on the freedom to provide services, guaranteed in Article 16 of Directive 2006/123. In the alternative, the Commission maintains that that requirement infringes Article 56 TFEU.
197. Hungary contests those arguments.

(ii) Findings of the Court
198. As a preliminary point, it should be noted that, in accordance with the second subparagraph of Article 16(1) of Directive 2006/123, the Member State in which the service is provided is to ensure, in particular, free exercise of a service activity within its territory.
199. In the present case, Article 76(1)(b) of the Law on higher education requires that the institutions concerned offer higher education in the State in which they have their seat.
200. When considered in the light of Directive 2006/123, such a requirement is, in so far as it imposes an additional condition on service providers that have their seat in another Member State, capable of restricting the right of such providers to the free exercise of higher education teaching activities in Hungary, if they wish first to carry on their activity in Hungary rather than in the Member State in which they have their seat, or if they plan to carry on such an activity only in Hungary.

(3) Whether there is justification

(i) Arguments of the parties
201. Hungary contends that the requirement that the institution concerned provide education in the Member State where it has its seat is necessary for the purposes of maintaining public order. In that regard, Hungary refers, *mutatis mutandis*, to its arguments in relation to the plea alleging infringement of Article 49 TFEU.

202. The Commission submits that Hungary has not demonstrated that the education services supplied on a temporary basis by higher education institutions established in a Member State had an effect on public order in Hungary, as nevertheless required by Article 16(3) of Directive 2006/123.

(ii) Findings of the Court

203. Under Article 16(3) of Directive 2006/123, the Member State to which the provider moves may impose requirements with regard to the provision of a service activity where these are justified, inter alia, for reasons of public policy and public security, and in accordance with paragraph 1 of Article 16.

204. It must, however, be recalled that, as is apparent from the case law cited in paragraph 181 of the present judgment, to which reference is made in recital 41 of Directive 2006/123, reasons of public policy and public security presuppose, in particular, that there is a genuine, present and sufficiently serious threat affecting a fundamental interest of society. As has been noted in paragraphs 154 and 182 of the present judgment, Hungary has not put forward any arguments that might establish, in a specific and detailed manner, how the exercise, within its territory, of higher education teaching activities by institutions that have their seat in another Member State constitute, should the requirement that the institution concerned provide education in the State where it has its seat not be met, a genuine, present and sufficiently serious threat affecting a fundamental interest of Hungarian society.

205. Accordingly, it must be held that that requirement cannot be justified in the light of Article 16(3) of Directive 2006/123.

206. It follows from the foregoing that, by adopting the measure provided for in Article 76(1)(b) of the Law on higher education, Hungary has, in so far as that provision applies to higher education institutions which have their seat in another Member State, failed to fulfil its obligations under Article 16 of Directive 2006/123. Consequently, there is no need to examine whether Hungary has infringed Article 56 TFEU, which the Commission raised only in the alternative.

207. Having regard to the foregoing considerations, it must be held that, by adopting the measure provided for in Article 76(1)(b) of the Law on higher education, Hungary has failed, in so far as that provision applies to higher education institutions which have their seat in a third country member of the WTO, to fulfil its obligations under Article XVII of the GATS and, in so far as the provision applies to higher

education institutions having their seat in another Member State, to fulfil its obligations under Article 49 TFEU and Article 16 of Directive 2006/123.

3. Article 13, Article 14(3) and Article 16 of the Charter

(a) Applicability of the Charter

(1) Arguments of the parties

208. The Commission submits that, when Member States perform their obligations under international agreements concluded by the Union, such as the GATS, they are "implementing Union law", within the meaning of Article 51(1) of the Charter, with the result that they are obliged to respect the provisions of the Charter.

209. Furthermore, in so far as Article 76(1)(b) of the Law on higher education restricts fundamental freedoms guaranteed by the FEU Treaty, Directive 2006/123 and the GATS, that provision must be compatible with the Charter.

210. Hungary contends that, first, a national measure which infringes the commitments undertaken by the Member States within the framework of the GATS cannot be considered part of the implementation of EU law, within the meaning of Article 51(1) of the Charter.

211. Second, given that, according to Hungary, neither the provisions of the FEU Treaty concerning the freedom to provide services nor the provisions of Directive 2006/123 apply in the present case, and that, therefore, the measures at issue do not constitute a restriction that infringes the fundamental freedoms laid down by the FEU Treaty or Directive 2006/123, they do not fall within the scope of EU law, and therefore the Charter is of no relevance.

(2) Findings of the Court

212. So far as the actions of the Member States are concerned, the scope of the Charter is defined in Article 51(1) thereof, according to which the provisions of the Charter are addressed to the Member States only "when they are implementing Union law".

213. In the present case, first, as has been noted in paragraph 71 of the present judgment, the GATS forms part of EU law. It follows that, when the Member States are performing their obligations under that agreement, including the obligation imposed in Article XVII(1) thereof, they must be considered to be implementing EU law, within the meaning of Article 51(1) of the Charter.

214. Second, where a Member State argues that a measure of which it is the author and which restricts a fundamental freedom guaranteed by the FEU Treaty is justified by an overriding reason in the public interest recognised by EU law, such a measure must be regarded as implementing EU law within the meaning of Article 51(1) of the Charter, such that it must comply with the fundamental rights enshrined in the Charter (judgment of 18 June 2020, *Commission v. Hungary (Transparency of associations)*, C-78/18, EU:C:2020:476, paragraph 101 and the case law cited). The same applies with respect to Article 16 of Directive 2006/123.

215. Consequently, the measures at issue must comply with the fundamental rights enshrined in the Charter.

216. In those circumstances, it is necessary to examine whether those measures limit the fundamental rights invoked by the Commission and, if so, whether they are nevertheless justified, as Hungary contends.

(b) Whether there are limitations on the fundamental rights concerned

(1) Arguments of the parties

217. According to the Commission, the measures at issue affect, in the first place, academic freedom, guaranteed in Article 13 of the Charter, and, in the second place, the freedom to found educational establishments and the freedom to conduct a business, enshrined, respectively, in Article 14(3) and in Article 16 of the Charter.

218. As regards academic freedom, the Commission considers those measures to affect the ability of the foreign higher education institutions concerned to conduct research freely in Hungary and to disseminate scientific knowledge and advances.

219. As regards the freedom to found educational establishments and to conduct a business, in the Commission's view, the measures at issue restrict the right of individuals to carry on a commercial activity and the right of undertakings to benefit from a certain stability with respect to their business.

220. Hungary contends, with regard to academic freedom, that the fact that a higher education institution must meet certain legal obligations does not affect the academic freedom of the institution concerned nor that of its staff. Such obligations do not inevitably affect the ability to undertake scientific activities, whether from the point of view of the institution or that of the staff.

221. So far as the freedom to found educational establishments and the freedom to conduct a business are concerned, Hungary does not

dispute, in essence, the fact that the measures at issue limit the exercise of the former.

(2) Findings of the Court

222. As regards, in the first place, academic freedom, this is enshrined in general terms in the second sentence of Article 13 of the Charter, according to which "academic freedom shall be respected".

223. Under Article 52(3) of the Charter, rights enshrined therein which correspond to rights guaranteed by the Convention for the Protection of Human Rights and Fundamental Freedoms, signed in Rome on 4 November 1950 ("the ECHR") must be given the same meaning and, at the very least, the same scope as those laid down by that convention.

224. It is true that the text of the ECHR makes no reference to academic freedom. However, it is apparent from the case law of the European Court of Human Rights that that freedom is associated, in particular, with the right to freedom of expression enshrined in Article 10 of the ECHR (ECtHR, 15 April 2014, *Hasan Yazıcı* v. *Turkey*, CE: ECHR:2014:0415JUD004087707, § 55 and 69, and ECtHR, 27 May 2014, *Mustafa Erdoğan and Others* v. *Turkey*, CE:ECHR:2014: 0527JUD000034604, § 40 and 46), as is also confirmed by the comments on Article 13 of the Charter in the Explanations relating to the Charter of Fundamental Rights (OJ 2007 C 303, p. 17).

225. From that specific perspective, academic freedom in research and in teaching should guarantee freedom of expression and of action, freedom to disseminate information and freedom to conduct research and to distribute knowledge and truth without restriction, although it should be made clear that that freedom is not restricted to academic or scientific research, but that it also extends to academics' freedom to express freely their views and opinions (ECtHR, 27 May 2014, *Mustafa Erdoğan and Others* v. *Turkey*, CE:ECHR:2014:0527JUD 000034604, § 40).

226. That being the case, as the Advocate General stated in points 145 and 146 of her Opinion, the concept of "academic freedom" must be understood more broadly.

227. In that regard, the Court considers it helpful, for the purposes of clarifying the various elements inherent in academic freedom and of determining whether the measures at issue constitute limitations on that freedom, to take into consideration the content of Recommendation 1762 (2006), adopted by the Parliamentary Assembly of the Council of Europe on 30 June 2006 and entitled "Academic freedom and university autonomy", from which it is

apparent that academic freedom also incorporates an institutional and organisational dimension, a link to an organisational structure being an essential prerequisite for teaching and research activities. Also relevant is point 18 of the Recommendation concerning the status of higher-education teaching personnel, adopted on 11 November 1997 by the General Conference of the United Nations Educational, Scientific and Cultural Organisation (UNESCO), meeting in Paris from 21 October to 12 November 1997, at its 29th session, according to which "autonomy is the institutional form of academic freedom and a necessary precondition to guarantee the proper fulfilment of the functions entrusted to higher-education teaching personnel and institutions". Point 19 of that recommendation makes clear that "Member States are under an obligation to protect higher education institutions from threats to their autonomy coming from any source".

228. In the light of the foregoing, it must be held that the measures at issue are capable of endangering the academic activity of the foreign higher education institutions concerned within the territory of Hungary and, therefore, of depriving the universities concerned of the autonomous organisational structure that is necessary for conducting their academic research and for carrying out their educational activities. Consequently, those measures are such as to limit the academic freedom protected in Article 13 of the Charter.

229. As regards, in the second place, the freedom to found educational establishments and the freedom to conduct a business, these are enshrined, respectively, in Article 14(3) and Article 16 of the Charter.

230. Under Article 14(3) of the Charter, the freedom to found educational establishments with due respect for democratic principles must be respected, in accordance with the national laws governing the exercise of such freedom.

231. Moreover, Article 16 of the Charter provides that the freedom to conduct a business in accordance with EU law and national laws and practices must be recognised.

232. As a preliminary point, it should be noted that, as is apparent from the Explanations relating to the Charter of Fundamental Rights, the freedom to found educational establishments, whether public or private, is guaranteed as one of the aspects of the freedom to conduct a business, and it is therefore appropriate to examine them together.

233. In that regard, it must be noted that the measures at issue are, depending on the circumstances, such as to render uncertain or to exclude the very possibility of founding a higher education institution, or of continuing to operate an existing higher education institution, in Hungary.

234. Consequently, those measures must be regarded as limiting both the freedom to found educational establishments guaranteed in Article 14(3) of the Charter and the freedom to conduct a business enshrined in Article 16 of the Charter.

(c) Whether there is justification

(1) Arguments of the parties
235. Hungary maintains that the measures at issue are justified in the light of the requirements set out in Article 52(1) of the Charter.
236. As regards, in particular, the freedom to found educational establishments and the freedom to conduct a business, Hungary submits that these must be exercised with due respect for democratic principles and within the framework of national provisions governing the exercise of those freedoms. Accordingly, a Member State cannot be accused of having introduced an unlawful limitation if the Member State is regulating an economic activity with the aim of enabling others to exercise those freedoms.
237. The Commission submits that the limitations—as a result of the measures at issue—on the freedoms enshrined, respectively, in Article 13, Article 14(3) and Article 16 of the Charter are not justified in the light of the requirements set out in Article 52(1) of the Charter.
238. According to the Commission, Hungary has not demonstrated, in the present case, that the limitations which the measures at issue place on academic freedom and the freedom to found educational establishments meet objectives of general interest recognised by the Union or the need to protect the rights and freedoms of others, nor has it demonstrated that those limitations are proportionate.

(2) Findings of the Court
239. Article 52(1) of the Charter provides that any limitation on the exercise of the rights and freedoms recognised by the Charter must be provided for by law and respect the essence of those rights and freedoms. Subject to the principle of proportionality, limitations may be made only if they are necessary and genuinely meet objectives of general interest recognised by the Union or the need to protect the rights and freedoms of others.
240. In the present case, the Court has concluded, in paragraphs 132, 138, 154, 155 and 189 of the present judgment, that the

measures at issue were not justified by any of the objectives of general interest recognised by the Union upon which Hungary relied.

241. It follows that those measures, which place limitations on the rights enshrined, respectively, in Article 13, Article 14(3) and Article 16 of the Charter, as the Court has ruled in paragraphs 228 and 234 of the present judgment, do not in any event meet those objectives of general interest.

242. Having regard to the foregoing considerations, it must be held that, by adopting the measures at issue, Hungary has failed to fulfil its obligations under Article 13, Article 14(3) and Article 16 of the Charter.

243. In the light of all of the foregoing considerations, it must be held that:

– by adopting the measure provided for in Article 76(1)(a) of the Law on higher education, Hungary has failed to fulfil its obligations under Article XVII of the GATS;
– by adopting the measure provided for in Article 76(1)(b) of the Law on higher education, Hungary has failed, in so far as that provision applies to higher education institutions which have their seat in a third country member of the WTO, to fulfil its obligations under Article XVII of the GATS and, in so far as the provision applies to higher education institutions having their seat in another Member State, to fulfil its obligations under Article 49 TFEU and Article 16 of Directive 2006/123; and
– by adopting the measures at issue, Hungary has failed to fulfil its obligations under Article 13, Article 14(3) and Article 16 of the Charter.

COSTS

244. Under Article 138(1) of the Rules of Procedure, the unsuccessful party is to be ordered to pay the costs if they have been applied for in the successful party's pleadings. In the present case, since Hungary has been unsuccessful, it must be ordered to pay the costs, in accordance with the form of order sought by the Commission.

On those grounds, the Court (Grand Chamber) hereby:

1. Declares that, by adopting the measure provided for in Article 76(1)(a) of Nemzeti felsőoktatásról szóló 2011. évi CCIV. törvény (Law No CCIV of 2011 on national higher education), as amended by Nemzeti felsőoktatásról szóló 2011. évi CCIV. törvény

módosításáról szóló 2017. évi XXV. törvény (Law No XXV of 2017 amending Law No CCIV of 2011 on national higher education), which makes the exercise, in Hungary, of teaching activities leading to a qualification by foreign higher education institutions situated outside the European Economic Area subject to the condition that the Government of Hungary and the government of the State in which the institution concerned has its seat have agreed to be bound by an international treaty, Hungary has failed to fulfil its obligations under Article XVII of the General Agreement on Trade in Services, in Annex 1B to the Agreement establishing the World Trade Organization, signed in Marrakesh and approved by Council Decision 94/800/EC of 22 December 1994 concerning the conclusion on behalf of the European Community, as regards matters within its competence, of the agreements reached in the Uruguay Round multilateral negotiations (1986-94);

2. Declares that, by adopting the measure provided for in Article 76(1)(b) of Nemzeti felsőoktatásról szóló 2011. évi CCIV. törvény (Law No CCIV of 2011 on national higher education), as amended by Nemzeti felsőoktatásról szóló 2011. évi CCIV. törvény módosításáról szóló 2017. évi XXV. törvény (Law No XXV of 2017 amending Law No CCIV of 2011 on national higher education), which makes the exercise, in Hungary, of the activities of foreign higher education institutions subject to the condition that they offer higher education in the State in which they have their seat, Hungary has failed, in so far as that provision applies to higher education institutions which have their seat in a third country member of the World Trade Organization, to fulfil its obligations under Article XVII of the General Agreement on Trade in Services, in Annex 1B to the Agreement establishing the World Trade Organization, signed in Marrakesh and approved by Decision 94/800, and, in so far as the provision applies to higher education institutions having their seat in another Member State, to fulfil its obligations under Article 49 TFEU and Article 16 of Directive 2006/123/EC of the European Parliament and of the Council of 12 December 2006 on services in the internal market;

3. Declares that, by adopting the measures provided for in Article 76(1)(a) and (b) of Nemzeti felsőoktatásról szóló 2011. évi CCIV. törvény (Law No CCIV of 2011 on national higher education), as amended by Nemzeti felsőoktatásról szóló 2011. évi CCIV. törvény módosításáról szóló 2017. évi XXV. törvény (Law No XXV of

2017 amending Law No CCIV of 2011 on national higher education), Hungary has failed to fulfil its obligations under Article 13, Article 14(3) and Article 16 of the Charter of Fundamental Rights of the European Union;

4. Orders Hungary to pay the costs.

[Report: EU:C:2020:792]

Human rights — Right to property — American Convention on Human Rights, 1969 — Article 2 — Obligation of States to adopt domestic legal provisions — Article 23(1) — Right to participate — State obligation to consult indigenous peoples on projects on communal property — Whether judgment on the merits requiring Argentina to include the right to prior consultation under its laws to ensure the right to indigenous communal property

International tribunals — Jurisdiction — Inter-American Court of Human Rights — Admissibility — Whether the Lhaka Honhat representatives' request for interpretation of the judgment on the merits admissible

INDIGENOUS COMMUNITIES OF THE LHAKA HONHAT
(OUR LAND) ASSOCIATION *v.* ARGENTINA[1]

Inter-American Court of Human Rights

Interpretation of the Judgment on Merits, Reparations and Costs.
24 *November* 2020

(Odio Benito, *President*; Pazmiño Freire, *Vice-President*; Vio Grossi, Sierra Porto, Ferrer Mac-Gregor Poisot, Pérez Manrique, *Judges*)

SUMMARY:[2] *The facts*:—On 13 August 2020, representatives of the Lhaka Honhat Association of Aboriginal Communities ("the Lhaka Honhat") requested the Inter-American Court of Human Rights ("the Court") to interpret its judgment on the merits, issued on 6 February 2020, which required, inter alia, the Argentine Republic ("Argentina"), to adopt appropriate laws and procedures to provide legal certainty to the right to indigenous communal property.[3]

The judgment arose from a case filed by the Lhaka Honhat, an indigenous community from Argentina, which alleged that Argentina had violated its right to communal property, by failing to (i) provide them adequate title to their land; (ii) properly demarcate the land; and (iii) prevent non-indigenous families from continuing to settle on the ancestral territory. The Court held that Argentina had violated the Lhaka Honhat's right to indigenous

---

[1] The victims were represented by the Lhaka Honhat (Our Land) Association of Aboriginal Communities and the Centro de Estudios Legales y Sociales.
[2] Prepared by Ms C. Kimeu.
[3] *Indigenous Communities of the Lhaka Honhat (Our Land) Association* v. *Argentina (Merits, Reparations and Costs)*, 201 ILR 141.

communal property, on the grounds raised above. It found that Argentina had failed to establish proper laws and procedures to facilitate indigenous territorial claims under its domestic legislation and directed it to adopt laws that would provide legal certainty on indigenous communal property rights.

Lhaka Honhat's representatives filed the present request for interpretation, asking the Court to clarify whether Argentina was obligated to include the right to prior consultation in the laws and procedures that the Court had directed it to adopt, as a means of ensuring the right to indigenous communal property. Argentina argued that the representatives' request for interpretation was inadmissible. It stated that its duty to ensure the right to consultation with indigenous communities was not in dispute, in light of its commitments under international human rights law, but argued that the Court had not specifically required it to legislate that right. As such, the victims' representatives' claim exceeded the scope of "interpretation of judgment" and sought to repeat the debate in order to expand the reparations that had been ordered. The Inter-American Commission on Human Rights agreed with the representatives that clarification of the scope of the Court's judgment on the issue was important.

Held (unanimously):—(1) The request for interpretation was admissible. It was submitted within the required time frame and the request for interpretation was appropriate, and useful in ensuring correct compliance with the Court's orders (paras. 6, 7, 17 and 18).

(2) The right to indigenous communal property could not be adequately guaranteed without ensuring the effective participation of indigenous peoples or communities in actions that might affect their territories. Prior, free and informed consultation guarantees were necessary elements of the right to indigenous communal property, and had to be included in the laws and measures that the State would adopt (paras. 24-30).

The following is the text of the judgment of the Court:

I. REQUEST FOR INTERPRETATION AND PROCEEDINGS BEFORE THE COURT

1. On February 6, 2020, the Inter-American Court delivered judgment in the instant case and this was notified to the parties and to the Inter-American Commission on Human Rights (hereinafter also "the Commission") on April 2 that year.

2. On August 13, 2020, the victims' representatives[1] submitted a request for interpretation concerning the scope of the provisions in the

---

[1] The victims' representatives are the Lhaka Honhat (Our Land) Association of Aboriginal Communities and the Centro de Estudios Legales y Sociales (CELS).

fifteenth operative paragraph of the judgment ordering the State to adopt the necessary legislative and/or any other measures to provide legal certainty to the right to indigenous communal property.

3. On August 14, 2020, pursuant to Article 68(2) of the Rules of Procedure and on the instruction of the President of the Court, the Court's Secretariat forwarded the said request for interpretation to the Argentine Republic (hereinafter also "the State" or "Argentina") and the Commission, and granted them until September 15, 2020, to present any written observations they deemed pertinent. On September 14 and 15, 2020, the State and the Commission, respectively, submitted their observations.

II. JURISDICTION

4. Article 67 of the American Convention establishes:

The judgment of the Court shall be final and not subject to appeal. In case of disagreement as to the meaning or scope of the judgment, the Court shall interpret it at the request of any of the parties, provided the request is made within ninety days from the date of notification of the judgment.

5. Pursuant to this article, the Inter-American Court is competent to interpret its judgments. According to Article 68(3) of the Rules of Procedure, when examining requests for interpretation and making the corresponding decisions, the Court should, if possible, have the same composition it had when delivering the respective judgment. On this occasion, the Court is composed of the same judges who delivered the judgment the interpretation of which has been requested.[2]

III. ADMISSIBILITY

6. The Court must verify whether the request presented by the representatives complies with the requirements established in the rules applicable to a request for interpretation of judgment; namely, Article 67 of the aforementioned Convention, and Article 68 of the Rules of Procedure. Also, Article 31(3) of the Rules of Procedure establishes that "[j]udgments and orders of the Court may not be contested in any way."

---

[2] Owing to the exceptional circumstances resulting from the COVID-19 pandemic, this judgment was deliberated and adopted during the Court's 138th regular session, which was held virtually using technological resources as established in the Court's Rules of Procedure.

7. The Court notes that the representatives presented their request for interpretation within the 90-day period established in Article 67 of the Convention. In this regard, it should be clarified that, when the judgment was notified on April 2, 2020, the procedural time frames had been suspended since March 17, 2020, pursuant to the provisions of Decision 1/20 of the Court. This suspension of time frames as a result of the COVID-19 pandemic, a well-known situation, was later extended until May 20, 2020, by the Court's Decision 2/20. Therefore the request for interpretation presented on August 13, 2020, was admissible as regards the time frame for its presentation. Regarding the other requirements, the Inter-American Court will analyze the merits of this request in the following chapter.

IV. ANALYSIS OF THE ADMISSIBILITY OF THE REQUEST FOR INTERPRETATION

8. The Court will examine the representatives' request to determine whether, based on the regulations and the standards developed in its case law, it is admissible to clarify the meaning or scope of any provision of the judgment.

9. The Court has indicated that a request for interpretation of judgment cannot be used as a means of contesting the decision whose interpretation is required. The exclusive purpose of this type of request is to determine the meaning of a ruling when any of the parties claims that the text of its operative paragraphs or of its considerations is unclear or imprecise, provided such considerations affect the said operative paragraphs. Consequently, a request for interpretation may not be used to seek the amendment or nullification of the judgment in question.[3]

10. The Court has also indicated that it is inadmissible to use a request for interpretation to submit considerations on factual and legal matters that have already been submitted at the proper procedural moment and on which the Court has already taken a decision,[4] or to expect the Court to re-assess matters that have been decided in the judgment.[5] Similarly, a request cannot be used to try and expand the

---

[3] *Cf. Case of Loayza Tamayo* v. *Peru. Interpretation of the judgment on merits.* Order of the Court of March 8, 1998. Series C No 47, paras. 12 and 16, and *Case of Rosadio Villavicencio* v. *Peru. Interpretation of the judgment on preliminary objections, merits, reparations and costs.* Judgment of October 8, 2020. Series C No 414, para. 11.

[4] *Cf. Case of Loayza Tamayo* v. *Peru,* para. 15, and *Case of Rosadio Villavicencio* v. *Peru,* para. 12.

[5] *Cf. Case of Salvador Chiriboga* v. *Ecuador. Interpretation of the judgment on reparations and costs.* Judgment of August 29, 2011. Series C No 230, para. 30, and *Case of Rosadio Villavicencio* v. *Peru,* para. 12.

scope of a measure of reparation that was ordered at the opportune procedural moment.[6]

11. The Inter-American Court will now examine the issue raised by the representatives. To this end, it will set out their arguments, as well as those of the State and the Commission, and then its own considerations.

A. Arguments of the parties and the Commission

12. The *representatives* requested clarification of the measure of reparation ordered in the fifteenth operative paragraph of the judgment, consisting in the adoption of "the necessary legislative and/or any other measures to provide legal certainty to the right to indigenous communal property, pursuant to paragraphs 354 to 357 of th[e] judgment." When doing so, they indicated that their request was for the Court to "clarify" whether what it had ordered "should specifically include the indigenous peoples' right to consultation." In this regard, "in order to avoid different interpretations of the State's obligations," they asked that the Court clarify the paragraphs of the judgment to which the fifteenth operative paragraph referred, as well as its paragraph 353.

13. The representatives indicated that "[t]he indigenous communities' right to consultation, in addition to its intrinsic significance, is critically important for the protection of the right to indigenous property, as well as for the protection of their other rights." They noted that the Court had determined violations of the right to property and to consultation of the indigenous communities who were the victims in the case. Therefore, they understood that it should be inferred that the legislative and/or other measures that the Court had ordered to ensure the right to property should "contain a specific section on the right to consultation," because the former right could not be ensured without the latter. They indicated that, despite this, "the judgment did not expressly mention this," which was the reason for the interpretation they were requesting.[7]

14. The *State* argued that the fact "that the Argentine Republic has the obligation to ensure the right to consultation of the indigenous

---

[6] Cf. *Case of Escher et al.* v. *Brazil. Interpretation of the judgment on Preliminary objections, merits, reparations and costs.* Judgment of November 20, 2009. Series C No 208, para. 11, and *Case of Rosadio Villavicencio* v. *Peru*, para. 12.

[7] The representatives also recalled that, during the proceedings, they had requested that the Court order, as a measure of reparation, the enactment of norms that ensured the right to consultation. They noted that their request was set forth in paragraph 351 of the judgment and was not explicitly denied therein.

communities is not in dispute, in light of the applicable commitments under international human rights law." It indicated that, nevertheless, the Court "has not included the duty of the Argentine State to legislate the right to consultation in general terms, so that the claim of the victims' representatives exceeds the scope of interpretation of judgment," because "it seeks to repeat the debate in order to expand the reparations that have already been ordered."

15. Argentina also argued that judgment should be understood in a "harmonious way, integrating [their] considerations and conclusions, [. . .] and it was inadmissible to do this in a biased manner." It considered that the Court:

Throughout its judgment, had taken a very clear position with regard to the right to free, prior and informed consultation of the indigenous communities in the case of projects to be executed on their territories, [. . .] and also had determined the need to adapt or enact laws and regulations that establish an adequate procedure to this end according to the circumstances of each case.[8]

Therefore, it argued that the decision adopted in the eighth operative paragraph[9] "complements the considerations and reasoning included throughout the judgment." Consequently, it understood that the representatives' request for interpretation was "inadmissible."

16. The *Commission* understood that the representatives' request sought to determine the "meaning or scope" of the fifteenth operative paragraph of the judgment and therefore "fell within the parameters" established by Article 68 of the Court's Rules of Procedure. It noted that, in paragraph 184 of the judgment, the Court had concluded that Argentina had failed to comply with the obligation to ensure adequate consultation mechanisms and that, in paragraph 328 of the judgment, the Court ordered the State to abstain from carrying out certain actions on the territory of the indigenous communities victims without prior and adequate consultation procedures. It also noted that "the Court determined, in paragraph 353 of the judgment that existing legal regulations in Argentina are insufficient to provide legal certainty to the right to indigenous communal property." Nevertheless, the

---

[8]   The State supported its assertion recalling the Court's considerations in paragraphs 173, 174, 175, 179, 328, 351, 352, 353 and 354, in footnote 334 corresponding to paragraph 355, and in the eighth operative paragraph.
[9]   The eighth operative paragraph of the judgment states: "The State shall refrain from implementing actions, public works or undertakings on the indigenous territory or that might affect its existence, value, use and enjoyment, without previously informing the indigenous communities that have been identified as victims, and conducting adequate, free and informed prior consultation, pursuant to the standards established in this judgment, as established in paragraphs 328 and 343 of this judgment."

Commission indicated that those determinations "do not have a specific parallel mention" in the fifteenth operative paragraph, which orders the adoption of legislative and/or other measures. Therefore, it "agree[d with the representatives in] the pertinence of clarifying the scope of the reparation ordered so as to have greater certainty and to facilitate its execution."

B. *Considerations of the Court*

17. The representatives asked the Court to clarify whether, pursuant to the measure ordered in the fifteenth operative paragraph of the judgment, the right to prior consultation was included among the aspects that should be established in the legislative and/or other measures that the State must adopt to provide legal certainty to the right to indigenous communal property. In particular, the representatives' request referred to whether the measures indicated should "contain a specific section on the right to consultation" (*supra* para. 13).

18. This Court understands that the request for interpretation is admissible and will now respond to it.[10] To this end, it recalls that, in its judgment it determined two aspects of the violation of the right to indigenous communal property: (a) the first, as can be seen from paragraphs 167 and 168 of the judgment, based on the failure to provide adequate title to the land, the failure to demarcate the property, and the continued presence of third parties, as well as the lack of appropriate laws to guarantee the right to communal property satisfactorily, and (b) the second, as established in its paragraph 184, owing to Argentina's failure to comply with "its obligation to ensure appropriate mechanisms for free, prior and informed consultation of the indigenous communities concerned," in relation to the construction of an international bridge. Then, among the diverse measures of reparation ordered, the Court established, in the fifteenth operative paragraph, the duty of the State to "adopt the necessary legislative and/or any other measures to provide legal certainty to the right to indigenous communal property, pursuant to paragraphs 354 to 357 of th[e] judgment."

---

[10] Additionally, the Court emphasizes that, although the State has argued the inadmissibility of the request for interpretation, it has done so while providing a response to it; namely, that the order given in the fifteenth operative paragraph does not include the duty "to legislate" on prior consultation (*supra* para. 14). However, while asserting the foregoing, Argentina argued that, in relation to the right to consultation, the judgment "has established the need to adapt or to issue regulations and laws that establish an adequate procedure" (*supra* para. 15). This leads to the understanding that the interpretation of the decision is appropriate and useful to ensure correct compliance with what was ordered.

19. First, the Court will review the order given to adopt legislative and/or other measures, the reasons for this order and its scope. Then, it will set forth its conclusion and clarification requested.

B.1. The order to adopt legislative and/or other measures

20. The Court noted, in paragraph 166 of the judgment, that, owing to "legal problems [. . .], the right to property of the indigenous communities in this case has not received effective protection." According to paragraphs 164 and 162 of the judgment, respectively, these legal problems consist in "[t]he failure of these [State] norms to address the issue of indigenous property adequately and sufficiently [as] inferred from national legislation following the 1994 constitutional reform"; in particular, with regard to "procedures for claiming indigenous lands." Therefore, in paragraph 168 of the judgment, the Court determined a violation of the right to indigenous communal property in relation not only to the obligations to respect and to ensure rights established in Article 1(1) of the Convention, but also in relation to the adoption of domestic legal provisions, established in Article 2 of this instrument.[11]

21. It was on this basis that, when establishing the corresponding measures of reparation, the Court found it appropriate to order the adoption of legislative and/or other measures, recalling, in paragraph 353 of the judgment—in the chapter on reparations—"that the existing legal regulations are insufficient to provide legal certainty to the right to indigenous communal property since they fail to establish specific procedures that are appropriate for this purpose."

22. Consequently in its fifteenth operative paragraph, the judgment established: "[t]he State, within a reasonable time, shall adopt the necessary legislative and/or any other measures to provide legal certainty to the right to indigenous communal property, pursuant to paragraphs 354 to 357 of th[e] judgment."

23. Accordingly, the purpose of this measure is to redress the insufficiency of domestic law that the Court had noted in relation to the right to indigenous communal property. This insufficiency refers to

---

[11]   It also did so in relation to the rights to judicial guarantees and to judicial protection, the standards for which establish the due process of law that must be observed in the mechanisms that the State must adopt to implement indigenous territorial rights. In this regard, paragraph 116 of the judgment indicates that, "in order to implement the territorial rights of the indigenous peoples, States must provide an effective mechanism by the adoption of the necessary legislative and administrative measures," and that this mechanism must "meet the requirements of due process established in Articles 8 and 25 of the American Convention."

the measures to claim indigenous communal property and to its recognition. As already indicated (*supra* para. 20), this is in accordance with the analysis made in paragraphs 158 to 166 of the judgment, under the heading "Impact of domestic law," and also, pursuant to the conclusion presented in the following paragraphs, 167 and 168.

24. Evidently, and notwithstanding the foregoing, the order given to adopt the necessary legislative and/or any other measures to provide legal certainty to the right to indigenous communal property, could not be executed adequately if this were to be done in a way that was incompatible with the right of the indigenous peoples and communities to prior, adequate, free and informed consultations, or disregarding this right. Therefore, in order to ensure the effective participation of indigenous peoples or communities in actions that may affect their territories, including by adequate consultation processes, it is a necessary element to guarantee the right to indigenous communal property.

25. The foregoing results from the terms of the judgment, paragraph 354 of which, while establishing the "order" to the State "within a reasonable time, to adopt the legislative and/or other measures necessary [. . .] to provide legal certainty to the human right to indigenous communal property," indicates that this should be done "pursuant to the guidelines indicated in th[e] judgment," expressly referring to its paragraphs 93 to 98, 115 and 116.

26. According to paragraph 98 of the judgment, the Court notes that States must refrain from carrying out actions that may "adversely affect the existence, value, use and enjoyment of [indigenous] territory," and "guarantee the right of the indigenous peoples to truly control and use their territory and natural resources [. . .] without any type of external interference from third parties."[12] As paragraph 94 of the judgment indicates:

[A]ny activities by the State or third parties that could "affect the integrity of the land and natural resources" should respect certain parameters that the State must guarantee: the real participation of the communities concerned; their reasonable benefit, and the prior execution of social and environmental impact assessment.[13]

---

[12] Similarly, later, in paragraph 115 of the judgment, the Court indicated, *inter alia*, that, in the "context" of the "legal certainty [of] the indigenous ownership of land," "the diverse and specific ways and means of control, ownership, use and enjoyment of the territories by the communities should be acknowledged, without interference from third parties."

[13] Paragraph 94 of the judgment, regarding the part transcribed, cites previous case law of the Court: *Case of the Saramaka People* v. *Suriname. Preliminary objections, merits, reparations and costs.* Judgment of November 28, 2007, Series C No 173, para. 129 and footnote 124.

27. Later, the judgment makes it clear that to "ensure the effective participation" of the indigenous peoples or communities, "in conformity with their customs and traditions," in the corresponding circumstances the State is required to conduct consultations, in good faith, using culturally acceptable procedures aimed at reaching agreements.[14] Due to the failure to comply with this obligation in relation to the construction of an international bridge, the Court determined that the State had failed to respect the process of prior, free and informed consultation and had therefore violated the rights to indigenous communal property and to the participation of the communities victims.[15] These considerations should be taken into account because, as this Court has already indicated, the correct procedure is "to make an integral reading of the judgment rather than considering each paragraph of the judgment as if it was independent from the others."[16]

28. Therefore, the guidelines referred to in paragraph 354 of the judgment (*supra* para. 25) include the effective participation of the indigenous communities with regard to the implementation of activities that could affect the integrity of the lands and natural resources, which, in the pertinent circumstances, results in the realization of prior, adequate, free and informed consultations.

29. Consequently, the legislative and/or other measures that the State should adopt, according to the fifteenth operative paragraph of the judgment, must be appropriate to provide adequate means for claiming and for recognition of indigenous communal property, in a way that ensures legal certainty to the right to communal property considering its different elements, which include the implementation of consultations and participation in them, pursuant to the preceding paragraphs.

---

[14] *Case of the Indigenous Communities members of the Lhaka Honhat (Our Land) Association v. Argentina. Merits, reparations and costs.* Judgment of February 6, 2020. Series C No 400, para. 174. This paragraph, in the part transcribed, cites, *inter alia*, previous case law of the Court: *Case of the Saramaka People v. Suriname*, para. 133; *Case of the Kichwa Indigenous People of Sarayaku v. Ecuador. Merits and reparations.* Judgment of June 27, 2012. Series C No 245, para. 186, and *Case of the Kaliña and Lokono Peoples v. Suriname. Merits, reparations and costs.* Judgment of November 25, 2015. Series C No 309, para. 201.

[15] *Cf. Case of the Indigenous Communities members of the Lhaka Honhat (Our Land) Association v. Argentina*, paras. 180 to 184.

[16] *Case of Pollo Rivera et al. v. Peru. Request for interpretation of the judgment on merits, reparations and costs.* Judgment of May 25, 2017. Series C No 335, para. 26, and *Case of Alvarado Espinoza et al. v. Mexico. Interpretation of the judgment on merits, reparations and costs.* Judgment of August 30, 2019. Series C No 381, para. 18.

B.2. Conclusion

30. Therefore, the Court, responding to the request for interpretation presented by the victims' representatives, stipulates the following: the measures that the State should adopt, pursuant to the fifteenth operative paragraph and paragraph 354 of the judgment, must be appropriate to provide adequate means for claiming and for recognition of indigenous communal property in a way that ensures legal certainty to the right to communal property considering the different elements that compose this right, and those established in the judgment pursuant to its paragraphs 93 to 98, 115 and 116, including, the "garant[ee of] the effective participation" of indigenous communities, through prior, free and informed consultation based on the considerations made in this judgment on interpretation.

V. OPERATIVE PARAGRAPHS

31. Therefore,

THE COURT,

pursuant to Article 67 of the American Convention on Human Rights and Articles 31(3) and 68 of its Rules of Procedure,

Decides:

Unanimously,

(1) To declare admissible the request presented by the victims' representatives for interpretation of the judgment on merits, reparations and costs delivered in the *Case of the Indigenous Communities members of the Lhaka Honhat (Our Land) Association* v. *Argentina*, pursuant to paragraphs 6, 7, 17 and 18 of this judgment on interpretation.

(2) To clarify, by interpretation, the judgment on merits, reparations and costs delivered in the *Case of the Indigenous Communities members of the Lhaka Honhat (Our Land) Association* v. *Argentina*, with regard to the reparation ordered in the fifteenth operative paragraph of that judgment, in the sense that the legislative and/or other measures that the State should adopt to provide legal certainty to the right to indigenous communal property should include, among the different elements that this right encompasses, prior, free and informed consultation, pursuant to the considerations contained in paragraphs 20 to 30 of this judgment on interpretation.

(3) To require the Secretariat of the Court to notify this interpretation judgment to the Argentine Republic, the representatives of the victims and the Inter-American Commission on Human Rights.

[Report: Inter-Am. Ct HR (Series C) No 420]

International tribunals — International Tribunal for the Law of the Sea ("ITLOS") — Constitution of a Special Chamber — Article 15, paragraph 2, of the Statute of the ITLOS, 1982

International tribunals — Jurisdiction — Preliminary objections to the jurisdiction of the Special Chamber — Article 294 of United Nations Convention on the Law of the Sea, 1982 ("UNCLOS") — Indispensable third party — Competence over the interpretation or application of UNCLOS — Paragraph 1 of Article 288 of UNCLOS — Sovereignty over the Chagos Archipelago — *Chagos* Arbitral Award of 18 March 2015 under Annex VII of UNCLOS — ICJ's *Chagos* Advisory Opinion of 25 February 2019 — Legal effects of determinations found in non-binding advisory opinions — United Nations General Assembly Resolution 73/295 of 22 May 2019 — Determination of the coastal State in application of Articles 74 and 83 of UNCLOS — Obligation to negotiate under Articles 74 and 83 of UNCLOS — Notion of dispute — Existence of a dispute between the Parties

International tribunals — Admissibility — Preliminary objection to the admissibility of the claim — Article 294 of United Nations Convention on the Law of the Sea, 1982 — Abuse of process

Dispute concerning Delimitation of the Maritime Boundary between Mauritius and Maldives in the Indian Ocean

(Mauritius/Maldives)[1]

International Tribunal for the Law of the Sea

---

[1] Mauritius was represented by Mr Dheerendra Kumar Dabee, GOSK, SC, Solicitor-General, Attorney General's Office, as Agent; Mr Jagdish Dharamchand Koonjul, GOSK, Ambassador and Permanent Representative of the Republic of Mauritius to the United Nations in New York, United States of America, as Co-Agent; Professor Philippe Sands QC, Mr Paul S. Reichler and Professor Pierre Klein, as Counsel and Advocates; Mr Remi Reichhold, Mr Andrew Loewenstein, Ms Diem Huang Ho, Mr Yuri Parkhomenko and Ms Anjolie Singh, as Counsel; Mr Shiu Ching Young Kim Fat, as Adviser; Mr Scott Edmonds and Mr Thomas Frogh, as Technical Advisers, and Ms Lea Main-Klingst, as Assistant. The Maldives was represented by Mr Ibrahim Riffath, Attorney General, as Agent; Ms Khadeeja Shabeen, Deputy Attorney General and Ms Salwa Habeeb, Senior State Counsel in the Office of the Attorney General, as Representatives; Professor Payam Akhavan, Professor Alan Boyle, Professor Jean-Marc Thouvenin, and Dr Naomi Hart, as Counsel and Advocates; Mr John Brown, as Technical Adviser; and Dr Justine Bendel, Mr Mitchell Lennan, and Ms Melina Antoniadis, as Assistants. The judgment of 28 April 2023 on the Merits will be reported in a future volume of the *International Law Reports*.

Preliminary Objections.   28 *January* 2021

(Paik, *President of the Special Chamber*; Jesus, Pawlak, Yanai,
Bouguetaia, Heidar, Chadha, *Judges*; Oxman, Schrijver,
Judges ad hoc)[2]

SUMMARY:[3] *The facts*:—On 24 September 2019, a Special Agreement
was concluded between the Parties to submit a dispute concerning the delimitation of the maritime boundary between them in the Indian Ocean to a
Special Chamber of the International Tribunal for the Law of the Sea ("the
Special Chamber"), in accordance with Article 15, paragraph 2, of the Statute
of the Tribunal, 1982. On 18 December 2019, the Maldives filed preliminary
objections to the jurisdiction of the Special Chamber and the admissibility of
the claims of Mauritius, in accordance with Article 294 of the United Nations
Convention on the Law of the Sea ("UNCLOS") and Article 97 of the Rules
of the International Tribunal for the Law of the Sea.

In 1814, Mauritius and its dependencies, including the Chagos
Archipelago, were ceded by France to the United Kingdom. Prior to
Mauritius' independence in 1968, the Chagos Archipelago was detached on
8 November 1965 by the United Kingdom, as provided in the British Indian
Ocean Territory Order. This prompted the United Nations General Assembly
("UNGA") to adopt on 16 December 1965 Resolution 2066 (XX) which
pointed out that the United Kingdom's steps were taken in contravention of
the UNGA Resolution 1514 (XV) entitled "Declaration on the Granting of
Independence to Colonial Countries and Peoples". Nevertheless, the Chagos
Archipelago remained under the administration of the United Kingdom after
Mauritius acceded to independence in 1968. According to the Maldives, the
United Kingdom had consistently claimed sovereignty over the Chagos
Archipelago since 1814, and reaffirmed it in 1965. Additionally, according
to the Maldives, Mauritius had claimed sovereignty over the Archipelago since
at least 1980.

On 1 April 2010, the United Kingdom announced the creation of a
marine protected area ("MPA") in and around the Chagos Archipelago, which
prompted Mauritius to institute arbitral proceedings against it under Annex
VII of UNCLOS, contesting the United Kingdom's status of coastal State
which would allow it to declare such a maritime zone. On 18 March 2015, the
arbitral tribunal rendered its Award and found that it lacked jurisdiction to
determine whether the United Kingdom was the coastal State and therefore
entitled to declare the MPA.[4] It concluded that it only had partial jurisdiction
to determine the compatibility of the MPA with certain UNCLOS provisions,

---

[2] Judges ad hoc Oxman and Schrijver were appointed, respectively, by Maldives and Mauritius
under Article 17 of the Statute of the Tribunal, 1982.
[3] Prepared by Ms J. Joly-Hébert.
[4] *Chagos Marine Protected Area (Republic of Mauritius* v. *United Kingdom) (Award)*, 162 ILR 1.

and that the United Kingdom was acting in breach of its obligations under the UNCLOS.[5]

Through Resolution 71/292, the UNGA requested an advisory opinion from the International Court of Justice ("ICJ") on certain questions related to the Chagos Archipelago, namely whether the process of decolonization of Mauritius had been lawfully completed when Mauritius became independent in 1968, in light of the prior separation of the Chagos Archipelago, and with regard to the consequences in international law of the continued administration of the Chagos Archipelago by the United Kingdom. On 25 February 2019, the ICJ rendered its opinion that the United Kingdom's continued administration of the Chagos Archipelago was an unlawful act of a continuing character.[6] It concluded that "the process of decolonization of Mauritius was not lawfully completed", that the United Kingdom was "under an obligation to bring to an end its administration of the Chagos Archipelago as rapidly as possible", and that "all Member States [were] under an obligation to co-operate with the United Nations in order to complete the decolonization of Mauritius."[7] On 22 May 2019, the UNGA adopted Resolution 73/295 which demanded that the United Kingdom "withdraw its colonial administration from the Chagos Archipelago unconditionally within a period of no more than six months from the adoption of the present resolution, thereby enabling Mauritius to complete the decolonization of its territory as rapidly as possible".

Mauritius and the Maldives had been engaged in discussions with regard to their maritime boundary and the delimitation of their continental shelf since 2010. Both States were Parties to UNCLOS. The Maldives raised five preliminary objections against the jurisdiction of the Special Chamber and the admissibility of Mauritius' claims.

Held:—All five preliminary objections raised by the Maldives (subparagraphs (1) to (5) of the *dispositif*) were rejected.

(1) The first two objections raised by the Maldives were considered together.

(a) On the basis of the conclusions reached in the *Chagos* Arbitral Award, the existence of a sovereignty dispute over the Chagos Archipelago between Mauritius and the United Kingdom was accepted. Nevertheless, the conclusions reached by the Arbitral Tribunal did not mean that the United Kingdom had been recognized as the coastal State in respect of the Chagos Archipelago. The Award could still have some relevance in its evaluation of whether

---

[5] *Chagos Marine Protected Area (Republic of Mauritius v. United Kingdom) (Award)*, 162 ILR 152-8.

[6] *Legal Consequences of the Separation of the Chagos Archipelago from Mauritius in 1965*, 192 ILR 84.

[7] *Legal Consequences of the Separation of the Chagos Archipelago from Mauritius in 1965*, 192 ILR 84, para. 183.

Mauritius could be considered as the State with an opposite or adjacent coast to the Maldives (paras. 79-80 and 128-39).

(b) The ICJ's findings in the *Chagos* Advisory Opinion had, in fact, clarified the issue of sovereignty over Chagos, and that the Special Chamber was competent to evaluate the consequences stemming from it. Even though advisory opinions were not considered to be legally binding, they could offer "an authoritative statement of international law" and "judicial determinations made in advisory opinions carr[ied] no less weight and authority than those in judgments". There was a close relationship between the decolonization and sovereignty of Mauritius, including the Chagos Archipelago, and that the ICJ's determinations could be interpreted as an acceptance of the sovereignty of Mauritius over the Chagos Archipelago (paras. 162-75, 188-92 and 202-6).

(c) Even though UNGA resolutions were not binding, the general functions of the UNGA with regard to decolonization meant that Resolution 73/295 was relevant to determine the legal status of Chagos, especially the UNGA's statement therein that the Chagos Archipelago "forms an integral part of the territory of Mauritius" (paras. 224-30).

(d) (unanimously) The first objection to jurisdiction was rejected. In light of the findings in the Arbitral Award, the Chagos Archipelago had been subjected to a special regime, under which Mauritius had certain rights. The continued claim of sovereignty of the United Kingdom over Chagos was contrary to the ICJ's findings in its Advisory Opinion, which had legal effect. Resolution 73/295 and the non-compliance of the United Kingdom with its terms further exemplified that the United Kingdom's claims over Chagos were contrary to the Advisory Opinion of the ICJ. Any remaining interests the United Kingdom may have retained over the Chagos Archipelago were not sufficient for this State to be considered as an indispensable third party to the proceedings (paras. 246-8).

(e) (by eight votes to one, Judge ad hoc Oxman dissenting) Moreover, Mauritius was to be considered as the coastal State in respect of the Chagos Archipelago for the purpose of the delimitation of a maritime boundary with the Maldives within the meaning of Article 74, paragraph 1, and Article 83, paragraph 1, of UNCLOS. The second objection by the Maldives was also rejected (paras. 249-51).

(2) (a) Article 74, paragraph 1, and Article 83, paragraph 1, comprised an obligation to negotiate in good faith, with the objective of reaching an agreement, even though such agreement may not be, in fact, reached. If States failed to reach an agreement, they could delimit their exclusive economic zone and continental shelf by resorting to the dispute settlement procedures found in Part XV of UNCLOS (paras. 267-75).

(b) (by eight votes to one, Judge ad hoc Oxman dissenting) The third objection to jurisdiction was rejected. The Parties had complied with the requirement to negotiate laid down in Articles 74 and 83 of UNCLOS. On 21 October 2010, the two States had met to discuss their delimitation. Mauritius had attempted, on several occasions, to negotiate with the Maldives. While the latter State had met Mauritius, it had refused to engage in meaningful negotiations, claiming that jurisdiction over Chagos was not being exercised by Mauritius. Nothing else could have been done on Mauritius' part to engage with the Maldives (paras. 283 and 288-93).

(3) (unanimously) The fourth objection to jurisdiction was rejected. The different national legislation of the Parties, namely Mauritius' Maritime Zones Act 1977 and the Maldives' Law No 30/76 of 1976, clearly demonstrated that their respective maritime claims to an exclusive economic zone and continental shelf beyond 200 nautical miles overlapped. Mauritius' formal protests with regard to the submissions made by the Maldives to the Commission on the Limits of the Continental Shelf ("CLCS") showed an opposition of views between the Parties. The dispute did not have to limit itself to the actual location of the maritime boundary. Finally, a dispute existed between the Parties long before the ICJ's *Chagos* Advisory Opinion. That dispute did not need to crystallize in the short window of time between the ICJ's Opinion and the commencement of the present proceedings. For all these reasons, a dispute on a point of law or fact, of which the respondent State was aware, existed between the Parties at the time of the filing of the notification (paras. 320-36).

(4) (a) (unanimously) The fifth objection to jurisdiction was rejected. Mauritius had resorted to the dispute settlement procedures found in Part XV in accordance with Article 74, paragraph 2, and Article 83, paragraph 2, of UNCLOS. Mauritius' claim concerned those provisions of UNCLOS and did not constitute an abuse of process (paras. 345-50).

(b) (by eight votes to one, Judge ad hoc Oxman dissenting) The Special Chamber had jurisdiction to adjudicate the dispute between Mauritius and the Maldives concerning the delimitation of their maritime boundary in the Indian Ocean and Mauritius' claim was admissible. It decided to defer to the proceedings on the merits questions concerning the extent to which it may exercise its jurisdiction (paras. 351-2 and 354).

(c) (unanimously) The consideration of Mauritius' claims in relation to Article 74, paragraph 3, and Article 83, paragraph 3, were deferred to the proceedings on the merits (paras. 353-4).

Joint Declaration of Judges ad hoc Oxman and Schrijver: (1) The Special Chamber in subparagraph (6) of the *dispositif* wisely deferred to the merits stage questions concerning the extent to which the Special Chamber might exercise its jurisdiction (para. 2).

(2) Subparagraph (7) of the *dispositif* referred to the claim of violation as found in paragraph 28 of the notification, but did not question the Parties' duty to comply with Article 74, paragraph 3, and Article 83, paragraph 3, of UNCLOS (para. 3).

Separate and Dissenting Opinion of Judge ad hoc Oxman: (1) The request to draw a maritime boundary between the Parties was not yet admissible. Articles

74, paragraph 3, and 83, paragraph 3, of UNCLOS applied to the Parties' activities in the zone within 200 nautical miles of the coast of both the Maldives and the Chagos Archipelago (para. 1).

(2) This case did not demonstrate the existence of a dispute with regard to the maritime boundary or the method to be used to fix it. Restraint accordingly had to be exercised; in the light of the history of the dispute opposing Mauritius to the United Kingdom, there was no need to draw other parties into this dispute (paras. 2 and 7).

(3) Paragraph 1 of Articles 74 and 83 did not require delimitation; only paragraph 2 of those Articles could compel delimitation, but did not necessarily do so as they did not impose a jurisdictional limitation as such. The term "reasonable period of time" could be understood as regulating the admissibility of a delimitation claim and offering some latitude. A case-specific analysis could be required to determine if the time had come for a fixed maritime boundary to be drawn, bearing in mind that the obligations found in paragraph 3 of Articles 74 and 83, relating to the conduct of States in the area of overlapping entitlements, remained applicable pending delimitation. Moreover, the existence of maritime overlapping entitlements did not mean that a dispute had arisen and had to be addressed under Part XV of UNCLOS, which referred not only to arbitration and adjudication, but to all dispute settlement procedures, including conciliation. Such disputes usually arose after a maritime boundary had been claimed or when a specific method of delimitation had been rejected by the other Party (paras. 9-17 and 43-9).

(4) Regarding the nature and scope of the dispute, while there were overlapping entitlements between Mauritius and the Maldives, neither Party had yet made any concrete proposal regarding delimitation. The differences of views between the States were evident from the Maldives' submissions to the CLCS. Mauritius' view regarding the effects of the ICJ's *Chagos* Advisory Opinion conflated the distinction between the authoritative nature of such opinions and their legally binding effects, as well as the distinction between the UNGA's capacity to deal with a subject-matter and the bindingness of its conclusions. By implying that the Special Chamber should have reached the same conclusions as the ICJ or those found in the UNGA's resolution with respect to the sovereignty of Chagos, it risked complicating the exercise by the General Assembly of its political functions and the exercise by the ICJ of its discretion with respect to requests for advisory opinions (paras. 18-33).

(5) Considering the formality and finality of boundaries, either land or maritime, paragraph 1 of Articles 74 and 83 of UNCLOS could not be interpreted as requiring a State to conduct negotiations on a maritime boundary when it declined to negotiate to avoid entanglement with a third State. Mauritius' request was not yet admissible, and the objections raised by the Maldives did not need to be decided (paras. 34-42).

The text of the judgment of the Special Chamber and the declaration and separate and dissenting opinion is set out as follows:

The following is the text of the judgment of the Special Chamber:[8]

TABLE OF CONTENTS

---

[8]   The text of the judgment is also available at DOI 10.1163/9789004516946_003.

I. INTRODUCTION

1. By letter dated 23 August 2019, the Solicitor-General of the Republic of Mauritius (hereinafter "Mauritius") informed the President of the International Tribunal for the Law of the Sea (hereinafter "the Tribunal") of the institution of arbitral proceedings by Mauritius against the Republic of the Maldives (hereinafter "the Maldives") on 18 June 2019, pursuant to Annex VII to the United Nations Convention on the Law of the Sea (hereinafter "the Convention"). Attached to that letter was the Notification and the Statement of the claim and grounds on which it is based (hereinafter "the Notification") of Mauritius dated 18 June 2019, instituting arbitral proceedings against the Maldives under Annex VII to the Convention "in the

dispute concerning the maritime boundary between Mauritius and Maldives".

2. Following consultations held by the President of the Tribunal with representatives of Mauritius and the Maldives in Hamburg on 17 September 2019, a Special Agreement was concluded between the two States on 24 September 2019 to submit the dispute concerning the delimitation of the maritime boundary between them in the Indian Ocean to a special chamber of the Tribunal to be formed pursuant to article 15, paragraph 2, of the Statute of the Tribunal (hereinafter "the Statute").

3. The Special Agreement and Notification between Mauritius and the Maldives dated 24 September 2019 (hereinafter "the Special Agreement"), in its relevant part, reads as follows:

Special Agreement and Notification

1. Pursuant to article 15, paragraph 2, of the Statute of the International Tribunal for the Law of the Sea (hereinafter "the Tribunal"), the Republic of Mauritius and the Republic of Maldives hereby record their agreement to submit to a special chamber of the Tribunal the dispute concerning the delimitation of the maritime boundary between them in the Indian Ocean. The agreement was reached on 24 September 2019, under the conditions reflected in the agreed Minutes of Consultations (17 September 2019), attached hereto.

2. The Republic of Mauritius and the Republic of Maldives further record their agreement that the special chamber shall be composed of the following nine individuals:

Judge Jin-Hyun Paik, as President
Judge José Luis Jesus
Judge Jean-Pierre Cot
Judge Shunji Yanai
Judge Boualem Bouguetaia
Judge Tomas Heidar
Judge Neeru Chadha
Mr Bernard Oxman, Judge ad hoc (Republic of Maldives)
Judge ad hoc to be chosen by the Republic of Mauritius

3. Receipt by the Registry of the Tribunal of the electronic copy of this Agreement and Notification signed by both Parties shall constitute the notification contemplated in article 55 of the Rules of the Tribunal. The date on which the Registry of the Tribunal has received this electronic copy will constitute the date of the institution of proceedings before the Tribunal. The original of the Special Agreement and Notification should be submitted to the Tribunal forthwith.

4. The Minutes of Consultations agreed between Mauritius and the Maldives on 17 September 2019 and attached to the Special Agreement read in their relevant part as follows:

3. During the consultations, the Parties agreed to transfer the arbitral proceedings instituted by Mauritius in the dispute concerning the delimitation of the maritime boundary between Mauritius and the Maldives in the Indian Ocean to a special chamber of the Tribunal to be formed pursuant to article 15, paragraph 2, of the Statute. The Parties agreed that the date of the institution of proceedings before the Tribunal is the date on which the Registry of the Tribunal has received the electronic copy of the Special Agreement and Notification signed by both Parties (see paragraph 3 of the Special Agreement and Notification). The proceedings of the special chamber of the Tribunal shall be governed by the provisions contained in the Statute and the Rules of the Tribunal.

4. The Parties agreed that the special chamber to be formed pursuant to article 15, paragraph 2, of the Statute shall be composed of nine members, two of whom will be judges ad hoc chosen by the Parties in accordance with article 17 of the Statute of the Tribunal. The composition of the special chamber will be determined by the Tribunal with the approval of the parties. In this respect, the Parties have agreed on the following names:

Judge Jin-Hyun Paik, as President
Judge José Luis Jesus
Judge Jean-Pierre Cot
Judge Shunji Yanai
Judge Boualem Bouguetaia
Judge Tomas Heidar
Judge Neeru Chadha

Mauritius has not yet chosen its judge ad hoc but will make its nomination in due course. Maldives has chosen Mr Bernard Oxman as judge ad hoc.

5. An electronic copy of the Special Agreement was received by the Registry on 24 September 2019 and the original was received on 7 October 2019. Pursuant to paragraph 3 of the Special Agreement, receipt by the Registry of the electronic copy of the Special Agreement signed by both Parties constituted the notification contemplated in article 55 of the Rules of the Tribunal (hereinafter "the Rules").

6. As stated in the Special Agreement, the Government of Mauritius had appointed Mr Dheerendra Kumar Dabee, GOSK, SC, Solicitor-General, as Agent for Mauritius, and the Government of the Maldives had appointed Mr Ibrahim Riffath, Attorney General, as Agent for the Maldives.

7. By Order dated 27 September 2019, the Tribunal decided to accede to the request of Mauritius and the Maldives to form a special

chamber of nine judges to deal with the dispute concerning delimitation of their maritime boundary in the Indian Ocean (hereinafter
"the Special Chamber"), and determined, with the approval of the
Parties, the composition of the Special Chamber as follows:

President	Paik
Judges	Jesus
	Cot
	Yanai
	Bouguetaia
	Heidar
	Chadha
Judge ad hoc	Oxman
Judge ad hoc	to be chosen by Mauritius.

8. In the Order, the Tribunal stated that, in the Special Agreement,
the Maldives had notified the Tribunal of its choice of Mr Bernard
Oxman to sit as judge ad hoc in the Special Chamber, and that no
objection to the choice of Mr Oxman as judge ad hoc appeared to the
Tribunal. The Tribunal also stated that, in the Special Agreement,
Mauritius had notified the Tribunal of its intention to choose a judge
ad hoc.

9. The Registrar transmitted a copy of the Order of 27 September
2019 to the Parties on the same date.

10. The case was entered in the List of Cases as Case No 28.

11. By letter dated 27 September 2019, the Registrar, pursuant to
the Agreement on Cooperation and Relationship between the United
Nations and the International Tribunal for the Law of the Sea of
18 December 1997 (hereinafter "the Relationship Agreement"), notified the Secretary-General of the United Nations of the institution of
proceedings. By a note verbale of the same date, the Registrar also
notified the States Parties to the Convention, in accordance with article
24, paragraph 3, of the Statute, of the institution of proceedings.

12. On 8 October 2019, in accordance with article 45 of the Rules,
telephone consultations were held by the President of the Special
Chamber with representatives of the Parties to ascertain their views
with regard to questions of procedure in respect of the case.

13. By letter dated 9 October 2019, the Agent of Mauritius
informed the Registrar that Mauritius had chosen Mr Nicolaas
Schrijver to sit as judge ad hoc in the case. The Registrar transmitted
a copy of the letter to the Maldives on the same date. No objection to
the choice of Mr Schrijver as judge ad hoc was raised by the Maldives,

and no objection appeared to the Special Chamber. Consequently, in accordance with article 19, paragraph 3, of the Rules, the Parties were informed by separate letters dated 4 November 2019 that Mr Schrijver would be admitted to participate in the proceedings as judge ad hoc, after having made the solemn declaration required under article 9 of the Rules.

14. Having ascertained the views of the Parties, by Order dated 10 October 2019, the President of the Special Chamber, in accordance with articles 59 and 61 of the Rules, fixed the following time-limits for the filing of the pleadings in the case: 9 April 2020 for the Memorial of Mauritius and 9 October 2020 for the Counter-Memorial of the Maldives. The Registrar transmitted a copy of the Order to the Parties on 10 October 2019.

15. By communication addressed to the Registrar and received on 18 December 2019, within the time-limit set by article 97, paragraph 1, of the Rules, the Maldives filed with the Special Chamber written preliminary objections "under article 294 of the Convention and article 97 of the Rules" to the jurisdiction of the Special Chamber and the admissibility of Mauritius' claims (hereinafter "the Preliminary Objections"). The Preliminary Objections were notified to Mauritius on the same date.

16. Upon receipt of the Preliminary Objections by the Registry, pursuant to article 97, paragraph 3, of the Rules, the proceedings on the merits were suspended, as noted in the Order of the President of the Special Chamber dated 19 December 2019.

17. By the same Order, the President of the Special Chamber fixed 17 February 2020 as the time-limit for Mauritius to file its written observations and submissions on the Preliminary Objections filed by the Maldives, and 17 April 2020 as the time-limit for the Maldives to file its written observations and submissions in reply. The Registrar transmitted a copy of the Order to the Parties on 19 December 2019.

18. Pursuant to the Relationship Agreement, the Registrar, by letter dated 18 December 2019, notified the Secretary-General of the United Nations of the Preliminary Objections filed by the Maldives in the case. By note verbale of the same date, the Registrar also notified the States Parties to the Convention of the Preliminary Objections.

19. In accordance with article 45 of the Rules, on 4 February 2020, the President of the Special Chamber held telephone consultations with the representatives of the Parties to ascertain their views with regard to questions of procedure in respect of the Preliminary Objections.

During these consultations, the Parties agreed that the hearing should take place from 24 to 27 June 2020.

20. Mauritius filed its written observations and submissions on the Preliminary Objections (hereinafter "the Observations") on 17 February 2020 and a copy thereof was transmitted to the Maldives on the same date.

21. The written observations and submissions in reply of the Maldives (hereinafter "the Reply") were filed on 15 April 2020 and a copy thereof was transmitted to Mauritius on the same date.

22. In light of the situation concerning the COVID-19 pandemic, including travel restrictions and safety considerations, by separate communications dated 7 May 2020, the Registrar sought the views of the Parties with regard to the feasibility of holding the hearing on the dates previously agreed.

23. The Maldives, by communication dated 8 May 2020, and Mauritius, by communication dated 13 May 2020, expressed their agreement that the hearing should take place during the week beginning 12 October 2020. The Registrar transmitted a copy of each communication to the other Party on 14 May 2020.

24. By Order dated 19 May 2020, the President of the Special Chamber, having ascertained the views of the Parties, fixed 13 October 2020 as the date for the opening of the oral proceedings. The Registrar transmitted a copy of the Order to the Parties on the same date.

25. By separate letters dated 28 July 2020, the Registrar, referring to the ongoing COVID-19 pandemic and the difficulty to organize an in-person hearing owing to health and safety concerns as well as travel and border restrictions, informed the Parties that the President of the Special Chamber was considering holding the hearing on the scheduled dates in hybrid format. The Registrar stated that a hearing in hybrid format would combine physical and virtual participation of members of the Special Chamber and representatives of the Parties.

26. The Maldives, by letter dated 4 August 2020, and Mauritius, by letter dated 6 August 2020, expressed their agreement that the hearing should be held in hybrid format. The Registrar transmitted a copy of each letter to the other Party on 7 August 2020.

27. By separate letters dated 13 August 2020, the Registrar informed the Parties that the President of the Special Chamber, having ascertained their views, had decided that the hearing would be conducted in hybrid format. On 19 August 2020, the Registrar informed the Parties by telephone of the intention of the members of the Special

Chamber, including the judges ad hoc, to participate in the hearing in person or remotely.

28. By letter dated 26 August 2020, the Registrar informed the Parties that Judge Cot had tendered his resignation as member of the Special Chamber by letter dated 26 August 2020 to the President of the Special Chamber with effect from that date, and that, accordingly, a vacancy had occurred in the Special Chamber. The Registrar also informed the Parties that the President of the Special Chamber wished to ascertain their views with regard to the Special Chamber's composition. Further to written consultations, the Parties agreed that Judge Pawlak should fill the vacancy left by the resignation of Judge Cot.

29. With regard to the information referred to in paragraph 27, the Maldives, by letter dated 26 August 2020, expressed concerns regarding the participation of the judges ad hoc in the proceedings "by different means". The Maldives stated that "[t]his could potentially undermine the fairness of the proceedings" and that "it is consistent with the practice of other international courts and tribunals for parties' respective appointed Judges to participate in hearings and deliberations on the same basis". Accordingly, the Maldives requested that, "if Judge ad hoc Oxman is to participate in the hearing remotely, then Judge ad hoc Schrijver should also be requested to participate remotely." A copy of the letter was transmitted by the Registrar to Mauritius on 27 August 2020.

30. By letter dated 31 August 2020, Mauritius opposed the Maldives' request. In the view of Mauritius, the Maldives' proposal "implies a differential treatment for one (or two) members of the Special Chamber from any of the others, and is inconsistent with the 'complete equality' of Judges ad hoc with other judges." With reference to article 17 of the Statute and article 8 of the Rules, Mauritius stated that "[t]he Statute and Rules of the Tribunal do not provide for any distinction of treatment as to these members of the Special Chamber." Mauritius also stated that it "[was] not aware of any precedent that supports … Maldives' proposal." In addition, Mauritius submitted that the Maldives "might have raised this matter at an earlier stage, when the question of a hybrid hearing was first raised, and the views of the parties were sought" but that "[i]t did not do so." A copy of the letter was transmitted by the Registrar to the Maldives on the same date.

31. On 1 September 2020, the President of the Special Chamber held telephone consultations with representatives of the Parties to

ascertain the views of the Parties regarding the organization of the hearing.

32. By letter dated 3 September 2020, the Maldives referred again to the issue of the participation of judges ad hoc in the proceedings, maintaining that it had "raised its concerns with the Registrar within two days of receiving the relevant information" and that "[t]here was no unreasonable delay whatsoever." In its letter, the Maldives also reiterated its request made on 26 August 2020. A copy of the letter was transmitted by the Registrar to Mauritius on 3 September 2020.

33. Mauritius responded by letter dated 4 September 2020, a copy of which the Registrar transmitted to the Maldives on the same day. In its letter, Mauritius referred to its previous arguments, stating, *inter alia*, that "all judges are equal" and that "ad hoc judges are to be treated no differently than sitting judges."

34. With regard to the participation of judges ad hoc in the hearing and meetings of the Special Chamber, pursuant to article 45 of the Rules, by letter to the Parties dated 8 September 2020, the President of the Special Chamber indicated that, "in light of the ongoing pandemic, both parties had agreed to hold the hearing in a hybrid format, in which members of the Special Chamber are allowed to participate either in person or remotely." He stated that "[s]uch format is based on the premise that there is no difference between the two modes of participation" and that "[a]ny suggestion to the contrary runs counter to this basic notion of a hybrid hearing." The President of the Special Chamber further stated that, in accordance with article 17, paragraph 6, of the Statute and article 8, paragraph 1, of the Rules, "ad hoc judges participate in a case 'on terms of complete equality' with the other judges" and that "[t]here is no ground whatsoever in the Statute or the Rules to treat ad hoc judges differently." He noted that "[i]t is up to each member of the Special Chamber, including judges ad hoc, to decide whether he or she participates in the hearing in person or remotely" and that he "fully respect[ed] the decision of each member in this regard." The President of the Special Chamber also assured the Parties that "each member, irrespective of his or her mode of participation, [would] be given an equal opportunity to participate fully in the proceedings of the Special Chamber."

35. By Order dated 15 September 2020, the Tribunal determined, with the approval of the Parties, that Judge Pawlak should fill the vacancy left by the resignation of Judge Cot and that as a result the composition of the Special Chamber formed to deal with this case was as follows:

President	Paik
Judges	Jesus
	Pawlak
	Yanai
	Bouguetaia
	Heidar
	Chadha
Judges ad hoc	Oxman
	Schrijver.

36. On 15 September 2020, the Registrar transmitted a copy of the Order to each Party.

37. By letter dated 6 October 2020 addressed to the President of the Special Chamber, received by the Registry on 7 October 2020, the Prime Minister of Mauritius notified the Special Chamber of the appointment of Mr Jagdish Dharamchand Koonjul, Ambassador and Permanent Representative of Mauritius to the United Nations in New York, as Co-Agent for Mauritius.

38. Prior to the opening of the oral proceedings, on 9 October 2020, the Agent of the Maldives and the Agent of Mauritius submitted to the Registry materials required under paragraph 14 of the Guidelines concerning the Preparation and Presentation of Cases before the Tribunal.

39. At a public sitting held in hybrid format on 12 October 2020, Mr Oxman and Mr Schrijver each made the solemn declaration required under article 9 of the Rules.

40. In accordance with article 68 of the Rules, on 12 October 2020, prior to the opening of the oral proceedings, the Special Chamber held initial deliberations in hybrid format.

41. On 12 October 2020, the President of the Special Chamber held consultations with representatives of the Parties at the premises of the Tribunal to ascertain the views of the Parties regarding the organization of the hearing.

42. Between 13 and 19 October 2020, the Special Chamber held four public sittings in hybrid format. At these sittings, the Special Chamber was addressed by the following:

For the Maldives: Mr Ibrahim Riffath,
as Agent;
Mr Payam Akhavan,
Mr Alan Boyle,
Mr Jean-Marc Thouvenin,

Ms Naomi Hart,
as Counsel and Advocates;
Ms Khadeeja Shabeen,
Ms Salwa Habeeb,
as Representatives;

For Mauritius: Mr Jagdish Dharamchand Koonjul,
as Co-Agent;
Mr Philippe Sands,
Mr Paul S. Reichler,
Mr Pierre Klein,
as Counsel and Advocates.

43. During the hearing, the Parties displayed a number of exhibits on screen, including maps and excerpts of documents.

44. The hearing was broadcast on the Internet as a webcast.

45. Pursuant to article 67, paragraph 2, of the Rules, copies of the pleadings and documents annexed thereto were made accessible to the public on the opening of the oral proceedings.

46. In accordance with article 86, paragraph 1, of the Rules, the transcript of the verbatim records of each public sitting was prepared by the Registry in the official languages of the Tribunal used during the hearing. In accordance with article 86, paragraph 4, of the Rules, copies of the transcripts of the said records were circulated to the judges sitting in the case and to the Parties. The transcripts were also made available to the public in electronic format.

47. By separate letters dated 15 October 2020, the Registrar communicated to the Parties, pursuant to article 76 of the Rules, a list of questions which the Special Chamber wished the Parties specially to address. These questions were as follows:

1. What were the legal considerations of the Parties in holding the first meeting on maritime delimitation and submission regarding the extended continental shelf of 21 October 2010 and in agreeing to "make bilateral arrangements on the overlapping area of extended continental shelf of the two States around the Chagos Archipelago" in the joint communiqué of 12 March 2011?

2. According to the Advisory Opinion of the International Court of Justice of 25 February 2019, "all Member States are under an obligation to co-operate with the United Nations in order to complete the decolonization of Mauritius." This obligation is further explained in paragraph 180 of the Advisory Opinion. Is this obligation relevant to the present case and, if so, how?

3. If delimitation were deferred for reasons indicated in the preliminary objections, what would be the obligations of the Parties under paragraph 3 of articles 74 and 83 of the Convention? Would there be jurisdiction with respect to those obligations?

48. Responses to the aforementioned questions were provided during the second round of oral pleadings by counsel for the Maldives on 17 October 2020, and by counsel for Mauritius on 19 October 2020.

49. By letter dated 16 October 2020 addressed to the President of the Special Chamber, the Agent of the Maldives, with reference to a statement made by counsel of Mauritius during the first round of oral pleadings, requested that the Maldives be allowed, pursuant to article 71 of the Rules, to submit additional documents. On the same date, the Agent of the Maldives transmitted to the Special Chamber the additional documents consisting of copies of three email communications between counsel for the Parties dated 27, 28 and 29 August 2019. On 17 October 2020, the Registrar transmitted the letter of 16 October 2020 and the additional documents to the Agent of Mauritius, in accordance with article 71 of the Rules, for comments the same day. By communication dated 17 October 2020, the Co-Agent of Mauritius informed the Special Chamber that Mauritius did not object to the Maldives' request.

50. By letter dated 17 October 2020, the Registrar informed the Agent of the Maldives that the documents submitted by the Maldives would be included in the case file and that the Maldives could refer to the documents in the second round of oral pleadings. A copy of the letter was transmitted to the Agent of Mauritius.

51. By letter dated 19 October 2020, the Co-Agent of Mauritius, pursuant to article 71, paragraph 4, of the Rules, provided comments on the new documents produced by the Maldives and submitted documents in support of his comments, consisting of copies of the three emails referred to in paragraph 49 and copies of further emails exchanged between counsel for the Parties during the period from 7 to 13 September 2019. By letter dated 19 October 2020, the Registrar transmitted Mauritius' letter and the attached documents to the Agent of the Maldives, indicating that, in accordance with article 71, paragraph 4, of the Rules, the letter and documents would form part of the case file and that Mauritius could refer to the documents in the second round of oral pleadings. A copy of the Registrar's letter was transmitted to the Agent of Mauritius.

52. By letter dated 19 October 2020, the Agent of the Maldives transmitted comments on the letter of Mauritius of 19 October 2020 and accompanying documents. A copy of the letter was transmitted to the Agent of Mauritius.

II. SUBMISSIONS OF THE PARTIES

53. In its Preliminary Objections, and in its Reply, the Maldives requested the Special Chamber to adjudge and declare that:

For the reasons set out in [the] Preliminary Objections ... it is without jurisdiction in respect of the claims submitted ... by the Republic of Mauritius. Additionally or alternatively, for the reasons set out in [the] Preliminary Objections, ... that the claims submitted ... by the Republic of Mauritius are inadmissible.

54. In its Observations, Mauritius requested the Special Chamber to rule that:

a. The Preliminary Objections raised by the Maldives are rejected;
b. It has jurisdiction to entertain the Application filed by Mauritius;
c. There is no bar to its exercise of that jurisdiction; and
d. It shall proceed to delimit the maritime boundary between Mauritius and the Maldives.

55. In accordance with article 75, paragraph 2, of the Rules, the following final submissions were presented by the Parties at the conclusion of the last statement made by each Party at the hearing:

On behalf of the Maldives:

In accordance with Article 75, paragraph 2, of the Rules of the Tribunal, and for the reasons set out during the written and oral phases of the pleadings, the Republic of Maldives requests the Special Chamber to adjudge and declare that it is without jurisdiction in respect of the claims submitted to the Special Chamber by the Republic of Mauritius. Additionally or alternatively, for the reasons set out during the written and oral phases of the pleadings, the Republic of Maldives requests the Special Chamber to adjudge and declare that the claims submitted to the Special Chamber by the Republic of Mauritius are inadmissible.

On behalf of Mauritius:

For the reasons set out in the Written Observations of Mauritius on the Preliminary Objections raised by the Republic of Maldives, dated 17 February 2020, and for the reasons set out in the oral pleadings of Mauritius during the hearings on 15 and 19 October 2020, the Republic of Mauritius respectfully requests the Special Chamber of the International Tribunal for the Law of the Sea to rule and adjudge that:

a. The Preliminary Objections raised by Maldives are rejected;
b. It has jurisdiction to entertain the Application filed by Mauritius;
c. There is no bar to its exercise of that jurisdiction; and
d. It shall proceed to delimit the maritime boundary between Mauritius and the Maldives.

III. FACTUAL BACKGROUND

56. Mauritius and the Maldives are States situated in the Indian Ocean. Both States consist of several islands. According to Mauritius, "[t]he territory of Mauritius includes, in addition to the main Island, *inter alia*, the Chagos Archipelago, which is located approximately 2,200 kilometres north-east of the main Island of Mauritius." Mauritius states that the Chagos Archipelago "is about 517 kilometres from Maldives".

57. In 1814, France, by the Treaty of Paris, ceded Mauritius and its dependencies to the United Kingdom. According to Mauritius, between 1814 and 1965, the United Kingdom administered the Chagos Archipelago as "a dependency of the colony of Mauritius."

58. In September 1965, a constitutional conference took place in London involving representatives of the colony of Mauritius and the United Kingdom. Mauritius submits that at that conference "the British Government made the independence of Mauritius conditional on Mauritian Ministers 'agreeing' to detachment [of the Chagos Archipelago], linking 'both matters in a possible package deal'", and that the British Prime Minister "procured the supposed but reluctant 'agreement' of Premier Ramgoolam [of Mauritius] and two of his colleagues to the detachment of the Chagos Archipelago." Mauritius notes that, when considering "the question of whether the people of Mauritius had given their consent to the detachment of a part of their territory", the International Court of Justice (hereinafter "the ICJ") found that it was "not possible to talk of an international agreement, when one of the parties to it, Mauritius, which is said to have ceded the territory to the United Kingdom, was under the authority of the latter."

59. On 8 November 1965, the United Kingdom adopted *The British Indian Ocean Territory Order*, which provided that the Chagos Archipelago, with certain other islands, "shall together form a separate colony which shall be known as the British Indian Ocean Territory." On 12 March 1968, Mauritius became an independent State. The United Kingdom continues to administer the Chagos Archipelago.

60. On 16 December 1965, the United Nations General Assembly (hereinafter "the UNGA") adopted resolution 2066 (XX) on the "Question of Mauritius", in which it noted "*with deep concern* that any step taken by the administering Power to detach certain islands from the Territory of Mauritius for the purpose of establishing a military base would be in contravention of the Declaration" (referring to the Declaration on the Granting of Independence to Colonial Countries and Peoples) and invited the "administering Power to take no action which would dismember the Territory of Mauritius and violate its territorial integrity".

61. According to the Maldives, since 1814 and following the establishment of the British Indian Ocean Territory (hereinafter "the BIOT") in 1965, "the United Kingdom has consistently claimed sovereignty over the Chagos Archipelago." The Maldives states that, "since at least 1980, Mauritius has claimed that it is sovereign over the Chagos Archipelago".

62. In a letter dated 19 June 2001 addressed to the Minister of Foreign Affairs of the Maldives, the Minister of Foreign Affairs and Regional Cooperation of Mauritius stated that Mauritius was "embarking on the exercise to delimit the Continental Shelf around the Chagos Archipelago" and asked the Maldives to "agree to preliminary negotiations being initiated at an early date." By a diplomatic note dated 18 July 2001, the Ministry of Foreign Affairs of the Maldives replied that:

As jurisdiction over the Chagos Archipelago is not exercised by the Government of Mauritius, the Government of Maldives feels that it would be inappropriate to initiate any discussions between the Government of Maldives and the Government of Mauritius regarding the delimitation of the boundary between the Maldives and the Chagos Archipelago.

63. According to Mauritius, in February 2010, the Maldives proposed "that Mauritius and Maldives hold discussions for the delimitation of the exclusive economic zone of [their] two countries." In a letter of 2 March 2010, addressed to the Minister of Foreign Affairs of the Maldives, the Minister of Foreign Affairs, Regional Integration and International Trade of Mauritius referred to the Maldives' proposal that "Mauritius and Maldives hold discussions for the delimitation of the exclusive economic zones of [their] two countries", adding that this proposal was "under active consideration by the relevant Mauritian authorities".

64. On 1 April 2010, the United Kingdom announced the creation of a marine protected area (hereinafter "the MPA") in and around the

Chagos Archipelago. On 20 December 2010, Mauritius instituted arbitral proceedings against the United Kingdom pursuant to Annex VII of the Convention, requesting the Arbitral Tribunal to adjudge and declare, in respect of the Chagos Archipelago, that:

(1) the United Kingdom is not entitled to declare an "MPA" or other maritime zones because it is not the "coastal State" within the meaning of *inter alia* Articles 2, 55, 56 and 76 of the Convention; and/or
(2) having regard to the commitments that it has made to Mauritius in relation to the Chagos Archipelago, the United Kingdom is not entitled unilaterally to declare an "MPA" or other maritime zones because Mauritius has rights as a "coastal State" within the meaning of *inter alia* Articles 56(1)(b)(iii) and 76(8) of the Convention; and/or

. . .

(4) The United Kingdom's purported "MPA" is incompatible with the substantive and procedural obligations of the United Kingdom under the Convention, including *inter alia* Articles 2, 55, 56, 63, 64, 194 and 300, as well as Article 7 of the Agreement for the Implementation of the Provisions of the United Nations Convention on the Law of the Sea of 10 December 1982 Relating to the Conservation and Management of Straddling Fish Stocks and Highly Migratory Fish Stocks of 4 August 1995.

(Arbitration regarding the Chagos Marine Protected Area between Mauritius and the United Kingdom of Great Britain and Northern Ireland, Award of 18 March 2015, RIAA, Vol. XXXI, p. 359, at pp. 440-1, para. 158)

65. On 26 July 2010, the Maldives made a submission to the Commission on the Limits of the Continental Shelf (hereinafter "the CLCS") pursuant to paragraph 8 of article 76 of the Convention. In a diplomatic note dated 21 September 2010, addressed to the Ministry of Foreign Affairs of the Maldives, the Ministry of Foreign Affairs, Regional Integration and International Trade of Mauritius noted that the Government of Mauritius was "agreeable to holding formal talks with the Government of . . . Maldives for the delimitation of the exclusive economic zones (EEZs) of Mauritius and Maldives." It also stated that Mauritius had taken note of the Maldives' submission to the CLCS and that "the holding of EEZ delimitation boundary talks [was] all the more relevant in the light of" that submission.

66. On 21 October 2010, a "first meeting on maritime delimitation and submission regarding the extended continental shelf between the Republic of Maldives and Republic of Mauritius" took place in Malé "to discuss a potential overlap of the extended continental shelf and to exchange views on maritime boundary delimitation between the two

respective States." According to the minutes of the meeting, which were signed by representatives of both States, the two sides "agreed to exchange coordinates of their respective base points as soon as possible in order to facilitate the eventual discussions on the maritime boundary." With regard to the Maldives' submission to the CLCS, the representative of the Maldives stated that the exclusive economic zone coordinates of "Mauritius in the Chagos region were not taken into consideration" and that "this would be rectified by an addendum to the submission".

67. From 11 to 13 March 2011, the President of the Maldives paid a State visit to Mauritius. A joint communiqué issued during this visit, on 12 March 2011, records that the Prime Minister of Mauritius and the President of the Maldives "agreed to make bilateral arrangements on the overlapping area of extended continental shelf of the two States around the Chagos Archipelago."

68. In a diplomatic note dated 24 March 2011, addressed to the Secretary-General of the United Nations, the Permanent Mission of Mauritius to the United Nations, referring to the Maldives' submission to the CLCS and the October 2010 meeting between the two countries, noted that "no addendum has up to now been filed with the Secretary-General of the United Nations" by the Maldives. The diplomatic note states that Mauritius "protests formally against the submission . . . in as much as the Extended Continental Shelf being claimed by . . . Maldives encroaches on the Exclusive Economic Zone of . . . Mauritius".

69. On 18 March 2015, the Arbitral Tribunal constituted pursuant to Annex VII to the Convention rendered its award in the *Arbitration regarding the Chagos Marine Protected Area* (hereinafter "the *Chagos* arbitral award"). The Arbitral Tribunal found, in relation to its jurisdiction, "that it lacks jurisdiction with respect to Mauritius' First and Second Submissions" (*Arbitration regarding the Chagos Marine Protected Area between Mauritius and the United Kingdom of Great Britain and Northern Ireland, Award of 18 March 2015, RIAA, Vol. XXXI*, p. 359, at p. 582, para. 547). It also found that it had jurisdiction pursuant to article 288, paragraph 1, and article 297, paragraph 1(c), of the Convention to consider Mauritius' Fourth Submission and the compatibility of the MPA with certain provisions of the Convention. In relation to the merits, the Arbitral Tribunal found that, in establishing the MPA surrounding the Chagos Archipelago, the United Kingdom breached its obligations under article 2, paragraph 3, article 56, paragraph 2, and article 194, paragraph 4, of the Convention.

70. In resolution 71/292 of 22 June 2017, the UNGA decided to request the ICJ, pursuant to article 65 of its Statute, to give an advisory opinion on the following questions:

(a) Was the process of decolonization of Mauritius lawfully completed when Mauritius was granted independence in 1968, following the separation of the Chagos Archipelago from Mauritius and having regard to international law, including obligations reflected in General Assembly resolutions 1514 (XV) of 14 December 1960, 2066 (XX) of 16 December 1965, 2232 (XXI) of 20 December 1966 and 2357 (XXII) of 19 December 1967?;

(b) What are the consequences under international law, including obligations reflected in the above-mentioned resolutions, arising from the continued administration by the United Kingdom of Great Britain and Northern Ireland of the Chagos Archipelago, including with respect to the inability of Mauritius to implement a programme for the resettlement on the Chagos Archipelago of its nationals, in particular those of Chagossian origin?

71. On 25 February 2019, the ICJ delivered its advisory opinion on the *Legal Consequences of the Separation of the Chagos Archipelago from Mauritius in 1965* (hereinafter "the *Chagos* advisory opinion"). The operative part of the *Chagos* advisory opinion provides as follows:

The Court,

. . .

(3) By thirteen votes to one,

> *Is of the opinion* that, having regard to international law, the process of decolonization of Mauritius was not lawfully completed when that country acceded to independence in 1968, following the separation of the Chagos Archipelago;

. . .

(4) By thirteen votes to one,

> *Is of the opinion* that the United Kingdom is under an obligation to bring to an end its administration of the Chagos Archipelago as rapidly as possible; . . .

(5) By thirteen votes to one,

> *Is of the opinion* that all Member States are under an obligation to co-operate with the United Nations in order to complete the decolonization of Mauritius.

. . .

(*Legal Consequences of the Separation of the Chagos Archipelago from Mauritius in 1965, Advisory Opinion, ICJ Reports 2019*, p. 95, at p. 140, para. 183)

72. Following the *Chagos* advisory opinion, in a diplomatic note dated 7 March 2019, addressed to the Permanent Mission of the Maldives to the United Nations, the Permanent Mission of Mauritius to the United Nations referred to the "meeting on maritime delimitation held between Mauritius and the Maldives in Malé in October 2010" and invited the Maldives "to a second round of discussions in the second week of April in Mauritius." The Maldives did not respond to that note.

73. In a communiqué of the Mauritian Prime Minister's Office of 30 April 2019, it was stated that it is "undeniable that the Republic of Mauritius is the sole State lawfully entitled to exercise sovereignty and sovereign rights in relation to the Chagos Archipelago and its maritime zones." On the other hand, on the same date, the United Kingdom Minister of State for Europe and the Americas stated that:

we have no doubt about our sovereignty over the Chagos Archipelago, which has been under continuous British sovereignty since 1814. Mauritius has never held sovereignty over the Archipelago and we do not recognise its claim. We have, however, made a long-standing commitment since 1965 to cede sovereignty of the territory to Mauritius when it is no longer required for defence purposes. We stand by that commitment.

74. On 22 May 2019, the UNGA adopted resolution 73/295 entitled "Advisory opinion of the International Court of Justice on the legal consequences of the separation of the Chagos Archipelago from Mauritius in 1965". In the resolution, the UNGA, *inter alia*,

Demands that the United Kingdom of Great Britain and Northern Ireland withdraw its colonial administration from the Chagos Archipelago unconditionally within a period of no more than six months from the adoption of the present resolution, thereby enabling Mauritius to complete the decolonization of its territory as rapidly as possible;

. . .

Calls upon all Member States to cooperate with the United Nations to ensure the completion of the decolonization of Mauritius as rapidly as possible, and to refrain from any action that will impede or delay the completion of the process of decolonization of Mauritius in accordance with the advisory opinion of the Court and the present resolution;

75. The resolution was adopted with 116 votes in favour, 6 against and 56 abstentions. Mauritius voted in favour of the resolution. The Maldives and the United Kingdom voted against.

76. The representative of the United Kingdom, commenting on that resolution before the UNGA on 22 May 2019, reiterated that

"[t]he United Kingdom is not in doubt about our sovereignty over the British Indian Ocean Territory" and that "[i]t has been under continuous British sovereignty since 1814."

77. The United Kingdom did not take any action on the demand of the UNGA within the period indicated in paragraph 3 of the abovementioned resolution.

IV. THE MALDIVES' PRELIMINARY OBJECTIONS TO JURISDICTION AND ADMISSIBILITY

78. Mauritius and the Maldives are both States Parties to the Convention, having ratified it on 4 November 1994 and 7 September 2000, respectively. In its Notification, Mauritius relied on articles 286 and 288, paragraph 1, of the Convention to found the jurisdiction of an arbitral tribunal to be constituted in accordance with Annex VII to the Convention. As noted in paragraph 2 of the present Judgment, by the Special Agreement, the Parties agreed to transfer their dispute to a special chamber of the Tribunal.

79. The Maldives raises five preliminary objections to the jurisdiction of the Special Chamber and the admissibility of Mauritius' claims. According to the Maldives' first preliminary objection, the United Kingdom is an indispensable third party to the present proceedings, and, as the United Kingdom is not a party to these proceedings, the Special Chamber does not have jurisdiction over the alleged dispute. In its second preliminary objection, the Maldives submits that the Special Chamber has no jurisdiction to determine the disputed issue of sovereignty over the Chagos Archipelago, which it would necessarily have to do if it were to determine Mauritius' claims in these proceedings. The Maldives contends in its third preliminary objection that, as Mauritius and the Maldives have not engaged, and cannot meaningfully engage, in the negotiations required by articles 74 and 83 of the Convention, the Special Chamber lacks jurisdiction. According to the Maldives' fourth preliminary objection, there is not, and cannot be, a dispute between Mauritius and the Maldives concerning its maritime boundary. Without such a dispute, the Special Chamber has no jurisdiction. Finally, the Maldives submits that Mauritius' claims constitute an abuse of process and should therefore be rejected as inadmissible at the preliminary objections phase.

80. The Special Chamber will now examine the above preliminary objections in the order presented by the Maldives.

V. FIRST PRELIMINARY OBJECTION: INDISPENSABLE THIRD PARTY

81. The Maldives' first preliminary objection is that the Special Chamber lacks jurisdiction "because an indispensable party, namely the United Kingdom, is absent in these proceedings and did not consent to be a party to them."

82. The Maldives maintains that, under the well-established Monetary Gold principle, "a court or tribunal cannot exercise its jurisdiction in the absence of an indispensable party". Referring to the findings of the ICJ and the Tribunal, the Maldives states that under the Monetary Gold principle: (1) a State not party to proceedings is an "indispensable party" when the decision between the parties cannot be reached without the court or tribunal examining the validity of the conduct of this State or its legal position; and (2) an international court or tribunal cannot exercise its jurisdiction in the absence of such an indispensable party.

83. The Maldives contends that the Monetary Gold principle plainly applies to the present case and prevents the Special Chamber from exercising jurisdiction. According to the Maldives, there is a long-standing and unresolved sovereignty dispute between Mauritius and the United Kingdom over the Chagos Archipelago. Thus, in order to entertain Mauritius' delimitation claims, the Special Chamber would necessarily be required to rule on those States' respective sovereignty claims. In other words, the subject matter of the Special Chamber's decision in the present case would necessarily entail a determination as to whether the United Kingdom is or is not sovereign over the Chagos Archipelago. However, in the view of the Maldives, the Special Chamber cannot make such a determination without the consent of the United Kingdom.

84. In this regard, the Maldives argues that the legal situation in the present case is strikingly similar to the *East Timor* case. In the latter case, the Maldives points out, the ICJ noted that the very subject matter of its decision would necessarily be a determination of whether Indonesia, which was not a party to the proceedings, "could or could not have acquired the power to enter into treaties on behalf of East Timor relating to the resources of its continental shelf" and concluded that it "could not make such a determination in the absence of the consent of Indonesia."

85. With respect to Mauritius' contention that the *Chagos* advisory opinion has already determined that the United Kingdom has no sovereign rights with regard to the Chagos Archipelago, so that the

Special Chamber should consider that the United Kingdom's claim to sovereignty or sovereign rights is not plausible, the Maldives claims that "the Special Chamber should acknowledge that the sovereignty dispute between the United Kingdom and Mauritius does exist and has not been resolved as a matter of fact."

86. According to the Maldives, despite the advisory opinion and the subsequent UNGA resolution 73/295, the United Kingdom "maintains its claim over Chagos, which it continues to administer as the British Indian Ocean Territory." The Maldives states that Mauritius acknowledges this fact and that Mauritius has "reiterate[ed] its view that the ICJ Advisory Opinion 'made clear that the Chagos Archipelago is, and has always been, a part of Mauritius'." Thus, in the Maldives' view, it is plain that the matter of sovereignty over the Chagos Archipelago remains in dispute between Mauritius and the United Kingdom.

87. Moreover, the Maldives submits that "Mauritius' present claims" also require the Special Chamber to rule on:

(a) Whether the ICJ gave an opinion on the sovereignty dispute; (b) Whether any such opinion is binding on the United Kingdom; (c) Whether the obligation on which the ICJ advised—namely, that the United Kingdom must bring an end to its administration of the Chagos Archipelago—means that Mauritius is entitled to exercise the rights of the "coastal State" and delimit a maritime boundary with the Maldives before the United Kingdom's administration has in fact been terminated; and (d) Whether the *Chagos Advisory Opinion* overruled the award in the *Chagos Marine Protected Area Arbitration* with the effect that that award no longer has *res judicata* effect between the United Kingdom and Mauritius.

88. As to whether the Monetary Gold principle applies in the context of decolonization, the Maldives asserts that the *East Timor* case

leaves no doubt that the principle applies with equal force even in the extreme case of aggression and annexation of a non-self-governing territory, in flagrant violation of obligations *erga omnes*. The context of decolonization is simply irrelevant; whether the UK is right or wrong is irrelevant; its consent to jurisdiction cannot be circumvented.

89. The Maldives concludes that a decision on Mauritius' maritime claims in the present proceedings would necessarily require the Special Chamber to rule on the United Kingdom's legal interests, which would not only be affected by, but would form the very subject matter of, this decision. Since the United Kingdom is absent from the present proceedings, the Maldives submits that the Special Chamber should decline jurisdiction.

90. While Mauritius "does not dispute that the *Monetary Gold* principle is 'a well-established procedural rule in international judicial proceedings'", it submits that "this principle has no application to the present case." Mauritius maintains that "[t]he *Monetary Gold* principle can have no application in circumstances where a third State has no rights."

91. According to Mauritius, the United Kingdom is plainly not an indispensable party in this case. It maintains that the United Kingdom is not even an interested party, because "it has no legal interest in the Chagos Archipelago, and therefore none that can be affected by a delimitation of the maritime boundary separating the Archipelago from the Maldives, which is the object of this case."

92. Mauritius submits that "[t]he bar for declining to exercise jurisdiction is very high", referring to the finding of the ICJ in *Monetary Gold Removed from Rome in 1943* that, "[i]n the present case, Albania's legal interests would not only be affected by a decision, but would form the very subject-matter of the decision." Mauritius argues that the subject matter of the Special Chamber's decision does not require it to make a prior determination of rights and obligations of the United Kingdom that would form the subject matter of the decision to be rendered as "[t]hat determination has already been made by the ICJ."

93. For Mauritius, "[t]he subject-matter of the present proceedings is the delimitation of a maritime area adjacent to insular features over which the United Kingdom, as the ICJ has made clear, has no plausible claim of sovereignty or sovereign rights." Mauritius submits that the United Kingdom is not an indispensable party to these proceedings because, as the ICJ determined, "the United Kingdom has no sovereignty, or sovereign rights, in respect of any part of the Chagos Archipelago."

94. According to Mauritius, since the United Kingdom has no sovereignty, or sovereign rights or other material rights, in respect of any part of the territory of Mauritius, it follows that "the United Kingdom has no rights that could in any way be affected by a delimitation of the maritime boundary between Mauritius and the Maldives."

95. Regarding the *East Timor* case, Mauritius submits that the ICJ, in that case, could not treat the resolutions of political organs, without more, as having resolved a dispute about the lawfulness of Indonesia's conduct and on that basis alone proceed to adjudicate Indonesia's rights in its absence. In contrast, "here we have the ICJ's authoritative, and correct, by admission, judicial determinations that directly address, and resolve, the legal status of the Chagos Archipelago as an integral part of Mauritius' territory."

96. Regarding the United Kingdom's sovereignty claim to the Chagos Archipelago after the ICJ rendered its advisory opinion, Mauritius contends that "the Maldives cannot hide behind fallacious assertions by the United Kingdom that, contrary to the Advisory Opinion, it has 'no doubt' about its sovereignty over the Chagos Archipelago." According to Mauritius, this gives more weight to "a defiant political statement by a recalcitrant State than to the Court's authoritative legal determination of the issue."

* * *

97. The Special Chamber recalls that the Tribunal stated in the *M/V "Norstar" Case* that the Monetary Gold principle is "a well-established procedural rule in international judicial proceedings" (*M/V "Norstar" (Panama v. Italy), Preliminary Objections, Judgment, ITLOS Reports 2016*, p. 44, at p. 84, para. 172). The Special Chamber notes in this regard that the Parties are in agreement as to the effect of the Monetary Gold principle. The Parties further agree that Mauritius' claims can be entertained only if the Special Chamber accepts that Mauritius, not the United Kingdom, has sovereignty over the Chagos Archipelago.

98. However, the Parties disagree as to whether the United Kingdom is an indispensable party to the present proceedings. While the Maldives argues that the United Kingdom is an indispensable party as there is an extant sovereignty dispute between the United Kingdom and Mauritius over the Chagos Archipelago, Mauritius contends that the United Kingdom is not such a party because the ICJ has already determined that it has no sovereignty, or sovereign rights, in respect of any part of the Chagos Archipelago. Thus the Parties' disagreement boils down to the question as to whether a sovereignty dispute between Mauritius and the United Kingdom over the Chagos Archipelago still exists or has been resolved.

99. Accordingly, if a sovereignty dispute over the Chagos Archipelago exists, the United Kingdom may be regarded as an indispensable party and the Monetary Gold principle would prevent the Special Chamber from exercising its jurisdiction. On the other hand, if such sovereignty dispute has been resolved in favour of Mauritius, the United Kingdom may not be regarded as an indispensable party and the Monetary Gold principle would not apply.

100. As the Special Chamber will examine below, the core issue of the second preliminary objection raised by the Maldives also concerns the legal status of the Chagos Archipelago. Therefore, this issue is central to both the first and the second preliminary objection. The Special Chamber observes that the Parties acknowledge that their entire

cases for both preliminary objections rest on the "core premise", namely that for the Maldives, the sovereignty dispute between Mauritius and the United Kingdom remains unresolved and that for Mauritius, the sovereignty issue has been resolved in its favour. It also observes that during the oral proceedings the Parties presented their arguments on the first and second preliminary objections in combination. The Special Chamber thus considers it appropriate to examine the two objections together insofar as the legal status of the Chagos Archipelago is concerned. Accordingly, the Special Chamber will proceed to the second preliminary objection of the Maldives and scrutinize the key issues common to these two preliminary objections. It will then give its findings on the first and second preliminary objections of the Maldives.

VI. SECOND PRELIMINARY OBJECTION: DISPUTED ISSUE OF SOVEREIGNTY

101. The Special Chamber will now turn to the second preliminary objection of the Maldives, namely that the Special Chamber has "no jurisdiction to determine the disputed issue of sovereignty over the Chagos Archipelago, which it would necessarily have to do if it were to determine Mauritius' claims in these proceedings."

102. In addressing this objection, the Special Chamber will begin by examining the scope of its jurisdiction under article 288, paragraph 1, of the Convention and the nature of the dispute submitted to it. It will then consider the question of the legal status of the Chagos Archipelago.

A. Scope of jurisdiction of the Special Chamber and nature of the dispute

103. The Maldives submits that the Special Chamber's "jurisdiction . . . is established by, and limited to, disputes 'concerning the interpretation or application of this Convention'" pursuant to article 288, paragraph 1, of the Convention. It further submits that a dispute over territorial sovereignty is clearly not a dispute concerning the interpretation or application of the Convention. According to the Maldives, "[t]he jurisprudence provides clear and consistent confirmation that disputes concerning sovereignty over land territory do not come within the jurisdiction of an UNCLOS tribunal" pursuant to article 288, paragraph 1, of the Convention. In support of its

submission, the Maldives refers to the findings of the arbitral tribunals in the *Chagos Marine Protected Area Arbitration*, the *South China Sea Arbitration* and *Coastal State Rights in the Black Sea, Sea of Azov and Kerch Strait* (hereinafter "*Coastal State Rights*").

104. As to the nature of the dispute submitted to the Special Chamber, the Maldives contends that the case before the Special Chamber "*primarily* concerns a long-standing and unresolved bilateral dispute between Mauritius and the United Kingdom about territorial sovereignty over the Chagos Archipelago". According to the Maldives, "[o]nly an 'opposite' or 'adjacent' state may bring proceedings" pursuant to articles 74 and 83 of the Convention. However, it argues that determining whether Mauritius is currently the State with the "opposite or adjacent coast" to the Maldives would inevitably require the Special Chamber "to determine (either expressly or implicitly) the dispute between Mauritius and the United Kingdom regarding sovereignty over the Chagos Archipelago."

105. The Maldives asserts that the Special Chamber has no jurisdiction to determine such a disputed issue of sovereignty, as "the question of whether Mauritius is the 'coastal State' in respect of the Chagos Archipelago is clearly not a dispute concerning the interpretation or application of UNCLOS" and thus is a matter that is manifestly outside the jurisdiction of the Special Chamber under article 288 of the Convention. Accordingly, the Maldives claims that the Special Chamber is without jurisdiction in respect of the claims of Mauritius.

106. For its part, Mauritius submits that the preliminary objection raised by the Maldives should be rejected as it offers no basis for the Special Chamber to decline to exercise its jurisdiction.

107. As to the scope of jurisdiction of the Special Chamber, Mauritius does not appear to contest that the jurisdiction of the Special Chamber is limited to disputes concerning the interpretation or application of the Convention and that a territorial dispute is not such a dispute.

108. As to the nature of the dispute submitted to the Special Chamber, Mauritius contends that "[t]he dispute concerns the delimitation of the Exclusive Economic Zone ("EEZ") and continental shelf of Mauritius with Maldives in the Indian Ocean." It states that it "does not seek, nor has it ever sought, to use these proceedings to settle a territorial dispute." In its view, there exists no dispute over territorial sovereignty that could prevent the Special Chamber from delimiting the maritime boundary between Mauritius and the Maldives. Mauritius argues that,

following the ICJ's Advisory Opinion of 25 February 2019 and UN General Assembly Resolution 73/295, Mauritius is recognised under international law, by the ICJ and the UN, as the coastal State that is opposite or adjacent to the Maldives for purposes of this maritime boundary delimitation.

Accordingly, for Mauritius, the subject matter of the present proceedings is the delimitation of a maritime area adjacent to the Chagos Archipelago over which "the United Kingdom, as the ICJ has made clear, has no plausible claim of sovereignty or sovereign rights."

* * *

109. Article 288, paragraph 1, of the Convention reads:

A court or tribunal referred to in article 287 shall have jurisdiction over any dispute concerning the interpretation or application of this Convention which is submitted to it in accordance with this Part.

It is thus clear that the jurisdiction of the Special Chamber is confined to "any dispute concerning the interpretation or application of [the] Convention".

110. The Special Chamber considers that a dispute, which requires the determination of a question of territorial sovereignty, may not be regarded as a dispute concerning the interpretation or application of the Convention under article 288, paragraph 1, of the Convention. In this regard, the Special Chamber recalls the following statement made by the Arbitral Tribunal in the *South China Sea Arbitration*:

The Convention, however, does not address the sovereignty of States over land territory. Accordingly, this Tribunal has not been asked to, and does not purport to, make any ruling as to which State enjoys sovereignty over any land territory in the South China Sea, in particular with respect to the disputes concerning sovereignty over the Spratly Islands or Scarborough Shoal.

(*The South China Sea Arbitration between the Republic of the Philippines and the People's Republic of China, Award of 12 July 2016, RIAA, Vol. XXXIII*, p. 153, at p. 184, para. 5)

111. The Special Chamber notes that the Parties appear to be in agreement that the jurisdiction of the Special Chamber is confined to a dispute concerning the interpretation or application of the Convention and that a territorial dispute is not such a dispute.

112. The Special Chamber will now examine the nature of the dispute submitted to it. In paragraphs 27 and 28 of the Notification, Mauritius makes the following claims:

27. Mauritius requests the Tribunal to delimit, in accordance with the principles and rules set forth in UNCLOS, the maritime boundary between Mauritius and Maldives in the Indian Ocean, in the EEZ and continental shelf, including the portion of the continental shelf pertaining to Mauritius that lies more than 200 nautical miles from the baselines from which its territorial sea is measured.

28. Mauritius also requests the Tribunal to declare that Maldives has violated its obligation to, pending agreement as provided for in paragraphs 1 of Articles 74 and 83 of UNCLOS, make every effort to enter into provisional arrangements of a practical nature and, during such transitional periods, not to jeopardize or hamper the reaching of the final agreement.

113. The Special Chamber notes that, given the geography of the area relevant to the present proceedings, in particular the location of the Chagos Archipelago, Mauritius' claims are based on the premise that it has sovereignty over the Chagos Archipelago and thus is the State with an opposite or adjacent coast to the Maldives within the meaning of article 74, paragraph 1, and article 83, paragraph 1, of the Convention and the State concerned within the meaning of paragraph 3 of the same articles. The Special Chamber further notes that the Parties are in agreement that Mauritius' claims are based on such premise.

114. However, the Parties disagree on the validity of the premise that Mauritius has sovereignty over the Chagos Archipelago. The Maldives argues that such premise is untenable in light of the long-standing, unresolved sovereignty dispute between Mauritius and the United Kingdom. For its part, Mauritius contends that such premise must be accepted by the Special Chamber as the advisory opinion of the ICJ has already determined that the United Kingdom has no rights as a sovereign over the Chagos Archipelago and has confirmed that, as a matter of international law, the Chagos Archipelago is an integral part of Mauritius, and Mauritius only. Mauritius adds that the Special Chamber is called upon simply to recognize and respect the ICJ's authoritative determination of this issue and proceed to delimit the maritime boundary between the Parties.

115. Therefore, the legal status of the Chagos Archipelago is at the core of the disagreement between the Parties with respect to the second preliminary objection. As noted above, it is also central to the disagreement between the Parties with respect to the first preliminary objection. Accordingly, the Special Chamber's examination of this question is pertinent to both the first and the second preliminary objection.

B. *Legal status of the Chagos Archipelago*

116. The Special Chamber will now turn to the question of the legal status of the Chagos Archipelago.

117. The Maldives claims that "the sovereignty dispute remains extant" and that "[u]ntil it is resolved there cannot be a dispute between the parties concerning a maritime boundary which they may or may not share." In support of its claim, the Maldives puts forward the following arguments. First, the *Chagos* arbitral award did not resolve the sovereignty dispute and remains *res judicata* between Mauritius and the United Kingdom. Second, the *Chagos* advisory opinion did not resolve the sovereignty dispute. Third, UNGA resolution 73/295 had no effect on the sovereignty dispute. Fourth, in any case, the sovereignty dispute between Mauritius and the United Kingdom exists as a matter of fact.

118. Mauritius submits that, in light of the ICJ advisory opinion, there is no issue of sovereignty over the Chagos Archipelago and that the Maldives' claim should accordingly be rejected.

119. The Special Chamber will examine the arguments advanced by the Parties with respect to the *Chagos* arbitral award, the *Chagos* advisory opinion, UNGA resolution 73/295 and the current status of the sovereignty dispute over the Chagos Archipelago.

1. *Arbitral award in the* Chagos Marine Protected Area Arbitration

120. The Special Chamber now turns to the question as to whether the *Chagos* arbitral award has any relevance or implication for the legal status of the Chagos Archipelago.

121. The Maldives argues that the Annex VII Arbitral Tribunal in the *Chagos Marine Protected Area Arbitration* found that a sovereignty dispute existed between Mauritius and the United Kingdom over the Chagos Archipelago and declined to resolve this dispute, finding that to do so would be outside its jurisdiction. The Maldives claims that "the 2015 arbitral award, according to which the territorial dispute between Mauritius and the United Kingdom does not concern the interpretation or application of the United Nations Convention on the Law of the Sea, remains fully relevant" and "possesses the 'finality' of decisions with *res judicata* effect."

122. The Maldives submits that, while the Arbitral Tribunal found that the parties' dispute with respect to Mauritius' first submission was properly characterized as relating to land sovereignty over the Chagos Archipelago, it held, however, that it could exercise jurisdiction over

Mauritius' fourth submission—namely, that the United Kingdom's declaration of the MPA violated its obligations under, *inter alia*, articles 2, 55, 56, 63, 64, 194 and 300 of the Convention. According to the Maldives, the Arbitral Tribunal concluded that the United Kingdom's declaration involved a breach of article 2, paragraph 3, article 56, paragraph 2, and article 194, paragraph 4, of the Convention "because, in exercising the powers of a coastal State, it had failed to consult with or have due regard to the interests of Mauritius." The Maldives claims that "[t]he tribunal's findings necessarily treat the United Kingdom as the relevant coastal State for the purpose of managing maritime zones around the Chagos Archipelago."

123. In the Maldives' view, therefore, "the *Chagos Marine Protected Area Arbitration* produced an award, with *res judicata* effect between Mauritius and the United Kingdom, to the effect that, at least until resolution of the sovereignty dispute, the United Kingdom is entitled to exercise the rights of a coastal State under UNCLOS in respect of the Chagos Archipelago".

124. As to Mauritius' argument concerning the difference between the *Chagos Marine Protected Area Arbitration* and the present case, the Maldives points out that it "advances no claim that the award in the *Chagos Marine Protected Area Arbitration* is *res judicata* between the parties to the present proceedings, so Mauritius' response is irrelevant."

125. Mauritius states that "it should be indisputable that the arbitral award could not have had *res judicata* effect on the question of who is the "coastal State" in respect of the Chagos Archipelago, because the Annex VII tribunal did not make any decision on that issue." It further states that, "[t]o the contrary, it decided, by a 3-2 vote, that it would not rule on that issue because it had no jurisdiction under the 1982 Convention to decide questions of land sovereignty." Mauritius adds that, "[i]n short, sovereignty over Chagos was not the *res* that was *judicata* in the Annex VII case."

126. Mauritius contends that it "is not seeking the same decision which it sought in the *Chagos MPA Arbitration*, or the ruling which the UN General Assembly sought in the Advisory Opinion concerning the Chagos Archipelago." According to Mauritius, there have been "critical developments" since the *Chagos* arbitral award was rendered, namely the ICJ's advisory opinion and UNGA resolution 73/295. Mauritius avers that "[t]hese make it clear that the Chagos Archipelago is an integral part of the territory of Mauritius, with the consequence that Mauritius—and Mauritius alone—is the coastal State for purposes of maritime delimitation with the Maldives."

127. Mauritius also points out that "[t]here is no identity between the relief sought or the issues determined in the *Chagos MPA Arbitration* and those now raised before the Special Chamber." It adds that "[t]hey are not based on the same set of facts, nor do they involve the same parties."

* * *

128. The Special Chamber is aware that, before the present dispute was submitted to it, the questions relating to the legal status of the Chagos Archipelago had been considered first by the Annex VII Arbitral Tribunal in relation to the dispute between Mauritius and the United Kingdom concerning the MPA established by the United Kingdom around the Chagos Archipelago, and then by the ICJ in relation to the request made by the UNGA for an advisory opinion regarding the decolonization of Mauritius.

129. The Parties make reference to, and rely on, the *Chagos* arbitral award and the *Chagos* advisory opinion in support of their respective claims. However, as was seen above and will be seen below, the Parties hold markedly different views as to the meaning and effect of the arbitral award and the advisory opinion.

130. The Special Chamber will begin with the examination of the *Chagos* arbitral award to assess whether it can shed light on the legal status of the Chagos Archipelago.

131. In the *Chagos Marine Protected Area Arbitration*, Mauritius made four submissions to claim that the establishment of the MPA around the Chagos Archipelago by the United Kingdom was in breach of the Convention. The submissions that may be relevant to the question the Special Chamber has to address are the first and fourth submissions.

132. The first submission of Mauritius reads as follows:

the United Kingdom is not entitled to declare an "MPA" or other maritime zones because it is not the "coastal State" within the meaning of *inter alia* Articles 2, 55, 56 and 76 of the Convention;

(*Arbitration regarding the Chagos Marine Protected Area between Mauritius and the United Kingdom of Great Britain and Northern Ireland, Award of 18 March 2015, RIAA, Vol. XXXI*, p. 359, at p. 440, para. 158)

The fourth submission reads:

The United Kingdom's purported "MPA" is incompatible with the substantive and procedural obligations of the United Kingdom under the Convention, including *inter alia* Articles 2, 55, 56, 63, 64, 194 and 300, as well as Article 7 of the Agreement for the Implementation of the Provisions of the United Nations Convention on the Law of the Sea of 10 December 1982 Relating to the Conservation and Management of Straddling Fish Stocks and Highly Migratory Fish Stocks of 4 August 1995. (*Ibid.*, at pp. 440-1, para. 158)

133. Regarding the first submission, the Arbitral Tribunal found that "a dispute between the Parties exists with respect to sovereignty over the Chagos Archipelago" and that "[t]he Parties' dispute regarding sovereignty over the Chagos Archipelago does not concern the interpretation or application of the Convention." Accordingly, the Arbitral Tribunal concluded that it had no jurisdiction to entertain Mauritius' first submission.

134. Thus, it is clear that the Arbitral Tribunal recognized the existence of a sovereignty dispute between Mauritius and the United Kingdom over the Chagos Archipelago, which, it concluded, it lacked jurisdiction to address. In this regard, it is worth noting what the Arbitral Tribunal observed about "the agreement between the United Kingdom and the Mauritius Council of Ministers in 1965 to the detachment of the Archipelago" (hereinafter "the 1965 Agreement"). According to the Arbitral Tribunal, the validity or otherwise of the 1965 Agreement was "a central element of the Parties' submissions on Mauritius' First and Second Submissions, sovereignty, and the identity of the coastal State" (*Arbitration regarding the Chagos Marine Protected Area between Mauritius and the United Kingdom of Great Britain and Northern Ireland, Award of 18 March 2015, RIAA, Vol. XXXI*, p. 359, at pp. 533-4, para. 418).

135. As to the fourth submission, the Arbitral Tribunal found that it had jurisdiction to consider Mauritius' fourth submission and the compatibility of the MPA with the following provisions of the Convention:

(a) Article 2(3) insofar as it relates to Mauritius' fishing rights in the territorial sea or to the United Kingdom's undertakings to return the Archipelago to Mauritius when no longer needed for defence purposes and to return the benefit of any minerals or oil discovered in or near the Chagos Archipelago to Mauritius;

(b) Article 56(2), insofar as it relates to the United Kingdom's undertakings to return the Archipelago to Mauritius when no longer needed for defence purposes and to return the benefit of any minerals or oil discovered in or near the Chagos Archipelago to Mauritius;

(*Arbitration regarding the Chagos Marine Protected Area between Mauritius and the United Kingdom of Great Britain and Northern Ireland, Award of 18 March 2015, RIAA, Vol. XXXI*, p. 359, at pp. 500-1, para. 323)

136. After finding that it had jurisdiction over the fourth submission of Mauritius, the Arbitral Tribunal noted that "the legal effect of the 1965 Agreement is also a central element of the Parties' submissions on Mauritius' Fourth Submission, insofar as it involves the Lancaster House Undertakings" (*Arbitration regarding the Chagos Marine Protected Area between Mauritius and the United Kingdom of Great Britain and Northern Ireland, Award of 18 March 2015, RIAA, Vol. XXXI*, p. 359, at p. 534, para. 419). The Arbitral Tribunal then found that "its jurisdiction with respect to Mauritius' Fourth Submission . . . permits it to interpret the 1965 Agreement to the extent necessary to establish the nature and scope of the United Kingdom's undertakings" (*Ibid.*). The Arbitral Tribunal went on to examine the legal status of the 1965 Agreement and the extent to which it was called upon to engage with Mauritius' arguments regarding its validity as well as the legal significance of the United Kingdom's repetition of its undertakings in the years following the independence of Mauritius.

137. On the basis of those examinations, the Arbitral Tribunal found:

(1) that the United Kingdom's undertaking to ensure that fishing rights in the Chagos Archipelago would remain available to Mauritius as far as practicable is legally binding insofar as it relates to the territorial sea;

(2) that the United Kingdom's undertaking to return the Chagos Archipelago to Mauritius when no longer needed for defence purposes is legally binding; and

(3) that the United Kingdom's undertaking to preserve the benefit of any minerals or oil discovered in or near the Chagos Archipelago for Mauritius is legally binding;

(*Arbitration regarding the Chagos Marine Protected Area between Mauritius and the United Kingdom of Great Britain and Northern Ireland, Award of 18 March 2015, RIAA, Vol. XXXI*, p. 359, at pp. 582-3, para. 547)

Accordingly, the Arbitral Tribunal declared that, in establishing the MPA surrounding the Chagos Archipelago, the United Kingdom breached its obligations under article 2, paragraph 3, article 56, paragraph 2, and article 194, paragraph 4, of the Convention.

138. In the view of the Special Chamber, the fact that the Arbitral Tribunal found that it had jurisdiction to consider the fourth submission of Mauritius and concluded that the United Kingdom had breached its obligations under the Convention does not mean that the Arbitral Tribunal recognized the United Kingdom as the coastal State with respect to the Chagos Archipelago, as the Maldives argues. On the

contrary, in addressing the first submission of Mauritius, the Arbitral Tribunal made it clear that it lacked jurisdiction to determine who has sovereignty over the Chagos Archipelago. With respect to the fourth submission, the main concern of the Arbitral Tribunal was, without prejudice to the question of sovereignty over the Chagos Archipelago, to consider whether the United Kingdom's declaration of the MPA was compatible with its obligations under the Convention. In this regard, the Arbitral Tribunal examined the 1965 Agreement to the extent necessary to establish the nature and scope of the United Kingdom's undertakings, and found them to be legally binding on the ground of estoppel "in view of their repeated reaffirmation after 1968" (*Arbitration regarding the Chagos Marine Protected Area between Mauritius and the United Kingdom of Great Britain and Northern Ireland, Award of 18 March 2015, RIAA, Vol. XXXI*, p. 359, at p. 548, para. 448). The Special Chamber, therefore, cannot accept the Maldives' contention that

the *Chagos Marine Protected Area Arbitration* produced an award, with *res judicata* effect between Mauritius and the United Kingdom, to the effect that, at least until resolution of the sovereignty dispute, the United Kingdom is entitled to exercise the rights of a coastal State under UNCLOS in respect of the Chagos Archipelago.

139. The Special Chamber considers that the *Chagos* arbitral award is of some relevance to the legal status of the Chagos Archipelago. While the Arbitral Tribunal recognized the existence of the sovereignty dispute over the Chagos Archipelago, it was unable to address it owing to its jurisdictional limitation as an Annex VII tribunal. On the other hand, in the Special Chamber's view, the Arbitral Tribunal's findings on the rights of Mauritius in respect of the Chagos Archipelago pursuant to the legally binding undertakings of the United Kingdom, such as fishing rights in the waters of the Archipelago, the right to the return of the Archipelago when no longer needed for defence purposes, and the right to the benefit of any minerals or oil discovered in or near the Archipelago, may play a role in the assessment of whether Mauritius can be regarded as the State with an opposite or adjacent coast to the Maldives for the purpose of maritime boundary delimitation. The Special Chamber will return to this issue when it comes to a conclusion below (see paragraph 246 below).

2. Advisory opinion on the Legal Consequences of the Separation of the Chagos Archipelago from Mauritius in 1965

140. The Special Chamber will now consider whether the *Chagos* advisory opinion has any relevance to, or implications for, the legal status of the Chagos Archipelago.

141. The Maldives submits that the *Chagos* advisory opinion did not, and could not, resolve the bilateral sovereignty dispute between Mauritius and the United Kingdom. The Maldives advances the following arguments in this regard. First, "[t]he ICJ was not asked to, and did not, provide advice on the sovereignty dispute, let alone the question of which State is the relevant coastal State for UNCLOS purposes". Second, resolution of the sovereignty dispute is not "an implied or necessary consequence of the ICJ's Advisory Opinion". Third, even if the ICJ had given advice on the sovereignty dispute, any such opinion would not have been binding on States. Fourth, the ICJ was not asked, had no power and did not purport to overrule the *Chagos* arbitral award.

142. For its part, Mauritius submits that "[t]here can be no doubt that the issue of sovereignty over the Chagos Archipelago has been disposed of by the Court in its Advisory Opinion, the conclusions of which carry legal consequences for all UN Member States and international institutions."

143. The Special Chamber will examine the issues raised by the Parties' arguments in the order presented by the Maldives. The Special Chamber will embark upon this task by first considering the nature of the questions posed to the ICJ and the scope and contents of the advisory opinion. It will then examine the consequences and legal effect of the advisory opinion. Finally, it will address the relationship between the *Chagos* arbitral award and the *Chagos* advisory opinion.

Questions posed to the ICJ and the scope and contents of the Chagos *advisory opinion*

144. The Maldives maintains that neither of the questions which the UNGA posed to the ICJ concerned sovereignty or required the ICJ to give an opinion on the sovereignty dispute between Mauritius and the United Kingdom. According to the Maldives, "[t]he questions posed to the Court made no mention of sovereignty whatsoever" and "[t]he Court made that much clear itself." The Maldives argues that the ICJ "expressly recognised that '[t]he General Assembly ha[d] not sought the Court's opinion to resolve a territorial dispute between two States'."

145. The Maldives points out that, in considering the first question, the ICJ found that,

[i]n Question (*a*), the General Assembly asks the Court to examine certain events which occurred between 1965 and 1968, and which fall within the framework of the process of decolonization of Mauritius as a non-self-governing territory. *It did not submit to the Court a bilateral dispute over sovereignty which might exist between the United Kingdom and Mauritius.*

146. The Maldives underscores that it was indeed specifically on the basis that it had not been asked to resolve the sovereignty dispute that the ICJ considered that "it could exercise jurisdiction to give the advisory opinion requested without 'circumventing the principle of consent by a State to the judicial settlement of its dispute with another State'."

147. The Maldives contends that the second question put to the ICJ is particularly instructive in this regard. It points out that the ICJ's answer was a short one, that "the United Kingdom has an obligation to bring to an end its administration of the Chagos Archipelago as rapidly as possible, and . . . all Member States must co-operate with the United Nations to complete the decolonization of Mauritius." The Maldives states that

[t]hose were the only legal consequences which the Court identified. At no point did the Court state that the UK suddenly lost sovereignty, let alone that Mauritius immediately became the exclusive sovereign and coastal State. The General Assembly had not asked for an opinion about sovereignty—only one about decolonization.

148. The Maldives considers that "Mauritius' claim that the ICJ decided the bilateral dispute could only be correct if the Court went beyond the legal questions put to it and exceeded its jurisdiction."

149. In this regard, the Maldives draws the attention of the Special Chamber to the attempts made by Mauritius, during the advisory proceedings, to invite the ICJ to "issue a sweeping opinion on territorial sovereignty and maritime boundary delimitation with the Maldives." First, according to the Maldives, Mauritius invited the ICJ to find that

sovereignty over the Chagos Archipelago is entirely derivative of, subsumed within, and determined by the question of whether decolonization has or has not been lawfully completed.

The Maldives contends that the ICJ declined to do so, "stating in clear terms that the UNGA had not asked it to resolve the sovereignty or territorial dispute between Mauritius and the United Kingdom." Second, Mauritius invited the ICJ to find that,

among the legal consequences of continued British administration of the Chagos Archipelago, was the obligation of the United Kingdom to "consult and cooperate with Mauritius *inter alia* to . . . allow Mauritius to proceed to a delimitation of its maritime boundaries with the Maldives."

The Maldives argues that the ICJ again declined Mauritius' invitation to "articulate even these consequences which are more modest than a sovereignty claim." In the Maldives' view, "the Court's silence" is certainly not consistent with the claim that the sovereignty dispute has been resolved in favour of Mauritius.

150. For the Maldives, "there is no clearer indication of Mauritius' mischaracterization of the Opinion than its repeated assertion that the Court concluded that the Chagos 'is, and always has been, a part of the territory of Mauritius.'" The Maldives emphasizes that the ICJ simply did not say this and that all it said was that, "*at the time of its detachment from Mauritius in 1965*, the Chagos Archipelago was clearly an integral part of that non-self-governing territory [i.e. Mauritius]".

151. With regard to the two passages which Mauritius claims indicate the ICJ's opinion that the Chagos Archipelago is currently part of Mauritius' sovereign territory, the Maldives asserts that, "[r]ead properly and in context, neither of the passages support that conclusion." First, regarding the passage stating that the United Kingdom must bring to an end its administration of the Chagos Archipelago so as to enable Mauritius to complete the "decolonization of its territory", the Maldives submits that, read in context, "the words . . . most readily refer to the United Kingdom's obligation to complete the decolonisation of the entire territory of Mauritius *as it stood in 1965.*" Second, as to the passage stating that the obligations arising under international law "require" the United Kingdom to respect the territorial integrity of that country, including the Chagos Archipelago, the Maldives is also of the view that, in context, the passage is best understood as a reference to the territorial integrity of Mauritius "as it stood in 1965", and the United Kingdom's obligation to complete the process of decolonization in respect of the entire territory.

152. Mauritius takes the position that

[t]he issue of whether the Chagos Archipelago is an integral part of the territory of Mauritius or whether it is a lawful colonial possession of the UK was resolved definitively, and as a matter of international law, by the International Court of Justice in its Advisory Opinion of 25 February 2019.

153. According to Mauritius, the passage of the advisory opinion, in which the ICJ notes that the General Assembly "did not submit to the Court a bilateral dispute over sovereignty which might exist between the United Kingdom and Mauritius", is far from supporting the Maldives' position that the advisory opinion did not, and could not, resolve the bilateral sovereignty dispute. Mauritius contends that, read in context, this and other passages of the advisory opinion to the same effect are "a repudiation of the argument put forward by the United Kingdom urging the Court to exercise its discretion and decline to

provide the opinion requested by the General Assembly." According to that argument, Mauritius notes, accepting the General Assembly's request would amount to circumventing the principle of consent.

154. However, Mauritius argues that the ICJ rejected the United Kingdom's objection and made clear that the questions posed did not concern a bilateral territorial dispute, since "[t]he issues raised by the request are located in the broader frame of reference of decolonization, including the General Assembly's role therein, from which those issues are inseparable."

155. For Mauritius, the ICJ left no doubt about which issues it considered inseparable from one another. Mauritius argues that the ICJ recognized that "the issue of whether the Chagos Archipelago forms an integral part of Mauritius was inseparable from the issue of the lawfulness of Mauritius' decolonization", and that its advisory opinion would necessarily address and resolve both issues. Mauritius notes that the ICJ thus continued in the next paragraph:

> However, the fact that the Court may have to pronounce on legal issues on which divergent views have been expressed by Mauritius and the United Kingdom does not mean that, by replying to the request, the Court is dealing with a bilateral dispute.

In Mauritius' view, in replying to the General Assembly's request, and deciding whether the decolonization of Mauritius had been lawfully completed, the ICJ was also determining which State had sovereignty over the Chagos Archipelago.

156. Mauritius contends that, contrary to the Maldives' claim, it did not "invite" the ICJ to find that the sovereignty issue was subsumed within the question of decolonization; nor did the ICJ reject an "invitation" from Mauritius which it never received. Rather, its argument before the ICJ was similar to that of the United Kingdom that "the underlying sovereignty dispute could not be separated from the question of decolonization, and that by answering the UNGA's questions on decolonization . . . the sovereignty issue would inevitably be resolved." In Mauritius' view, it is of paramount significance that, "faced with these entirely congruent views by the two main protagonists in the Advisory Proceedings, on the consequences of answering the questions, the Court chose to do so."

157. Mauritius argues that decolonization always implicates sovereignty, because "the end result of decolonization is independence, and the exercise of sovereignty by the newly independent State over the entirety of the former colonial territory." Thus, in Mauritius' view, in answering the question as to whether the decolonization of Mauritius

had been lawfully completed, the ICJ clearly understood that, "in so doing, it was determining which State was the lawful sovereign over Chagos."

158. Mauritius notes that, as regards the General Assembly's first question, the ICJ determined that

the United Kingdom's detachment of the Archipelago was unlawful and without legal consequences, having violated fundamental rules of international law, including the right to self-determination and the corollary right to territorial integrity, which were a part of customary international law at the time the purported detachment occurred.

As the detachment was unlawful, Mauritius argues, it follows that the United Kingdom has no rights in respect of the Chagos Archipelago.

159. Mauritius asserts that what made the decolonization of Mauritius incomplete was the United Kingdom's failure to fulfil its obligation "to respect the territorial integrity of that country, including the Chagos Archipelago." According to Mauritius, "[t]here can be no clearer determination, that as a matter of international law, the Archipelago is an integral part of the territory of Mauritius."

160. In Mauritius' view, there are equally clear determinations in the ICJ's answer to the General Assembly's second question regarding the legal consequences arising from the failure to complete the decolonization of Mauritius. According to Mauritius, in response to this question, the ICJ determined that, "because the UK continued to occupy and administer Chagos after Mauritius achieved independence as a sovereign State, the UK was engaged in 'an unlawful act of a continuing character.'" As a consequence, "the United Kingdom's continued administration of the Chagos Archipelago constitutes a wrongful act entailing the international responsibility of that State." The United Kingdom accordingly is "under an obligation to bring an end to its administration of the Chagos Archipelago as rapidly as possible, thereby enabling Mauritius to complete the decolonization of its territory in a manner consistent with the right of peoples to self-determination." In light of this language, Mauritius avers, "the only conclusion that can be drawn is that in the Court's view Mauritius alone is sovereign over Chagos".

161. In this regard, Mauritius draws attention to the specific words used in two passages of the advisory opinion. First, as seen above, the ICJ determined that the United Kingdom is obligated to bring an end to its administration of the Chagos Archipelago "so as to enable '*Mauritius* to complete the decolonization of *its territory* . . .'."

Second, the ICJ used the present tense when holding that the "obligations arising under international law ... *require* the United Kingdom ... to respect the territorial integrity of *that country* [*i.e.,* Mauritius] including the Chagos Archipelago." Mauritius states that the ICJ "did not refer to the obligation as one that was limited to a past moment". It asserts that the words admit of only a single interpretation: the ICJ concluded that "the Chagos Archipelago is an integral part of the territory of Mauritius, and that Mauritius alone is sovereign over all of its territory, including the Chagos Archipelago."

* * *

162. The questions put by the UNGA to the ICJ for an advisory opinion are as follows:

(a) Was the process of decolonization of Mauritius lawfully completed when Mauritius was granted independence in 1968, following the separation of the Chagos Archipelago from Mauritius and having regard to international law, including obligations reflected in General Assembly resolutions 1514 (XV) of 14 December 1960, 2066 (XX) of 16 December 1965, 2232 (XXI) of 20 December 1966 and 2357 (XXII) of 19 December 1967?;

(b) What are the consequences under international law, including obligations reflected in the above-mentioned resolutions, arising from the continued administration by the United Kingdom of Great Britain and Northern Ireland of the Chagos Archipelago, including with respect to the inability of Mauritius to implement a programme for the resettlement on the Chagos Archipelago of its nationals, in particular those of Chagossian origin?

163. The Special Chamber notes that the questions posed by the General Assembly are concerned with the lawfulness of the process of decolonization of Mauritius and the consequences under international law arising from the United Kingdom's continued administration of the Chagos Archipelago.

164. The Special Chamber further notes that both Parties refer to the findings of the ICJ that, in making a request for an advisory opinion, the General Assembly "has not sought the Court's opinion to resolve a territorial dispute between two States" and "did not submit to the Court a bilateral dispute over sovereignty which might exist between the United Kingdom and Mauritius" (*Legal Consequences of the Separation of the Chagos Archipelago from Mauritius in 1965, Advisory Opinion, ICJ Reports 2019*, p. 95, at p. 117, para. 86, and at p. 129, para. 136).

165. However, the Parties differ as to the meaning and implication of these findings. The Maldives is of the view that, given the nature of

the questions posed, the ICJ did not, and could not, address the sovereignty dispute between the United Kingdom and Mauritius. On the other hand, Mauritius' view is that the ICJ stated so because "the issues raised by the request were 'located in the broader frame of reference of decolonization'" and that, in answering the questions about the decolonization of Mauritius and its consequences, the ICJ also determined the sovereignty issue over the Chagos Archipelago.

166. In the Special Chamber's view, the pronouncement that the General Assembly did not submit to the ICJ a bilateral dispute over sovereignty does not necessarily carry with it the inference that the advisory opinion therefore has no relevance or implication for the issue of sovereignty. Given the close relationship between decolonization and sovereignty, such inference is far from evident. The Special Chamber notes that the ICJ itself denied such inference when it stated that "the fact that the Court may have to pronounce on legal issues on which divergent views have been expressed by Mauritius and the United Kingdom does not mean that, by replying to the request, the Court is dealing with a bilateral dispute" (*Legal Consequences of the Separation of the Chagos Archipelago from Mauritius in 1965, Advisory Opinion, ICJ Reports 2019*, p. 95, at p. 118, para. 89).

167. The Special Chamber will next examine whether the advisory opinion has, expressly or implicitly, addressed the sovereignty dispute over the Chagos Archipelago. The Special Chamber notes that the Parties hold diametrically opposed views as to this question. While the Maldives contends that the advisory opinion does not and cannot resolve the sovereignty dispute between Mauritius and the United Kingdom, Mauritius asserts that the advisory opinion has conclusively resolved the sovereignty issue in favour of Mauritius.

168. As an initial matter, the Special Chamber notes that the principle of consent by a State to the judicial settlement of its dispute with another State is fundamental to international judicial proceedings. It would be contrary to the principle of consent to accept the proposition that international courts or tribunals, through contentious or advisory proceedings, can resolve a bilateral dispute without the consent of a party to the dispute. However, this does not mean that the advisory opinion could not entail implications for the disputed issue of sovereignty.

169. The Special Chamber will now consider paragraphs in the *Chagos* advisory opinion which are of particular relevance in this regard.

170. With respect to the first question posed by the General Assembly, the relevant paragraphs are:

170. . . . at the time of its detachment from Mauritius in 1965, the Chagos Archipelago was clearly an integral part of that non-self-governing territory.
. . .

172. . . . Having reviewed the circumstances in which the Council of Ministers of the colony of Mauritius agreed in principle to the detachment of the Chagos Archipelago on the basis of the Lancaster House agreement, the Court considers that this detachment was not based on the free and genuine expression of the will of the people concerned.

173. . . . The Court considers that the obligations arising under international law and reflected in the resolutions adopted by the General Assembly during the process of decolonization of Mauritius require the United Kingdom, as the administering Power, to respect the territorial integrity of that country, including the Chagos Archipelago.

174. The Court concludes that, as a result of the Chagos Archipelago's unlawful detachment and its incorporation into a new colony, known as the BIOT, the process of decolonization of Mauritius was not lawfully completed when Mauritius acceded to independence in 1968.

(*Legal Consequences of the Separation of the Chagos Archipelago from Mauritius in 1965, Advisory Opinion, ICJ Reports 2019*, p. 95, at pp. 136-7)

171. Thus, the ICJ determined that the detachment of the Chagos Archipelago, which was clearly an integral part of Mauritius in 1965, was not based on the free and genuine expression of the will of the people concerned and consequently the process of decolonization of Mauritius was not lawfully completed. The Special Chamber notes that the ICJ made these determinations after reviewing the circumstances in which the Council of Ministers of the colony of Mauritius agreed in principle to the detachment of the Chagos Archipelago on the basis of the 1965 Agreement, the validity or otherwise of which, as stated above (see paragraph 134 above), the Arbitral Tribunal in the *Chagos Marine Protected Area Arbitration* noted was "a central element" of the parties' submissions on sovereignty. Thus, these determinations could have implications for the issue of sovereignty over the Chagos Archipelago.

172. With respect to the second question of the General Assembly, the relevant paragraphs of the advisory opinion are:

177. The Court having found that the decolonization of Mauritius was not conducted in a manner consistent with the right of peoples to self-determination, it follows that the United Kingdom's continued administration of the Chagos Archipelago constitutes a wrongful act entailing the international responsibility of that State . . . It is an unlawful act of a continuing character which arose as a result of the separation of the Chagos Archipelago from Mauritius.

178. Accordingly, the United Kingdom is under an obligation to bring an end to its administration of the Chagos Archipelago as rapidly as possible,

thereby enabling Mauritius to complete the decolonization of its territory in a manner consistent with the right of peoples to self-determination.

179. The modalities necessary for ensuring the completion of the decolonization of Mauritius fall within the remit of the United Nations General Assembly, in the exercise of its function relating to decolonization.
. . .

180. Since respect for the right to self-determination is an obligation *erga omnes*, all States have a legal interest in protecting that right ... The Court considers that, while it is for the General Assembly to pronounce on the modalities required to ensure the completion of the decolonization of Mauritius, all Member States must co-operate with the United Nations to put those modalities into effect.
. . .

182. ... the Court concludes that the United Kingdom has an obligation to bring to an end its administration of the Chagos Archipelago as rapidly as possible, and that all Member States must co-operate with the United Nations to complete the decolonization of Mauritius.

(*Legal Consequences of the Separation of the Chagos Archipelago from Mauritius in 1965, Advisory Opinion, ICJ Reports 2019*, p. 95, at pp. 138-40)

173. The ICJ thus determined that the United Kingdom's continued administration of the Chagos Archipelago is an unlawful act of a continuing character, entailing its international responsibility, and must be brought to an end as rapidly as possible. The Special Chamber considers that these determinations, together with those previously mentioned, have unmistakable implications for the United Kingdom's claim to sovereignty over the Chagos Archipelago. In the Special Chamber's view, such claim is contrary to the determinations made by the ICJ that the detachment of the Chagos Archipelago was unlawful and that the United Kingdom's continued administration of the Chagos Archipelago constitutes an unlawful act of a continuing character.

174. The ICJ's determinations may also entail considerable implications for the sovereignty claim of Mauritius, whose territory, as the ICJ found, included the Chagos Archipelago at the time of its unlawful detachment by the United Kingdom. In particular, the ICJ determined that "the obligations arising under international law and reflected in the resolutions adopted by the General Assembly during the process of decolonization of Mauritius *require* the United Kingdom, as the administering Power, to respect the *territorial integrity of that country, including the Chagos Archipelago*" (emphasis added by the Special Chamber) (*Legal Consequences of the Separation of the Chagos Archipelago from Mauritius*

in 1965, Advisory Opinion, ICJ Reports 2019, p. 95, at p. 137, para. 173). In the Special Chamber's view, this can be interpreted as suggesting Mauritius' sovereignty over the Chagos Archipelago. The same may be said of the determination that "the United Kingdom is under an obligation to bring an end to its administration of the Chagos Archipelago as rapidly as possible, thereby enabling Mauritius to complete the *decolonization of its territory* in a manner consistent with the right of peoples to self-determination" (emphasis added by the Special Chamber) (*Ibid.*, at p. 139, para. 178). The Special Chamber also notes that the process of decolonization has yet to be completed and that in this regard the ICJ stated that "[t]he modalities necessary for ensuring the completion of the decolonization of Mauritius" were left with the UNGA (*Ibid.*, at p. 139, para. 179).

175. The Special Chamber will take into account its findings above, together with other relevant factors, in assessing the legal status of the Chagos Archipelago. On the basis of that assessment, the Special Chamber will give its conclusion as to whether Mauritius can be regarded as the State with an opposite or adjacent coast to the Maldives for the purpose of maritime boundary delimitation under article 74, paragraph 1, and article 83, paragraph 1, of the Convention.

Consequences of the Chagos *advisory opinion*

176. The Maldives further submits that the resolution of the sovereignty dispute is not "an implied or necessary consequence" of the *Chagos* advisory opinion.

177. Refuting Mauritius' argument that "the Opinion can be taken to have resolved the sovereignty dispute by necessary implication", the Maldives contends that Mauritius' case requires the Special Chamber to assume that "the Court, without saying so, agreed with Mauritius' submissions on the consequences of the decolonisation questions for the sovereignty dispute." However, the Maldives argues that the ICJ's refusal to make such statements is consistent with the fact that "it had not been requested to give an opinion on these matters and did not consider that the consequences suggested by Mauritius flowed from its opinion."

178. In this regard, the Maldives presents three arguments. First, according to the Maldives, whatever Mauritius' own interpretation is, it cannot deny that there is a dispute between Mauritius and the United Kingdom over the consequences of the advisory opinion for the sovereignty dispute between them. The Maldives maintains that, while it considers its interpretation of the advisory opinion to be correct, it does not matter whether it has interpreted the advisory opinion correctly or

not because "the correct interpretation of the Advisory Opinion is not a matter concerning the interpretation or application of UNCLOS. It is plainly outside the scope of this Chamber's jurisdiction."

179. Second, the Maldives submits that, "on its face, Mauritius' claim that the *Chagos* Advisory Opinion resolved the sovereignty dispute by necessary implication is not convincing." In the Maldives' view, as a matter of international legal principle, it is not the case that "an administering State which bears an obligation to complete the process of decolonisation in respect of a given territory is immediately stripped of sovereignty over that territory." The existence of such an obligation is thus neither necessarily nor automatically accompanied by an instant loss of sovereignty.

180. Third, the Maldives contends that neither the advisory opinion on *Legal Consequences for States of the Continued Presence of South Africa in Namibia (South West Africa) notwithstanding Security Council Resolution 276 (1970)* (hereinafter "the *Namibia* advisory opinion") nor the *Western Sahara* advisory opinion, to which Mauritius referred, assist Mauritius in establishing that "the sovereignty dispute was resolved as a necessary consequence of the *Chagos* Advisory Opinion." The Maldives asserts that the factual and legal situations addressed in these advisory opinions are distinguishable in crucial respects.

181. The Maldives argues that the *Namibia* advisory opinion was not "dispositive on the issue of sovereignty" as Mauritius alleges. According to the Maldives, what was at issue in that case was the extent of South Africa's obligations as a mandatory power, not a claim to sovereignty which it had never made. In contrast, there is no dispute that the United Kingdom historically possessed sovereignty over Mauritius when it was a colony. Thus, once the mandate agreement had been lawfully terminated, South Africa had no right or title of any kind to administer Namibia. However, that is not the case with the United Kingdom. In the Maldives' view, "[t]he *Chagos* Advisory Opinion makes clear that the right of administration remains with the United Kingdom until it departs." In addition, the Maldives argues that, while there was a binding Security Council resolution to ensure that all States were compelled to recognize the illegality and invalidity of South Africa's presence in Namibia, there is no Security Council resolution to such effect relating to the Chagos Archipelago. For these reasons, the Maldives contends, the ICJ did not draw a comparison between the situation in the Chagos Archipelago and that of Namibia, or refer in any other way to the *Namibia* advisory opinion when giving its opinion on the consequences of the United Kingdom's continued administration of the Chagos Archipelago.

182. As regards the *Western Sahara* advisory opinion, the Maldives is of the view that, contrary to Mauritius' claim, the ICJ rejected Spain's objection to the advisory proceedings precisely because "rendering the opinion sought would *not* resolve a bilateral sovereignty dispute or otherwise affect Spain's rights as the administering power of Western Sahara." The Maldives adds that, to the extent that the ICJ gave an opinion on sovereignty, it was in the context of answering the second question posed, which directly required the ICJ to consider the question of historic sovereignty over, or any other legal ties with, Western Sahara. According to the Maldives, as an asserted historical tie of sovereignty was the very subject matter of the second question, there was no need to "extrapolate from the Court's express statements what the implied consequences were for sovereignty . . ., which is what Mauritius is asking the Special Chamber to do in the present proceedings." The Maldives adds that the *Western Sahara* advisory opinion confirms that "the obligation to complete decolonization is not one and the same as territorial sovereignty; the Court can issue an opinion on the former without any necessary or implied consequences for the latter."

183. Mauritius maintains that, as a consequence of the *Chagos* advisory opinion,

Mauritius is the only State entitled to claim sovereignty over Chagos; the United Kingdom has no sovereignty in respect of the Archipelago; and, insofar as these proceedings are concerned, it has no legal rights that could be affected by a delimitation of the maritime boundary between the Archipelago and the Maldives.

184. As regards the Maldives' interpretation of the advisory opinion, Mauritius asserts that, "[i]n essence, the Maldives invites the Special Chamber . . . to disregard and effectively overrule the ICJ's authoritative determination that the United Kingdom has no lawful basis to claim sovereignty or sovereign rights in regard to the Chagos Archipelago." In this regard, Mauritius argues that "there is no tenable basis for the Special Chamber to place itself in direct opposition to the ICJ and the UN General Assembly." In proceeding to delimit the overlapping maritime zones of Mauritius and the Maldives, Mauritius contends, the Special Chamber "is asked to do no more than respect the territorial integrity of Mauritius, as confirmed by the Court."

185. Mauritius refutes the Maldives' claim that, as a matter of international legal principle, the existence of an obligation to complete decolonization is not necessarily accompanied by an instant loss of sovereignty. Mauritius contends that the Maldives cites not a single authority for the existence of such an alleged "legal principle". On the

contrary, according to Mauritius, "[r]ecognising even the plausibility of the United Kingdom's claim of sovereignty over the Chagos Archipelago as a result of its wrongful detachment from Mauritius would transgress the general principle of international law of *ex injuria non oritur jus*".

186. In support of its argument that the advisory opinion disposed of the issue of sovereignty, Mauritius refers to the *Namibia* advisory opinion of the ICJ. Mauritius notes that, following that advisory opinion, the United Nations Council for South-West Africa, which was established in 1967 by the General Assembly with the function of administering the territory until it gained independence, continued to act in pursuance of the powers and duties granted to it by the United Nations, despite the fact that South Africa denied access to the territory. According to Mauritius, this demonstrated "the immediate and authoritative legal effect of the ICJ's Advisory Opinion, notwithstanding the protestations of South Africa."

187. Referring to the *Western Sahara* advisory opinion, Mauritius asserts that the ICJ determined that it should issue an advisory opinion because the request fundamentally raised a question of decolonization, and "the matter of sovereignty was subsumed within and incidental to that question." Similarly, according to Mauritius, the matter referred to the ICJ in the *Chagos* advisory proceedings concerned decolonization, but "once the lawfulness of decolonisation is determined, the question of territorial sovereignty no longer arises."

* * *

188. The Special Chamber considers that decolonization of a territory entails considerable consequences regarding the question of sovereignty over the territory, as decolonization and territorial sovereignty are closely interrelated. To what extent decolonization may implicate territorial sovereignty depends on the particular circumstances of each case.

189. In the Special Chamber's view, the decolonization and sovereignty of Mauritius, including the Chagos Archipelago, are inseparably related. This was recognized by the Arbitral Tribunal in the *Chagos* arbitral award when it stated that the validity or otherwise of the "1965 Agreement" was "a central element of the Parties' submissions on Mauritius' First and Second Submissions, sovereignty, and the identity of the coastal State" (see paragraph 134 above). This was also implied when the ICJ stated in the *Chagos* advisory opinion that "[t]he issues raised by the request are located in the broader frame of reference of decolonization, including the General Assembly's role therein, from

which those issues are inseparable" (*Legal Consequences of the Separation of the Chagos Archipelago from Mauritius in 1965, Advisory Opinion, ICJ Reports 2019*, p. 95, at p. 118, para. 88).

190. As regards the Maldives' first argument, the Special Chamber does not consider that the Parties' disagreement on the consequences of the *Chagos* advisory opinion falls outside its jurisdiction. Under article 288, paragraph 4, of the Convention, the Special Chamber has the competence to decide its own jurisdiction. In this regard, whether the *Chagos* advisory opinion has clarified the legal status of the Chagos Archipelago is a question central to the jurisdiction of the Special Chamber. Accordingly, the Special Chamber is competent to assess the Parties' dispute as to the consequences of the advisory opinion to the extent necessary to determine its jurisdiction.

191. With respect to the Maldives' argument that the obligation to complete the process of decolonization is neither necessarily nor automatically accompanied by an instant loss of sovereignty, the Special Chamber considers that the relevant question is whether this would be the case in the specific circumstances of the decolonization of Mauritius rather than whether it is valid as a general proposition. In the case of Mauritius, as noted above, the issues of decolonization and sovereignty are inseparably related so that a decision on decolonization may necessarily implicate sovereignty.

192. Regarding the *Namibia* and *Western Sahara* advisory opinions referred to by the Parties to support their views as to the consequences of decolonization for sovereignty, the Special Chamber notes that, as the circumstances of the two cases are different from those of the present case, it is difficult to draw any meaningful inference from them to support either the view of the Maldives or that of Mauritius.

Legal effect of the Chagos *advisory opinion*

193. The Maldives argues that even if the ICJ had given an opinion on the sovereignty dispute, any such opinion would not have been binding on States.

194. The Maldives states that the Parties are in agreement that advisory opinions do not have binding effect. The Maldives also states that the ICJ itself has confirmed on numerous occasions that its advisory opinions are not binding even on the organs which request them, let alone on other entities such as States. Additionally, the Maldives expresses the view that, "whatever authority advisory opinions may have in jurisprudence as abstract statements of international law, they are not a means of binding States in specific disputes through the backdoor."

195. As for the *Chagos* advisory opinion, the Maldives asserts that, "even if the Court had purported to advise on the sovereignty dispute, its opinion did not have binding force on the UNGA or any State (including the United Kingdom and the Maldives)".

196. With respect to the two cases decided by the Court of Justice of the European Union (hereinafter "the CJEU") to which Mauritius refers (see paragraph 199 below), the Maldives submits that neither of the cases supports Mauritius' position. According to the Maldives, although it is possible for the CJEU to resolve inter-State disputes, it was not performing this role in either of those cases. In addition, the Maldives argues that in neither of the cases did the CJEU's Grand Chamber or the CJEU suggest that an advisory opinion of the ICJ was "binding on it or on any EU organ or Member State."

197. Mauritius maintains that, while an advisory opinion is not binding as such, this does not mean that it is devoid of legal effects. According to Mauritius, when the ICJ gives an advisory opinion, it provides "an authoritative statement of the law in relation to the issues to which the advisory proceedings give rise." As the ICJ is the principal judicial organ of the United Nations, the statement of law made in advisory opinions is considered authoritative.

198. Referring to scholarly views on this matter, Mauritius argues that the pronouncements made by the ICJ in advisory opinions are considered to be on an equal footing with those made in judgments as integral components of its jurisprudence. It further argues that, although compliance may not be obligatory in respect of an opinion itself, States are bound and obliged to comply with the law, as declared and defined by the ICJ, whether in contentious cases or advisory opinions.

199. Mauritius is of the view that "legal determinations made by the ICJ in its advisory opinions are accepted as binding and dispositive statements of the law by other international courts and tribunals." In this regard, it refers to two cases decided by the CJEU. In *Council of the European Union* v. *Front Polisario* (Case C-104/16P), Mauritius contends, the CJEU accepted as conclusive as a matter of international law the ICJ's determination in its advisory opinion in the *Western Sahara* case. Likewise, in *Organisation juive européenne and Vignoble Psagot Ltd* v. *Ministre de l'Économie et des Finances* (Case C-363/18), the CJEU applied the factual and legal findings of the ICJ in the advisory opinion on the *Legal Consequences of a Wall in the Occupied Palestinian Territory* (hereinafter "the *Wall* advisory opinion"). Accordingly, Mauritius emphasizes that, even though the *Western Sahara* and *Wall* advisory opinions were not binding as such on Morocco or Israel, all

States, including the two States concerned, were bound by "the rules of international law identified and applied by the Court."

200. Referring to the *Chagos* advisory opinion, Mauritius argues that it is "replete with references to the legal obligations by which the United Kingdom, and other States, are legally bound" and that "[s]uch legal obligations are, indeed, binding, even if the Advisory Opinion itself, *per se*, is not."

201. Mauritius further argues that the advisory opinion of 2019 has been accepted and approved by the General Assembly. According to Mauritius, it is "the law recognized by the United Nations" and

continues to be so although the Government of the country that is unlawfully administering the Chagos Archipelago has declined to accept it as binding upon it, and although it has acted in disregard of the international obligations as declared by the Court in that Opinion.

* * *

202. The Special Chamber notes that it is generally recognized that advisory opinions of the ICJ cannot be considered legally binding. As the ICJ itself stated in the advisory opinion on *Interpretation of Peace Treaties with Bulgaria, Hungary and Romania*, "[t]he Court's reply is only of an advisory character: as such, it has no binding force" (*Interpretation of Peace Treaties with Bulgaria, Hungary and Romania, First Phase, Advisory Opinion, ICJ Reports 1950*, p. 65, at p. 71; see also *Request for Advisory Opinion submitted by the Sub-Regional Fisheries Commission, Advisory Opinion, 2 April 2015, ITLOS Reports 2015*, p. 4, at. p. 26, para. 76). However, it is equally recognized that an advisory opinion entails an authoritative statement of international law on the questions with which it deals.

203. In this regard, the Special Chamber finds it necessary to draw a distinction between the binding character and the authoritative nature of an advisory opinion of the ICJ. An advisory opinion is not binding because even the requesting entity is not obligated to comply with it in the same way as parties to contentious proceedings are obligated to comply with a judgment. However, judicial determinations made in advisory opinions carry no less weight and authority than those in judgments because they are made with the same rigour and scrutiny by the "principal judicial organ" of the United Nations with competence in matters of international law.

204. The Special Chamber notes in this regard that the CJEU, while it did not suggest that an advisory opinion of the ICJ is "binding", attached due importance to the legal and factual determinations made by the ICJ in its advisory opinions.

205. In the Special Chamber's view, determinations made by the ICJ in an advisory opinion cannot be disregarded simply because the advisory opinion is not binding. This is true of the ICJ's determinations in the *Chagos* advisory opinion, *inter alia*, that the process of decolonization of Mauritius was not lawfully completed when that country acceded to independence in 1968, following the separation of the Chagos Archipelago, and that the United Kingdom is under an obligation to bring to an end its administration of the Chagos Archipelago as rapidly as possible. The Special Chamber considers that those determinations do have legal effect.

206. The Special Chamber, accordingly, recognizes those determinations, and takes them into consideration in assessing the legal status of the Chagos Archipelago.

Relationship between the Chagos *arbitral award and the* Chagos *advisory opinion*

207. In support of its argument that the advisory opinion did not resolve the sovereignty dispute over the Chagos Archipelago, the Maldives contends that "[t]he ICJ was not asked, had no authority, and did not purport to overrule" the *Chagos* arbitral award.

208. The Maldives notes that the Arbitral Tribunal found that a sovereignty dispute existed between Mauritius and the United Kingdom over the Chagos Archipelago and that such dispute did not concern the interpretation or application of the Convention. The Maldives argues that the Arbitral Tribunal "found unanimously in 2015 that the UK was entitled to exercise the powers of a coastal State in respect of the Chagos Archipelago in accordance with UNCLOS".

209. According to the Maldives, these findings have *res judicata* effect as between Mauritius and the United Kingdom, and the ICJ "could not have considered itself to be overturning an existing award with binding effect". In the Maldives' view, therefore, the advisory opinion did not resolve the extant bilateral sovereignty dispute and did not overrule the Arbitral Tribunal's findings on the power of the United Kingdom to act as a coastal State.

210. Mauritius contends that the Maldives' argument is the same as that of the United Kingdom in the advisory proceedings, which was rejected by the ICJ. According to Mauritius, the ICJ found that "the arbitral award did not have *res judicata* effect in respect of any of the issues that were submitted to it by the General Assembly."

211. Mauritius underlines that the ICJ had no need to override or overrule the arbitral award because the issues decided by the Arbitral

Tribunal were not the same as those before the ICJ. Mauritius points out that "[t]he fact that the Annex VII tribunal decided not to decide the "coastal State" issue only underscores that there was no decision on this issue for the ICJ to overrule."

212. Mauritius also states that the ICJ, which was not subject to the jurisdictional limitation under the Convention, was thus free to "opine on the lawfulness of Mauritius' decolonization and whether the Chagos Archipelago was an integral part of Mauritius' territory, before and after independence, without treading on the arbitral tribunal's turf."

* * *

213. The Special Chamber notes that the premise of the Maldives' contention is that the Arbitral Tribunal rendered an award with *res judicata* effect regarding the existence of a sovereignty dispute between Mauritius and the United Kingdom as well as which State is entitled to exercise the power of the coastal State in respect of the Chagos Archipelago (see paragraphs 121-3 above).

214. As the Special Chamber noted in paragraph 133 above, the Arbitral Tribunal in the *Chagos Marine Protected Area Arbitration* found that a sovereignty dispute existed between Mauritius and the United Kingdom over the Chagos Archipelago and that it lacked jurisdiction to entertain said dispute. Unlike the Arbitral Tribunal, whose jurisdiction was limited to disputes concerning the interpretation or application of the Convention under article 288, paragraph 1, of the Convention, the ICJ, in rendering its advisory opinion, had no such jurisdictional limitation. Consequently, it proceeded to examine issues relating to the decolonization of Mauritius and concluded, *inter alia*, that the detachment of the Chagos Archipelago from Mauritius was unlawful. Irrespective of whether or not the advisory opinion has resolved the sovereignty dispute, therefore, there is no question of the advisory opinion overruling the arbitral award, since, as the ICJ stated, "the issues that were determined by the Arbitral Tribunal in the *Arbitration regarding the Chagos Marine Protected Area* . . . are not the same as those that are before the Court in these proceedings" (*Legal Consequences of the Separation of the Chagos Archipelago from Mauritius in 1965, Advisory Opinion, ICJ Reports 2019*, p. 95, at p. 116, para. 81).

215. The Special Chamber, in paragraph 138 above, did not accept the Maldives' claim that the Arbitral Tribunal determined, with *res judicata* effect between Mauritius and the United Kingdom, that, until the sovereignty dispute is resolved, the United Kingdom is entitled to exercise the rights of a coastal State under the Convention in respect of the Chagos Archipelago. Accordingly, it is plain that, regardless of

whether or not the advisory opinion has resolved the sovereignty dispute, there can be no question of the advisory opinion overruling the arbitral award, as there was no determination in the award to that effect.

3. United Nations General Assembly resolution 73/295

216. The Special Chamber will now turn to the relevance or implications of UNGA resolution 73/295 for the legal status of the Chagos Archipelago.

217. The Maldives maintains that UNGA resolution 73/295 had no effect on the sovereignty dispute. According to the Maldives, it is a purely political statement, not an instrument with binding force or capable of being construed as "an amplification or authoritative interpretation of the *Chagos* Advisory Opinion".

218. Referring to the contents of the resolution, the Maldives states that the word "sovereignty" appears nowhere in the text. In its view, the resolution did not purport to resolve, and was not capable of resolving, the sovereignty dispute. In particular, the Maldives contends, in stating that "[t]he Chagos Archipelago forms an integral part of the territory of Mauritius", the resolution went further than the advisory opinion, which found only that the Chagos Archipelago was an integral part of Mauritius "at the time of its detachment from Mauritius in 1965".

219. The Maldives maintains that "[t]he UNGA Resolution does not provide evidence that the sovereignty dispute between Mauritius and the United Kingdom has been resolved, for three reasons." First, the General Assembly resolution is not binding on States in its own right; second, it cannot be read as amplifying or providing an authoritative interpretation of the *Chagos* advisory opinion; and third, as a matter of fact, it is clear that sovereignty over the Chagos Archipelago has remained in dispute since the resolution was passed. Therefore, the Maldives submits, there is no basis for "assuming that Mauritius and the United Kingdom have accepted it as resolving their dispute."

220. Mauritius notes that, following the advisory opinion, the General Assembly adopted resolution 73/295, in which it welcomed and endorsed the advisory opinion. Mauritius further notes that the resolution affirmed, *inter alia*, that "in accordance with the advisory opinion of the Court", the Chagos Archipelago forms an integral part of Mauritius. It adds that the General Assembly also "demand[ed]" that the United Kingdom "withdraw its colonial administration from the Chagos Archipelago unconditionally within a period of no more than six months from the adoption of the present resolution" and "call[ed] upon" all Member States to "refrain from any action that [would]

impede or delay the completion of the process of decolonization of Mauritius in accordance with the advisory opinion of the International Court of Justice and the present resolution."

221. Mauritius submits in this regard that "sovereignty inevitably pertains to the State of which the territory is an integral part" and that

[f]ollowing the ICJ's Advisory Opinion and UN General Assembly Resolution 73/295, it is now beyond doubt that the United Kingdom's detachment of the Chagos Archipelago violated international law, and that it has no sovereignty or sovereign rights in regard to the Archipelago.

Mauritius further submits that, notwithstanding the General Assembly's demand, the United Kingdom has refused to cease its internationally wrongful act and its unlawful administration of the Chagos Archipelago, in violation of Mauritius' sovereignty, continues.

222. Regarding the obligations of the Maldives under resolution 73/295, Mauritius argues that, as a matter of international law, the Maldives is under an obligation to cooperate with the United Nations to complete the decolonization of Mauritius and that "[t]he resolution thus prohibits the UK from impeding Mauritius' effort to negotiate a maritime boundary with the Maldives, and it prohibits the Maldives from invoking the UK's sovereignty claim to delay such negotiation."

223. Mauritius further argues that the Special Chamber "too is asked to do that which is laid out at paragraphs 6 and 7" of UNGA resolution 73/295, namely:

to recognize that the Chagos Archipelago forms an integral part of the territory of Mauritius, to support the decolonization of Mauritius as rapidly as possible, and to refrain from impeding that process by recognizing, or giving effect to any measure taken by or on behalf of, the "British Indian Ocean Territory".

* * *

224. The Special Chamber recalls the statements of the ICJ in the *South West Africa* case that UNGA resolutions "subject to certain exceptions . . . are not binding, but only recommendatory in character" and that "[t]he persuasive force of Assembly resolutions can indeed be very considerable," yet the General Assembly "operates on the political not the legal level: it does not make these resolutions binding in law" (*South West Africa (Ethiopia* v. *South Africa; Liberia* v. *South Africa), Second Phase, Judgment, ICJ Reports 1966*, p. 6, at pp. 50-1, para. 98; see also *Dispute Concerning Coastal State Rights in the Black Sea, Sea of Azov and Kerch Strait (Ukraine* v. *Russian Federation)*, Award on Preliminary Objections, para. 172).

225. The Special Chamber also recalls the statement of the Arbitral Tribunal in its award on *Coastal State Rights* that "the effect of factual and legal determination made in UNGA resolutions depends largely on their content and the conditions and context of their adoption. So does the weight to be given to such resolutions by an international court or tribunal" (*Dispute Concerning Coastal State Rights in the Black Sea, Sea of Azov and Kerch Strait (Ukraine* v. *Russian Federation)*, Award on Preliminary Objections, para. 174).

226. Resolution 73/295 was adopted by the General Assembly after it received the *Chagos* advisory opinion. It should be noted in this regard that, in the advisory opinion, the ICJ emphasized the functions of the General Assembly with regard to decolonization, in particular the "crucial role" which it has played in the work of the United Nations on decolonization (*Legal Consequences of the Separation of the Chagos Archipelago from Mauritius in 1965, Advisory Opinion, ICJ Reports 2019*, p. 95, at p. 135, para. 163). It should also be noted that the ICJ stated in that context that "[t]he modalities necessary for ensuring the completion of the decolonization of Mauritius fall within the remit of the United Nations General Assembly, in the exercise of its functions relating to decolonization" (*Ibid.*, at p. 139, para. 179). The ICJ went on to state that, "while it is for the General Assembly to pronounce on the modalities required to ensure the completion of the decolonization of Mauritius, all Member States must co-operate with the United Nations to put those modalities into effect" (*Ibid.*, at p. 139, para. 180).

227. The General Assembly has thus been entrusted to take necessary steps toward the completion of the decolonization of Mauritius. In light of the general functions of the General Assembly on decolonization and the specific task of the decolonization of Mauritius with which it was entrusted, the Special Chamber considers that resolution 73/295 is relevant to assessing the legal status of the Chagos Archipelago.

228. In resolution 73/295, the General Assembly affirmed, "in accordance with the advisory opinion of the Court", that: "[t]he Chagos Archipelago forms an integral part of the territory of Mauritius". The Special Chamber considers that this affirmation is the General Assembly's view of the advisory opinion.

229. In the resolution, the General Assembly demanded that

the United Kingdom ... withdraw its colonial administration from the Chagos Archipelago unconditionally within a period of no more than six months from the adoption of the present resolution, thereby enabling Mauritius to complete the decolonization of its territory as rapidly as possible.

The Special Chamber notes that this demand was made as one of the "modalities" for ensuring the completion of the decolonization of Mauritius pursuant to the advisory opinion. In the Special Chamber's view, the fact that the time-limit set by the General Assembly has passed without the United Kingdom complying with the demand further strengthens the Special Chamber's finding as to the United Kingdom's claim to sovereignty over the Chagos Archipelago noted in paragraph 173 above.

230. With respect to the argument made by Mauritius that the obligations under paragraphs 6 and 7 of UNGA resolution 73/295 also apply to the Special Chamber, neither the language of the resolution nor the practice of the General Assembly suggests that the reference to "international, regional and intergovernmental organizations, including those established by treaty", in paragraph 7 of the resolution, is directed to the Special Chamber or any other international court or tribunal in light of the independent exercise of their adjudicatory functions.

4. Current status of the sovereignty dispute

231. The Special Chamber will now turn to the Parties' disagreement as to the current status of the sovereignty dispute over the Chagos Archipelago.

232. According to the Maldives, it is beyond doubt that there is a sovereignty dispute between the United Kingdom and Mauritius as a matter of fact. The Maldives submits that, "despite the Advisory Opinion and the General Assembly resolution, the UK maintains its claim over Chagos, which it continues to administer as the British Indian Ocean Territory." In the Maldives' view, Mauritius acknowledges this fact, and has publicly opposed the United Kingdom's sovereignty claim. It adds that, plainly, the question of sovereignty remains in dispute between Mauritius and the United Kingdom.

233. In support of its claim, the Maldives advances the following three arguments. First, the Maldives contends that, in order for a dispute to exist, a court or tribunal must assess whether there is "a disagreement on a point of law or fact, a conflict of legal views or of interests" between the parties. In the present case, according to the Maldives, "it is clear that a dispute, as this concept is defined by the well-established and widely accepted jurisprudence ... exists with respect to sovereignty over the Chagos Archipelago." It adds that it is a fact that the United Kingdom has asserted its sovereignty claim over the Chagos Archipelago both before and after the ICJ rendered its advisory opinion and that Mauritius has opposed the United

Kingdom's sovereignty claim. Thus, the Maldives submits, there is no doubt about the factual existence of a dispute between the United Kingdom and Mauritius as to which of them is sovereign over the Chagos Archipelago.

234. Second, the Maldives submits that the plausibility or implausibility of the United Kingdom's legal position is irrelevant to the determination of whether or not a dispute exists. Referring to the *Coastal State Rights* case, the Maldives contends, the jurisprudence shows that, contrary to Mauritius' assertion, the Special Chamber should not enter into an analysis of whether the United Kingdom's sovereignty claim over the Chagos Archipelago is "plausible", but must only assess whether it exists.

235. Third, the Maldives argues that in any event Mauritius has not established that the United Kingdom's sovereignty claim is implausible. According to the Maldives, "if the Special Chamber were to find ... that it *should* consider the plausibility of the United Kingdom's claim, it should reach the conclusion that that claim is (at the very least) plausible."

236. The Maldives adds that "the recognition by the Special Chamber of the existence of a sovereignty dispute between the United Kingdom and Mauritius would not imply a recognition that the United Kingdom's claim is well-founded." Furthermore, by declining jurisdiction, the Special Chamber would simply act in accordance with the true scope and legal effect of the advisory opinion, as well as the established principles of international law on the competence of courts and tribunals under such circumstances.

237. Mauritius contends that, "in light of the ICJ's Advisory Opinion, there exists no dispute over territorial sovereignty that could prevent the Special Chamber from delimiting the maritime boundary between Mauritius and the Maldives." In its view, "[t]he fact that the United Kingdom, for political reasons, chooses to continue to make claims that have no basis in international law ... cannot bar the Special Chamber from exercising its jurisdiction in these proceedings."

238. Mauritius states that "[t]he fact that the United Kingdom, in defiance of the Court's ruling, is attempting to maintain a claim to sovereignty over the Chagos Archipelago does not mean that that claim is plausible or even arguable." Mauritius also states that any assertion of such rights by the United Kingdom is manifestly contrary to international law and that it is unarguable. According to Mauritius, "these words, whether uttered by the UK or echoed by the Maldives, are, in the end, only assertions" and "cannot, as a matter of law, establish the existence of a dispute, especially after the dispute has

been resolved by the authoritative pronouncement of an international court or tribunal."

239. Mauritius explains that it does "not contend that the UK's continued assertion of sovereignty over Chagos should be disregarded because it is implausible—though it is." It argues that "it is irrelevant because the issue of sovereignty has already been resolved by the ICJ's determination that Chagos is an integral part of the territory of Mauritius, and that the UK's ongoing administration is unlawful, and must be terminated", and that there is thus no unresolved sovereignty dispute.

240. Mauritius submits that the present case is not one in which the Special Chamber is required to make a determination on competing territorial claims over the Chagos Archipelago, because the ICJ has conclusively determined in its advisory opinion that the Archipelago is part of the territory of Mauritius.

241. Referring to the *Coastal State Rights* case, Mauritius contends that, unlike Mauritius in the present case, Ukraine could not point to any authoritative judicial or legal determination to support a claim that its sovereignty was undisputed. According to Mauritius, "[u]nlike this Special Chamber, the Annex VII tribunal in that case would have had to determine for itself which State was sovereign over the territory; it considered the question without any prior judicial determination of this issue to rely upon." On the other hand, Mauritius relies in this case on "what both sides have agreed is an authoritative and correct legal determination by the ICJ." Mauritius asserts that there is "a world of difference" between relying on the opinion of the ICJ and relying on the resolutions of political organs of the United Nations.

* * *

242. The Special Chamber notes that it is beyond doubt that there had been a long-standing sovereignty dispute between Mauritius and the United Kingdom over the Chagos Archipelago. As noted above, this was confirmed by the Arbitral Tribunal in the *Chagos* arbitral award.

243. However, the key question in the present proceedings is whether the legal status of the Chagos Archipelago has been clarified by the advisory opinion of the ICJ. In the view of the Special Chamber, therefore, the fact that the United Kingdom and Mauritius continue to make their respective claims to the Chagos Archipelago is beside the point. If, indeed, the ICJ has determined that the Chagos Archipelago is a part of the territory of Mauritius, as Mauritius argues, the continued claim of the United Kingdom to sovereignty over the Chagos

Archipelago cannot be considered anything more than "a mere asser-tion". However, such assertion does not prove the existence of a dispute. As the Special Chamber recalls,

it is not sufficient for one party to a contentious case to assert that a dispute exists with the other party. A mere assertion is not sufficient to prove the existence of a dispute any more than a mere denial of the existence of the dispute proves its non-existence.

(*South West Africa* cases (*Ethiopia* v. *South Africa; Liberia* v. *South Africa*), *Preliminary Objections, Judgment, ICJ Reports 1962*, p. 319, at p. 328)

244. The Special Chamber sees a difference between the present case and the *Coastal State Rights* case, upon which the Maldives relies to buttress its position. In the latter case, the Annex VII Arbitral Tribunal did not have the benefit of prior authoritative determination of the main issues relating to sovereignty claims to Crimea by any judicial body. However, that does not seem to be the case in the present proceedings.

245. In light of the advisory opinion, which determined, *inter alia*, the United Kingdom's continued administration of the Chagos Archipelago to be an unlawful act of a continuing character, the Special Chamber does not find convincing the Maldives' argument as to the matter-of-fact existence of a sovereignty dispute over the Chagos Archipelago.

5. Summary of key findings

246. The Special Chamber summarizes its findings relevant to the legal status of the Chagos Archipelago as follows:

While the Arbitral Tribunal in the *Chagos* arbitral award recognized the existence of a sovereignty dispute between the United Kingdom and Mauritius over the Chagos Archipelago, it found that it lacked jurisdiction to address said dispute. On the other hand, the Arbitral Tribunal recognized, without prejudice to the question of sovereignty, that Mauritius had certain rights in respect of the Chagos Archipelago, including fishing rights, the right to its return when no longer needed for defence purposes and the right to the benefit of minerals or oil discovered. This demonstrates that, aside from the question of sovereignty, the Chagos Archipelago has been subject to a special regime, according to which Mauritius is entitled to certain maritime rights;

The determinations made by the ICJ with respect to the issues of the decolonization of Mauritius in the *Chagos* advisory opinion have legal effect and clear implications for the legal status of the Chagos Archipelago. The United Kingdom's continued claim to sovereignty over the Chagos Archipelago is contrary to those determinations. While the process of decolonization has yet to be completed, Mauritius' sovereignty over the Chagos Archipelago can be inferred from the ICJ's determinations;

Resolution 73/295 of the General Assembly, within the remit of which the modalities necessary for ensuring the completion of the decolonization of Mauritius fall, demanded that the United Kingdom withdraw its administration over the Chagos Archipelago within six months from its adoption. The fact that the time-limit set by the General Assembly has passed without the United Kingdom complying with this demand further strengthens the Special Chamber's finding that its claim to sovereignty over the Chagos Archipelago is contrary to the authoritative determinations made in the advisory opinion.

C. Conclusions of the Special Chamber concerning the first and the second preliminary objection

1. With respect to the first preliminary objection

247. In light of the above findings, the Special Chamber considers that, whatever interests the United Kingdom may still have with respect to the Chagos Archipelago, they would not render the United Kingdom a State with sufficient legal interests, let alone an indispensable third party, that would be affected by the delimitation of the maritime boundary around the Chagos Archipelago. In the Special Chamber's view, it is inconceivable that the United Kingdom, whose administration over the Chagos Archipelago constitutes a wrongful act of a continuing character and thus must be brought to an end as rapidly as possible, and yet who has failed to do so, can have any legal interests in permanently disposing of maritime zones around the Chagos Archipelago by delimitation.

248. For these reasons, the Special Chamber concludes that the United Kingdom is not an indispensable party to the present proceedings. Accordingly, the first preliminary objection of the Maldives is rejected.

2. With respect to the second preliminary objection

249. The question the Special Chamber has to answer is whether Mauritius is the State with an opposite or adjacent coast to the Maldives in respect of the Chagos Archipelago within the meaning of article 74, paragraph 1, and article 83, paragraph 1, of the Convention.

250. The Special Chamber considers that the above findings as a whole provide it with sufficient basis to conclude that Mauritius can be regarded as the coastal State in respect of the Chagos Archipelago for the purpose of the delimitation of a maritime boundary even before the

process of the decolonization of Mauritius is completed. In the Special Chamber's view, to treat Mauritius as such State is consistent with the determinations made in the *Chagos* arbitral award, and, in particular, the determinations made in the *Chagos* advisory opinion which were acted upon by UNGA resolution 73/295.

251. For these reasons, in the circumstances of the present case, the Special Chamber is satisfied that Mauritius can be regarded as the State with an opposite or adjacent coast to the Maldives within the meaning of article 74, paragraph 1, and article 83, paragraph 1, of the Convention and the concerned State within the meaning of paragraph 3 of the same articles. Accordingly, the second preliminary objection of the Maldives is rejected.

VII. THIRD PRELIMINARY OBJECTION: REQUIREMENT UNDER ARTICLES 74 AND 83 OF THE CONVENTION

252. The Special Chamber will now consider the Maldives' third preliminary objection that "Articles 74 and 83 of UNCLOS stipulate that negotiations between the parties are a procedural precondition to jurisdiction" and that "this precondition has not been—and cannot meaningfully be—fulfilled in the present case."

A. *Interpretation of articles 74 and 83 of the Convention*

253. The Special Chamber will first examine the question as to whether articles 74 and 83 of the Convention oblige States Parties to the Convention to engage in maritime boundary negotiations prior to having recourse to compulsory dispute settlement.

254. The Maldives argues that,

[p]ursuant to the plain terms of Articles 74 and 83, *before* resorting to the procedures provided for in Part XV, States with opposite or adjacent coasts are under a mandatory obligation to negotiate with a view to effecting "by agreement" the relevant delimitation. It is only once such negotiations have been engaged in, and the attempt to reach an agreement has failed, that either State can resort to the procedures provided for in Part XV UNCLOS.

255. Relying on the Judgment in the *Dispute concerning delimitation of the maritime boundary between Ghana and Côte d'Ivoire in the Atlantic Ocean* (hereinafter "*Ghana/Côte d'Ivoire*"), the Maldives observes that the Special Chamber in that case stated that "the obligation under article 83, paragraph 1, of the Convention to reach an agreement on delimitation necessarily entails negotiations to this effect." The

Maldives observes further that the Special Chamber emphasized "that the obligation to negotiate in good faith occupies a prominent place in the Convention, as well as in general international law."

256. The Maldives explains that "[i]t is, of course, recognised that Articles 74 and 83 'do not require that delimitation negotiations should be successful', but 'like all similar obligations to negotiate in international law, the negotiations have to be conducted in good faith'."

257. According to the Maldives, this requires, *inter alia*, States to conduct themselves with a view to actually reaching an agreement. It notes that "in the *Gulf of Maine* case the ICJ referred to the 'duty to negotiate with a view to reaching agreement, and to do so in good faith, with a genuine intention to achieve a positive result'."

258. The Maldives argues that

[t]he fact that the precondition of negotiation appears outside of but before Part XV ... strengthens the Maldives' argument that the subsequent Part XV procedures are only relevant where negotiations under Parts V and VI have been first exhausted. That was the clear intention of the drafters. States Parties should not rush to adversarial litigation. They are entitled to invoke Part XV, and, in particular, compulsory procedures entailing binding decisions under Section 2, only where negotiations have failed.

259. Referring to articles 74 and 83 of the Convention, the Maldives argues that in the case law from the ICJ the obligation of negotiation contained in these provisions has been interpreted as a precondition to jurisdiction. In this regard, the Maldives refers to the decision of the ICJ on preliminary objections in *Maritime Delimitation in the Indian Ocean* (hereinafter "*Somalia* v. *Kenya*"). According to the Maldives,

[t]he Court accepted that "Article 83, paragraph 1, of UNCLOS, in providing that delimitation shall be effected by way of agreement, requires that there be negotiations conducted in good faith" before the parties resorted to the dispute resolution procedures in Part XV of UNCLOS .... In other words, good faith negotiations were required *before* either party resorted to Part XV dispute resolution, and a failure to do so would prevent the Court from exercising jurisdiction.

260. Responding to Mauritius' argument that articles 74 and 83 are not located in Part XV but in Parts V and VI of the Convention, the Maldives submits that "Mauritius has not pointed to any rule of treaty interpretation—and there is none—that says that all jurisdictional requirements must be contained in the same part of a treaty that sets out the dispute resolution procedures."

261. With respect to Mauritius' claim that the only procedural precondition for exercise of the Special Chamber's jurisdiction is contained in article 283, the Maldives contends that "article 283 concerns a different obligation. It requires States to exchange views once a dispute has arisen. It does not contain an obligation to negotiate."

262. Mauritius argues that articles 74 and 83 of the Convention impose no obligation to negotiate as a jurisdictional precondition to invoking the procedures provided for in Part XV of the Convention. The position of Mauritius is that

Articles 74 and 83 do not establish conditions for the exercise of jurisdiction. Rather, they set out two interrelated *substantive* obligations: (1) a State may not unilaterally delimit its EEZ or continental shelf but must do so by agreement with another State; and (2) failing to reach such agreement, the States concerned must resort to the procedures provided for in Part XV of the Convention.

263. Mauritius refutes the assertion of the Maldives that articles 74 and 83 of the Convention "require that Mauritius must negotiate with the Maldives prior to commencing proceedings to delimit the maritime boundary under Part XV of the Convention." According to Mauritius,

[t]here is no such requirement. Articles 74 and 83 set out substantive obligations. The only procedural precondition for exercise of the Special Chamber's jurisdiction is contained in Article 283. Mauritius has scrupulously complied with the requirements of Article 283, and the Maldives has not asserted otherwise.

264. Mauritius observes that articles 74 and 83 are located not in Part XV of the Convention, which governs the settlement of disputes, but in Parts V and VI, which concern States' substantive obligations in relation to the exclusive economic zone and continental shelf.

265. Mauritius argues that

courts and tribunals that have exercised jurisdiction under UNCLOS to delimit maritime boundaries . . . have never found—or even considered—that a separate obligation to negotiate, rather than merely an exchange [of] views, emanating from Articles 74 and 83, must be satisfied before ITLOS or an Annex VII tribunal may exercise jurisdiction.

266. Referring to the decision of the Special Chamber in *Ghana/Côte d'Ivoire*, Mauritius submits that the "Special Chamber interpreted and applied Article 83(1) as imposing a *substantive* obligation 'to reach an agreement on delimitation,' which can be achieved through negotiations conducted in good faith."

* * *

267. Articles 74 and 83 of the Convention provide in relevant parts:

1. The delimitation of the [exclusive economic zone/continental shelf] between States with opposite or adjacent coasts shall be effected by agreement on the basis of international law, as referred to in Article 38 of the Statute of the International Court of Justice, in order to achieve an equitable solution.

2. If no agreement can be reached within a reasonable period of time, the States concerned shall resort to the procedures provided for in Part XV.

268. The Special Chamber will first interpret these provisions before applying them to the facts and circumstances of the present preliminary objections proceedings. The Special Chamber observes that articles 74 and 83 of the Convention are identical in their content, differing only in respect of the designation of the maritime area to which they apply. It will therefore address them together.

269. These articles apply respectively to areas where the entitlements of two coastal States to an exclusive economic zone in accordance with article 57 of the Convention overlap and to areas where their entitlements to a continental shelf in accordance with article 76 of the Convention overlap. Article 74, paragraph 1, and article 83, paragraph 1, of the Convention establish an obligation for States with opposite or adjacent coasts to effect the delimitation of the exclusive economic zone and the continental shelf by agreement. Paragraph 2 imposes an obligation on them to resort to the procedures provided for in Part XV of the Convention, if no agreement can be reached within a reasonable period of time.

270. In this regard, the Special Chamber recalls the following statement of the ICJ:

By its terms, Article 83, paragraph 1, of UNCLOS sets out the manner in which delimitation of the continental shelf is to be effected by States parties thereto, namely by way of agreement as distinct from unilateral action; it is a provision on the establishment of a maritime boundary between States with opposite or adjacent coasts in respect of the continental shelf, which does not prescribe the method for the settlement of any dispute relating to the delimitation of the continental shelf. This is made clear by paragraph 2 of Article 83, which requires that, if no agreement can be reached within a reasonable time, the States concerned shall resort to the dispute settlement procedures of Part XV, entitled "Settlement of disputes".

(*Maritime Delimitation in the Indian Ocean (Somalia* v. *Kenya), Preliminary Objections, Judgment, ICJ Reports 2017*, p. 3, at p. 37, para. 90)

271. The Special Chamber wishes to state that the main purpose of article 74, paragraphs 1 and 2, and article 83, paragraphs 1 and 2, of the Convention is to ensure that, where States with opposite or adjacent coasts are confronted with overlapping claims regarding the exclusive economic zone and the continental shelf, no State shall settle its maritime limits unilaterally and such limits shall rather be effected by agreement between the States concerned or by resorting to the procedures provided for in Part XV, if no agreement can be reached within a reasonable period of time.

272. In the Special Chamber's view, these means—reaching an agreement through negotiation or resorting to Part XV of the Convention—are both conducive to achieving "an equitable solution" in the delimitation of the exclusive economic zone and the continental shelf, on the basis of international law, as referred to in Article 38 of the Statute of the ICJ, as opposed to unilateral delimitation carried out by the States concerned.

273. The Special Chamber considers that article 74, paragraph 1, and article 83, paragraph 1, of the Convention entail an obligation to negotiate in good faith with a view to reaching an agreement on delimitation. However, this obligation does not require the States concerned to reach such agreement. As the ICJ stated in *Somalia* v. *Kenya*,

Article 83, paragraph 1, of UNCLOS, in providing that delimitation shall be effected by way of agreement, requires that there be negotiations conducted in good faith, but not that they should be successful.

(*Maritime Delimitation in the Indian Ocean (Somalia v. Kenya), Preliminary Objections, Judgment, ICJ Reports 2017*, p. 3, at p. 37, para. 90)

274. In the Special Chamber's view, there can be a number of reasons for which the States concerned cannot reach an agreement. They may not be able to do so after exhaustive negotiations or because one State refuses to negotiate or withdraws from negotiations after initially engaging in them. If no agreement can be reached within a reasonable period of time, the States concerned are required to resort to the dispute settlement procedures of Part XV rather than carrying out unilateral delimitation.

275. In the view of the Special Chamber, article 74, paragraphs 1 and 2, and article 83, paragraphs 1 and 2, of the Convention, in a mutually reinforcing way, establish substantive obligations for the States concerned not to delimit their exclusive economic zones and continental shelves unilaterally but to do so by way of agreement or, failing such agreement, by resorting to the dispute settlement procedures under Part XV of the Convention.

B. Application of articles 74 and 83 of the Convention

276. The Special Chamber now turns to the issue of whether the Parties engaged in negotiations concerning their maritime boundary.

277. The Maldives maintains that "bilateral negotiations between Mauritius and the Maldives addressing delimitation of the EEZ and continental shelf have not taken place." It acknowledges, however, that "Mauritius has in the past requested that the Maldives meet to discuss a maritime boundary delimitation." The Maldives considers that, in circumstances where the sovereignty dispute between Mauritius and the United Kingdom remains unresolved, Mauritius and the Maldives cannot meaningfully engage in the negotiations mandated by articles 74 and 83 of the Convention.

278. The Maldives is of the view that, until such dispute is settled, it "is unable to negotiate a maritime boundary agreement with Mauritius" and that, "[f]or the same reasons, it is neither possible nor appropriate for the parties to seek to negotiate the provisional arrangements envisaged by Articles 74(3) and 83(3)."

279. With respect to the first meeting on maritime delimitation and the submission regarding the extended continental shelf of 21 October 2010 and the joint communiqué of 12 March 2011, the Maldives submits, in its response to the first question posed by the Special Chamber (see paragraph 47 above), that these bilateral exchanges were of "a strictly diplomatic nature with a view to exploring possible solutions to a potential overlap of the Parties' extended continental shelf."

280. The Maldives maintains that the procedural precondition mandated in articles 74 and 83 of the Convention has not been fulfilled and therefore the Special Chamber is unable to exercise jurisdiction.

281. Mauritius contends that, before it "commenced these proceedings under Part XV, Mauritius and the Maldives *did* engage in negotiations in regard to the disputed maritime boundary, and failed to reach an agreement." It states that the Maldives' allegation that no negotiations took place is belied by the diplomatic record. According to Mauritius, "[t]his record confirms that the Parties attempted to delimit by agreement their overlapping claims in the EEZ and continental shelf, until the Maldives unilaterally ended the negotiations."

282. Mauritius outlines several steps that were taken in this regard, namely:

On 21 September 2010, Mauritius objected to the maritime claims depicted in the Maldives' submission to the CLCS. Mauritius welcomed the Maldives' proposal to "hold discussions for the delimitation of the exclusive economic zones of the two countries," asserting that "the holding of EEZ delimitations boundary talks are all the more relevant in the light of this submission" in order to resolve the two States' overlapping claims.

283. Mauritius explains that

[s]hortly thereafter, on 21 October 2010, the Parties met to address delimitation of their maritime boundary. The meeting was convened expressly "to discuss a potential overlap of the extended continental shelf and to exchange views on maritime boundary delimitation between the two States." In the course of the meeting, the Maldives confirmed the existence of a dispute over the maritime boundary: It recognised that in its "submission to the CLCS the exclusive economic zone (EEZ) coordinates of the Republic of Mauritius in the Chagos region were not taken into consideration."

Mauritius states that the Maldives then "assured the Mauritius side that this would be rectified by an addendum to the submission of the Republic of Maldives which would be prepared by the Expert in consultation with the Government of Mauritius." Recognizing the existence of overlapping claims, according to Mauritius, the Maldives further "agreed that both sides [would] work jointly on the area of the overlap". Mauritius asserts that, "despite having recognised the overlap and the dispute to which it gave rise, the Maldives failed to take any further steps to address the situation, notwithstanding its undertakings to do so."

284. Mauritius adds that

[t]he Maldives' conduct caused Mauritius to send a diplomatic note to the United Nations Secretary-General on 24 March 2011. In the note, Mauritius: "protest[ed] formally against the submission made by the Republic of Maldives in as much as the Extended Continental Shelf being claimed by the Republic of Maldives encroaches on the Exclusive Economic Zone of the Republic of Mauritius." The matter remained unresolved for the following eight years.

285. In response to the first question posed by the Special Chamber (see paragraph 47 above), Mauritius submits that the meeting of 21 October 2010, together with the joint communiqué of 12 March 2011, reflects "the momentum behind the two States at that time with a view to arriving at an agreement on the delimitation of their maritime boundary."

286. Mauritius states that,

[o]n 7 March 2019, following the ICJ's Advisory Opinion of 5 February 2019, and with the objective of resolving its dispute with the Maldives over the course of the maritime boundary in the area adjacent to the Chagos

Archipelago, Mauritius again "invit[ed] the Maldives authorities to a second round of discussions." Mauritius requested an early confirmation that the Maldives would participate in the proposed negotiations, which Mauritius suggested could take place in April 2019. The Maldives did not respond. As of the date of these Observations, the Maldives still has not responded.

287. Mauritius claims that recourse to judicial dispute settlement methods under Part XV of the Convention is justified because the maritime delimitation dispute between it and Maldives is manifestly one that cannot be settled by agreement. In particular, it argues that,

[b]ecause the delimitation of the EEZ and continental shelf cannot be reached by agreement as prescribed by paragraph 1 of [a]rticles 74 and 83, paragraph 2 of those provisions requires the Maldives and Mauritius, as the next step, to "resort to the procedures provided for in Part XV".

* * *

288. The Special Chamber notes that, on the basis of the records before it, Mauritius, on several occasions, attempted to engage the Maldives in negotiations concerning the delimitation of their claimed overlapping exclusive economic zones and continental shelves.

289. These records also show that, while the Maldives at times had shown interest in meeting and even had met with Mauritius "to discuss a potential overlap of the extended continental shelf and to exchange views on maritime boundary delimitation between the two respective States", the Maldives, for most of the time, refused to negotiate with Mauritius, arguing that,

[a]s jurisdiction over the Chagos Archipelago is not exercised by the Government of Mauritius, the Government of Maldives feels that it would be inappropriate to initiate any discussions between the Government of Maldives and the Government of Mauritius regarding the delimitation of the boundary between the Maldives and the Chagos Archipelago.

290. By persisting in its position that, "in circumstances where the sovereignty dispute between Mauritius and the United Kingdom remains unresolved, Mauritius and the Maldives ... cannot meaning-fully engage ... in the negotiations mandated by Articles 74 and 83 UNCLOS", the Maldives demonstrates that "no agreement can be reached within a reasonable period of time", whatever time could have been reserved for that negotiation.

291. In particular, by not responding to Mauritius' invitation of 7 March 2019, to a second round of discussions following the *Chagos* advisory opinion, it became clear that there was nothing more that Mauritius could have accomplished in insisting on having delimitation

negotiations with the Maldives. This is confirmed by the Maldives' own admission during the hearing that "no amount of unilateral attempts by Mauritius to commence maritime delimitation negotiations [in respect of the Chagos Archipelago] can change the fact that those negotiations, as things stand today, would not be meaningful and could not achieve an agreement."

292. The Special Chamber is of the view that, in situations in which "no agreement can be reached", to resort to the procedures of Part XV of the Convention, as set out in paragraph 2 of each of articles 74 and 83, is not only justified but also an obligation of the States concerned.

293. On the basis of the foregoing, the Special Chamber concludes that the obligation under article 74, paragraph 1, and article 83, paragraph 1, of the Convention has been fulfilled. Accordingly, the third preliminary objection of the Maldives is rejected.

VIII. FOURTH PRELIMINARY OBJECTION: EXISTENCE OF A DISPUTE

294. The Special Chamber now turns to the Maldives' preliminary objection that "there is no maritime boundary dispute between the Parties, and the [Special Chamber] manifestly lacks jurisdiction over this case."

295. The Maldives submits that "UNCLOS Article 288(1) makes explicit that only disputes concerning the interpretation or application of UNCLOS fall within the Tribunal's jurisdiction" and that "[a] claim will concern 'the interpretation or application' of Articles 74(1) and 83(1) only if it addresses the 'delimitation of the exclusive economic zone [or continental shelf] between States with opposite or adjacent coasts'."

296. The Maldives further submits that Mauritius' claim to be a State with a relevant opposite or adjacent coast to the Maldives is predicated on its assertion that it has sovereignty over the Chagos Archipelago, which is disputed by the United Kingdom. For the Maldives, there can be no dispute between the Maldives and Mauritius over maritime delimitation until such time as Mauritius becomes the undisputed opposite coastal State within the meaning of article 74, paragraph 1, and article 83, paragraph 1, of the Convention.

297. The Maldives argues "[a]dditionally and alternatively" that,

even if the sovereignty dispute did not bar the existence of a valid dispute over maritime delimitation as claimed by Mauritius, ... it is manifest that there was no maritime boundary dispute between Mauritius and the Maldives at the time that proceedings under Part XV of UNCLOS were initiated.

It contends that

> Mauritius . . . must demonstrate that . . . the parties held clearly opposite views in respect of the delimitation of the maritime boundary between Mauritius and the Maldives in the Indian Ocean in the EEZ and the continental shelf, and that such views had been expressed with sufficient clarity.

According to the Maldives, Mauritius has not provided any evidence of a dispute, consisting of positively opposed claims as to their respective maritime zones, between the Parties.

298. The Maldives maintains that it is insufficient merely to show that there could be a potential dispute because of notional overlap between the Parties' maximum possible entitlements. It argues that "[a] dispute requires disagreement on where the actual maritime boundary should lie; otherwise, any State with an adjacent coast, or an opposite coast less than 400 nautical miles from another State's coast, could be hauled before ITLOS."

299. The Maldives submits that the Notification of Mauritius has not pointed to any dispute or positive opposition between the Parties regarding their respective maritime boundary claims. Furthermore, none of the exchanges between the Maldives and Mauritius referred to in the Notification establish that a dispute exists.

300. The Maldives further submits that

> the Special Agreement dated 24 September 2019 by which the parties submitted Mauritius' claim to a special chamber does not establish the existence of a dispute. First, it was made after the critical date (18 June 2019, when Mauritius filed its case) and second, it was made without prejudice to the Maldives' right to make objections to jurisdiction, including as regards whether a dispute existed at all. Accordingly, no dispute had crystallised at the critical date, and the Tribunal lacks jurisdiction over Mauritius' claims.

301. Regarding the crystallization of the dispute, the Maldives contends that,

> even on Mauritius' own theory that the International Court's Advisory Opinion somehow granted it sovereignty, less than four months elapsed before Mauritius filed its Notification and Statement of Claim. A dispute would need to have crystallized during this brief window.

302. Regarding legislation adopted by the Parties, the Maldives maintains that it "does not establish the existence of a dispute . . . For one thing, the legislation did not create a dispute of sufficient clarity to ground the Special Chamber's jurisdiction. This much is evident from the Parties' subsequent diplomatic exchanges". Furthermore, according to the Maldives, its legislation

does not purport to set down an immutable maritime boundary claim either in respect of its EEZ or its continental shelf. It merely sets out as a point of departure the maximum extent of the Maldives' entitlement to an EEZ under UNCLOS, subject to agreement with relevant opposing or adjacent coastal States.

In its view, the mere existence of an overlap is not evidence of a dispute. Referring to "the so-called 'official depictions of overlapping boundary claims'", the Maldives contends that Mauritius has presented none of these.

303. The Maldives argues that, in subsequent diplomatic exchanges, the Parties spoke of a potential dispute which they might attempt to pre-empt through negotiations and that there were no claims affirmatively opposed and rejected.

304. Referring to the meeting between the Parties on 21 October 2010, the Maldives contends that the meeting concerned its submission to the CLCS a few months earlier and that, in the meeting, "Mauritius stated only that 'to the north of the Chagos Archipelago there is an area of *potential overlap* of the extended continental shelf of the Republic of Maldives and the Republic of Mauritius'." It adds that, during the meeting, "both sides agreed that they would 'exchange coordinates of their respective base points ... in order to facilitate the eventual discussions on the maritime boundary'." For the Maldives, this was a mere expression of intention to discuss a maritime boundary in the future. It argues that its

offer to amend its submission to the CLCS was not evidence of opposing claims: all that the Maldives' representative stated was that the Maldives' CLCS submission would in due course be amended "in consultation with the Government of the Republic of Mauritius".

305. With reference to the joint communiqué of 12 March 2011, the Maldives submits that it "states that the Parties 'agreed to make bilateral arrangements on the overlapping area of extended continental shelf' between them." In the view of the Maldives, this is obviously an intention to cooperate before a dispute is crystallized.

306. As to the diplomatic note sent by Mauritius to the Secretary-General of the United Nations on 24 March 2011, the Maldives asserts that this note made only vague statements about Maldives' submission not taking into account the exclusive economic zone around the Chagos Archipelago without any clarification as to an area of overlapping claims.

307. In response to the third question posed by the Special Chamber (see paragraph 47 above), the Maldives expresses its view on Mauritius' claim in relation to article 74, paragraph 3, and article 83, paragraph 3, of the Convention stated in paragraph 28 of the Notification. In particular, the Maldives argues that any claim relating to either of these obligations would be outside the jurisdiction of the Special Chamber, as Mauritius has never produced any evidence and never even suggested that

it has either invited the Maldives to enter into negotiations concerning any provisional arrangements of a practical nature or that the Maldives is carrying out any unilateral activities causing irreparable prejudice to Mauritius that would require such negotiations.

308. For its part, Mauritius rejects the contention of the Maldives that "there cannot exist any valid dispute as regards maritime delimitation between Mauritius and the Maldives until the dispute between Mauritius and the United Kingdom concerning the sovereignty over the Chagos Archipelago is resolved". For Mauritius, "[t]his is simply another iteration of the Maldives' erroneous argument that sovereignty over the Chagos Archipelago is uncertain merely because the United Kingdom continues to assert a claim."

309. Mauritius submits that the evidence confirms that a dispute in regard to the course of the maritime boundary in the area adjacent to the Chagos Archipelago has existed between the Parties since at least 2010. According to Mauritius,

[t]here is plainly a dispute: this is manifested, *inter alia*, in the Parties' respective national maritime laws and their submissions to the United Nations, which evidence their overlapping maritime claims. Further, the Maldives has, in the course of the Parties' maritime boundary negotiations, explicitly acknowledged the existence of a boundary dispute.

310. Mauritius further submits that the objection of the Maldives "that when Mauritius filed its Notification and Statement of Claim on 18 June 2019, it did so in the absence of a dispute between the Parties in respect of the maritime boundary in the EEZ and continental shelf" has no factual or legal support.

311. In response to the contention of the Maldives that there has been no "positive opposition between the Parties regarding their respective maritime boundary claims", Mauritius asserts that the untenable nature of this argument is revealed by the contemporaneous official documents and communications between the Parties, including official depictions of overlapping boundary claims.

312. As to the crystallization of the dispute, Mauritius contends that

[t]he dispute between the two Parties to these proceedings concerning the extent of their maritime areas does not date from only recently, or even from the filing of the document instituting proceedings by the Republic of Mauritius, as the other Party seems to be suggesting. The evidence in the file shows that the existence of this dispute is clearly established and that the overlapping of their respective claims was recognized by the Parties themselves as of 2010.

313. Regarding the argument of the Maldives that a dispute would need to have crystallized during the "brief window" after the ICJ had rendered the Advisory Opinion and before Mauritius had filed its Notification, Mauritius maintains that it is

entirely without merit. The Court clearly found that the separation of Chagos was not consistent with international law when it took place in 1965 and that those islands have, at all times, continued to be part of the territory of the Republic of Mauritius. That was clearly also the case in 2010-11, when the exchanges . . . took place.

314. With respect to legislation adopted by the Parties, Mauritius submits that overlaying the maritime claims made by the two States, as they appear in their respective legislation, leaves no doubt as to the fact that they necessarily create a conflict affecting an area of some 96,000 square kilometres. In its view, graphic representations illustrate the extent of the Parties' claims and the fact that those claims inevitably create a situation of conflict. According to Mauritius, this state of affairs was, moreover, confirmed in no uncertain terms by the Parties themselves in the course of their exchanges on the delimitation of their maritime areas.

315. Referring to the meeting between the Parties on 21 October 2010, Mauritius states that it "was convened expressly 'to discuss a potential overlap of the extended continental shelf and to exchange views on maritime boundary delimitation between the two States.'" Mauritius contends that,

[i]n the course of the meeting, the Maldives confirmed the existence of a dispute over the maritime boundary: It recognised that in its "submission to the CLCS the exclusive economic zone (EEZ) coordinates of the Republic of Mauritius in the Chagos region were not taken into consideration." The Maldives then "assured the Mauritius side that this would be rectified by an addendum to the submission of the Republic of Maldives which would be prepared by the Expert in consultation with the Government of Mauritius." Recognising the existence of overlapping claims, the Maldives further "agreed that both sides will work jointly on the area of the overlap."

316. Mauritius argues that, in subsequent exchanges between the Parties, including the joint communiqué of 12 March 2011, the disappearance of the qualifier "potential" is confirmed and reference is made clearly and exclusively to an established overlapping area between the maritime zones of the two States.

317. Mauritius asserts that,

despite having recognised the overlap and the dispute to which it gave rise, the Maldives failed to take any further steps to address the situation, notwithstanding its undertakings to do so. The Maldives' conduct caused Mauritius to send a diplomatic note to the United Nations Secretary-General on 24 March 2011. In the note, Mauritius: "protest[ed] formally against the submission made by the Republic of Maldives in as much as the Extended Continental Shelf being claimed by the Republic of Maldives encroaches on the Exclusive Economic Zone of the Republic of Mauritius."

318. Mauritius contends that, even if it were assumed that the extent of the area of overlap resulting from the Parties' opposing claims must be specified for a dispute to be deemed to exist, which it does not think to be the case, all the ingredients were thus present, from that moment, in order to determine precisely the contours of the area of overlap. It adds that,

[w]hat the note from Mauritius strikingly confirms is the existence of an established disagreement between the two States over the extent of their respective maritime areas. When a State protests formally, at the highest possible multilateral level, against claims put forward by another State to maritime areas which it deems to fall within its jurisdiction, it is proclaiming—to the world, what is more—the existence of a dispute between the States in question.

319. In response to the third question posed by the Special Chamber (see paragraph 47 above), Mauritius expresses its view that "there is no bar to the exercise by this Special Chamber of jurisdiction in relation to the Parties' obligations under paragraph 3 of articles 74 and 83." Mauritius adds that if, however, the Special Chamber finds that it cannot exercise jurisdiction to delimit the Parties' maritime boundaries, "then we have difficulty in seeing how it could exercise jurisdiction in relation to those obligations."

* * *

320. The Special Chamber notes that the Maldives' objection under consideration is based on two principal arguments. First, the Maldives argues that there can be no dispute between it and Mauritius over maritime delimitation until such time as Mauritius becomes the

undisputed State with an opposite coast to the Maldives within the meaning of article 74, paragraph 1, and article 83, paragraph 1, of the Convention. Second, the Maldives argues that there was no dispute, consisting of positively opposed claims as to their respective maritime zones, between it and Mauritius when the proceedings under Part XV of the Convention were initiated.

321. With respect to the first argument, the Special Chamber notes that it concluded in paragraph 251 above that it is satisfied that Mauritius can be regarded as the State with an opposite or adjacent coast to the Maldives within the meaning of article 74, paragraph 1, and article 83, paragraph 1, of the Convention. The Special Chamber, therefore, finds that this argument is without a basis.

322. With respect to the second argument, the Special Chamber recalls the jurisprudence of the Tribunal to the effect that, for it to have jurisdiction *ratione materiae* to entertain a case, "a dispute concerning the interpretation or application of the Convention between the Parties must have existed at the time of the filing of the Application" (*M/V "Norstar" (Panama v. Italy), Preliminary Objections, Judgment, ITLOS Reports 2016*, p. 44, at p. 65, para. 84; see also *M/V "Louisa" (Saint Vincent and the Grenadines* v. *Kingdom of Spain), Judgment, ITLOS Reports 2013*, p. 4, at p. 46, para. 151).

323. The Special Chamber notes that, in the *Southern Bluefin Tuna Cases*, the Tribunal stated that

a dispute is a "disagreement on a point of law or fact, a conflict of legal views or of interests" (*Mavrommatis Palestine Concessions, Judgment No 2, 1924, PCIJ, Series A, No 2*, p. 11), and "[i]t must be shown that the claim of one party is positively opposed by the other" (*South West Africa, Preliminary Objections, Judgment, ICJ Reports 1962*, p. 328).

(*Southern Bluefin Tuna (New Zealand* v. *Japan; Australia* v. *Japan), Provisional Measures, Order of 27 August 1999, ITLOS Reports 1999*, p. 280, at p. 293, para. 44; see also *M/V "Norstar" (Panama* v. *Italy), Preliminary Objections, Judgment, ITLOS Reports 2016*, p. 44, at pp. 65-6, para. 85)

324. The Special Chamber further notes that, in *Obligations concerning Negotiations relating to Cessation of the Nuclear Arms Race and to Nuclear Disarmament*, the ICJ held that, in order for a dispute to exist,

[t]he evidence must show that the parties "hold clearly opposite views" with respect to the issue brought before the Court ... As reflected in previous decisions of the Court in which the existence of a dispute was under consideration, a dispute exists when it is demonstrated, on the basis of the evidence, that the respondent was aware, or could not have been unaware, that its views were "positively opposed" by the applicant (*Alleged Violations of Sovereign*

Rights and Maritime Spaces in the Caribbean Sea (Nicaragua v. Colombia), Preliminary Objections, Judgment, ICJ Reports 2016 (I), p. 26, para. 73; *Application of the International Convention on the Elimination of All Forms of Racial Discrimination (Georgia v. Russian Federation), Preliminary Objections, Judgment, ICJ Reports 2011 (I)*, p. 99, para. 61, pp. 109-10, para. 87, p. 117, para. 104).

(*Obligations concerning Negotiations relating to Cessation of the Nuclear Arms Race and to Nuclear Disarmament (Marshall Islands v. United Kingdom), Preliminary Objections, Judgment, ICJ Reports 2016*, p. 833, at pp. 850-1, para. 41)

325. The Special Chamber observes that, by its Maritime Zones Act of 1977, Mauritius declared an exclusive economic zone extending to a distance of 200 nautical miles from the baseline (section 6) and a continental shelf extending to the outer edge of the continental margin, or to a distance of 200 nautical miles from the baseline where the outer edge does not extend up to that distance (section 5). This was reaffirmed in Mauritius' Maritime Zones Act of 2005 (sections 14 and 18).

326. By Law No 30/76 of 1976, the Maldives declared an exclusive economic zone, indicating the coordinates of its outer limits. In its Maritime Zones Act No 6/96 of 1996, which repealed Law No 30/76, the Maldives declared an exclusive economic zone extending up to 200 nautical miles from the archipelagic baselines (section 6). Section 7 of this Act further provides that

[i]n the event that the exclusive economic zone of Maldives as determined under section 6 of this Act overlaps with the exclusive economic zone of another State, this Act does not prohibit the Government of Maldives from entering into an agreement with that State as regards the area of overlapping and delimiting the exclusive economic zone of Maldives for the said area of overlapping.

327. The Special Chamber notes that it is clear from the national legislation adopted by the Parties that their respective claims to an exclusive economic zone in the relevant area overlap. This is further illustrated by the graphic representations made by Mauritius in these proceedings.

328. The Special Chamber observes that, on 26 July 2010, the Maldives submitted information to the CLCS on the limits of the continental shelf beyond 200 nautical miles from the baselines from which the breadth of its territorial sea is measured.

329. The Special Chamber notes that the Parties met on 21 October 2010 "to discuss a potential overlap of the extended continental shelf and to exchange views on maritime boundary

delimitation between the two respective States." According to the Minutes of the meeting,

[r]egarding the submission of the Republic of Maldives on the extended continental shelf to the Commission on the Limits of the Continental Shelf (CLCS), [the Minister of Foreign Affairs of the Maldives] said that the Expert working on the submission of Maldives has acknowledged that in the submission to the CLCS the exclusive economic zone (EEZ) coordinates of the Republic of Mauritius in the Chagos region were not taken into consideration. He assured the Mauritius side that this would be rectified by an addendum to the submission of the Republic of Maldives which would be prepared by the Expert in consultation with the Government of the Republic of Mauritius.

330. At the same meeting, Mauritius stated "that the Mauritius side also noted that to the north of the Chagos archipelago there is an area of potential overlap of the extended continental shelf of the Republic of Maldives and the Republic of Mauritius". The Maldives "agreed that both sides will work jointly on the area of overlap." In a joint communiqué of 12 March 2011, following a meeting between the President of the Maldives and the Prime Minister of Mauritius, the Parties "agreed to make bilateral arrangements on the overlapping area of extended continental shelf of the two States around the Chagos Archipelago."

331. The Special Chamber notes that, despite the assurance by the Maldives that an addendum to its submission to the CLCS would be made to take into consideration the coordinates of Mauritius' exclusive economic zone, no such addendum was submitted. As a consequence, Mauritius sent a diplomatic note to the Secretary-General of the United Nations on 24 March 2011, "protest[ing] formally against the submission made by the Republic of Maldives in as much as the Extended Continental Shelf being claimed by the Republic of Maldives encroaches on the Exclusive Economic Zone of the Republic of Mauritius."

332. In the view of the Special Chamber, it is clear from the above that there is an overlap between the claim of the Maldives to a continental shelf beyond 200 nautical miles and the claim of Mauritius to an exclusive economic zone in the relevant area. In light of the formal protest of Mauritius, in its diplomatic note of 24 March 2011, to the submission by the Maldives to the CLCS, the Parties clearly hold opposite views and the claim of the Maldives is positively opposed by Mauritius.

333. The Special Chamber cannot accept the Maldives' argument that "[a] dispute requires disagreement on where the actual maritime boundary should lie". In the Special Chamber's view, maritime delimitation disputes are not limited to disagreement concerning the location

of the actual maritime boundary and may arise in various other forms and situations.

334. The Special Chamber notes the contention of the Maldives that a dispute would need to have crystallized during the "brief window" after the ICJ had rendered the *Chagos* advisory opinion and before Mauritius had filed its Notification. In the view of the Special Chamber, it is clear from the above that a disagreement existed between the Parties regarding maritime delimitation long before the *Chagos* advisory opinion was rendered. While the Maldives may have been justified in having reservations with respect to the existence of a dispute between it and Mauritius before the ICJ rendered the advisory opinion, this is no longer the case now that the advisory opinion has been rendered. In this regard, the Special Chamber also takes note of the invitation by Mauritius to the Maldives to a second round of discussions on maritime delimitation in a diplomatic note of 7 March 2019, to which the Maldives did not respond. As the ICJ stated,

the existence of a dispute may be inferred from the failure of a State to respond to a claim in circumstances where a response is called for.

(*Application of the International Convention on the Elimination of All Forms of Racial Discrimination (Georgia v. Russian Federation), Preliminary Objections, Judgment, ICJ Reports 2011*, p. 70, at p. 84, para. 30; see also *Obligations concerning Negotiations relating to Cessation of the Nuclear Arms Race and to Nuclear Disarmament (Marshall Islands v. India), Jurisdiction and Admissibility, Judgment, ICJ Reports 2016*, p. 255, at p. 271, para. 37; *Obligations concerning Negotiations relating to Cessation of the Nuclear Arms Race and to Nuclear Disarmament (Marshall Islands v. Pakistan), Jurisdiction and Admissibility, Judgment, ICJ Reports 2016*, p. 552, at p. 567, para. 37; *Obligations concerning Negotiations relating to Cessation of the Nuclear Arms Race and to Nuclear Disarmament (Marshall Islands v. United Kingdom), Preliminary Objections, Judgment, ICJ Reports 2016*, p. 833, at p. 850, para. 40)

335. The Special Chamber, therefore, concludes that in the present case a dispute existed between the Parties concerning the delimitation of their maritime boundary at the time of the filing of the Notification.

336. Accordingly, the fourth preliminary objection of the Maldives is rejected.

IX. FIFTH PRELIMINARY OBJECTION: ABUSE OF PROCESS

337. The Special Chamber now turns to the Maldives' preliminary objection that "Mauritius' claims are inadmissible because they constitute an abuse of process."

338. The Maldives submits that it founds this objection on the well-established procedural rule according to which a claim will be inadmissible and an international court or tribunal must refrain from exercising jurisdiction if the claimant's application constitutes an abuse of process. In this regard, it refers, *inter alia*, to the case law of the ICJ.

339. The Maldives argues that,

[h]aving failed in the *Chagos Marine Protected Area Arbitration* to obtain a judicial decision against the United Kingdom stating that Mauritius has sovereignty over the Chagos Archipelago, Mauritius now tries to secure the same outcome by initiating UNCLOS proceedings against the Maldives, a third party to the bilateral sovereignty dispute.

In the Maldives' view,

[t]he use of maritime boundary proceedings in order to promote its claim to sovereignty over the Chagos Archipelago is a clear attempt by Mauritius to "use proceedings for aims alien to the ones for which the procedural rights at stake have been granted".

It maintains that "[u]sing UNCLOS compulsory procedures to obtain a ruling on a territorial dispute with a third State is the very definition of an abuse of process."

340. The Maldives disagrees with the position of Mauritius that, by raising preliminary objections in these proceedings, the Maldives has acted inconsistently with the "obligation to co-operate with the United Nations in order to complete the decolonization of Mauritius" stated in the *Chagos* advisory opinion. The Maldives, in its response to the second question posed by the Special Chamber (see paragraph 47 above), submits that "the raising of preliminary objections . . . is not in any way inconsistent with its obligation to cooperate in the decolonization of Mauritius."

341. Mauritius contends that the Maldives' objection based on an alleged abuse of process by Mauritius is itself vexatious, and, like all its other preliminary objections, unfounded. Mauritius further contends that it may be that the case law of the ICJ includes instances in which the principle of abuse of process has been invoked. It adds, however, that the Court has never once found the conditions for an application of the principle to be satisfied.

342. Mauritius submits that the Maldives' objection "is patently frivolous" and "echoes the same refrain as the other, equally baseless objections: that Mauritius seeks adjudication of a territorial dispute between itself and the United Kingdom, a dispute over which the Special Chamber may not exercise jurisdiction."

343. Mauritius asserts that it does not seek a ruling on sovereignty over the Chagos Archipelago and that such a ruling has already been issued by the ICJ. It further asserts that "the Maldives' reliance on the decision in the *Chagos MPA Arbitration* to demonstrate an alleged abuse of process by Mauritius is entirely ill-founded" since

[t]here is no identity between the relief sought or the issues determined in the *Chagos MPA Arbitration* and those now raised before the Special Chamber. They are not based on the same set of facts, nor do they involve the same parties. The task of the Special Chamber is the delimitation of the maritime boundary between the Maldives and Mauritius.

344. In response to the second question posed by the Special Chamber (see paragraph 47 above), Mauritius submits that the Maldives, by raising a preliminary objection which is based on the argument that the United Kingdom is an indispensable third party to the present proceedings, is taking action in violation of the advisory opinion and UNGA resolution 73/295. According to Mauritius, "[i]f any party has committed an abuse of process, it is the Maldives."

* * *

345. The Special Chamber concluded in paragraph 293 above that the obligation under article 74, paragraph 1, and article 83, paragraph 1, of the Convention has been fulfilled. It concluded further in paragraph 335 above that a dispute existed between the Parties concerning the delimitation of their maritime boundary at the time of the filing of the Notification.

346. Article 74, paragraph 2, and article 83, paragraph 2, of the Convention each provide that, "[i]f no agreement can be reached within a reasonable period of time, the States concerned *shall* resort to the procedures provided for in Part XV" (emphasis added by the Special Chamber).

347. The Special Chamber notes that, by filing its Notification on 18 June 2019, Mauritius resorted to the dispute settlement procedures provided for in Part XV of the Convention, in accordance with article 74, paragraph 2, and article 83, paragraph 2, of the Convention.

348. The Special Chamber recalls that Mauritius' claims, as set out in paragraphs 27 and 28 of the Notification, read as follows:

27. Mauritius requests the Tribunal to delimit, in accordance with the principles and rules set forth in UNCLOS, the maritime boundary between Mauritius and Maldives in the Indian Ocean, in the EEZ and continental shelf, including the portion of the continental shelf pertaining to Mauritius that lies more than 200 nautical miles from the baselines from which its territorial sea is measured.

28. Mauritius also requests the Tribunal to declare that Maldives has violated its obligation to, pending agreement as provided for in paragraphs 1 of Articles 74 and 83 of UNCLOS, make every effort to enter into provisional arrangements of a practical nature and, during such transitional periods, not to jeopardize or hamper the reaching of the final agreement.

As is evident from the above, Mauritius' claims are confined to articles 74 and 83 of the Convention.

349. The Special Chamber, therefore, does not consider that Mauritius' claims constitute an abuse of process.

350. Accordingly, the fifth preliminary objection of the Maldives is rejected.

X. CONCLUSIONS ON JURISDICTION AND ADMISSIBILITY

351. For the above reasons, the Special Chamber concludes that it has jurisdiction to adjudicate upon the dispute concerning the delimitation of the maritime boundary between the Parties in the Indian Ocean and that the claim submitted by Mauritius in this regard is admissible.

352. The Special Chamber finds it appropriate to defer to the proceedings on the merits questions concerning the extent to which it may exercise its jurisdiction over the above dispute, including questions arising under article 76 of the Convention.

353. Regarding the Parties' views in relation to Mauritius' claim stated in paragraph 28 of its Notification concerning the obligations under article 74, paragraph 3, and article 83, paragraph 3, of the Convention (see paragraphs 307 and 319 above), the Special Chamber finds it appropriate to reserve this matter for consideration and decision in the proceedings on the merits, as this point has not yet been fully argued by the Parties.

XI. OPERATIVE PROVISIONS

354. For the above reasons, the Special Chamber

(1) Unanimously,
    Rejects the first preliminary objection raised by the Maldives on the grounds that the United Kingdom is an indispensable third party to the present proceedings.

(2) By 8 votes to 1,
Rejects the second preliminary objection raised by the
Maldives on the grounds that the Special Chamber lacks juris-
diction to determine the disputed issue of sovereignty over the
Chagos Archipelago.

IN FAVOUR: Judge Paik, *President of the Special Chamber; Judges*
Jesus, Pawlak, Yanai, Bouguetaia, Heidar, Chadha; *Judge ad
hoc* Schrijver;
AGAINST: *Judge ad hoc* Oxman.

(3) By 8 votes to 1,
Rejects the third preliminary objection raised by the Maldives
relating to articles 74 and 83 of the Convention.

IN FAVOUR: Judge Paik, *President of the Special Chamber; Judges*
Jesus, Pawlak, Yanai, Bouguetaia, Heidar, Chadha; *Judge ad
hoc* Schrijver;
AGAINST: *Judge ad hoc* Oxman.

(4) Unanimously,
Rejects the fourth preliminary objection raised by the Maldives
based on the non-existence of a dispute between the Parties.

(5) Unanimously,
Rejects the fifth preliminary objection raised by the Maldives
based on an abuse of process.

(6) By 8 votes to 1,
Finds that it has jurisdiction to adjudicate upon the dispute
submitted to it by the Parties concerning the delimitation of
the maritime boundary between them in the Indian Ocean and
that the claim submitted by Mauritius in this regard is admissible; *defers*, however, to the proceedings on the merits questions regarding the extent to which the Special Chamber may
exercise its jurisdiction, including questions arising under article 76 of the Convention.

IN FAVOUR: Judge Paik, *President of the Special Chamber; Judges*
Jesus, Pawlak, Yanai, Bouguetaia, Heidar, Chadha; *Judge ad
hoc* Schrijver;
AGAINST: *Judge ad hoc* Oxman.

(7) Unanimously,
Reserves for consideration and decision in the proceedings on
the merits the question of jurisdiction and admissibility with

respect to Mauritius' claim stated in paragraph 28 of its Notification concerning the obligations under article 74, paragraph 3, and article 83, paragraph 3, of the Convention.

Judges ad hoc Oxman and Schrijver, availing themselves of the right conferred on them by article 125, paragraph 2, of the Rules of the Tribunal, append their joint declaration to the Judgment of the Special Chamber.

Judge ad hoc Oxman, availing himself of the right conferred on him by article 30, paragraph 3, of the Statute of the Tribunal, appends his separate and dissenting opinion to the Judgment of the Special Chamber.

JOINT DECLARATION OF JUDGES AD HOC OXMAN AND SCHRIJVER[1]

[1] Consideration of preliminary objections to jurisdiction and admissibility prior to the submission of pleadings on the merits serves the useful purpose of obviating the need to expend the effort necessary to prepare those pleadings in the event that the preliminary objections are upheld. It does, however, mean that on certain issues limited information is available regarding the factual and legal predicates for the claims, and that the parties may not necessarily raise and address all relevant questions at this stage.

[2] The Judgment, wisely in our view, in subparagraph (6) of the *dispositif* defers to the proceedings on the merits questions regarding the extent to which the Special Chamber may exercise its jurisdiction, including questions arising under article 76 of the Convention.

[3] Subparagraph (7) of the *dispositif* reserves for consideration and decision in the proceedings on the merits the question of jurisdiction and admissibility relating to Mauritius' claim stated in paragraph 28 of the Notification. We wish to record our view that subparagraph (7) refers to the claim of violation set forth in paragraph 28 of the Notification, and does not call into question the duty of the Parties to comply with paragraph 3 of article 74 and paragraph 3 of article 83 of the Convention. We trust they will do so in a spirit of understanding and co-operation.

[4] Lastly, pursuant to the rules and practices of the Tribunal, matters concerning scheduling and the hybrid nature of these

---

[1 The paragraph numbers have been inserted by the editors.]

proceedings were addressed by the President of the Special Chamber in consultation with the Parties. Each of us first learned in the latter part of December 2020 of the communications to which reference is made in paragraphs 29 to 34 of the Judgment. We wish to express our appreciation to the President, the Registry, and the Parties for their discretion in this regard.

SEPARATE AND DISSENTING OPINION OF JUDGE AD HOC OXMAN

1. I believe that the request of Mauritius for judicial determination of a permanent maritime boundary is not yet admissible. I also believe that paragraph 3 of article 74 and paragraph 3 of article 83 apply to the activities of the Parties in the area that is within 200 nautical miles of the coast of both the Maldives and the Chagos Archipelago. The reasons are set forth below.

* * *

2. The record in this case does not reveal a dispute regarding the location of a maritime boundary, or the method to be used to determine its location, that is comparable to the delimitation disputes that have been submitted for binding determination by an international court or tribunal on numerous occasions since proceedings were instituted before the International Court of Justice (hereinafter "the ICJ") over a half century ago in the *North Sea Continental Shelf* cases, or indeed since the *Grisbådarna* arbitration over a century ago.

3. The Notification and the Statement of the claim and grounds on which it is based (hereinafter "the Notification") avers that "[d]espite the efforts of Mauritius to engage Maldives in negotiations to agree upon a maritime boundary, other than agreeing to attend a single meeting in October 2010, Maldives has declined to participate in such negotiations." It goes on to indicate that proceedings were accordingly instituted by Mauritius under the compulsory jurisdiction provisions of Section 2 of Part XV of the United Nations Convention on the Law of the Sea (hereinafter "the Convention").

4. At the outset of the hearing, the Agent of the Maldives explained the reasons for its reluctance to accept Mauritius' invitation to engage in delimitation negotiations with respect to areas off the coast of the Chagos Archipelago. Those reasons relate to a principle to which reference is made in numerous maritime delimitation cases, namely, to cite one example, that coastal State

maritime rights derive from the coastal State's sovereignty over the land, a principle which can be summarized as "the land dominates the sea" ... Following this approach, sovereignty over the islands needs to be determined prior to and independently from maritime delimitation.

(*Territorial and Maritime Dispute between Nicaragua and Honduras in the Caribbean Sea (Nicaragua v. Honduras), Judgment, ICJ Reports 2007*, p. 659, at p. 699, para. 126) (hereinafter "*Nicaragua v. Honduras*")

This Tribunal referred to the principle that the land dominates the sea in its first maritime delimitation judgment (*Delimitation of the Maritime Boundary in the Bay of Bengal (Bangladesh/Myanmar), Judgment, ITLOS Reports 2012*, p. 4, at p. 56, para. 185).

5. The Agent of the Maldives stated that it "cannot be expected to take sides" in a dispute between Mauritius and the United Kingdom regarding the Chagos Archipelago, "a conflict which is not of our making" and "a dispute in which the Maldives has repeatedly stated that it does not wish to interfere." He explained that the Maldives "is understandably reluctant to become entangled in a controversial dispute with two States with which it enjoys important and friendly relations," noting in this regard that since 2011 "the Maldives has adopted a policy of refraining from bilateral talks with either party to the exclusion of the other." He observed that if there were no such dispute, "there would be no issue with delimitation. The Maldives would eagerly negotiate an agreement on the maritime boundary."

6. The history of the dispute between Mauritius and the United Kingdom regarding the Chagos Archipelago is recounted in the *Chagos* arbitral award (*Arbitration regarding the Chagos Marine Protected Area between Mauritius and the United Kingdom of Great Britain and Northern Ireland, Award of 18 March 2015, RIAA, Vol. XXXI*, p. 359, at pp. 383-440, paras. 54-157) (hereinafter "the *Chagos Arbitral Award*") and in the *Chagos* advisory opinion (*Legal Consequences of the Separation of the Chagos Archipelago from Mauritius in 1965, Advisory Opinion, ICJ Reports 2019*, p. 95, at pp. 107-11, paras. 25-53) (hereinafter "the *Chagos Advisory Opinion*").

7. There is nothing unusual in international relations about trying to avoid being drawn into a dispute between other parties. A compendium of State practice to this effect, having consumed volumes, might still be incomplete. Such restraint may have desirable effects with respect to the maintenance of public order in general, and the prevention of aggravation and extension of disputes in particular. So much so that, absent countervailing rights and duties, the law may

even encourage such restraint (see Declaration on Principles of International Law concerning Friendly Relations and Co-operation among States in accordance with the Charter of the United Nations, UNGA resolution 2625 (XXV), 24 October 1970 ("States parties to an international dispute, *as well as other States*, shall refrain from any action which may aggravate the situation") (emphasis added)).

8. The question is whether the relevant provisions of the Convention compel a State to negotiate a maritime boundary notwithstanding the foregoing concerns and, in this connection, whether the compulsory dispute-settlement provisions of the Convention may be used directly or indirectly to achieve that result. These issues arise in the context of the requests for relief by Mauritius set forth respectively in paragraphs 27 and 28 of the Notification, namely:

to delimit . . . the maritime boundary between Mauritius and Maldives . . . in the EEZ and continental shelf, including the portion of the continental shelf pertaining to Mauritius that lies more than 200 nautical miles from the baselines from which the breadth of its territorial sea is measured

and

to declare that Maldives has violated its obligation to, pending agreement as provided for in paragraph 1 of Articles 74 and 83 of UNCLOS, make every effort to enter into provisional arrangements of a practical nature and, during such transitional periods, not to jeopardize or hamper the reaching of the final agreement.

Article 74 and article 83

9. Both of the foregoing claims relate to article 74 and article 83 of the Convention, the former article addressing the exclusive economic zone ("EEZ") and the latter the continental shelf in identical terms. The four paragraphs of each of these articles provide as follows:

1. The delimitation of the [exclusive economic zone] [continental shelf] between States with opposite or adjacent coasts shall be effected by agreement on the basis of international law, as referred to in Article 38 of the Statute of the International Court of Justice, in order to achieve an equitable solution.

2. If no agreement can be reached within a reasonable period of time, the States concerned shall resort to the procedures provided for in Part XV.

3. Pending agreement as provided for in paragraph 1, the States concerned, in a spirit of understanding and cooperation, shall make every effort to enter into provisional arrangements of a practical nature and, during this transitional period, not to jeopardize or hamper the reaching of the final agreement. Such arrangements shall be without prejudice to the final delimitation.

4. Where there is an agreement in force between the States concerned, questions relating to the delimitation of the [exclusive economic zone] [continental shelf] shall be determined in accordance with the provisions of that agreement.

10. The four paragraphs of article 74 and of article 83 of the Convention address both the substantive and procedural consequences of overlapping entitlements under article 57 and article 76, respectively. Article 74 and article 83 contemplate determination of a maritime boundary that ordinarily divides the overlapping entitlements. That is an outcome whose benefits arise from applying the same geographic allocation to all affected entitlements and duties. The fact that delimitation may not in itself adequately address regulatory needs is made clear with respect to living resources by article 63, paragraph 1, article 64, paragraph 1, article 66, paragraph 4, and article 67, paragraph 3; with respect to pollution by article 194, paragraph 2, article 208, paragraph 4, and article 210, paragraph 5; and with respect to both as well as marine scientific research by article 123. Also, many delimitation agreements contain special clauses regarding deposits in the seabed and subsoil of non-living resources, especially those in fluid form, that are traversed by a boundary.

11. "Article 83, paragraph 1, of UNCLOS, in providing that delimitation shall be effected by way of agreement, requires that there be negotiations conducted in good faith, but not that they should be successful" (*Maritime Delimitation in the Indian Ocean (Somalia v. Kenya), Preliminary Objections, Judgment, ICJ Reports 2017*, p. 3, at p. 37, para. 90; see *Delimitation of the Maritime Boundary in the Atlantic Ocean (Ghana/Côte d'Ivoire), Judgment, ITLOS Reports 2017*, p. 4, at p. 162, para. 604) (hereinafter "the *Ghana/Côte d'Ivoire Judgment*").[1] One might add that the first judgment of the ICJ on delimitation of the continental shelf contains an oft-cited passage concerning the duty to negotiate (*North Sea Continental Shelf Cases (Federal Republic of Germany v. Denmark; Federal Republic of Germany v. Netherlands), Judgment, ICJ Reports 1969*, p. 3, at p. 87, para. 85(a)).

12. The agreements referred to in paragraphs 1 and 4 of article 74 and paragraphs 1 and 4 of article 83 may provide for joint or cooperative implementation of some or all of the coastal State rights with respect to some or all of the area of overlap. The existence of such agreements illustrates the fact that paragraph 1 does not necessarily require delimitation.

---

[1]   See Judgment, para. 273.

13. A further illustration may be found in the ubiquity of overlapping entitlements that have yet to be delimited, decades after the adoption and entry into force of the Convention. That does not mean that the coastal States concerned are in breach of the Convention. It also does not mean that the undelimited areas are not regulated by article 74 and article 83. What it means is that the areas of overlap are governed by paragraph 3 of those articles. The number and significance of these undelimited areas, and the fact that some are the object of serious political differences, suggest caution in considering limitations on the scope and application of paragraph 3 of those articles. The rules on how to live with unresolved issues are of no less importance than the rules on how to resolve them.

14. Only paragraph 2 of article 74 and paragraph 2 of article 83 may, but do not necessarily, compel delimitation. Some States have exercised the specific right under article 298, paragraph 1(a)(i), to exclude "disputes concerning the interpretation or application of articles 15, 74 and 83 relating to sea boundary delimitations" from compulsory arbitration or adjudication under the Convention. Whatever the jurisdictional constraints on a court or tribunal to which a delimitation dispute has been submitted, it also should be borne in mind that paragraph 2 of article 74 and paragraph 2 of article 83 refer to all of the dispute-settlement procedures provided for in Part XV, not just arbitration and adjudication. A possible consequence of applying those paragraphs is agreement on conciliation under article 284 or submission of the dispute to compulsory conciliation by one party under article 298, paragraph 1(a)(i). That may result, and indeed has resulted, in much more than simple delimitation (see *Timor Sea Conciliation between Timor-Leste and Australia*, Report and Recommendations of 9 May 2018, paras. 303-6, Annex 28: Maritime Boundary Treaty, Arts. 2, 4, 7, Annex B) (PCA Case No 2016-10) (hereinafter "the *Timor Sea Conciliation*").

15. Mauritius suggests that paragraph 2 of article 74 and paragraph 2 of article 83 impose no jurisdictional requirement additional to that contained in Part XV, notably article 283, paragraph 1. Were there any doubt about the importance and relevance of paragraph 2 of article 74 and paragraph 2 of article 83, it should be noted that their "reasonable period of time" requirement is repeated in article 298, paragraph 1(a)(i), as a condition for compulsory conciliation of a delimitation dispute that is excluded from arbitration or adjudication by a declaration under that article. In the first such conciliation, the refusal of a State to negotiate on delimitation was examined in the light of that

condition (*Timor Sea Conciliation*, Decision on Australia's Objections to Competence of 19 September 2016, paras. 77-82).

16. The reference to a reasonable period of time in the cited provisions makes clear that the existence of overlapping entitlements under article 57 and article 76 does not, in itself, mean that a delimitation dispute has yet arisen that is ready to be addressed under Part XV in general, and Sections 2 and 3 of that part in particular. Such a dispute typically arises after one party claims or proposes a maritime boundary or a method of delimitation that the other party rejects. Even then, one might need to draw a distinction between a continuing negotiation and an impasse.

17. Paragraph 2 of article 74 and paragraph 2 of article 83 need not be regarded as imposing a jurisdictional limitation as such. The "reasonable period of time" requirement set forth in those paragraphs might better be regarded as regulating the admissibility of a delimitation claim arising in the specific context of paragraph 1 of each of those articles, with which it is directly associated. Those articles are found in Parts V and VI of the Convention on the EEZ and continental shelf, not Part XV on settlement of disputes. Jurisdiction over a dispute concerning the interpretation or application of those articles is not necessarily predicated on Part XV, as article 282 makes clear. The wording of the "reasonable period of time" requirement appears to confer some latitude. The process presumably entails a case-specific evaluation directed to a question the answer to which will determine whether it is yet time for a court or tribunal to step in and establish a permanent maritime boundary itself, bearing in mind that the alternative is not a legal vacuum: paragraph 3 of each of those articles continues to regulate conduct within the area of overlapping entitlements pending delimitation.

The nature and scope of the dispute

18. The record in this case indicates that there is an area of overlapping entitlements that is within 200 nautical miles (nm) of the coasts of both the Maldives and the Chagos Archipelago. The map that accompanies the executive summary of the Maldives' submission to the Commission on the Limits of the Continental Shelf (hereinafter "the CLCS") indicates that the Maldives regards its entitlements as extending into that area.[2] Mauritius depicts its entitlements as

---

[2] The map is reproduced in Mauritius, Written Observations on the Preliminary Objections, Vol. 1, at p. 32 (Figure 3).

extending into that area as well. The location of this area of overlap may be ascertained with reasonable clarity, as Mauritius illustrated from its perspective in its Written Observations.[3] It encompasses a discrete portion of the respective 200-mile zones at their far reaches, even taking into account the use of different basepoints to which reference was made in these proceedings.

19. There appears to be no evidence in the record that either Party made a concrete delimitation proposal with respect to that area of overlap prior to the institution of proceedings in this case. During the first round of oral proceedings, the Co-Agent of Mauritius showed a map that illustrates its view of the area of overlap within 200 nm and depicts a line running midway through it that is labelled "Potential Median Line".[4] There is, however, no indication that such a line had been claimed by Mauritius or proposed to the Maldives as either a permanent maritime boundary or a provisional limit.

20. The record does indicate the emergence of a difference between the Parties with respect to the submission of the Maldives to the CLCS. Such submissions concern the seaward limits of continental shelf entitlements beyond 200 nm under article 76, not delimitation of overlapping entitlements under article 83. The absence of delimitation is relevant to CLCS submissions because the CLCS, under its Rules of Procedure, may decline to review a submission without the consent of a State with potentially overlapping entitlements. While CLCS Rule 46 and Annex I to its Rules of Procedure speak of disputes in this context, the CLCS is not a dispute-settlement body and the reference to "land or maritime disputes" is much broader than a legal dispute with respect to delimitation.[5] Sometimes the State with potentially

---

[3] Mauritius, Written Observations on the Preliminary Objections, Vol. 1, at p. 34 (Figure 4).
[4] A copy of that map is appended at the end of this opinion.
[5] Rule 46 provides as follows:

1. In case there is a dispute in the delimitation of the continental shelf between opposite or adjacent States or in other cases of unresolved land or maritime disputes, submissions may be made and shall be considered in accordance with Annex I to these Rules.
2. The actions of the Commission shall not prejudice matters relating to the delimitation of boundaries between States.

   Annex I to the Rules provides in pertinent part:

5. (a) In cases where a land or maritime dispute exists, the Commission shall not consider and qualify a submission made by any of the States concerned in the dispute. However, the Commission may consider one or more submissions in the areas under dispute with prior consent given by all States that are parties to such a dispute.
   (b) The submissions made before the Commission and the recommendations approved by the Commission thereon shall not prejudice the position of States which are parties to a land or maritime dispute.

overlapping entitlements consents to consideration of the submission by the CLCS on the understanding that this is without prejudice to the question of delimitation. Sometimes it does not consent and the CLCS does not proceed.

21. The map that accompanies the executive summary of the submission of the Maldives illustrates the continental shelf entitlements of the Maldives in the area beyond 200 nm from its coast whose outer limits it is submitting for review by the CLCS under article 76, paragraph 8, and Annex II. That map reveals that the submission with respect to the continental shelf entitlements of the Maldives beyond 200 nm from its coast is not intended to extend within the EEZ of other States, whose limits are illustrated in yellow. In this regard the map depicts a 200-mile EEZ measured from the Chagos Archipelago.[6]

22. Mauritius informed the Maldives that there was an error in the map's depiction of the precise location of the 200-mile limit measured from the Chagos Archipelago, so that there is an area of limited size where the continental shelf entitlement beyond 200 nm from its coast that is illustrated by the Maldives overlaps with the area within 200 nm of the Chagos Archipelago as measured by Mauritius. When the Maldives failed to amend the map, Mauritius transmitted a note to the CLCS protesting the encroachment into its EEZ of the extended continental shelf entitlement depicted in the map.[7]

23. While the note addresses overlapping claims of entitlement, it does not address delimitation as such.[8] This is confirmed by the map shown by the Co-Agent of Mauritius during the first round of oral proceedings: the "Potential Median Line" is located only within 200 nm of both coasts.[9]

24. It is accordingly apparent, as previously noted, that this case is not before the Special Chamber because of a difference between the Parties regarding how overlapping entitlements should be delimited. It is here because one of the Parties has declined to proceed with delimitation negotiations. The reasons for doing so help to define the nature and scope of the dispute between the Parties.

25. The preliminary objections and the arguments of the Parties focus largely on the question of jurisdiction to decide on the status of the Chagos Archipelago in order to determine whether Mauritius is the

---

[6]   See note 2 *supra*.
[7]   See Judgment, paras. 66, 68.
[8]   See Judgment, paras. 331-3.
[9]   See note 4 *supra*.

State with opposite or adjacent coasts to which paragraph 1 of article 74 and paragraph 1 of article 83 refer.[10] Approaching that issue frontally engages the established jurisprudence that eschews the exercise of jurisdiction over issues regarding rights to land territory in proceedings under the compulsory jurisdiction provisions of Section 2 of Part XV of the United Nations Convention on the Law of the Sea (see *Arbitration regarding the delimitation of the maritime boundary between Guyana and Suriname, Award of 17 September 2007, RIAA, Vol. XXX*, p. 1, at pp. 42-5, paras. 174-81, p. 86, paras. 307-8; *Chagos Arbitral Award*, at pp. 458-60, paras. 214-21; *South China Sea Arbitration between the Republic of the Philippines and the People's Republic of China, Award of 12 July 2016, RIAA, Vol. XXXIII*, p. 153, at pp. 184-5, para. 5 (hereinafter *"South China Sea Arbitral Award"*);[11] *Arbitration concerning Coastal State Rights in the Black Sea, Sea of Azov, and Kerch Strait between Ukraine and the Russian Federation, Award concerning Preliminary Objections of the Russian Federation of 21 February 2020*, PCA Case No 2017-06 at pp. 48-9, para. 156, p. 59, para. 197) (hereinafter "the *Coastal State Rights Arbitral Award*").

26. The *South China Sea* award makes a similar point with respect to the territorial claims of third States as well (*South China Sea Arbitral Award*, at p. 239, para. 157). This is one of the reasons given for concluding that the third-State claimants are not indispensable parties (*ibid.*). Although the situations are different, that reasoning tends to suggest that the predicate for the second preliminary objection subsumes the predicate for the first in this case (see *Monetary Gold Removed from Rome in 1943 (Italy v. France, United Kingdom and United States of America), Preliminary Question, Judgment, ICJ Reports 1954*, p. 19, at p. 32 ("Albania's legal interests . . . would form the very subject-matter of the decision")).

27. Mauritius asserts at the outset of its Written Observations, "The existence of the ICJ Advisory Opinion and the UN General Assembly Resolution are matters of fact, which, as shown below, are determinative of the legal issues raised by the Maldives' Preliminary Objections." Mauritius thereby invites the Special Chamber to avoid the question of the existence of jurisdiction to determine disputed rights to land territory by attributing conclusive prescriptive and, in practical effect, *res judicata* consequences to the advisory opinion and the ensuing General Assembly resolution 73/295 of 22 May 2019. In doing so,

---

[10]   See Judgment, para. 115.
[11]   See Judgment, para. 110.

Mauritius attempts to avoid the distinction between the authoritative nature of an advisory opinion of the ICJ and its legally binding effect, and the distinction between the competence of the General Assembly to deal with a matter and the legally binding effect of its conclusions. It may be noted in this regard that General Assembly resolution 73/295, like the General Assembly resolutions unsuccessfully invoked by Ukraine in the *Coastal State Rights* arbitration, was "not adopted unanimously or by consensus but with many States abstaining or voting against" it (see *Coastal State Rights Arbitral Award*, at p. 54, para. 175).[12]

28. Even if Mauritius correctly perceives the intended meaning of the advisory opinion and the ensuing General Assembly resolution, its understanding of their legal effects is clearly not embraced by the United Kingdom.[13] In this regard the question before the Special Chamber is not whether that difference would constitute a dispute for purposes of satisfying the requirements for adjudication.[14] The question is whether the issue posed is outside its jurisdiction.

29. It is not apparent how, or why, the established jurisprudence, which eschews the exercise of compulsory jurisdiction under the Convention with respect to issues regarding rights to land territory, can be or should be avoided where there is a disagreement regarding the legal effect of a treaty, or judgment, award, or advisory opinion, or resolution of an international organization that addresses such rights.[15] The *Coastal State Rights* award suggests otherwise:

if the Arbitral Tribunal were to accept Ukraine's interpretation of those UNGA resolutions as correct, it would *ipso facto* imply that the Arbitral Tribunal finds that Crimea is part of Ukraine's territory. However, it has no jurisdiction to do so.

(*Coastal State Rights Arbitral Award*, p. 54, para. 176)

It is not clear why that logic should not apply to the *Chagos* advisory opinion as well. Shortly after the hearing on preliminary objections in the present proceedings, the ICJ rendered a judgment in which it noted the close connection for jurisdictional purposes between a boundary dispute and a dispute regarding an arbitral award concerning the boundary (*Arbitral Award of 3 October 1899 (Guyana v. Venezuela), Judgment on Jurisdiction*, para. 130, to be published in *ICJ Reports 2020*).

---

12 See Judgment, para. 75.
13 See Judgment, paras. 73, 75-7.
14 But see Judgment, para. 243.
15 But see Judgment, para. 190.

30. Approaching the issue of the status of the Chagos Archipelago frontally also magnifies the scope of the dispute between the Parties to this case. Mauritius maintains that its sovereignty over the Chagos Archipelago is beyond dispute as a matter of law. The Maldives, noting that there is in fact a dispute between Mauritius and the United Kingdom regarding the Chagos Archipelago, declines to be drawn into that dispute. The differences between these positions are narrower than the arguments concerning the jurisdictional objections may suggest.[16] It is possible to apply article 74 and article 83 only where these positions necessarily conflict, that is to the narrow questions that are unavoidably in dispute between the Parties at this juncture.

31. This would be far from the first case where a court or tribunal took such a restrained approach. That does not mean that every case is necessarily best approached in this way. But prior to the institution of proceedings in this case, the ICJ in its advisory opinion addressed, in a manner and to an extent that the Court deemed appropriate, the nature and implications of basic principles invoked by Mauritius in the present proceedings, and made clear that it is for the United Nations General Assembly to consider the ensuing steps (*Chagos Advisory Opinion*, at p. 139, para. 179).

32. The question before the Special Chamber is not whether it should reach the same conclusion on the merits with respect to the status of the Chagos Archipelago as that which is expressed in or implied by the advisory opinion or the ensuing General Assembly resolution. That would require adjudicating the merits of the claims to the islands, which would run counter to the jurisdictional limitations recognized by the existing jurisprudence. Rather in this case, Mauritius invites the Special Chamber to treat the territorial dispute as resolved by the Advisory Opinion and the ensuing General Assembly action. Quite apart from its underlying analytical challenges, accepting that invitation risks complicating the exercise by the General Assembly of its political functions and the exercise by the ICJ of its discretion with respect to requests for advisory opinions.

33. The advisory opinion states "that all Member States are under an obligation to co-operate with the United Nations in order to complete the decolonization of Mauritius" (para. 183(5)). It does not necessarily follow that this precludes the Maldives from declining to negotiate a maritime boundary with Mauritius for the time being. A more fulsome observation in this regard might, without questioning the authority or importance of the statement, nevertheless question

---

[16] Cf. Judgment, para. 114.

whether its interpretation or application is within the jurisdiction of the Special Chamber, referring in this connection to the existing jurisprudence eschewing the exercise of jurisdiction under Section 2 of Part XV of the Convention with respect to issues regarding rights to land territory. In this connection it might be noted that questions regarding the right of self-determination and decolonization were addressed by the Third United Nations Conference on the Law of the Sea in resolution III rather than in the text of the Convention, that there is no reference to that resolution in the text of the Convention, that such matters are beyond the scope of the substantive and dispute-settlement obligations accepted by the States Parties in consenting to be bound by the Convention, and that the references to international law in article 74, article 83, and article 293 are not open-ended invitations to conclude otherwise.

The request for judicial determination of a permanent maritime boundary

34. It is difficult to reach a conclusion that there is jurisdiction to proceed with delimitation in this case that is compatible not only with a cautious view of the legally binding effect of the ICJ advisory opinion and ensuing General Assembly resolution but that is also compatible at the same time with a restrained view of the Special Chamber's jurisdiction to pronounce on rights to land territory. The two are in tension with each other, pulling in opposite directions in that context. There is little if anything in the record of this case to suggest that there is a need for a permanent maritime boundary to divide the area of overlapping entitlements that is pressing enough to require such an undertaking at present. In my view, it is preferable to consider alternatives under articles 74 and 83 that avoid foreclosing such action in the future if need be, and that for the time being restrain the activities of the Parties in the area of overlapping entitlements.

35. The object of paragraph 1 of article 74 and of paragraph 1 of article 83 is a maritime boundary. Land and maritime boundaries share the characteristics of formality and finality, whatever the conceptual distinctions between them (see *Maritime Delimitation in the Black Sea (Romania v. Ukraine), Judgment, ICJ Reports 2009*, p. 61, para. 217). The "establishment of a permanent maritime boundary is a matter of grave importance" (*Nicaragua v. Honduras*, at p. 659, para. 253).

Whether it is a land frontier or a boundary line in the continental shelf that is in question, the process is essentially the same, and inevitably involves the same element of stability and permanence, and is subject to the rule excluding boundary agreements from fundamental change of circumstances. (*Aegean Sea Continental Shelf (Greece* v. *Turkey), Judgment, ICJ Reports 1978*, p. 3, at pp. 35-6, para. 85; see Vienna Convention on the Law of Treaties, Art. 62, para. 2(a))

36. These characteristics amplify the differences between the Parties to this case. These characteristics also suggest that paragraph 1 of article 74 and paragraph 1 of article 83 should not be interpreted to require a State to negotiate on a permanent maritime boundary when it declines to do so on the grounds that this would require it to become entangled in a disagreement between other States that exists in fact with respect to the territory of which the opposite or adjacent coast forms part. From this it should ordinarily follow that the "reasonable period of time" referred to in paragraph 2 for reaching agreement under paragraph 1 has not yet elapsed. Otherwise, in situations of failure to negotiate, one would impose the same result as would obtain in the absence of a reasonable justification.

37. In the Timor Sea Conciliation, the Conciliation Commission did not accept Australia's asserted justifications for declining to negotiate on delimitation, and accordingly concluded that a reasonable period of time had elapsed under article 298, paragraph 1(a)(i) (*Timor Sea Conciliation*, Decision on Australia's Objections to Competence, paras. 77-82). It is evident that Australia's objective in that context was to preclude delimitation. It may be assumed for purposes of the present case that a comparable refusal to negotiate under paragraph 1 of article 74 and paragraph 1 of article 83 would ordinarily mean that a reasonable period of time had elapsed under paragraph 2.

38. The Maldives has made clear that its reluctance to negotiate a maritime boundary is based on its desire not to be drawn into a dispute between other States that is not of its making and to which it is not party. The Maldives has also indicated that it is prepared to proceed with delimitation negotiations once the dispute between the other States is resolved. As previously noted, that position in my view merits respect for important reasons of public order.

39. The effect to be accorded the reluctance of the Maldives to negotiate a permanent maritime boundary is not logically contingent on the legal merits of the respective positions taken by the disputing parties. Territorial claimants not infrequently insist that opposing claims are mere assertions that merit no legal cognizance; whether that view is or is not correct says little if anything about the posture of a

third State that seeks to avoid entanglement in the disagreement. Nor is the effect to be accorded the reluctance of the Maldives to negotiate logically contingent on any particular characterization of the disagreement between Mauritius and the United Kingdom, be it one over territorial sovereignty or one over completion of the process of decolonization as envisaged in the ICJ advisory opinion and General Assembly resolution 73/295. Indeed, resolution III of the Third United Nations Conference on the Law of the Sea suggests that it could be both.

40. A conclusion for the foregoing reasons that the request of Mauritius for judicial determination of a permanent maritime boundary is not yet admissible renders it unnecessary to address and decide on each of the preliminary objections with regard to that claim. This in itself, in my view, is a helpful consequence of resolving in the foregoing manner the narrow questions that necessarily divide the Parties to this case.

41. The issue thereby decided under paragraphs 1 and 2 of article 74 and paragraphs 1 and 2 of article 83 is the effect of the position of the Maldives with respect to the negotiation of a maritime boundary under paragraph 1, not that of the sovereignty claim of another State. There is ample evidence in the record of this case that the Maldives' explanation of the reason for its reluctance to negotiate a maritime boundary with Mauritius is not a mere fabrication or pretext for precluding delimitation (see *Coastal State Rights Arbitral Award*, at p. 57, para. 189). No additional pronouncement on the existence, let alone the merits, of a territorial dispute regarding the Chagos Archipelago is required.[17] That in turn avoids the risk of calling into question the coherence of the jurisprudence regarding jurisdiction to determine rights to land territory in proceedings instituted under the compulsory jurisdiction provisions of Section 2 of Part XV of the Convention.

42. A decision on jurisdiction and admissibility in this case need not, and preferably should not, amplify the dispute between the Parties by treating their basic positions of principle as being in fundamental and unavoidable conflict. Alternative inferences need not be excluded where this is unnecessary to decide the question. It might be maintained that the conclusion that a reasonable period of time for negotiation under paragraph 1 of article 74 and paragraph 1 of article 83 has not yet elapsed implies that Mauritius is the State with an opposite or

---

17   Compare Judgment, paras. 243, 245.

adjacent coast under those paragraphs; it also might be maintained that all that is decided is that paragraph 1 does not require the Maldives to negotiate with Mauritius on a final boundary when the Maldives declines to do so pending resolution of a dispute regarding territory of which the opposite or adjacent coast forms part.

Obligations under paragraph 3 of article 74 and paragraph 3 of article 83

43. The conclusion, for the foregoing reasons, that the request of Mauritius for judicial determination of a permanent maritime boundary is not yet admissible would not necessarily mean that the Parties have no obligations under paragraph 3 of article 74 and paragraph 3 of article 83 pending delimitation.

44. The more flexible word "arrangements" in paragraph 3 may be compared with the more formal word "agreement" in paragraph 1 of each of those articles. The contrast is marked. The function of paragraph 3 is not delimitation, but rather management of the situation pending delimitation. It provides the basis for self-restraint and enhances both the willingness and the ability of governments to forestall and resist pressures for destabilizing action.

45. Paragraph 3 specifies two obligations in this regard (see *Ghana/ Côte d'Ivoire Judgment*, at p. 166, para. 626). One is to make every effort to enter into provisional arrangements of a practical nature with the other party, on the understanding that such arrangements are without prejudice to the final delimitation. The other is to make every effort not to jeopardize or hamper the reaching of the final agreement. The latter obligation might be satisfied either by unilateral self-restraint or by provisional arrangements with the other party or both.

46. One may reasonably assume that the term "States concerned" in paragraph 3 of article 74 and paragraph 3 of article 83 includes the "States with opposite or adjacent coasts" referred to in paragraph 1. But that need not necessarily limit the application of paragraph 3. The immediate context for the interpretation of the words "States concerned" in paragraph 3 is that paragraph. Its function is different from that of paragraph 1. It is not apparent why the words "[p]ending agreement as provided for in paragraph 1" cannot be understood to embrace an impediment to agreement such as that which led the Maldives to decline to negotiate a maritime boundary for the time being.

47. It is neither logically necessary nor consistent with the overall structure of article 74 and article 83 to conclude that relieving the Maldives for the time being of its obligation to negotiate under

paragraph 1, in order to avoid being drawn into a dispute between other States, also relieves both Parties of their obligations under paragraph 3. While negotiating a permanent maritime boundary may be difficult to reconcile with a policy of avoiding involvement in a dispute between other States regarding land territory of which the opposite or adjacent coast forms part, that need not be the case with respect to self-restraint and informal arrangements. Self-restraint may be unilateral, need not be directed explicitly to any given State, and need not apply to all of the area in which the 200-mile zones overlap. The fact that both Parties are also flag States with respect to certain activities may provide a convenient basis for affirmative cooperation in a manner that avoids prejudice to either's position.

48. In its Written Observations, the Maldives asserts that the *Chagos* arbitral award "retains *res judicata* force between the United Kingdom and Mauritius." Similarly, counsel for the Maldives states that the award remains "pleinement pertinente" and has "le 'caractère définitif' des décisions revêtues de l'autorité de la chose jugée." From that perspective, the reasons advanced by the Maldives for declining to negotiate a boundary under paragraph 1 of article 74 and paragraph 1 of article 83, and its jurisdictional objections in regard to the judicial determination of a permanent maritime boundary, need not extend to the question of its obligations under paragraph 3 with respect to the legal interests of Mauritius identified in the *Chagos* arbitral award. In addition to a reversionary interest in the Chagos Archipelago itself, these interests include both fishing and the benefit of any minerals or oil discovered in or near the Chagos Archipelago (see *Chagos Arbitral Award* at pp. 539-42, paras. 429-34, p. 548, para. 448, pp. 550-1, para. 453). The inclusion of these legal interests as objects of the obligations of the Maldives under paragraph 3 would be consistent with the object and purpose of that paragraph, and would thereby embrace what are widely regarded as the principal economic benefits of EEZ and continental shelf entitlements.

49. Accordingly, I agree that the legal interests of Mauritius identified in the *Chagos* arbitral award may play a role in this case.[18] In my opinion that role is best directed to paragraph 3 of article 74 and paragraph 3 of article 83. The text of those paragraphs and their object and purpose lend themselves to flexible application of a transitional nature that, to the extent required, may be addressed in geographic and substantive detail.

---

[18] See Judgment, para. 139.

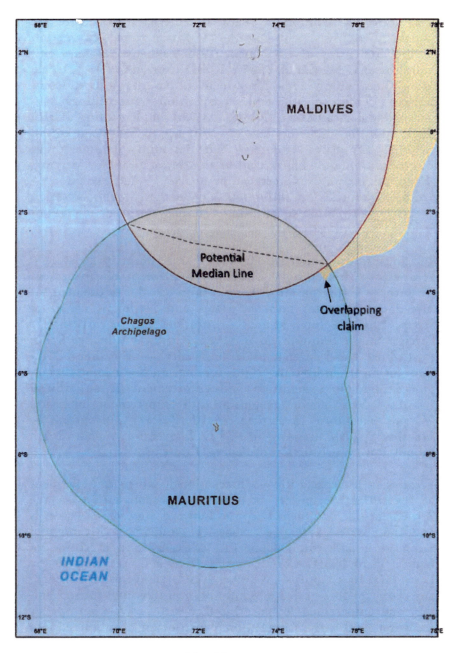

Mauritius map

[Report: *ITLOS Reports 2020-2021*, p. 17]

Arbitration — Arbitration award — International Centre for
Settlement of Investment Disputes — International Convention
on the Settlement of Investment Disputes between States and
Nationals of Other States, 1965 ("ICSID Convention") — Article
54 — Recognition and enforcement of award — Distinction
between enforcement and recognition proceedings —
International Arbitration Act 1974 (Cth) implementing ICSID
Convention in domestic law — Whether ICSID Convention
excluding any claim for foreign State immunity in proceedings
for recognition and enforcement of an arbitral award — Meaning
of recognition and enforcement in Article 54 and execution in
Article 55 of ICSID Convention — Whether Spain's accession
to ICSID Convention constituting a submission to jurisdiction of
Federal Court of Australia

Relationship of international law and municipal law —
Treaties — International Centre for Settlement of Investment
Disputes — International Convention on the Settlement of
Investment Disputes between States and Nationals of Other
States, 1965 — International Arbitration Act 1974 (Cth) —
Foreign States Immunities Act 1985 (Cth) — Whether Spain
entitled to plead foreign State immunity — Whether ICSID
Convention excluding any claim for foreign State immunity in
proceedings for recognition and enforcement of an arbitral
award — Meaning of recognition and enforcement in Article
54 and execution in Article 55 of ICSID Convention —
Whether Spain's accession to ICSID Convention constituting a
submission to jurisdiction of Federal Court of Australia

Treaties — Interpretation — International Centre for Settlement
of Investment Disputes — International Convention on the
Settlement of Investment Disputes between States and Nationals
of Other States, 1965 — Articles 54 and 55 — Meaning of
recognition and enforcement in Article 54 and execution in
Article 55 of ICSID Convention — Vienna Convention on the
Law of Treaties, 1969 — Whether ICSID Convention excluding
any claim for foreign State immunity in proceedings for recognition and enforcement of an arbitral award — Whether Spain's
accession to ICSID Convention constituting a submission to
jurisdiction of Federal Court of Australia

State immunity — Foreign States Immunities Act 1985 (Cth) — Exceptions to immunity — Exception where foreign State agreeing by treaty to submit to jurisdiction — International Centre for Settlement of Investment Disputes — Spain acceding to international Convention on the Settlement of Investment Disputes between States and Nationals of Other States, 1965 ("ICSID Convention") — Whether constituting submission to jurisdiction of Federal Court of Australia — Whether Spain entitled to plead foreign State immunity — Whether ICSID Convention excluding any claim for foreign State immunity in proceedings for recognition and enforcement of an arbitral award

Jurisdiction — State immunity — Foreign States Immunities Act 1985 (Cth) — International Centre for Settlement of Investment Disputes — International Convention on the Settlement of Investment Disputes between States and Nationals of Other States, 1965 — Spain acceding to ICSID Convention — Whether constituting submission to jurisdiction of Federal Court of Australia — Whether Spain entitled to plead foreign State immunity — Whether Federal Court of Australia having jurisdiction — The law of Australia

KINGDOM OF SPAIN *v.* INFRASTRUCTURE SERVICES
LUXEMBOURG S.à.r.l.[1]

([2023] HCA 11)

Australia, High Court.   12 *April* 2023

(Kiefel, *Chief Justice*; Gageler, Gordon, Edelman, Steward, Gleeson and Jagot, *Justices*)

SUMMARY:[2] *The facts*:—Infrastructure Services Luxembourg S.à.r.l. and Energia Termosolar BV ("the respondents") maintained that they had invested EUR 139,500,000 in solar power generation projects within the territory of the appellant, the Kingdom of Spain ("Spain"). They claimed that they had been encouraged to do so by a subsidy programme which was

---

[1]   The appellant was represented by Dr C. S. Ward SC and Mr P. F. Santucci, instructed by K&L Gates. The respondent was represented by Mr B. W. Walker SC, Mr J. A. Hogan-Doran SC and Mr C. W. Brown, instructed by Norton Rose Fulbright.
[2]   Prepared by Mr D. Peterson.

subsequently withdrawn. The respondents alleged that the withdrawal of the subsidies contravened the Energy Charter Treaty, 1994 ("the ECT") pursuant to which Spain had also agreed to consent to the submission of disputes to arbitration under the Convention on the Settlement of Disputes between States and Nationals of Other States, 1965 ("the ICSID Convention") to which Australia was also a Party. The respondents commenced arbitration proceedings against Spain under the ICSID Convention.

The arbitrators awarded the respondents EUR 101,000,000 with interest. The respondents applied to the Federal Court of Australia for an order that Spain pay that amount with interest. Spain contested the Court's jurisdiction on the basis that it was immune from suit as a foreign State under Section 9 of the Foreign States Immunities Act 1985 (Cth) ("the Immunities Act"). However, Section 10(2), read with Section 3, of the Immunities Act provided an exception to immunity where a foreign State had agreed by treaty to submit itself to the jurisdiction.[3] At first instance, the judge rejected Spain's plea of foreign State immunity, accepting that Spain's accession to the ICSID Convention constituted an agreement by treaty to submit itself to the Federal Court's jurisdiction. Spain appealed. The Full Court of the Federal Court of Australia held that immunity from proceedings for recognition of the award had been waived by Spain's entry into the ICSID Convention, although immunity from execution and perhaps enforcement had not. Ultimately, the Full Court held that the orders of the primary judge went too far by requiring Spain to do something and made orders that the arbitral award be recognized as binding of Spain but that nothing in the order should be construed as derogating from any law relating to the immunity of Spain from execution.[4]

On appeal to the High Court of Australia, the questions before the Court were whether Spain's agreement to Articles 53-5 of the ICSID Convention involved a waiver of foreign State immunity from the jurisdiction of the courts of Australia, and if so, whether Spain's amenability to the jurisdiction was limited to "bare recognition" of the award, or the "recognition" and "enforcement" of the award.

Held (unanimously):—Spain's appeal was dismissed with costs.

(1) If an international agreement did not expressly use the word "waiver", the inference that an express term involved a waiver of immunity would only be drawn if the implication was clear from the words used and the context. The rule that waiver of immunity by treaty must always be express was well-established in international law. However, there was ambiguity regarding the meaning of the term "express". The international authorities

---

[3] The text of Section 10(2) appears at para. 14 of the judgment.
[4] 196 ILR 593.

that insisted upon express waiver of immunity in a treaty should not be understood as denying the ordinary and natural role of implications in elucidating the meaning of the express words of the treaty. The insistence that a waiver be "express" should be understood as requiring that the expression of the waiver be derived from the express words of the international agreement, whether as an express term or as a term implied for reasons which included necessity. Thus, the insistence that a waiver of immunity in an international agreement must be "express" is an insistence that any inference of a waiver of immunity must be drawn with great care when interpreting the express words of that agreement in context. It does not deny that implications are almost invariably contained in any expressed words of a treaty (paras. 19-26).

(2) There was no basis to interpret Section 10(2) of the Immunities Act as excluding the possibility of a waiver of immunity being evidenced by implications inferred from the express words of a treaty in their context and in light of their purpose. A high level of clarity and necessity was required before inferring that a foreign State had waived its immunity in a treaty as it was so unusual and the consequences were so significant. Under Section 10(2) the mere fact that a State was Party to an agreement was not sufficient to waive immunity from jurisdiction; submission, and thus waiver, were "by agreement". Section 10(2) therefore aligned with the approach taken to waiver of immunity in the United States, where general immunity from jurisdiction did not apply if the foreign State waived its immunity either explicitly or by implication, the latter only arising rarely and where the waiver was unmistakable (paras. 27-9).

(3) The words "recognition", "enforcement" and "execution" had been used in vague, overlapping, and interchangeable contexts within treaties related to international arbitration. In contrast, Articles 53-5 of the ICSID Convention used the terms separately and with different meanings. Pursuant to Article 54(1) the obligation to "recognize" was expressed to apply to the entirety of an award made under the Convention and was to be no more than an obligation to recognize the award as binding. The obligation to "enforce" was expressed to apply only to the pecuniary obligations imposed by the award and went no further than to oblige a Contracting State to enforce those pecuniary obligations within its territories as if the award were a final judgment of a court in that State. These obligations were severable and a Party to an arbitral award might seek "recognition" by a competent court of a Contracting State without necessarily also seeking "enforcement" of the pecuniary obligations imposed by the award. Pursuant to Articles 54(3) and 55 enforcement was a matter to be governed by the domestic law of the Contracting State and none of the obligations imposed extended so far as to derogate from the domestic law of the Contracting State concerning foreign State immunity from execution. This interpretation accorded with interpretations within the United States and the United Kingdom (paras. 42-8).

(4) There was no relevant difference between the English, French and Spanish texts of Articles 53-5 of the ICSID Convention. A literal interpretation of the French and Spanish texts might have suggested that those texts treated enforcement as synonymous with execution, leading to a conflict between the texts. If such a conflict existed it would have been resolved by applying the rule that if an apparent difference in meaning arose then the meaning which best reconciled the texts, having regard to the object and purpose of the treaty, should be adopted. The better approach was to proceed on the basis that there was no difference in meaning between the texts that required reconciliation. The French and Spanish texts were to be understood against the background of the civilian process of *exequatur* which encompasses both recognition and the step by which a court granted an arbitral award the force of a judgment of the domestic court. The real distinction within Articles 54 and 55 of the French and Spanish texts of the ICSID Convention was therefore between recognition and enforcement by *exequatur* in Article 54 and enforcement as execution in Article 55 (paras. 59-66).

(5) The express terms of Article 54(1) of the ICSID Convention involved a waiver of immunity from jurisdiction in relation to the recognition and enforcement of arbitral awards. Spain's interpretation would have required the text of Articles 53-5 of the ICSID Convention to be read in a contorted manner. These difficulties were compounded when the ordinary meaning of Article 54 was understood in light of its object and purpose, which included mitigating sovereign risk. The purpose of Article 54 was to enable Contracting States to obtain effective remedies against private investors and to ensure parity with the obligations between Contracting States because it was otherwise assumed that participating nation States would abide by arbitral outcomes. This assumption was most explicit in Article 53(1), which restated customary international law, that each Party "shall abide by and comply with the terms of the award" (paras. 67-73).

The following is the text of the judgment of the Court:

Introduction

1. The respondents, relying on provisions of the Energy Charter Treaty (1994),[1] commenced arbitration against the Kingdom of Spain ("Spain") under the Convention on the Settlement of Investment Disputes between States and Nationals of Other States (1965) ("the ICSID Convention"),[2] to which Spain is a party. Chapter IV of the

---

[1]   2080 UNTS 95, Art. 26.
[2]   575 UNTS 159.

ICSID Convention, entitled "Arbitration", provides in Section 1 for an arbitral tribunal to hear and determine disputes between State parties and nationals of other State parties upon request.[3]

2. The respondents obtained an arbitral award of €101 million. They brought proceedings in the Federal Court of Australia seeking "to enforce [that] award under section 35(4) of the International Arbitration Act 1974 [(Cth)]" and seeking orders including that Spain pay them €101 million together with interest on that sum. Section 35(4) of that Act provides that, with leave, the Federal Court can enforce an award "as if the award were a judgment or order of that court".

3. The Foreign States Immunities Act 1985 (Cth) provides that a foreign State is immune from the jurisdiction of the courts of Australia, except as provided by that Act.[4] One circumstance where this immunity does not apply is where the foreign State has submitted to the jurisdiction, including by agreement.[5] An "agreement" is defined to include a treaty.[6] The relevant treaty in this case is the ICSID Convention.

4. As a party to the ICSID Convention, Spain agreed to the provisions in Ch IV which include, in Section 6, three articles concerning "Recognition and Enforcement of the Award": Arts. 53, 54 and 55. Article 53 relevantly provides for the binding nature of the award. Article 54 relevantly provides for recognition of the award by a Contracting State as binding, enforcement of the award within a Contracting State as if it were a final judgment of a court in that State, and execution of the award which is to be governed by the laws of the State concerning execution. And Art. 55 relevantly provides that nothing in Art. 54 shall be construed as derogating from the law in force in a Contracting State relating to immunity of a foreign State from execution.

5. The primary judge in the Federal Court (Stewart J) held that Spain's agreement to these articles constituted a waiver of its immunity from recognition and enforcement, but not from execution, of the award by the Court.[7] His Honour made orders against Spain including an order that Spain "pay the applicants €101 [million]".

---

[3] ICSID Convention, Art. 36.
[4] Foreign States Immunities Act 1985 (Cth), s 9.
[5] Foreign States Immunities Act 1985 (Cth), ss 10(1), 10(2).
[6] Foreign States Immunities Act 1985 (Cth), s 3.
[7] Eiser Infrastructure Ltd v. Kingdom of Spain (2020) 142 ACSR 616 at 648 [175], 649 [179]-[181].

6. On appeal, the Full Court of the Federal Court of Australia (Allsop CJ, Perram and Moshinsky JJ) held that immunity from a proceeding for recognition had been waived by Spain's entry into the ICSID Convention (and concomitant agreement to Arts. 54 and 55), although immunity from court processes of execution, and perhaps also from enforcement, had not.[8] The Full Court concluded that the orders of the primary judge went too far by "requiring Spain to do something".[9] The Full Court made new orders including, in broad terms, an order recognising the award as binding on Spain, as well as that "judgment be entered" against Spain for €101 million, but providing that nothing in that order "shall be construed as derogating from the effect of any law relating to immunity of [Spain] from execution".[10]

7. The two issues raised on this appeal by Spain are: (i) whether Spain's agreement to Arts. 53-5 of the ICSID Convention involved any waiver of foreign State immunity from the jurisdiction of the courts of Australia (Spain being the subject of a binding ICSID arbitral award); and (ii) if so, whether Spain's amenability to jurisdiction is limited to "bare recognition" of the award, or to "recognition" and "enforcement" of the award, and whether the orders made by the Full Court amounted to enforcement.

8. For the reasons below, given that Spain was the subject of a binding ICSID arbitral award, the effect of Spain's agreement to Arts. 53-5 amounted to a waiver of foreign State immunity from the jurisdiction of the courts of Australia to recognise and enforce, but not to execute, the award. The orders made by each of the primary judge and the Full Court are properly characterised as orders for recognition and enforcement. Spain's challenge to the orders of the Full Court should not be accepted. The orders of the Full Court should not be disturbed.

9. This conclusion leaves unaffected any foreign State immunity enjoyed by Spain in relation to execution. Spain's agreement to Arts. 53-5 did not amount to a waiver of its immunity from court processes concerning execution. No issue arises in this proceeding concerning the scope of that immunity, including any exceptions to that immunity, such as where the execution relates to commercial property.[11]

---

[8]	*Kingdom of Spain* v. *Infrastructure Services Luxembourg Sàrl* (2021) 284 FCR 319 at 322 [1], 323 [6], 324 [9], 327-8 [22], [25], 345 [118].

[9]	*Kingdom of Spain* v. *Infrastructure Services Luxembourg Sàrl* (2021) 284 FCR 319 at 336 [65]. See also at 322 [1], 324 [10], 345 [118].

[10]	*Kingdom of Spain* v. *Infrastructure Services Luxembourg Sàrl [No 3]* (2021) 392 ALR 443 at 450-1.

[11]	Foreign States Immunities Act 1985 (Cth), s 32. See also s 33.

10. The issues raised on this appeal are addressed below as follows. The starting point is to explain the operation in the Foreign States Immunities Act of the concept of foreign State immunity from jurisdiction and the manner in which that immunity can be waived. Then it is necessary to explain the extent to which Spain, as the subject of a binding ICSID arbitral award, waived its foreign State immunity under the Foreign States Immunities Act by entry into the ICSID Convention. The primary issues concerning the extent of Spain's waiver of foreign State immunity are: (i) the background, purpose, and general operation of the ICSID Convention; (ii) the meaning of each of the concepts of recognition, enforcement, and execution in Arts. 53-5; and (iii) the extent to which the words of Arts. 53-5 of the ICSID Convention constitute "express" agreement by a foreign State party to waive its immunity from the jurisdiction of the courts of Australia.

Foreign State immunity from jurisdiction

11. The Explanatory Memorandum to the Bill which became the Foreign States Immunities Act explains that the proposed legislation was "based upon a report and recommendations of the Law Reform Commission ... which involved a thorough review of developments in other countries and at the international level, including the work of the International Law Commission".[12] As will be seen, the Australian Law Reform Commission drew from international legal rules and principles governing the existence of foreign State immunity from jurisdiction and the waiver of that immunity.

12. Part II of the Foreign States Immunities Act provides for a general regime of immunity of foreign States from jurisdiction. Section 9 provides that, subject to the Act, "a foreign State is immune from the jurisdiction of the courts of Australia in a proceeding". The term "jurisdiction" is used in this context to describe "the amenability of a defendant to the process of Australian courts" so that Australian courts "will not by their process make the foreign State against its will a party to a legal proceeding".[13]

---

[12] Australia, House of Representatives, Foreign States Immunities Bill 1985, Explanatory Memorandum at 2, citing Australian Law Reform Commission, *Foreign State Immunity*, Report No 24 (1984). See also Australia, House of Representatives, *Parliamentary Debates* (Hansard), 21 August 1985 at 141.

[13] *PT Garuda Indonesia Ltd* v. *Australian Competition and Consumer Commission* (2012) 247 CLR 240 at 247 [17]. See also *Firebird Global Master Fund II Ltd* v. *Republic of Nauru* (2015) 258 CLR 31 at 47-8 [35].

13. The Foreign States Immunities Act contains a further, particular, regime in Pt IV concerning immunity from any process or order of an Australian court in respect of execution over property. This relevantly includes, in s 30, a process or order "for the satisfaction or enforcement of a judgment, order or arbitration award". In the Federal Court, the processes of court relating to execution include the issue of any writ or warrant of execution for which the Sheriff of the Court is responsible.[14]

Waiver of foreign State immunity from jurisdiction

(i) Waiver of general and specific immunities from jurisdiction

14. The general and specific foreign State immunities from jurisdiction do not apply when those immunities have been waived. The provisions for waiver in relation to the general and specific immunities respectively are contained in ss 10(2) and 31(1) of the Foreign States Immunities Act. Section 10(2) provides:

A foreign State may submit to the jurisdiction at any time, whether by agreement or otherwise, but a foreign State shall not be taken to have so submitted by reason only that it is a party to an agreement the proper law of which is the law of Australia.

Section 31(1) provides:

A foreign State may at any time by agreement waive the application of section 30 in relation to property, but it shall not be taken to have done so by reason only that it has submitted to the jurisdiction.

15. This appeal concerns whether, pursuant to s 10 of the Foreign States Immunities Act, Spain's entry into the ICSID Convention, and concomitant agreement to Arts. 53-5 of that Convention, constituted a waiver of its immunity from Australian court processes concerning recognition and enforcement of a binding ICSID arbitral award (necessarily consequent upon agreement to arbitrate).

(ii) Interpreting s 10(2) consistently with international law

16. A "long standing" principle of interpretation is that statutory provisions should be interpreted, so far as possible, to be consistent

---

[14] Federal Court of Australia Act 1976 (Cth), s 18P(1).

with international law.[15] This is particularly so where a provision, like s 10 of the Foreign States Immunities Act, seeks to give effect to matters of international law.[16]

17. In reliance upon international law, Spain submitted that s 10 of the Foreign States Immunities Act only permits an Australian court to recognise a waiver of foreign State immunity from jurisdiction in a treaty if the words of that treaty contain an "express", and not an "implied", waiver. It was said that this requirement reflected a principle of international law that waiver of immunity by treaty must always be express, and that this was recognised by the Report of the Australian Law Reform Commission which was the foundation for the Foreign States Immunities Act. In that report, the Australian Law Reform Commission said that in a treaty:[17]

[t]he need for clarity and certainty entails that a waiver be express, rather than being ... inferred from such things as the fact that Australian law was chosen, or determined to be, the proper law of the contract.

18. The extent to which this statement should be understood to reject the possibility of any implication of waiver of foreign State immunity from jurisdiction in a treaty is doubtful. Earlier in the same report, the Australian Law Reform Commission seemingly acknowledged the possibility of an implied waiver of immunity, referring to circumstances "in which parties either explicitly or (arguably) impliedly waive foreign state immunity".[18] It is necessary, therefore, to consider more closely the international law principle—that waiver of immunity in an international agreement must be "express"—against which s 10(2) falls to be interpreted.

(iii) An international law principle that waiver of immunity in an international agreement must be express

19. As Spain submitted, it has been said that "[t]he rule that waiver of immunity by treaty must always be express is well established in international law".[19] That "rule" was enunciated by the International

---

[15] *Al-Kateb* v. *Godwin* (2004) 219 CLR 562 at 589 [63]. See also *Jumbunna Coal Mine, No Liability* v. *Victorian Coal Miners' Association* (1908) 6 CLR 309 at 363; *Polites* v. *Commonwealth* (1945) 70 CLR 60 at 68-9, 77, 80-1; *Minister for Immigration and Ethnic Affairs* v. *Teoh* (1995) 183 CLR 273 at 287; *Kartinyeri* v. *Commonwealth* (1998) 195 CLR 337 at 384 [97].
[16] *Firebird Global Master Fund II Ltd* v. *Republic of Nauru* (2015) 258 CLR 31 at 50 [44].
[17] Australian Law Reform Commission, *Foreign State Immunity*, Report No 24 (1984) at 44 [79].
[18] Australian Law Reform Commission, *Foreign State Immunity*, Report No 24 (1984) at 44 [79].
[19] McLachlan, "*Pinochet* Revisited" (2002) 51 *International and Comparative Law Quarterly* 959 at 961, fn 20.

Court of Justice in the *Case Concerning Armed Activities on the Territory of the Congo (Democratic Republic of the Congo* v. *Uganda).*[20] In that case, the International Court of Justice said that "waivers or renunciations of claims or rights must either be [(i)] express or [(ii)] unequivocally implied from the conduct of the State alleged to have waived or renounced its right".

20. There is no doubt concerning the second category to which the International Court of Justice referred. An example is the "universally recognised rule that commencement of proceedings by a foreign state constitutes a waiver of immunity with respect to those proceedings".[21] As to the first category, namely where the waiver is constituted by words of a treaty rather than by conduct, the point made by the International Court of Justice is that those words must "express" waiver.

21. A similar requirement for a waiver of immunity in a treaty to be "express" can be seen in numerous treaties of widespread operation. Article 32(2) of the Vienna Convention on Diplomatic Relations (1961)[22] provides that a waiver of immunity from jurisdiction of diplomatic agents "must always be express". Article 2 of the European Convention on State Immunity (1972)[23] relevantly provides that a Contracting State cannot claim immunity from the jurisdiction of a court of another Contracting State if it has undertaken to submit to the jurisdiction of that court by "international agreement" or "an express term contained in a contract in writing". In the Explanatory Report to the latter Convention,[24] the drafters observe that Art. 2, as a whole, "concerns cases in which a Contracting State has expressly undertaken to submit to the jurisdiction of a foreign court".

22. This principle of international law was reflected in Lord Millett's and Lord Goff of Chieveley's judgments in *R* v. *Bow Street Magistrate; Ex parte Pinochet [No 3].*[25] In that case, their Lordships considered a provision concerning waiver of immunity by agreement, similarly worded to s 10(2) of the Foreign States Immunities Act.[26]

---

[20]   *ICJ Reports 2005*, 168 at 266 [293].
[21]   Australian Law Reform Commission, *Foreign State Immunity*, Report No 24 (1984) at 45 [81]. See also *Rothschild* v. *Queen of Portugal* (1839) 3 Y & C Ex 594 [160 ER 838]; United Nations Convention on Jurisdictional Immunities of States and Their Property (2004), Art. 8(1) (not yet entered into force).
[22]   500 UNTS 95.
[23]   1495 UNTS 181.
[24]   Council of Europe, *Explanatory Report to the European Convention on State Immunity* (1972) at 5 [21].
[25]   [2000] 1 AC 147.
[26]   State Immunity Act 1978 (UK), s 2(2).

Lord Goff accepted that a waiver of immunity could occur by implication from conduct outside the terms of a treaty, such as by taking steps in proceedings concerning the merits of the case.[27] However, Lord Goff said that in the interpretation of a treaty, "consent by a state party to the exercise of jurisdiction against it must ... be express".[28] One source relied upon by Lord Goff for this reasoning was the 1991 Report of the International Law Commission which said that customary international law and international usage required waiver of immunity to be "expressed ... in no uncertain terms".[29] Similarly, Lord Millett said that it was not in dispute that "where [State immunity] is waived by treaty or convention the waiver must be express".[30]

(iv) The meaning of the international law principle that waiver of immunity in a treaty be express

23. There is some ambiguity about what these numerous statements mean by their insistence that a waiver of immunity in a treaty be "express". Part of the difficulty is a lack of clarity in legal discourse generally about what is meant by "express" meaning.[31] Properly understood, express meaning can include implications, which constitute the unexpressed content of a statement or term and which are identified by inference.[32]

24. An express term of an agreement involves words that are "openly uttered" either orally or in writing.[33] The meaning of an express term is derived primarily from the content of the words expressed. It contrasts with an implied term, the meaning of which is derived primarily by inference from the conduct of the parties to the agreement and the circumstances in light of the express terms. There can sometimes be difficulty in distinguishing between the two types of terms, because often the imprecision of language means that inferences are required to understand an express term.[34] Even the words of the most carefully

---

[27] [2000] 1 AC 147 at 215, citing *Oppenheim's International Law*, 9th ed (1992), vol 1 at 351-5. Consistently with this, see Crawford, *Brownlie's Principles of Public International Law*, 9th ed (2019) at 486.

[28] [2000] 1 AC 147 at 216.

[29] United Nations General Assembly, *Report of the International Law Commission on the work of its forty-third session* (1991) at 53.

[30] [2000] 1 AC 147 at 268.

[31] See Wilmot-Smith, "Express and Implied Terms" (2023) 43 *Oxford Journal of Legal Studies* 54.

[32] *Macquarie Dictionary*, 7th ed (2017), vol 1 at 762, "implication", sense 1, 2 and especially 3.

[33] See Blackstone, *Commentaries on the Laws of England* (1766), bk 2, ch 30 at 443.

[34] Wilmot-Smith, "Express and Implied Terms" (2023) 43 *Oxford Journal of Legal Studies* 54 at 58-9. See also Wilson and Sperber, *Meaning and Relevance* (2012) at 149-68.

drafted international instrument are built upon a foundation of pre-suppositions and necessary implicatures and explicatures. The international authorities that insist upon express waiver of immunity in a treaty should not be understood as denying the ordinary and natural role of implications in elucidating the meaning of the express words of the treaty.

25. The insistence that the waiver be "express" should be understood as requiring only that the expression of waiver be *derived* from the express words of the international agreement, whether as an express term or as a term implied for reasons including necessity. For instance, Lord Goff's statement in *Pinochet [No 3]* that consent must be "express" was based on his acceptance of the submissions of Dr Collins,[35] including that "[a] term can only be [recognised as] implied [in] a treaty for necessity, not to give the treaty maximum effect".[36] In *Li* v. *Zhou*,[37] this point was made in the context of rejecting a claim of waiver by a foreign State of immunity from proceedings, where the claim was based on alleged agreement by the foreign State in a treaty[38] to waive the immunity. Basten JA (with whom Bathurst CJ and Beazley P agreed) said that even if the express terms of the treaty did not manifest submission to jurisdiction, it is possible that "language and context may give rise to a necessary implication to similar effect" if that implication is "readily derived from the [express] terms".[39]

26. In this sense, the insistence by international authority that a waiver of immunity in an international agreement must be "express" is an insistence that any inference of a waiver of immunity must be drawn with great care when interpreting the express words of that agreement in context. It does not deny that implications are almost invariably contained in any (expressed) words of a treaty. As senior counsel for Spain rightly put the point in oral submissions: "[T]here must be implications that surround every textual passage. The question is: what are those implications, and what level of clarity about the implication is required?" Accordingly, if an international agreement does not expressly use the word "waiver", the inference that an express term involves a waiver of immunity will only be drawn if the implication is clear from the words used and the context. In words quoted by Lord

[35] Later, Lord Collins of Mapesbury.
[36] [2000] 1 AC 147 at 176, 216.
[37] (2014) 87 NSWLR 20.
[38] Convention against Torture and Other Cruel, Inhuman or Degrading Treatment or Punishment (1984) 1465 UNTS 85.
[39] (2014) 87 NSWLR 20 at 31 [38].

Goff in *Pinochet [No 3]* from the International Law Commission's commentary upon (what were then) the draft articles on jurisdictional immunities of States and their property, there is "no room" to recognise an implication of "consent of an unwilling state which has not expressed its consent in a clear and recognisable manner".[40] And as Rehnquist CJ said, delivering the opinion of the Supreme Court of the United States in *Argentine Republic* v. *Amerada Hess Shipping Corp,*[41] a foreign State will not waive its immunity merely "by signing an international agreement that contains no mention of a waiver of immunity to suit in United States courts or even the availability of a cause of action in the United States". This reflects the "political principle that those who are independent and autonomous cannot, except by consent, exercise authority over, or establish an external source of authority over, others of independent and autonomous status".[42]

(v) *The proper approach to waiver in s 10(2) of the Foreign States Immunities Act*

27. Against this background of international law, there is no basis to interpret s 10(2) of the Foreign States Immunities Act as requiring a novel approach to interpretation that would exclude the possibility of a waiver of immunity being evidenced by implications inferred from the express words of a treaty in their context and in light of their purpose.

28. A high level of clarity and necessity are required before inferring that a foreign State has waived its immunity in a treaty because it is so unusual,[43] and the consequence is so significant. Hence, s 10(2) makes clear that the mere fact that a State "is a party to an agreement the proper law of which is the law of Australia" is not sufficient to waive immunity from jurisdiction. But s 10(2) expressly refers to submission (and thus waiver) "by agreement".

29. For these reasons, and contrary to Spain's submissions, s 10(2) of the Foreign States Immunities Act aligns with the approach taken to waiver of immunity in the United States, where the general immunity

---

[40] [2000] 1 AC 147 at 215, quoting United Nations General Assembly, *Report of the International Law Commission on the work of its forty-third session* (1991) at 49 [8].

[41] (1989) 488 US 428 at 442-3.

[42] *Li* v. *Zhou* (2014) 87 NSWLR 20 at 30 [37], referring to Charlesworth and Chinkin, *The Boundaries of International Law: A Feminist Analysis* (2000) at 124, 145.

[43] Australian Law Reform Commission, *Foreign State Immunity*, Report No 24 (1984) at 44 [79]: "The Commission is not aware of any existing bilateral treaties which contain a waiver of immunity from jurisdiction of Australian courts."

of a foreign State from jurisdiction[44] does not apply if the foreign State "waived its immunity either explicitly or by implication",[45] and where it has been accepted that words said to evidence waiver by implication must be "construed narrowly",[46] as well as that waiver "is rarely accomplished by implication"[47] and only arises where "the waiver was unmistakeable".[48] The waiver in s 10(2) is unmistakable.

The background, purpose, and operation of the ICSID Convention

30. In 1960, in a paper entitled "The Promotion of the International Flow of Private Capital", the Secretary-General of the United Nations called for the establishment of "special international arbitration machinery for foreign investments".[49] The ICSID Convention was the response to that call. It arose from the work of the World Bank, and in particular from the remarkable efforts of Mr Aron Broches, General Counsel of the Bank from 1959 to 1979.[50] Mr Broches was rightly described by the primary judge as "the principal architect" of the ICSID Convention,[51] which was developed in the spirit of the Bretton Woods Conference of 1944.

31. In the *History of the ICSID Convention*,[52] it is explained how it had become "increasingly clear" during the 1960s that the growth plans

---

[44] Foreign Sovereign Immunities Act of 1976 (28 USC § 1604).

[45] Foreign Sovereign Immunities Act of 1976 (28 USC § 1605(a)(1)).

[46] *Blue Ridge Investments LLC* v. *Republic of Argentina* (2013) 735 F 3d 72 at 84, quoting *Cabiri* v. *Government of the Republic of Ghana* (1999) 165 F 3d 193 at 201. See also *In re Tamimi* (1999) 176 F 3d 274 at 278, citing *Frolova* v. *Union of Soviet Socialist Republics* (1985) 761 F 2d 370 at 377, *Joseph* v. *Office of the Consulate General of Nigeria* (1987) 830 F 2d 1018 at 1022, and *Foremost-McKesson Inc.* v. *Islamic Republic of Iran* (1990) 905 F 2d 438 at 444.

[47] *In re Tamimi* (1999) 176 F 3d 274 at 278.

[48] *Cabiri* v. *Government of the Republic of Ghana* (1999) 165 F 3d 193 at 201, quoting *Shapiro* v. *Republic of Bolivia* (1991) 930 F 2d 1013 at 1017.

[49] See International Centre for Settlement of Investment Disputes, *History of the ICSID Convention: Documents Concerning the Origin and the Formulation of the Convention on the Settlement of Investment Disputes between States and Nationals of Other States* (1970), vol 1 at 2, fn 3, referring to Secretary-General of the United Nations, *The Promotion of the International Flow of Private Capital* (1960) at [170]-[171], [200], [203].

[50] Broches, "Awards Rendered Pursuant to the ICSID Convention: Binding Force, Finality, Recognition, Enforcement, Execution" (1987) 2 *ICSID Review—Foreign Investment Law Journal* 287 at 287.

[51] *Eiser Infrastructure Ltd* v. *Kingdom of Spain* (2020) 142 ACSR 616 at 639 [122], citing Schreuer, *The ICSID Convention: A Commentary*, 2nd ed (2009) at 2 [2]. See also *Schreuer's Commentary on the ICSID Convention*, 3rd ed (2022), vol 1 at 2 [2].

[52] International Centre for Settlement of Investment Disputes, *History of the ICSID Convention: Documents Concerning the Origin and the Formulation of the Convention on the Settlement of Investment Disputes between States and Nationals of Other States* (1970), vol 1 at 2.

of developing countries would need to rely upon international private investment as well as external government sources:

To encourage such investments, the competent international organizations considered several schemes designed to remove some of the uncertainties and obstacles that faced investors in any foreign country and in particular in many of the States that had only recently attained independence and self-government and whose need for outside capital was greatest.

32. Following Mr Broches' preparation of the Preliminary Draft of the ICSID Convention, a series of consultative meetings were held in Addis Ababa (December 1963), Santiago de Chile (February 1964), Geneva (February 1964) and Bangkok (April-May 1964), with representatives from a large number of countries (usually lawyers).[53] The summary record of proceedings of the first consultative meeting at Addis Ababa records Mr Broches as repeating the concern of developing countries that one of the most serious impediments to the flow of private capital was "the fear of investors that their investment would be exposed to political risks such as outright expropriation, government interference and non-observance by the host government of contractual undertakings on the basis of which the investment had been made".[54]

33. The consultative meetings gave rise to a Revised Draft which was then the subject of intensive deliberation by a special legal committee convened in Washington (from November to December 1964). The ICSID Convention was concluded in March 1965 and entered into force in 1966. It now has 165 State parties.

34. The primary purpose of the ICSID Convention was, and remains, to promote the flow of private capital to sovereign nations, especially developing countries, by the mitigation of sovereign risk.[55] The ICSID Convention mitigates risk by giving private investors, upon default by a country, an arbitral remedy which is intended to provide certainty. As was observed in the 1965 Report of the Executive Directors of the International Bank for Reconstruction and

---

[53] International Centre for Settlement of Investment Disputes, *History of the ICSID Convention: Documents Concerning the Origin and the Formulation of the Convention on the Settlement of Investment Disputes between States and Nationals of Other States* (1968), vol 2-1 at 557.

[54] International Centre for Settlement of Investment Disputes, *History of the ICSID Convention: Documents Concerning the Origin and the Formulation of the Convention on the Settlement of Investment Disputes between States and Nationals of Other States* (1968), vol 2-1 at 240.

[55] International Bank for Reconstruction and Development, *Report of the Executive Directors on the Convention on the Settlement of Investment Disputes between States and Nationals of Other States* (1965) at 40-1 [9], [12]-[13].

Development on the ICSID Convention,[56] the ICSID Convention serves the cause of economic development by its "creation of an institution designed to facilitate the settlement of disputes between States and foreign investors" in order to promote "an atmosphere of mutual confidence and thus stimulat[e] a larger flow of private international capital into those countries which wish to attract it".

35. The preamble to the ICSID Convention begins by referring to "the need for international cooperation for economic development, and the role of private international investment therein" and refers to "the possibility that from time to time disputes may arise in connection with such investment between Contracting States and nationals of other Contracting States".[57] In Ch I, the ICSID Convention establishes the International Centre for Settlement of Investment Disputes. In Ch II, the ICSID Convention establishes the jurisdiction of the Centre, which broadly extends to any legal dispute arising directly out of an investment between a Contracting State and a national of another Contracting State. Chapter III deals with conciliation.

36. Chapter IV of the ICSID Convention is concerned with arbitration. It provides for the constitution, powers, and functions of an arbitral tribunal. It also provides a process by which any Contracting State or any national of a Contracting State may institute arbitration proceedings following a request in writing. This was the procedure followed by the respondents in initiating their arbitration against Spain. Section 6 of Ch IV is concerned with "Recognition and Enforcement of the Award". It contains three Articles—Arts. 53, 54 and 55—the meaning of which is the central issue on this appeal.

37. In Australia, the International Arbitration Act gives effect to the ICSID Convention.[58] Section 32 gives the force of law in Australia to relevant provisions in the ICSID Convention, including Arts. 53-5, with the words and expressions in Pt IV of the International Arbitration Act having the same meaning as they do in the ICSID Convention.[59] Section 33 provides that an award under the ICSID Convention is binding on a party to the investment dispute to which the award relates. Section 34 provides that other laws relating to the recognition and enforcement of arbitral awards, including Pts II and III of the International Arbitration Act, do not apply. As will be discussed

---

[56] International Bank for Reconstruction and Development, *Report of the Executive Directors on the Convention on the Settlement of Investment Disputes between States and Nationals of Other States* (1965) at 40 [9].
[57] See also International Arbitration Act 1974 (Cth), Sch 3.
[58] International Arbitration Act 1974 (Cth), s 2D(f), Sch 3.
[59] International Arbitration Act 1974 (Cth), s 31(2).

below, s 35 provides that the Federal Court is designated as "the competent court" for the purposes of Art. 54 of the ICSID Convention,[60] and that awards may be "enforced in the Federal Court of Australia with the leave of that court as if the award were a judgment or order of that court".[61]

The meaning of recognition, enforcement, and execution in the ICSID Convention, Arts. 53-5

(i) Principles of treaty interpretation

38. The text of an international agreement or treaty is not interpreted according to particular domestic rules of interpretation, which might have slight variations from country to country.[62] Rather, as is reflected by the approach taken in Australia, a treaty should have the same meaning for all of the States which are party to it.[63] The general principles of treaty interpretation are contained in the Vienna Convention on the Law of Treaties (1969).[64] Although the Vienna Convention on the Law of Treaties post-dates the ICSID Convention, it is widely accepted that, in the respects relevant to this appeal, the Vienna Convention was declaratory of customary international law.[65]

39. Article 31(1) of the Vienna Convention on the Law of Treaties provides that a treaty must be interpreted "in good faith in accordance with the ordinary meaning to be given to the terms of the treaty in their context and in the light of its object and purpose". Article 32 provides that extrinsic sources, including the *travaux préparatoires*, may be used to confirm the meaning or to determine the meaning when it is ambiguous or obscure or leads to a manifestly absurd or unreasonable

---

[60] International Arbitration Act 1974 (Cth), s 35(3).

[61] International Arbitration Act 1974 (Cth), s 35(4).

[62] *Povey* v. *Qantas Airways Ltd* (2005) 223 CLR 189 at 211 [60].

[63] *Shipping Corporation of India Ltd* v. *Gamlen Chemical Co A/Asia Pty Ltd* (1980) 147 CLR 142 at 159; *Great China Metal Industries Co Ltd* v. *Malaysian International Shipping Corporation, Berhad* (1998) 196 CLR 161 at 186 [71], 213 [137]; *Siemens Ltd* v. *Schenker International (Australia) Pty Ltd* (2004) 216 CLR 418 at 466-7 [153]-[154]; *Povey* v. *Qantas Airways Ltd* (2005) 223 CLR 189 at 202 [25]; *Basfar* v. *Wong* [2023] AC 33 at 55 [16].

[64] 1155 UNTS 331. See *Commonwealth* v. *Tasmania (The Tasmanian Dam Case)* (1983) 158 CLR 1 at 93, 222; *Thiel* v. *Federal Commissioner of Taxation* (1990) 171 CLR 338 at 356; *Applicant A* v. *Minister for Immigration and Ethnic Affairs* (1997) 190 CLR 225 at 240, 251-2; *Povey* v. *Qantas Airways Ltd* (2005) 223 CLR 189 at 202 [24], 211 [60]; *Maloney* v. *The Queen* (2013) 252 CLR 168 at 180-1 [14], 255-6 [235]; *Macoun* v. *Federal Commissioner of Taxation* (2015) 257 CLR 519 at 539 [69].

[65] See *Territorial Dispute (Libyan Arab Jamahiriya* v. *Chad), ICJ Reports 1994*, 6 at 21-2 [41]. See also *Tasmanian Dam Case* (1983) 158 CLR 1 at 93-4, 222-3; *Thiel* v. *Federal Commissioner of Taxation* (1990) 171 CLR 338 at 356; *Golder Case* (1975) 57 ILR 200 at 213-14.

result. Article 33(1) provides that if a treaty has been authenticated in two or more languages, then the text is equally authoritative in each language unless the treaty provides, or the parties agree, otherwise. However, under Art. 33(4), if an apparent difference in meaning arises between the equally authoritative authentic texts, then the meaning that should be adopted is that which best reconciles the texts, having regard to the object and purpose of the treaty.

(ii) The terms of Arts. 53-5

40. Articles 53-5 of the ICSID Convention, which have the force of law in Australia,[66] are a central plank in giving effect to the primary object of the ICSID Convention: to encourage private international investment including by mitigating sovereign risk and providing an investor with the "legal security required for an investment decision".[67]

41. Articles 53-5 provide as follows:

Recognition and enforcement of the award

Article 53

(1) The award shall be binding on the parties and shall not be subject to any appeal or to any other remedy except those provided for in this Convention. Each party shall abide by and comply with the terms of the award except to the extent that enforcement shall have been stayed pursuant to the relevant provisions of this Convention.

(2) For the purposes of this Section, "award" shall include any decision interpreting, revising or annulling such award pursuant to Articles 50, 51 or 52.

Article 54

(1) Each Contracting State shall recognize an award rendered pursuant to this Convention as binding and enforce the pecuniary obligations imposed by that award within its territories as if it were a final judgment of a court in that State. A Contracting State with a federal constitution may enforce such an award in or through its federal courts and may provide that such courts shall treat the award as if it were a final judgment of the courts of a constituent state.

---

[66] International Arbitration Act 1974 (Cth), ss 31 (definition of "Investment Convention"), 32.

[67] See, eg, *Schreuer's Commentary on the ICSID Convention*, 3rd ed (2022), vol 1 at 7. See also International Bank for Reconstruction and Development, *Report of the Executive Directors on the Convention on the Settlement of Investment Disputes between States and Nationals of Other States* (1965) at 40-1 [9]-[13].

(2) A party seeking recognition or enforcement in the territories of a Contracting State shall furnish to a competent court or other authority which such State shall have designated for this purpose a copy of the award certified by the Secretary-General. Each Contracting State shall notify the Secretary-General of the designation of the competent court or other authority for this purpose and of any subsequent change in such designation.

(3) Execution of the award shall be governed by the laws concerning the execution of judgments in force in the State in whose territories such execution is sought.

Article 55

Nothing in Article 54 shall be construed as derogating from the law in force in any Contracting State relating to immunity of that State or of any foreign State from execution.

(iii) The textual meaning of recognition, enforcement, and execution

42. In some contexts pertaining to international arbitration, the English words "recognition", "enforcement", and "execution" have been used in vague, overlapping and even interchangeable senses. In the Convention on the Execution of Foreign Arbitral Awards (1927),[68] for example, the word "execution" appeared in the title as a broad description of the subject matter of substantive obligations framed in terms of "recognition" and "enforcement". The Convention on the Recognition and Enforcement of Foreign Arbitral Awards (1958),[69] as a further example, does not define either term and makes no reference to "execution", although the French title uses the word "*exécution*" in place of the English "enforcement". In common parlance, as leading arbitration practitioners and arbitrators have observed, "enforcement" is sometimes used "loosely" to extend to "execution".[70] For instance, F A Mann used the term "enforcement" not merely to mean "turning the award into a judgment or a title equivalent to a judgment by providing it with an *exequatur* or some similar judicial certificate" but also to extend to "execution in the accepted sense of the term".[71]

---

[68] 92 LNTS 301.
[69] 330 UNTS 3.
[70] See Reed, Paulsson and Blackaby, *Guide to ICSID Arbitration*, 2nd ed (2011) at 179-80; Juratowitch, "Waiver of State Immunity and Enforcement of Arbitral Awards" (2016) 6 *Asian Journal of International Law* 199 at 218. See also Broches, "Awards Rendered Pursuant to the ICSID Convention: Binding Force, Finality, Recognition, Enforcement, Execution" (1987) 2 *ICSID Review—Foreign Investment Law Journal* 287 at 318.
[71] Mann, "State Contracts and International Arbitration" (1967) 42 *British Yearbook of International Law* 1 at 18.

43. Within the structure of Arts. 53-5 of the ICSID Convention, in contrast, the words "recognition", "enforcement", and "execution" can be seen to be used separately and with different meanings. The distinction between "recognition" and "enforcement" is apparent in the two distinct obligations that are imposed on a Contracting State by the first sentence of Art. 54(1). The subject matter of each obligation is different and the extent of each obligation is identified separately with precision. The obligation to "recognize" is expressed to apply to the entirety of "an award rendered pursuant to this Convention" and to be no more than an obligation to recognise the award "as binding". The obligation to "enforce" is expressed to apply only to "the pecuniary obligations imposed by [the] award" and to go no further than to oblige the Contracting State to enforce those pecuniary obligations within its territories "as if [the award] were a final judgment of a court in that State". The disjunctive "or" in Art. 54(2) makes plain that those two obligations imposed by Art. 54(1) are severable, in that a party to an arbitral award might seek "recognition" by a competent court of a Contracting State without necessarily also seeking "enforcement" of the pecuniary obligations imposed by that award.

44. The further distinction between "recognition" and "enforcement", on the one hand, and "execution", on the other hand, is then drawn out in Arts. 53-4 and Art. 55. This is seen in the provision by Art. 54(3) that execution is a matter to be governed by the domestic law of the Contracting State, and by Art. 55 that none of the international obligations imposed by Art. 54 extend so far as to derogate from the domestic law of the Contracting State concerning State immunity or foreign State immunity from execution. In particular, Art. 55 spells out that the obligation to "enforce" the pecuniary obligations imposed by an award as if the award were a final judgment of a court in the Contracting State stops short of an obligation to ensure their execution. Whether or not enforcement against a State party to an award can lead to execution is left entirely to be determined under the domestic law of the Contracting State concerning State immunity or foreign State immunity from execution.

45. That usage of the words "recognition", "enforcement", and "execution" in the context of Arts. 53-5 of the ICSID Convention aligns with the precise definitions adopted in the recently approved version of the proposed *Restatement of the Law: The US Law of International Commercial and Investor–State Arbitration*, which described "terminological confusion" that may result when these "analytically distinct" concepts are not distinguished and

"recognition" is used to mean "enforcement" or "enforcement" is used to mean "execution".[72] Consistently with the usage in the context of Arts. 53-5, the proposed *Restatement* defines "recognition" as the court's "determination . . . that an international arbitral award is entitled to be treated as binding",[73] involving the court's "acceptance of the award's binding character and its preclusive effects".[74] It describes "enforcement" as "the legal process by which an international award is reduced to a judgment of a court that enjoys the same status as any judgment of that court".[75] It defines "execution" as "the means by which a judgment enforcing an international arbitral award is given effect"[76] and explains that "[t]he execution process commonly involves measures taken against the property of the judgment debtor by a law-enforcement official . . . acting pursuant to a writ of execution".[77]

46. The distinction so drawn between "recognition" and "enforcement" accords with reasoning of Lord Rodger (with whom Lords Bingham, Hope, Walker and Neuberger agreed) in *Clarke* v. *Fennoscandia Ltd*[78] relating to the recognition of a foreign judgment. The distinction also accords with the reasoning of French CJ and Gageler J in *TCL Air Conditioner (Zhongshan) Co Ltd* v. *Judges of the Federal Court of Australia*[79] in the context of examining Art. 35 of the UNCITRAL Model Law on International Commercial Arbitration,[80] which relevantly provides that an arbitral award "shall be recognized as binding and, upon application in writing to the competent court, shall be enforced". Their Honours there observed that an appropriate order for the Federal Court to make on an application for "enforcement" of

---

[72] American Law Institute, *Restatement of the Law: The US Law of International Commercial and Investor–State Arbitration*, Proposed Final Draft (2019) § 1.1, Note n. See also § 1.1, Note nn.
[73] American Law Institute, *Restatement of the Law: The US Law of International Commercial and Investor–State Arbitration*, Proposed Final Draft (2019) § 1.1(nn).
[74] American Law Institute, *Restatement of the Law: The US Law of International Commercial and Investor–State Arbitration*, Proposed Final Draft (2019) § 1.1, Note nn.
[75] American Law Institute, *Restatement of the Law: The US Law of International Commercial and Investor–State Arbitration*, Proposed Final Draft (2019) § 1.1, Note m, § 1.1(m). See also Collins (ed), *Dicey, Morris and Collins on the Conflict of Laws*, 15th ed (2012), vol 1 at 678 [14-028].
[76] American Law Institute, *Restatement of the Law: The US Law of International Commercial and Investor–State Arbitration*, Proposed Final Draft (2019) § 1.1(n).
[77] American Law Institute, *Restatement of the Law: The US Law of International Commercial and Investor–State Arbitration*, Proposed Final Draft (2019) § 1.1, Comment n. See also Juratowitch, "Waiver of State Immunity and Enforcement of Arbitral Awards" (2016) 6 *Asian Journal of International Law* 199 at 218.
[78] 2008 SC (HL) 122 at 126 [18], 127 [21]-[22]. See also Briggs, *The Conflict of Laws*, 4th ed (2019) at 129.
[79] (2013) 251 CLR 533 at 551-2 [19]-[23].
[80] Adopted by UNCITRAL on 21 June 1985 and amended by UNCITRAL on 7 July 2006.

an arbitral award "would be an order that the arbitral award be enforced as if [it] were a judgment or order of the Federal Court".[81] It has been noted elsewhere in relation to Art. 35(1) of the UNCITRAL Model Law that "the possibility of ordering actual enforcement measures [ie execution] [i]s not a prerequisite for such a declaration of enforceability".[82]

47. Moreover, the drawing of a distinction between "enforcement" and "execution" accords with the construction of Arts. 53-5 of the ICSID Convention proffered by Mr Broches writing academically some years after it had entered into force.[83] Mr Broches noted that "enforce" standing alone in Art. 54(1) "might be considered as including execution" but he said that Art. 54(3) "which deals separately with execution makes clear that that is not the intention". He nevertheless acknowledged that "a slight awkwardness remains" and that Art. 54(1) might have been clearer had it been drafted to state that an award "shall be recognized as binding by each Contracting State, and the pecuniary obligations imposed by the award shall be enforceable within the territories of each such State, as if it were a final judgment of one of its courts". Importantly, he explained the substantive distinction being drawn through the making of the linguistic distinction between "enforcement" and "execution" within the structure of Arts. 53-5 as "the distinction between enforceability which is governed and decreed by the Convention and its implementation by execution which is governed by domestic law".

48. Both the linguistic distinction between "enforcement" and "execution" and the substantively intended effect of the linguistic distinction as identified by Mr Broches are borne out by the *travaux préparatoires* to the ICSID Convention.

(iv) Confirmation of these meanings in the travaux préparatoires

49. Following the preparation of a working paper on the ICSID Convention by Mr Broches and his team, a meeting was held on 20 September 1963 to receive comments from the Executive

---

[81] *TCL Air Conditioner (Zhongshan) Co Ltd* v. *Judges of the Federal Court of Australia* (2013) 251 CLR 533 at 552 [24].

[82] United Nations Commission on International Trade Law, *UNCITRAL 2012 Digest of Case Law on the Model Law on International Commercial Arbitration* (2012) at 170, citing Bayerisches Oberstes Landesgericht, Germany, 4 Z Sch 31/99, 27 June 1999.

[83] See Broches, "Awards Rendered Pursuant to the ICSID Convention: Binding Force, Finality, Recognition, Enforcement, Execution" (1987) 2 *ICSID Review—Foreign Investment Law Journal* 287 at 318.

Directors.[84] The minutes of the meeting record Mr Broches' explanation that it was "desirable to have a very clear provision . . . which required that each Contracting State recognize an award of a tribunal as binding and enforce it within its territories as if that award were a final judgment of the courts of that State".[85] Mr Broches saw clarity, and "quite a step forward", in: (i) requiring recognition, namely that "each Contracting State recognize an award of a tribunal as binding"; (ii) requiring enforcement, namely that each Contracting State "enforce [an award] within its territories as if that award were a final judgment of the courts in that State"; (iii) recognising that "[i]n general" forced execution "would not be possible"[86] where the term "execution" was used to describe "seizing [the foreign State's] property and selling it in forced execution".

50. The provision as framed to give effect to the approach Mr Broches outlined ultimately became Art. 54 of the ICSID Convention. As it appeared in the Preliminary Draft, which was the subject of the consultative meetings in Addis Ababa, Santiago, Geneva and Bangkok, the precursor to Art. 54 simply provided that "[e]ach Contracting State shall recognize an award . . . as binding and enforce it within its territories as if it were a final judgment of the courts of that State".[87]

51. Referring to the provision as then appearing in the Preliminary Draft, in introductory remarks at the commencement of each consultative meeting, Mr Broches said that he "wished to make it clear that where, as in most countries, the law of State [i]mmunity from execution would prevent enforcement against a State as opposed to execution against a private party, the Convention would leave that law unaffected" and that "[a]ll the Convention would do would be to place an arbitral award rendered pursuant to it on the same footing as a final judgment of the national [c]ourts". He spelt out the result: "[i]f such judgment could be enforced under the domestic law in question, so

[84] International Centre for Settlement of Investment Disputes, *History of the ICSID Convention: Documents Concerning the Origin and the Formulation of the Convention on the Settlement of Investment Disputes between States and Nationals of Other States* (1968), vol 2-1 at 174.
[85] International Centre for Settlement of Investment Disputes, *History of the ICSID Convention: Documents Concerning the Origin and the Formulation of the Convention on the Settlement of Investment Disputes between States and Nationals of Other States* (1968), vol 2-1 at 177 [12].
[86] International Centre for Settlement of Investment Disputes, *History of the ICSID Convention: Documents Concerning the Origin and the Formulation of the Convention on the Settlement of Investment Disputes between States and Nationals of Other States* (1968), vol 2-1 at 177 [12].
[87] International Centre for Settlement of Investment Disputes, *History of the ICSID Convention: Documents Concerning the Origin and the Formulation of the Convention on the Settlement of Investment Disputes between States and Nationals of Other States* (1968), vol 2-1 at 218.

could the award; if that judgment could not be so enforced, neither could the award".[88]

52. In a discussion at the Santiago meeting on the impact of the provision as appearing in the Preliminary Draft on State immunity, Mr Broches volunteered that the insertion of a further provision might be warranted to make the position "completely clear"[89] and noted that it had "been suggested that it might be useful to distinguish between recognition of awards as binding and their execution"[90]. Picking up on that language at the Geneva meeting, and referring back to the Santiago meeting, Mr Broches noted that the view had been expressed that the provision as appearing in the Preliminary Draft "would force a modification in State practice and law on the question of a State's immunity from execution". He said that he thought that view was "unfounded", but added that "an express proviso removing any doubt as to the intent of the section might be inserted".[91]

53. When subsequently explaining the language of the provision as then appearing in the Preliminary Draft at the Bangkok meeting, Mr Broches spoke with more precision.[92] He said that it "dealt with two problems". He said that the first was the obligation of each Contracting State "to recognize an award ... as binding". He added that "the intent of the provision" in that first respect might have been better reflected if the word "accept" had been used in place of "recognize" given that "[w]hat was contemplated in [that] part of the sentence was the force of the award as [a] res judicata ... defence in resisting an action ... in the ordinary courts of a State, on a matter already determined in arbitral proceedings" under the ICSID Convention. He said that the second part was the obligation of each Contracting State "to enforce the award within [its] territories". He added that "the intent of the provision" in that second respect "might be better

---

[88] International Centre for Settlement of Investment Disputes, *History of the ICSID Convention: Documents Concerning the Origin and the Formulation of the Convention on the Settlement of Investment Disputes between States and Nationals of Other States* (1968), vol 2-1 at 242, 372, 464-5. See also 304.

[89] International Centre for Settlement of Investment Disputes, *History of the ICSID Convention: Documents Concerning the Origin and the Formulation of the Convention on the Settlement of Investment Disputes between States and Nationals of Other States* (1968), vol 2-1 at 343.

[90] International Centre for Settlement of Investment Disputes, *History of the ICSID Convention: Documents Concerning the Origin and the Formulation of the Convention on the Settlement of Investment Disputes between States and Nationals of Other States* (1968), vol 2-1 at 347.

[91] International Centre for Settlement of Investment Disputes, *History of the ICSID Convention: Documents Concerning the Origin and the Formulation of the Convention on the Settlement of Investment Disputes between States and Nationals of Other States* (1968), vol 2-1 at 428.

[92] International Centre for Settlement of Investment Disputes, *History of the ICSID Convention: Documents Concerning the Origin and the Formulation of the Convention on the Settlement of Investment Disputes between States and Nationals of Other States* (1968), vol 2-1 at 519.

expressed if the words 'recognize . . . and enforce it' were substituted by 'recognize as enforceable'".

54. In a report summarising the issues which had been raised in relation to the Preliminary Draft during the consultative meetings, Mr Broches referred to issues having been raised about the effect of the provision on State immunity.[93] He explained that "[b]y providing that the award could be enforced as if it were a final judgment of a local court", the provision "implicitly imported the limitation on enforcement which in most countries existed with respect to enforcement of court decisions against Sovereigns". "However", he added, "this point might be made explicit in order to allay the fears expressed by several delegations".

55. The fears concerning State immunity to which Mr Broches referred were allayed by the insertion into the Revised Draft of the provision which was soon to become Art. 55 of the ICSID Convention.[94] Picking up on the suggestion concerning terminology which had been noted at the Geneva meeting, the provision expressed the intended preservation of State immunity in terms of "immunity . . . from execution".

56. In the subsequent deliberation of the legal committee in Washington, the principle of enforcement which was to be embodied in Art. 54 of the ICSID Convention—requiring an award to be equated with a final decision—"survived [an] onslaught" of opposition.[95] The draft of Art. 54 underwent a measure of refinement, including by the limitation of the obligation of enforcement in Art. 54(1) to the enforcement of pecuniary obligations and by the insertion of what would become Art. 54(3), which also picked up on the language of "execution". Article 55, which Mr Broches described at a meeting of the legal committee in December 1964 as a mere "clarification",[96] emerged substantially unaltered.

---

[93] International Centre for Settlement of Investment Disputes, *History of the ICSID Convention: Documents Concerning the Origin and the Formulation of the Convention on the Settlement of Investment Disputes between States and Nationals of Other States* (1968), vol 2-1 at 575.

[94] International Centre for Settlement of Investment Disputes, *History of the ICSID Convention: Documents Concerning the Origin and the Formulation of the Convention on the Settlement of Investment Disputes between States and Nationals of Other States* (1968), vol 2-1 at 637.

[95] Broches, "Awards Rendered Pursuant to the ICSID Convention: Binding Force, Finality, Recognition, Enforcement, Execution" (1987) 2 *ICSID Review—Foreign Investment Law Journal* 287 at 316.

[96] International Centre for Settlement of Investment Disputes, *History of the ICSID Convention: Documents Concerning the Origin and the Formulation of the Convention on the Settlement of Investment Disputes between States and Nationals of Other States* (1968), vol 2-2 at 905.

57. Mr Broches provided a succinct summary of the result in a memorandum to the Executive Directors on 19 January 1965. He wrote:[97]

Article 54 requires Contracting States to equate an award rendered pursuant to the Convention with a final judgment of its own courts. It does not require them to go beyond that and to undertake forcible execution of awards rendered pursuant to the Convention in cases in which final judgments could not be executed. In order to leave no doubt on this point Article 55 provides that nothing in Article 54 shall be construed as derogating from the law in force in any Contracting State relating to immunity of that State or of any foreign State from execution.

58. Those remarks were reproduced in the accompanying Report of the Executive Directors on the ICSID Convention when it was published on 18 March 1965 and submitted to governments by the World Bank.[98]

(v) French and Spanish texts of Arts. 53-5

59. Despite the English text of Arts. 53-5 embodying, clearly enough, a distinction between recognition, enforcement, and execution, with those concepts used in the senses described above, account must be taken of the fact that the ICSID Convention was done in French and Spanish, as well as English, and all three texts are equally authentic and authoritative.[99] As Perram J observed in the Full Court, referring to a point made by Professor Schreuer,[100] a difficulty that arises in interpreting Arts. 53-5 is that the French and Spanish texts, respectively, use the words *exécution* and *ejecución*, and similar forms, wherever the words "enforce", "enforcement", *or* "execution" are used in the English text.[101] By contrast, in the French and Spanish texts,

---

[97] International Centre for Settlement of Investment Disputes, *History of the ICSID Convention: Documents Concerning the Origin and the Formulation of the Convention on the Settlement of Investment Disputes between States and Nationals of Other States* (1968), vol 2-2 at 963 [44].

[98] International Bank for Reconstruction and Development, *Report of the Executive Directors on the Convention on the Settlement of Investment Disputes between States and Nationals of Other States* (1965) at [43]. See also International Centre for Settlement of Investment Disputes, *History of the ICSID Convention: Documents Concerning the Origin and the Formulation of the Convention on the Settlement of Investment Disputes between States and Nationals of Other States* (1968), vol 2-2 at 1041, 1083.

[99] See ICSID Convention, testimonium. See also Vienna Convention on the Law of Treaties (1969), Art. 33(1).

[100] Schreuer, *The ICSID Convention: A Commentary*, 2nd ed (2009) at 1134-5. See also *Schreuer's Commentary on the ICSID Convention*, 3rd ed (2022), vol 2 at 1493-4.

[101] *Kingdom of Spain* v. *Infrastructure Services Luxembourg Sàrl* (2021) 284 FCR 319 at 338 [79], 339-40 [88].

respectively, *reconnaissance* and *reconocimiento*, and similar forms, are used where the English text uses "recognition" and "recognize".

60. A purely literal comparison of the French and Spanish texts with the English text might suggest that the French and Spanish texts are treating enforcement as synonymous with execution. If that were correct, then there would be a conflict between the French and Spanish texts (where enforcement and execution would have the same meaning) and the English text (where enforcement and execution have different meanings).

61. If such conflict existed, it would be resolved by applying the rule that if an apparent difference in meaning arises, then the meaning that should be adopted is that which best reconciles the texts, having regard to the object and purpose of the treaty. In taking this approach, Professor Schreuer[102] reasoned that since there was no explanation for the inconsistency in the drafting history of the ICSID Convention, the interpretation that best reconciled the three texts was to treat "enforcement" and "execution" as having the same meaning in the English text. This would mean that the preservation of immunity from court processes relating to execution in Art. 55 would extend also to enforcement. But once enforcement in Art. 54 is understood to be the process of granting an award the status of a judgment of a domestic court, the reasoning of Professor Schreuer is not consonant with the purpose of the ICSID Convention, particularly Arts. 53-5. The object and purpose of the ICSID Convention, which includes mitigating sovereign risk, would not favour a reconciliation of any differences in the texts by extending the application of laws concerning foreign State immunity beyond execution to enforcement (as that concept, in English, is used in Art. 54).

62. The better approach is to proceed on the basis that there is no difference in meaning between the texts that requires reconciliation. The French and Spanish texts are, of course, to be understood against the background of the civilian process of *exequatur*, which encompasses both recognition and the step by which a court grants an arbitral award the force of (that is, the same status as) a judgment of the domestic court.[103] The function of the *exequatur* is thus both to recognise the

---

[102] *Schreuer's Commentary on the ICSID Convention*, 3rd ed (2022), vol 2 at 1493.
[103] Juratowitch, "Waiver of State Immunity and Enforcement of Arbitral Awards" (2016) 6 *Asian Journal of International Law* 199 at 217-18. See also Reed, Paulsson and Blackaby, *Guide to ICSID Arbitration*, 2nd ed (2011) at 179-80.

arbitral award and to render the award enforceable in the territory of the issuing State.[104]

63. The literal conflation in the French and Spanish texts of "enforcement" and "execution" reflects what Allsop CJ described as "a penumbra or range of meaning in the words *exécution* and *ejecu[ción]* to encompass a non-execution procedure of enforcement".[105] In other words, *exécution* and *ejecución* slide between the meanings of enforcement and execution, in the loose sense described above, so that they are used in Art. 54 to refer to the process of *exequatur* or enforcement (granting an award the force of a judgment of the court), but are used in Art. 55 in the different sense of execution (subsequent effectuation of the judgment).

64. The real distinction within the French and Spanish texts of Arts. 54 and 55 is therefore between, on the one hand, recognition and enforcement by *exequatur* in Art. 54 and, on the other hand, "enforcement" as execution in Art. 55. This is consistent with the description by the Special Rapporteur in the Second Report on Jurisdictional Immunities of States and their Property[106] to the International Law Commission of "the practice of the French courts in which a strict distinction was drawn between recognition of arbitral awards and actual execution of the awards". The report then quotes a decision of the Tribunal de grand instance of Paris from 1970 which treated recognition as including enforcement, namely all steps "up to and including the procedure for granting an *exequatur* which was necessary for the award to acquire full force".[107]

65. The same approach, treating recognition and enforcement as loosely interchangeable but separate from the immunity from execution, was taken by the Court of Cassation, in *SOABI (Seutin) v. Senegal*.[108] There, the Court quashed a decision of the Court of Appeal of Paris which had held that SOABI failed to demonstrate that "enforcement" against Senegal would not conflict with the State's immunity from execution. In the English translation of the report, *exequatur* was described by the Court of Cassation as "recognition", which the Court held "does not constitute a measure of execution".

---

[104] See *Jurisdictional Immunities of the State (Germany v. Italy: Greece Intervening) ICJ Reports 2012*, 99 at 150 [125], 151 [128], referred to in *Firebird Global Master Fund II Ltd v. Republic of Nauru* (2015) 258 CLR 31 at 50-1 [47]-[48].

[105] *Kingdom of Spain v. Infrastructure Services Luxembourg Sàrl* (2021) 284 FCR 319 at 324 [9].

[106] United Nations General Assembly, *Second Report on Jurisdictional Immunities of States and their Property* (1989) at 12 [15].

[107] *Socialist Federal Republic of Yugoslavia v. Société Européenne d'Études et d'Entreprises* (1970) 65 ILR 46.

[108] (1991) 30 ILM 1167.

Again, the process of *exequatur*—which combines recognition and enforcement, as the preliminary measures to be taken before execution—can be seen in the English translation of the decision in *Benvenuti et Bonfant S.à.r.l.* v. *Government of the People's Republic of the Congo.*[109] In that decision, the Court of Appeal of Paris described Art. 54 as "lay[ing] down a simplified procedure for obtaining an *exequatur*" and, after quoting Art. 55, said that "[t]he order granting an *exequatur* for an arbitral award does not, however, constitute a measure of execution but simply a preliminary measure prior to measures of execution".

66. For these reasons, there is no real difference between the English text of Arts. 53-5, and the French and Spanish texts (at least not in respect of the important distinction between recognition and enforcement, on the one hand, and execution, on the other).

Waiver of immunity from court processes concerning recognition or enforcement in Art. 54

(i) The text and purpose of Art. 54

67. Spain's primary submission on this appeal was that Art. 54 is not concerned with awards sought to be enforced against a State in a foreign court. Spain argued that the express words of Art. 54 are not sufficiently clear to amount to a waiver of immunity from court processes concerning recognition or enforcement.

68. Spain's primary submission concerning the interpretation of Art. 54(1) was that, in its application in Australia, it contemplated recognition and enforcement in three circumstances: (i) if a State had an award against an investor and sought recognition and enforcement in an Australian court; (ii) if an investor had an award against Australia (which is not entitled to foreign State immunity in Australia) and sought recognition and enforcement against Australia in an Australian court; and (iii) if an investor had an award against a foreign State and sought recognition and enforcement against the foreign State in an Australian court and the foreign State chose to waive immunity over the proceeding. Spain argued that since Art. 54(1) said nothing "expressly" about a waiver of immunity from jurisdiction by a foreign State, there should be no inference drawn that a foreign State had waived that immunity by agreement to Art. 54(1).

[109] (1981) 65 ILR 88 at 91.

69. Spain's submission requires the text of Arts. 53-5 to be read in a contorted manner. In light of the effect of the provision in Art. 53 that awards shall be "binding" on Contracting States, together with the preservation in Art. 55 of immunity from execution only (subject to the laws of Contracting States), it would distort the terms of Art. 54(1) to require separate conduct that amounted to a waiver of immunity before an award could be recognised and enforced against a foreign State. On Spain's interpretation, Art. 55 would also be inaccurate, because Art. 54(1) would then preserve to a Contracting State a much greater immunity than merely immunity from execution subject to the laws of the Contracting State.

70. Spain submitted that since Arts. 53 and 54(2) make no reference to execution, and since Art. 54(3) leaves execution (and any immunity from execution) to be governed by the laws of the jurisdiction in which execution is sought, Art. 55 would be redundant or surplus on the interpretation we prefer. This possible surplusage of Art. 55 is, however, a consequence of the plain meaning of "execution" in Art. 55 which, as explained above, must be adopted as a matter of text, principle, context, and purpose. The view that Art. 55 has no independent work to do, other than reinforcement of the limits in Arts. 53 and 54, is also supported by the *travaux préparatoires* to the ICSID Convention, to which reference has already been made.

71. The textual difficulties with Spain's primary submission are compounded when the ordinary meaning of Art. 54(1) is understood, as the Vienna Convention on the Law of Treaties requires, in light of its object and purpose, which includes mitigating sovereign risk. Although Spain correctly submitted that the main reason for the inclusion of Art. 54 was to ensure that Contracting States were able to obtain effective remedies against private investors,[110] this was to ensure parity with the obligations of the Contracting States because it was otherwise assumed that participating nation states would abide by arbitral outcomes. This assumption is most explicit in the provision in Art. 53(1), restating customary international law[111] that each party, that is each Contracting State, "shall abide by and comply with the

---

[110] See the discussion at the consultative meeting in Geneva: International Centre for Settlement of Investment Disputes, *History of the ICSID Convention: Documents Concerning the Origin and the Formulation of the Convention on the Settlement of Investment Disputes between States and Nationals of Other States* (1968), vol 2-1 at 424.

[111] Broches, "Awards Rendered Pursuant to the ICSID Convention: Binding Force, Finality, Recognition, Enforcement, Execution" (1987) 2 *ICSID Review—Foreign Investment Law Journal* 287 at 289.

terms of the award", except to the extent to which the terms are stayed. In that sense, Art. 53 is the "primary provision".[112]

72. The assumption of parity was also recorded in the summary record of proceedings of the consultative meeting held at Santiago, where Mr Broches observed that the provision that became Art. 54 "was intended to protect the interests of the host States which while they were themselves internationally bound to comply with the award, might want an effective assurance that the private party would be compelled to do the same".[113] Again, following the last consultative meeting in Bangkok, a Chairman's Report prepared by Mr Broches referred to Art. 54 as "establishing equality not only of rights, but also of obligations, between State[s] and investors".[114] All of the drafts leading to the ICSID Convention thus referred "to recognition and enforcement against the parties in equal terms, without distinguishing between investors and host States". Giving effect to that purpose, the terms of Art. 54 do "not distinguish between the recognition and enforcement of awards against investors, on the one side, and against host States, on the other".[115]

73. In light of the object and purpose of the ICSID Convention, Professor van den Berg has observed that a curiosity of the ICSID Convention is not that it requires recognition and enforcement of awards against foreign States, but that a foreign State which has agreed to arbitration is not deemed to also accept the consequence of execution. He explains the result—that Contracting States waive their immunity from jurisdiction in relation to recognition and enforcement but not any immunity that they have from execution—on the basis of political and economic considerations:[116]

Execution is commonly felt to be a "more intensive interference with the rights of a State." From the eco[n]omic point of view, restrictive immunity principles applied to execution could result in foreign States refraining from investment in countries in which they know their property could be subject to execution. (footnote omitted)

---

[112] Broches, "Awards Rendered Pursuant to the ICSID Convention: Binding Force, Finality, Recognition, Enforcement, Execution" (1987) 2 *ICSID Review—Foreign Investment Law Journal* 287 at 302.

[113] International Centre for Settlement of Investment Disputes, *History of the ICSID Convention: Documents Concerning the Origin and the Formulation of the Convention on the Settlement of Investment Disputes between States and Nationals of Other States* (1968), vol 2-1 at 347.

[114] International Centre for Settlement of Investment Disputes, *History of the ICSID Convention: Documents Concerning the Origin and the Formulation of the Convention on the Settlement of Investment Disputes between States and Nationals of Other States* (1968), vol 2-1 at 574.

[115] *Schreuer's Commentary on the ICSID Convention*, 3rd ed (2022), vol 2 at 1474.

[116] Van den Berg, "Recent Enforcement Problems under the New York and ICSID Conventions" (1989) 5 *Arbitration International* 2 at 13.

(ii) International authority

74. As explained above, there is no real distinction between the United States provision permitting a waiver of immunity to be identified "either explicitly or by implication" and s 10(2) of the Foreign States Immunities Act permitting a waiver of immunity "by agreement". And, consistently with the caution that is required before drawing inferences of a waiver of immunity, United States courts have concluded, sometimes saying that they had little or no doubt,[117] that entry into the ICSID Convention involves a waiver of immunity from jurisdiction.[118]

75. The conclusion that the express terms of Art. 54(1) involve a waiver of immunity from jurisdiction in relation to recognition and enforcement is also supported by the 1991 Report of the International Law Commission which, as explained above, was relied upon by Lord Goff in *Pinochet [No 3]*[119] for his Lordship's cautious approach to inferences supporting a waiver of immunity. That report referred to a rule of customary international law that a waiver of immunity be "expressed ... in no uncertain terms".[120] The International Law Commission gave examples of State practice where a State "has previously expressed its consent to such jurisdiction in the provision of a treaty or an international agreement".[121] One of those examples was the ICSID Convention.

Spain's alternative submission: Waiver limited to bare recognition

76. Alternatively, Spain argued that Art. 54 contemplates only a waiver of immunity from court processes relating to recognition, and not enforcement, relying heavily on the French and Spanish texts which use execution and enforcement interchangeably. In this respect, Spain submitted that the orders of the Full Court went beyond bare recognition.

---

[117] *Liberian Eastern Timber Corporation* v. *Government of the Republic of Liberia* (1986) 650 F Supp 73 at 76; *Continental Casualty Company* v. *Argentine Republic* (2012) 893 F Supp 2d 747 at 751.

[118] *Blue Ridge Investments LLC* v. *Republic of Argentina* (2013) 735 F 3d 72 at 84-5; *Mobil Cerro Negro Ltd* v. *Bolivarian Republic of Venezuela* (2017) 863 F 3d 96 at 113; *Micula* v. *Government of Romania* (2019) 404 F Supp 3d 265 at 277.

[119] [2000] 1 AC 147 at 216.

[120] United Nations General Assembly, *Report of the International Law Commission on the work of its forty-third session* (1991) at 53.

[121] United Nations General Assembly, *Report of the International Law Commission on the work of its forty-third session* (1991) at 52, fn 89, referring to United Nations, *Materials on Jurisdictional Immunities of States and their Property* (1982) at 150-78.

77. The only matter supporting Spain's alternative submission, that any waiver of immunity from jurisdiction should be confined to recognition, is the different linguistic phrasing used in the French and Spanish texts of Arts. 53-5. But, for the reasons explained above, the materials before this Court strongly militate against any conclusion that the French and Spanish texts of Arts. 53-5 were intended to mean, or have been interpreted to mean, anything different from the English text. No basis has been shown to conclude that those texts bear a different meaning from the English text, preserving, subject to the laws of a Contracting State, the immunity from court processes relating to enforcement and not merely immunity from court processes relating to execution.

Decision of the Court of Justice of the European Union in Republic of Moldova v. Komstroy LLC

78. A final, although not fully developed, submission by Spain concerned the effect of the decision of the Court of Justice of the European Union in *Republic of Moldova* v. *Komstroy LLC*.[122] In that case, the European Court of Justice applied the earlier decision of *Slovak Republic* v. *Achmea BV*[123] and decided that the agreement to arbitrate in the Energy Charter Treaty must be interpreted as not being applicable to disputes between a member state of the European Union and an investor of another member state where the dispute concerned an investment by the investor in the first member state.[124]

79. Spain's contention was that this Court would "take cognisance" of *Komstroy* in identifying whether Spain had agreed to submit to the jurisdiction of the Australian courts for the purposes of the Foreign States Immunities Act. That contention must fail because the relevant agreement arose from Spain's entry into the ICSID Convention, which included its agreement as to the consequences of an award rendered pursuant to the ICSID Convention.

Conclusion

80. The appeal should be dismissed with costs. It is unnecessary to consider any further the grounds in the notice of contention, which were raised by the respondents only in the event that they were

---

[122] [2021] 4 WLR 132.
[123] [2018] 4 WLR 87.
[124] [2021] 4 WLR 132 at [66].

unsuccessful on their primary submissions. No notice of any application for costs was given to the European Commission so there should be no order as to costs against the European Commission in relation to its unsuccessful application for leave to appear as amicus curiae.

[Reports: (2023) 275 CLR 292; (2023) 408 ALR 58;
(2023) 97 ALJR 276]

International criminal law — Crimes against humanity — Widespread and systematic attack against civilian population — Torture — Severe deprivation of liberty — Syria — Civil unrest — Syrian general intelligence service — Defendant employed in Syrian general intelligence service — Germany — Defendant Syrian refugee now located in Germany — German Code of Crimes against International Law — Whether defendant committed crimes against international law — Whether defendant aided in crimes against humanity — Whether defendant arresting protestors subsequently subjected to torture aided a crime against humanity — Whether defendant arresting protestors subsequently subjected to severe deprivation of liberty aided a crime against humanity

War and armed conflict — Non-international armed conflict — Syrian civil war — War crimes and crimes against humanity — Torture and ill-treatment of detainees — The law of Germany

JUDGMENT AGAINST A SUSPECTED EMPLOYEE OF THE SYRIAN SECRET SERVICE FOR AIDING AND ABETTING A CRIME AGAINST HUMANITY

(Case No 1 StE 3/21)

Federal Republic of Germany, Koblenz Higher Regional Court. 24 *February* 2021

SUMMARY:[1] *The facts*:—The defendant was a Syrian national born in Damascus in May 1976. In July 1996 he joined the Syrian general intelligence service where he attained the rank of sergeant major and served until his desertion in January 2012. From February 2010, the defendant primarily served in Branch 251, a branch of the General Intelligence Directorate that was responsible for the internal security of Damascus and Rif Dimashq. During the outbreak of conflict and civil unrest in Syria in early 2011, Branch 251 was responsible for combating protests in Damascus and Rif Dimashq and carried out the majority of arrests in those areas. According to evidence presented before the Koblenz Higher Regional Court ("the Court"), on arrival at the location of Branch 251, detainees were subjected to significant abuse and ill-treatment, including torture, sexual violence and physical abuse.

---

[1] Prepared by Mr D. Peterson.

In September or October of 2011, a demonstration occurred that was attended by 3,000 to 6,000 demonstrators. Some 1,000 security forces, including the defendant, were deployed to keep the demonstrators under control. The defendant, and a subgroup of 250 intelligence officers, were ordered to shoot at the demonstrators. The defendant did not follow these orders, but upon seeing the demonstrators fleeing he joined the security forces in making arrests and placing those in detention on buses. Thirty demonstrators were transported to Branch 251 in Damascus on buses while the defendant was on board. Many of the detainees were beaten on board the buses, and when they arrived at the location of Branch 251, they faced severe abuse and ill-treatment. The detainees were held for several days and were subjected to torture, while their arbitrary detention failed to meet minimum rule of law standards.

In January 2012, the defendant deserted the intelligence service after escorting an armed convey of refrigerated trucks that was transporting corpses, the majority of whom had died in intelligence service prisons, to a mass grave. At an unknown point in time, he fled Syria and travelled to Greece via Turkey, where he remained until April 2018. He subsequently flew, with his wife and five children, from Greece to Germany, where one of his sons, who was a minor at the time, was already residing. During the process of applying for asylum in Germany, the defendant made a number of self-incriminatory statements, including that he had witnessed, but not participated in, people being beaten and killed while detained at Branch 251. In August 2018 the defendant was questioned as part of a structural investigation by the Federal Public Prosecutor's Office into unknown offenders suspected of violating the German Code of Crimes against International Law ("CCAIL") connected with the civil war in Syria. In February 2019, the defendant was arrested and ultimately charged with a suspected violation of Section 7(1) Nos 5 and 9 and (2) of the CCAIL for aiding a crime against humanity in the form of torture and severe deprivation of liberty with respect to the arrest and subsequent treatment of thirty demonstrators detained by the defendant in September or October of 2011.

Held:—The defendant was guilty of aiding a crime against humanity in the form of torture and severe deprivation of liberty. He was sentenced to a term of imprisonment of four years and six months.

(1) The thirty demonstrators who were arrested and taken to Branch 251 with the defendant's assistance were subject to severe physical and psychological ill-treatment. However, it was not possible to establish that any of the thirty specific demonstrators died as a result of their ill-treatment or detention conditions or that they were subjected to sexual assault (para. 433).

(2) The defendant knew the purpose of the specific operation against the demonstrators in Douma, and that the arrested demonstrators were to be taken to Branch 251. He was also aware of the nature of the ill-treatment and detention conditions which awaited them, that their arrest was arbitrary and

lacked any basis in the rule of law. It was not conceivable that he could have remained unaware of the function of the operation against the demonstrators, even if the Court was unable to establish that the defendant had himself engaged in any specific actions. He was well-aware of the general situation in Syria over the course of 2011, up until the operation which was the subject of the criminal proceedings, and it was extremely likely that he knew from the outset the purpose of such operations. During police questioning the defendant had explicitly stated that orders had been issued to kill demonstrators, including during the demonstration in Douma (paras. 434-8).

(3) Circumstantial evidence justified the conclusion that the defendant had willingly participated in putting down the demonstration and transporting demonstrators to Branch 251. The evidence was not sufficient to establish that, at the time of the incident, the defendant had found himself in a predicament which would have prevented him from stepping back from the act due to a present threat to his own life or limb, or threats to close relatives (paras. 439-47).

(4) Openly refusing to carry out orders would have had serious negative consequences for the defendant. However, during each phase of the operation, the defendant would have been able to stop taking part by feigning acute symptoms of illness or injury or by taking advantage of the turmoil out in the field by absconding. Given the severity of the offence, it was reasonable to expect the defendant to accept the risk of subjecting himself to suspicion and the organisational and financial challenges linked to abruptly defecting. The assertions of the defendant that he had wanted to wait until certain unspecified regions had fallen to the opposition before he fled did not alter this fact. There was therefore no subjective state of necessity which the defendant was seeking to evade, and it was not unreasonable to expect him to act in a rule-based manner (paras. 448-9 and 464).

(5) The events in Syria from late April 2011 onwards had constituted a widespread and systematic attack directed against a civilian population within the meaning of Section 7(1) of the CCAIL. The Syrian government and its subordinate authorities had used massive force against protestors, the opposition, civil society activists, and civilians, making the broad majority of civilians subject to increasingly planned and arbitrary state violence from March 2011. From April 2011, the attack had become widespread and systematic, as evidenced by the large number of civilian victims and country-wide approach to the persistent and escalating use of violence (paras. 451-6).

(6) Within the context of the overall widespread and systematic attack directed against the civilian population, all of the demonstrators who had been arrested with the assistance of the defendant and taken to Branch 251 had been subjected to torture within the meaning of Section 7(1) No 5 of the CCAIL and deprived of their liberty within the meaning of Section 7(1) No 9. While it was not possible to establish the specific manner in which the demonstrators were treated in Branch 251, it had been established that their treatment significantly exceeded the threshold of "substantial" ill-treatment

and that they were all subjected to severe beatings as soon as they arrived and were subsequently exposed to further physical abuse and inhumane conditions of detention. Their deprivation of liberty had been without basis in law or in the rule of law, and had lasted for a not inconsiderable length of time, which unquestionably surpassed the threshold of "severe" (paras. 457-61).

(7) The individual acts committed against the demonstrators had been part of the overall offence of a widespread and systematic attack directed against the civilian population. Where individual acts were factually, temporally and spatially linked, their functional link to the same overall offence within the meaning of Section 7(1) of the CCAIL meant that they constituted a single entity for the purposes of legal assessment (para. 462).

(8) The defendant had aided the main offence by committing an individual act against the thirty individuals who had been arrested. He had contributed to the main offence by arresting the victims and taking them to Branch 251, enabling the elements of the offence set out in Section 7(1) Nos 5 and 9 of the CCAIL to be realized. It could not, however, be assumed, in the absence of further evidence, that the defendant had provided even mental support to the other acts committed as part of the attack directed against the civilian population (para. 463).

(9) The sentence took account of the defendant's contribution to the discovery of the offence, and other mitigating circumstances including that the offending was considered to be less serious due to the reduced illegality of aiding, rather than committing, an act. Particular emphasis was placed on the fact that it was defendants' own statements prior to the preliminary investigation that led to charges being laid, and that the defendant had voluntarily renounced his work in the Syrian intelligence service. These factors had been balanced against the incriminating circumstances of the number of victims of the act, whose torture and deprivation of liberty the defendant had aided (paras. 468-87).

The following is the text of the judgment of the Court:[2]

TABLE OF CONTENTS

---

[2] The paragraph numbers have been inserted by the editors.

REASONS

A. FINDINGS

I. Findings as to the person of the Defendant

[1] The Defendant was born in Damascus on 25 May 1976 and is a Syrian national. He grew up in eastern Syria; his hometown is the town of Muhasan in the Deir ez-Zor Governorate. The Defendant has at least four siblings—an older and a younger brother and two sisters. His

father died on an unascertainable date. His mother and his younger brother are in Turkey. One of his sisters lives with her family in Greece; his other sister lives in Damascus.

[2] The Defendant attended school in his hometown and left at the end of Year 12 without any qualifications. From 1994 to 1996 he then lived with two brothers and an uncle in Damascus, in the district of al-Midan. On 10 July 1996, aged 20, the Defendant joined the Syrian general intelligence service and served in it until he deserted in early January 2012. He continued to live in Damascus whilst serving in the general intelligence service; for some of the time he lived in accommodation provided by the intelligence service. The Defendant pursued the non-commissioned officer career path and attained the rank of sergeant major. The places and nature of his work within the intelligence service are addressed in section II (Findings as to the substance of the case). The act which is the subject of the present proceedings occurred in September or October 2011.

[3] The Defendant deserted on 5 January 2012 and returned to his hometown of Muhasan, where he remained for an unknown period of time; his wife and their then four children did not go with him and initially remained in Damascus. The intelligence service enquired with his wife and his brother as to his whereabouts. It was not possible to establish with any certainty either when the Defendant rejoined his family, who had also travelled to eastern Syria at an unknown point in time, or when he left Syria, and whether he left together with his family or not. At any rate, the Defendant travelled to Greece via Turkey, where, by his own account, he remained for quite some time. On 25 April 2018 he, his wife and five of their six children flew from Greece to Germany. Entry was granted for the purpose of family reunification, since . . . [C], one of the Defendant's sons who was a minor at the time, had been sent on ahead and was already in Germany.

[4] The Defendant and his wife filed an asylum application in Germany on 9 May 2018. On 2 August 2018 he was issued with a certificate confirming permission to stay for a limited time (*Aufenthaltsgestattung*) so as to be able to undergo the asylum procedure, which has not been concluded to date. The Defendant and his family were first placed in a reception centre in . . . [a]. In the summer of 2018 he was assigned an apartment at . . . [b] Street in . . . [c], where he lived with his wife and children—except his eldest son . . . [D]— until his arrest. The Defendant and his family receive basic social security benefits (*Grundsicherung*) in Germany under the Asylum Seekers Benefits Act (*Asyl-bewerberleistungsgesetz*, AsylbLG).

[5] The Defendant is a Sunni Muslim. He has been married to . . . [E], who was born on . . . 1977, since 1 September 1998. The couple

has six children: a son, . . . [D], born on . . . 1999; a daughter, . . . [F], born in Damascus on . . . 2001; a son, . . . [C], born in Damascus on . . . 2002; a daughter, . . . [G], born in Damascus on . . . 2005; a son, . . . [H], who, according to civil status certificates issued in Syria, was born in Deir ez-Zor on . . . 2014; and a daughter, . . . [J], who, according to records, was born in Deir ez-Zor on . . . 2015. The Defendant's eldest daughter, . . . [F], suffers from muscle atrophy and is a wheelchair user.

[6] The Defendant has a criminal record in Germany. By summary penalty order issued by . . . [a] Local Court on 24 July 2018 (case no 8143 Js 20064/18 - Cs), which became final and binding on 1 September 2018, he was sentenced to pay a fine of 20 daily rates of €5 each; the penalty has been fully enforced. The ruling had its basis in the fact that, during an argument between the Defendant's son and another child in a reception centre for asylum seekers in . . . [a] on 26 May 2018, the Defendant punched the other child in the face.

[7] In the context of the present proceedings, the Defendant was arrested and placed in remand detention on 12 February 2019 on the basis of an arrest warrant issued by the investigating judge at the Federal Court of Justice on 7 February 2019 (case no 4 BGs 25/19). He was released from remand detention on 17 May 2019 after the investigating judge at the Federal Court of Justice, by order of that same day (case no 4 BGs 128/19), held that the Defendant's self-incriminatory witness statement was inadmissible and, on that basis, denied that there was a strong suspicion of an offence having been committed and thus revoked the arrest warrant. The Federal Public Prosecutor General (*Generalbundesanwalt*, GBA) filed a complaint against that order, on the basis of which the Third Criminal Panel at the Federal Court of Justice, by order of 6 June 2019 (case no StB 14/19), set aside the investigating judge's aforementioned order and amended the original arrest warrant dated 7 February 2019 by limiting the extent of the act regarding which there was a strong suspicion of an offence having been committed. On 25 August 2019 the Defendant was then again placed in remand detention, where he has remained ever since.

II. Findings as to the substance of the case

1. General political and social developments in Syria up to 2011

(a) History: Political and social structure

[8] The population of Syria, which has been an independent state since the end of the French mandate in 1946, is divided into various

ethnic and religious groups: Muslim Sunnis make up the largest population group (approx. 60-70% in 2011); Muslim Alawites account for another, significantly smaller, group (approx. 11% in 2011); the remainder of the population is made up of Christian, Shia Muslim, Druse, Jewish and Yazidi minorities. Since independence, the Alawite minority had grown to become the most influential political and social demographic group. The reasons for this are its early support for the French mandate and the fact that a disproportionate number of this demographic joined the Syrian Army, in which they still account for the majority of the officers. The membership of the Ba'ath Party, which was later installed as the ruling party, was also dominated by Alawites. On account of President Hafez al-Assad and President Bashar al-Assad having since appointed mainly Alawite confidants and relatives to positions of leadership, Alawites are also significantly overrepresented in the country's administration, military and business sector. Nevertheless, there are also a few Sunnis who have achieved positions of leadership, which is attributable to both their qualifications and strategic efforts to ensure ethnic and religious diversity, at least in the eyes of the general public. Examples of high-ranking Sunni functionaries include Hassan Turkmani, who was Minister of Defence up until 2009 and subsequently a key adviser to the President (he was killed in a bomb attack in 2012); Hisham Ikhtiyar, who was Director of the General Intelligence Directorate up until 2005 and later security chief in the Ba'ath Party; and, allegedly, Ali Mamlouk, Director of the General Intelligence Directorate. President Bashar al-Assad and close family members are also married to Sunnis.

[9] The initial objective of the Ba'ath Party, which was originally founded on an Arab nationalist programme and in opposition to the colonial powers, was to establish an Arab and socialist community in Syria, Lebanon and Iraq which was independent of other countries. Following a military coup in 1963 it became the ruling party. In 1973 the Ba'ath Party was written into the Syrian constitution as the leading party in the Syrian state. Positions within the state leadership are reserved for its members. In 2010, two-thirds of the members of the Syrian parliament belonged to the Baath Party and other bloc parties. Larger organisations, business associations and trade unions are close to the Party; membership of the Party increased the chances of obtaining state concessions such as business licences, being admitted to university or promotion within the public service. The Ba'ath Party has increasingly lost its originally socialist, pan-Arab ideology in pursuit of clientelist policies which shore up the government.

[10] Following a second coup in 1970, Hafez al-Assad, then Minister of Defence, assumed power as President of Syria, which he remained until his death in June 2000. He was succeeded by his son Bashar al-Assad, who was aged 34 at the time and is still President of Syria today. After the new president had at first publicly made a case for social change, more democracy and reforms, cautious measures relating to social liberalisation and the political opening of society (known as the "Damascus Spring") were then implemented: political prisoners were released, for instance, independent newspapers were authorised, detention centres were closed, the founding of human rights organisations was accepted and mobile phone networks and the internet were authorised. The President also launched an anti-corruption campaign. However, as early as the summer of 2001 the Syrian government reverted to its repressive line and arrested numerous government critics. As had been the case under Hafez al-Assad, it was specifically the intelligence services which were used to enforce government policies. In 2004, for example, the security forces cracked down on a Kurdish uprising in north-eastern Syria; 14 people died and numerous people were injured.

[11] Following the Iraq War, Syria sought closer foreign policy ties with Iran. At the same time, the Syrian government made efforts to improve its relations with the international community.

(b) Exercise of power: Role of the Syrian security apparatus
[12] (aa) Following the military coup in 1963, Syria moved from being a pluralist, liberal society and form of government towards an autocratic, repressive regime which, ultimately, took on dictatorial traits owing to the, in effect, one-person rule which was upheld by violent means. The state of emergency in effect since the coup, which Bashar al-Assad did not lift until April 2011 (albeit without any noticeable actual changes), enabled bans to be imposed on assemblies, newspapers and political parties and further powers to be assigned to the security apparatus, in particular making it easier for people to be arrested and detained. The security authorities, for instance, were empowered to imprison, without a court order, any person who posed a threat to public security or order. People who were politically unwelcome were increasingly subjected to arbitrary arrest and for the most part placed in prisons run by the intelligence services.

[13] Although torture was banned under the constitution applicable from 1973, it was an oft-deployed means of extorting information and of intimidation. People often died in detention facilities, either as a consequence of the conditions of detention and ill-treatment or by

hanging, specifically of prisoners who were accused of committing assaults or attacks on members of the government or government facilities. During an incident which became known as the "Hama Massacre", Hafez al-Assad in [1982; translator's note: the year is missing in the source text] ordered the army to bomb the city of Hama, which was predominantly occupied by opposition groups, mainly the so-called Muslim Brotherhood; between 4,000 and 40,000 civilians died during the operation. After Bashar al-Assad came to power and the country experienced a period of political and social opening up, large numbers of political opponents were once more imprisoned from the summer of 2001 on and the President reverted to his father's repressive policies. As had been the case under Hafez al-Assad's rule, it was impossible for a credible opposition movement to establish itself in time for the elections, which were at least formally conducted. Civil society and political initiatives were monitored and controlled using police state means, that is unless they were banned from the outset; human rights activists were prohibited from leaving the country. Print media and the internet were controlled and censored by the government. In the world of business, contracts and licences (e.g. for mobile networks) were awarded to a network of families who were loyal to the government or related to the President, such as those awarded to the group of companies owned by Rami Makhlouf, a cousin of Bashar al-Assad. When it came to modernisation measures and infrastructure-building, those regions were favoured which were regarded as loyal to the government or which promised the government a particularly large economic profit.

[14] Ever since Hafez al-Assad's time in power, resistance to the government was nipped in the bud by the intelligence services, which were omnipresent in both urban areas and rural regions. The system of recruited informants which permeated the whole of society gave rise to a climate of mistrust and fear in the country.

[15] (bb) One of the key instruments of power used by the Syrian state leadership has, since Hafez al-Assad's rule, been the extensive intelligence apparatus (*mukhabarat*), which was and is responsible for surveillance of the population, for information-gathering at the political and social level and for applying repressive measures to that end, such as searches, arrests and interrogations, in some cases using the most serious of physical violence. Owing to the long-standing state of emergency, the intelligence services in effect had wide-ranging executive powers without any basis in law. Within the regime they had a great deal of authority; they were less of a subordinate part of the Syrian administrative and security apparatus and more autonomous

institutions which reported directly to the head of state and directly
served to secure his rule. The services' official remit includes exposing
and preventing anti-government activities and combating terrorism
and extremism.

[16] The National Security Bureau (NSB) was established to control
and coordinate the work of the intelligence services, which are structured much like the military. The commanders of the intelligence
agencies, amongst others, hold office in the Bureau. The Central
Crisis Management Cell (CCMC), which is presented in detail in the
following, was set up in March 2011. The intelligence services, whose
jurisdictions sometimes overlap, are formed of

- the General Intelligence Directorate, which is directly subordinate to
  the President,
- the Military Intelligence Directorate, which reports to the Minister
  of Defence,
- the Air Force Intelligence Directorate, which also reports to the
  Minister of Defence,
- the Technical Intelligence Service, which is likewise assigned to the
  Ministry of Defence and
- the Political Security Directorate, which is subordinate to the
  Ministry of the Interior.

[17] Each of the intelligence services is divided into branches, which
are usually assigned a three-digit number; some branches have sub-
branches, which are assigned two-digit numbers. Most of the services
have a network of regional offices which covers the entire country. The
General Intelligence Directorate, the Military Intelligence Directorate
and the Air Force Intelligence Directorate, for instance, have both
central organisational units and regional units with branches and field
offices in each province. Besides the branches which are assigned
administrative tasks, those which are responsible for undercover investigations and those responsible for gathering information on social
media, the General, the Military and the Air Force Intelligence
Directorates at any rate have branches with executive powers which
can take direct and violent action against people and institutions.
Although they are not part of the military, their members, particularly
those at the management level, have military titles. The individual
services and their branches are generally headed by generals and sub-
branches by officers of the rank of colonel and lieutenant colonel.

[18] The level of control exercised by the intelligence services ranged
from monitoring public spaces and public events to observing political
organisations, universities, businesses and religious communities to

conducting surveillance of individual public servants and religious dignitaries. The General Intelligence Directorate focused on monitoring the Syrian population, primarily in the Damascus region. The Military Intelligence Directorate was officially responsible for ensuring the security of the armed forces—including as part of foreign intelligence activities—and the Political Security Directorate for political and religious surveillance. The Air Force Intelligence Directorate was linked to the Syrian Air Force by name only. It derives its name from the fact that Hafez al-Assad was a member of the Air Force and he eventually turned it into his personal security agency; it was responsible for securing air traffic and, primarily, for controlling the opposition. Further, the intelligence services were all tasked with "counterterrorism" and countering opponents of the regime.

[19] The intelligence services had their own detention facilities, including in their regional field offices, in which those arrested were held, including for longer periods, without formal proceedings, and in which interrogations were conducted and torture was used to extort information. This was generally done before prisoners were transferred to normal detention facilities such as the civilian prison in Adra or the military prison in Mezzeh. Methods of torture (which were even given their own names) had already been systematically used whilst Hafez al-Assad was in power. They included hitting a person all over the body with cables or sticks; hitting or whipping the soles of the feet (*fallaqa*); forcing someone into a car tyre and then hitting them whilst thus immobilised (*dulab*); beating a person who was shackled to a wooden board ("Flying Carpet"); hanging a person up by the hands so that their toes barely touch the floor, thereby applying violence to the person thus incapacitated (*shabeh*); shackling a person to a chair which has a moveable backrest and whose movement causes the spine to be overstretched ("German Chair"); burning, chemically burning or scalding body parts; electric shocks; means of humiliation; refusing to allow a person to go to the toilet; and sleep, water and food deprivation. Time and again prisoners died as a result of such ill-treatment and general conditions of detention.

[20] The picture which emerges in terms of the period up until the start of the protests in the spring of 2011 is that the intelligence services used targeted arrests and abuse to move against prominent members of the opposition, the press or groups regarded as critical of the state, for example the Muslim Brotherhood or politically active members of the Kurdish community. It is only in the period after this that a move towards a wide-ranging and extensive approach to dealing with large parts of the civilian population is discernible.

[21] (cc) The Syrian Army is a conscript army. Elite units responsible for securing existing power structures of which particular mention
should be made include the Republican Guard, which is directly
subordinate to the President, and the 4th Division, of which the
President's brother, Maher al-Assad, was commander, at any rate
in 2011.

[22] (dd) Besides the intelligence services and regular armed forces,
the Syrian regime also drew on paramilitary units and pro-government
militias to exercise control over the population. Particular weight was
not, however, attached to their activities until the start of the protest
movement and unrest in the spring of 2011. Special mention should be
made of the *"shabiha"* (the name derives from the Arabic word *shab-
biha*, meaning "phantoms, ghosts"), initially a loose network of people
close to the regime who regarded themselves as the unofficial arm of the
state and evolved into a kind of shadow economy with organised crime-
like structures serving their own enrichment. They were under the
protection of the aforementioned Rami Makhlouf, a cousin of
President Bashar al-Assad. Following the onset of the unrest in the
spring of 2011, the *shabiha* played a key role in implementing measures
to stifle the uprising and persecuting opposition forces.

2. Start of the conflict in Syria and its course from early 2011 to mid-2012

(a) "Arab Spring": Gathering momentum of civil-society protest in Syria
[23] Beginning primarily in Tunisia, from late 2010 onwards a civil-
society pro-democracy movement gathered increasing momentum in
North African countries and countries in the Middle East. It became
known in the media and academic circles as the "Arab Spring", or
"Arabellion". Social media posts, demonstrations and other types of
rallies were used in these countries, some of which were under autocratic rule, to protest against political and social ills, corruption and
mismanagement; this led to some political changes in these countries.
The political slogan used across all the countries affected was "The
people want to bring down the regime". Both the regime in Syria and
independent observers considered it unlikely that these protests would
cross over into Syria.

[24] However, sympathy for the protest movement did also grow in
Syria. Increasing support for ideas which were critical of the government was already being voiced on the internet in early 2011.
Encouraged by developments in other Arab countries, the willingness
to publicly criticise the Syrian government subsequently grew; key

groups involved in this were made up of established members of the opposition, parts of the younger, internet-savvy generation, who were able to access information critical of the government despite the informational restrictions, and economically disadvantaged demographic groups who were not benefitting from the clientelist system of government. Owing to the government's increasing use of force, the number of those who turned against it grew in the further course of the conflict, in particular amongst the relatives of those who were arrested or of other victims of previous protests. Mosques attended by Sunni Muslims came to symbolise the movement and served as the starting point for demonstrations, especially following Friday prayers, which are mandatory for practising Muslims. As the security authorities focused their activities on these times and places, the repressive measures turned further parts of the Sunni majority population against the Syrian regime and the predominantly Alawite security forces, since from that time on the measures also appeared to be sectarian.

(b) *Course of the conflict*
[25] (aa) The first small-scale rallies against corruption and poverty and for more democratic rights were held across parts of Syria in February 2011. These gatherings were peaceful, and the security forces did not initially intervene. In early March 2011 a group of 10- to 15-year-old children wrote anti-government graffiti on the walls of houses in Daraa in south-western Syria. They used slogans such as "The people want the regime to fall", which had already been used in other countries. The children were arrested. When they were released from prison a few days later and exhibited obvious signs of torture, the incident attracted the attention of both national social media and the international press, which led to a wave of demonstrations across various parts of the country.

[26] In response to the imprisonment and ill-treatment of these children, protests were held in Damascus on 15 March 2011 in the historic Al-Hamidiya Souq (covered market). These were followed over the next few days by a silent rally attended by some 150 people, around 30 of whom were arrested. On Friday, 18 March 2011, protesters gathered in Daraa, Baniyas, Homs and Deir ez-Zor following midday prayers and held demonstrations. These were already considerably bigger, and were met with violence on the part of the security forces who were drafted in. The consequence was that hundreds of people were injured and at least two people died. Rallies were regularly held thereafter, mainly on Fridays, which grew to number several thousand people, especially in the cities of Damascus, Homs, Daraa and Douma.

The security forces responded by firing tear gas and live ammunition. On 23 March 2011 the security forces used firearms against demonstrators in Daraa who had assembled at the city's Al-Omari Mosque; a number of people died, though it was not possible to determine exactly how many. Following Friday prayers on 25 March 2011, a demonstration held at the Umayyad Mosque in Damascus was violently broken up. A likewise as yet undefined number of demonstrators were killed on 1 April 2011 in the Damascus area as well as in Douma to the north-east of the capital when the security forces fired their guns at them. Numerous other demonstrators were also arrested.

[27] The overwhelming majority of the demonstrations and rallies were peaceful. The usually unarmed demonstrators carried palm and olive branches, for instance, as a sign of their peaceful intentions. Some, though, also threw stones. There were arson attacks against buildings linked to the government, for example an office belonging to the Ba'ath Party, during riots in Daraa.

[28] (bb) The Syrian regime pursued various strategies in parallel in response to the growing number of protests.

[29] (1) Official statements released by the government and printed in pro-government newspapers claimed that the protests were in fact uprisings which were being controlled from abroad and sought to destabilise the Syrian state. Throughout the whole of 2011 there were repeated denials that demonstrators had been killed by the security forces. To disinform the (global) public, press events were used to present members of the security forces, who had allegedly been injured, in hospital. The aim was to suggest that it was the demonstrators who were resorting to violence.

[30] (2) At the same time, Bashar al-Assad appeared to reach out to the protesters by announcing reforms and having some of the members of the security forces' leadership replaced. In early April 2011 the state of emergency was lifted and the order given to release imprisoned demonstrators. Further, legislative amendments were made to meet the demands of some population groups. For instance, stateless Kurds were granted Syrian nationality and the ban on teachers wearing the full-face veil was lifted. In the period which followed, the Syrian government also adopted a conciliatory tone and announced—including in response to international protests in the face of the violence perpetrated against the civilian population—that it wanted to enter into dialogue with the opposition and had plans to draft a new constitution. In late July and early August 2011, Bashar al-Assad did in fact enact laws allowing other political parties alongside the Ba'ath Party and granting greater freedom of expression in the media.

[31] (3) On the other hand, and unbeknownst to the general public, as from late March 2011 the conditions were being put in place at the highest governmental level permitting security personnel to use more force, both in quantitative and qualitative terms. An ad hoc body comprising the highest-ranking security force leaders was set up, for instance, in response to the situation escalating in March 2011. The Central Crisis Management Cell (CCMC) reported directly to President Bashar al-Assad. Its permanent members included the Deputy Head of the Ba'ath Party Regional Command, Mohammed Said Bekheitan, the Minister of Defence, the Minister of the Interior and the heads of the various intelligence services, as well as, on a rotating basis, other government representatives. The CCMC was the highest governing body, even above the military and intelligence services, and set general policies on dealing with future protests by means of orders issued centrally to all the security forces. Its orders and instructions were mainly organisational in nature and encompassed the intelligence services and Ba'ath Party structures. The aim was, from mid-April 2011 at the latest, to violently suppress the protest movement through armed intervention on the part of the security forces in order to prevent the destabilisation and possible overthrow of the regime.

[32] (i) The CCMC met several times in April 2011. At one such meeting on or shortly before 18 April 2011, the following decision was taken after the "security situation" and the "political situation" were discussed:

1. The phase of tolerance and meeting of demands is over, as the saboteurs and conspirators have relied too much on our policy to that effect, they have raised the ceiling of their demands, stepped up their hostile courses of action, used all the means of agitation and weapons available and fomented sectarian conflicts.
2. Various strategies must be applied to confront the demonstrators, those who pose a threat to security and the saboteurs, including the following:
   (a) No release of any arrested persons whatsoever and their handover to the judicial authorities.
   (b) An armed response to those who take up arms against the state, though care is to be taken not to endanger civilians.
   (c) Instructions to be issued to seize unregistered motorcycles and registered motorcycles used by armed individuals as a means of agitation or as a means of transport (the regions and details to be coordinated with the Ministry of the Interior).
   (d) The arrest of known offenders without any raids, their imprisonment and handover to the judicial authorities.
   (e) Mechanisms for dealing with rallies:

- The police, backed by the security apparatus, are to be prepared and equipped to deal with demonstrations. Likewise, the Party and organisations are to be prepared to confront demonstrations, where necessary and as the situation requires.
- The Armed Forces are only to be involved in an emergency and only to deal with predetermined tasks.
- Tasks, competences and mechanisms for cooperation between the various agencies are to be precisely determined.

3. In the regions, supreme bodies comprising a leader, a high-ranking military officer and a security officer are to be established for planning, implementation and leadership purposes. All the military, security and party agencies within their region will be subordinate to them. They include
   - a body for the central region.
   - a body for the coastal region.
   - the central crisis management agency to take on this task in Damascus and Rif Dimashq [note by the Division of the Crimes against International Law: the governorate which encompasses the region around Damascus].

4. Preferential treatment is to be given to the central region, whilst the remaining regions must be pacified.

5. The Party apparatus (Party organisations, popular organisations and professional trade unions) is assigned the following role:
   - Training of designated forces to confront demonstrators and in the use of weapons.
   - Continuous, rotating presence at the various Party headquarters.
   - Holding ready limited reserves within the Party apparatus and its organisations which can be enlarged in each governorate depending on the situation.
   - Involvement in confronting hostile demonstrations.
   - Organising supportive rallies, as and when required and depending on the situation in each governorate.
   - Monitoring the situation in the population and reporting suspects and agitators, possibly also arresting them and handing them over to the security authorities and Army.
   - Structuring trained forces into units which have a leadership to ensure that their interventions are structured and organised.

6. A meeting is to be held with the trade unions at which they are to be told what their tasks are and they are to be informed that anyone who does not comply will be held accountable under the Trade Unions Act and other general legislation.

7. University presidents are to be notified that students are to be informed that rallies at universities are prohibited by law and anyone who does not comply will be expelled.

8. The role of the media:
   - Civilian and military media delegations are to be deployed at the scenes of the protests and are to film events there so that the recordings made

can be swiftly broadcast—following editing and the addition of the
relevant commentary by a specialised media agency, preferably one
acting with the involvement of the political administration of the
Armed Forces. There is to be ongoing coordination with the security
authorities and the Armed Forces.

- Banners, terms and phrases shown in the broadcast footage are to be
reviewed and that which is insalubrious is to be deleted; concepts and
terminology referring to offences under the criminal law are to be used.
- The use of creative methods when responding to hostile media which
are backed by audio-visual documentation.
- Explanation of cases which are to be regarded as unlawful.
- It is to be made clear to both citizens and the saboteurs that we are on
the cusp of a period in which the law must be precisely and relentlessly
applied to maintain the safety and security of the state, its citizens and
public order.
- The main focus is to be placed on unmasking the saboteurs and their
condemnation by all sections of the population.

9. A special assembly of the Central Crisis Management Cell is to be held to
make preparations for confronting any demonstrations on Friday.

[33] (ii) The CCMC met again on 20 April 2011 and, according to
the minutes of the meeting, "continued to assess the security situation".
The following was determined and agreed upon:

1. The facts show that persons who carry out demonstrations, rallies,
murders, killings and acts of sabotage are further refining their methods
and plans in order to terrorise citizens and force them to join them. They
are using all the methods known to them to destroy citizens' trust in the
state and its abilities to fight these individuals. They are planning to hold
demonstrations in several towns and cities on Friday. It is likely that they
will attempt to widen their demonstrations to include other towns and
cities and to foment sectarian discord.

2. It is necessary to launch a new phase to combat the conspirators and to
use force against them from now on. It is important to win the battle and
to demonstrate the state's strength and capabilities.

3. Detailed plans are being prepared to counter likely armed and unarmed
demonstrations and rallies, in particular in the regions of Daraa,
Damascus, Rif Dimashq and Homs. These plans will be drawn up today
and tomorrow under the supervision of the National Security Bureau.
The Armed Forces are asked to provide the necessary support with the
agreement of Army command (as per instructions issued).

4. The General Command of the Army and the Armed Forces must put
forward comprehensive plans. These plans are being drawn up on the
basis of a scenario in which the demonstrations and hostile actions will
continue to spread across all the provinces. All measures will be taken and
cooperation with the enforcing agencies will be put in place to be able to

carry out these measures in full or in part, depending on the prevailing situation.

5. Some military units will be mobilised as per instructions issued.

6. The Armed Forces will publish a statement concerning the murders and killings of members of the military which is to mention that the offenders will be pursued by all available means and tried in court so that they receive their just punishment.

7. Depending on the situation, all the methods and means detailed will be applied where a region is encircled, raids are carried out against suspects or a hostile demonstration is combated. (Pursuant to the instructions issued during the meeting.)

8. Suspects are to be arrested who, based on instructions from abroad, have participated in acts of sabotage, killings, the planning of serious crimes and inciting discord.

9. The security authorities will focus on investigations, interrogations and tracking in order to obtain documented results and to present them in the media.

10. The deceased are to be buried without assemblies and demonstrations. The relatives of the deceased must commit to this before the corpses are released to them.

11. The Central Crisis Management Cell to meet on a daily basis.

12. Students who take part in demonstrations will be exmatriculated pursuant to university rules and regulations.

13. According to the instructions of the Minister of the Interior, bicycles may not be taken into towns and cities.

14. Emphasis is hereby put on item no 8 of the minutes of the last meeting concerning the role of the media and coordination with the political administration of the Armed Forces, the Office of Moral Guidance in the Ministry of the Interior.

15. The supreme leadership committees and the governor of Daraa will be notified of the general situation and decisions taken.

16. In accordance with the proposal made by the Minister of Defence, the Ministry of the Interior will receive all the support it needs.

17. The Deputy Regional Secretary of the Ba'ath Party will coordinate the role of the Party and its organisations in the plans drawn up. He is to pass on instructions to the Party and its organisations in line with applicable provisions.

18. Emphasis is to be put on the citizens' demands that the state take action against the conspirators and win the battle so that citizens and their children are protected and can continue to go about their everyday life in safety.

19. The people's committees are to be dissolved.

[34] (iii) Notwithstanding the linguistic smokescreen of bureaucratic, trivialising phrases which give a semblance that the rule of law applies, these decisions contain clear instructions to use force, including

lethal force, against protesters with the full participation of governmental authorities, security forces and the Ba'ath Party's apparatus. Given the CCMC's status and that of its members, the decisions were binding on all security organs across the whole of Syria and were passed down the chain of command to those security forces which implemented them.

[35] The objective of these decisions was to crush the protests at all costs using the force of arms in order to stabilise the regime and to stop participants and permanently deter the population as a whole from engaging in any further activities. Despite the wording used in the meeting held on 18 April 2011 (see 2(b) of the minutes cited in the above)—that attention was to be paid to ensuring that no civilians came to any harm—the order was given to use the force of arms and it was not only accepted that demonstrators (who were regarded as non-civilian insurgents) would be killed and injured, the purpose was that this was to act as a deterrent. It is likewise clear from these decisions that, according to the will of the state leadership, the objective behind the further strategy adopted vis-à-vis the civilian population was to nip future protests or uprisings in the bud by force. This encompassed the persecution, arrest, torture and killing of those people who allegedly took part in protests or who were only allegedly linked to such protests. In actual fact, and authorised by the state leadership, the decisions acted as a licence for the security forces to take violent action against the alleged opponents of the regime without prior verification of any suspicion and without judicial proceedings.

[36] The instructions were passed on and interpreted in this sense. The military, intelligence services and other parts of the security apparatus were instructed across the respective hierarchical levels and acted accordingly from that point on. Based on the decisions taken by the CCMC, a more systematic approach was thus adopted, meaning that protest rallies were broken up, including with the use of a considerable degree of armed force, and as many as possible of the surviving demonstrators were arrested and taken in waiting vehicles to detention facilities operated by the intelligence services, where they were detained for various lengths of time and subjected to ongoing ill-treatment, in some cases leading to death. Demonstrators who fled the violence were pursued by the security forces and arrested. A large number of people were also arrested and abducted at the many checkpoints which were set up across the country and during large-scale raids, some of which covered entire city districts. Sometimes people who were entirely uninvolved were caught up in these measures. The aim of the subsequent torture and ill-treatment by the security authorities was, first, to

gather information, in particular about organisations and further planned protests, and, second, to intimidate the population and punish those arrested.

[37] (iv) Further meetings of the CCMC were subsequently held, though both their subject matter and the content of any further decisions adopted cannot be established. At a meeting held on 5 August 2011 the order was given to "organise daily campaigns to be carried out jointly by the military and security authorities concerning security sectors deemed by them to be of security-related priority". "All the security branches" were required to participate in such measures "in order to storm the places where those who committed the crimes of sabotage, murder and attacks against citizens and their property and against state institutions are being sought". These people were to be arrested; individual areas were to be "cleansed" of those who were wanted. The orders issued on 5 August 2011 also related to the fact that the results of investigations, in particular information about searches, were to be submitted to the Head of the National Security Bureau on a daily basis. Further, the names were to be reported of any members of the security forces who "acted negligently when confronted with the armed gangs or whose weapons were taken off them".

[38] (cc) The predominantly peaceful demonstrations continued in April 2011 and the number of participants successively increased, to which the state responded with increasing violence. The demonstrations regularly, but not always, took place on a Friday; in most cases there were fatalities. The security forces were henceforth instructed to use firearms to break up the demonstrations, and they used live ammunition against civilians without warning. The security forces also responded violently during funerals held for activists who had died, which took on the guise of rallies. Neither when applying physical violence or using their firearms, nor when arresting people was any distinction drawn between whether the civilians present were protesting activists, devout mosque-goers or grieving relatives attending a funeral. In addition, some of the demonstrators who were injured by the security forces were denied medical assistance in that ambulances were prevented from attending to them and medical staff were (also) shot at. In Daraa and in Homs, security forces were posted at the entrance to hospitals to stop alleged opponents of the regime entering.

[39] On 22 April 2011 at least 100 civilians were shot and killed by government forces during demonstrations held across various parts of the country; numerous others were injured. The demonstrations were broken up by security forces; numerous arrests were made. A few days

later the city of Daraa was surrounded, besieged and finally stormed by government forces, which included army tank units and snipers. Numerous people died in the city, which had its supply of water, food and health care cut off; there were also fatalities during demonstrations outside the city and when citizens from the surrounding area attempted to bring water and food to the civilians in the besieged city. Despite holding up placards to indicate that they only wanted to provide help, the security forces deployed there used live ammunition without warning to shoot at the helpers and demonstrators. A total of at least 200 people died. In late April the security forces carried out other operations in other parts of the country during which there were fatalities. Numerous arrests were made in the city of Douma during extensive raids.

[40] In the following months the protest movement grew to a six-figure number of active participants, as a result of which the extent of state repression also increased. In July 2011 alone a four-figure number of civilians died at the hands of the state. The security forces on the one hand focused on those towns and cities which were regarded as the opposition's strongholds. In late July 2011, for instance, government forces stormed the city of Hama, resulting in the deaths of several hundred people. In September 2011 the city of Douma was sur-rounded by the military and its infrastructure (i.e. electricity and water supplies and food transports) was disrupted; numerous arrests were made, too. The security forces also erected increasing numbers of checkpoints to conduct identity checks; they had lists of the names of people who were to be arrested. Firearms were from then on used against demonstrators, and members of the opposition were also sub-jected to arbitrary abuse at these checkpoints.

[41] The security forces had orders to break up gatherings of more than eight civilians by force of arms. Searches specifically targeted the leaders of the protest movement. The extensive waves of arrests led to massive overcrowding in state detention facilities, in which detainees were subjected to arbitrary violence and torture, sometimes leading to death. Conditions in the prisons run by the intelligence services were characterised by a lack of water and food, sleep deprivation and catastrophic hygiene conditions.

[42] (dd) As of September 2011 the protests, which had up until then been peaceful, became increasingly more combative. The Free Syrian Army (FSA) was founded; the majority of its initial members were soldiers who had deserted the regular army. Members of the opposition forces subsequently carried out isolated attacks against government buildings. From early 2012 onwards there were armed

clashes between government forces and militant opposition groups. At the same time, civilians continued to hold mass demonstrations which were entirely peaceful but which the security forces nevertheless continued to move against using firearms and physical violence. *Shabiha* militias were increasingly drawn on to combat the demonstrations. Large numbers of demonstrators were still being killed and arbitrarily arrested. The situation escalated to such an extent that soldiers who refused to shoot at unarmed demonstrators were themselves shot dead by intelligence service staff "in the second row". Defectors and others who refused to obey orders were arrested.

[43] There was a short period of détente in early 2012. After the Arab League had exerted diplomatic pressure on Syria in late 2011 by threatening to suspend its membership, the Syrian government agreed to implement measures which the League had proposed. In December 2011 the Arab League sent around 160 observers to Syria. At the turn of the year the Syrian government withdrew its military, including tanks and heavy weapons, from Syrian towns and cities and released around 3,500 prisoners. Nevertheless, civilians were still being killed by government forces at demonstrations held during this period.

[44] The biggest demonstration to be held in the Syrian capital since the start of the conflict was held in the Mezzeh district of Damascus in February 2012. The security forces deployed there shot dead at least one person and used tear gas and stun grenades to disperse the demonstration. Dozens of demonstrators were arrested. In February 2012 Syrian troops also attacked the city of Homs. Numerous civilians, including journalists, died. The government ascribed a massacre of civilians in Homs to armed terrorist groups; opposition activists, by contrast, claimed that the Syrian Army and pro-government militias were responsible. In March and April 2012, 95 civilians died as a result of acts of violence committed by government forces in Idlib, where numerous arbitrary arrests were also made. More than 100 civilians were killed by pro-government militia in Houla on 31 May 2012. At least 55 people were killed in the village of Al-Qubeir near Hama following an act of violence by an armed pro-government group. At the end of July 2012, the Syrian Army or pro-government forces began shooting at civilians wanting to cross the Jordanian border; at least one person died. In late August 2012 more than 200 civilians were discovered in the suburb of Darya in Damascus; they had been shot dead by security forces during house raids.

[45] As the conflict developed, it became increasingly militarised. The Syrian Air Force, for instance, bombed districts of Damascus and other cities in the area around the capital which were more oppositional

or were occupied by members of the Free Syrian Army; cluster and incendiary bombs were used, too. From mid-2012 onwards the fighting escalated on both sides to such an extent that the conflict can be regarded as a civil war from then on. Notwithstanding this, there were still peaceful oppositional structures and civil protests in regions controlled by the Syrian state.

(c) Involved state actors and institutions: Strategy and victims
[46] (aa) Following the outbreak of the conflict, the Syrian regime availed itself of the same institutions and forces which it had already had at its disposal before then; they were merely increased in number. General military and paramilitary units, in particular the *shabiha* militia, were deployed. The intelligence services made up a substantial proportion of the security forces used to combat the protest movement; as a direct instrument for securing power, their remit did not change in the early days of the conflict. After the start of the clashes, the intelligence services' activities focused on this domestic task. The General Intelligence Directorate, the Military Intelligence Directorate and the Air Force Intelligence Directorate in particular were used as operational forces. It was above all Branches 215, 227, 291 and 235 ("Palestine Branch") of the Military Intelligence Directorate which were involved in crushing the protest movement, as were the "Mezzeh Airport" and "Bab Touma" Branches of the Air Force Intelligence Directorate. Branch 285 and Branch 251 were operative branches within the General Intelligence Directorate; the latter is of relevance in relation to the Defendant's concrete contribution to the act which is the subject of the present proceedings (see section A.II.3 [Branch 251 and Sub-branch 40 of the Syrian General Intelligence Directorate], below, for details).
[47] The General Intelligence Directorate and the Military Intelligence Directorate each had between 8,000 and 10,000 full-time employees. The Political Security Directorate and the Air Force Intelligence Directorate both had between 5,000 and 6,000 full-time employees. It is not possible to reliably establish how many forces were deployed in the context of individual operations against demonstrations. However, an at least three-figure number of military and intelligence service forces were typically deployed to cordon off roads, to fire tear gas and live ammunition at demonstrations, subsequently to go into the demonstration armed with striking implements, to injure and arrest demonstrators and take them to detention facilities. At the same time, adjoining streets were searched for those who were fleeing or who were suspected of having participated in the demonstration—often merely on the basis of their age and place of residence.

[48] From the start of the demonstrations in February 2011, which were initially held only sporadically, the intelligence service branches sought to establish how and by whom the protests were being organised; participants were arrested and interrogated under torture to that end. They continued to carry out the tasks previously assigned to them, that is, intimidating and pursuing opposition forces, but these were now deliberately extended to encompass those who organised and supported the protest movement in the streets and on social media. From late April 2011 at the latest, the involved security forces within the military or militarised structures were instructed to coordinate their actions against the demonstrators. Further, members of the intelligence services in particular were involved in conducting raids and house searches and making arrests. Moreover, the intelligence services set up a growing number of checkpoints in inner cities and along thoroughfares in rural areas at which people were likewise searched and arrests were made.

[49] At the start of the conflict the Syrian Army was between 200,000 and 300,000 people strong and had an additional 300,000 reservists; the majority were conscripts. In the period up until the spring of 2012 some 60,000 soldiers deserted the army by fleeing abroad or later joining the Free Syrian Army because they objected to the attacks against the civilian population. Higher-ranking, often Alawite, officers generally stayed on in the regular Syrian Army. The Republican Guard, which was deployed to protect the government in the area around Damascus, and the 4th Division, which was subordinate to the President's brother, Maher al-Assad, were regarded as elite units loyal to the regime and were mainly made up of Alawites. They were the two preferred units when it came to suppressing the protest movement and were involved in making arrests, carrying out house raids and injuring and killing demonstrators. A distinction must be drawn between them and the regular army units whose soldiers, including conscripts, were deployed to attack unarmed demonstrators on the pretext that they were combating Salafists, terrorists and criminals. This led to increasing numbers of people deserting and defecting. In the second half of 2012, pro-government militias which had already provided support to the armed and intelligence forces in 2011 were incorporated into the new National Defence Forces (NDF).

[50] The Military Police were primarily responsible for administrative tasks, such as photographing and documenting those who died. For example, from March 2011 at the latest the Military Police's photographic service was instructed to systematically record those demonstrators or prisoners who were killed. It was this work which

resulted in the creation of 26,938 image files which were smuggled out of the country by a military photographer who deserted (known as "Caesar") and which contained photographs of a total of 6,821 corpses. Most of the people in the photographs, the majority of whom showed signs of emaciation and ill-treatment, had died in the intelligence service branches in the period between May 2011 and August 2013 and were photographed by the Military Police's photographers shortly after they died. The Military Police were, however, also responsible for transporting prisoners from prison to court and for the military field courts (which were also responsible for passing sentence on political prisoners). Following brief sham trials, these courts imposed penalties, usually based on confessions extorted under torture, which could go as far as the death penalty.

[51] (bb) From March 2011 onwards, the security authorities arrested large numbers of people in the course of violently breaking up demonstrations, during house searches and raids and at checkpoints. Those arrested were usually carried off to detention centres in buses and then detained there for various lengths of time—from a few days to years—without an arrest warrant or other formal proceedings.

[52] The Syrian regime used existing civilian, military and intelligence service prisons as detention facilities. They were significantly overcrowded owing to the large numbers of people being detained there. Prisons such as Tadmur Military Prison, which had closed sometime around 2001, were reopened. Important bigger prisons included the civilian prison in Adra, to which prisoners were transferred for long periods of detention, and a prison in Saydnaya operated by the military. Further, the intelligence services ran a large number of prisons, including facilities in the provinces, which formed a network across the whole of the country. These facilities served as reception centres for those who were arrested. However, people were sometimes detained there for months or even years. The General Intelligence Directorate at any rate had prisons in Branches 251 and 285. Of the remaining intelligence services, it was above all the Military Intelligence Directorate and the Air Force Intelligence Directorate which were involved in arresting, torturing and killing actual or alleged opponents of the regime—the former in Branch 235, also known as the "Palestine Branch", which had become notorious amongst the population. The Military Intelligence Directorate operated a total of 10 detention facilities, including five in Damascus. The Air Force Intelligence Directorate was responsible for at least two prisons. The Political Security Directorate operated a prison in the Mezzeh district of Damascus.

416 GERMANY (KOBLENZ HIGHER REGIONAL COURT)

[53] The conditions of detention in the facilities operated by the intelligence services were characterised by a shortage of food and medical assistance, overcrowding and the resulting insufficient opportunity to exercise and lack of places to sleep, catastrophic hygiene conditions owing to pest infestation and insufficient opportunity to wash or change one's clothing, the arbitrary use of violence and enormous mental stress on account of the uncertainty as to one's fate and constantly hearing the screams of other prisoners who were being abused in neighbouring rooms by day and by night. Prisoners were regularly and systematically tortured during their interrogations in the intelligence services' facilities. Those torture methods were applied which had already been "trialled" within the Syrian intelligence apparatus before the start of the conflict: prisoners were physically restrained—sometimes in a car tyre (a technique known as *dulab*) or on a board (known as the "Flying Carpet")— and then beaten all over their body with or without an implement, especially the soles of the feet (known as *fallaqa*), they were hung up by the wrists (known as *shabeh*) and their body and spine were over-stretched (known as the "German Chair"). They were also subjected to electric shocks, burning and scalding, their fingernails and toenails were extracted; other methods which were down to the sadistic ingenuity of those carrying out the measure were sometimes used as well. Sexual violence against both men and women was widespread; it especially served to humiliate the victim and could go as far as rape. Whilst at the start of the conflict torture was primarily used to extract information, from May 2011 onwards the detention facilities were less interested in gathering intelligence and more in breaking actual or alleged members of the opposition, deterring them from engaging in further activities and thereby stifling the protest movement.

[54] The detention facilities in the Greater Damascus area included the military hospitals in Tishreen (also known as "607"), Harasta and Mezzeh (also known as "601"). Prior to the conflict, they had only ever been used to treat soldiers and their relatives. When the protest movement started the military hospitals began to be repurposed and were then also used to house and ill-treat alleged opposition patients. Initially, the focus was still on treating these people, too, but from April 2011 the security forces and medical staff themselves increasingly began massively abusing the injured prisoners or demonstrators who were admitted. From 2012 the military hospitals had a twofold remit: besides units which provided conventional treatments which were reserved for those loyal to the regime, there were customised wards in which the admitted prisoners were shackled to hospital beds and tortured—in some cases to death. As a result, the civilian population

sometimes dreaded the military hospitals more than the prisons operated by the intelligence services.

[55] (cc) At the same time, the military hospitals formed an important part of the infrastructure for dealing with corpses. From March 2011 they continuously served as a collection point for deceased prisoners, who were documented by military physicians and photographers. The corpses of those prisoners who died in prisons and intelligence service facilities or who were killed on the street were taken to the military hospitals. The corpses—most of them naked or only clad in their underwear and bearing traces of malnourishment and/or torture—were amassed there together with the corpses of those who died in the military hospitals and were temporarily put in cold storage. As the number of corpses exceeded the capacities of the cold storage facilities, the bodies were soon simply laid out in large halls or courtyards. The dead were bureaucratically recorded: numbers designating the place of detention and death (generally the figure assigned to the intelligence service sub-branch) and a prisoner number were either written on a note which was stuck to the corpse or written onto the corpse's skin using a felt marker. A forensic expert employed by the hospitals wrote a brief report which generally recorded a false natural cause of death such as heart failure or respiratory arrest, issued the death certificates and himself included an additional registration number on the note or the deceased's body. Military photographers from the Military Police were then called in to take several photographs to document each of the corpses. The photographs and reports were then placed together in a dossier. This documentation system was to serve the purpose of government internal checks, specifically to make it possible to trace the fate of each prisoner and ensure that they were not released following payment of a bribe.

[56] At the start, at least 10 corpses a day were recorded in this way in Damascus alone, but that figure soon rose to at least 50 a day. After being catalogued in the manner described, the corpses were transported in refrigerated vehicles and trucks, sometimes on semitrailer trucks, from the collection points in Damascus and Rif Dimashq to mass graves dug specifically for this purpose in the surrounding region (Najha and al-Quteifa). After their origin had been documented once more by administrative officials recruited to that end, the deceased were then tipped into the graves. This treatment of the killed civilians began in May 2011 at the latest when the numbers of victims of the conflict rose significantly.

[57] (dd) Given the lack of reliable counts, the dynamic developments and the lack of neutral observers, it is not possible to determine

precisely how many civilians died, were injured, imprisoned or suffered harm in another way during various phases of the conflict on account of state measures carried out by the Syrian security authorities. The Division bases its assessment, in the Defendant's favour, on figures which are at the lower end of the available estimates. According to these estimates, at least 2,000 civilians died between the start of the conflict and July 2011 and at least 5,000 civilians died in the period between the start of the conflict and December 2011. By May 2012 more than 10,000 people had died during the unrest. Multiples of these numbers of people were abducted from demonstrations, checkpoints, from work, their home or from hospital and taken to prisons operated by the intelligence services, where they were systematically subjected to, in some cases, the most serious abuse using the established torture methods. The number of dead continued to increase throughout 2012 as the conflict continued.

(d) Summary
[58] As has been established (see section A.II.1 [General political and social development in Syria up until 2011]), the foundation for the Syrian regime's course of action against the growing protest movement after February 2011 had already been laid in the 1970s on the basis of the established autocratic political system in Syria which was backed by an extensive and repressive security apparatus. The political leadership had sufficient forces at its disposal within the army, intelligence services and paramilitary units so as to be able to take violent action across the whole of the country against citizens who were critical of the government. The political system was geared to just that; it had for decades already been oppressing the political opposition and, in isolated cases, imposing violent "penal measures" to which a large number of people fell victim. Extrajudicial detention facilities were available across the country, and methods for controlling business and society and the police-state persecution and torture of individual activists were trialled.
[59] As has also been established (see section A.II.2 [Start of the conflict in Syria and its course from early 2011 to mid-2012]), the protest movement was met with tried and tested repressive measures as soon as the "Arab Spring" crossed over into Syria in February 2011, although the security authorities initially limited themselves to violently dispersing demonstrations and making arbitrary arrests in what were, at that time, still isolated incidents. In late April 2011 at the latest the protests spilled across the whole of the country, and rallies were at any rate held in the provincial capitals. At the same time, the measures

applied by the security authorities were massively extended both in terms of quality and quantity in that they were able to "break up" demonstrations by violent means, that is including the fatal use of firearms, and to make extensive arrests, up to thousands per day, and then to subsequently torture those detained in the various detention facilities. Checks and arrests were also made at the countrywide network of checkpoints; entire urban districts which were regarded as oppositional were violently brought under control by being sealed off and raided. Violence was not only used in isolated and random cases, but also as part of a wide-ranging strategy aimed at bringing the Syrian civilian population into line and "educating" it to be loyal to the government. This use of violence was organised and planned on the basis of the decisions taken in April by the highest executive body (the CCMC), which was established to that end; the decisions relating to the use of force, the making of arrests and the ill-treatment of those detained were implemented by being passed down the government hierarchy as far as those who were required to execute the relevant measures.

[60] In anticipation of its legal assessment (see section C.I.1 [Widespread and systematic attack directed against a civilian population]), taking the above findings as a whole the Division sees a wide variety of facts and circumstances which constitute an attack against the Syrian civilian population such that they were linked to the killing, extralegal deprivation of liberty and torture of a large number of civilians. This attack served to shore up the Syrian government and was used as a means of retaining power and suppressing anti-government political endeavours. In the light of the centralised decisions adopted by the CCMC, this attack was also both systematic and widespread as of late April 2011 at the latest.

3. Branch 251 and Sub-branch 40 of the Syrian General Intelligence Directorate

[61] (a) Before the conflict began, the remit of the General Intelligence Directorate (also known colloquially as "State Security") encompassed counterintelligence, surveillance of the Syrian population at home and abroad, monitoring the Syrian business sector, fighting corruption and surveillance of foreign institutions in Syria. As from the spring of 2011 its focus turned to "counterterrorism", which was interpreted to mean the suppression of oppositional groups and groups critical of the regime. The agency initially had between 10,000 and 30,000 full-time employees. The Directorate was divided into

12 central units in Damascus—a central branch and 11 special branches—plus 13 regional branches. Branches subordinate to the General Intelligence Directorate included Branch 251, which is the subject of the present proceedings, and a training academy in Najha, a suburb of Damascus, analysis, technology and counterintelligence branches, and a central investigation branch (also known as "Branch 285"). The latter was located in the centre of Damascus, in the district of Kafr Sousa. From 16 July 2005 to 24 July 2012 the General Intelligence Directorate was headed by Major General Ali Mamlouk and then from 24 July 2012 by Major General Dib Zaitoun.

[62] Branch 251 was one of the branches of the General Intelligence Directorate based in Damascus with responsibility for the "internal security" of the governorates of Damascus and Rif Dimashq. It had between 2,500 and 3,000 employees. After the outbreak of the conflict it was in effect responsible for combating protests in this area, for carrying out the majority of the waves of arrests in Damascus and Rif Dimashq and putting up road blocks in these areas. Branch 251 is located in the built-up city centre of Damascus, on Baghdad Street close to the Red Crescent Hospital. It covers an extensive area which is bounded either by walls or road blocks and includes a spacious garden area and car park. Because it is located in the al-Khatib district of the city it is also known informally to locals as the "Al-Khatib Branch". Branch 251 essentially comprises two at least three-storey buildings on either side of an inner courtyard which house offices and interrogation rooms.

[63] In 2011 and 2012 at any rate there was a prison in the basement of one of the buildings belonging to Branch 251 which had several communal cells measuring between 10 and 40 square metres plus small single cells measuring no more than 1 by 2 metres. There were also recreational rooms for the prison guards, interrogation rooms and an open interrogation area in the basement. In early 2012 the prison was extended to include subterranean rooms underneath the garden in order to create additional room for the number of prisoners, which grew rapidly in the period after March 2011. The officers' offices and interrogation rooms were, by contrast, located in the upper storeys of Branch 251, to which the prisoners were taken from the prison tract. In 2011 and 2012 Branch 251 was headed by Major General Tawfiq Younes. The former Co-Defendant . . . [K] was head of Branch 251's Interrogation (Sub-)Branch until 2012.

[64] Sub-branch 40 was formally assigned and subordinate to Branch 251. It acted as a rapid response unit in the field and was deployed to carry out raids, set up and operate checkpoints, make

arrests, conduct house searches and, especially in the further course of 2011, to break up demonstrations critical of the regime ("sweep and thug squad"); its jurisdiction covered the governorates of Damascus and Rif Dimashq. Despite formally being a sub-branch, it enjoyed a certain degree of autonomy as it was headed by Hafez Makhlouf, a maternal cousin of Bashar al-Assad who had especially close ties with the highest decision-making echelons of the Syrian regime. Although it was officially under the command of Branch 251, the sub-branch operated largely independently. It had its own office building in the Jisr al-Abyad district of Damascus and its own detention facility. It provided assistance to Branch 251, primarily by transporting prisoners there. Staff were handpicked; key requirements made of those employed there were physical fitness and loyalty to the regime.

[65] (b) When Sub-branch 40 was deployed to deal with demonstrations and other protests, to conduct house searches and at checkpoints, some of those detained were taken to its own premises for a short time, where they were regularly exposed to both interrogation and ill-treatment. After remaining there for a short while (though rarely for more than one day) in transit, as it were, they were then taken to Branch 251, where they faced torture and longer periods of detention. In other cases, those arrested by Sub-branch 40 were taken straight to Branch 251 and left under its control, often after having been abused in the buses used to transport them.

[66] On arrival in Branch 251, the detainees were driven into the courtyard between the two parts of the building and the overwhelming majority of them were forced to run the gauntlet of massive abuse after disembarking; often they were maltreated with baton- and whip-like implements for long periods of up to several hours. Some of them already died at this point. Staff cynically called this introductory treatment a "welcome party". The abducted were then taken or pushed into the prison cellar, where they were forced to undress and were searched—including rectally—for hidden objects.

[67] The detainees were held in the basement of Branch 251; men and women were housed separately, mainly in communal cells, though from April 2011 onwards these were so overcrowded that those detained there could only sleep in rotation, huddled together and staggered on the floor; sometimes they were forced to stand. Often the only source of fresh air in the cells, which were either not or only entirely insufficiently ventilated, was the gap under the cell door. This meant that detainees were only able to breathe in extremely stifling air or even suffered oxygen deficiency. The cells either had only a single toilet with a water flush which was not partitioned off, or detainees

were taken to the toilet by guards at specific predetermined times. Some cells had a skylight up into the courtyard, whilst others only had artificial lighting which was never switched off, meaning that detainees were unable to tell day from night. Since they hardly had any opportunity to wash and change their clothes, the hygiene conditions were catastrophic. Pests such as lice were ever-present in the cells. Prisoners who were already injured when they arrived or who suffered injuries as a result of the torture inflicted received no or only inadequate medical care. Open wounds became infected; injuries and illnesses usually went untreated. Alternatively, detainees were placed in one of the very small single cells which measured only around 1 by 2 metres and into which two or more prisoners were often crammed together. Detainees were generally not given enough food to eat, which led to their rapidly losing weight and strength. Day and night they were exposed to the cries of pain of the other prisoners who were being tortured in neighbouring interrogation rooms or in open areas. Prisoners who were led out of the communal cell regularly returned with injuries and visible signs of torture. This and the uncertainty about their own fate meant prisoners were under enormous mental strain, which went as far as persistent existential mortal fear.

[68] The fear of being subjected to ill-treatment generally proved well-founded, as, after a waiting period, each new prisoner was taken to at least one interrogation either in the prison area or one of the interrogation officers' offices in the upper storeys of the building, where they were then subjected to torture. In the majority of cases this meant being beaten on the soles of the feet with a belt or cable (known as *fallaqa*), which caused swelling and lacerations as well as extreme pain walking (which detainees were then forced to do by the guards), being hung up by the wrists (known as *shabeh*), electric shocks, burning and scalding, arbitrary beatings with or without implements and being kicked all over the body. Often, the ill-treatment did not end when detainees made (false) confessions or had information extorted from them, either because they did not have the desired information or because the ill-treatment, a form of humiliation and deterrent, was an end in itself. Prison guards also administered beatings without cause or because prisoners broke the rules, for instance if they talked without permission to do so. On some occasions men as well as women were also subjected to sexual violence in the form of rape or touching or beating of their sexual organs; threats of sexual violence against spouses or family members were also issued. Only those prisoners who were deliberately arrested alone, who were well-known celebrities or personally known to staff were, in exceptional cases, spared such direct physical abuse.

[69] Relatives were not notified where family members were being detained. Nor were detainees themselves told how long they would be detained. They were also regularly left in the dark about what charges were actually being brought against them and the reason for their detention.

[70] (c) According to their jurisdiction and actual activities, as of the spring of 2011 Branch 251 and Sub-branch 40 were closely involved in suppressing the protest movement. Along with other intelligence services, they formed an integral part of the Syrian regime's violent strategy: They arrested masses of alleged or actual opponents of the regime, disbanded demonstrations, arbitrarily abducted demonstrators and systematically tortured them.

4. Defendant's contribution to the offence

(a) Defendant's function within the Syrian intelligence service: Conduct prior to the offence

[71] The Defendant joined the Syrian general intelligence service on 10 July 1996, at the age of 20. He first underwent basic training at the training base in Najha, a suburb of Damascus, in the General Intelligence Directorate's Branch 295. Besides undergoing physical training, he was instructed in the fundamentals of basic military operations and the use of various weapons systems, including pistols, sniper rifles and explosives. After one and a half years (i.e. from early 1998) he himself worked as a trainer until February 2010. In 2004 and 2005 he underwent "counterterrorism" training which was supported by Russian military experts, during which he was taught how to storm buildings in big cities, how to construct and combat ambushes, engage in street fighting, kidnap armed and unarmed people, make arrests and provide personal security.

[72] From February 2010 the Defendant was assigned to Branch 251 of the General Intelligence Directorate. He was at least predominantly deployed in the Branch's main site on Baghdad Street in Damascus. He was first employed in the "Religious Branch", where he was responsible for information-gathering in mosques, amongst other things. The objective was to investigate the political attitudes of the imams preaching there and what those attending the mosque said—possibly against the government; these spying activities included collecting other personal information about those attending events there. The Defendant wrote reports about this work which were passed to his superiors for further use. He then spent five months working in one of the sub-branches assigned to the city of Al-Zabadani, in the Rif

Dimashq governorate, where he did office work. As this work bored him, he returned, at his own request, to the "Religious Branch" for two months. After this he was transferred to Sub-branch 40, where he served from July 2011 until he deserted on 5 January 2012. The Defendant belonged to a unit of the sub-branch which was deployed mainly in Douma, at least for a time.

[73] During his many years in the Syrian general intelligence service, when he primarily served in various sub-branches of Branch 251, the Defendant became well-acquainted with the modus operandi of the Syrian intelligence services, especially of Branch 251. The Defendant knew that, even before the start of the Arab Spring in February 2011, the intelligence services were used both as a means to spy on the civilian population and for the purpose of political repression. He was aware of what Branch 251 was tasked with, of the buildings located on Baghdad Street, including the subterranean prison, of the conditions of detention there and the fact that prisoners were tortured to extort information or simply as a means of intimidation. The Defendant also knew that conditions in the branch had drastically deteriorated for its prisoners after March 2011 because extensive arbitrary arrests were being made, a large number of previous prisoners were then being detained in the facility and they were systematically ill-treated there, in particular that they were subjected to the arbitrary behaviour of the violent guards and to torture. Finally, the Defendant was not unaware that, from late April 2011 at the latest, a wide-ranging attack to suppress the Syrian oppositional movement and intimidate the population by violently intervening in demonstrations, with many resulting injured and dead and mass arrests was in train and was being controlled by the leadership of the security authorities. It cannot be ruled out that the Defendant maintained a certain inner distance to all that was going on, but he nevertheless continued in his job in order to earn his living.

(b) Contribution to the offence in September/October 2011
[74] In September or October 2011 a demonstration attended by around 3,000 to 6,000 demonstrators was held near the Al-Kabeer Mosque in the city of Douma south of Damascus. The demonstrators were peaceful; they sat on the road or danced. Some 1,000 security forces were deployed to keep them under control, including members of the Ministry of the Interior, the Air Force Intelligence Directorate and various sub-branches of Branch 251. Sub-branch 40 sent some 250 men, including the Defendant, who was equipped with a firearm.

[75] The members of Sub-branch 40 at any rate were ordered to shoot at the demonstrators, to pursue and arrest them. Hafez Makhlouf himself arrived in an off-road vehicle, hurled insults at the demonstrators, told the security staff, "If you love the President, you'll shoot these traitors" and then himself started firing his automatic pistol. He hit at least five people, at least three of whom died. Intelligence service staff also began to shoot at the demonstrators. The Defendant did not follow suit, but backed off a little. The demonstrators thereupon attempted to flee. The security forces, including the Defendant, pursued them, combed the streets, arrested many of the demonstrators and put them on buses which were ready and waiting.

[76] A total of 30 demonstrators were then transported from Douma to Branch 251 in Damascus in a convoy of at least two buses; the Defendant accompanied and secured the journey. Many of those arrested were already beaten whilst in the buses; it was not possible to establish whether the Defendant participated in this. Once they arrived in the courtyard of Branch 251, the detainees were forced off the bus and severely beaten on their way into the building; amongst other things, they were beaten with metal pipes by new recruits. The Division was also unable to establish whether the Defendant himself ill-treated the detained demonstrators.

[77] The detainees were held in Branch 251 by force for a minimum of several days; all of them were tortured during their stay there. Besides the violence which without exception they all had to endure immediately on arrival in Branch 251, during their subsequent internment and interrogations the overwhelming majority were subjected to systematic physical violence, that is beatings all over their body and to the soles of their feet with implements, which caused significant pain. The conditions of detention were typical for the branch: the prisoners were all held in the subterranean cells, some of which had no daylight, in extremely cramped conditions, without sufficient food, under catastrophic hygiene conditions in pest-infected rooms, without the means to engage in personal hygiene and with only limited opportunity to relieve themselves. They were all forced to endure listening, at all times of the day and night, to the cries of pain and the entreaties of others who were being tortured in neighbouring interrogation rooms. None of the prisoners was told why they were being detained and for how long. Each of the prisoners was left entirely in the dark as to their future fate, especially when it would be their "turn" to be subjected to brutal mistreatment, the effects of which they constantly saw in others. None of them knew whether

and, if so, when they would leave the prison alive again. Their relatives were not informed of their fate.

[78] Just like their subsequent detention, which lasted at least several days, the demonstrators' arrest was also arbitrary, without individualised grounds and an order which met minimum rule-of-law standards. Neither was the justification for their detention reviewed by an independent body during their imprisonment. The sole basis for these arrests were catch-all instructions issued by the executive (i.e. the security authorities) to break up demonstrations by force and detain those taking part to prevent further oppositional endeavours.

[79] As he was a member of Sub-branch 40, which was tasked with suppressing the opposition movement and was deployed as a rapid response and arrest unit, the Defendant knew that the purpose of the operation against the demonstration was to arbitrarily arrest and abduct those taking part. He was aware that he would be required to take demonstrators to "his" Branch 251. Based on his many years of working in Branch 251 and the building it occupied and what he had become aware was going on there, he knew what awaited the demonstrators there, in particular that they would be subjected to systematic physical abuse, atrocious detention conditions and extreme mental stress, which began with brutal beatings during the customary "welcome party". Finally, the Defendant was also aware that there was no procedure which could even approximately have provided a rule-of-law basis to legitimise the demonstrators' imprisonment. Owing to the political situation and events in Syria, which were generally known, in particular, though, on account of his intelligence service activities, the Defendant knew that this incident was part of a series of attacks being carried out across the country from late April 2011 against civilian demonstrators and alleged or actual members of the opposition. And this notwithstanding the fact that he had begun to tell his relatives that he disassociated himself from the Syrian regime.

[80] In order to be able to continue his work in the intelligence service, which secured his own and his family's living, the Defendant became reconciled to participating in putting down the demonstration and arresting the demonstrators. He was not faced with any subjective dilemma, but freely chose to stay in his job until he deserted several months after the incident. Notwithstanding this, had he been willing not to participate in the act, the Defendant would have had sufficient opportunity to do so. For instance, he could have feigned illness after receiving orders relating to the operation, or either feigned indisposition or an injury whilst the operation was ongoing. In contrast to, for instance, ordinary soldiers, who were

constantly under surveillance during operations against demonstrations, especially by the intelligence services, the Defendant also had the opportunity, on account of his freedom of movement during the demonstration and in the adjoining streets, to make off and turn his back on the intelligence service.

(c) Conduct after the fact
[81] The Defendant continued his active service in Sub-branch 40 until he deserted on 5 January 2012. Early one morning around late 2011/early 2012 he escorted an armed convoy of refrigerated trucks transporting around 50 to 60 corpses to a mass grave near Najha in the vicinity of Damascus. After passing checkpoints, the corpses, the majority of which at any rate were people who had died in intelligence service prisons and branches, were thrown into a mass grave which had been excavated by a digger.

B. EVALUATION OF EVIDENCE

I. Statements by the Defendant

[82] At the main hearing the Defendant testified neither as to his person nor as to the substance of the case. He did, however, have his defence counsel submit a statement to the Division which he himself had written. Before the preliminary investigation was instituted, he had made statements—including self-incriminating statements—during his hearing before the Federal Office for Migration and Refugees (*Bundesamt für Migration und Flüchtlinge*, BAMF) and during subsequent questioning as a witness by the Federal Criminal Police Office (*Bundeskriminalamt*, BKA). More specifically:

1. Defendant's written statement

[83] During the main hearing on 9 December 2020, the Defendant had his defence counsel submit a three-page handwritten statement he had drafted to the Division. In that statement he detailed the impression which the "Caesar Files" had made on him, that is photographs (which had previously been inspected in the main hearing) depicting dead people, most of whom had previously been tortured and were emaciated. He also addressed the question of why, in his opinion, it had not been possible to break with the intelligence service at an earlier point in time. The Defendant did not permit any follow-up questions to his statement.

[84] In essence, the Defendant submitted the following in writing:

The Defendant thanked the forensic expert for his remarkable work and detailed description of the physical and mental torture which the prisoners had suffered. He also thanked the Syrian hero given the alias "Caesar" for his involvement in exposing the crimes committed by the Assad regime and his sectarian gangs. The images were upsetting, shocking, painful and extremely frightening, he wrote. They had pained and saddened his heart. During the presentation his whole body had shaken in shock and grief for the victims, the Defendant wrote. Anger and hate towards the criminal Assad regime and all his helpers had filled his head and his heart. Sometimes he had had to avert his gaze. The Defendant gave his assurance that he had never before seen 99% of the images shown in the courtroom; the remaining 1% he had seen on Al-Jazeera or other Arab news broadcasters. He wrote that he had to think about those of his relatives who had been detained in the regime's prisons since the start of the revolution. Seven of his relatives, dozens of his people and hundreds of citizens of his hometown Muhasan had been taken to prison; he was not aware of the fate of any of them since then. The Defendant wrote that he had looked at the images in the courtroom and searched them for his relatives. On his way back to prison from the courthouse he had been overcome with grief and pain, he wrote; he had wept bitterly. The Defendant wrote that he had thought about the detainees, their families and the millions of Syrians who had been expelled merely because they had called for freedom, justice, equality and democracy. Bashar al-Assad and most of the members of his religious denomination, including civilians and mercenary troops from other countries, were the real criminals who were still committing their crimes against innocent Syrians. Like every Syrian, the Defendant, who loved his country and his people, wished that they—first and foremost the dictator Bashar al-Assad and his family—would be held to account by being brought before international courts.

[85] As far as his situation as a member of the Syrian security service was concerned, the Defendant wrote that he was no different from all the other members of the Sunni denomination: They were entirely powerless, especially since the start of the revolution in Syria. It was undisputed that 90% of the revolutionaries were members of the Sunni denomination, to which he also belonged. Since the outbreak of the revolution the regime had regarded them with distrust and as a constant threat, the Defendant wrote. Many "of us", he wrote, were kept away from important and sensitive posts or were removed from their posts. Many, including himself, had had their personal weapons and security passes taken away. Colleagues of other denominations had been ordered to monitor them at work, had watched their every step, every word, every look and even every breath, he wrote. They had waited for the merest indication that someone was aligned with the

revolution "so as to arrest us". He, and all the others who had been in a similar position, had therefore been left with only one of the following options:

– Openly defy orders given by superiors, as a consequence of which he would have been accused of refusal of duty and collaborating with demonstrators. The result of this course of action would have been imprisonment and, usually, execution.
– Dissociate himself from the regime and immediately flee without regard for his wife and four children. The result of this course of action would have been that his wife and children would have been arrested and tortured until he returned and was executed.
– The right and safest option for him and his family was to hold out for a few months until some regions were no longer under the control of the regime or until it was possible to cross the border into a neighbouring country, then to dissociate himself from the regime and secretly flee with his family.

[86] On 5 January 2012 the Defendant had chosen the latter option, he wrote. He asked whether his love for his wife and his children was a mistake for which he deserved to be punished.

2. Statements made in the asylum procedure

[87] The Defendant had already provided information—including that of a self-incriminatory nature—in the course of his asylum procedure, more specifically at his hearing on 9 May 2018 at the local branch of the Federal Office for Migration and Refugees in . . . [t]. This information was provided to the Division by Witness . . . [L] and Witness . . . [M], who conducted the hearing on behalf of the agency, and—as regards the accuracy of the translation—by Witness . . . [N], the interpreter used on that occasion. According to Witness . . . [N], there had been no difficulties communicating with the Defendant. The Division therefore has no reason to doubt that the Defendant gave the statements as reported by the witnesses and recorded in the transcript.

[88] (a) At his hearing the Defendant had first stated his denomination, his place of origin in Syria, his family circumstances, his school education and his places of residence up until he joined the Syrian intelligence service as set out in section A.I above (Findings as to the person of the Defendant).

[89] (b) From 10 July 1996 until 5 January 2012 he had, as he further stated, been a member of an intelligence service and had ultimately risen to the rank of sergeant major. Sometimes he had lived

in intelligence service accommodation. He had undergone two years of training in Najha, a suburb of Damascus. This had included weapons training, military strategy and physical fitness, he stated. He had been trained to use rifles and guns, including Russian "Mikarov" (the Division assumes that the reference here is to Russian "Makarov" pistols), weapons made by Braun (the reference here is possibly to "Browning"), a sniper rifle, various types of bombs and a bazooka. He had undergone training to become a trainer, he stated. This had included three days in the desert after which you either stayed out there or had to walk 120 kilometres without a break.

[90] The Defendant stated that he had then worked as a trainer in Najha up until 2010. Thereafter, that is up until he deserted in early 2012, he had been deployed in the intelligence Branch 251 on Baghdad Street in Damascus. He had first worked in the "Religious Branch" there. Over the course of five months he had learned about all the various religions in Syria and had been responsible for the districts of "Mukhain Al-Yarmouk, Palestine Road, Hajar al-Aswad and Al-Kadem" in Damascus. The Defendant stated that he had been responsible for information-gathering in all the mosques, in particular for finding out what was being taught in the mosques. He had attended Friday prayers to see what was being preached and to find out each imam's orientation ("strategy"), that is whether he was inciting protest against the government, for instance. He had also "recorded data" on people. He had handed over the reports he made about this to his superior in the branch, Lieutenant Colonel Kamal Al-Ahmad.

[91] The Defendant further stated that he worked for the "Al-Zabadani" Branch for a while. He had wanted to leave the job because "office work isn't really my thing". Lieutenant Colonel Kamal Al-Ahmad had wanted him to return to his branch, which he had then done for two months. After that he was "moved" to a "dangerous branch", Branch 40. He worked there, in the vicinity of Bashar al-Assad's home, from July 2011 up until 5 January 2012, he stated. The branch was like a Mafia-style grouping; once you were in, you could not leave. It was headed by Hafez Makhlouf, a cousin of Assad.

[92] When asked whether he himself had witnessed crimes, attacks or abuse, the Defendant replied that he had seen people being beaten (including on the head) as a result of which some of them had died. That had "also" been done by people in Branch 251. When people had emerged after Friday prayers and had demonstrated, the security forces had come on the scene. Hafez Makhlouf had shot and killed five people on one such occasion; that was in Douma in August or September 2011. Also, corpses had been transported away from the prison in "our

branch", he reported. It was underground in the "251 building". He himself had not been involved in this. Orders had been given by Brigadier General Tawfiq Younes, the Defendant said.

[93] (c) The Defendant stated that he deserted on 5 January 2012. As his motivation for doing so and also as his grounds for seeking asylum, the Defendant stated that he had been ordered by the intelligence service to kill civilians. He was required to arrest demonstrators, in particular to drag the ringleaders of the demonstrations into a car and take them away. In late 2011 he had been ordered to fight civilians who were supposedly against the government and armed. Three of his colleagues had already died doing so. The Defendant stated that he had not wanted to kill any of his compatriots and had decided to go to Deir ez-Zor.

[94] In January 2012, the Defendant stated, he therefore first fled to Muhasan, his home village, where he had gone into hiding for six months, moving house every day or two. His wife and his children had remained in Damascus; "they" (the reference here is obviously to members of the intelligence service) had made unofficial enquiries with his wife and his brother. The intelligence service had also found out that he, the Defendant, was staying in his home village. One of his brothers and one of his brothers-in-law had then helped his wife leave Damascus and go to "Qudsaya", where she had gone into hiding in an uncle's house. Attempts had been made to arrest his wife; she had then used a cousin's identity card to go to be with the Defendant. He himself had learned from a cousin about threats which had been made by the intelligence service; this had, ultimately, been the reason why he had decided to leave the country. When his parents' house was to be attacked from the air, he had fled with his family to the village of Abo Hassan. When asked why he had chosen to go back to his home village, which was known to the intelligence services, the Defendant replied that the government had not known that his parents' house was in Muhasan.

[95] The Defendant stated that after he had left the village, his parents' house had in fact been shot at, but not been hit. He himself had seen this, he said. When asked, the Defendant stated that he returned to the village after having taken his family to safety because the house in Abo Hassan was too small for all of them.

[96] (d) Lastly, the Defendant stated that he left Syria on 12 February 2013. After that he spent three years in the "Haran" refugee camp in Turkey and entered Greece on 20 February 2016. He spent two years, two months and four days in a camp near Thessaloniki without filing an asylum application there, he said. Both

his leaving to go to Turkey and his journey from Turkey to Greece had
been organised by a people smuggler.

3. Police questioning as a witness

[97] The Defendant was, moreover, questioned as a witness on
16 August 2018 as part of a structural investigation
(*Strukturermittlungsverfahren*) conducted by the Federal Public
Prosecutor's Office (*Bundesanwaltschaft*) into unknown offenders on
suspicion of a violation of the German Code of Crimes against
International Law (*Völkerstraf-gesetzbuch*, VStGB) in connection with
the civil war in Syria. The circumstances and content of this police
questioning, in particular the Defendant's statement, were relayed to
the Division by investigators ... [O] and ... [P], who are witnesses in
the present proceedings, and by the interpreter employed on that
occasion, Witness ... [Q]. On that basis, the Division came to the
firm conviction that the Defendant testified during his questioning by
the police as set out in the following. In particular, according to
Witness ... [Q], there were no problems communicating with him.
The information which the Defendant provided for the record was
translated back for him from German to Arabic; he made some
handwritten corrections to the translation.

[98] (a) The particulars which the Defendant furnished as regards
his childhood and youth were identical to those he had previously
furnished during his hearing before the Federal Office for Migration
and Refugees. Regarding his relatives he stated that one of his sisters
still lives in Damascus.

[99] (b) The Defendant stated that he joined the intelligence service
on 10 September 1996. He worked in the General Intelligence
Directorate, also known as "State Security". The Defendant stated that
he was based at Kafr Sousa in Damascus. The Defendant further
provided information about his training and deployment up until
February 2010 as presented in section A.I above (Findings as to the
person of the Defendant), particularly in relation to his basic training
and work as a trainer. The Defendant described himself as a very good
trainer. This was the reason why he was allowed to continue working as
a trainer for a long time, he stated. He had mainly instructed trainees as
part of their "physical training". The Defendant revealed that he had
been a tough trainer: "You had to force people to put up with more."
But that was not all he had done. He underwent "counterterrorism"
training, for which he received an award, he stated. The training was
watched over by "Russian experts". He was taught

how to storm buildings, even multi-storey ones. That included storming buildings in big cities with large populations and out in the countryside. We were trained to identify and combat ambushes, as well as to set them up ourselves. We were trained how to kidnap both armed and unarmed people and to make arrests. We also learned how to protect important people.

[100] Conducting interrogations had not been part of his training, the Defendant stated. That had been the task of the investigation branches, in particular Branch 285.

[101] In February 2010, the Defendant stated, he transferred to Branch 251, also known as the "Internal Branch" or "Al-Khatib". It was located on Baghdad Street in the al-Khatib district of Damascus, opposite the Red Crescent Hospital. He had performed his duties in various sub-branches of Branch 251. He was first deployed in the "Religions" unit, which was based in the building on Baghdad Street. He spent one month working in the sub-branch responsible for Zabadani, possibly in June 2011, he stated. At that point the unrest had already been ongoing for three months. He had not liked working in the branch, which was why he had applied to be transferred back to the "Religions" unit. In July 2011, the Defendant stated, he had then, finally, "moved" to Sub-branch 40. This was in Jisr al-Abyad in Damascus.

[102] The Defendant provided details about Branch 251 in the "al-Khatib" district of Damascus on Baghdad Street, specifically how the buildings were arranged and the location of the subterranean prison in the basement of one of the buildings. He stated that the sub-branch for religions was located in the building opposite. The Defendant described the location of various other sub-branches and the site of an ammunitions depot in the group of buildings. The two buildings were around 8 metres apart; there was a cafeteria situated between them. "Before the war," the Defendant stated, the buildings were secured by two barriers, and afterwards more extensively. Further, the Defendant provided the names of the heads of some of the branches in January 2012.

[103] (c) As regards the overall political situation and the work of the intelligence services, the Defendant stated that "the intelligence services had committed crimes against humanity even before the start of the unrest". Other religions had been discriminated against in the intelligence services; Sunnis in particular had always been disadvantaged or punished more severely for less serious offences. Road blocks were put up in August 2011, he stated. After the start of the unrest, orders had been issued to shoot and kill civilian demonstrators. The Defendant stated that the regime maintained contacts with Islamist groups such as Jund al-Sham, a militia in Lebanon.

[104] The regime used "tricks", the Defendant stated. In late 2011, for example, a delegation of the Arab League was supposed to visit the prisons. Upon the orders of the head of the branch, Tawfiq Younes, its inmates had been relocated and the prison had been filled with staff members who were to pretend to be prisoners. Weapons had also been "planted" on demonstrators so as to justify the regime's actions. Members of the intelligence service were taken to a hospital, the Defendant stated, where bandages were applied to them to make them look like they were injured. The aim was to suggest that they had been attacked by demonstrators. Media representatives had interviewed the alleged injured in the Al-Mujtahid Hospital, he reported.

[105] (d) The Defendant stated the following as regards core aspects of the offence as established:

[106] Orders were issued to shoot and kill civilian demonstrators. He was in Sub-branch 40 when he received them, he said. This was in 2011, possibly in September or October. There had been demonstrations by the Al-Kabeer Mosque. The demonstrators had planned not to allow themselves to be dispersed. They sat on the road, although some also danced. They remained peaceful. There had been chants of "Bashar go home" and "The people want to bring down the regime".

[107] The Defendant had, he stated, seen with his own eyes how the head of his sub-branch, Hafez Makhlouf, had pulled up and got out of his Mercedes off-road vehicle; he had thrown insults at the demonstrators and then shot at them with an automatic pistol, using up an entire round of shots. Five people were hit; three of them had immediately slumped down dead and another two had at any rate been close to death. Others were injured and were able to flee. The dead were taken to the Red Crescent Hospital, the Defendant stated. Hafez Makhlouf ordered everyone to use their weapons. He said: "If you love the President, you'll shoot the traitors." Six or seven people who were directly subordinate to him had then opened fire.

[108] There had been a total of between 3,000 and 6,000 demonstrators and 1,000 members of the security forces, including around 250 from Sub-branch 40, the Defendant stated. They had been joined by members of other sub-branches, in particular the sub-branch responsible for Douma commanded by Samer Breidi, plus people from the Air Force Intelligence Directorate and the Ministry of the Interior.

[109] The Defendant stated that he had not shot at the demonstrators but had stepped back so that nobody would notice. Together with others ("we") he had combed the streets when the demonstrators "scarpered". It was especially those who had wanted to film something on their mobile phone who had been taken away. Lots of

demonstrators were arrested and later died, he stated. People who had had nothing to do with the demonstration were also arrested. They were taken to Branch 251 in buses and were already beaten on their way from the site of the demonstration to the branch's offices, he said. The buses had parked between the two buildings. "Most of the deaths" had occurred in front of the Branch 251 building. New recruits, amongst others, armed with metal pipes were deployed there, and they had beaten those arrested on their way from where the bus was parked into the building. The demonstrators, stooped and hooded, were walked to the subterranean prison by the recruits. The Defendant stated that he was present at the demonstration and during the demonstrators' transportation and admission and himself saw everything. "When the buses came for the demonstrators the beatings weren't so bad. It wasn't until [they] arrived at Branch 251 that they were severely beaten." It had been the security forces and his colleagues who had beaten the demonstrators on the buses; he had not joined in, he said.

[110] Once the demonstrators had arrived at Branch 251 they were taken into the basement, and most of them had not come out again, the Defendant stated. Some of them were transferred to Branch 285, especially when the prison was overcrowded. Before the start of the conflict, detainees were taken straight to court.

[111] (e) Regarding the torture and abuse of prisoners in Branch 251, the Defendant further reported that after the start of the unrest in October 2011 he had himself once been in the prison in Branch 251. People screaming and crying on account of being tortured could be heard in the prison. The Defendant stated the following in this regard: "The torture did not stop until the prisoner passed out." The head of the prison, Abu Ali, was responsible for the torture. The Defendant had not spoken about the torture with his colleague, ... [R], who had shown him around the prison. "It was normality. Even when dead people were brought out of the prison, that was nothing special." When asked, the Defendant stated that he had seen dead bodies being brought out of the prison in Branch 251 both before and after the start of the unrest. For instance, one dead body had been taken out of the prison and another person had been beaten over the head and killed with a metal bar after getting off a bus. This was one or two months before he was deployed at the demonstration in Douma in September or October 2011.

[112] The screams of those being tortured could even be heard in the branch's cafeteria because they were very loud, the Defendant stated. People had been arrested and tortured even before the start of the unrest: "Before the unrest, when someone had taken part in a

demonstration they were taken to the prison and their back was scalded with a water kettle. There were always electrocutions. That's how it was in all the branches." When asked what had changed in the prison after the start of the unrest, the Defendant explained that the punishments had become more severe and the guards had been able to do what they wanted. The prisoners had been tortured in the branch until they were transferred elsewhere. Sometimes the guards had taken prisoners upstairs, where they were meant to shout that they revered the President. After April 2011, prisoners often had their leg broken so that they could not go back to demonstrating, the Defendant stated.

[113] The prison in the basement, which measured between 300 and 400 square metres, was designed to hold 100 prisoners; in actual fact there were 400 or more people in it. The Defendant stated that he had worked this out based on the number of people who arrived there and the number of buses. They had arrived "sometimes (...) on a daily basis, sometimes twice a day". Other people who were arrested were also put in the prison. He had sporadically seen people being released, he said. Between April 2011 and mid-May 2011, those who were arrested on a Friday were already released on Saturday or Sunday. Prisoners were transferred to Branch 285 two or three times a week "when our prison was full".

[114] (f) The Defendant stated that he deserted in January 2012. He returned to Deir ez-Zor and stayed with relatives in Muhasan until February 2013. Sometime between 9 and 13 February 2013 he illegally crossed the Syrian-Turkish border and then stayed in a refugee camp near Urfa. On 20 February 2016 he left Turkey and went to Greece, where he stayed until 25 April 2018. He then flew from Athens to Germany. He was given an entry visa because an underage son of his was living in Germany.

4. *Admissibility*

[115] The Division considers the statements the Defendant made during his hearing before the Federal Office for Migration and Refugees on 9 May 2018 to be fully admissible. In the opinion of the Division, the statements he made during his police questioning as a witness on 16 August 2018 are partly admissible; the Division used the statements up to and including those in the first paragraph on page 13 of the transcript of the interview as the basis for its assessment and has therefore only rendered these in the above.

[116] (a) Pursuant to section 8(3) sentence 1 no 3 of the Asylum Act (*Asylgesetz*, AsylG), the statements which the Defendant made

during his hearing before the Federal Office for Migration and Refugees may on principle be used in the criminal proceedings. There was also no failure to inform the Defendant of his rights which would result in his statements being inadmissible.

[117] The Division considers the statements which the Defendant made during his hearing to be insufficient in and of themselves to establish an initial suspicion which would have made him appear to be accused of concrete offences and which could have meant—that is, if the relevant duties to give instructions had applied—that he should have been informed of his rights, in particular as to the charge made against him, his being at liberty to testify and his right to consult defence counsel. The job which he admitted to having done whilst working in Sub-branch 40 of the Syrian General Intelligence Directorate is not sufficient in that regard. Besides, the hearing conducted as part of the asylum procedure does not constitute an examination which can be enforced with means of compulsion pursuant to provisions under the law of criminal procedure, in particular sections 55, 136, 161 and 163a of the Code of Criminal Procedure (*Strafprozeßordnung*, StPO). This is on account of the purpose of such a hearing, which serves to assert the individual rights of a person seeking asylum and thus in principle differs from the purpose of hearings conducted as part of criminal proceedings. It is only to that extent that someone is under the (non-enforceable) obligation to cooperate (see section 15(2) no 1, section 25(1) sentence 1 of the Asylum Act), which does not encompass the obligation to incriminate oneself with facts relevant to criminal law matters. Therefore, even based on a broad, functional definition of what an "examination" is, this does not constitute an examination by the state in the course of which facts which could be detrimental in criminal proceedings could be inadmissible if sufficient instruction was not given (see Decisions of the Federal Court of Justice in Criminal Matters (BGHSt) 36, 328; Bavarian Higher Regional Court *NStZ* 2020, 684; Düsseldorf Higher Regional Court *NStZ* 1992, 349; Hamm Higher Regional Court *NStZ* 1989, 187; Gleß, in: Löwe-Rosenberg, *StPO*, 27th ed., section 136 margin no 12, with further references).

[118] (b) The Division considers the statements which the Defendant made during his police questioning on 16 August 2018, that is up to and including the first paragraph on page 13 of the transcript, to be admissible, even though the Defendant had up until that point not been instructed about the fact that he could possibly have the status of an accused but was merely questioned as a witness. Up until that point in the police interview, the level of suspicion raised

against him had not grown to such an extent that the prosecuting authorities, in particular officers ... [P] and ... [O], who conducted the questioning, would have had to question him as an accused and inform him of his rights. No facts came to light during the main hearing which could justify any other assessment.

[119] The Division thus follows the principles established by the Federal Court of Justice and their application to this matter (Federal Court of Justice, Order of 6 June 2019—StB 14/19; Decisions of the Federal Court of Justice in Criminal Matters 64, 89). The Division sees no reason, either in fact or in law, to assume any inadmissibility beyond that. In particular, there were no indications to suggest that either the Federal Public Prosecutor's Office or the Federal Criminal Police Office was intending to prosecute the Defendant, which would have been contrary to his status as a witness, consequently that the investigating officers deliberately deceived the Defendant as to his status as an accused. From an objective point of view, too, there is no evidence that there were any other indications that the Defendant had the status of an accused before the point in time assumed in the aforementioned ruling from which he should have been informed that he was an accused.

[120] The Division heard Witness ... [P] and Witness ... [O] in their capacity as the police investigators leading the Federal Criminal Police Office's investigation in this regard. They reported on the context in which the police questioning was conducted, the course of the investigation and what they knew at various stages. By their own account, up until the start of the interview there had only been unspecific indications and these solely resulted from what the Defendant had said during his hearing before the Federal Office for Migration and Refugees on 9 May 2018. There was no further evidence or proof that the Defendant had committed any concrete offences, they testified. In particular, it had not been possible to deduce any from the intelligence service passes which he had presented in the asylum procedure. Accordingly, as the witnesses stated, the purpose of the police interview had not been to question the Defendant as an offender and to convict him. Rather, the primary objective had been to gather information about the tasks, structures and responsibilities of Branch 251 and Sub-branch 40 of the General Intelligence Directorate and about the local situation, conditions and procedures applied within Branch 251. It was only in the course of the questioning—about the content and status of which the Federal Public Prosecutor's representative was informed—that the Defendant had provided more and more details about his involvement in arresting demonstrators and their fate after arriving at Branch 251.

[121] The files confirm the witnesses' account as regards the state of the investigation. To the Division's knowledge, objectively speaking, no concrete suspicions which could have led to the assumption that the Defendant had been involved in criminal activities were available before the police questioning began. Based on the evidence available to it, the Division also shares the assessment that the suspicion that the Defendant may have had the status of an accused had only deepened in the course of the police questioning. It assumes this occurred from the point at which the Defendant made the statements as reported in the first paragraph on page 13 of the record of his questioning by the police. It was only based on the information which followed that it became clear, that is in the sense of a concrete and serious suspicion that an offence had been committed, that the Defendant had probably himself been involved in crimes against humanity by dint of his own actions. Accordingly, the Division has in the above only reported these statements which the Defendant made up to that point in his police interview and only uses these to that extent as the basis for its assessment of the accusation made against him.

II. Re the findings as to the general political and social situation in Syria: Domestic structure and security services in the period up to 2011

1. General political and social developments in Syria up to 2011

[122] (a) The findings as to the general political and social developments in Syria up to the start of the protest movement in the spring of 2011 are in essence based on the expert report rendered to the Division by the ethnologist and expert witness . . . [Th], which in turn is based on a large number of verified sources in academic publications, the press (including the Arabic press), from non-governmental organisations (NGOs) and official announcements by the Syrian government. The Division had no reason to doubt the expert's report, details of which are corroborated by a large amount of other evidence (see (b) and (c) below).

[123] (b) Expert . . . [Th]'s insights concur with statements made by several, mainly expert, witnesses and are supplemented by these.

[124] (aa) The Division therefore drew on statements made by the following witnesses, which are here presented in summary:

[125] (1) Expert Witness . . . [S] is a Syrian lawyer, journalist and human rights activist who was politically active in opposition in Syria before and after the start of the protest movement. He is currently head of a centre for media and freedom of speech which he founded in

France in 2004. He is co-author of yearly reports on the human rights situation in Syria. The witness was on several occasions detained in various branches of the Syrian intelligence service, including the Military Intelligence Directorate and, for three and a half years, in the Air Force Intelligence Directorate and the 4th Division. He was subjected to torture in the 4th Division and the Air Force Intelligence Directorate.

[126] The witness first outlined the history of Syria since independence. In the witness's opinion, its lack of democratic structures has its origin in the alliance between Syria and Egypt from 1958 to 1961 to form the United Arab Republic, in consequence of which the independent press and independent political parties were lost. This paved the way for the coup of 1963 and the rise of the Ba'ath Party, the witness stated. The coup had also boosted the importance of the military and thus, indirectly, propelled Hafez al-Assad, then Minister of Defence, to power. The witness further provided details about the declaration of the state of emergency, the introduction, in 1973, of a constitution which conferred wide-ranging presidential powers and about the Ba'ath Party's monopoly as the leading institution in the state and society. In the course of these developments, instruments had been created which conferred wide-ranging de facto powers for controlling society. Ultimately, a security apparatus, which had been given free rein, had replaced governmental institutions. The Hama Massacre, which had directly affected between 16,000 and 60,000 people, was ultimately directed against the whole of Syrian civil society because it had made it clear that the security apparatus no longer knew any bounds when it came to maintaining the political status quo, the witness stated. Further, violent attacks resulting in many deaths had, in particular, occurred in the period between 1979 and 1989 in the course of the conflict with the Muslim Brotherhood and the breaking up of the trade unions and left-wing movements.

[127] According to the witness, all the other governmental bodies were subordinate to and at the disposal of the security authorities; all independent organisations were broken up. Social control began early on: children aged between six and 12 years of age joined the "Ba'ath Youth", after which—from the age of 12—they joined the "Revolutionary Youth", a youth organisation which was also part of the Ba'ath Party. The purpose of these organisations was political indoctrination.

[128] When Bashar al-Assad assumed power, he had, ultimately, found a "broken society" with no press and no parliament, the witness

said. Civil society was borne by individuals, especially lawyers, although they were only permitted to engage in very limited activities. Bashar al-Assad was installed as his father's successor because his older brother, who had originally been prepared for this role, had died in an accident. In the witness's view, even during Hafez al-Assad's time in power there was no fully functional state structure, only a "family business" with inherited power.

[129] Moreover, Witness ... [S] testified as to Bashar al-Assad's attempts to introduce reforms, although these were pursued without any underlying statutory changes. The President had tried to window-dress the continuing policy of repression; it was just that "make-up was applied to the face of tyranny". The trend had already been reversed in August 2001, the witness stated, when activists were arrested and cultural and political forums were broken up. Hopes that the United States would force through political changes in Syria following the end of the Iraq War were dashed, he said. Foreign policy measures, which ultimately only served to maintain power, included support for jihadist endeavours in Iraq, fanning the flames of an alleged Arab-Kurdish conflict and rapprochement with Iran. On the other hand, the witness stated, there had been unsuccessful attempts to incorporate Syria into the international community, for example through official visits from the European Union.

[130] As far as domestic policy was concerned, the regime had used the security apparatus to take resolute action against the opposition; for example, demonstrations had already been broken up and demonstrators arrested back in 2004. The intelligence services had taken targeted action against the circle of political activists, which was actually small. Branch 285 of the General Intelligence Directorate was responsible for blocking unwelcome internet portals. Wide-ranging privatisations and corruption had created a shadow economy.

[131] Amongst other things, the witness's knowledgeable explanations, which were based on his personal experience, provide proof of the fact that the historically established and extensive powers of the security organs had already created the structural conditions necessary for massive and widespread action to be taken against the protest movement from April 2011 on.

[132] (2) Expert Witness ... [T], a Syrian lawyer and human rights activist, also described how, in his own experience, which goes as far back as the 1970s, those who were politically unwelcome were subjected to arbitrary chicanery and imprisonment. He himself was imprisoned in various branches of the intelligence services in 1978, 1986, 1989 and 2006 and was, in the intervening periods, summoned

to be interrogated on countless occasions. He was accused of fabricated offences such as homicide and theft.

[133] It was especially in 1978 that members of the peaceful opposition had died under torture, the witness testified. Some 3,000 people disappeared in the aftermath of the Hama Massacre in 1982. The aim was to strike at the whole of society. The witness explained that it was normal to move against the peaceful opposition under the pretext of fighting extremists. In the end, though, it was the government which was an extremist organisation and was fighting society, the witness stated.

[134] Alawites held key posts in government and the services, but there had also been many high-ranking Sunnis within the security apparatus, the witness testified. It had been difficult for them to progress as far as head of a branch. In the experience of Witness ... [T], Sunnis in the security services had been more brutal than Alawites because they had had to prove their loyalty, something he himself had experienced whilst he was imprisoned and also learned from former prisoners whom he had represented as a lawyer.

[135] (3) Expert Witness ... [U] is a former Syrian opposition politician and currently a politician-in-exile and businessman. He was elected to the Syrian Parliament in 1994 and was for a long time regarded as the country's most prominent dissident and critic of the Assad governments.

[136] The witness in particular reported on the economic and political situation in the period in which power transferred from Hafez to Bashar al-Assad and on his personal experience of having to assert himself as a member of the opposition and "free entrepreneur" against those families who were protected by the state, like the Makhloufs. He gave the Division an insight into the origins and ultimate failure of the Damascus Spring of 2001, of which he was one of the initiators. They had believed, at the time, that it would be possible to fight corruption and change the economy. The witness stated that he had believed that could be achieved by strengthening civil society, and he had, in vain, used his time as a Member of Parliament to get critical civil-society organisations and gatherings licensed. He had organised numerous gatherings in an open forum to create a national platform for exchange. In the end, the forum had had to be closed on the intervention of the intelligence services. When he had himself continued it without a permit, he was taken to prison on 5 September 2001. He lost all his assets and was sentenced to five years' imprisonment. The charges brought against him were "incitement of the people, violent system change and undermining public opinion".

However, as a Member of Parliament he had enjoyed privileges in prison.

[137] In 2006, Witness ... [U] stated, he was again imprisoned in the Al-Khatib Branch for one day. He was also kept under surveillance by the police and intelligence service and had had to report regularly to the Al-Khatib Branch. When attending the intelligence service branches he had also been subjected to physical abuse. Finally, he was again arrested in 2008 and spent two and a half years in the prison in Adra. After serving his sentence, Ali Mamlouk and Tawfiq Younes, high-ranking intelligence service staff had intimated that he should in future refrain from engaging in political activities. A new page was being turned; he would not get away so lightly the next time, he was told. He had then, with a heavy heart, given up his civil-society engagement in Syria.

[138] When asked about relations between Alawites and Sunnis in Syria, Witness ... [U] stated that the Alawites were the "real bosses in Syria, especially in the intelligence service", but that one also heard that members of other religions were more brutal because they had to outdo the Alawites and get their backing.

[139] (4) Witness ... [V] was employed in the German Embassy in Damascus up until 2012, amongst other things as a translator, and then in the Stiftung Wissenschaft und Politik (SWP) in Berlin. She testified that the Syrian intelligence services had already been using torture back in 2011. She had learned of cases which were described in documents she had translated, that is of maltreatment using a bastinado, blows to the soles of the feet and the "German Chair" method, which involved breaking a person's spine. People had also died whilst being interrogated, in particular as a result of brutal beatings, she stated.

[140] (5) Expert Witness ... [W], a journalist and Islamic scholar who had studied in Syria, amongst other places, had dealt with political developments in Syria in his publications since the 1990s and conducted on-site research during numerous visits. His knowledge is based on analyses of publications and on numerous conversations with members of civil society and oppositional groups he knew from the past and with whom he was in contact on account of spending time in the country and through Syrians living in exile.

[141] Witness ... [W] explained that even whilst Hafez al-Assad was in power and nearly continuously during the handover of power to Bashar al-Assad abuse inflicted by the security authorities had been part of everyday life in Syria and the intelligence services had played a prominent role, sometimes holding competing powers. In particular, it was common knowledge even before 2011 "that the regime makes

arrests, torments and kills. Everyone knew it, it was nothing new". Even in the late 1970s and in the 1980s there had been uprisings which had been crushed, especially those by the Muslim Brotherhood in Hama. The army had shelled the city and killed 15,000 people. At that time, though, the dissident scene was small and, so the regime thought, harmless. "If no-one takes to the streets, nothing will happen."

[142] The period before 2011 was, the witness stated, in no way comparable to what happened after that. However, "conditions were already set within the apparatus for the greatest of cruelty"; before, though, it had not been the case that "people were killed by the dozen". As far as working for the regime was concerned, in the witness's opinion, those who had chosen a career path in the government could not do anything other than adapt to the conditions which prevailed in the dictatorship. It had been dominated by Alawites; as a Sunni you had to prove yourself, to cooperate in the repression as required by the state; as a Sunni, you had to be "the first to say that more people have to be arrested".

[143] (6) Other witnesses whom the Division chiefly examined regarding their experience as former employees or victims of the regime occasionally made reference to how they perceived the Syrian political system.

[144] Witness ... [X], for instance, who was later imprisoned on several occasions in various facilities run by the security apparatus for being an anti-government activist, told of a climate of fear which existed during her childhood and teenage years in the 1980s. She remembered an incident whilst she was in Year Four at primary school when she had told her friends some things her father had said which were critical of the regime. The next day security forces had paid a visit to her school.

[145] A witness who was examined anonymously by the Division on 16 December 2020 (Witness Z 16/12/2020) was imprisoned in Branch 251 in 2012. By her own account, she was a member of the Syrian upper class and an active member of the opposition. She pointed out, as regards the allocation of positions of power amongst religious and population groups, that the Syrian regime was not made up only of Alawites. High-ranking government posts, such as those of prime minister, president of the parliament and vice-president, had been held by Sunnis, she stated. Although Alawites generally held positions of leadership within the security authorities, Sunnis had also held other higher-ranking posts in the administration.

[146] Witness ... [Y], a long-time employee of the General Intelligence Directorate, confirmed this in essence. He testified that

Sunnis had also been able to hold executive positions, although a distinction needed to be drawn between normal posts within authorities and sensitive posts within the security apparatus. Although the statements made by this witness, whose testimony chiefly concerned the period after the start of the conflict and his observations as to the conditions in Branch 251 and Sub-branch 40, were inconsistent (see section B.III.1 [General course of the conflict as from 2011], (c)(bb), for details), the Division took this specific part of his statement to be true and used it as the basis for its assessment since, in contrast to the statements he made regarding the situation after the start of the conflict, he consistently testified in the preliminary investigation and before the Division, he gave a nuanced representation of the facts and his observations were consistent with those of Witness Z 16/12/2020.

[147] (bb) The individual observations made by the witnesses designated in the above corroborate the assessment that, in the period prior to the internal conflict, Syria had evolved socially and politically into an autocratic one-party state with a president as the dominant leadership personality. The political leadership relied, on the one hand, on a clientelist system in which people and families close to it took on prominent positions in business and in government and, on the other hand, on a widespread and extensive security apparatus whose task it was to surveille and suppress any and all oppositional endeavours. The witnesses gave graphic accounts of how this had included the use of violence towards prisoners, in particular torture and extralegal killings, as well as measures to retain power which were known to the general public. This effectively prevented the establishment of a pluralist civil society. Efforts to open up society, which were partly motivated by foreign policy considerations, did not last long. As regards the excessively violent approach which was later adopted, the coherent picture which emerges is that an organisational infrastructure and know-how was already in place—for example prisons where critics of the regime could be imprisoned and means of inflicting systematic physical abuse—and that all that was needed was for the army and intelligence services to be given the relevant orders for these activities, which they had practised for many years, to be extended qualitatively and quantitatively across the whole protest movement. The political developments as presented by the witnesses demonstrate that the Syrian state leadership had, ultimately, continued the pattern of conflict management which it had rehearsed over many years and had, in the government's opinion, been successful, that is violent repression and confrontation.

[148] The witness statements present a multi-layered overall picture as regards the religious/ethnic balance of power within the Syrian state apparatus. Whilst historically and after the Assad family assumed power the Alawite religious community generally held a more privileged position and was overrepresented in key government posts (in particular security-related leadership positions), members of other religious communities, Sunnis in particular—who were in the majority in the population—also held executive posts. It appears reasonable to assume that these Sunnis were under pressure because they had to prove that they were especially loyal to the regime. However, it also appears plausible that, in view of the large majority of Sunnis in the population, the regime also appointed them to positions within the extensive security apparatus and had to elevate them to higher-ranking posts in order to keep the peace in society.

[149] (c) The Division also relied on circumstantial evidence presented in reports published in November 2011 and March 2012 by an independent international commission of inquiry established by the Human Rights Council of the United Nations on the basis of events in Syria as from March 2011 (see section B.III.1 [General course of the conflict as from 2011], (e)(aa), for details). The account of historical and social developments in Syria presented in summary in these reports is consistent with the statements made by the experts and witnesses cited in the above. The reports in particular confirm the autocratic rule of the al-Assad family following the military coup in 1971; the repeal of civil rights under the decades-long state of emergency; the Syrian Ba'ath Party's dominance over and controlling influence on politics and society; human rights violations like the attack by Syrian security forces on the city of Hama in 1982 and reports of an estimated death toll of between 10,000 and 25,000; and state repression in the previous four decades (i.e. prior to 2011) against actual or alleged opponents of the regime who were imprisoned, tortured and sentenced to terms of imprisonment based on unspecific charges. Surveillance and suppression were carried out by an extensive security apparatus; political life and an autonomous civil society were massively restricted as a result.

2. Exercise of power, structure and remit of the Syrian intelligence services

[150] (a) In terms of the findings as to the structure, evolution and activities of the Syrian intelligence services and other parts of the Syrian security apparatus in the period before 2011, the Division bases its findings on a statement submitted by the Federal Intelligence Service

(*Bundesnachrichtendienst*, BND) dated 16 June 2016 regarding the structure of the Syrian intelligence services, on the report submitted by the expert . . . [Th] and on the statements made by Witness . . . [Z], who holds a senior position within the Commission for International Justice and Accountability (CIJA), an NGO investigating aspects of the Syrian conflict.

[151] The Division is not aware of the Federal Intelligence Service's sources. The insights provided by the expert . . . [Th] are based on an analysis of a wide variety of sources, including specialist publications, press releases and publications by international and human rights organisations. The insights provided by Expert Witness . . . [Z] are based on a systematic analysis of anonymised surveys of a large number of victims and members of the Syrian regime which the CIJA has conducted since the start of the internal Syrian conflict. Even though the names of the anonymised witnesses and thus the witnesses them-selves were not known even to the Division, Witness . . . [Z] gave a detailed description of how the surveys were standardised and how the information provided was documented in relation to the anonymised witnesses and analysed in order to be able to assess the conflict situation and the course of the conflict (see section B.III.2 [Central Crisis Management Cell], (a), for details). The evidence is consistent with the findings as to the structure, scope and remit of the intelligence services. The Division also gained the impression that the external structure of the intelligence services and their extensive resources were already in place before 2011 and were used as a tool to stabilise the political machinery of power and that the services were drawn on to massively and violently suppress the conflict.

[152] (b) A number of Syrian witnesses also testified in detail, consistent with what was reported in the above and, in some cases, based on their own experience regarding the history, structure and activities of the Syrian intelligence services.

[153] (aa) For example, Expert Witness . . . [S] traced the historical evolution of the intelligence services as follows: the oldest of the intelli-gence services, the Military Intelligence Directorate, was established back in the 1950s. It was, the expert witness reported, succeeded in the 1960s by the General Intelligence Directorate (known colloquially as "State Security"). The Air Force Intelligence Directorate was the youngest service, and was established in the 1970s. The expert witness reported that the services had always been responsible for suppressing the opposition by means of arbitrary arrests, torture or "disappear-ances". It was also a well-known fact in Syrian society that the services engaged in torture. It was especially following the violent events of the

1980s, for instance the crushing of the Muslim Brotherhood movement or of the Communist Workers' Party, that the modus operandi, including individual torture methods, had come to light. The regime itself had let the people know it in order to scare them. The witness reported that torture techniques had also been a part of a general culture, as it were. Means of inflicting abuse such as *dulab, shabeh* and the "Flying Carpet" were regularly being used even before 2011. People had died in the intelligence service branches even before the conflict began, the witness stated.

[154] (bb) Witness ... [T] corroborated this. Back in the 1970s individuals who were out of favour were arrested by the intelligence services and then tortured or simply made to disappear. There had been no court proceedings. The witness himself was imprisoned and tortured in 1978 in Branches 251 and 285 of the Syrian General Intelligence Directorate; in 2006 he was kidnapped in broad daylight and taken to Branch 285. At that time torture had been run of the mill in the branches, as he himself had noted. The witness was also aware of this on account of what imprisoned clients of his had told him (he is a lawyer). According to the witness, the fact that the Syrian security apparatus was using torture was already common knowledge before 2011 and described as especially well-known amongst members of the security authorities.

[155] The witness—who is well-informed as to these matters given that he is a lawyer—also testified that employees of the intelligence services had themselves been protected against any criminal prosecution whatsoever on account of their activities. For instance, it was prohibited by law from bringing charges against security officials, and employees could only be prosecuted with the authorisation of the head of the relevant central branch.

[156] (cc) Witness ... [U] described the tasks of the intelligence services such that the system relied on their intelligence and that they served to maintain political control. After 1963, he said, the Syrian system was founded on "absolution, isolation and violence". There was no intelligence service which did not use torture, he stated.

[157] (dd) By his own account, the anonymously examined Witness Z 28/07/16 spent 21 years working in the otherwise unspecified "central branch" in the General Intelligence Directorate. The witness outlined how the intelligence services were divided up into the general intelligence service, the military intelligence service, a "political" intelligence service and the air force intelligence service. The "political" intelligence service was affiliated to the Ministry of the Interior, he reported. The general intelligence service had between 30,000 and

50,000 employees across the whole of Syria. Up until his death in 2012, it had been headed by Ali Mamlouk, then by Dib Zaitoun, the witness stated.

[158] Torture existed in all the intelligence services, the witness testified. In his experience there had been no interrogation during which prisoners had not suffered ill-treatment. The presumption of innocence until proven guilty did not apply, he said. Further, as previously established, the witness testified, in relation to the methods of torture applied, that the intelligence services all used the same techniques. The interrogations had also usually followed the same procedure: Prisoners were shackled and then taken by a guard to be questioned by an interrogator. The interrogator ordered the torture to be inflicted by the guards either verbally or by means of a hand signal. Sometimes the methods to be applied were also ordered in writing using coded wording such as "enhanced investigations". It had also been customary to smuggle spies into prison cells or to intimidate and "flip" prisoners, especially political opponents, based on fake criminal charges.

[159] (c) The report published in November 2011 by the United Nations Human Rights Council (see section B.III.1 [General course of the conflict as from 2011], (e)(aa)(1), for details) also describes the structure of the Syrian security authorities and corroborates the afore-mentioned evidence. Emphasis should be placed on the existence of elite units in the army—in particular the Republican Guard and the 4th Division—which were under the direct command of the President, on a multitude of different intelligence services with overlapping juris-dictions and pro-government militias such as the *shabiha* and those comprising members of the Ba'ath Party. The Division drew on this information as circumstantial evidence.

III. Re the findings as to the start of the conflict and its course as from 2011: The actors and victims

[160] The findings as to the course of the conflict, the involved actors and institutions and the numbers of victims are based on the overall picture which emerges on the basis of the evidence gathered by the Division in that regard. This comprised the expert report rendered by the expert ... [Th], who was also heard in this regard, the state-ments made by the expert witnesses ... [V], ... [W], ... [Z], ... [S], ... [T] and ... [U] and several reports published by international and human rights organisations. Information was also provided by Witness Z 28/07/16, a former member of the regime, by witnesses ... [AA] and ... [Y] and a large number of victim witnesses

who were imprisoned in Branch 251, many of whom were first arrested by members of Sub-branch 40. The Division attaches particular evidential value to the CCMC documents dating back to April 2011 which were made available to it by the CIJA by way of the Federal Criminal Police Office. The number and condition of the people killed in the course of the conflict, their bureaucratic documentation and eventual burial in mass graves are impressively borne out by the "Caesar Files", by statements made by Witness ... [BB] and Witness Z 30/07/19, who were involved in documenting the burials, and by an analysis of satellite images of mass graves.

More specifically:

1. General course of the conflict as from 2011

[161] (a) Expert Witness ... [Th] was also able to set out the general course of the internal Syrian conflict after the "Arab Spring" spilled over into Syria in February 2011; she detailed its chronology and escalation based on an extensive analysis of the source material available in relation to these aspects. The expert was, in particular, able to provide an overview of individual documented incidents which occurred in an escalating sequence between the spring of 2011 and mid-2012. Notwithstanding the overall coherent picture as regards the course of the conflict and the state's response which she was able to present, the expert did point out that, because of the lack of opportunity to conduct independent surveys and freely engage in her journalistic activities, any numbers, in particular the numbers of victims, are fraught with uncertainty. The Division follows the expert's explanations, which are confirmed and supplemented by a large amount of other evidence, and took them as the basis for its assessment.

[162] As regards the intelligence services' involvement in the conflict, the Division likewise relies on the expert report rendered by Expert Witness ... [Th], on the report dated 16 June 2016 submitted by the Federal Intelligence Service and on information provided by Expert Witness ... [Z], which are not only consistent as regards the formal competences of the individual intelligence services and their position within the Syrian state apparatus, but also as regards their actual status and remit during the protest movement and the civil war as from 2011. According to the above, the findings made as to the external structure of the Syrian intelligence services had not changed in 2011. Together with the military and militias, they constituted essential elements of the security apparatus which were used to quash the protest movement.

[163] (b) As regards the circumstances and developments as from 2011, the Division also heard the witnesses designated in the following (some of whom have already been listed in the above) who held views and engaged in activities which were critical of the regime. Taken together, their testimonies provide a consistent overall picture of how the security forces responded, from the outset, in a violent, ultimately coordinated and escalating manner, to the protest movement as from February 2011. These statements consolidate the picture that the Syrian regime had, from the outset, wanted to violently suppress efforts by those critical of the regime and that a significant increase in the use of force, both qualitatively and quantitatively, on the part of the state was discernible from late April 2011 onwards.

[164] (aa) On account of his involvement in oppositional activities, Expert Witness ... [S] (see section B.II.1 [General political and social developments in Syria up to 2011], (b)(aa)(1), above) was also able to provide details about events as a consequence of the Syrian protest movement and its suppression. He himself sometimes took part in protests and demonstrations; sometimes he was able to systematically collect information within the organisation he headed in order to gain a picture of the political security situation.

[165] The witness described in detail how the Arab Spring, which began in Tunisia and Egypt, spilled over into Syria. At the start, people had expressed their approval and solidarity online, then came a wave of demonstrations. The witness named individual demonstrations at the start of the protest movement, including one in front of the Libyan Embassy during which the security forces cracked down on demonstrators after first filming them, then hitting them with clubs and arresting them. Saturday, 5 February 2011 was proclaimed as the Day of Syrian Rage; sit-ins were held in Damascus und Aleppo. The witness himself and other prominent individuals, for instance Witness ... [T], were subsequently summoned to the Internal State Security Branch and interrogated, he testified. He was questioned by Tawfiq Younes himself, he said. State Security had accused him of inciting demonstrations. Another demonstration was held in front of the Syrian Ministry of the Interior on 6 March 2011; when images of people who had been arrested were held up, the security people had gone on the attack, ripped up the images and struck the demonstrators hard. Blood was shed, the witness reported. Two people had held on to a philosophy lecturer he knew and hit his head against an electricity pylon. On 15 March 2011 a fairly large demonstration was held in Damascus during which a large number of people were arrested; the day after that a sit-in was held in an attempt to get those arrested

released. The witness stated that he had taken part in the sit-in and was again arrested. Although these protests were entirely peaceful—described as "standing around peacefully in front of the Ministry of the Interior in Damascus"—a large number of security forces had charged at the protesters and started hitting them. More than 30 people, including women, were arrested. There were also well-known incidents in which children had written graffiti on walls and had then been arrested and tortured.

[166] The security services were, the witness testified, well-prepared to quash the opposition movement; the country was divided up into sectors and each sector was assigned to a specific intelligence service branch. No shots were fired in Damascus in February and March 2011, but firearms were already used in Daraa on 18 March 2011, resulting in the first civilian victims. Although the demonstrators had made civil demands, the security forces' response had been extremely violent. In the witness's assessment, a decision had been taken to use force against demonstrators and not to give in to their demands.

[167] From April 2011 onwards, the witness testified, reports of the use of firearms became commonplace, first in Homs, then in Damascus, then across the whole of the country. Mass arbitrary arrests were made across entire regions, too. The security forces had begun to use force systematically by, for instance, using live ammunition against demonstrators. The witness, who was himself arrested as early as 22 March 2011, recalled hearing reports about a Friday demonstration in Damascus in April 2011 during which demonstrators had died and others had been arrested by the security forces. On 29 April 2011 a large demonstration in Douma was broken up and dozens of people were killed. In June 2011 live ammunition was used to shoot at people who were staging a sit-in; demonstrators were killed on that occasion, too, the witness stated. It was during this period that the city of Daraa was besieged by the military, whereupon there had been demonstrations to express solidarity, which in turn were put down by force. The witness testified that he remembered the dates because they had been recorded in the documentation centre he operated based on reports by those who took part. It had generally been difficult to establish how many victims there had been exactly.

[168] The mostly young people were subjected to systematic torture and humiliation following their arrest. Whilst at the start of the protests those arrested were detained in prison for only a day or a few days, they were later kept in prison for a month. Those who were released told the witness that they would rather die than have to go through anything like that again.

[169] The security forces' modus operandi was consistent with public statements made by the Syrian President, the witness testified. For instance, Bashar al-Assad had said the following, or words to that effect, in a public speech on 30 March 2011: "If you want open war, then so be it." In April 2011 Syria had then got to the point "where it exploded". The witness had tried in the course of his work for a human rights organisation to document human rights violations, until, that is, all the members of the organisation were themselves arrested.

[170] As regards the modus operandi of the Syrian intelligence apparatus, the witness reported that there were several changes compared to the period before the protests began. Although arrests and torture were already omnipresent before the start of the protest movement, the number of people who were imprisoned and who were killed drastically increased in 2011 as the activities of the intelligence services were not directed solely against the smaller oppositional groups as they had been in the period before that. The way in which torture was used also changed, he stated. The witness himself was able to observe the difference, because he was arrested both before and after 2011. Before, torture was used to extort information, he stated. The abuse had ended as soon as the prisoner revealed all the information. From 2011, torture was used more as a punishment, in retaliation and a means of liquidating people or breaking them psychologically. There was torture without interrogations, he stated. During his period in detention with the Air Force Intelligence Directorate the witness had himself seen a prisoner who had been hung up pleading in vain to be let down so that he could confess; the guards had not been interested. Critics of the regime had suffered abuse, as had people who were arrested accidentally, for example as a result of mistaken identity. The aim, the witness stated, was to keep society under control "whatever the cost". The intelligence services had, ultimately, been given free rein. They had been able to do "what they wanted"; no rules applied. The witness himself had been able to observe this on the several occasions when he himself was detained, latterly between April and October 2012 in the 4th Division.

[171] (bb) Consistent with this, Expert Witness . . . [T] testified, on the basis of his work as a lawyer and his contact with a large number of people who were persecuted by the Syrian authorities, that the security authorities changed their modus operandi after the protests began in 2011. The regime became more and more nervous in the spring of 2011 as the protest movement grew into civil unrest, he stated. Its response became more and more brutal. The witness illustrated this based on protests held from February 2011 onwards which he knew

about because they concerned his release, amongst other things, and because members of his family had taken part and demonstrators had been beaten with sticks during the event and arrested. Whilst, previously, the task had been to torture members of the opposition in order to extort information from them, after 2011 the focus had no longer been on information-gathering but on retaliation and deterrence. Clients whom the witness had tried to defend were asked "Do you want freedom?" and then tortured if they answered "Yes". The idea was to exact revenge, the witness stated. The number of people who were arrested had risen to an alarming degree. Whilst before 2011 maybe 3,000 people had been in prison at the same time, and ultimately brought before the State Security court, from 2011 hundreds of people were being arrested every day. The intelligence services' powers also changed, the witness stated. Before 2011 only key branches such as Branch 251 had been given free rein in terms of the conduct of investigations and making of arrests whilst others had only been permitted to act on the orders of the government. From 2011 onwards, though, each intelligence service branch was able to do what it wanted. Torture methods became more brutal. People were, for example, shackled to a chair without a seat and a candle was placed underneath. Such techniques had not been used before 2011, the witness testified.

[172] According to the witness, everyone whom the security apparatus got its hands on was tortured. Beatings were a matter of course even whilst those arrested were being transported to the relevant intelligence service branch; upon arrival, institutionalised "welcome parties" were held. The witness had himself seen them. In the period since 2006 he was imprisoned for a total of five years and spent five days in Branch 285 of the General Intelligence Directorate shortly before being released in May 2011. There was a communal cell there measuring 4 by 5 metres which had been completely overcrowded with 50 to 60 people in it; the people were "glued to each other", he said. By day and night he had heard the screams of those being tortured.

[173] There was never anyone who was taken to prison who was not beaten, the witness stated. At most, it was well-known members of the opposition or media representatives who were spared severe torture for fear that this could lead to further unrest. In such cases, special orders were issued as to how to deal with these people. There were also occasions when members of the opposition were arrested with the intention of getting them to work as informants for the government; they were not subjected to ill-treatment either.

[174] As regards the situation in prisons operated by the intelligence services in 2011, the witness's clients had told him about cells in which

there was hardly any space to stand up ("There was only enough space for your own foot."). Prisoners had broken down, hallucinated and eventually lost their mind. As there was no ventilation, prisoners had serious difficulty breathing. People had died and then been deliberately left in the cells until their bodies began to decompose. It had not been possible to cover up any wounds, the witness stated. Referring to 2011, though without being able to recall the exact time and place, he said that a friend had reported that 17 people had died during the 27 days he spent in prison. The food, that is slices of bread, potatoes, a little jam, had sometimes simply been thrown into the cells. As he was a lawyer, the witness had met the prisoners on their way from the security facilities to court; they were usually injured, barefoot and sometimes only clad in their underwear. He met people who weighed 40 kilogrammes who used to weigh 80 kilogrammes.

[175] Sexual violence against men as well as women was widespread after 2011, although only few of the survivors were willing to speak openly about it. This form of violence was specifically used to humiliate both the prisoners and their relatives. According to incidents reported to the witness, prisoners were raped in front of their relatives. He himself had helped women get an abortion following their release.

[176] (cc) Expert Witness ... [W] travelled to Syria as part of his job as a journalist, including in 2011 and 2012. He testified that he had tried to find out how the political opposition and demonstrations were organised and to what extent the government pronouncements that the protest movement was organised by terrorist groups, primarily Islamist terrorist groups, were true. Later on in the conflict he had attempted to conduct research into the mass killings and the "collection points" for corpses which then gradually came to light.

[177] The witness testified that at the start of the protests in February and March 2011 the demonstrations tended to be more like spontaneous flashmobs. The regime had responded in different ways in different places. Whilst those taking part in Damascus were "only" arrested, firearms were already being used at an early stage in Homs. The witness said he attended one of the demonstrations; young men had stood in the middle of the street and women, children and the elderly had stood on the edges because that made it easier for them to flee. "People know they're going to a peaceful demo but have to reckon with being shot at." In February and March 2011 there had been situations "in which people were just beaten, others where they were shot at". In the latter case, however, the regime had let it be known that it was not the security forces who had opened fire and had presented weapons in the media which had allegedly been used against the

security forces. The witness had himself heard shots being fired in Homs in August 2011 and had seen people in hospital with gunshot wounds who themselves said they had been at a demonstration. As early as April or May 2011 there had been 200 arrests following a demonstration in Homs.

[178] The witness himself saw arrests being made, he stated. He testified that on one occasion he was travelling on a coach when one of the other passengers had been singled out at a checkpoint: "A sack was put over his head and he was driven away in van." Many people had told him about arrests being made in the streets or at demonstrations. He stated that at the start those arrested were beaten and tortured; they had "disappeared for a while", but most of them were released and told not to take part in demonstrations again.

[179] The regime's response then became increasingly more brutal, the witness testified. In June 2011 "you knew that the intelligence service would come and open fire on those who came". The sequence of events had been disturbing: "On Fridays there was a demo at which people were shot and killed, on Saturday they were buried and then shots were also fired at the funerals, then things were quiet from Sunday to Thursday, and then on Friday it started all over again. But that didn't deter people. Quite the opposite, demonstrations were being held in more and more places." In December 2011 there were shootings at a checkpoint in Homs. From 2012, those who were arrested often did not come back. In December 2011, the witness stated, there were also clusters of snipers from which "shots were fired at anyone who went out into the street"; this was the case in those districts of Homs which were said to be oppositional, for instance. In 2012 and 2013 it was then normal for people to be shot at. The demonstrators, he said, had begun to arm themselves in order to protect the demonstrations. The witness also testified in detail about the massacre in Houla on 31 May 2012 such that, contrary to statements released by the government stating the opposite and according to his own research, it was down to the excessive use of force on the part of the Syrian security forces. More and more armed units—including in some cases the heavily armed army—had come to the demonstrations, although responsibility for making arrests lay with the intelligence services.

[180] The role of the intelligence services also changed in the course of the conflict, the witness stated. In the past their role had mainly been to gather intelligence, but now they mainly had an executive function. Whilst in the past the different intelligence services had competed against each other, they then engaged in coordinated action. For

example, there had been lists of wanted persons which the services shared amongst themselves. It had often been difficult to assign the security forces to individual agencies at checkpoints and when demonstrations were being quashed—"people in uniform wearing sneakers" came along—and these were regularly members of the intelligence services and the army. In the past the services had each had different characteristics, the witness stated. The Air Force Intelligence Directorate and the Military Intelligence Directorate had been the worst and the Political Intelligence Directorate had been regarded as reasonably civil. In the course of the conflict they had then progressively aligned themselves, the witness testified. Sadistic terror had to all intents and purposes been politically stage-managed; according to the witness's research, Ali Mamlouk, the head of the General Intelligence Directorate, had a central, coordinating role in this.

[181] Finally, the witness also gave testimony about his meetings with, amongst others, former employees of the regime concerning how and why people defected. He stated that defectors could roughly be divided into three groups: "Those who left in 2011 were heroes. Those who left in 2012 didn't like the brutality of it. Those who left in late 2012 were opportunists, though, because this was regarded as rather late in the day." The later people defected, the more it was assumed they had only gone so as not to be left on the wrong side when the regime collapsed, as was expected to happen. The first people had already deserted in the summer of 2011.

[182] (dd) Witness . . . [U], a prominent Syrian opposition politician, testified that he took part in several demonstrations in the spring of 2011. He recalled one of the first rallies to be held in front of the Ministry of the Interior on 15 March 2011 during which participants were beaten by the intelligence services and around 40 of them were arrested. The witness always took part in the Friday demonstrations there, he stated. On 7 May 2011 he himself was attacked and beaten by members of the intelligence service "until blood was drawn". He was then taken to the prison in Adra, he testified. Hundreds of people were arrested and then also beaten. According to what he himself saw, new groups had been formed within the intelligence services to crush the uprisings and these had been specially recruited to conduct operations directed against the protesters. There had also been—possibly staged— counter-demonstrations by Alawites during which they—armed with axes, large knives and iron bars—had chanted slogans against the demonstrators ("Bashar, don't worry, there are people who drink blood.").

[183] In the first six weeks after the start of the protest movement, which the witness estimated to be 15 March 2011, the government

had, he believed, not yet issued instructions to violently quash the demonstrations. Afterwards, though, the level of violence had significantly increased. The attack against himself on 7 May 2011 could also have been fatal, he stated, because he had been hit over the head with an iron rod and had barely been able to shield himself using his arm, which was broken during the attack. Based on the witness's knowledge of the structure of the Syrian machinery of power, this could not have been done without orders issued by a centralised authority.

[184] (ee) Witness ... [CC], a cousin of the Defendant and an oppositional publicist, testified that from late February 2011 the security services had been put on a state of alert and reinforced so as to be able to prevent demonstrations happening; the Defendant himself had told him that. The witness gave testimony about a demonstration held in Douma on 25 March 2011. The participants had gathered outside a mosque; a counterdemonstration organised by the regime had been led towards them. There was violence at demonstrations from late April 2011 onwards, the witness stated. Demonstrators taking part in a rally at that time were encircled; soldiers and members of the security authorities got out of vehicles and attacked the demonstrators with batons, giving them beatings "the like of which he'd never seen in his life before". Many people were arrested, he stated. The regime had institutionalised violence at such an early stage, as was evident from the rising number of casualties amongst those taking part in the Friday demonstrations (whom the witness called "martyrs"). It was after that that the level of violence had increased. As regards his own detention in the Palestine Branch as from 8 April 2011, the witness reported that he himself was not ill-treated there on account of his position and that he was released after one day. Other prisoners, though, had been kicked and beaten; he had constantly heard people screaming during his time there. He himself was merely insulted, he testified. Sympathy had been shown for the work of intellectuals and members of the opposition, and attempts had been made to recruit him as an informant.

[185] (c) The Division also heard former regime staff who likewise testified as to the course of the conflict and the activities of the involved Syrian security forces.

[186] (aa) Based on experience gained as a long-time employee of the General Intelligence Directorate, Witness Z 28/07/16, who was examined anonymously, stated that the security forces had free rein after the start of the unrest and were given more and more competences as the popular movement grew. Each branch was, ultimately, able to do what it wanted. A kind of "state of emergency" was imposed, on

account of which everyone who opposed the regime was regarded as a traitor. The charges levelled against prisoners were a foregone conclusion; the only thing left to be done was for them to be confirmed and signed by the prisoners. Members of the regime who defied instructions were also regarded as traitors. As the witness experienced for himself, officers were transferred elsewhere or to another service or were interrogated as to their motivation. At any rate, defying orders was dangerous, he stated. Usually, however, those working in the intelligence service did not dare leave, including owing to the advantages they had as members of the intelligence service.

[187] On account of the numerous arrests made at demonstrations, the number of prisoners in the intelligence services' individual branches grew in the course of the conflict, the witness stated. The interrogation methods changed, they had been "crazy". He was aware that the General Intelligence Directorate's Branch 285 was the central agency for the whole of Syria and responsible for interrogations and that people were hung up from the ceiling there so that the tips of their toes just about touched the floor. Those who were interrogated were maltreated with electric shocks, the witness testified, and had hot water poured over them. Cigarettes were stubbed out on their skin and their head was pushed under water. There were cases, the witness stated, in which prisoners were forced to wear shoes containing nails, or in which male prisoners had their penis tied off with a piece of string, in the worst case they were hung up by the string. After having had their penis tied off, the prisoners were forced to drink water. The witness knew of one case in which a man's penis was cut off with a pair of pliers. Men were brutally raped using a wooden stick. There were cases in which a three-figure number of prisoners were placed in tiny cells measuring 4 by 4 metres, he reported. Prisoners spent many days in the cells without being interrogated, after which they were merely tortured. Such methods were first applied "during the revolution", the witness said, to humiliate the prisoners. When, finally, the order was given to shoot at people in the streets it was no longer important whether people died in their cells either.

[188] Around three months after the start of the movement, instructions came "from above", the witness stated, to put down the demonstrations using all means available, including using firearms. The orders were given "by Assad"; "everything" was to be shot at. This was probably the case as of late May 2011, as the unrest had begun in March. There had, to the witness's knowledge, been no armed groups of opponents of the regime until 2012. It was only then that the people had begun to turn violently against the regime.

[189] The Division sees no reasons not to take the witness's statement to be true, since it concurs with the statement he made in the preliminary investigation, which was detailed and lacked any incriminatory or exonerating tendency.

[190] (bb) By his own account, Witness ... [Y] is a former member of the intelligence service who worked in various branches of the Syrian General Intelligence Directorate for 30 years, including 13 years (between 1985 and late 1998) in Branch 251. From 2008 to early 2016 he held a senior post in Information Branch 255 of the General Intelligence Directorate.

[191] (1) The witness stated, with regard to his work at the start of the internal Syrian conflict, that he was responsible for scanning and archiving documents. He said that this involved some 10,000 pages per day, the content of which he could barely recall. He had compiled statistics, he reported. He handled reports and lists of people who were arrested or wanted. The documents also described how someone was to be arrested and interrogated, for instance "using all methods and means".

[192] The witness stated that he knew that many branches of the intelligence services brutishly tortured detainees. It already started when the arrest was made. For example, in Branch 285 people were hit with rifle butts, batons and iron bars. He himself saw more than 15 people who were killed; they had "bled profusely", were carried away. That was at the start of the uprising, which, according to the witness, was on 15 March 2011. Instructions had been issued to use force; they were "strict and hard", although some officers had tried to temper them. Torture had already been inflicted prior to the start of the conflict, but not to the same extent and not in the same way.

[193] Further, the witness testified as to the religious/ethnic division of power in Syria. He provided a nuanced picture of the period up to the outbreak of the conflict (see section B.II.1 [General political and social developments in Syria up to 2011], (b)(aa)(6), above). During his police interview the witness had provided a "rank order" of religions which applied in the period after the start of the protest movement; the Alawites ranked first, followed by the Sunnis. He stated during his examination at the main hearing that he had changed his views on the matter and then gave different information. The witness then stated that once the conflict began the Alawites had seized all the power. A low-ranking Alawite had suddenly been able to have command over a Sunni; he was also able to tell a much higher-ranking Sunni what to do. The Alawites, the witness stated, had no longer trusted any of the other religions. Although

high-ranking Sunnis were allowed to continue in post, they were under observation by the Alawites.

[194] The witness also reported that, although he was only an office clerk working at a computer in the Information Branch, he had been called on to help quash demonstrations. He had refused to do so and had had to give reasons. He had undergone in-house questioning. In the end, the witness defected, though he had needed time to prepare his escape, he stated. He had wanted to sell all his worldly possessions and get his family out of Syria first. When his son and his son's wife fled, he, too, was questioned.

[195] (2) The Division critically assessed the information provided by this witness, who also gave detailed testimony on how the deceased were treated (see section B.III.3 [Number, documentation and treatment of those killed: Mass graves], (b)(dd), below) and on the internal structure of Branch 251 and Sub-branch 40 (see sections B.IV.1 [Branch 251], (a)(cc), and B.IV.2 [Sub-branch 40], (a)(cc), below).

[196] The witness had already pointed out in the course of his police questioning that he could not remember any details about his past because he was "mentally and socially under a lot of pressure". His examination at the main hearing was laboured at first; the witness gave evasive answers. At first, the witness's statement in the main hearing alternated between containing detailed, specific information and general claims and attributions, for instance as regards the relationship between Alawites and Sunnis and the role which Sub-branch 40 played after the conflict broke out. The witness was not initially able to provide any information about the intelligence services' modus operandi during the conflict. It appeared inconsistent that he remembered certain documents concerning the former Co-Defendant . . . [K], which he himself stated he had had his hand on and the general gist of the content of which he was able to relate, although when the Division made general enquiries about whether he had also handled interrogation transcripts he cited a general lack of capacity to remember anything given the large number of documents. Also, his testimony was often strikingly different to what he had said during his questioning by the police in the preliminary investigation. The Division gained the impression that the witness answered questions selectively and tendentiously and that he was possibly attempting to dispel any suspicion of his own involvement, which he feared would be raised. The witness also had a clear tendency to exonerate both of the then co-defendants.

[197] When he was confronted with this behaviour, the witness stated that they had been "difficult times" in Syria which had "broken

everything inside him". Since then he had difficulty remembering things and had "forgotten everything". In Germany he frequently fell into a state of shock during which he would even forget his own name. Finally, the witness asked his legal counsel to explain that he and his family felt they were in danger on account of his giving testimony. He had found correspondence from the Division in connection with his summons open in his letterbox. His sister was sent a summons in Syria, he stated. It was suggested to her that she should remind him, Witness ... [Y], that his siblings were still in Syria. "Friends" had also approached him with "advice", which he had in fact regarded as threats.

[198] However, following the Division's intervention, a break and a discussion between the witness and his legal counsel, the witness gave testimony considerably more candidly than had previously been the case, for instance as regards details of the documents he had seen, even though he had not been able to remember any of them earlier. It was then that he gave the testimony as set out in the above regarding torture and instructions issued in the intelligence service branches to carry it out. The Division took these statements the witness made to be truthful, as they were then detailed, concurred with what the witness had stated during the preliminary investigation, were explained when follow-up questions were asked and were, in the Division's assessment, based on his own experience. The Division attaches particular importance to testimony being consistent, since the danger to which the witness referred had not been addressed in the preliminary investigation.

[199] In contrast, the Division is unable to believe the witness's statements regarding the shift in the balance of power which took place between the religious groups in Syria. Although the outcome of the taking of evidence so far also suggests that Alawites played a dominant role, nowhere else has any account been given of a second significant shift in power at the start of the Syrian conflict. In contrast to his description, which was still nuanced in the course of the preliminary investigation, the witness then described developments in a very generalised and drastic manner. He himself is an Ishmaelite and described this religious group as the one which was the most discriminated against. The Division thus has very clear indications that, in order to exonerate himself, the witness presented a view of things which was based on self-interest and did not correspond to the facts; it is thus not able to take into account the witness's statements in this regard.

[200] (cc) Witness ... [AA], a guard in Branch 251, stated that there was a marked increase in the number of prisoners arriving in

buses from April 2011 on, and that they further increased up until August 2012. Sometimes one vehicle arrived every day, sometimes two or three arrived on several consecutive days. The largest transports were usually made on Fridays because that was the day when the demonstrations were held.

[201] (d) It was against the backdrop of their own oppositional activities, their having taken part in demonstrations, being arrested in other contexts or their general observations regarding the escalating conflict after February 2011 that witnesses ... [DD], ... [EE], ... [FF], ... [GG], ... [HH], ... [N], ... [X], ... [JJ], Z 25/11/2020 and ... [KK]—who were all examined by the Division and were detained in Branch 251 and, in some cases, before that in Sub-branch 40, and whose testimony primarily concerned their detention (see section B.IV.1 [Branch 251], (d), below)—and Witness "Sami" were able to testify. Naturally, their observations only constitute snapshots of overall events, albeit their own; taken together, though, they provide an overall picture of a systematically violent modus operandi on the part of the cooperating Syrian security forces, and not only against alleged members of the opposition or those taking part in the protest movement but also against only supposed protesters. The Division had no reason to doubt the truthfulness of the detailed and discernibly experience-based statements made by the witnesses referred to in the following.

– As Witness ... [DD] reported, the number of arrests increased dramatically in 2011. The aim was to intimidate people by making mass arrests and to stop them taking to the streets again. Many peaceful activists were killed, she stated. Nevertheless, the proportion of people who were killed was small compared to those who were arrested. Later, that is from 2012, fewer people were arrested, but many of them were killed.

– Witness ... [EE], a director and documentary filmmaker, had attempted to document the protest movement from the start by "grabbing a camera" and taking to the streets with the demonstrators. At the start, he stated, the demonstrations were organised "on the fly" at different locations in an attempt to evade the security forces. The use of tear gas and batons and the firing of shots could be made out on the footage, which was later confiscated. The rallies were infiltrated by the security forces, the witness reported, who pretended to be demonstrators and kidnapped those taking part. By his own account, in addition to being carried off to Branch 251, the witness was detained in the Air Force Intelligence Directorate for three months from late March 2011 on and after that in other intelligence service branches, too. He had suffered considerable injuries through beatings and being maltreated with razorblades. He also saw children in detention in the Air Force Intelligence Directorate, he stated. During interrogations conducted in August 2011 in connection with the footage he had recorded he was subjected to massive slapping, elbowing and kicking. Following his detention in Branch 251 in September 2011 he was taken to various other branches of the intelligence services, including Branch 285 of the General Intelligence Directorate and a field office in Najha. Like all the other prisoners, he suffered abuse in the form of punches and beatings with rifle butts and cables, he reported.

- Witness ... [FF] reported about demonstrations he took part in from 15 March 2011 on, first in Damascus and then in Harasta. The regime had used force from day one, he testified. Two weeks after first taking part in a demonstration (i.e. in early April 2011), live ammunition began to be used. He was nearly killed himself once when a shot narrowly missed his head. A participant whom he had been talking to about the fear of dying was shot dead shortly after right next to him. The demonstrations remained peaceful, he reported; he had filmed them in order to record the fact that people who were demonstrating peacefully were being shot at. Once, the entire region of Harasta was stormed and its streets were combed. The witness's own detentions were aimed specifically at gathering information about members of the opposition and his own activity as an anti-government blogger and publicist. In reference to the time he spent in Branch 285 of the General Intelligence Directorate from October 2011 subsequent to his detention in Branch 251, the witness testified that massive amounts of torture had occurred there (as well). He was forced to stand up for 24 hours. He was doused with water and then an air-conditioning unit was pointed at him to cool him down. He was made to lie down on the ground, after which guards trampled all over him. The witness reported that he was hit with belts. Other prisoners were hung up by their hands outside in the blazing sun or deliberately hit over the head. Friends told him what it was like in the central prison in Adra, where men were raped using a bottle or stick and had their penis tied off and scalded with hot water.

- Witness ... [GG] reported that he took part in a demonstration in Douma on 25 March 2011 and then regularly in other demonstrations elsewhere. As he was a doctor, he also tried to get medicines delivered to regions which were besieged. There was, he reported, never a rally at which the security forces did not use force. They had already been shot at by the police at the demonstration on 25 March 2011. At another protest rally (the date of which he could not narrow down more precisely than to sometime in 2011) he had helped a man "get a shot out of his thigh". Demonstrators were regularly arrested, he stated. Typically, as the witness reported, participants were beaten with sticks and the butts of guns, pushed to the ground, after which they were blindfolded and had their hands tied behind their back with cable ties. They were then shoved into cars with their head down. The witness heard those who were released tell of torture; others who were arrested simply disappeared. The security forces involved in this belonged to the army and the intelligence services. Uniformed officers wearing black boots belonged to the army and security forces wearing trainers (whether in uniform or not) were in the intelligence services or paramilitary forces controlled by the intelligence services. The security forces were normally armed with Kalashnikovs. In August 2011, the witness stated, he was detained by the Palestine Branch for 23 hours. He was beaten but there was no real interrogation. He was again arrested in September/October 2011 and taken to Branches 251 and 285. In Branch 285 he was crammed into a cell measuring 4.5 by 5.5 metres with 85 other prisoners. There were prisoners with open wounds and broken bones who cried out in pain. He himself contracted a bad eye infection which was not treated, he stated.

– Witness . . . [HH] reported on his arbitrary arrest in July 2012 at a checkpoint manned by a militia. The only reason he was arrested was that he was from Aleppo. Immediately after his arrest he was taken somewhere unknown to him and was locked up with a lot of people. He and the others were doused with petrol, after which a security officer threatened to light a cigarette. Whilst being relocated he was repeatedly beaten, especially at several checkpoints, he stated. During his subsequent stays in Branches 251 and 285 he was also beaten and kicked.

– Witness . . . [N] reported on his arbitrary arrest on 26 August 2011 during a raid in Damascus. He was first taken to a detention facility belonging to the "10th Division", where he was subjected to brutal beatings which caused extensive wounds on his back, he stated. After a period in the "Al-Khatib Branch" he was then transferred to the military hospital in Harasta on account of his injuries, although he received no treatment there. In fact, that was where "the torture really started". Like other prisoners, he was chained to the bed, whipped, and cut and injured with a blade. The ill-treatment lasted three days; he sometimes lost consciousness. The torture was indescribable, he said. Another prisoner, for instance, said that his hand hurt, whereupon it was chopped off. Instructions were issued to dump the witness out in the street, severely injured ("You can toss him. He's done for.").

– By her own account, Witness ... [X] was active in an opposition group and detained in various facilities operated by the regime a total of five times between November 2011 and March 2014. She took part in demonstrations from June 2011, all of which had been peaceful, she said. Nevertheless, the security forces had arrested anyone they could get their hands on. Often they had arrested people who only happened to be at the mosque and had only gone there to say their prayers. That was why, she reported, the demonstrations were organised as five-minute "flash demos". She herself had not seen any live ammunition being used in Damascus, apart from at a funeral, but she had heard that it was being used in the surrounding area. The security forces wore military uniform although they were neither members of the regular police nor of the army. Before her first arrest in November 2011, the witness stated, she had taken part in one of the demonstrations in Damascus which were mainly held on Fridays. After a few minutes, security forces from the Air Force Intelligence Directorate had appeared. As she had seen a 12-year-old boy being beaten, she herself was arrested and abused in a police station along with other women and men. After the Syrian Army shelled Homs, she, in February 2012, helped to collect medicines for those who were injured in the city. Torture existed in each of the facilities in which she was detained, she reported. In February 2012, she also saw dead people in Branch 285 of the General Intelligence Directorate and in the summer of 2012 in the prison run by the Air Force Intelligence Directorate. Other women also told her about the systematic use of rape in the facilities operated by the intelligence services and at checkpoints. Sometimes it was used as a means of humiliation and to exert pressure on the women's husbands: "Women were raped in front of their husband's eyes to get the husband to confess."

– Witness ... [JJ] testified that, in September 2012 following his detention in Branch 251, he was taken to the central office of the General Intelligence Directorate in Kafr Sousa and, along with the other detainees, subjected to continuous beatings there. It was

common knowledge that torture was applied in the branches,
he stated.

- Witness Z 25/11/2020, who was examined anonymously on 25 and
26 November 2020, testified that he took part in a demonstration in
Douma on 18 March 2011. A large number of security forces from
various agencies armed with Kalashnikovs arrived in their vehicles.
They broke up the demonstration and used brutal force against the
demonstrators. They beat them and dragged them into waiting
buses, the witness stated. The same happened at a sit-in in front of
the municipal authorities that same day. The security forces had shot
dead 11 people that day. The witness himself was arrested a week
later for taking part in the demonstration and for being an activist,
he stated. After his release he took part in the funeral procession for
those who were killed, he reported.

- By his own account, Witness . . . [KK] was one of the activists who
was involved in organising the demonstrations held in Raqqa in
spring 2011. The first demonstration was held there on
25 March 2011, after which demonstrations took place twice a
week, he reported. They had printed details on leaflets in a coordination office and then distributed the leaflets. Sometimes the security
forces, especially the *shabiha* units, were already waiting at the place
where a demonstration was to be held and tried to stop it happening,
then they began breaking up the demonstration using batons. The
witness had, however, not witnessed anyone dying at a demonstration until 2012. He was working in an NGO because he wanted to
promote democratic structures and civil-society engagement. That
was why he was wanted and was imprisoned on several occasions: by
the military intelligence service in Raqqa in May 2011, by the
criminal police in Raqqa in November 2011 and then by the
military police in May 2012, after which he was transferred to the
Al-Khatib and Palestine branches, amongst others.

- The statement which Witness "Sami" made to the police—which is
primarily of relevance in relation to the "Caesar Files"—was communicated to the Division through its hearing of the investigating
officer. The witness stated that "at the start of the revolution" (which
he said was mid-March 2011) he took part in demonstrations in his
hometown of Qaboun in the Greater Damascus area. He himself
saw demonstrators being shot dead there. The other demonstrators
were not able to recover the dead bodies from the streets, but had to
flee. On another occasion he witnessed a demonstrator being shot at,
after which she was paralysed. He saw many people arrested during

that period, he stated. On one occasion alone around 40 people were arrested in his hometown, he testified. Even taking into account the fact that it was not possible to directly examine the witness, the Division did not doubt the truthfulness of his detailed statement, which according to the officer questioning him was given candidly and without any communication problems.

[202] (e) The Division supplementally adduced a number of reports on the course of the conflict which are consistent with the direct evidence supplied by the witnesses and experts to which it gave precedence in its assessment, thereby confirming it circumstantially.

[203] (aa) Reports published by an international commission of inquiry set up by a United Nations body describe the course of the conflict in a manner which supports the outcome of the taking of evidence.

[204] (1) In the light of the result of a fact-finding mission in September 2011 and the worsening of the human rights situation in Syria it revealed, the United Nations Human Rights Council set up an independent international commission of inquiry which reported on events in Syria in November 2011. According to the report, it is based on face-to-face interviews with victims of and other witnesses to events after March 2011.

[205] In sum, the report finds that there were a limited number of protests in February 2011 around issues such as poverty, corruption, freedom of speech, democratic participation and the release of political prisoners, which were linked to calls for economic and political reforms. In Daraa they were also held in response to the detention and torture of a group of children, which then spread across the entire country; the report mentions Latakia, Baniyas, Damascus, Deir ez-Zor, Homs, Hama and Idlib. Extensive military-like operations took place in Daraa on 25 April 2011, which soon spread across the whole country and involved increasingly violent conduct on the part of the state security forces. In November 2011 the Office of the United Nations High Commissioner for Human Rights (OHCHR) assumed that at least 3,500 civilians had been killed by security forces in the period since March 2011. Thousands more had been detained and tortured, with most of the victims being in Homs, Hama and Daraa. The violence had escalated until, in around November 2011, military and security forces had carried out operations in various cities against public assemblies and funeral processions in the course of which tanks had also been deployed and 260 civilians had been killed within a short space of time.

[206] The report goes on to deal in detail with official statements issued by the Syrian government, the founding of the "Free Syrian Army" and the response of foreign countries. In a section headed "Excessive use of force and extrajudicial executions" details are provided of how government forces shot indiscriminately at unarmed demonstrators when quelling the protests, hitting them in the upper body and the head. Defectors reported that they had received orders to shoot at unarmed people without warning. In some instances, demonstrators were ordered to disperse and warnings were given before the shooting began. Joint operations between the military, security forces and militias with "shoot-to-kill" orders and numerous fatalities, including children, were held in Latakia in mid-April 2011. One defector gave details of orders which were issued under the guise of cracking down on "armed conspirators and terrorists". There had been a peaceful demonstration at which participants had called for freedom and carried olive branches. The demonstrators had been shot at with machine guns and other weapons. There had been dead and injured people on the ground afterwards. Helpers who had tried to take food, water and medicines to people in the city of Daraa on 29 April 2011 had been ambushed and more than 40 people, including women and children, had been killed.

[207] The report goes on to describe the deployment of snipers, the setting up and use of force at checkpoints, the blockading of cities and city districts followed by house raids, and the killing, by security forces posted behind them, of conscripts who had fired into the air instead of shooting at demonstrators. The report also describes the mass arrest of demonstrators and of civilians in large-scale raids, for example in the city of Baniyas on 7 May 2011. These arrests targeted activists and journalists. Detainees were "routinely tortured". In addition, thousands went missing or disappeared. The report also describes cases of people being abducted and then disappearing. Family members had never heard from them again and were advised by the state authorities to forget about them.

[208] Another section in the report deals with the use of systematic torture: beatings with sticks and cables; electroshocks; having to endure stress positions for days on end; food, water and sleep deprivation; overcrowded cells; and sexual violence, that is rape and maltreatment of the genital organs. There are reports of torture and killings, including of minors, and of their being taken to intelligence service facilities. Those who tried to leave the country were likewise subjected to lethal force. The report mentions cases of people being shot and killed trying to cross the Syrian border in August and September 2011.

[209] Finally, the report explains that witness testimonies revealed that the security forces' operations were highly coordinated. Various units carried out concerted actions. The operations were carried out on the orders of high-ranking officers (colonels or brigadier generals), including the order to open fire on unarmed demonstrators.

[210] (2) A second report dated February 2012 gives an update on the chronology of events. This report, too, was based on statements made by unnamed witnesses, on publicly accessible sources and government documents. According to the report, the situation had become increasingly violent and polarised. The peaceful protests against the government had continued, as had the security forces' violent response—backed by Bashar al-Assad, according to whom the top priority was still to "restore security and fight terrorism with an iron fist". At the same time, the Free Syrian Army carried out its first operations against the government forces—although these were initially only defensive in nature. According to the Syrian government, 2,131 civilians were killed in the period from March to December 2011, although according to other sources there were 6,399 civilian deaths and 1,680 deaths of army defectors in the period from March 2011 to February 2012. The report also cites military operations in January and February 2012 carried out in residential areas— citing villages around Idlib, in Homs, Al-Zabadani, Rif Dimashq, Khaldieh and Hama—which included bombardment with heavy weapons leading to large numbers of civilian deaths. "Shoot-to-kill" orders were still being issued against peaceful demonstrators. Arbitrary arrests were still being made on a grand scale, mainly by encircling demonstrations and taking those arrested away in buses and trucks to the intelligence services' detention facilities. Besides, entire urban districts were sealed off by intelligence services, elite army units and/or *shabiha* militia and raids were conducted in the course of which a large number of people were arrested. Military hospital wings were transformed into torture centres. Doctors and medical staff in the civilian hospitals clandestinely treated the injured and sick and were then likely to be arrested themselves.

[211] Another United Nations report entitled "Out of sight, out of mind: Deaths in detention in the Syrian Arab Republic", which was published in February 2016 by a committee set up by the Human Rights Council, describes in detail a pattern which, in the committee's assessment, became established across the country in the period after March 2011, namely of the mass arrest of civilians or their enforced disappearance, their lack of contact with relatives and deaths by torture in government prisons.

[212] (3) The Division is aware that the above-mentioned documents are not able to act as direct evidence of the human rights violations they describe. In particular, the Division was not in a position itself to verify the information provided by the witnesses, whom the report does not name. Given the institutions which compiled the reports and the wide-ranging description of their bases and limitations—emphasis is placed on the fact that the Syrian government denied the authors of the report the opportunity to see the situation on the ground for themselves—the Division nevertheless regards them as circumstantial evidence of the intensifying government response to the largely peaceful protests, which in April 2011 tipped over into systematic, countrywide arbitrary arrests, torture and killings.

[213] (bb) The Division similarly drew on reports by the NGOs Human Rights Watch and Amnesty International as circumstantial evidence, which by their own account were based on personal interviews with numerous victim witnesses of the internal Syrian conflict. It was not possible to verify these sources either. The evidence therefore had to be treated with caution.

[214] (1) The report entitled "We've Never Seen Such Horror: Crimes Against Humanity by Syrian Security Forces" traces the sequence of violent responses by the Syrian security forces and cites the number of dead from the start of the protest movement. It focuses on events in the governorate of Daraa in the period between 18 and 22 May 2011. According to its authors, the report is based on 50 interviews with local residents and people who were staying there at the time and on an analysis of generally accessible press releases.

[215] According to the authors of the report, the protest movement was still quite insignificant in February 2011. They regard the start of the protests proper to be the arrest and torture of 15 children and teenagers in Daraa and the protest rallies held in Daraa in response to that as from 18 March 2011. These were attended by several thousand civilians and centred around the Al-Omari Mosque in Daraa. The report lists further protests held between 23 and 25 March 2011 which resulted in the deaths of more than 30 protesters. According to the report, at least 12 people died during protests held in Latakia on 26 March 2011. At first, government representatives were sent to the city to try to calm and pacify the situation, and Bashar al-Assad publicly pledged to enact reforms and promised to establish a committee of inquiry, but the violence had then escalated in April 2011. Starting on Friday, 1 April 2011, thousands of protesters had taken to the streets. Between eight and 15 people died during a demonstration against the government held in Douma. Subsequently, mass demonstrations were

472   GERMANY (KOBLENZ HIGHER REGIONAL COURT)

held every Friday in bigger towns and cities across the whole of Syria, including in Daraa, Baniyas, Homs, Harasta, Latakia, Idlib and Qamishli. Twenty-five people were killed in Daraa on 8 April 2011 and 34 during protests and funeral processions on 22 and 23 April 2011. Across the country, 22 April 2011 was the most deadly day thus far, with a total of 110 victims. On the one hand, witnesses concurred in their reports of cases in which crowds were shot at with live ammunition and automatic weapons after tear gas was first used and shots were fired into the air. On the other hand, though, there were also already reports of cases in which shots were fired without prior warning. The targets had been the demonstrators as well as the helpers who had wanted to help the injured. From late March 2011 onwards, snipers placed on the roofs of government buildings in Daraa had also fired at protesters' heads, throats and upper bodies.

[216] The report goes on to describe in detail how security forces carried out large-scale sweep operations against those cities and villages which were regarded as hotbeds of the protests. On 25 April 2011, for instance, security and military forces had moved into Daraa in armoured personnel carriers, had shelled the city for 16 hours and then set up numerous checkpoints and posted snipers on the roofs of buildings. The electricity supply and all communications were cut off. The security forces opened fire on anyone who tried to leave the house. Later, hundreds of people were arrested in their homes. The city was then placed under military control and residents experienced shortages of supplies. There were more than 200 deaths, including of residents in neighbouring cities who had, on 29 April 2011, attempted to help the besieged people and then themselves come under fire from the security forces without prior warning. This pattern was repeated in several places: on 25 April 2011 the security forces also surrounded Douma, on 1 May 2011 Al-Zabadani, then on 6 May 2011 Baniyas and various districts of Homs. The report also details military operations in smaller towns and how many demonstrators were killed in May 2011 and where. Mention is also made of people who wanted to provide medical assistance who were prevented from doing so or were shot at.

[217] (2) By its own account, the report entitled "Torture Archipelago", published in July 2012, is based on 200 interviews conducted by Human Rights Watch staff, including with members of the Syrian security services who defected. The interviewees stated that they had witnessed ill-treatment and conditions in the intelligence service prisons. Based on this, the report lists the individual organisations in the security apparatus (*mukhabarat*) and 27 detention centres

assigned to them by name, name of the intelligence service branch office and torture methods applied there. The torture techniques to which the interviewees were subjected or which they observed are presented by means of a detailed description and, in some cases, using key words. The interviewed victims are listed by code name, the date of the interview and the date, branch office and place where they were detained.

[218] (3) The Amnesty International report "'It breaks the human': Torture, disease and death in Syria's prisons" focuses on people who were imprisoned by the Syrian regime in the period 2011 to 2015 and is based on interviews with more than 60 former detainees and staff in a military hospital. The report describes the conditions in detention centres operated by the Syrian intelligence service and in the prison in Saydnaya and the torture techniques used there.

[219] (4) The Division feels there is a sufficient basis for drawing on the research presented in the above reports, at least circumstantially. Even though it was, again, not possible to verify the cited sources, in view of the detailed descriptions the reports contain—which, in essence, concur with the information the Division obtained from the witnesses and experts it examined—it feels it is out of the question that the reports, taken as a whole, are based on inaccurate findings, even though the reliability of individual observations should be called into question.

2. Central Crisis Management Cell

[220] Witness . . . [Z] described in detail the status, tasks, composition and activities of the Central Crisis Management Cell (CCMC), the highest-ranking central coordinating body which was established in the light of the protest movement. His statements are confirmed by witnesses . . . [T], . . . [S] and Z 28/07/16.

[221] (a) Witness . . . [Z], an American lawyer who was involved in prosecuting war crimes committed in the former Yugoslavia, holds a senior position within the international NGO Commission for International Justice and Accountability (CIJA), which was established as a foundation under Dutch law in 2012 against the backdrop of the conflict in Syria. According to the witness, the NGO is funded by various countries, including Germany, Canada, the United States of America, the United Kingdom and the Netherlands. They have no influence on the work done by the CIJA. More senior members of staff are recruited from amongst those who have, in the course of working for courts, gained experience in international criminal prosecution, for

instance lawyers, former public prosecutors and analysts who conducted investigations in Rwanda, the former Yugoslavia, Cambodia
and Sierra Leone. According to the witness, the organisation's founders
had already begun collecting witness statements and written documents
relating to the internal Syrian conflict back in 2011 so as to be able to
make them available to courts at a later date. This work had, the
witness stated, essentially involved conducting interviews and documenting a large number of witness statements—from both civilian
victims and former members of the regime and other eyewitnesses—
most of which were made anonymously. The majority of these people
were still in Syria, the witness stated. The witness interviews were all
conducted based on a set protocol. Each witness was instructed about
the fact that their testimony might possibly become the subject matter
of criminal proceedings and that they had to tell the truth. Witnesses
were then able to speak freely without being guided by a CIJA staff
member. Dossiers were compiled once all the different statements were
systematised. Witness ... [Z] presented examples of transcripts of
witness statements to illustrate the procedure followed.

[222] According to Witness ... [Z], more than 2,500 witnesses
were interviewed; the survey for the most part covered the years
2011 and 2012. Further, more than 800,000 pages from a large
number of original documents relating to the military and Syrian
intelligence service were "got out" during the subsequent civil war.
In practical terms, the work had involved local CIJA staff going into an
area as soon as armed groups had left it. They then looked for
documents, including on electronic data carriers, in former government
buildings and took them to a safe place. The documents were then
scanned, archived and barcoded in order to be able to traceably
document their origin and content as sources.

[223] Witness ... [Z] stated that reliable information about the
establishment, activity and staffing of the Central Crisis Management
Cell was secured in this way. As its name already suggested, the body
was set up to engage in crisis management, he testified. Its task was to
standardise the strategy applied by all the involved government organisations in relation to fighting the conflict. Accordingly, the body was
made up of individuals who already held positions of leadership in—
from the regime's perspective—maintaining order. Formally, it was
aligned to the Syrian Ba'ath Party. The witness stated that the
CCMC comprised the heads of the individual intelligence services,
the Minister of the Interior, the Minister of Defence and, on an ad
hoc basis, other ministers. Ultimately, it was the regime's hard response
to the growing protest movement. Its objective was to standardise the

security authorities' escalating operations. According to the witness, the CCMC was chaired by Mohammad Said Bekheitan up until October 2011, then by Hassan Turkmani. Members included Ali Mamlouk (Head of the General Intelligence Directorate), Jamil Hassan (Head of the Air Force Intelligence Directorate), Mohammed Dib Zaitoun (Head of the Political Security Directorate) and Abdel-Fatah Qudsiyeh (Head of the Military Intelligence Directorate). Minister of the Interior Mohammad al-Shaar and Minister of the Defence Dawoud Rajiha also belonged to it.

[224] The ascertained CCMC documents dated April 2011 were taken from a government building in Idlib by a CIJA member of staff in 2015 in the manner described above. The member of staff was a Syrian living in that region, not a member of the government. He had gained access to the office after the Syrian regime staff left Idlib. The ascertained document dated August 2011 was taken from the Military Intelligence Directorate office in Raqqa. It, too, was found by a member of staff after the regime pulled out.

[225] Witness ... [Z] also testified that, according to credible information provided by regime staff, decisions were passed along information chains down to the provinces, including smaller units in the army and security authorities, for implementation. Specifically, all of the intelligence services, army command posts and police stations had been involved in passing on instructions. In support of this the witness presented further documents. In a letter dated 8 August 2011, the sub-branches affiliated to Branch 243 were ordered by the head of branch to conduct daily raids and patrols and to arrest demonstrators and other people they held responsible for the protests. In another letter dated 22 August 2011, which made reference to a circular issued by the Ministry of the Interior on 16 August 2011, the head of the Political Intelligence Service in Raqqa informed the Ministry of the Interior that detailed measures which had been ordered—such as a common approach to certain city districts and the arrest of "incendiaries" and those taking part in demonstrations—had been implemented. Expressions comparable to the ascertained letters written by the CCMC are used in the letter.

[226] (b) Some of the documents, which can be attributed to the CCMC by dint of their content, and which were inspected and translated, are direct transcripts of one of the meetings of the CCMC, others relay orders issued by the CCMC. It is also evident that each document was transmitted by fax.

[227] One document dated 20 April 2011 is headed "Circular" and, according to its letterhead, was written by the General Command of

the Army and Armed Forces and the Head of Branch 294 of the (most likely Military) Intelligence Directorate. According to other headers, it is "Strictly Confidential" and "Urgent" and addressed to the head of the branch. The document cross-references a letter by a regional commander concerning a meeting of the CCMC. The body had met on 18 April 2011 and taken various decisions which were subsequently detailed in the document dated 20 April 2011 and are reproduced in the Findings. At the end of the document there are two illegible signatures, one of which is headed "Head of the Intelligence Branch". A seal at the bottom of the document bears the words "General Army Command" and the—otherwise illegible—label "Intelligence Branch". Reference is also made to a distribution list which includes the branch offices of the intelligence service branch and the request "Please make all necessary arrangements".

[228] Another document, also dated 20 April 2011, is headed "An Arab Nation with an Eternal Message". According to the sender's address, it was written by the Syrian leadership of the Ba'ath Party. The document is also marked "Strictly Confidential" and "Only to be Kept with the Officer Responsible". This is followed by the heading "Minutes of the Meeting". According to the body of the text, the CCMC, "chaired by Comrade General Secretary", met on 20 April 2011 and "continued its analysis of the security policy situation". There follows a list of orders and (alleged) facts as reproduced by the Division in the Findings. The document concludes "Please take note and implement in accordance with jurisdiction" and is signed by the Deputy Regional Secretary of the Ba'ath Party.

[229] The last document, dated 6 August 2011, also bears the heading "An Arab Nation with an Eternal Message" and is marked "Strictly Confidential—Urgent". According to the letterhead, it was also written by the leadership of the Syrian Ba'ath Party and is addressed to "Comrade Head of the Party's Branch Office in the Governorate of Hama, Rif Dimashq, Deir ez-Zor, Homs, Idlib and Daraa" in his function as "Head of the Security Committee". It goes on to list the decisions which the CCMC took at its meeting on 5 August 2011 (these are reproduced in summary form in the Division's Findings). The letter closes with the words "Please implement what is required to bring the crisis to a swift conclusion, to return to safety and security and peace for our citizens". The signature is followed by the words "Comrade Head of the National Security Bureau".

[230] (c) Further witnesses confirmed the existence and function of the CCMC, as well as, in some cases, the instructions issued to use force.

[231] According to Witness . . . [S], the CCMC's objective was to get a coordinated "grip on" the demonstrations. He testified that overarching orders to put down the uprisings were issued to the intelligence services, the police, sometimes even the press. The members of the CCMC included Dib Zaitoun (Head of the National Security Bureau), Jamal Hassan (Head of the Air Force Intelligence Directorate), Ali Mamlouk (Head of the General Intelligence Directorate), the Minister of Defence and the Minister of the Interior. The CCMC was set up in late March or early April 2011, the witness stated. Witness . . . [T] confirmed its existence.

[232] Witness Z 28/07/16 testified that the Cell—which he initially described as the "Directorate for Emergencies" and the "Cell for Dealing with Emergencies" but which, when confronted with this testimony, he confirmed was the CCMC—was composed of the leaders of the security services, in particular the heads of the intelligence services Bachtiar (National Security Bureau), Mamlouk (General Intelligence Directorate) and Hassan (Air Force Intelligence Directorate). The Cell was established on the basis of a decree issued by President Assad in order to get the popular movement, which was perceived as a crisis, under control. The witness stated that there were security branches in other places below the level of the Crisis Cell, meaning that every town or city was involved. The CCMC had issued specific instructions. From the start this included instructions to arrest people who were communicating via social media in order to silence them, the witness stated. Another order issued by the Crisis Cell was addressed to the branches in the provinces. They were to put pressure on traders so that they, in turn, would pass it on to the rest of the population. Finally, there had also been coded orders to use force, for instance, to "take the necessary steps" and "blot out the resistance". The witness himself had, some three months after the unrest, seen orders to use targeted force against demonstrators. In his recollection this was in May 2011.

[233] (d) Taking the above as a whole, the Division has no doubts as regards the establishment, composition and function of the CCMC. It also takes the documents submitted by Witness . . . [Z] to be authentic and uses them as the basis for its assessment. There are no indications which cast doubt on the methods applied by the CIJA as described by Witness . . . [Z]. The witness detailed the origin of the information about the course of the conflict which was available to him and about the Syrian security apparatus, and he backed this up with numerous documents. The documents he presented containing orders issued by the CCMC fit with the hierarchy and power structure in the

Syrian state, in particular the function of the Ba'ath Party, which pervades the machinery of power. Especially in view of the fragmentary nature of the recorded decisions, in particular their only being available as forwarded circulars, and their coded wording, the Division also found no indication that these could be—interest-driven—forgeries. It is also easy to bring the CCMC's orders into line chronologically with the course of the conflict as presented directly to the Division by the witnesses and experts.

3. Number, documentation and treatment of those killed: Mass graves

[234] That the Syrian regime had large numbers of people killed from April 2011 on at the latest, that it bureaucratically documented this and had the bodies buried in mass graves also follows from the testimony given by former employees of the regime, from satellite images of alleged mass graves and from the origin and analysis of a large number of photographs of corpses (the "Caesar Files"). At the same time, evidence is thereby furnished of the fact that a substantial proportion of those who were killed originated from the branches of the intelligence services, including the General Intelligence Directorate.

[235] (a) The documentation of the dead by a Syrian military photographer ("Caesar") as ordered from late spring 2011 on provides key evidence of the systematic and extensive killing of those arrested in the intelligence services' prisons. The 26,938 image files which "Caesar" secretly secured and took out of the country depict the corpses of 6,821 people, who were each photographed more than once; the majority of the people bore signs of emaciation and of injuries caused by torture. The corpses had numbers on them which shed light on their origin. The numbers were either written on the person's skin with a felt-tip pen or on notes on their body.

[236] (aa) The Division was not able to directly examine the military photographer known by the alias "Caesar", as he lives abroad at an unknown location. A friend of "Caesar" who also lives abroad under an unknown identity and who is known to the Division only by the alias "Sami" was involved in securing, storing and sending the image files out of Syria; he was not prepared to undergo witness examination. However, the Division was able to gain a sufficient impression of the origin, content and authenticity of the image files by examining both Witness . . . [LL], who was in contact with "Caesar" and "Sami" in 2014 and documented and edited their work, and Witness . . . [O], who conducted the police questioning of "Sami" during the preliminary investigation, on the basis of a plausibility

report on the image files produced by a foreign forensic expert, by
inspecting a part of the photographs taken by "Caesar" and by means of
an overall forensic assessment of the photographs conducted by the
expert ... [R].

[237] (bb) Witness ... [LL], a French journalist and publicist who
was examined by the Division, was able to enter into contact with
"Sami" in 2014 via intermediaries and, also, through him, with
"Caesar" in the course of her work as a journalist, which regularly took
her to Arab states, including to Syria in 2012. Based on interviews with
both men regarding the origin of the image files and other research she
conducted, Witness ... [LL] published a book entitled "Codename
Caesar: In the Heart of the Syrian Death Machine". The witness
"Sami" was questioned on 9 November 2017 as part of the structural
investigation conducted by the Federal Public Prosecutor's Office. The
content of his statements was relayed to the Division by Witness ...
[O], a police investigator.

[238] (1) The Division does not doubt that Witness ... [LL] and
Witness ... [O], whom it examined in person, testified truthfully.
In particular, Witness ... [LL] testified in detail about how she made
contact with the witness "Caesar". This was done through an editorial
assignment, its incorporation into the book project she was working
on at the time, gaining the trust of a chain of intermediaries, including "Sami", a key confidant of "Caesar". She was able to conduct a
detailed interview with "Sami", she stated, and it was he who, ultimately, helped her establish contact with "Caesar". After telephoning
with "Caesar" via Skype, she had several face-to-face meetings with
him. The witness also comprehensibly explained what she understood
"Caesar"'s motivation to be for documenting the photographs: Syria
was a country of absentees; the photographs provided both an insight
into the fate of a large number of people who disappeared and
invaluable help to their relatives.

[239] The particulars which Witness ... [LL] and Witness ... [O]
provided about the witnesses "Caesar" and "Sami" were detailed, both
consistent in themselves and with each other and plausible. Taken
together with the other evidence in this complex of evidence, they
form a consistent overall picture. In particular, the expert's analysis of
the photographs (see (cc) and (ee), below) proves the accuracy of the
information. The mass burials of dead bodies bearing numbers (see (b),
below), which various former employees of the regime described as
well, also confirm what "Caesar" and "Sami" reported. Finally, the fact
that Witness ... [T]—who, in turn, relies on information given to him
by clients as part of his work as a Syrian lawyer and victim

representative—confirmed both the tasks of the Syrian military photographers before and after the start of the conflict and the numerical recording of those killed by means of notes stuck on their corpses or written on their skin circumstantially speaks to its truthfulness.

[240] (2) Based on the information provided by "Caesar" and "Sami", as relayed by Witness ... [LL] and Witness ... [O], the Division draws on the following facts in its assessment:

[241] Up until he fled Syria in August 2013, "Caesar" was a senior member of the military photography staff in the Syrian military police. Both the photographic documentation department and the military police were based in the Qaboun district of Damascus. As part of his original job, "Caesar" and his staff were required to document the members of the military who died or were injured as a result of an accident, crime or combat action. He was also responsible for the military hospitals in Mezzeh and Tishreen in and near Damascus, though not for the other military hospital in Harasta.

[242] From spring 2011 the subject matter of this documentation work changed. In March 2011, "Caesar"'s attention was drawn by a staff member to images showing civilians who had been shot and killed. Shortly thereafter he himself was called by the forensic medicine department to go the military hospital in Tishreen, subsequently also to that in Mezzeh, and was commissioned with documenting the corpses lying in the courtyard there, which bore the signs of torture and ill-treatment. He was required to take several photographs of each, that is four to five per corpse. The bodies had already been divided into groups of "martyrs" (which were identified by their real names and of which there were only a few), "detainees" and "terrorists". The corpses categorised as "detainees" and "terrorists" had numbers on them, either written on their skin using a felt-tip pen or on an attached piece of paper. A number or letter identified the intelligence service branch in which a person had died—for instance "J" for "Jawiyya" (= air) to designate the Air Force Intelligence Directorate. Another number sequence comprised a prisoner number used to identify the person and a report number issued by the military hospitals' forensic medicine department which was assigned to the corpses in ascending order up to 5,000 after which the numbering started over with the addition of a letter. In a few isolated cases the dead had no numbers on them.

[243] A forensic expert of the rank of colonel who was responsible for the Tishreen and Mezzeh hospitals was routinely required to record the physical characteristics of the corpses and to write a brief postmortem report. A military photographer was called in, too. After assigning a forensic number, the photographer was required to take several

photographs (generally between three and five) of each corpse. The forensic medicine department was then required to compile dossiers on the deceased, to which the photographs taken by the military photographers were added.

[244] In the assessment of both "Caesar" and "Sami" there were two reasons why the Syrian authorities compiled these documents. First, it was important, for bureaucratic reasons, to be able to issue a death certificate citing a natural cause of death which could, if required, be passed on to the victim's relatives. Second, the documents served internal control purposes, in that they ensured that the fate of those detained could be unequivocally verified, that is that they had, in fact, been killed and had not been released, as a result of corruption, for instance.

[245] After "Caesar" first became aware, in March 2011, of civilian deaths, he contacted "Sami", a friend, and reported that he had received photographs of tortured corpses from his employees ("I'm getting photos that are so terrible."). In the opinion of both men, the state of the corpses which were laid out in the hospital courtyards did not concur with the medical report which "Caesar" had received from the hospitals' forensic medicine department. There had in the past already been similar, but—according to "Caesar"—"not such brutal" photographic material. Once "Caesar" had smuggled the image files out of his office on data carriers, he and "Sami" decided that he would continue his work so that both of them could collate photographic material and get it out of the country. "Caesar" and "Sami" wanted to let the public know what was happening to the large numbers of people who were disappearing in Syria at that time and to secure evidence. They both expected the Syrian regime to fall imminently and those who belonged to it to be prosecuted. Following this organisational phase, from May 2011 "Caesar" and "Sami" cooperated such that "Caesar" secretly stored, on USB sticks and memory cards, the photographs which he had taken or which he obtained from his employees, he smuggled them out of the authority and took them to "Sami", who then stored them in various file folders on a PC and deleted the files on the storage media, which he passed back to "Caesar". At the start, i.e. in May 2011, the image files contained pictures of only a few corpses. However, they quickly increased in number to 10 to 20 per day. By 2012, around 50 to 70 corpses were being documented each day by the military photographers in Damascus.

[246] Given the security situation and the fact that the internet was being monitored in Syria, getting the photographic material and files out of the country proved difficult and was the reason why different

routes were used and why there were then different versions of the data. In 2012, "Sami" had intermediaries compress the images (down to 250 to 300 KB per image) and upload them to the online platform Google Drive. After fleeing to Lebanon in July 2013, he was also given a hard drive which had been smuggled into Lebanon by the Free Syrian Army and which contained another compressed version of the photographs. Once he was in Jordan, and subsequently in Turkey, "Sami" then put the photographs into chronological order based on the numbers applied to the corpses. He then renamed the files and had intermediaries pass them on to the British law firm Carter-Ruck and Co., who in turn commissioned experts with carrying out a plausibility check. The original, uncompressed files (1 to 1.3 MB per image), in their original order, were first stored on an external hard drive and taken to Syrian territory controlled by the Free Syrian Army and then also uploaded to the Google Drive platform. These files were made available to the law firm, too. A meeting with forensic experts whom the law firm had commissioned was held in Qatar in early 2014. "Caesar", who fled Syria in late September 2013, smuggled photographic material comprising another 1,500 images taken in July and August 2013 out of the country on a USB stick.

[247] In the light of this sequence of events, which it was not possible to determine any more precisely given that the Division was not able to directly examine the witnesses "Caesar" and "Sami", it assumes, in terms of chronology and number, that "Caesar" had for the first time become aware of suspicious—though initially only isolated—corpses in March 2011 which provided an indication of abuse and killings by the Syrian security forces, that image files relating to between 10 and 20 corpses were secured each day as from May 2011 and that the number of photographs taken up until the end of the recording period in August 2013 successively increased. Given the total number of deceased people photographed (6,821), this sequence of events was readily consistent. Based on the statements made by the expert . . . [R] as set out in the following, the Division assumes that the people depicted generally died only a few days, up to a maximum of a few weeks, before the photographs were taken.

[248] (cc) As Witness . . . [LL] confirmed before the Division, the London-based law firm Carter-Ruck and Co. to whom, according to "Caesar" and "Sami", the image files were passed, commissioned a body of inquiry with conducting a forensic analysis. The body included, as its chairperson, Sir Desmond de Silva (former Chief Prosecutor of the Special Court for Sierra Leone) as well as Prof. David Crane (former first Chief Prosecutor of the Special Court for

Sierra Leone), Prof. Geoffrey Nice (former Lead Prosecutor of the Former President of Yugoslavia at the International Criminal Tribunal for the Former Yugoslavia), Dr Stuart Hamilton (an expert in forensic pathology), Prof. Susan Black (Professor of Anatomy and Forensic Anthropology) and Stephen Cole (technical director of a forensics investigation company). According to the investigation report, the experts had the opportunity to interview the witness "Caesar" in January 2014 after which they were able to assess the authenticity of the photographs.

[249] According to their written statements, after analysing a sample of the 5,500 photographs of a total of 835 deceased persons, 3,500 of them in detail, and comparing the statements made by "Caesar" and "Sami" concerning the origin of the images, the experts came to the conclusion that the witnesses' descriptions were consistent with the injuries as established which were depicted on the images made available. The corpses in the photographs exhibited signs of strangulation, beatings, emaciation and injuries caused by electric shocks. Overall, the picture emerged, the experts concluded, that the deceased had very likely died of unnatural causes, specifically as a result of ill-treatment and torture, even though fatal injuries were, ultimately, only found in a minority of the cases investigated. Making a value-based assessment, the experts come to the conclusion that the material they analysed constitutes "evidence of the systematic torture and killing of detainees by actors in the Syrian government".

[250] (dd) Witness … [O], who led the police investigation, explained the origin of the photographs, which were printed out in the course of the present proceedings and were available on data carriers. According to him, they are the uncompressed data sets which were taken out of the country via the internet, supplemented by files which "Caesar" created in July and August 2013 and which were then passed on by "Sami" in September 2017 to the Federal Public Prosecutor General via intermediaries in Liechtenstein. According to Witness … [O], these data were also made available to the expert … [R], who had already been commissioned as part of the preliminary investigation.

[251] The Division inspected a selection of the photographs. In its layperson's assessment, the overwhelming majority of them depict the corpses of naked young men lying on, for instance, either tarpaulins or dusty ground in an outdoor area. The corpses, some of which are severely emaciated, show signs of different kinds of injuries, including open wounds and, in the majority of cases, significant bruising and abrasions, some extensive, some also longitudinal, which could be an

indication of beatings or whippings. The eyes of some of the corpses were missing. Further, the Division had access to an example of a form which the witness "Caesar" had photographed and, according to Witness . . . [LL], passed on to her. According to its introductory text, the form served to document a death and was "issued on behalf of the military public prosecution service".

[252] (ee) All the photographs were subjected to a forensic examination by the experienced court expert . . . [R], who heads a forensic medicine institute in Germany. By way of his vivid and impactful presentation, which was backed up by photographic material taken from the "Caesar Files", the expert gave his comprehensive expert opinion, which included brief descriptions of the people depicted in the photographs, including their age, sex and prominent features, a translation and a systematic representation of the numbers visible on the corpses, a description of the general condition of those depicted in the photographs, signs of ill-treatment, torture and the use of violence, and the presumed cause of death. The expert drew attention to the limitations of any diagnosis done on the basis of assessing photographs, which is no substitute for a postmortem, on the basis of only partial views of the bodies being available and the limitations of enlarging the photographic material. He gave examples of case histories based on individual images.

[253] According to the expert, the majority of the photographs depict naked males lying on their back in an outdoor area. There are a total of 26,938 image files showing a total of 6,821 distinguishable individuals. Based on the numbering of the corpses, their origin can be broken down as follows:

(Sub-)Branch	No of image files	No of people
215	13,801	3,551
216	1,108	292
220	210	50
227	8,001	2,049
235	482	127
248	206	54
251	446	110
Air Force ("Air")	1,515	352
Military Police	177	46
Unknown	601	116
Miscellaneous	391	74

[254] The photographs showed 6,820 men and one woman, the expert stated. They were judged to include 329 very young people, possibly adolescents, 2,342 people of a young age, 2,178 middle-aged people, 1,215 people of advanced age, 531 old people and 226 people whose age could not be determined. The overwhelming majority of the deceased had been photographed lying on stoney or sandy ground, the expert reported; some of them had blankets or tarpaulins under them. In some cases obvious injuries had been covered with clothing. The majority of the faces were well-documented; where their eyes were missing this was due to them having been eaten by birds or insects following death. A total of 3,912 people were photographed in their underwear, another 1,547 were naked, the rest were fully or partially clothed, although their clothes were dirty and threadbare. One in 20 showed signs of professional medical treatment such as bandages. In some cases the bodies suggested that the person had died shortly after emergency surgery following ballistic trauma.

[255] According to the expert, the photographs had obviously served less as medical documentation and more the general, rather superficial, "registration" of the bodies. The fact that a systematic approach had been applied when taking the photographs in order to create a typical "set" for each body—an overview, details of the head and neck area and the upper and lower half of the body—tended to suggest that instructions had been issued to that effect or that the same photographer had been used.

[256] The expert explained in detail that, from an expert forensic medical perspective, it was to be assumed that all the photographs did in fact depict dead human bodies, although clear signs of death in the form of livor mortis, rigor mortis, putrefaction changes or injuries which were not compatible with life could be identified in only 88.6% of the cases. A large number of the people depicted in the photographs showed signs of the consequences of ill-treatment in the form of mainly blunt injuries, the expert reported, for instance stroke marks (i.e. parallel erythema stripes) together with burst capillary bleeding and haematomas. These could only have been caused by very severe, unbridled blows to the body, which would also have caused severe pain and even meant the person lost consciousness. The expert believed that sticks, pipes, cables and similar items had likely been used for these beatings. Moreover, numerous bodies had large haematomas on the legs and feet, indicating that these areas of the body had been subjected to targeted blows. Besides stick-like implements, flat objects had been used as well. The intensity of the blows suggested systematic ill-treatment through beating or kicking, the expert stated. In some

cases the impact marks blended into one another so that it was not possible to count the number of blows to the body. Based on the images of the injuries, the expert stated, it was also plausible that the people had been hit severely and several times whilst physically restrained. Judging by their outward appearance, many of the injuries were explainable by having been inflicted simultaneously. In a few cases it was evident that fingernails or toenails had been removed by mechanical means, in the expert's assessment an extremely painful process.

[257] In many other cases the expert found indications of suffocation following the application of mechanical pressure to the neck, in particular significant force to the throat, in some cases with extensive haematomas across the entire neck area together with large abrasions, which could have been caused by massive beating and kicking of the neck or else someone standing on the person's neck, he reported. The course of the haemorrhages suggested that cane-like objects had been pushed against the neck, possibly from behind. The expert explained that the massiveness of the ill-treatment could have led to both compression of the trachea and larynx on account of haemorrhaging and swelling and to ligation of the carotid veins. In some cases, whitish foam was visible on and around the mouth, a sign of suffocation or drowning. The expert described the mechanical dislocation of the airways as a manner of death which was accompanied by a massive fear of dying ("a feeling of annihilation").

[258] A little over half of the people depicted in the photographs had such injuries, the expert stated. Apart from these injuries, more than 60% of those depicted were in an at times considerably reduced state in terms of their general, nutritional and health condition. Their bodies showed signs of extensive emaciation and wasting, which, in the expert's assessment, was most likely a consequence of food deprivation. Numerous bodies also had very severe signs of malnutrition together with severe weight loss owing to the body using up body fat and to muscle atrophy. It was in some cases obvious, the expert explained, that the people had starved to death. This was specifically to be assumed on the basis of the pronounced emaciation of the body which caused the skeleton to protrude and generalised muscle atrophy. The expert described starving to death as a lengthy process with a considerable amount of painful paraesthesia. Many bodies also had signs of extensive skin diseases, such as were caused by a lengthy and extensive lack of hygiene in combination with injuries, malnutrition and parasite infestation. It was obvious, the expert reported, that many of the people depicted in the photographs had needed urgent medical care and treatment but had not received it. The expert also drew attention to

the multitude of signs of shackling on their wrists, plus strap-like injuries and evidence of blindfolds.

[259] Some of the bodies had no or only minimal externally visible injuries or diminution, the expert reported. Since the majority were young and middle-aged men, who also showed no signs of any fatal illness, then, in view of the context in which the photographs had been taken, they could have suffered asphyxiation, for example owing to a lack of oxygen in the air or interventions involving gas, poison, drowning or suffocation by gently covering the respiratory organs. A few of the bodies showed signs of ballistic trauma following gunshot wounds or wounds caused by an explosion; in a few cases numerous bullet wounds in one region of the body or signs of close-range gunshots could also be considered to have been caused by execution. A few corpses (52) showed signs of (electro-)thermic impacts. None of the bodies could be regarded as having suffered a natural cause of death.

[260] As regards time of death, the expert explained that storing the corpses outside and the absence of any green discolouration in the area around the lower abdomen, which already occurs at an outdoor temperature of 21 degrees, was either an indication that the corpses had first been kept in cold storage or that death had occurred just before the photographs were taken.

[261] The Division follows the expert's findings and uses them as the basis for its assessment. These findings, for each of which the expert gave detailed oral explanations and which were evidently based on his experience and expertise, were the result of a meticulous investigation and comprehensive explanation of the photographic material—some of which the Division inspected whilst the expert report was being rendered—and are consistent with it.

[262] (ff) In the light of the above, the Division has no doubts as to the authenticity and origin of the photographs as presented by the witnesses ... [LL] and ... [O] and indirectly by the witnesses "Caesar" and "Sami". In its assessment, the photographs prove that, from May 2011, a large number of deaths occurred in the Syrian regime's various intelligence service branches on account of detainees being tortured to death, being killed by food deprivation or suffocation, or being executed there.

[263] (b) Numerous witnesses corroborate the large number, documentation and treatment of the corpses of the victims of the regime.

[264] (aa) Expert Witness ... [W] testified that he had met two witnesses in the course of his research who reported that there was a "handling facility for corpses" in Homs. They had, he stated, explained that the corpses had numbers on them, were photographed and

registered. This was in early 2012; the witnesses were interviewed in April 2012. One of them was young and was deployed as a conscript; he gave the impression of being very distressed. He had, the Expert Witness reported, described having to pack body parts into plastic bags in a military hospital. From early March 2012 on, corpses had been brought in on an ongoing basis and formed metres-high piles in a courtyard. He was required to photograph the corpses, attach numbers to them and then pack them up. A doctor who defected had described the collection point in a similar manner, the witness stated. The dead originated from a district of Homs, which had declared its independence, from checkpoints and a large number came from prisons, especially those operated by the Military Intelligence Directorate and the Air Force Intelligence Directorate. Between 30 and 400 corpses were delivered every day, sometimes in a truck. The hospitals in Tishreen and Harasta were also well-known in that regard. Another person the Expert Witness talked to reported being allowed to search for his brother's corpse. Because he was a person with influence he was assigned several security personnel so that he could spend hours looking through the corpses. According to Expert Witness . . . [W], the person he talked to was unable to provide any further proof, though.

[265] The Division regards this statement as evidence of a system which was applied across the country and which was geared to recording a large number of people who died at the hands of the security authorities.

[266] (bb) By his own account, Witness Z 30/07/19, who was already examined anonymously in the course of the preliminary investigation, was a member of the administrative staff in the cemeteries department in Damascus. He testified that he was recruited by senior officers in the security services in May or June 2011 and that he and 10 to 15 employees he had to nominate were tasked with assisting in the burial of corpses in mass graves. He himself had had to document the corpses which were delivered. He had done this job from 2011 until 2017, he said.

[267] (1) The witness stated that, when he first began this job in May or June 2011, he and a group of employees from his agency were sent to the military hospitals in Tishreen and Harasta, where refrigerated trucks were waiting to transport corpses. The trucks were driven to a place he did not at first recognise. During a second phase of his job he then received lists several times a week, was picked up from his place of work by a patrol and taken to mass graves. Large trenches up to 6 metres deep had been dug there into which the corpses were tipped. Eventually, he drove himself and his staff members there in a minivan

which they were provided with; they were required to check the lists they were handed by the drivers of the trucks in which the corpses were delivered. He and his staff were given a vehicle which belonged to the intelligence service (a Nissan Sunny) so that they would not be stopped at checkpoints. The witness stated that this work, which did not change over the next few years, had begun four to five months after he took on the original job, that is between September and November 2011.

[268] The witness stated that the regular transports from the military hospitals in Harasta and Tishreen had arrived at the mass graves around twice a week. That was where the corpses which originated from the branches accumulated. Corpses came in from all the branches. The witness named "State Security", which he said included an "Administration" he did not designate any more precisely, the "Al-Khatib Branch" and Sub-branch 40, the Palestine Branch, branches in the regions, Branch 215 and patrol branches belonging to the Air Force Intelligence Directorate. The corpses had numbers written on their forehead or chest, he testified. They then drove to the mass graves which were in Najha (around 14 kilometres south of the centre of Damascus out towards the airport) and al-Quteifa (alternative spelling "Al-Qutayfah") around 40 kilometres north-east of the city centre on the motorway heading towards Homs. He had heard from a digger operator that there was another mass grave near Mezzeh Military Airport for which the Air Force Intelligence Directorate was responsible and about a cemetery operated by the 4th Division; the digger operator had excavated pits there, amongst other places. The burials which the witness was part of took place at night. They left around 4:00 or 5:00 hrs, he stated, and returned between 8:00 and 9:00 hrs.

[269] The cemeteries were depots which were not accessible to civilians and which were enclosed—in al-Quteifa by a mound of earth around 2 to 3 metres high and in Najha by a wall around 7 to 8 metres in height. The witness stated that they had had to pass two checkpoints. There were armed security service patrols on the sites of the cemeteries. He himself had stayed away from the actual graves. However, he had spoken to digger operators who had talked of excavated areas which were up to 6 metres deep. The drivers of the refrigerated trucks and his other staff members had also talked about the trenches which were dug and which he himself had also seen. The refrigerated trucks were bigger than a freight container, the witness stated, and approximately 11 metres long. They had each held between 700 to 750 corpses, which were stacked up inside. The trenches were between 100 and 200 metres long and between 2 and 3 metres wide; some were only 50 metres long. Each of the trenches was big enough

for between 20 and 50 truckloads. When a truck arrived, the doors were opened, the corpses were pulled out and thrown into the trenches haphazardly. The stench was abominable, the witness reported. Those of his staff members who had had to handle the corpses had usually worn a gown and a mask, but the work had still made them ill. His staff reported that the corpses, which were all naked, were covered in blue impact marks and bloody wounds. They had seen the signs of torture, such as wounds resulting from electroshocks and extracted fingernails, sometimes strangulation marks, presumably from execution by hanging. Some corpses were handcuffed and shackled using cable ties. The penis of one male corpse had been cut off. There were also corpses of women and children. The witness himself had once seen a dead woman who was holding a dead child. He had nearly broken down at the sight of it.

[270] The staff tasked with unloading the corpses also reported that some of the bodies were already decomposed and that their faces were no longer recognisable, the witness testified. This was due to chemicals having been applied to the faces, amongst other things. Some of the bodies were "burst open"; the staff saw "floods of blood and maggots" when they emptied the trucks. The witness said he could smell the stench from 100 metres away. The first time he was unable to eat anything for several days. It was only the corpses from the hospital which had smelled so badly, not those from the prison in Saydnaya, because they had been executed the same night, as an escort officer had told him. There had, the witness stated, also been cases in which the people executed were still alive and an officer had given the order to run them over with an earthmover.

[271] The witness's task had been to "add corpses to the lists". He was given the lists by the officers who escorted the vehicles delivering them and the refrigerated trucks. At the burial site the witness then entered in the documents the date, the origin of the individual corpses (i.e. the intelligence service branch) and the total number of dead as told to him. For example, he was told "Palestine Branch, put down 150!" or "Sub-branch 40, put down 100!". His staff told him that the corpses also bore a number, that is the number of the branch. He had to hand the completed lists over to an officer following the burial. Before that he made a copy which was to be passed on to his supervisor. According to the numbers attached to the corpses and the documents he was given, the corpses had arrived from all sorts of intelligence service branches, including the Al-Khatib Branch. Such deliveries of dead bodies were usually made twice a month in 2011 and 2012, the witness stated, sometimes once a month, though, or not at all.

[272] The witness was not able to provide more precise figures for the number of victims. According to what he reported during his police questioning, between 3,500 and 5,000 corpses were delivered from the Al-Khatib Branch and Sub-branch 40 between June and December 2011. At the main hearing the witness, emphasising that he was unable to provide any exact figures, estimated that the figure was between 3,000 and 5,000 dead throughout the whole of 2011. During the preliminary investigation he had put the total number of those buried in the period between 2011 and 2017 at between 1 and 1.7 million. At the main hearing he stated that on an unknown date an officer had quoted a figure of one million dead. Based on what his staff reported, though, the witness himself considered that between two and three million was also possible.

[273] The witness was not able to provide accurate information as to how often per week he was deployed to do this work. There were at least two regular deliveries per week from the military hospitals, he stated. Then there were also the special transports of those executed in the prison in Saydnaya and special transports after which the burials had been supervised by high-ranking officers. It was the staff he had to bring along to carry out these tasks who had to take the corpses out of the trucks, the witness stated. They were all civilian administrative staff, he reported, and were forced to work there.

[274] (2) Owing to his still vivid memories of events, the witness was visibly moved whilst making his statement before the Division and stated that he still had nightmares about them. Because it put a noticeable psychological strain on him, the examination had to be interrupted and continued on the next day of the main hearing. In the Division's assessment, even though the witness evidenced under-standable uncertainties as regards the number of transported corpses and deceased persons and their administrative/technical documentation, this in no way affects the credibility of what he said, which is otherwise consistent with the outcome of the investigation. The witness made discernible efforts to recall memories from years ago. His testimony before the Division was initially rather jumbled, fragmentary and gen-eralised. However, when asked follow-up questions he was always able to provide more concrete, structured information which formed a logical picture and was consistent with what the witness had stated in the preliminary investigation. Occasional inconsistences—for instance when the witness first stated that he was collected and driven to the mass graves and then later corrected himself and said that a vehicle had been made available to them—were of minor relevance and easily explained by the many years he spent doing his job and his changing workflows.

[275] The witness's statement forcefully demonstrates the industrialised "processing", as it were, of people killed by the Syrian security services the longer the conflict went on in the form of their continuous collection, registration and, ultimately, disposal in mass graves which were dug over many years at considerable, machine-assisted effort. Consistent with what the witness stated, and also in view of the outcome of the taking of evidence in the "Caesar" complex (which is consistent with the processes described by the witness), the Division concludes, as regards the chronology of events, that the witness and other staff in his authority were recruited as early as May or June 2011 and that the number of corpses continually grew after that until it plateaued at a high level in the second half of 2011. It is not possible to put a concrete figure on the number of victims of the regime who were buried in mass graves. In view of the frequency of the transports which the witness reported and their capacity, however, it can be assumed that from mid-2011 there were at least 5,000 deaths per month and that the numbers likely increased after that.

[276] (cc) Witness ... [BB], a trained computer scientist and member of the intelligence service of the rank of lieutenant, worked for the Syrian general intelligence service between November 2010 and early 2012. By his own account, he initially worked in the "Information Branch" and then, from 15 November 2010 to late 2012, in the "mailroom" in Branch 295 in the Najha field office south of Damascus.

[277] (1) The witness testified that, from some point in the second half of 2011 which he was not able to specify more precisely, he had in the course of his work in the mailroom in Branch 295 regularly received papers listing deceased persons which were used to announce the transports of corpses. These lists were passed on to him from hospitals, for instance the Harasta Hospital or Hospital No 601. They included the number of dead and, for each dead person, an identification number, a number to indicate the intelligence service branch they originated from and a date. The papers, the witness stated, bore the stamp of one of the forensic experts employed in the military hospitals. The names of the dead were not included. The numbers of the branches cited were mainly 215, 235, 251, 285 and 293; the numbers referred to the intelligence service branches from which the deceased originated. The lists were intended for the head of Branch 295, although the witness had also been able to read them. The lists, the structure of which the witness provided a sketch of during the main hearing, served the preparation of the burials, he stated.

[278] The witness stated that Branch 295 was responsible for the whole region and thus also for the graves. The lists were not received on

a daily basis but cumulatively for 50 to 100 people, sometimes considerably more. They were assigned to the refrigerated trucks and checked against their content. The numbers on the corpses had to be kept distinct from the numbers which were given out to those relatives who wanted to find out what had happened to the deceased, the witness stated. These numbers were chosen at random and communicated in pretence only. They were just as fake as the information which was given to the families that the victims had died a natural death. The witness also stated that the corpses transported to the mass graves had come exclusively from Damascus and its surrounding area. Most of them had come from the intelligence service branches. But corpses were also delivered straight from the Mezzeh, Tishreen and Harasta military hospitals.

[279] Between 50 and 300 corpses were taken early in the morning (around 4:00 hrs) in refrigerated trucks to preprepared mass graves excavated by diggers near Najha, which the witness identified on a satellite map. Between April 2011 and January 2012 the lists to which he had access had included more than 8,400 dead. There were two mass graves, he stated. One was primarily for people who had been executed and for fallen soldiers. Another was reserved for those who died in the intelligence service prisons. The witness stated that he had not had direct access to the mass graves. However, he was able to watch the diggers excavating them from an elevated position in the cemetery. The area was cordoned off and separately guarded "by Iranians". The drivers of the trucks transporting the corpses had special authorisation to pass through checkpoints.

[280] (2) The Division considers this witness, too, to be credible and his statements to be believable. The witness reported openly about his career within the intelligence service, including that he had wanted to study to become an officer but had not been accepted. By his own account, the witness was reticent to testify on account of pressure being exerted on his family. However, when he was asked follow-up questions he was, although sometimes laboriously, then repeatedly able to provide detailed information which was consistent in itself and concurred with the outcome of the taking of evidence as to the fate of those killed and their documentation. The witness was able to pinpoint the exact location of the mass graves on aerial photographs. The local conditions are consistent with the analysis of satellite images conducted by the Federal Criminal Police Office. Further, at the main hearing the witness was able clearly to explain the sketches he had already made during his police questioning relating to the location of Branch 295 and the mass graves. Besides, in contrast to what he stated

regarding his acquaintanceship and meeting with the Defendant (see section B.V [Re the findings as to the person of the Defendant], (1)(c), below), there were otherwise no substantial discrepancies compared to what he stated during his questioning by the police.

[281] However, the discrepancies as to the Defendant himself do not undermine the credibility of the witness's testimony, since the Division gained the certain impression that he had kept other facts concerning the Defendant a secret for fear of what would happen to his relatives given the targeted threats made by members of the Defendant's family, which he described in detail (see section B.VI [Re the findings as to the Defendant's concrete contribution to the offence], (1)(c), for details). Further, based on the totality of information provided by the witness, the Division takes as its basis that in addition to his office job in a mailroom he was also responsible for receiving reports about the delivered corpses for further administrative processing.

[282] (3) The information provided by this witness, too, confirms the picture that the corpses of killed detainees from the intelligence service branches were amassed at central locations, in particular the military hospitals, where they were recorded before they were loaded onto refrigerated trucks or other vehicles, driven to mass graves and buried there. The lists of the dead to which the witness testified and which obviously originated from a forensic expert or his office fit with the photographic record provided by the "Caesar Files" and the bureaucratic documentation of those killed which it likewise evidences.

[283] (dd) Witness . . . [Y], a former employee of the Syrian General Intelligence Directorate who worked in a documentation office in Kafr Sousa operated by intelligence headquarters in 2011 and 2012, stated that numerous people died in the intelligence service prisons. He knew that to be the case in Branch 285 in particular. He had seen corpses in the Branch's courtyard. There were refrigerated trucks in which corpses were transported, he stated. The bodies came from the intelligence service field offices, were collected there and taken to an "administrative centre". The witness learned this from talking to colleagues, he said. Besides, a register of deaths was kept which was only intended for the administration. The witness stated that the dead had been treated in this way "since the start of the uprising", which he said was March 2011. He also saw corpses in the military hospital in Harasta. They were just lying around on the floor, exposed to the sun, he said. One of the corpses had visible signs of torture. Relatives were usually not informed when someone had died, the witness reported. Enquiries were either ignored or answered to the effect that the person had never

been detained. Relatives were also sometimes falsely informed that prisoners had died of a natural cause.

[284] As already presented in the above (see section B.III.1 [General course of the conflict as from 2011], (c)(bb)), the Division critically assessed the testimony given by Witness … [Y] on account of his possibly being influenced by others and his tendentious self-exculpatory statements. Nevertheless, the aforementioned particulars are consistent with what he stated in the preliminary investigation. They are detailed and in keeping with what he was able to learn in the course of carrying out his duties. The Division therefore takes them to be true and uses them as its basis.

[285] (ee) Finally, Witness Z 28/07/16, a former employee in the General Intelligence Directorate, also stated that people who died in the intelligence service branches were taken to hospitals and stored in refrigerated trucks there. When they ran out of space, the bodies were simply thrown onto the ground. Certificates were issued stating that the people had died of an illness. Lists were drawn up, the corpses were each marked with a number, photographed and then taken to mass graves. Hardly any of the corpses were ever handed over to their families, the witness testified.

[286] (c) The analysis of aerial photographs of the region around Damascus which was done by the Federal Criminal Police Office is consistent with the aforementioned witnesses' statements and with the large number of dead to be buried which also follows from the "Caesar" complex.

[287] According to Witness … [MM], who was involved in the investigation, after Witness Z 30/07/19 gave testimony aerial photographs were inspected for signs of the mass graves which the witness had said were in al-Quteifa. The witness had indicated to the Federal Criminal Police Office its location on a section of a map, at the coordinates 33.756887 and 36.603874. Satellite and aerial photographs of the area in question which are available on Google Maps and Apple's image service were then secured; an area which had been worked on was visible on these photographs. Some of the area, which was enclosed by earth deposits, had been levelled and some of it had mounds of earth on it. On the right-hand (eastern) side of the higher resolution images provided by the Apple service it was possible to make out what was likely a digger and a long, narrow pit which, according to the indicated scale, was around 100 metres long. The Division convinced itself of this fact by inspecting the images, to which reference is hereby made pursuant to section 267(1) sentence 3 of the Code of Criminal Procedure (case files Vol. III.5, pp. 483-5 regarding images 1 to 6).

[288] The Division is conscious of the fact that the evidential value of these images is diminished because, as Witness ... [MM] also testified, it is not possible to establish when they were taken. The witness, however, also testified that the Federal Criminal Police Office had commissioned the German Aerospace Centre (*Deutsches Zentrum für Luft- und Raumfahrt*) with conducting a time series analysis. The analysis included a photograph dated January 2016 which was almost identical to the secured images, meaning that it could be assumed that the photographs were taken around the turn of 2015/16. The time series study also showed that pits which had been dug over the years had again and again been filled in, others had been dug and a wall had finally been erected around the area. The pits were up to 120 metres long and between 3 and 5 metres wide. It also emerged that the worked area increased in size from 19,000 square metres in 2014 to 40,000 square metres in August 2019.

[289] The Division is convinced that these are the mass graves which the witnesses described. The photographs provide proof of their existence at least from 2014 on and circumstantially confirm the information provided by the witnesses relating to the period before that. To the extent that no structural changes could be determined in the area in the period before 2014, this does not contradict what the witnesses stated, especially since, according to Witness ... [MM], there was a second, considerably larger, area close by which had not yet been investigated.

[290] (d) The Division evaluates the outcome of the taking of evidence presented in (a) to (c) above to mean that the Syrian regime was responsible for the deaths of a growing number of people who were killed during protests and in prisons and intelligence service branches in the period after April/May 2011 and that it wanted to "dispose of" them in secret on a massive scale, thereby disregarding the peace and honour of the dead and the individuality of the deceased. Documenting those killed did not serve their individualisation but was merely a bureaucratic means of controlling the implemented procedures and of preventing rescue measures enabled by corruption. This ties in with the fact that relatives were prevented from searching for people who had disappeared by being given arbitrarily assigned numbers. The evidence fits seamlessly into the chronological sequence of the conflict's escalation. It proves that, in line with the instructions which the leadership handed down to the security authorities and which were implemented by them, from late April 2011 at the latest violent action was taken against protests by the civilian population, leading to a rapidly growing number of fatalities.

4. Military hospitals

[291] Proof that the military hospitals in Harasta, Tishreen and Mezzeh were also involved in the ill-treatment of those who were detained and that they at the same time served as collection and documentation points for those who were murdered in various intelligence service branches is provided in Expert Witness . . . [Th]'s presentation, in particular, though, by the outcome of the taking of evidence presented in the above regarding the origin and subject of the "Caesar Files". Further, Witness . . . [N] described his own torture and the ill-treatment of other prisoners who were taken to Harasta Military Hospital. Witness Z 30/07/19, who was present when those who were murdered were buried in mass graves in the vicinity of Damascus and who added the dead to lists, described the military hospitals as the origin of the corpses. Witness . . . [T] testified that prisoners who survived had reported that detainees who were sick were taken to military hospitals, tortured and murdered there. It depended on the geographical location, the witness stated. As Branches 215 and 248 were close to the military hospital in Mezzeh, injured and sick people as well as corpses were taken there. Branches 251, 227 and 235 were closer to the hospitals in Harasta and Tishreen, which was why they had then been responsible for them.

IV. Re the findings as to Branch 251 and Sub-branch 40 of the Syrian General Intelligence Directorate

1. Branch 251

[292] The Division used the statement provided by the Federal Intelligence Service dated 16 June 2016 as the basis for its assessment as to how Branch 251 fit within the organisational structure of the Syrian General Intelligence Directorate. As regards the Branch's remit, its real estate properties, the prevailing conditions of detention and the treatment of prisoners in the course of the conflict in 2011 and 2012, the Division drew on the information provided by former employees of the regime and statements made by expert witnesses who worked as publicists or were members of the opposition. It was on the basis of either their work within the Syrian intelligence service or the Branch itself or based on knowledge acquired by other means in the course of their many years of political or media activities that these witnesses were able to provide detailed information on the modus operandi of Branch 251 and the conditions which prevailed there. Further, the Division used the statements, already presented in the above, made by the

Defendant during his police questioning as a witness concerning the observations he made relating to the Branch as the basis for its assessment.

[293] The information provided by a large number of witnesses detained in Branch 251 was of key importance over and above that. Based on their own observations, these witnesses were able to give the Division a powerful, often devastating, insight into the conditions which prevailed in the Branch and how those detained there were treated.

[294] (a) In sum, former employees of the regime testified as follows before the Division:

[295] (aa) By his own account, Witness Z 28/07/16, who was examined anonymously, worked in an unspecified office of the General Intelligence Directorate for 21 years. He provided comprehensive details concerning Branch 251's organisational structure and remit.

[296] (1) According to the witness, Branch 251 was one of the General Intelligence Directorate's central branches responsible for the province of Damascus. Besides its branch number, it was also referred to informally as the "Al-Khatib Branch" and "Internal Branch". It was a security branch responsible for Damascus and Rif Dimashq. The branch had diverse other responsibilities beyond that, too, the witness stated: there were various sub-branches, such as those responsible for interrogations, students, workers, political parties, weapons, religions; an economic sub-branch; a sub-branch responsible for the security of ministries; and Sub-branch 40, which was responsible for patrols. Further, the witnesses stated, there was also an external sub-branch and field offices across the regions. Essentially, its objective was to monitor political parties and groups, including by means of infiltration, and to engage in preventative work so that they were unable to harm the government. Whilst the other branches of the General Intelligence Directorate were housed in a single complex of buildings in Kafr Sousa in Damascus, Branch 251 was the only one to be based elsewhere, the witness reported. It was close to the Red Crescent Hospital. Historically, it had been under the leadership of Major General Mohammed Nasif. According to the witness, he was succeeded by Lieutenant General Tawfiq Younes, who he believed was still in charge today. Branch 251 operated independently, the witness stated, although formally it was part of the central branch of the General Intelligence Directorate. The witness drew up an organisational chart of Branch 251 to which he added the names of the respective senior officers.

[297] Branch 251, including its field offices, had between 2,500 and 3,000 employees, the witness further stated. It employed around

50 interrogators who worked in shifts. Interrogations were carried out continuously throughout the day and night. The Branch had various prisons, the witness reported. A distinction had to be drawn between the central prison in the basement of the branch and prisons located elsewhere. The latter were assigned to the sub-branches, which were responsible for arresting people who were then eventually taken to the Branch. Branch 251 had the worst reputation in the whole of Syria. That had always been the case, even before "the start of events", and was still the case.

[298] According to the witness, suspects were specifically taken to Branch 251 so that they could be interrogated there. Its role was similar to that of Branch 285, the central interrogation branch for the whole of Syria. It was where the investigative work done by all the cities and governorates in Syria was collated and then shared with the head of the intelligence service, Ali Mamlouk. Accordingly, prisoners were sometimes transferred from Branch 251 to the central branch so that investigations could continue there.

[299] The hierarchy within a branch was such that there was a head of branch, a deputy head of branch and a head of the interrogation sub-branch; interrogators were lower down in the hierarchy. Torture was ordered by the respective head of the interrogation sub-branch, who was in turn given orders by the head of branch. According to the witness, where this was done in writing, coded wording was used, such as "rigorous interrogation methods". At the end of the interrogation a decision was taken about what was to be done with a prisoner, that is whether he was to be taken to a prison or whether further investigations were necessary. The interrogator submitted a suggestion to the head of branch.

[300] The prisoners detained in the prisons belonging to Branch 251 were treated in a similar way to those held in other intelligence service prisons. A "welcome party" was held when they arrived, the witness stated. This meant that whoever was arrested was beaten and kicked by every member of staff from when they were arrested until they arrived in their cell. The means of torture applied in Branch 251 were similar to those used in other facilities, the witness stated. Syria did not apply the principle of innocent until proven guilty; everyone was guilty from the outset. If an interrogator did not like an answer, then torture was inflicted. You could say that there was not a single interrogation of a detained person either in Branch 251 or in Branch 285 which did not involve torture. The outcome was a foregone conclusion, the witness stated, which was merely supposed to be confirmed by the interrogation. Prisoners had no civil rights whilst they

were in the branch. They were, for instance, only allowed to use the toilet if a guard gave them permission to do so. Prisoners often soiled themselves as a result. Sick or injured prisoners were not treated, the witness reported. They were left lying until they died.

[301] (2) The Division largely uses the witness's testimony as the basis for its assessment. Owing to the danger he was in, the witness was permitted not to provide any details which could reveal his identity, and he thus made general reference to his knowledge being based on his many years of working for the intelligence service and to the fact that he himself had observed the conditions of detention which prevailed in the branch and certain orders issued by decision-makers. In view of the comprehensive and detailed information he provided, the Division is nevertheless not concerned that the witness gave false testimony, specifically that he may have played down or artificially dramatised the conditions. As regards the witness's report of the appalling conditions in the intelligence service branches, he provided additional details which were confirmed by many other witnesses, both those close to the regime and those critical of the regime. The Division only treated with caution the evaluative statements which the witness made, for instance when he described Branch 251 as the "most terrible" in the Syrian intelligence service, especially since such ascriptions conflicted with other things he said, for instance that the intelligence services' modi operandi had become aligned over the course of the conflict.

[302] (bb) By his own account, Witness ... [AA] was an officer in Branch 251's guard units and thus responsible for some of the guards deployed there. He worked there in 2011 and 2012 until he deserted on 5 August 2012. His task was to guard the outside of the branch. In the course of his work he had got to know officers working inside the branch. He had also seen the prisoners being brought there.

[303] (1) According to the witness, Branch 251 is the general intelligence service's security branch which is responsible for Harasta and Douma, amongst other cities. The witness provided precise details as to where the branch was located on Baghdad Street in Damascus near the Red Crescent Hospital. The property was enclosed by a wall; there was a checkpoint and a barrier at the entrance, he stated. As the witness explained using a sketch, the branch covered a large area which included parking for staff and an inner area comprising two multi-storey buildings and a courtyard. The buildings housed the sub-branches. Those in charge of the interrogation sub-branch had offices above the prison, which was in the basement. The witness also provided details about those who were in charge of the branch and sub-branches.

[304] After the start of the unrest, the number of employees, which the witness put at between 80 and 100, doubled. The witness initially stated that this was in late 2011, but after further consideration said it was March 2011 and that the number of prisoners taken there increased in April 2011. From that point on, between one and three vehicles had arrived daily, he stated. From the start of the unrest prisoners who were arrested at demonstrations and taken to the branch in buses were subjected to beatings on the square in front of the branch for between half an hour and up to four hours. Instruments such as batons and tasers were used, he reported. When the latter were used, prisoners simply fell to the ground. The detentions and admissions did not stop throughout the entire period of unrest.

[305] The witness stated that when he was on duty and he crossed the courtyard to go to the canteen or to a dormitory he heard cries of pain through the cellar windows in the underground prison and those who were being tortured pleading for the ill-treatment to stop ("For pity's sake, I didn't do anything"). On occasion he also saw a blind-folded prisoner walking across the square with a guard. A friend had told him about the conditions in the prison, which he had himself never been in. The witness himself had not seen the torture which was taking place in the offices or in the basement, he stated. However, he had heard told that the prisoners were beaten and treated badly in other ways too. They were in a catastrophic state when they were released. He also once witnessed a lifeless person being taken away during the night.

[306] Prisoners had arrived from Douma, too, almost on a daily basis. The witness remembered one occasion in particular when arrested demonstrators came in from Douma in buses which seated 15 to 20 people. There were also times when up to 40 people were crammed into a bus on arrival.

[307] (2) The Division also largely based its assessment on the information provided by this witness. To the extent that it was based on what he himself experienced, the witness vividly described things and at the same time plausibly justified why he—a guard deployed outside, though in a senior function—was not able to provide any extensive particulars. His statement thus to a large extent corresponded with the information which he had already given during his hearing before the Federal Office for Migration and Refugees—as relayed by Witness ... [NN]—and during his questioning by the Federal Criminal Police Office—as relayed by witnesses ... [OO] and ... [P]. The Division was not able to accept the witness's estimate as to how many people were working in the branch. This is already hardly

compatible with the size of the building and the number of sub-branches housed in it and also stands in contradiction to the more plausible information provided by Witness Z 28/07/16.

[308] (cc) Witness ... [Y] is a former member of the intelligence service with 30 years of experience working in the Syrian general intelligence service, including 13 years between 1985 and late 1998 in Branch 251 (see section B.III.1 [General course of the conflict as from 2011], (c)(bb), above). He stated that Branch 251, which he described as the "internal branch", was headed by Major General Tawfiq Younes in 2011 and 2012. The former Co-Defendant ... [K] was head of the interrogation sub-branch. According to the witness, the Branch had property which comprised two building complexes in the centre of Damascus on Baghdad Street near a hospital. The prison was extended in 2011. The witness described in detail the multi-storey building complex and the allocation of the offices belonging to the sub-branches there. In the course of his archiving work he had seen the minutes of meetings held in Branch 251 containing proposals regarding the arrest and treatment of detainees. Sometimes the "continuation of detention" was proposed, sometimes the coded wording "expand the interrogation" was used. Occasionally an order was given to release a detainee. The witness also explained a sketch which he had drawn in the preliminary investigation and used to recount a typical report drawn up in Branch 251. A report included the following, for instance: "It was determined that [name] participated in demonstrations." This was followed by a summary of the outcome of the investigation across several pages which was to be passed on to the head of the branch. It concluded with the proposal that detention or imprisonment continue. There was no explicit written instruction to apply torture, only to gather information "by whatever means". Torture was undoubtedly used in Branch 251, the witness stated. He also recalled two deaths.

[309] The Division held the witness's aforementioned statement to be true despite the specifics already described in the above (see section B.III.1 [General course of the conflict as from 2011], (c)(bb)) and drew on it for its assessment. For example, the witness had initially given contradictory testimony and was, on the one hand, able to recall certain documents concerning the former Co-Defendant ... [K]—which by his own account had passed through his hands and the content of which he was able to recount—but, on the other hand, when asked generalised follow-up questions by the Division as to whether interrogation records had also passed through his hands, he had claimed a general lack of ability to recall such things on account of the large

number of documents. However, after discussing the reasons for this behaviour, the witness was prepared to provide further particulars and testified as to details contained in documents relating to Branch 251 which he had initially allegedly not been able to remember but which he was then able to present in detail, consistent with what he had stated in the preliminary investigation, and was able to further explain when asked follow-up questions. The Division thus assessed the information provided as based in fact. It also regarded the detailed description of the site, its structural features and the organisational structure of Branch 251, which the witness described, as based on his own observations, since it was provided in as much detail as and was consistent with statements made by other witnesses.

[310] (b) In sum, other witnesses who also acquired expert knowledge based on their work and experience testified as follows:

[311] (aa) Expert Witness … [S] also testified as regards the "Al-Khatib" Branch. He stated that the branch was one of Syria's most important intelligence service branches and to all intents and purposes had its fingers in every pie. The head of the branch was one of the President's key confidants. The witness sought to prove this using an example, namely original documents in which an official in the branch had banned a sizeable cultural event shortly before it was to start although it had already been authorised. The witness had been issued with a travel ban by the branch. Employees in the branch had also prevented him from being re-admitted to practise as a lawyer. The branch was tasked with guaranteeing political security by broadly controlling all areas of life, he stated, for instance by having sub-branches which were responsible for political parties and students. Employees in the branch were already being deployed to deal with sit-ins and demonstrations in February and March 2011, the witness reported. Torture was used continuously in the branch. The witness cited the *dulab* method (being forced into a tyre and beaten) as an example.

[312] (bb) Expert Witness … [T] testified that Branch 251 had executive functions and was responsible for arrests and interrogations. It was a branch of the state security with 10 sub-branches in the provinces and other sub-branches which were responsible specifically for Damascus and Rif Dimashq. The expert witness stated that the branch was the intelligence services' internal administration and had a coordinating role. Tawfiq Younes, a loyal leader, was its head, he stated. Branch 251 and its sub-branches were responsible for most of the arrests made.

[313] By contrast, Branch 285 was the central interrogation branch, the witness stated. That was where most of the prisoners were

transferred from Branch 251. As he, the witness, had himself been detained in Branch 285 for a while, he had noted the terrible condition the prisoners were in when they came from Branch 251. Clients had told him, in 2011, about the terrible conditions there and about the fact that a large number of prisoners were taken to Branch 251, sometimes 500 a day. He in particular recalled one report, according to which a group of imprisoned women were humiliated by having to sit naked in an area where they were visible to everyone. The witness was also able to describe the location and structure of the branch on account of himself being detained there on several occasions in 1978, 2005 and 2006.

[314] (cc) By his own account, Witness ... [U] was himself kept under observation and arrested by Branch 251. The "Al-Khatib Branch" was, he said, the branch responsible for internal matters. Its task had been to keep an eye on the activities of important people, in particular business people, and to stop those who were out of favour engaging in political activities. This was something he himself had experienced. The branch was originally established by Mohammed Nasif, who was close to Hafez al-Assad, and had been used to exercise control and obtain information by infiltrating government ministries. The branch had also been responsible for monitoring the chambers of trade and industry.

[315] It was, the witness stated, a well-known fact that torture existed in the branch, as it was in the other intelligence service branches. When he was himself detained there in February 2006, the witness had seen implements of torture such as sticks, whips and equipment used to hang people up. He himself had been taken to a room in which people had suffered torture. This had been a tacit warning to him. The witness also described the location of the branch on Baghdad Street in Damascus and said that it was very well known amongst people living in the city. At the start of the protest movement in spring 2011 he had himself witnessed the head of the branch, Tawfiq Younes, drive up to a rally in front of the Ministry of the Interior and address him.

[316] (dd) Expert Witness ... [W] reported that Branch 251 was well-known in Syria and that the people he had talked to as part of his research had been afraid of ending up there. It was also a well-known fact that the branch was not designed for prisoners to stay there for a long time but that it was only supposed to serve as a way station.

[317] (c) As an interim conclusion, the Division assesses the above statements as follows:

[318] According to the details provided by the aforementioned witnesses, which are in essence consistent, Branch 251 had a special

status within the overall organisational structure of the Syrian General Intelligence Directorate. This was already outwardly visible on account of its size and the fact that it was located on a separate property and not together with the other branches of the general intelligence service based in the Kafr Sousa district of Damascus, and not least that it was well-known amongst the Syrian public, as is consistently reported. Whilst the entire general intelligence service was established to uphold the existing power structure, Branch 251, with its executive functions and investigative and coordinating tasks, had wide-ranging competences when it came to monitoring society as a whole. Its core task was the surveillance and suppression of anti-government endeavours across the whole of society. Accordingly, the branch played a key role when it came to crushing the Syrian protest movement. The branch was, at least in Damascus and Rif Dimashq, involved in receiving and interrogating those arrested, then passing them on to other agencies, in particular to Branch 285 at the General Intelligence Directorate's headquarters.

[319] It can already be assumed, based on the consistent statements made by the above-mentioned witnesses, that systematic torture was applied in the branch using the available equipment and based on well-practised cooperation across all levels in the hierarchy, and that those who participated in demonstrations who were taken there were regularly subjected to ill-treatment, sometimes over long periods, when they arrived in the courtyard. The individual statements paint a picture which is consistent with the outcome of the taking of evidence as to the general evolution of the conflict, namely that prisoners were subjected to deliberate humiliation and ill-treatment in the branch in order to deter them from ever taking part in protests again. The multitude of admissions which the witnesses described are consistent with the increase in the number of arrests following the suppression of the protest movement from March 2011 on and permit the conclusion that the cells in the branch were massively overcrowded. Taken together with the outcome of the taking of evidence as to the general course of the conflict and the violent quashing of the protests which was coordinated by the upper echelons of the Syrian machinery of power, the branch, a prominent institution within the Syrian security authorities, fit into processes which were directed against the civilian population. Based on the branch's central importance and its involvement in the conflict, the Division is also convinced that the decisions taken by the coordinating office, the CCMC, reached the branch and were implemented by it.

[320] (d) The witnesses ... [EE], ... [FF], ... [PP], ... [DD], ... [GG], ... [N], Z 25/11/2020, ... [QQ], ... [RR], ... [SS] and

Z 13/01/2021, who were all detained in Branch 251, specifically gave detailed testimony relating to the prevailing conditions and the use of torture there, as well as to the layout of the branch, with its prison in the basement.

[321] (aa) The Division saw no reason to doubt the truthfulness of the statements made by any of the witnesses examined at the main hearing. All the witnesses, some of whom had to deal with the serious consequences of their traumatising detention and ill-treatment, gave detailed testimony regarding their abduction and the conditions in Branch 251, and their testimonies are to a large extent consistent with what they stated in the preliminary investigation. Any uncertainties which arose in relation to details of the witnesses' usually long period of detention (e.g. the order of the cells) can be explained by the passage of nearly 10 years since then and by the things the witnesses experienced and had to process. These uncertainties did not give cause to doubt any of the witnesses' recollections, since what they recalled essentially did not change and was consistent with the testimonies of the other witnesses. Where the witnesses were not able to specify when and in which facility they made certain observations, then given that they were arrested on several occasions or successively placed in different detention facilities, the Division did not ascribe the relevant part of the statement to Branch 251. The majority of their descriptions were characterised by an astounding level of objectivity and were based on no vindictive motivation. By the same token, the majority of the witnesses were visibly moved when they recalled the life-changing experiences they had in detention. In some instances the main hearing had to be interrupted so that the witness under examination could collect themselves and continue giving their testimony.

[322] The Division is certain that each of the witnesses was in fact detained in Branch 251, since when they were asked about this they were able to back up why they were able to identify it, that is either based on their own knowledge of the site in the centre of Damascus or on account of information given to them by other prisoners during their detention. Also, all the witnesses drew sketches of the extensive underground prison in Branch 251, with its row of individual cells, several fairly large communal cells, interrogation rooms and an open, central area. The Division was able to examine and the witnesses were able to explain these sketches. Both the male and female witnesses stated that women and men were housed separately in the branch. The witnesses also all concurred in testifying that relatives were not informed about their whereabouts. Those witnesses who were examined anonymously did so because those of their relatives who are still in

the government-controlled part of Syria had been threatened with repressive measures if the witnesses gave testimony in the present proceedings. Other witnesses, too, who were not examined anonymously reported that they had cause for such concerns.

[323] (bb) More specifically, the witnesses testified as follows, in sum:

[324] (1) Witness ... [EE], a Syrian director and documentary filmmaker, was arrested in August 2011 after having earlier been detained with the Air Force Intelligence Directorate. After various stopovers, he was detained in Branch 251. Although the witness had, in the course of his police questioning, stated that he had been detained in October 2011, he later corrected himself when he remembered that he had spent his birthday in the branch, which was on 20 September. He was arrested on account of statements he made which were critical of the regime and documentary films he had made about the military and intelligence services using force against the civilian population. After he was arrested at the airport in Damascus shortly before planning to flee the country following a tip-off, he spent time in transit in various other intelligence service branches before finally being taken to the "Al-Khatib Branch".

[325] The witness stated that he spent some of August and the whole of September 2011 in the branch, that is around two months in total. When he arrived as part of a collective transport he was abused by being punched and hit with rifle butts in the courtyard of the branch during a "welcome party". Amongst other things, someone held on to his head whilst he was punched in the face. After that he was detained in the prison in the basement. There was an area there for torture from where there had been constant screams "that weren't normal", he testified. He himself was beaten with bare hands and batons ("my whole body was bruised") and then taken to an overcrowded communal cell measuring an estimated 30 square metres in which there were 200 to 300 people. The witness stated that he spent two to three days there; the rest of the time he spent in isolation in a small single cell. He recalled fellow inmates who had serious injuries, for instance a very old man who had been beaten up ("blood everywhere, his body swollen") and a 14-year-old boy who was taken away and then brought back with his feet bleeding. Other prisoners suffered even more severe injuries to their feet and back, and their faces were swollen, too, the witness testified. There were people who were sick but were not given any medical treatment and who were no longer able to move. His fellow inmates had tried to stop the bleeding as best they could once people were brought back after being tortured. Most of his fellow

inmates in the communal cell had injuries, he stated; you could see the consequences of the torture all over their faces. Some suffered broken bones. Detainees also had breathing difficulties on account of the stuffy air, the witness stated. Some people were half-dead. There were prisoners lying motionless on the floor in the corridors. The witness had constantly heard the screams of those being tortured, including women and adolescents.

[326] The witness was, he stated, taken away for questioning on the second day and was able to see, through the thin blindfold he was made to wear, that there were people lying on the floor who were being beaten up and that some of them were no longer moving. He was interrogated in the basement, where he was made to kneel and keep his head down. He was asked about the films he had made which were critical of the regime. He was not yet beaten, but threatened with being beaten, he stated. Also, he had heard the screams of other people being tortured coming from "all sides" of the open interrogation area. Immediately after this interrogation he was beaten up, the witness testified, then shackled and tortured nearly every day. During his second interrogation, when he was no longer asked any specific questions, his back and feet were beaten with a cable. On another occasion he was hung up high enough so that only the tips of his toes touched the ground. He was beaten whilst in this position and eventually lost consciousness. The witness stated that he still had problems with his legs on account of this ill-treatment. Other prisoners told him that they had suffered similar things. They reported about the *dulab* (tyre) method, too. Once, when he was lying on the floor, a stick was thrust into his anus. This caused significant damage and he subsequently had to undergo surgery. The choice and sequence of torture methods was arbitrary: "Blows to the legs, thighs and lower legs, blows with cables to the hands, back, legs. Blows to the feet with a baton, kicks." Once he had been jumped up and down on. Cable ties were tied so tightly round his wrists that he later started having problems using his hands, the witness stated. Although he was hardly able to walk on account of suffering blows to the soles of his feet, the guards had forced him to do so. The only clothing he had had on during his period in prison were his underpants. The witness thought that the staff there were given broad leeway to do what they wanted with the prisoners.

[327] As regards the general detention conditions, Witness . . . E] testified that the prisoners were given far too little food and that some of it was rotten. They were given olives, potatoes and bread, which was often mouldy. Everyone in the communal cell had to sleep sitting up. As there was not enough space, some of the prisoners fell asleep

standing up and then fell over. They were only allowed to go to the toilet at specific times, the witness testified. The rest of the time they had to hold it in. When the witness had once knocked because he needed to relieve himself he was beaten. The supply of water came from the toilet, he stated. The guards counted and then you had to decide whether you wanted to use the water out of a hose to wash or whether to drink it. The air in the cells was very bad, the witness testified. It stank of blood and mould. There was no medical care, and the prisoners had to improvise to help each other out. There was no daylight in the communal cell; only the single cell had a small window. The witness testified that he constantly thought he would be executed and that his time in prison caused him mental health problems.

[328] (2) Witness . . . [FF], a blogger critical of the regime who was active in Syria up until 2011, was arrested on 24 October 2011 and, following a stopover in Sub-branch 40, was taken to Branch 251, where he spent between 10 and 15 days until he was transferred to Branch 285. He was not, he stated, beaten whilst being admitted (alone) to Branch 251. The cell in the basement which he was detained in measured 2.5 by 3 metres. There were initially 12 to 20 people in it, later 25 people. The cell was so overcrowded, the witness stated, that you had to "dovetail" so as to be able to sleep. Later it was only possible to sleep lying on one's side. The prisoners drank the water in the toilet, he said. They were given food twice a day, though only very meagre portions. The food they were given for 15 people was only enough for five people at most. They were given rice, olives and small quantities of jam, all of bad quality. As there was no daylight in the cell, only artificial lighting which was kept on at all times, it was impossible to tell day from night. The first thing the other prisoners asked him when he arrived was what time it was.

[329] The witness stated that he had to kneel with his eyes blind-folded throughout his six interrogations in total. Whenever the interro-gator was not satisfied with an answer he gave he received blows to the soles of his feet and to his back, either with a belt or a four-wire cable. On one occasion he was beaten in this way before the interrogation as a form of intimidation. He was interrogated about his job; several of the interrogations had taken place in a corridor in the basement, though twice also in a separate room in the presence of an officer. On one such occasion the officer had said to the guard: "Either you get the names out of him or you'll go in his place." After being beaten, his feet had swollen up and were extremely painful for a long time. He was unable to walk, the witness stated. Once he was taken to a torture room without a blindfold. There was a table and military bed inside and

"dozens of torture instruments, military belts and batons". An interrogator had entered the room holding a pair of pliers. The witness said he knew from his fellow inmates that they were used to pull out people's fingernails. But that had not happened to him, the witness stated. He was no longer able to say whether—as he had testified during his police questioning in October 2018—he had seen the rings used to hang people up in Branch 251 or in other detention centres. There had also, the witness testified, been arbitrary group punishments, for instance if someone in the cell talked without permission. The guard had then come in and ordered everyone to turn to face the wall; he then proceeded to beat the prisoners, especially on their feet.

[330] The other prisoners were treated in the same way as he was, some of them worse, though. Some of them had bleeding feet. The witness himself saw a prisoner being ill-treated for quite a long time out in the corridor, he stated. Prisoners were made to kneel for days on end, were doused with water and beaten in passing. That was something he had observed through an air vent in the door. As a result, the prisoners' knees became infected. The wounds on one fellow inmate's knees were so bad that you could see his bones sticking out. Cables with exposed copper wires at the end were deliberately used to hit people, causing flesh to be ripped out of their bodies. There was no medical treatment, the witness stated. There was only someone who had come by and handed out paracetamol, sometimes an antibiotic. The witness stated that his fellow inmates were aged between 16 and 70. He had also heard female voices in other rooms.

[331] The witness testified that he was transferred when the subject of the interrogations became more complicated, when it concerned his acquaintances with other members of the opposition, for instance. He was taken to Branch 285, the main interrogation centre. He was tortured there, too. In the end, he was transferred to the prison in Adra.

[332] (3) Witness ... [PP] was detained on several occasions in different security authority facilities, including twice in Branch 251. The first time, which was sometime in August 2011, he was kept in the branch for several days, though he was not able to say exactly when that was.

[333] The witness stated that he was a civil servant in an administrative branch and also ran a shop in the town of Al-Zabadani. He was arrested at a roadblock there under false pretences, that is for smuggling Israelis into the country and being on the run. He was first taken to the State Security sub-branch in Al-Zabadani, where there was a small prison, then to the 4th Division, on arrival at which he was made to

walk between two rows of soldiers, who hit him and kicked him. Finally, he and other prisoners were taken in buses to the Al-Khatib Branch. Whilst being interrogated there he was initially shackled and made to kneel down with his eyes blindfolded. Owing to his being a civil servant he had, however, then been allowed to take off both the shackles and the blindfold. Because the interrogator recognised him, he was released shortly afterwards, the witness stated. During his period in detention he was aware of other prisoners being interrogated and beaten; you could tell when they returned to the cell. They were hardly able to walk and had wounds on their back. The *dulab* (tyre) method was used as a means of torture, too, he testified.

[334] The witness was no longer able to say exactly when he was detained the second time in Branch 251, only that he remembered being released in early 2013. He had been in an extremely bad state afterwards, unable even to remember his own name. The witness, who appeared very anxious during his examination by the Division, felt unable to continue answering questions. They were "like riddles" to him. The witness stated that he feared for his family, who had stayed in Syria.

[335] (4) Witness . . . [DD] was detained in Branch 251 from 2 to 16 May 2011 and from 12 to 19 April 2012. During her first period in detention she was repeatedly beaten, she stated. This was "normal" there even though no specific orders had been given to that effect. She was beaten with bare hands; on one occasion a taser was used on her, she said. The witness stated that she was interrogated about the organisers of a demonstration she had taken part in and that she was beaten from behind during the interrogation if they did not like the answer she gave. She was detained in the basement in a tiny single cell measuring 60 by 170 to 190 centimetres ("as big as a grave"). It was impossible to tell night from day; artificial lighting was kept on all the time. She had constantly heard the screams of prisoners being tortured ("terrible voices, and the whip striking the body"). She had heard one person say "I'll tell you everything". Shortly afterwards, though, the person had again been hit. On another occasion someone had been carried out of an interrogation room. The witness herself was shackled and interrogated in the basement of the branch with her eyes blindfolded on several occasions. She was only permitted to go to the toilet once a day, and was insulted and beaten whilst doing so, she testified. On one such occasion she also saw men being beaten with iron bars. Female inmates had talked about being sexually harassed, she stated.

[336] They had been given bread and olives to eat, though much too little. The witness stated that she was unable to eat any of it. She

vividly described how one lived in a constant state of fear: "You're in a grave, can't see anything, have no contact with the world outside, you only hear the screams of people being beaten." Sometimes the other prisoners were no longer able to handle it all and broke down. Fellow prisoners had told of their torture using the *shabeh* (hanging up) and *dulab* (tyres) methods and electric shocks. Cigarettes were stubbed out on one prisoner's knee, the witness testified. One of her acquaintances was still unable to walk six months after spending time in detention there. The hygiene conditions had been atrocious. There were insects everywhere, the witness testified, and the detainees had developed skin conditions; there was no soap. The witness said that she had to use her socks as sanitary protection.

[337] Following her second arrest the witness was slapped across the face on arrival in the courtyard in the branch. She was threatened, saw a room which stank terribly and in which she saw instruments of torture such as cables and sticks and traces of blood on the floor and walls. Later, the loudest screams were heard coming from that room, she stated. She had herself witnessed a woman who was detained with her having to watch her (adult) children being tortured. She herself was interrogated by the former Co-Defendant ... [K] on the top floor of the building, she testified. The conditions of detention and torture had essentially been the same as during her first period of detention.

[338] (5) By his own account, Witness ... [GG], a doctor and musical artist, had been an anti-government activist since March 2011, and was, he stated, arrested in Douma on 30 September 2011 together with other people whilst looking for a demonstration which did not take place owing to the strong military presence. They were picked up by members of the army, he stated, beaten whilst still out in the street and then taken by bus straight to the Al-Khatib Branch. The witness stated that he remained there for five days and was then taken to Branch 285, from where he was taken to court on 16 October 2011 and subsequently released.

[339] The beating he received in the street was already so severe that one of his ribs had cracked, the witness testified. Those arrested were made to lie down whilst being transported to the prison. Their hair was set on fire and then put out by being urinated on. On arrival at the branch, they were made to undress in a large hall in which there were several tables and officers standing behind them and had to do a squat as a "security measure" so that their anus and genital area could be searched for concealed items.

[340] The witness stated that he was placed in a cell measuring between 2 by 3 metres and 4 by 3 metres. There were between eight

and 10 prisoners in it. He had been in a great deal of pain on account of his broken rib and had had a cough and breathing difficulties, too. He also had open wounds on his back and was unable to lie down because of the pain they caused. He was given no medical treatment, he stated. Daylight fell into the cell through a small skylight. The detention conditions were characterised by a lack of food—a potato and a quarter of a slice of bread per day—as a result of which he lost 17 kilogrammes during the short period he spent in detention. The witness stated that he was interrogated a total of three times on the same floor on which his cell was located. His eyes were blindfolded. During his first interrogation he had tried to only give away information about people he knew were already "toast": "To avoid the blows, you try to give information that can do as little harm as possible to others." He was made to lie on his stomach with his feet facing up into the air. Then he was beaten on the soles of his feet, his lower legs and thighs, always in the same place so that it hurt all the more. He was beaten with a belt, cable or hose, the witness testified. The implements with which he was beaten caused different kinds of wounds. Each interrogation lasted 30 to 45 minutes, he stated. When the interrogator gave a signal, the guard hit him 10 to 12 times. This seemed to him to be a systematic process. His feet had swollen up so that it was very hard for him to walk; it was extremely painful. Other prisoners had told him that they had been tortured using the *shabeh* method (hanging up by the wrists).

[341] The witness stated that he was not aware of what exactly he was accused of. It seemed to him that the aim of the torture was not to get any information but to systematically intimidate demonstrators and the population. The subsequent court proceedings had been a farce, he said. He was asked why he had been looking for a demonstration, had said nothing and was simply released.

[342] (6) Witness . . . [N], who ran a car wash in Damascus, was arrested there on 26 August 2011 during a large-scale raid. He was first taken to the "10th Division", where he was beaten severely against the legs and back. He had suffered deep wounds, mainly on his back, which bled profusely. After a few days he was then shackled and— gagged with an aubergine stuffed in his mouth—taken in a bus with other prisoners to the Al-Khatib Branch. He remained there for four to five days, he stated.

[343] On arrival at the branch he and the other prisoners were made to sit on the floor in a row. Then they were struck with blows. This lasted two hours, he testified. When forced to undress in the prison cellar he was given one beating for each item of clothing he took off.

The detention room was overcrowded; it had 400 people in it. It was already impossible to sit down, the witness stated. As it was below ground level, it had been impossible to tell day from night. The air was stifling. There was one toilet which had a vent. People went there just to get some air, he said.

[344] During a later interrogation he was confronted with an entirely fabricated accusation ("Why did you blow up the convoy in Homs?"), was accused of lying, dragged out of the interrogation room on the orders of the interrogator ("Take him out and educate him.") and then beaten outside the room. The interrogator then continued to question him and, after the interrogation was over, ordered the guard to clean the floor, because it had been soiled by the witness's bleeding wounds. Whilst waiting he was beaten in passing, he stated. Next to the interrogation room was a kitchen which was used as a waiting room. Through the window in the kitchen he was able to see more prisoners arriving at the branch. Other prisoners in the cell were taken aback by his wounds, which bled profusely, smelled bad and oozed black blood, he stated. They had laid him down in a corner and not touched him because he was in a lot of pain. He had received no medical care. He had only been allowed out once to get some fresh air, during which he was laid down in the courtyard of the branch. During another interrogation the interrogator was unable to stand the smell of him, he testified. During his detention in the "Al-Khatib Branch" he had constantly heard loud screaming. However, that had already been the case during his stay in the 10th Division and then again in the military hospital.

[345] Finally, the witness stated, he was taken to the military hospital in Harasta on account of his injuries. However, he was not treated there, but subjected to further and worse abuse. He was put in a vehicle and thrown out of it onto the street, where he was left, unable to move ("There were flies on my body. I no longer had the strength to shoo them away. I wished I was six feet under."). It was only by chance that he was rescued by a taxi driver, the witness stated. He underwent several operations in Jordan to treat the extensive, deep wounds on his back. The Division was able to get an impression of the extent of the wounds by inspecting a photograph.

[346] (7) Witness Z 25/11/2020, who was examined anonymously on 25 and 26 November 2020, was detained in the Al-Khatib Branch from 25 March 2011 to 1 April 2011 and again from 5 April 2012 to 10 June 2012. After being arrested on 25 March 2011 he and others who were arrested with him were beaten and then taken to the branch in buses. A welcome party was held there, which involved brutal

beatings, the witness testified. They were made to walk along a corridor of security forces beating down on them. He himself was struck 10 times in the face with a stick, which damaged one of his eyes so that he was unable to see through it for six months. Some of his teeth were also broken, he stated. He was subsequently kicked so hard by one of the security officials in the branch that two of his ribs broke. After that he had great difficulty breathing, he said. He was taken to Al-Mujtahid Hospital in Damascus for a medical examination—shackled in a wheelchair and constantly subjected to the insults of and spitting by the Branch 251 staff who accompanied him. There he was simply told that his eye was "finished". The prescriptions he was given were ripped up in front of his eyes by the security officials who escorted him. He was detained in a room with 70 other prisoners which measured around 70 square metres. The interrogators' rooms were opposite it, he stated. He had constantly heard screams coming from them and from one specific torture room. The people were all gaunt, he said. "The food was bad, the people had wounds, it was hell."

[347] The methods of torture applied were blows with sticks and belts, and victims were also restrained in tyres, the witness stated. The *fallaqa* method involved a person's feet being restrained by a guard using a wooden device and a strip of cloth so that another guard could hit them with a belt. The witness had noticed a fellow inmate's fingers bleeding, no doubt because his fingernails had been pulled out. The witness himself was also ill-treated during his interrogations. Interrogations were held in those storeys in the branch which were above ground, in one of the officers' offices, where the witness was beaten and kicked in the stomach. "When you feel the fresh air you know you're in one of the officers' offices." Other interrogations were conducted in the basement, where the *fallaqa* method was applied in a room whose walls were full of blood. There the employee who beat him also asked the questions. The witness was made to sign papers before his release in which he pledged, amongst other things, to no longer take part in any demonstrations.

[348] When he was again arrested on 5 April 2012, the witness stated, he was placed in a large, overcrowded room with around 350 people and later in a smaller, dark cell with some 50 prisoners, which was also overcrowded. One of the detention cells was underneath what used to be a garden, which he had been able to see through a skylight. He was beaten there, too, he said. The witness stated that he saw a seriously injured person with wounds on their stomach and infected feet teeming with maggots. The person was not moving and was carried out. He heard that the person had died. Another person

had gone mad after being made to stand up for four days. The witness further stated that the "Al-Khatib" branch in Damascus was widely known and infamous.

[349] (8) Witness . . . [SS], a doctor in a hospital, was arrested on 21 August 2011 after being informed on and was then taken to the Al-Khatib Branch. During his numerous interrogations—during which he was made to kneel, was bound and blindfolded—he was accused of speaking ill of the government, of having arranged to take part in demonstrations and of having been in contact with Mossad, the Israeli secret service. He had in fact taken part in demonstrations, the witness testified, and he and a friend had wanted to help the population of the city of Daraa, which had been surrounded by security forces. Both the interrogators and the guards hit him, the witness stated, to extract information. He was, for instance, made to lie down during the interrogation and the soles of his feet were whipped with cables. He was also slapped across the face. Instructions were issued about how he was to be tortured ("We're not getting anywhere with the cable, fetch some wood."). The witness stated that he overheard friends of his being ill-treated and interrogated at the same time; presumably that had been the interrogators' intention.

[350] The witness was first kept in a single cell measuring 180 by 80 centimetres ("It feels like a tomb, you have no contact with anyone."). Later he was transferred to a communal cell in which most of the prisoners were from Harasta and Douma. This cell measured 3 to 3.5 by 3 metres, he stated. The number of fellow prisoners in the cell varied; sometimes there were between 30 and 50 of them. One night so many new prisoners were brought in that they were not all able to sleep lying on their back. He did not know how often this happened ("You're really scared, it's hard to remember exactly, maybe seven to 10 times."). Other prisoners were also ill-treated, he stated. The witness recalled a prisoner with a mental illness who was treated particularly brutally. New prisoners were beaten out in the square in front of the cells during "welcome parties", he reported. When a ventilator had short-circuited all the prisoners in the cell had been punished collectively by being beaten for at least an hour. You could hear people who were being tortured screaming, the witness stated. They were not given enough food and it was of bad quality; the blankets were full of lice. Prisoners had to use the toilet quickly, at fixed times, the witness stated. The medical care was very bad. A diabetic, for instance, was given insulin, whilst another prisoner who had severe toothache was only given a glass of salt water. People were mentally broken, lived in fear and uncertainty ("You never know in Syria how long you'll be in

prison."). After spending 77 days in the Al-Khatib Branch he was taken to another branch in Kafr Sousa. Later he was given a document, which was submitted to the Division, stating that the witness was accused of "harming the state through misinformation, undermining the nation's morale, as well as involvement and participation in demonstrations".

[351] (9) By his own account, a witness who was examined anonymously on 13 January 2021 (Witness Z 13/01/2021), a former opposition activist in Syria, was arrested along with other people at a demonstration on 8 December 2011, after which they were taken to Branch 251 in buses via a stopover in Sub-branch 40. The witness described how he was already beaten up and ill-treated with electric shocks to the foot whilst in the Sub-branch 40 building. On the way to the Al-Khatib Branch and after arriving there the prisoners were also subjected to arbitrary beatings, the witness stated. A 16-year-old boy had a screw pushed into his back on the journey there. Even the member of staff in the branch who removed the cable ties used to bind them hit him, the witness said, with the cutters. The witness said that he was shoved into the cell, hit the floor and lost consciousness. During his interrogations his back was whipped.

[352] The conditions of detention were bad, the witness stated. Some of the new arrivals were covered in blood and had to be carried into the cell. No-one had looked after a man living with epilepsy. The food consisted of a few olives and a little bread and jam. Sometimes arguments broke out over the food, he said. He himself had lost a lot of weight during his time in detention. Screaming could constantly be heard. The witness stated that he remained in the branch for seven days. The fear was the worst, he said. He had kept wondering when his life would be over ("They could always call my name and then I won't come back.").

[353] The witness stated that he was arrested once more on 5 April 2012 and again taken to the Al-Khatib Branch after another stopover in Sub-branch 40, where he was ill-treated using the *fallaqa* method, for example. He was first put in a huge cell there with 200 prisoners, later in a smaller one with 65 people which measured 4 by 5 metres. All the cells were overcrowded, the witness stated. They appeared to him to be a converted canteen and a former interrogation room. Sometimes the prisoners had to sleep standing up. Some fellow inmates had lost their mind and hallucinated owing to the lack of sleep. There was also a 14-year-old in the cell who was regularly tortured by having the soles of his feet beaten. Again, the medical care available had been inadequate. The witness himself had a high fever and was given an injection to treat it, he stated.

[354] (10) The statements made to the police by Witness ... [QQ] and Witness ... [RR], who live abroad and were not available for examination in person, were relayed to the Division by Witness ... [O] and Witness ... [TT], both police investigators. They described the context in which the questioning and interpretation took place, based on which the Division does not doubt that the witnesses made the statements during their police questioning as recounted and recorded by the investigators. Given the memorable details which both witness statements included and the fact that they are otherwise consistent with the outcome of the taking of evidence, the Division also found the following particulars as to the substance of the case to be accurate and used them as the basis for its assessment:

[355] According to the statement he made to the police, Witness ... [QQ] was a member of an oppositional political movement and co-organiser of the first demonstrations held in February 2011. He was then arrested on 19 February 2011 and taken to the Al-Khatib Branch. He spent a total of eight months and 20 days in detention. He spent around two months of that time in a single cell in the branch's cellar prison. Because his cell was kept in constant darkness, he was unable to tell one day from the next. His interrogations had revolved around his role in the opposition movement, his social media posts and the names of other members of his organisation. As he failed to cooperate, he was ill-treated as from his second interrogation, he reported. His back and legs were beaten with a cable, and his feet were also beaten with a spiked iron rod. The witness stated that he was forced into a tyre and beaten whilst immobilised in it. Afterwards he was made to stand facing the wall out in a corridor. Everyone who passed him hit him. The blows to the soles of his feet meant he was unable to tread on them. He was also hung up by his wrists, as a result of which his arms had swollen up, and his arm was also burned during this procedure. The witness stated that he lost consciousness whilst this torture was being inflicted. He was also aware of fellow prisoners being tortured, for example an Iraqi man who was doused with water and then tormented with electric shocks. After around one month in detention, the atmosphere in the branch had become more agitated because more and more people kept arriving there. At that time the screams of those being tortured had very often been heard, the witness said. In the end, he was taken to Branch 285.

[356] According to the statement he made to the police, Witness ... [RR] spent several days in the Al-Khatib Branch in May 2011. He was placed in a cell there which measured 2 by 1 to 1.5 metres. A large rat had entered the cell through a slit in the door, he said. During his

interrogations—which were based on his being accused of participating in demonstrations, news he posted online and contacts with members of the opposition and abroad—he was beaten using the *fallaqa* method, for instance. He was also tortured after his interrogations. He was then forced to lie down and was kicked and beaten. The witness stated that he heard men screaming in the torture rooms and, coming from the opposite direction, the screams of women. In the end, he was taken to Kafr Sousa and released there.

[357] (11) By their own accounts, witnesses ... [HH], ... [UU], ... [X], ... [JJ], ... [KK] and Witness Z 16/12/2020, who was examined anonymously on 16 December 2020, were detained in Branch 251 at different times in the course of 2012. Their statements concerning the detention conditions and ill-treatment of prisoners— which are of only subordinate relevance given the time of the commission of the offence as established—do not give rise to any significant discrepancies in relation to what the witnesses who were already detained in 2011 observed. The witnesses at any rate testified consistently when it came to their descriptions of the conditions in the branch and especially its location in Damascus and the layout of the underground prison, which they based on sketches they had drawn.

[358] For instance, Witness ... [HH], who was imprisoned in July 2012, reported having his toes beaten with a cable during his interrogations and arbitrary punishments being meted out against other prisoners. It was only possible to sleep in a sitting position in the overcrowded, stinking and damp communal cell, which had more than 300 people in it, he stated. The food had by no means been sufficient to feed everyone. He had lost 15 kilogrammes in weight. Screaming could constantly be heard, he testified.

[359] Witness Z 16/12/2020, who was arrested in May 2012, reported that she was crammed into a single cell measuring 2 by 1 metres for 21 days together with a woman who was eight months pregnant. The sounds of torture being inflicted could be heard. She had observed the welcome beatings which the newly arrived prisoners received, she stated. Women had traces of torture, too. The guards had gone into the men's communal cell at night and beaten up the prisoners. She herself had lost 8 kilogrammes in weight during her 35 days in detention on account of the small amounts of food they were given and the quality of the food (e.g. mouldy bread). They were allowed to go to the toilet at the guards' discretion, she testified. After a large number of women were arrested she was taken with them to a communal cell, which was in an extremely bad condition ("dirt, no air, bad smell"), infested with lice, cockroaches, rats and moths and so

overcrowded that it was not possible for everyone to sleep at the same time. She was temporarily transferred to Branch 285 for a few days. During her interrogations, the witness testified, a guard who was known amongst the prisoners for being particularly brutal (*Abu Ghadab* = "Father of Wrath") had threatened her by striking the floor next to her with a whip. The witness ascribed the fact that she was given preferential treatment and was not herself beaten to her special social status. She did not go into any further detail in that regard because otherwise her anonymity would have been jeopardised.

[360] By his own account, Witness … [UU] was arbitrarily arrested, together with many others, by members of the military during a raid in the village of Al-Abbadeh in Rif Dimashq on 4 February 2012. Even the mayor and imam were amongst those arrested. After being taken to the Al-Khatib Branch, he and numerous other people were first hit with fists, hoses and whips on arrival and then again and again inside the branch. There were communal punishments if anyone talked in the cell, the witness testified. You constantly heard prisoners who were being tortured shouting and pleading, he said. The light was kept on all the time; it was impossible to tell day from night. Again and again people were put into the cell, some of them with horrible traces of torture, he said. A boy aged between 10 and 15 years old who had a gunshot wound to his leg was also brought in and was nevertheless beaten. A man who was over 70 years old was also beaten. During his own interrogation the witness was told to confess, after which the interrogator had beaten his legs. He suffered a fractured leg as a result, the witness stated, and the ensuing wound had immediately become infected. He then said things that were not true and signed a blank sheet of paper. People slept on top of each other in the cell, he testified. The food had been "just about enough to stay alive". The witness stated that the worst thing about his time in prison was the uncertainty as to what was going to happen to them. After spending between 10 and 15 days in the branch and a short period in another prison, he was brought before a judge, had his hand stamped and was allowed to leave.

[361] Witness … [X] testified that she was arrested on the night of 4 February 2012, taken to the Al-Khatib Branch and detained there for three days. The reason was her work as an activist. She and others had collected medicines to help those who were injured during a bombard-ment of Homs. She was interrogated every day about her political activities, she testified. She was beaten immediately following her arrest and whilst being taken to be interrogated in the branch. There was a place near her cell in the basement where the imprisoned men were

abused. Their screams could be heard all the time, the witness stated. A man who had had to endure particularly brutal torture had suddenly gone mute. Usually at least two people were tortured at the same time, the witness said. The staff were more violent towards the men than towards the women, she testified. She herself was also verbally harassed and threatened with sexual violence, and one guard had deliberately touched her breast. She was placed in a small single cell with two other people; it measured 1.80 by 1 metre. Even when the witness had her period there was no means for her to practice feminine hygiene, she stated.

[362] According to his statement, Witness . . . [JJ] was arrested on 4 September 2012 at a checkpoint in the immediate vicinity of the Al-Khatib Branch. The witness told of a completely overcrowded cell with more than 200 people in it and not enough space for everyone to sit or lie down, with artificial lighting permanently on, without enough to drink and eat, stifling air and not enough opportunities to relieve themselves. According to the witness, it was an underground cell which had subsequently been added to the prison. He was interrogated several times, during which he was shackled and had to kneel blindfolded in front of the interrogating officer. During the interrogations his legs were sometimes physically restrained, and on each occasion he was hit with a belt or a cable for a long time and immeasurably painfully on the soles of his feet. One of his feet became infected afterwards, he stated. Fellow inmates had injuries, open wounds, some of them had been shot at during demonstrations. Many also had skin conditions, he testified.

[363] By his own account, Witness . . . [KK] was arrested in Raqqa in early May 2012 and, following stopovers in Deir ez-Zor, Homs and at the military police in Al-Qaboun, he was taken to the Al-Khatib Branch, where he was detained for three to four days. On arrival, he stated, they were all made to turn to face the wall and were beaten. The cells were overcrowded. The prisoners had rashes and allergies, their clothes were covered in pests, the witness said. The air was very humid on account of the overcrowding; there was no ventilation. All day they had heard the "really loud" screams of those being tortured. His fellow prisoners told him about electric shocks and the *shabeh* method. Most of the people in his cell exhibited signs of torture, he stated. Some had broken bones, swellings from the blows to the body, traces on their wrists after being hung up. The witness himself was interrogated and beaten on several occasions, he testified—including all over his body with an object like a fan belt. The interrogations were conducted in one of the upper storeys in the building, where the stench had not been quite so bad. When he gave an answer they did not like, the witness

stated, he was slapped across the face, kicked and beaten. He was repeatedly made to crouch down and then severely beaten whilst in that position.

[364] (cc) In synopsis, the Division's evaluation of the statements presented in the above is as follows:

[365] The witnesses' individual observations together create the overall picture that the processes and treatment of prisoners on arrival in Branch 251 differed quite considerably, for example as regards the length of detention in the branch, which was between a few days and up to months and years—though in some cases the latter was only based on hearsay. The type of detention ranged from (very) small single cells to communal cells the size of rooms or big halls whose occupancy was described as full to so overcrowded that it was impossible to lie down and even difficult to breathe. Cells were described as having no daylight or as having daylight, though in the latter case only through small openings. The choice of torture methods also followed no discernible pattern, with the exception of *fallaqa*, the preferred method during interrogations. For the rest, the type of ill-treatment applied in individual cases also varied and ranged from "standardised" torture techniques to sadistic excesses; in organisational terms, Branch 251 was geared to inflicting torture given its specially equipped "torture rooms", instruments for tormenting people and established procedures, for example involving the interrogator and the employee carrying out the ill-treatment. The frequency and objective of the interrogations and the waiting periods between them, which were agonising for prisoners, also differed considerably from one prisoner to the next.

[366] The lack of a verifiable, targeted procedure within the otherwise bureaucratised Syrian state structure, including within its security apparatus, is an indication that when the protest movement began the security authorities were faced with having to "process" a large number of prisoners without regard to a specific charge in each individual case and that their facilities were not equipped to deal with them and they therefore sometimes had to improvise when it came to the ill-treatment of detainees. The different types of abuse suggest that the guards exacting it were given free rein; sometimes they were driven by sadistic ingenuity. Justifications for the detentions were concocted through forced confessions. This is consistent with the approach adopted by the security authorities as described by other witnesses in relation to the general course of the conflict, namely that it served the purpose of collective punishment and deterrence.

[367] The variations in the treatment of those who were abducted to Branch 251 and exposed to the prevailing conditions there, who

were consciously left in the dark about the reason for their imprisonment and their future fate, paint a picture of arbitrariness. However, regardless of all these differences, the witness statements powerfully showed that the branch was characterised by the inhumane treatment of all those who were detained there and by a climate of massive violence and fear. It was especially the prisoners who were detained in the subterranean prison area who were exposed to random treatment by the guards in charge of it. Almost without exception attempts were made to extort testimonies from the prisoners by means of torture. On the other hand, though, in some cases there was no recognisable link between the brutal ill-treatment and any information-gathering purposes. This led to violent excesses with life-threatening consequences for the victims, including on account of the lack of medical treatment.

[368] Overall, the witness statements allow the safe conclusion to be drawn that those who were abducted to Branch 251, at least from April 2011 on, were exposed to systematic and brutal physical and sexual violence, to inhumane conditions of detention as a result of massive overcrowding, a lack of hygiene, not being allowed to go to the toilet often enough, insufficient food and drink, and massive mental pressure, amongst other things on account of constantly hearing the screams of their fellow prisoners who were being tortured and seeing the, in some cases, seriously injured tortured fellow prisoners in their own cell.

[369] The treatment the witnesses described is also consistent with the objective pursued by the Syrian apparatus of power, namely to use unspecific, broadly diversified violence against the civilian population for the purpose of intimidation and deterrence. The Division assumes that the aforementioned conditions, in particular the use of torture, were at any rate intended for all those who were detained arbitrarily at demonstrations and rallies and during raids. The Division found that exceptions—that is when no direct physical violence was used—were only made in the case of individuals who were specifically detained, had gained a certain degree of prominence or in the case of prisoners who turned out to be acquainted with an employee.

[370] Finally, the Division takes from the statements made by Witness ... [Y], Witness ... [AA] and Witness Z 25/11/2020 that the subterranean prison in the branch was extended before April 2012 to house additional detention rooms underneath an outdoor area. This appears to have been a consequence of the rapid growth in the number of prisoners in the branch after the start of the protest movement which the majority of the witnesses noted.

2. Sub-branch 40

[371] Taking the statements of various witnesses together, the Division was also able to gain a picture of the activities which Sub-branch 40 engaged in.

[372] (a) The information provided by the following witnesses was important in that regard:

[373] (aa) Witness Z 28/07/16, a former long-standing employee of the general intelligence service, testified that Sub-branch 40 was part of Branch 251 and was called the "Patrol Branch" or "Counterterrorism Branch". After Hafez Makhlouf took charge of it, Sub-Branch 40 gained a very bad reputation. According to the witness, Makhlouf had lots of people arrested and, as he was a cousin of Bashar al-Assad, had had free rein.

[374] Sub-branch 40 was responsible, the witnesses reported, for patrolling Damascus. When Branch 251 was looking for a specific person, Sub-branch 40 was responsible for arresting that person and taking them to Branch 251. However, it had often overstepped its competence. For example, those arrested were also interrogated in Sub-branch 40 and not always taken to Branch 251 but, based on a decision given by Hafez Makhlouf, were instead taken straight to Branch 285, for instance. Sub-branch 40 had around 100 to 200 members of staff, the witness stated; its head had an office in Branch 251. The witness stated that he had heard that people had died at the hands of Sub-branch 40.

[375] (bb) Witness . . . [AA], a senior officer in the guards in Branch 251, testified that the staff in Sub-branch 40 were responsible for making arrests on behalf of Branch 251. The unit carried out additional patrols and manned checkpoints, he stated. The only time they had anything to do with Branch 251 was when they took prisoners there. The witness stated that once during his training he had become aware that staff were being recruited for the sub-branch. Certain physical attributes were required, he stated. Besides, applicants' curriculum vitae had to be flawless in terms of evidencing a clear loyalty to the regime. It was always volunteers who were recruited, not conscripts. The branch was also particularly important on account of its head, Hafez Makhlouf, being the son of one of Bashar al-Assad's aunts, the witness stated.

[376] (cc) Witness . . . [Y], a former long-standing employee in the general intelligence service, described Sub-branch 40 as being part of Branch 251's interrogation sub-branch. However, he also described the opposite as being the case, that is that the interrogation sub-branch was

part of Sub-branch 40. At any rate, the person actually making the decisions was Hafez Makhlouf, who was responsible for issuing orders to the heads of interrogation in Branch 251, the witness stated. Ultimately, Makhlouf was the de facto head of the entire general intelligence service. Its formal head, Major General Ali Mamlouk, had come down from his office to receive Makhlouf. Makhlouf had issued instructions relating to the arrest of demonstrators and the length of their detention. The witness was there when Makhlouf issued the order to arrest all of the 1,000 people attending a rally next to a mosque.

[377] As detailed in the above (see section B.III.1 [General course of the conflict as from 2011], (c)(bb)), the Division had reservations about unreservedly accepting Witness ... [Y]'s statement. Besides the general inconsistencies in the witness's statements, it was striking that, in regard to his testimony concerning Sub-branch 40, he claimed to know specifics about the internal power structure within Branch 251 and Sub-branch 40 even though he left the branch in 1998 and then worked in the General Intelligence Directorate's headquarters, which was located elsewhere; his job was also limited to archiving documents. When asked follow-up questions, the witness was also unable to provide any concrete information about what concrete facts his assessment was based on and on which occasion he had supposedly made his observations. That, however, is the basis which would have been necessary to be able to make the assumption that the commander of a sub-unit with hundreds of staff across two hierarchical levels was the de facto head of what was—according to statements made by other witnesses—the most important Syrian intelligence service. The head of the General Intelligence Directorate receiving the head of Sub-branch 40 is not sufficient to prove that. Moreover, the outcome of the taking of evidence does not support the witness's claim either. It only proves that Hafez Makhlouf acted on his own authority when managing the sub-branch under his control and that this went unchallenged owing to his close ties with the head of the regime.

[378] (dd) Expert Witness ... [T] also assigned Sub-branch 40 to Branch 251 and described it as being responsible for Douma. Sub-branch 40 took its instructions from Branch 251, he stated. People were arrested by the sub-branch and taken to Branch 251, some of them after being interrogated. Sub-branch 40 did not have its own large prison, which was why the majority of the prisoners were handed straight over to Branch 251. Hafez Makhlouf, a cousin of the President, was head of the sub-branch, he stated. He was very influential, but subordinate to Branch 251, which was much bigger. The

witness stated that in Branch 251 the interrogations were carried out by its staff.

[379] (ee) Expert Witness ... [S] also testified that Sub-branch 40 was subordinate to Branch 251 and that it carried out specific functions for the branch. Several of his colleagues were arrested by the branch, he stated. Hafez Makhlouf, a cousin of Bashar al-Assad, was its head, which was why the branch was of particular importance within the security services. The sub-branch was responsible for the Damascus region, the witness stated, but had got involved in matters beyond its remit on account of its head's status.

[380] (ff) Witness ... [A] testified that Sub-branch 40 had a reputation for being particularly brutal under Hafez Makhlouf's leadership. The witness described it as an instrument of power whose purpose was to crush demonstrations and torture prisoners. This was common knowledge, he stated.

[381] (gg) Expert Witness ... [Z] (see section B.III.2 [Central Crisis Management Cell], (a), above) testified that, as far as he was aware, Sub-branch 40 was part of Branch 251. The sub-branch was known as the "City Branch" and the "Jisr al-Abyad" Branch. It was referred to as especially powerful and infamous. What was notable was that news from Sub-branch 40 was addressed directly to other branches and not, as was customary, sent via the head of Branch 251. Branch 251's letterhead was always used in such cases, the witness reported.

[382] (hh) The majority of the victims of the regime already referred to in the above who were abducted to Branch 251 and ill-treated there testified that they had first been arrested by Sub-branch 40 and briefly detained in premises which belonged to this unit.

[383] Witness ... [DD] was arrested on 2 May 2011 by members of Sub-branch 40 at a demonstration by women in Douma, was abducted to premises belonging to the sub-branch and then taken from there to Branch 251. She reported that Sub-branch 40 was also known as "Hafez Makhlouf". The men who had taken her away had beaten her and "touched" her "in sensitive places". She spent two hours in Sub-branch 40, she stated, without being interrogated there. After her second arrest on 12 April 2012 at a sit-in in front of the Syrian parliament as part of the "Stop the Killing" campaign, she was also first taken to Sub-branch 40, the witness stated. The security forces were ready and waiting and knew they were coming. They had immediately started arresting the women at the demonstration. Whilst in Sub-branch 40 she was subjected to "brutish blows" with cudgels, the witness testified. She and the others who were taken there with her were beaten, spat at and insulted for an hour. After a stopover in

Sub-branch 40, she was then taken in a van to Branch 251. The witness described the location of Sub-branch 40 as being on a road called "White Bridge" (= "Jisr al-Abyad"). It had a big iron gate, an open courtyard and was surrounded by residential buildings, she said.

[384] Before being taken on to Branch 251, Witness . . . [FF] was also, by his own account, arrested by alleged members of Sub-branch 40 on 24 October 2011 and spent two to three hours in its premises. Upon being arrested his laptop had been taken off him. Whilst in the sub-branch, the witness stated, he was briefly asked about his Facebook account. It was a well-known fact that the branch was headed by Hafez Makhlouf, a brother of the influential businessman Rami Makhlouf and a cousin of Bashar al-Assad. It was also a well-known fact that the sub-branch was responsible for making arrests and storming buildings "on behalf of Branch 251".

[385] According to her testimony, Witness Z 16/12/2020 was arrested on 4 May 2012 in Damascus together with others and taken to Sub-branch 40. Plain-clothes security forces had stormed into her office at gunpoint, had searched it, checked identity cards and blindfolded the men or pulled their t-shirt over their head. The men who were arrested with her were beaten once they arrived in the sub-branch, she reported. She was taken to see an acquaintance being tortured (he was being beaten and tormented with electric shocks) in order to force her to reveal her email and Facebook access details. She spent one night in Sub-branch 40, she testified, and was then driven to Branch 251 and beaten on the way there.

[386] Witness Z 25/11/2020 testified that he was arrested on 4 May 2012 by Sub-branch 40 staff and taken to the sub-branch's building in the Jisr al-Abyad district of Damascus. He was greeted with blows and spent a day there before being taken to Branch 251, he stated.

[387] According to the statement he made to the police, which was relayed to the Division by the police investigator, Witness . . . [RR] was summoned to Sub-branch 40 in the Jisr al-Abyad district of Damascus in May 2011 and questioned there about Facebook posts which were critical of the regime. After the witness pointed out that he was in contact with the President's media spokesperson, he was released. He was told to come back the next day, was shackled and taken to the Al-Khatib Branch.

[388] (b) The overall picture which emerges from the particulars presented in the above confirms the picture that Sub-branch 40 primarily had executive functions and was responsible for making arrests, carrying out searches and raids and crushing demonstrations and that it passed those arrested on to Branch 251, where their further fate was decided.

Sub-branch 40 also had its own premises with a small detention facility in the Jisr al-Abyad district of Damascus. Sub-branch 40 already conducted preliminary investigatory acts there, such as examining seized objects and questioning those arrested. It was not possible to establish whether this was based on any formal or appropriated competence.

[389] According to the concurring statements of all the witnesses, Sub-branch 40 had a special status on account of its remit, but especially on account of its head being well-known and his close ties with the government. Based on the particulars provided by the witnesses, it can be concluded that Sub-branch 40 was used as a flexible tool for rapidly and effectively combating the protest movement, at any rate in the Greater Damascus area. Witness … [AA]'s description of the special requirements made as to the physical fitness and loyalty to the regime of those working in the sub-branch can already be brought into line with the tasks assigned to it. The Division also takes as the basis for its assessment the fact that the head of Sub-branch 40, Hafez Makhlouf, used his special status on account of being a relation of President Bashar al-Assad to act on his own authority, which can easily be reconciled with the fact that the structure of the Syrian state was founded on close personal ties and loyalties. The Division also holds it to be true that, like the other heads of the sub-branches, the head of Sub-branch 40 had his own office in Branch 251, as Witness Z 28/05/16 testified. By contrast, it was not possible to confirm on the basis of the statements made by the witnesses, that, as Witness … [Y] claims, Hafez Makhlouf held a dominant position within Branch 251 or even within the general intelligence service as a whole. This would, rather, contrast with the fact that Sub-branch 40 was housed in separate premises and that, according to all the other witnesses' statements, its role was only to provide support (by arresting and delivering alleged critics of the regime) and that Branch 251 operated autonomously, as former members of the regime and witnesses detained in Branch 251 consistently explained.

[390] Finally, in accordance with the witnesses' statements, the Division was also able to use as the basis for its assessment the fact that Sub-branch 40, like all the other branches and sub-branches of the intelligence services involved in handling prisoners, treated detainees in a manner which was characterised by violence.

V. Re the findings as to the person of the Defendant

[391] (a) The findings as to the Defendant's family circumstances and his career are essentially based on the statements he himself made during his hearing before the Federal Office for Migration and

Refugees on 9 May 2018 and during his subsequent police questioning as a witness on 16 August 2018. On both occasions the Defendant outlined his family background and training in a mutually consistent manner. Witness . . . [CC], a cousin of the Defendant, confirmed this information to the extent that he himself had knowledge thereof. In particular, he testified that the Defendant grew up in the village of Muhasan (alternative spelling: Mouhassan) and that he later attended secondary school. The witness learned that the Defendant had deserted in early January 2012 from the latter's older brother. The Defendant had also been officially reported as missing, he stated.

[392] Details concerning the Defendant's family circumstances, especially the number and age of his children and his marriage, are based on excerpts from the Defendant's family booklet (containing extracts from the Syrian civil registry records), which was handed over to the Federal Office for Migration and Refugees by the Defendant and then added to his Foreigner's File (*Ausländerakte*).

[393] (b) The Division was able to make only very few determinations regarding the period between the Defendant's defecting in January 2012 and his entering Germany.

[394] It is just as difficult to establish with any certainty where the Defendant stayed and for how long in each case prior to his entering Germany as it is to establish when and where the Defendant's family rejoined him. It is, in particular, still unclear when the Defendant left Syria for Turkey and whether and, if so, when he met his family again in Syria and whether he left the country together with his family. Here, too, the available information was mainly provided by the Defendant himself. During his hearing before the Federal Office for Migration and Refugees the Defendant described in detail how he had first gone on his own to his home village after deserting on 5 January 2012 whilst his family had initially stayed on in Damascus, but then joined him. However, his statements regarding his moving between various villages, alleged targeted attacks against his home village and his parents' house and his witnessing of such attacks, despite having previously left the village, are rather inconclusive. It also seems implausible that the Defendant's parents' house would have been the target of shelling in response to his defection. The Defendant provided no information about where his family was staying, whom he claims very generally to have "got to safety". He only used singular pronouns when describing subsequent events, especially his leaving to go to Turkey, i.e. that "he" left. The Defendant also provided little information during his police questioning as a witness and only regarding himself, but not regarding the fate of his family after his defection.

[395] It is also striking that after arriving in Germany the Defendant presented excerpts from his family booklet which were dated 4 February 2016 and had been issued by the Syrian Ministry of the Interior, "Directorate General for Civil Matters", each with a German translation done by a translation agency in Damascus on 12 April 2016. This could be an indication that the Defendant's family, or some family members, were still in Damascus in April 2016 and were preparing to flee to Germany, or that they were at least able to obtain the documents and have them translated with the help of intermediaries. More generally, it appears problematic that the Defendant, who had been reported missing, claimed that he was actually able to get documents on his civil status issued by the Syrian authorities. Above all, though, the fact that the Syrian civil status documents the Defendant was carrying with him cite 1 January 2014 and 1 January 2015 respectively as the dates of birth of two of his children and Deir ez-Zor as their place of birth indicates that the Defendant and his family stayed in Syria for longer. Should this be true, the Defendant would most likely still have been in Syria in 2014.

[396] In the light of the above, the Division is not in a position to take at face value the date of his leaving to go to Turkey, which the Defendant narrowed down both during his hearing before the Federal Office for Migration and Refugees and during his police questioning as a witness very precisely to having been between mid-February 2012 and 12 February 2012 in the case of the latter and between 9 and 13 February 2012 in the case of the former. The same applies to the date on which he crossed the Turkish border into Greece, which he consistently stated on both occasions was on 20 February 2016.

[397] (c) The date of the Defendant's entry into Germany and information about his living circumstances here are based on the Foreigner's File kept by the foreigners authority in ... [c] on the Defendant, the content of which was relayed by Witness ... [VV], and, as regards the asylum procedure, on statements provided by Witness ... [L] and Witness ... [M], who work in the Federal Office for Migration and Refugees. This in particular concerns the course and status of the asylum procedure, the circumstances of the Defendant's entry into Germany, his family's assignment to a reception centre and their final allocation of an apartment in ... [c].

[398] The findings as to the Defendant's previous conviction are based on an extract from the Federal Central Criminal Register (*Bundeszentralregister*) pertaining to him and the summary penalty order issued to him by ... [a] Local Court on 24 July 2018. Findings concerning enforcement of the aforementioned order are

based on information relating to payments made by the Defendant which is on file. According to the final order made by ... [t] Public Prosecution Office, the Defendant's fine has been paid in full and the case is closed. Other proceedings based on the charge that the Defendant "injured two Afghan nationals living in a neighbouring property by punching them" on 7 July 2018 were terminated. The dates and circumstances of the Defendant's arrest, release from prison and renewed arrest were submitted to the Division by police officers ... [P] and ...[S], who were involved in the case. According to their statements, the Defendant's imprisonment, and especially his second arrest, came as a complete surprise to him. During his first arrest the Defendant believed there must be some misunderstanding, and during the second he complained about heart and breathing problems, which were possibly psychosomatic.

VI. Re the findings as to the Defendant's concrete contribution to the offence

1. Defendant's career in the Syrian intelligence service

[399] The findings made regarding the Defendant's joining the Syrian intelligence service, the work he did there, the branches he worked for and his service grade are largely based on information he himself gave during his hearing before the Federal Office for Migration and Refugees and during his questioning as a witness before the Federal Criminal Police Office. They are also based on several pieces of evidence and circumstantial evidence which corroborate the information about the work the Defendant did.

[400] (a) The Division does not doubt the truthfulness of the information which the Defendant himself gave. It already appears credible in and of itself. The information was detailed and coherent, consistent on both occasions on which the Defendant made a statement, even though the focus of each varied, and, in the light of the fact that he willingly and with unconcealed pride reported about his successful work as a "tough" trainer, for instance, it also appears to be based on his own experience. The Defendant discernibly did not attempt to window-dress the function of the intelligence service and the work he did in it, especially since the reason for his ultimately deserting and seeking asylum related to that work. In view of the depth of detail he provided in relation to his training and his office and operative work, in particular the act itself, the Division also rules out the possibility that the Defendant may have exaggerated his career

history and the work he did. One possible explanation for why he might falsely incriminate himself would be an attempt to establish a reason for claiming asylum. However, the circumstances of his desertion and subsequent persecution would have already been sufficient for this. Besides, the Defendant provided further details during his questioning as a witness by the Federal Criminal Police Office which did not promise to give him any advantage in relation to his asylum application or otherwise.

[401] Finally, the Defendant also explicitly confirmed that he worked for the Syrian security forces in the written statement which was submitted to the Division, in which he wrote, in general terms, that he had had no alternative but to continue his work for the time being, though he did not provide any further details about what that work entailed.

[402] (b) The work the Defendant did and the date of his desertion are confirmed by the statement made by Witness ... [CC], a cousin of the Defendant, that is the son of one of the Defendant's father's sisters.

[403] (aa) The witness first reported on his own political attitude to the situation at the time in Syria. By his own account, he had already been politically active during the Damascus Spring, had attended meetings and discussions organised by the opposition and had subsequently written political articles. In March 2011, the witness stated, he had taken part in demonstrations and seen the security forces in action. On 8 April 2011 he himself was first arrested for one day by the intelligence service (the so-called Palestine Branch) during a demonstration in the Kafr Sousa district of Damascus and then interrogated. Following a personal meeting with the head of branch, he was released without suffering any ill-treatment. He was described as an educated person and treated better than other prisoners, who were insulted and called terrorists and beaten. The witness was forced to reveal his Facebook access data and email passwords and was warned not to engage in any more anti-government activities. At the same time he was offered the opportunity to cooperate by spying on the opposition.

[404] As regards the Defendant, the witness testified that, after attending secondary school, he had joined the security forces or the Ministry of the Interior as a volunteer. He had, ultimately, progressed to the rank of staff sergeant or sergeant major. The Defendant worked for the "State Security", the witness stated, though he, the witness, did not know exactly what it belonged to. At any rate, his work involved monitoring people and various political groups. The organisation served the preservation of power, the witness stated.

[405] The Defendant first underwent six months of basic training, the witness testified. After graduating from university in 2001, the witness had opened a dental practice in Al-Dachadile, south of Damascus. During this time he had from time to time met with the Defendant, who was also living in that area and whose family members had come to him for dental treatment. At that time the Defendant was a sports trainer in the State Security in Najha. Later, the Defendant told the witness that he had transferred to the "Branch for Religious Affairs", where he was responsible for monitoring Friday sermons and the preachers. The Defendant had told the witness that in political terms he was definitely "for the revolution". When the Defendant came to the witness's practice in early February or early March 2011, they had talked about the situation in the security forces. The Defendant reported that they were on the highest alert and knew that the revolution was coming. He, the witness, had heard that the Defendant had warned a person called "Atassi", who was meant to be arrested. He heard this from one of the Defendant's brothers and then again shortly before his examination in the main hearing. The witness did not have the impression that the Defendant had wanted to harm anyone, otherwise he would have broken off contact with him. Many employees in the security services had come to him for treatment, the witness stated. You could tell people apart.

[406] The Defendant did not tell the witness much about his other activities. Nevertheless, it was clear that the security people "always went out on Fridays" and kept those places where the demonstrations were expected to take place under surveillance. From 2011, the Defendant's job, by his own account, no longer followed the same old routine. The regime had mobilised all its forces to fight the revolution. The Defendant had once told him about an incident involving a bus full of detainees, he stated. One of the Defendant's colleagues had taken a stick so that he could join in the "welcome party". The Defendant had been "angry" about that, because "something like that" was not "his thing". The Defendant had repeatedly mentioned the name Hafez Makhlouf and his rigorousness and brutality. Makhlouf had used firearms, too. One time, Hafez Makhlouf had got out of his jeep, put his foot on its running board and started to shoot at the demonstrators. That was what the Defendant had told him.

[407] The witness testified that he was not exactly sure whether the Defendant had worked in Sub-branch 40. The Defendant or one of his brothers might possibly have told him that. At any rate, the Defendant himself had talked a lot about Hafez Makhlouf. For

example, that he expected his employees to be loyal. It was public knowledge that Makhlouf was head of Sub-branch 40, the witness stated. When asked what reputation the sub-branch had, the witness replied that such sub-branches were a "kind of butcher's shop for slaughtering humans", that people were beaten and tortured there and that a sub-branch headed by Hafez Makhlouf must have been "hell". The Defendant had also told the witness that there had been a lot of distrust within the sub-branch. The staff, especially the Sunnis, had their service weapons taken off them and were only re-issued them when there were demonstrations.

[408] The Defendant had already spoken of a possible "dissociation" (i.e. desertion) in August or September 2011, the witness testified. But he had first wanted to take care of his family, he said. On 5 January 2012 the witness had been told personally by the Defendant's eldest brother that he had deserted. A "communiqué" had also been published that the Defendant was missing. According to the witness, that was standard procedure in the authorities.

[409] (bb) The Division believes the witness. No indications came to light that he may not have spoken the truth about his own political activities and detention. The information he obtained from the Defendant about his career and work also appears credible.

[410] It was apparent that the witness was trying to remember the encounters he had had with the Defendant, some of which were a long time ago, and what the Defendant had said on those occasions; he openly admitted to gaps in his memory and uncertainties, but was, on the other hand, also able to provide details regarding specific circumstances. He had also indicated that he dissociated himself from the security forces, whom he, based on his own experience, described in general terms as "butcher's shops". The Division naturally saw occasion to doubt the witness's attitude towards the Defendant, which sometimes seemed quite uncritical, given the witness's own work in the opposition, his own experience of being in detention and the, in his own words, brutal reputation of the sub-branch of which Hafez Makhlouf was head. When asked about this, the witness responded that he did not see any contradiction in that. The Defendant had again and again signalled that he clearly supported the revolution. The witness had believed him when he assured him that he rejected the regime. When confronted with the charges brought, the witness stated that he was simply unaware of such details, especially since he had not met the Defendant on a regular basis. When asked whether his own lenient treatment following his arrest on 8 April 2011 could have been down to the Defendant having interceded for him, the witness

vehemently denied this and explained that his arrest had been reported on social media.

[411] Even though certain exculpatory tendencies were discernible in his statement, especially in terms of the witness being unable to provide any tangible indications that the Defendant was critical of the regime, as he had reported, this does not, in the opinion of the Division, call what was stated into question. It is, first, obvious that the Defendant, knowing that his cousin was critical of the regime and involved in oppositional work, had glossed over his own work and presented himself as being inclined towards the "revolution". The Division therefore assumes that the Defendant did in fact tell the witness those things which the latter described. The same goes for the talk the witness testified to having had with the Defendant back in mid-2011 about his deserting. Second, Witness ... [CC]'s favourable attitude towards the Defendant fits seamlessly into the statements made by a number of witnesses—even though some of them had themselves been victims of the most serious attacks—who called for a more nuanced approach to be taken to former employees of the regime, especially those who deserted. It is, furthermore, understandable that the witness found himself in a conflict of loyalties between his oppositional work on the one hand and his kinship with the Defendant on the other, and that he wanted to believe what the Defendant said. The Division does not, therefore, assume that the witness deliberately wanted to exonerate the Defendant on account of their close family relationship, but that he simply recounted the Defendant's explanations truthfully without, though, being able to verify them himself.

[412] (cc) Overall, the witness's account confirms the career within the Syrian intelligence service which the Defendant himself described, sometimes including details regarding his various deployments. In view of what the Defendant told Witness ... [CC], the Division cannot rule out that the Defendant took a critical view of events as from 2011, even though this was not revealed in any ascertainable action on the part of the Defendant. Nevertheless, the alleged "warning" issued to an individual before their upcoming arrest, which Witness ... [CC] reported, is too vague for the Division to be able to use it as an establishable fact in its assessment. The witness was only able to relate key words in regard to that which he, in turn, had heard from third parties, in particular one of the Defendant's brothers.

[413] (c) Witness ... [BB]'s testimony also confirms the Defendant's active operative work in the Syrian intelligence service up to the end of 2011 and the fact that before that he had worked as a trainer.

[414] (aa) By his own account, Witness . . . [BB] was employed in Information Branch 255 of the Syrian General Intelligence Directorate in the period between November 2010 and early 2012. He had also worked in Training Branch 295 of the General Intelligence Directorate, in the field office in Najha, south of Damascus. As already set out in the above (see section B.III.3 [Number, documentation and treatment of those killed: Mass graves], (b)(cc)), the witness did administrative work in relation to the transports of corpses to mass graves in the southern environs of Damascus. On the occasion of one such transport the witness had recognised the Defendant as a member of the escort team of guards.

[415] During his examination by the Division, the witness described Branch 295 of the Syrian General Intelligence Directorate as a training branch and thus confirmed what the Defendant had said regarding the start of his career in the intelligence service. He was able to indicate the location of the branch in Najha, south of Damascus, on a map, including training grounds and accommodation for trainees. The witness also stated that he came from the same region as the Defendant, i.e. Muhasan. In contrast to what he had stated during his police questioning, the witness stated that he did not know the Defendant from when he was in Branch 295. However, he met the Defendant at a crossroads when the Defendant was escorting a refrigerated truck together with a total of 10 intelligence service staff in a pickup. There had been around 50 to 60 corpses in the truck, the witness testified. The Defendant and the others had been armed with guns. The witness was not able to say whether they were machine guns, as he had stated during his police interview, "also because of the pressure he was under". When asked how he knew the Defendant, the witness responded that one of his colleagues had mentioned the Defendant's name. He also knew from colleagues that the Defendant had worked for the State Security. The witness recognised the Defendant at the main hearing.

[416] In his police interviews on 24 July and 14 August 2019, which were relayed to the Division by witnesses . . . [P] and . . . [MM], Witness . . . [BB] testified extensively, although some of what he said contradicted the testimony he gave in the main hearing. In the light of the back translation which was done of his interviews, the signatures on each page of the transcript and handwritten corrections made by the witness, the Division rules out any communication issues. The witness also himself testified at the main hearing that he had been able to make himself understood. In the matter itself, Witness . . . [BB] stated during his police questioning that he knew the Defendant. He stated that he

met him for the first time in Branch 295 when he, the Defendant, was deployed in the State Security in Douma. The Defendant was there for a training course. As a member of the field office in Douma, the Defendant was responsible for crushing the demonstrations held there, according to the witness's recollection in a position of leadership.

[417] The witness also provided details during his police interview regarding the time when he met the Defendant again and his work in relation to the transports of corpses. The Defendant's name was indicated on the written notice of a transport of corpses, for instance. The witness had received from his unit a file with a list of the dead transported to the mass graves, he stated. He had also been informed by telephone of the vehicles which would be used and their registration numbers. He and the Defendant met at a crossroads near Branch 295, at 5:00 hrs, when a refrigerated truck and two pickups with mounted machine guns had pulled up. He recognised the Defendant as a former acquaintance. He, the witness, had merely greeted him. After they had exchanged a password, he had waved the transport through. The encounter lasted around 15 minutes. The convoy then drove towards a mass grave which was being guarded by "Iranians". As the witness recalled, this was in 2012.

[418] (bb) The Division uses as the basis for its assessment the statements which the witness made during the main hearing (see section B.III.3 [Number, documentation and treatment of those killed: Mass graves], (b)(cc), above) and, in addition, those he made during his police questioning.

[419] It was evident at the main hearing that the witness had not wanted to confirm various statements he had made during his police questioning, even though they were true, because he was afraid. He refused to provide further details regarding his acquaintance with the Defendant, citing the stereotypical reason that he was unable to remember. It was not possible to get any further explanations as to the gaps in his memory out of the witness, even when he was confronted with what he had said during his police questioning. At the same time, the witness admitted at the main hearing that his family, who were still in Syria, had been threatened by distant members of the Defendant's family. According to statements made by the police investigator (Witness ... [P]), Witness ... [BB] had already approached the Federal Criminal Police Office after his questioning by the police because his family was being threatened and he no longer wished to provide any more information.

[420] The witness's testimony in the main hearing regarding his acquaintance with the Defendant was not plausible, lacked detail and

was manifestly given as a pretext. For instance, the claim that he had seen the Defendant only once, fleetingly, and had picked him out amongst a large number of escorts when a convey passed by, appears hardly compatible with having a concrete memory of the Defendant after 10 years. The witness not only recognised him physically at the main hearing: during his questioning by the police he had already spontaneously identified him in a photo line-up and reasonably explained that he knew him from when they had both previously worked in Branch 295. According to the police investigators—Witness . . . [P] and Witness . . . [MM]—Witness . . . [BB] had shown willing to provide information during his police questioning on 24 July and 14 August 2019 and had given detailed information about the properties which belonged to Branch 295, the two mass graves, his own work, the content of the lists of dead people which he took receipt of and the delivery of corpses, amongst other things. He had also explained, when asked various follow-up questions, where he had got to know the Defendant and what tasks his job involved. The witness merely evidenced uncertainty when it came to assigning the numbers of the branches and assigning the individual branches to the different Syrian intelligence services. As already stated in the above, the witness, who was correctly informed of his rights, had the statements he made at his police interviews translated back to him. He signed these translations and made a few handwritten corrections. The witness was asked during the main hearing whether there had been any communication difficulties, which he claimed was not the case.

[421] All the above speaks to the fact that the witness deliberately sought to distance himself from providing detailed information relating to the Defendant in the main hearing although he had given it correctly during the preliminary investigation. As to the testimony the witness gave at the main hearing that he was no longer able to recall any details of what he had previously observed, the Division therefore based its assessment on the statements he made during his questioning by the police.

[422] (cc) As a result, the witness's statement first confirms the work the Defendant did in a branch of the General Intelligence Directorate which was responsible for Douma, whose remit included quashing demonstrations in the city. As Witness . . . [BB] himself left the intelligence service in early 2012 and the encounter with the Defendant was in 2012, the witness statement proves that the Defendant was still working for the Syrian intelligence service, evidently Sub-branch 40, at the turn of the year 2011/12.

[423] (d) The Division further concludes from several documents that the Defendant worked for Branch 251 of the Syrian General

Intelligence Directorate. An old official pass which the Defendant brought with him to Germany and which was added to his Foreigner's File was issued by the "general military and armed forces leadership" in 1997. It describes him as a "sergeant" and the nature of his service as "volunteer".

[424] Another official pass issued to the Defendant as an employee of the Syrian General Intelligence Directorate derives from an analysis of the Defendant's mobile phone on which photographs of the document were stored, as the Division was told by Witness ... [P], who conducted the analysis. The words "Syrian Arab Republic" are written on the front of the pass, and it is signed "General Intelligence Service" in Latin and Arabic letters. There is also a photograph of the Defendant, below which is written in Arabic script "Head of the Directorate of the General Intelligence Service". The word "Security" is also written in block capitals on the front of the pass, which also bears a pass number and a stylised eagle with the Syrian flag. The Defendant's name, an abbreviation of his service rank of "non-commissioned officer" is written on the back of the pass, as is "Branch 251"; there is also a section which refers to the type of weapon he was issued, which has been left blank, a pass number and the date of issue, that is March 2010. Further, the pass bears the request to authorities to render assistance to the holder of the pass.

2. Concrete participation in the offence: Conduct after the fact

[425] The findings as to the Defendant's concrete participation in the offence as established are likewise primarily based on the information he gave during his hearing before the Federal Office for Migration and Refugees on 9 May 2018 and during his police questioning as a witness on 16 August 2018, insofar as it is not inadmissible. The particulars which the Defendant gave on both occasions were relayed at the main hearing by witnesses ... [L], ... [M], ... [P] and ... [O], who also gave testimony regarding the context in which the hearing and the questioning were conducted.

[426] (a) The events which the Defendant described during his police questioning as a witness and his own involvement in putting down the demonstration in Douma in September or October 2011 are consistent and sufficiently detailed. No inconsistencies or other particularities emerged which could support the assumption that the Defendant wrongfully incriminated himself. This also applies in view of the fact that although the Defendant had reported the incident, though without stating that he himself was directly involved, he had

already reported about the demonstration and the firing of shots by
Hafez Makhlouf during his hearing before the Federal Office for
Migration and Refugees. There is no indication that the Defendant
may have given further incorrect specific details about the incident at
the hearing before the Federal Criminal Police Office because he
thought it would be to his advantage, for instance.

[427] The putting down of the demonstration in Douma in
September or October 2011 as described by the Defendant fits seamlessly into the picture which emerged concerning the course and
escalation of events in Syria in 2011, namely that the violent approach
to countering demonstrations using impact weapons and firearms and
the arbitrary arrest of demonstrators and their transfer to detention
facilities operated by the security authorities was one of the methods
which was regularly used by the Syrian regime from April 2011 at the
latest in an attempt to crush the protest movement by force. The taking
of arrested people to Branch 251 in buses and their reception there—an
orgy of violence cynically called a "welcome party"—is confirmed by
Witness Z 28/07/16, Witness . . . [AA] and several victim witnesses.
This, too, indicates that the Defendant's testimony is based on his
own experience.

[428] Likewise, as already presented in the above (see section B.III.2
[Central Crisis Management Cell]), it is certain that Sub-branch
40 acted as a "snatch and thug squad" in the field on behalf of
Branch 251, possibly also for other branches of the Syrian general
intelligence service, and that it was called to crush demonstrations,
make arrests and take those arrested to the Branch, meaning that the
incident also falls within the remit and actual tasks of this intelligence
unit. Witness . . . [AA] confirmed that Sub-branch 40 was specifically
responsible for Douma. The fact that those arrested were taken straight
to the Branch, that is without a stopover in the Sub-branch, also does
not represent a special case given what the witnesses giving testimony
about its activities reported.

[429] Finally, the incident is backed up by the statement made by
Witness . . . [CC] (see section B.VI.1 [Defendant's career in the Syrian
intelligence service], (b)). According to that witness, the Defendant,
who was still in Syria at the time, told him about an incident involving
at least one bus carrying detainees and a "welcome party" which one of
the Defendant's colleagues was involved in. The witness stated that the
Defendant also mentioned Hafez Makhlouf's involvement in this
incident, that is that he had got out of his jeep and shot at the
demonstrators. In view of this original detail, the Division does not
doubt that what the Defendant reported to the witness refers to the

incident which is the subject of the act, namely the putting down of the demonstration in Douma.

[430] (b) As regards the number of demonstrators who were arrested with the Defendant's assistance and taken to Branch 251, the Division assumes, in the Defendant's favour, that there were (only) 30 people.

[431] The Defendant quoted a precise number of people neither during his hearing before the Federal Office for Migration and Refugees nor during his questioning as a witness, that is to the extent that they were admissible. He did, however, state that those arrested were taken in "buses" to the branch. The Division thus assumes, in the Defendant's favour, a minimum of two vehicles.

[432] Witness ... [AA], a guard in Branch 251, reported that those arrested, especially in Douma, regularly arrived at Branch 251 in buses. According to him, the smaller buses could take 15 to 20 people. Sometimes, though, as far as he could see they were overcrowded. Based on this, the Division assumes, in the Defendant's favour, that the number of prisoners transported in each bus was 15, which adds up to a total of 30 people.

[433] (c) The Division takes as its basis that, given the standard treatment meted out to people who were arrested and taken to Branch 251, all the demonstrators who were taken there with the Defendant's assistance were also subjected to the severest physical and psychological ill-treatment in Branch 251 and exposed to the conditions which prevailed there at the time of the commission of the act and that they were detained there for at least several days. There were no indications that individual people who were arrested were, by way of exception, given preferential treatment. Such indications are also implausible because those who were taken to Branch 251 were arbitrarily arrested protesters and not deliberately arrested known critics of the regime. It is, though, only the latter who may, with a certain degree of probability, have been privileged, whilst people who were subjected to mass arbitrary arrest could expect deterrent, violent treatment in line with the security authorities' objective. By contrast, it is not possible to establish that any of these 30 specific demonstrators who were taken to Branch 251 died whilst they were there as a result of the ill-treatment or detention conditions, or that they were subjected to sexual assault.

[434] (d) As regards the subjective part of the offence, the Division takes as its basis that the Defendant knew both about what tasks were assigned to Sub-branch 40 and about the escalation of events happening out in the streets, including the growing intensity of the

attacks by the security forces. He also knew about the purpose of the specific operation against the demonstrators in Douma and knew that the arrested demonstrators were to be taken to Branch 251. He was aware both of the nature of the ill-treatment and detention conditions which awaited them there and of the fact that their arbitrary arrest lacked any rule-of-law basis. The Division concludes this from the following:

[435] In September 2011 the Defendant had already been working in Sub-branch 40 for three months. For that reason, its remit and actual operations were already known to him, including on account of his previous experience over many years of working in the intelligence service. As the sub-branch's only task was to act as a "snatch squad" by controlling the streets, carrying out searches and arrests, breaking up rallies and taking those arrested to detention facilities, including one in Sub-branch 40, it is simply not conceivable that he could have remained unaware of its function, even though the Division was not able to establish that the Defendant himself engaged in any other concrete actions. This is especially true given that the majority of the witnesses, both those critical of and those close to the regime, were able to provide information about the sub-branch based on their general knowledge about the prevailing situation within the Syrian security apparatus. The fact that the Defendant was already well informed before he transferred to the sub-branch can be derived circumstantially from the chronological description of his work in the intelligence service which he gave the Federal Office for Migration and Refugees: he described it in general terms as "dangerous". Witnesses who worked within the intelligence service whom the Division examined— Witness ... [AA], Witness ... [BB], Witness ... [Y] and Witness Z 28/07/19—were also able to explain, even though they were of lower rank, the structure of the intelligence services and the tasks and competences of at least their own branch.

[436] The Defendant was likewise well aware of the general situation in Syria over the course of 2011 up until the operation which is the subject of the act. Incidents which occurred from February 2011 onwards in the aftermath of the Arab Spring, the spreading demonstrations and their violent suppression by the security authorities were common knowledge in Syria. According to the statements made by the expert witnesses ... [S] and ... [T], the Syrian population was, in particular, well aware that the Syrian government was already availing itself of the services of the intelligence apparatus and other security forces even when Hafez al-Assad was still in power in order to intimidate oppositional forces by making arrests and using force and to

deter them from engaging in their activities. Apart from brief periods during which conditions were relaxed, nothing changed under Bashar al-Assad's rule. The events in Douma and subsequently across the whole of the country from February 2011 had drastic consequences and, even though the Syrian regime made efforts not to have them reported in the press, reports of them were disseminated on social media and foreign websites. There is no reason to assume that the Defendant was unaware of what was common knowledge in Syria. Above all, on account of his work within the Syrian intelligence apparatus, which was specifically involved in suppressing the burgeoning civil movement, the Defendant had an insider's view of the extent of the efforts undertaken in that regard. His training and the tasks assigned to him—ranging from his military-style training to his own work as a trainer, which was oriented to responding violently to opponents of the regime, to spying on mosques, responsibility for the surveillance of a specific district of Damascus and to his transfer to Sub-branch 40, which was in particular responsible for the direct use of force on the streets—were geared to identifying and suppressing oppositional efforts. The fact that he knew about the general situation in Syria also results from the statement made by Witness ... [CC], who reported about meetings either in February or March 2011 in which the Defendant had indicated his sympathy for the opposition movement.

[437] Even against this backdrop it is extremely likely that the Defendant knew from the outset what the purpose was of operations such as the one established here against the demonstration in Douma. In addition, the Defendant explicitly stated during his police questioning as a witness that, since "the start of the unrest", orders had been issued to kill demonstrators and, when asked a follow-up question, he made specific reference to the demonstration in Douma which is the subject of the act. The wording the Defendant used to describe how he had received such orders in relation to the demonstration, including information about the demonstrators' planned behaviour ("They will sit there and not be moved."), permits the conclusion that the Defendant was already informed ahead of the demonstration about the operation and its purpose. In the light of the scope of the operation and required coordination—the Defendant explained that 250 people belonging to Sub-branch 40 alone were involved—it is also to be assumed that instructions were given ahead of the demonstration about the precise remit and what was expected of him. This especially since the Defendant, a higher-ranking non-commissioned officer, ranked higher than the enlisted personnel. Accordingly, the Defendant was

also aware that the people arrested at the demonstration were to be taken to Branch 251.

[438] Finally, the Defendant also knew that, after being taken to Branch 251, those arrested would be subjected to the ill-treatment, torture and inhumane detention conditions established in the above. Taking together all the statements made by all the Syrian witnesses who were examined, the conditions in, tasks of and procedures applied in the detention facilities operated by the Syrian intelligence service were common knowledge amongst the general public in Syria. Witnesses . . . [BB], . . . [AA] and Z 28/07/16, who were employed in the intelligence services, were able to provide detailed insights in that regard. Especially since the Defendant was a sergeant major, and thus not of a low rank, it can be ruled out that these circumstances were unknown to him. This is especially true since various witnesses, including Witness . . . [DD] and Witness . . . [FF], had already reported about the ill-treatment of detainees in stopover facilities belonging to Sub-branch 40 in Damascus. The Division therefore takes as the basis for its assessment that the Defendant was well informed about the conditions in the branch both based on his own observations and what his colleagues told him. He had already spent time working in Branch 251 from February 2010 on, had thus been in and out of the premises belonging to the branch and had heard the screams of those being tortured, which, according to the testimony he gave during his police questioning, could even be heard in the cafeteria there. By his own account, the Defendant visited the prison in the branch, although it cannot be ruled out that this was after the incident which is the subject of the act. He was also able to report about the methods of torture used. According to his own testimony, the Defendant not only knew that torture existed in Branch 251 even before the unrest, i.e. before March 2011, he was even able to state during his police questioning what had changed after the unrest: "The punishments increased and the guards were able to do what they wanted."

[439] It was not possible to establish with any certainty what the Defendant's motives were for ultimately defecting. The Division assumes, in the Defendant's favour, that, as he had already asserted during his hearing before the Federal Office for Migration and Refugees, he ultimately turned his back on his work for the regime because he resented the fact that he was increasingly being required to use force against demonstrators. It would seem natural that the fact that the clashes with demonstrators and other opponents of the regime had become more extensive and more brutal also played a role in this, and that, owing to the foreseeable militarisation of the conflict, continuing

in his job in the intelligence service would have had considerable risks for the Defendant. As established in the above, on account of his involvement in the transportation of corpses the Defendant was also aware that the crushing of the protest movement led to large numbers of victims.

[440] (e) By contrast, the Division is unable to establish that at the time of the incident which is the subject of the act the Defendant found himself in a predicament which would have prevented him stepping back from the act on account of a present threat to his own life or limb or on account of relevant threats to his close relatives, and that that was the only reason or one of the reasons why he committed the act.

[441] (aa) The Division already cannot identify any will on the part of the Defendant to commit the act to avoid serious disadvantages for himself or third parties close to him. Rather, it assumes, based on various circumstantial facts, that the Defendant participated willingly and without any inner conflict in putting down the demonstration and transporting demonstrators to Branch 251.

[442] (1) After having worked in the intelligence service for many years, the Defendant was already aware of the methods applied by the security services against opposition movements in the period before February 2011. From the general media, in particular though on account of his being part of Branch 251, he also knew that it was primarily the intelligence services which were deployed to put down the anti-government protests, preferentially Sub-branch 40, which acted as a rapid response unit. Sub-branch 40 was, therefore, involved as from February 2011, consequently before the incident which is the subject of the act. Even though the Defendant was not initially employed in Sub-branch 40 and it is not possible to establish that he subsequently took part in such operations—with the exception of his contribution to the offence as established—it can be ruled out that he was unaware of them, especially given his status as a high-ranking non-commissioned officer. In the light of the fact that instructions which were issued on the basis of decisions taken by the CCMC from April 2011 onwards were being passed down to the intelligence services, that is to begin systematically using—even lethal—force, the Defendant was also aware, from May 2011 onwards, that the security situation was escalating. When he joined Sub-branch 40 in July 2011 he was, therefore, aware of what awaited him there.

[443] Even though it is not possible to establish that the Defendant's original transfer to Sub-branch 40 was primarily down to his own efforts, according to the statement given by Witness . . .

[AA], his deployment did presuppose the relevant aptitude and especial loyalty to the regime. It is thus to be ruled out that this occurred against the Defendant's declared will, especially since he had a dislike of mere office work and had himself been successful in his efforts to be allowed to return to the "operative business" of the intelligence service, as is evident from the statement he made during his hearing before the Federal Office for Migration and Refugees. In particular, given what he knew about the work of the sub-branch, the Defendant could have opposed his transfer. There is just as little evidence of this as there is of any specific efforts on his part to leave the sub-branch again or, if need be, to desert in the months following his transfer in which, in view of the intensification of the protests on the one hand and the more brutal response of the security forces on the other, the Defendant had quickly got an idea of what his new job entailed. Nor does the Defendant assert any such thing in the written statement he submitted to the Division.

[444] (2) It cannot be assumed that it would not have been possible for the Defendant to leave the service before the start of 2012.

[445] Based on the outcome of the taking of evidence, the Division cannot initially take as its basis that, as he claims in his written statement, the Defendant was subject to wide-ranging monitoring merely on account of his Sunni denomination and that this had massively restricted his options. According to the consistent statements made by Expert Witness . . . [Th] and several other witnesses (some of them expert witnesses), Alawites held the highest leadership positions, especially within the security authorities. However, there is no evidence to suggest that this predominance also pertained to the ranks of non-commissioned officers and enlisted personnel. Rather, the same evidence indicates that Syrians of the Sunni faith were also employed in the Syrian authorities, including in the security forces, and that, given that Sunnis make up the overwhelming majority of the Syrian population, it stands to reason that they were in the majority. There are no factual indications to suggest that Sunnis were subjected to monitoring merely on account of the protest movement, especially since such monitoring was de facto hardly implementable. The fact that, by his own account, the Defendant, a Sunni, was selected as late as July 2011 to do work in the sub-branch which, in the eyes of the regime, was especially important and sensitive and that he was able to remain in post despite the conflict escalating is not consistent with a particular mistrust of Sunnis in Sub-branch 40 in general and of the Defendant in particular. Rather, shortly before he deserted, the Defendant was entrusted with the armed escort of a transport of corpses, which was subject to especial secrecy.

[446] Other concrete obstacles to his deserting at an earlier point in time are not apparent. It is to be assumed that the financial circumstances of the Defendant, a higher-ranking non-commissioned officer, had been stable for quite some time and that this would have permitted him to leave his service, if necessary also to defect and to use the financial means available to him to organise his smuggling out of the country. The possibility of fleeing to his home village, which would have proved a risk for him after deserting the intelligence service on account of having to pass through both opposition-held and government-held regions, would have already and equally been open to him in mid-2011. By his own account, after he did in fact leave in early 2012 his family initially continued to live in Damascus largely without any repercussions, meaning that the assumption that deserting before the offence would have put them in considerable danger is also without basis in fact. Seen overall, it is not apparent what prevented the Defendant from fleeing to his village at an earlier point in time in order to possibly begin planning his efforts to leave the country from there.

[447] (3) From all the above the Division concludes that at the time of the offence the Defendant was in fact not yet willing to defect. Rather, his continuing to work in Sub-branch 40, which also secured his livelihood and that of his family, indicates that the Defendant had at least reconciled himself to his new tasks and performed his duties voluntarily, at any rate up until the end of 2011. In his written statement, too, the Defendant describes that he did not finally decide to desert until January 2012. The Division therefore takes that as the basis for its assessment.

[448] (bb) It is, further, not apparent that the Defendant would not, objectively speaking, simply have had any reasonable opportunities not to take part in the concrete offence. The Division does not fail to recognise that openly refusing to carry out orders would have had serious negative consequences for the Defendant, which could possibly have gone as far as his own arrest and placement in one of the intelligence service's prisons. During each phase of the operation—that is when it was announced prior to the journey to the site of deployment, during that journey and whilst in the field—the Defendant would, however, have been able to stop taking part by feigning acute symptoms of illness or an injury. In view of the turmoil out in the field, as he himself described it, the fact that numerous units and branches were deployed and demonstrators were pursued through the streets of Douma, the Defendant could also have taken advantage of the situation and absconded. In view of the severity of the offence (i.e. arresting and transporting innocent people to a prison where torture

was enforced), it would also have been within reason to expect him to accept the risk of subjecting himself to the suspicion that he had turned his back on the regime which that entailed, as well as the organisational and financial challenges linked to defecting so abruptly.

[449] The assertion the Defendant made in his written statement regarding the fact that he had first wanted to wait until (unspecified) regions fell into the hands of the opposition so that he could then flee does not alter this fact. The route which a former member of the intelligence service had to take to get to the Turkish border— through opposition-held areas—was no less dangerous than that which took him through a government-held area, which he would have had to pass through first anyway. Witnesses "Sami" and "Caesar" made statements which were passed to the Division by witnesses ... [LL] and ... [O] to the effect that "Caesar" had to pass through a rebel-held area on his way to work and was often subjected to checks, and that working for the Syrian regime had proved to be extremely dangerous.

C. LEGAL ASSESSMENT

[450] The Defendant is criminally liable for the established act of aiding a crime against humanity in the form of torture and severe deprivation of liberty.

I. Re the conditions of section 7 of the Code of Crimes against International Law

1. Widespread and systematic attack directed against a civilian population

[451] In the Division's assessment, the events in Syria from late April 2011 onwards constitute both a widespread and a systematic attack directed against a civilian population within the meaning of the attributes set out in section 7(1) of the Code of Crimes against International Law (CCAIL).

[452] (a) Following the legal definition in Article 7 para. (2) point (a) of the Rome Statute of the International Criminal Court (Rome Statute), "an attack directed against any civilian population" means a course of conduct involving the multiple commission, in the context of an overall act, of the alternatives listed in section 7(1) nos 1 to 10 of the CCAIL. The attack must be carried out by a collective, though not necessarily a state one. A "civilian population" is defined as a larger

group of people who share distinguishing features—for instance living in the same geographical area or having a shared political will—on account of which they come under attack. A state's own civilian population can be a relevant object of such an offence, too. The defining feature is that the measures are not directed primarily against individual victims of the act, as individual personalities, but against them as members of a group. The attack need not be directed against an entire population living in a particular area. Rather, it is sufficient for the attack to be directed against a significant number of individuals (see Decisions of the Federal Court of Justice in Criminal Matters 64, 10, margin no 164; Federal Court of Justice, Order of 3 February 2021—AK 50/20, margin no 32; Werle, in: *Münchener Kommentar*, *StGB*, 3rd ed., section 7 of the CCAIL, margin no 15, 21, with further references).

[453] A "widespread attack" is defined as a course of action applied on a large scale with a large number of victims. An attack is "systematic" if the use of violence is organised and executed according to plan in the sense of consistent actions (Decisions of the Federal Court of Justice in Criminal Matters 55, 137, margin no 27; Federal Court of Justice, Order of 3 February 2021—AK 50/20, margin no 32, with further references).

[454] (b) Judged on this basis, the actions of the Syrian regime from late April 2011 onwards meet the conditions of the attributes set out in section 7(1) of the CCAIL in relation to the act. According to the findings as established, the security forces already used violence against peaceful demonstrators and other, including alleged, members of the opposition as of March 2011. Whilst initially only a few individual protests were affected by the at first only isolated signs that the Arab Spring had crossed over into Syria and by the subsequent response to certain measures undertaken by the Syrian regime, the more the peaceful civilian movement grew the more violent the Syrian authorities responded, particularly the army and the intelligence services, which took action against the movement by means of organised and numerous arrests, long periods of detention, torture and also the killing of actual or alleged opponents of the regime.

[455] The massive force which the Syrian government and its subordinate authorities used against those taking part in the protest movement, against supposed or actual members of the opposition and civil society activists and against civilians who were entirely uninvolved served the politically motivated suppression of the protests by directly breaking them up and intimidating the population and thus also ensuring that the government under Bashar al-Assad retained power.

The Division thus regards the collective entity acting and leading the attack to be the Syrian state leadership and those within the security authorities responsible for giving and implementing instructions, in particular the state intelligence services. The object of the attack was the broad majority of civilians who had actually or were even only suspected of having joined the protest movement or of being critical of the Syrian government. They were subjected to increasingly planned and generally arbitrary state violence as from March 2011. This at least fulfils the elements of the offence under section 7(1) nos 1, 5, 6 and 9 of the CCAIL.

[456] From late April 2011 onwards the attack also was to be assessed as widespread and systematic. The fact that, from that point in time, the violent course of action adopted by the security forces was controlled centrally by those with the highest political and military responsibility in the President's circle within an executive body set up to that end establishes the systematic nature of the attack. The large number (i.e. thousands per month) of civilian victims—considered by the Division as both those who were killed directly by the security forces at demonstrations, checkpoints or elsewhere and those who were abducted to the state-run detention facilities and ill-treated there—and the persistent use of violence, which continued to escalate in the following months, and the countrywide approach, in particular in bigger towns and cities such as Greater Damascus, Douma, Daraa and Homs, evidence a multitude of acts of violence which meet the elements of the offence and constitute a widespread attack.

2. Main offence: Torture and severe deprivation of liberty

[457] Within the context of the overall act directed against the civilian population, all the demonstrators who were arrested with the Defendant's assistance and taken to Branch 251 were subjected to torture within the meaning of section 7(1) no 5 of the CCAIL by those employed in the branch and were severely deprived of their liberty within the meaning of section 7(1) no 9 of the CCAIL.

[458] (a) Anyone who, in the context of an overall act, tortures a person in his or her custody or otherwise under his or her control by causing that person substantial physical or mental harm or suffering where such harm or suffering does not arise only from sanctions which are compatible with international law commits the elements of the alternative set out in section 7(1) no 5 of the CCAIL. To be "substantial", that harm or suffering requires a sufficiently large degree of

impairment caused by the act and is to be assessed taking account of all the facts and circumstances of the case, in particular the nature of the act and its context. Lasting damage to health or extreme pain are, however, not necessary, nor is a degree of severity comparable to that required under section 226 of the Criminal Code (*Strafgesetzbuch*, StGB) (Decisions of the Federal Court of Justice in Criminal Matters 64, 89, margin no 63; Federal Court of Justice, Order of 5 September 2019—AK 47/19, margin no 38, Order of 25 September 2018—StB 40/18, margin no 22, and Order of 17 November 2016—AK 54/16, margin no 27). Massive psychological impairment can also lead to an act being classed as torture (see Federal Court of Justice, Order of 6 June 2019—StB 14/19, margin no 64; see also Article 1(1) of the UN Convention Against Torture; European Court of Human Rights *NJW* 2010, 3145, 3146).

[459] In the present case the Division was not able to establish in what specific manner the demonstrators, whose individual identities are not known, were treated in Branch 251. However, it was possible to establish that all the demonstrators were subjected to severe beatings as soon as they arrived there and that they were subsequently exposed to further physical abuse whilst inside the branch, at the very least that they were beaten. Taking this together with the inhumane conditions of detention as established, the fact that the detainees constantly heard loud cries of pain coming from their fellow inmates and the terrifying, gruelling uncertainty about their own impending treatment, the Division considers that the suffering of each victim significantly exceeded the threshold of "substantial".

[460] (b) At the same time, the imprisonment of the demonstrators who were arrested with the Defendant's assistance constitutes severe deprivation of physical liberty in contravention of a general rule of international law within the meaning of section 7(1) no 9 of the CCAIL. Following Article 7 para. (1) point (e) of the Rome Statute, this is assumed to be the case where a victim is prevented, without a legal basis which is recognisable under international law, from leaving the place where they are being held. "Severe" requires that all the facts and circumstances of the case be considered, in particular including the length and circumstances of the deprivation of liberty (see Bundestag Printed Papers 14/8524, p. 22; Werle, loc. cit., section 7 of the CCAIL, margin no 103 ff.).

[461] The Division considers the deprivation of liberty which each of those detained in Branch 251 unquestionably endured to be severe. It was in each case executed without basis in law, nor was an individual order issued which even remotely followed the rule of law. Those who

were arrested were not told the reason therefor. They were neither instructed about the legal remedies available to them nor granted legal counsel. Relatives were not notified and those concerned were not told how long they would be spending in detention, which for them was thus an unforeseeable length of time. The circumstances of detention were characterised by excessive violence and inhumane general conditions of detention. Also, their detention lasted a not inconsiderable time. Even though it cannot be ruled out that some of the 30 people who were arrested may only have been detained in Branch 251 for the comparatively short space of time of a few days, the deprivation of liberty weighs heavily in view of the other serious circumstances which made spending even a short period in the branch intolerable.

[462] (c) The fact that the individual acts committed against those who were arrested functionally fit seamlessly into the overall offence of a widespread and systematic attack directed against the civilian population (which was already ongoing in the period in which the acts were committed) and are linked to it requires no further elaboration. The main offenders who ordered and carried out the individual instances of torture and deprivations of liberty in Branch 251 are responsible only for one act in the legal sense. If (as is the case here) individual acts are factually, temporally and spatially linked, then their functional link to the same overall offence within the meaning of section 7(1) of the CCAIL means they constitute a single entity for the purpose of the legal assessment (Decisions of the Federal Court of Justice in Criminal Matters 64, 89, margin no 53; Werle, loc. cit., section 7 of the CCAIL, margin no 141).

II. Defendant's aiding of the offence

[463] The Defendant aided the main offence within the meaning of section 27 of the Criminal Code by committing an individual act against the 30 individuals who were arrested. He promoted the main offence by contributing, by means of a unitary act, to the victims being arrested and taken to Branch 251. This enabled the elements of the offence set out in section 7(1) nos 5 and 9 of the CCAIL to be realised in the first place. It cannot, by contrast, be assumed, in the absence of the provision of any concrete support, that the Defendant provided even mental support to the other acts committed as part of the attack directed against the civilian population, even though these were committed in the intelligence service branches to which he belonged (see Decisions of the Federal Court of Justice in Criminal Matters 64, 89).

III. Justification and culpability

[464] The Defendant also acted unlawfully and culpably. To the extent that he invokes necessity as defence, which precludes culpability, within the meaning of section 35 of the Criminal Code in the matter, the conditions of that provision are not met. As has been established, the Division does not consider there to have been a subjective state of necessity in the sense of a predicament which the Defendant would have wished to evade. Furthermore, it was, objectively speaking, not unreasonable to expect him to act in a rule-based manner. It is not apparent that it would have been impossible, or at any rate possible only at unjustifiable risk, for the Defendant not to commit the act. In view of the severity of the offence, the Division considers that greater expectations are to be placed on the Defendant when it comes to conscientiously examining how to avoid committing the act and doing all that is in his power in that regard—including accepting risks and personal constraints. This also applies because the Defendant, a long-standing employee of the intelligence service, was aware of the tasks assigned to Sub-branch 40, and there are no indications that he had previously made any provision to avoid participating in crimes under international criminal law.

[465] However, no such scrutiny and endeavours to avoid involvement in the act are discernible. Rather, as established, even in the situation itself alternatives were available to the Defendant, and it is not plausible why he had to postpone fleeing, which he did without his family, until January 2012.

IV. Obstacles to prosecution

[466] There are no obstacles to prosecution. In particular, the Defendant cannot rely on his immunity as a functionary (in the widest sense of the word) of another state (see Federal Court of Justice *NJW* 2021, 1326).

D. SENTENCING

I. Overview

[467] At the sentencing stage the Division was first required to determine the range of punishment. Taking, as its point of departure, the standard range of punishment under section 7(1) of the CCAIL, it was required to assess whether in consideration of all the relevant criteria regardless of the types of mitigating circumstances established

by law—in the present case the Defendant's status as an aider pursuant to section 27(2) sentence 2 and section 49(1) of the Criminal Code and possible contribution to discovery (*Aufklärungshilfe*) pursuant to section 46b and section 49(1) of the Criminal Code—or taking them into account (section 50 of the Criminal Code) it could assume a less serious case pursuant to section 7(2) of the CCAIL. It concluded that, taking account of the mitigating circumstance under section 27(2) of the Criminal Code, this did constitute a less serious case pursuant to section 7(2) of the CCAIL and it (again) mitigated the resulting range of punishment pursuant to section 46b of the Criminal Code. On the basis of this range of punishment, the Division weighed up the facts and circumstances which spoke for and those which spoke against the Defendant and set the individual sentence of imprisonment as set out in the operative part of this judgment. More specifically:

II. Range of punishment

1. Section 7(1) of the Code of Crimes against International Law

[468] Section 7(1) of the CCAIL provides for a term of imprisonment of not less than five years for cases of torture pursuant to section 7(1) no 5 of the CCAIL; it provides for a term of imprisonment of not less than two years for severe deprivation of liberty pursuant to section 7(1) no 9 of the CCAIL. Since the main offence which the Defendant aided also falls within the scope of section 7(1) no 5 of the CCAIL, a (standard) range of punishment of between five and 15 years was first to be taken as a basis (section 52(2) sentence 1, section 38(2) of the Criminal Code).

2. Section 7(2) of the Code of Crimes against International Law, section 27(2) of the Criminal Code

[469] The Division then considered whether a less serious case was to be assumed pursuant to section 7(2) of the CCAIL, that is a range of punishment of between two and 15 years. A less serious case exists where the overall offence, including all the subjective aspects and the offender's personality, deviates to such a significant degree from the average of normal cases that it appears necessary to apply the exceptional range of punishment, whereby an overall assessment of all the key exonerating and incriminating facts and circumstances must be conducted regardless of whether they are part of the act itself, whether they accompany, precede or succeed it. If the individual exonerating sentencing criteria are not sufficient to assume that there is a less serious

case, then account is also to be taken of those facts and circumstances which, taken on their own, already constitute one of the types of mitigating circumstances established by law.

[470] A key factor which the Division had to take into account, in the Defendant's favour, was the fact that he incriminated himself during both his hearing before the Federal Office for Migration and Refugees and during his subsequent questioning by the police as a witness and that his conviction to a decisive extent relies on the statements which he himself made. Even though the Defendant did not plead to the charge at the main hearing, the written statement he submitted to the Division constitutes a partial confession which also counts in his favour given that in it he admitted that he worked for the Syrian intelligence service. Another exonerating fact is that, at the time of his contributing to the offence, the Defendant was part of a military-like command structure and was, in consequence, under a certain amount of pressure to act. Finally, the Division had to take account, in his favour, of the fact that, measured in terms of the course of the internal Syrian conflict, he voluntarily turned his back on his job in the intelligence service at a comparatively early point in time, that is in early 2012, and that he fled, thereby accepting risks to himself and his family. The Division further assumes, in the Defendant's favour, that he had—even before he deserted—already distanced himself inwardly from his work for the regime and the attacks directed against the civilian population carried out by the Syrian security authorities, which increased both in terms of their extent and brutality in the course of 2011. Besides, at the time of the act the Defendant had no criminal record. The act was committed nine and a half years ago. In view of the fine of 20 daily rates which was imposed by . . . [a] Local Court—and which could, in principle, form part of a cumulative sentence but has already been fully enforced—there was no reason, in view of the nature of this penalty, to make a hardship allowance (see Federal Court of Justice *NStZ-RR* 2008, 370; *StV* 2020, 838; Order of 5 May 2021—6 StR 15/21).

[471] As regards what counts against him, the Division took account of the large number of people whom the Defendant handed over to the prison in Branch 251. In that prison the detainees were exposed to treatment which, in view of the intolerable conditions of detention and systematic torture inflicted, could hardly be surpassed in terms of its inhumanity and therefore weighs heavily, even when measured against the elements of the offence in section 7(1) no 5 of the CCAIL—as the Defendant was well aware even though he did not himself abuse the victims. The fact that the Defendant aided an offence

which simultaneously meets two of the conditions under section 7(1) of the CCAIL constitutes an aggravating circumstance. Further, account had to be taken of the fact that the attack directed against the civilian population, in the context of which the Defendant committed this offence, already at the point when he contributed to the act (as the Defendant knew) which already cumulatively fulfilled the attributes listed in section 7(1) of the CCAIL in terms of its ruthlessness and brutality and on account of the attack being widespread across the entire state and encompassing the civilian population as a whole, and that as a result it had reached a level which went beyond the average case. Finally, the Defendant must take responsibility for the fact that, knowing that, even then, opponents of the regime were being treated brutally and extralegally by the intelligence apparatus, he had many years before the offence made himself available to the regime, and that his own work was not limited to office work but was extended, at his own request, to include operative spying activities and that, ultimately, he worked for a period of six months in a sub-branch which was involved in the Syrian regime's repressive measures on a continuous basis, in which crimes pursuant to section 7 of the CCAIL were committed on an ongoing basis, in that opponents of the regime were arrested, abused and admitted, and which was well-known and infamous on that account.

[472] Considering these facts and circumstances alone the Division does not find the general mitigating circumstances to predominate to such a degree that this aspect in and of itself would justify applying the range of punishment set out in section 7(2) of the CCAIL. The decisive factor in this regard is the high degree of unlawfulness of the act. This can only be mitigated if account is further taken of the fact that the Defendant is not accused of having committed the act but merely of aiding it; on these grounds alone, the range of punishment must be shifted pursuant to section 27(2) and section 49(1) of the Criminal Code. Taking account of this circumstance together with the other aforementioned aspects which exonerate and incriminate the Defendant, the Division considers the act to constitute a less serious case and took as the basis for its assessment such a less serious case rather than shifting the range of punishment pursuant to section 49 of the Criminal Code, which there would otherwise have been occasion to do. It was no longer necessary to incorporate the contribution to discovery (see section D.II.3 [Section 46b of the Criminal Code], below) for this to be the case. In assuming a less serious case, the Division is aware that, applying section 49 of the Criminal Code as opposed to section 7(2) of the CCAIL would lower the maximum

penalty to 11 years and three months, although the lower threshold is the same in each case. On an overall assessment and in view of the fact that the penalty to be imposed will not be drawn from the upper part of the range of punishment, and in view of the further mitigation pursuant to sections 46b and 49 of the Criminal Code, which is still to be undertaken, the Division nevertheless considers that assuming a less serious case takes appropriate account of the act, the Defendant's self-incrimination, his turning his back on the regime and the other aforementioned aspects.

3. Section 46b of the Criminal Code

[473] In view of the statements which the Defendant made in the preliminary investigation, the Division saw occasion to examine whether a further shift in the range of punishment pursuant to sections 46b and 49 of the Criminal Code was necessary, and concluded that this was the case.

[474] (a) The contribution to discovery relates to the former Co-Defendant ... [K], whose case was separated from the Defendant's in February 2021 and is being continued separately after the main hearing was conducted jointly up to that point. As regards the question of the penalty to be imposed, the Division thus makes additional determinations which were not used in relation to the finding of guilt but are presented in the following; they are based on the Defendant's questioning as a witness by the Federal Criminal Police Office on 16 August 2018. During that questioning the Defendant gave further testimony which significantly incriminates the former Co-Defendant ... [K] as the allegedly co-responsible executive officer in Branch 251 and which was included in the admitted indictment against the Co-Defendant. The Division does not believe that it is prohibited from using this testimony, even beyond the point in time which is relevant for its admissibility in terms of the verdict of guilty, since the Defendant's contribution to discovery could otherwise possibly not be taken into account owing to a failure to inform him of his rights as an accused and a ban on using the statement which serves the purpose of his protection.

[475] As the Defendant's investigating officers at the time—witnesses ... [O] and ... [P]—testified, the Defendant provided detailed information about Branch 251 of the Syrian General Intelligence Directorate during his police questioning on 16 August 2018. He testified as to which districts of the city the branch was responsible for after the start of the unrest (Douma and

Harasta). The branch also operated checkpoints, he stated, at which arrests were regularly made. Further, the Defendant gave the names of senior officers, including the former Co-Defendant . . . [K]. The orders relevant to operations carried out by Sub-branch 40 came from Branch 251, he reported. It was in particular those arrested people who had allegedly had "information" who were taken to Branch 251. The "investigators" were responsible for them there, that is in the sub-branch for investigations headed by . . . [K]. The Defendant further provided information about the former Co-Defendant's tasks. He was responsible for information-gathering, he stated. The Defendant cited typical examples of questions which the investigators put to the demonstrators, such as "Who's supporting you?", "Who's funding you?" and "Who's organising these demonstrations?". The information had been got out of the demonstrators "using blows, *shabeh*, *dulab*, the Flying Carpet and the German Chair", by making the prisoners stand up for a long time (by binding them) and by depriving them of food. Such torture methods were applied in the basement of Branch 251, the Defendant stated. He also sketched the former Co-Defendant . . . [K]'s office, the distance between the office and the prison, and cross-sections and floorplans of the branch. He also stated how many staff were subordinate to . . . [K]. According to the Defendant, the prison in Branch 251 was also part of the former Co-Defendant's interrogation branch; the Defendant described him as a "very experienced investigator". The Defendant also stated that, on an occasion of which he otherwise had no specific recollection, the former Co-Defendant . . . [K] had refused to beat demonstrators after their arrest.

[476] As regards the number of prisoners who were taken to Branch 251, the Defendant stated that since the start of the conflict buses carrying prisoners had arrived on a daily basis, sometimes twice a day. The prison, which was designed to house around 100 prisoners, had been completely overcrowded with 400 prisoners, he stated. Prisoners had constantly had to be transferred to Branch 285.

[477] As regards deaths in Branch 251, the Defendant testified that he had on one occasion seen a prisoner being hit over the head with a metal rod by a guard after getting out of the bus on arrival at Branch 251 and dying as a result. He also stated that people had often died "during the investigation work" in Branch 251. They had then been taken out of the cellar prison at night wrapped in blankets and taken away, either to a cemetery in Najha or a hospital. Between May and June 2011 he had observed 10 dead bodies being taken out of the cellar.

[478] (b) The police investigators, witnesses ... [O] and ... [P], testified in relation to their taking account of the statements which the Defendant made at the time of the preliminary investigation against the then Co-Defendant ... [K]. The Defendant's statements were used in the preliminary investigation against the former Co-Defendant ... [K]. On the basis of the Federal Public Prosecutor General's indictment of 18 October 2019, which the Division admitted, the Co-Defendant ... [K] is charged with, amongst other things, having both killed 58 people out of base motives and tortured at least 4,000 people in the context of a widespread and systematic attack directed against a civilian population. As regards the attribution of these offences, the indictment most importantly refers to the prominent position which the former Co-Defendant ... [K] held as head of investigations in Branch 251 of the Syrian General Intelligence Directorate. As regards the killings with which he has been charged, accusations of acts to the detriment of 11 victims are based solely on the Defendant's statement.

[479] The information regarding the structure of and tasks assigned to Branch 251 and regarding the former Co-Defendant ... [K] himself is also of considerable relevance when it comes to assessing the charges against the Co-Defendant—even beyond the contribution to the act with which the Defendant is charged. As was already apparent to the Division in the context of the joint taking of evidence against both defendants, knowledge of the internal organisational structures and competences could only be obtained by taking as a whole generally accessible sources, expert analyses, revealing individual observations by victim witnesses and the statements of former employees of the regime, which were particularly important, with more wide-ranging and immediate observations from their vantage point within their area of work. Naturally, those witnesses who at least sometimes worked in the same area and at the same time are of particular relevance. Besides the Defendant, only Witness ... [AA] (who was deployed as a guard and was thus, given this function, limited as to the observations he could make) and Witness ... [Y] (the quality of whose statement, however, varied considerably) were available from Branch 251.

[480] The Defendant's statements are not inadmissible in the ongoing proceedings against the Co-Defendant ... [K].

[481] (c) The Division considers the Defendant's statements to contribute to discovery within the meaning of section 46b(1) sentence 1 no 1 of the Criminal Code. The act of which the former Co-Defendant is accused is one pursuant to section 100a(2) no 10(b) of the Code of Criminal Procedure. Although, on account of his contribution to the offence, the Defendant is also a participant in the crime

under international criminal law of which the Co-Defendant is accused, his contribution to discovery goes significantly beyond his own contribution to the act, which is limited to one act of arresting and delivering prisoners (section 46b(1) sentence 3 of the Criminal Code). On account of how they are intertwined in the context of a unitary attack directed against a civilian population and their spatial and situational overlapping within the same branch of the intelligence service, there is also a sufficient link between the offence of which the Defendant is accused and the offence of which the former Co-Defendant is accused. This is the case because the knowledge thereof was ultimately revealed before the main proceedings were opened against the Defendant. The fact that the Defendant made no further statements in the main hearing does not preclude the assumption of a contribution to discovery within the meaning of section 46b of the Criminal Code (Federal Court of Justice *NStZ* 2009, 394; Order of 2 June 1988—2 StR 248/88; Maier, in: *Münchener Kommentar, StGB,* 4th ed., section 46b margin no 30). In the same way, it cannot be assumed that the Defendant did not act voluntarily within the meaning of section 46b(1) sentence 1 no 1 of the Criminal Code as a consequence of his obligation to testify as a witness in criminal proceedings (see Decisions of the Federal Court of Justice in Criminal Matters 55, 153, 155), especially since, as an accused, he would have been able, at least in part, to refuse to testify.

[482] (d) When conducting the overall assessment begun on this basis (see Decisions of the Federal Court of Justice in Criminal Matters 55, 153) as to whether the Defendant should benefit from the mitigation of sentence pursuant to section 46b of the Criminal Code, the Division took particular account of the circumstances listed in section 46b(2) of the Criminal Code. The nature and extent of the facts disclosed are to be regarded as particularly important. As presented in the above, other evidence regarding the structure of the Syrian intelligence service and its remit in the burgeoning internal Syrian conflict as from February 2011 was already available in the preliminary investigation against the former Co-Defendant ... [K], including, specifically, the expert reports rendered by the German Federal Intelligence Service and by Expert ... [Th] and the statements made by former employees of the Syrian regime, that is witnesses Z 28/07/16, ... [Y], ... [N] and ... [BB]. However, the only witnesses who were from Branch 251 and were able to provide information—albeit insufficient information—about the former Co-Defendant ... [K], were Witness ... [Y] and Witness ... [AA]. The Defendant's nuanced statements as to the Co-Defendant's tasks and person were thus of great significance.

[483] In the Division's assessment, however, what weighs even more heavily is the fact that the Defendant was able to give testimony regarding killings in the branch, which—insofar as the former Co-Defendant ... [K] is charged with their commission—are based only on his testimony and might possibly only be provable by him. Notwithstanding the fact that the killings form part of a unitary overall act pursuant to section 7(1) of the CCAIL, they constitute a violation of the highest individual rights. The severity of the offence and the significance of the contribution to discovery are therefore to be regarded as very great. In addition, this is a significantly more serious wrong than the Defendant's own contribution to the act, since the Defendant cannot be proven to have aided the killing of any person, for instance. The Defendant provided all the information willingly during his police questioning, despite his evidently incriminating himself; he also gave testimony about other members of the regime and their work, in relation to which preliminary investigations are not yet pending. Insofar as the Defendant was unable to cooperate further with the investigating authorities and did not repeat his incriminations at the main hearing, then in view of the special nature of the information, some of which cannot be used, and the considerable amount of self-incrimination which is inevitably linked to such a wide-ranging revelation, this does not constitute a decisive factor which speaks against assuming that the range of punishment should be shifted.

[484] 4. As a result, the Division thus assumed the range of punishment in section 7(2) of the CCAIL as mitigated pursuant to section 49(1) of the Criminal Code. It was consequently required to draw the term of imprisonment to be imposed from a range of punishment of imprisonment of between six months and 11 years and three months.

III. Sentencing in the narrower sense

[485] When determining the term of imprisonment to be imposed, the Division considered and weighed up anew all the previously mentioned sentencing criteria. The Division again took account of the Defendant's contribution to discovery, which in itself leads to a shift in the range of punishment, and the mitigating circumstances drawn upon in making the assumption that this constituted a less serious case, in particular the reduced unlawfulness of merely aiding rather than committing the act. However, it attached less importance to these two aspects in its assessment. Particular emphasis again deserves to be placed on the fact that if the Defendant had not made his own

statements prior to the preliminary investigation then no charges would have been brought and no conviction made, and on the Defendant's voluntary and comparatively early renunciation of his work in the intelligence service in Syria. What is particularly incriminating is the number of victims of the act, whose torture and deprivation of liberty the Defendant aided.

[486] After weighing up all the aforementioned reasons, the Division imposes a term of imprisonment of

four years and six months

[487] as a penalty which is appropriate to the act and the Defendant's guilt.

E. COSTS: NEGOTIATED AGREEMENT

[488] The decision as to costs is based on section 465 of the Code of Criminal Procedure.

[489] This judgment was not preceded by a negotiated agreement (section 257c of the Code of Criminal Procedure).

[Report: English translation supplied by the German Federal Ministry of Justice]

Arbitration — International Convention on the Settlement of Investment Disputes between States and Nationals of Other States, 1965 ("ICSID Convention") — Energy Charter Treaty, 1994 — Article 26 — Arbitration proceedings initiated against a Member State of the European Union under ICSID Convention for violation of Energy Charter Treaty — Intra-EU arbitration — Where arbitration initiated under ICSID by entity registered within EU Member State against another EU Member State — Compatibility of ICSID Convention and Energy Charter Treaty with EU law — Primacy of EU law — Whether ICSID tribunal part of court system of EU — Whether Article 26 of Energy Charter Treaty applicable in intra-EU arbitral proceeding — Whether EU Member States must have capacity to review arbitral proceedings that consider EU law — Whether German courts can review arbitral proceedings initiated under ICSID

Relationship of international law and municipal law — International Convention on the Settlement of Investment Disputes between States and Nationals of Other States, 1965 — Energy Charter Treaty, 1994 — Treaty on the Functioning of the European Union, 2007 — Arbitration proceedings initiated against European Union Member State under ICSID Convention for violation of Energy Charter Treaty — Intra-EU arbitration — Where arbitration initiated under ICSID by entity registered within EU Member State against another EU Member State — Compatibility of ICSID Convention and Energy Charter Treaty with EU law — Primacy of EU law — Whether ICSID tribunal part of court system of EU — Whether Article 26 of Energy Charter Treaty applicable in intra-EU arbitral proceeding — Whether EU Member States must have capacity to review arbitral proceedings that consider EU law — The law of Germany

ENERGY CHARTER TREATY CASE

(Case No I ZB 43/22)

Federal Republic of Germany, Federal Court of Justice (BGH). 27 *July* 2023

(Koch, *Presiding Judge*; Feddersen, Pohl, Schmaltz and Odörfer, *Judges*)

SUMMARY:[1] *The facts*:—The defendants were investors in wind and solar energy with registered offices in Ireland. They claimed that a change in legislation in Germany had harmed their planned investments. On 30 April 2021, they filed a request for arbitration against Germany before the International Centre for Settlement of Investment Disputes ("ICSID") under the Convention on the Settlement of Investment Disputes between States and Nationals of Other States, 1965 ("ICSID Convention") for alleged violations of the Energy Charter Treaty, 1994 ("ECT").

In August 2021, Germany filed an application before the Berlin Higher Regional Court for a declaration of inadmissibility for the arbitration proceedings initiated by the defendants. The Berlin Higher Regional Court dismissed Germany's application declaring that it was inadmissible. The application was dismissed on the basis that the ICSID Convention was a closed legal system with its own procedural rules, meaning that no other legal remedies were admissible and that it was for the ICSID arbitral tribunal to decide on its own jurisdiction. The Regional Court further held that it was for the ICSID arbitral tribunal to decide whether Germany's consent under Article 26 of the ECT was valid in an intra-European Union ("EU") investment dispute.

Germany appealed this decision, with the Federal Court of Justice ("the Court") considering whether pursuant to Section 1025(2) of the German Code of Civil Procedure, Germany's application under Section 1032(2) of the Code was admissible. In considering the admissibility of Germany's application, the Court considered whether a review of arbitral proceedings initiated under the ICSID Convention was required by EU law, and compatible with Article 41 of the ICSID Convention. Similarly, the Court considered the compatibility of the ECT, and ICSID Convention, to arbitration proceedings between an EU Member State and an entity registered within the jurisdiction of another EU Member. Of concern was whether these conventions preserved the primacy of EU law within an intra-EU arbitral proceeding.

Held:—The order of the Berlin Higher Regional Court was set aside. The arbitration proceedings instituted by the defendants were inadmissible.

(1) Pursuant to Section 1025(2) of the German Code of Civil Procedure, German courts had international jurisdiction. The intention of the German legislature in adopting the German Code of Civil Procedure was to ensure that it was possible to seise the German courts in cases listed in Section 1025(2) of the Code, which included arbitration cases which took place abroad. The intention that the German courts should have global jurisdiction applied equally in delocalized arbitration proceedings under the ICSID Convention and in arbitration proceedings that took place abroad (paras. 24-48).

---

[1] Prepared by Mr D. Peterson.

(2) Pursuant to an application under Section 1032(2) of the German Code of Civil Procedure, an ordinary court could review arbitral proceedings to determine whether an effective arbitration agreement existed, whether it was practicable, and whether the subject matter of the arbitration proceedings fell within the scope of the agreement. The Court could carry out this review even where arbitration proceedings had been initiated under the ICSID Convention. The blocking effect of Article 41 of the ICSID Convention with respect to proceedings before ordinary courts exceptionally did not apply in the present case due to the primacy of EU law (para. 52).

(3) The ICSID Convention ranked as a simple federal law in the German legal order. Where domestic laws with the same status were in conflict, the principles of *lex posterior* and *lex specialis* applied. The principle of the German Constitution's openness to international law required that domestic laws should be interpreted, where possible, to avoid conflict with Germany's obligations under international law. However, this did not result in a constitutional obligation to comply with every provision of international law without limitation (para. 55).

(4) Under domestic German arbitration law, and the UNCITRAL Model Law on International Commercial Arbitration, 1985, ordinary courts could be called upon to review and support arbitration proceedings. The ICSID Convention deliberately deviated from involving ordinary courts in that manner. In ICSID arbitration proceedings, there was generally no subsequent review of the decision on jurisdiction by ordinary courts and thus no final decision-making competence for such courts. According to the ICSID Convention, the examination of jurisdictional competence was to be carried out exclusively within the framework of the arbitration proceedings themselves. If the ICSID Convention was looked at in isolation, it would therefore preclude the present proceedings initiated under Section 1032(2) of the German Code of Civil Procedure (paras. 56-65).

(5) However, due to the primacy of EU law, intra-EU investor–State arbitration proceedings initiated under the ICSID Convention on the basis of Article 26 of the ECT were a special case where, exceptionally, the blocking effect of Article 41(1) of the ICSID Convention did not prevent an application under Section 1032(2) of the German Code of Civil Procedure from being admissible. The supremacy of EU law required domestic courts to ensure the full effect of the provisions of EU law. They were therefore obliged to exercise their own decision-making power to disapply any conflicting domestic provision (paras. 66-8).

(6) An ICSID award would be incompatible with EU law if the arbitration clause underlying the arbitration proceedings called into question the respect of EU law. An arbitral award that was incompatible with EU law in this way could not have any effect and could not be enforced. A court of a Member State involved in the compulsory enforcement of such an ICSID award was under an obligation not to apply the award and consequently could not have

enforced it under any circumstances. In the intra-EU context, a review of an ICSID award by an ordinary court was required, contrary to the provisions of the ICSID Convention (paras. 69-81).

(7) The primacy of EU law over Article 41 of the ICSID Convention was not excluded by Article 351(1) of the Treaty on the Functioning of the European Union, 2007 ("TFEU"). Article 351(1) TFEU, which permitted derogations from EU law in specific circumstances, had to be interpreted narrowly as it permitted, if certain requirements were met, derogations from EU law. It only covered agreements concluded before 1 January 1958 or, in the case of States that acceded thereafter, agreements concluded before the date of their accession. In the present case, the relevant agreements were concluded after these dates and therefore the exceptions in Article 351(1) were not applicable (paras. 83-6).

(8) The arbitral proceedings initiated by the defendants were inadmissible due to a lack of an effective arbitration agreement. Pursuant to Articles 267 and 344 of the TFEU, the arbitral clause contained within Article 26 of the ECT was not applicable to intra-EU investor–State arbitration, nor could an arbitration agreement be based on Article 25 of the ICSID Convention. According to the case law of the Court of Justice of the European Union ("the CJEU"), because the EU was a Party itself to the ECT, the ECT had a dual nature as an agreement under international law and as a legal act of the EU. According to these principles, in an intra-EU investor–State arbitration the dispute resolution mechanism in Article 26 of the ECT violated EU law (paras. 95-100 and 103-6).

(9) Whether it was compatible with EU law for an investor to bring an action before an arbitral tribunal depended on whether the dispute on which the arbitral tribunal had to rule related to the interpretation or application of EU law. If it did, then its compatibility depended on whether the arbitral tribunal could be regarded as a court or tribunal entitled to request a preliminary ruling from the CJEU under Article 267 of the TFEU, or whether the award was subject to review by a court or tribunal of a Member State. According to the case law of the CJEU, an ICSID arbitral tribunal did not belong to the court system of the EU as it was not a court that was entitled to request a preliminary ruling, and pursuant to Articles 53 and 54 of the ICSID Convention, an ICSID award was not subject to a sufficient review by a court or a tribunal of a Member State (paras. 101-9 and 131).

(10) The requirement for consent to arbitration through an arbitration agreement could not be based on Article 25(1) of the ICSID Convention. Pursuant to paragraph 7 of the preamble to the ICSID Convention, Contracting States had declared that the mere ratification, acceptance or approval of the Convention did not imply an obligation to submit a particular dispute to conciliation or arbitration without consent. Accordingly, Article 25(1) of the ICSID Convention required written consent to establish the competence of an ICSID arbitral tribunal (para. 110).

The following is the text of the judgment of the Court:

On the applicant's appeal, the order of the Berlin Higher Regional Court—12th Civil Senate—of 28 April 2022 is set aside.

It is declared that the arbitration proceedings instituted by the defendants against the applicant before the International Centre for Settlement of Investment Disputes under file number ICSID ARB/21/26 are inadmissible.

The defendants are ordered to pay the costs of the proceedings.

The value of the subject matter of the appeal is set at € 30 million.

GROUNDS

1. A. The applicant is the Federal Republic of Germany (hereinafter also "Germany"). The 1st defendant and its two subsidiaries, the 2nd and 3rd defendants, have their registered offices in Ireland. The 2nd defendant holds 100% of the shares in each of the 4th, 5th and 6th defendants, all of which have their registered offices in Germany.

2. The defendants are investors in the field of wind and solar energy. They contended that a change in the legislation in Germany had harmed their planned investments, and on 30 April 2021 they filed a request for arbitration against the applicant with the International Centre for Settlement of Investment Disputes (hereinafter "ICSID" or "the Centre") on the basis of the Energy Charter Treaty. Those proceedings were registered on 13 May 2021 under file no ICSID ARB/21/26. The defendants quantify their claims at (...).

3. The arbitral tribunal was constituted on 14 September 2021. On 18 January 2022, in an interim decision, it rejected the application of the applicant here to dismiss the arbitration claim as manifestly unfounded.

4. The Energy Charter Treaty is a multilateral agreement on cooperation in the energy sector that has been ratified by 49 States as well as the European Union (EU) and the European Atomic Energy Community (Euratom) and entered into force on 16 April 1998. Since that day the Energy Charter Treaty has also been in force in Germany (Federal Law Gazette II 1998 p. 3009; hereinafter referred to as "ECT"), having been approved by way of an Act dated 20 December 1996 (Federal Law Gazette II 1997 p. 4). In Ireland, the Treaty entered into force on 14 July 1999.

5. In Article 10 ECT, the contracting parties affirm that they will promote and protect investments by creating stable, equitable, favourable and transparent conditions for investors of other contracting States.

Article 13 ECT grants protection against expropriation without compensation, among other things. Both provisions can be found in Part III of the Energy Charter Treaty. Article 26 ECT enables an investor from a contracting State to bring a claim against another contracting state for possible violations of the Energy Charter Treaty by way of arbitration proceedings. This Article states the following (excerpts):

(1) Disputes between a Contracting Party and an Investor of another Contracting Party relating to an Investment of the latter in the Area of the former, which concern an alleged breach of an obligation of the former under Part III shall, if possible, be settled amicably.

(2) If such disputes cannot be settled according to the provisions of paragraph (1) within a period of three months from the date on which either party to the dispute requested amicable settlement, the Investor party to the dispute may choose to submit it for resolution:

(a) to the courts or administrative tribunals of the Contracting Party party to the dispute;
(b) in accordance with any applicable, previously agreed dispute settlement procedure; or
(c) in accordance with the following paragraphs of this Article.

(3) (a) Subject only to subparagraphs (b) and (c), each Contracting Party hereby gives its unconditional consent to the submission of a dispute to international arbitration or conciliation in accordance with the provisions of this Article.

(4) In the event that an Investor chooses to submit the dispute for resolution under subparagraph (2)(c), the Investor shall further provide its consent in writing for the dispute to be submitted to:

(a) (i) The International Centre for Settlement of Investment Disputes, established pursuant to the Convention on the Settlement of Investment Disputes between States and Nationals of other States opened for signature at Washington, 18 March 1965 (hereinafter referred to as the "ICSID Convention"), if the Contracting Party of the Investor and the Contracting Party party to the dispute are both parties to the ICSID Convention; or

(5) (a) The consent given in paragraph (3) together with the written consent of the Investor given pursuant to paragraph (4) shall be considered to satisfy the requirement for:
    (i) written consent of the parties to a dispute for purposes of Chapter II of the ICSID Convention and for purposes of the Additional Facility Rules; ...

(6) A tribunal established under paragraph (4) shall decide the issues in dispute in accordance with this Treaty and applicable rules and principles of international law ...

6. The Convention of 18 March 1965 on the Settlement of Investment Disputes between States and Nationals of Other States (hereinafter "ICSID Convention") established an International Centre for the Settlement of Investment Disputes, the purpose of which is to provide conciliation and arbitration facilities for the settlement of investment disputes between contracting states and nationals of other contracting states in accordance with the provisions of the Convention (Article 1 ICSID Convention). The German Parliament (*Bundestag*) approved the ICSID Convention by passing the Act of 25 February 1969 (Federal Law Gazette II p. 369; hereinafter "InvStreitBeilG"); the Convention entered into force on 18 May 1969 (Federal Law Gazette II p. 1191). Ireland ratified the ICSID Convention in April 1981. It entered into force on 7 May 1981.

7. In its application, filed with the Berlin Higher Regional Court on 17 August 2021, the applicant sought a declaration of inadmissibility of the arbitration proceedings initiated with file number ICSID ARB/21/26. The Berlin Higher Regional Court dismissed the application (IPRax 2023, 77). The applicant is appealing this decision and the defendants have requested that that appeal be dismissed.

8. B. The Berlin Higher Regional Court gave the following reasons for dismissing the application as inadmissible:

9. It held that recourse to the ordinary courts was available; moreover, it held that the Berlin Higher Regional Court also had local jurisdiction. However, although the application for a declaration of the inadmissibility of the arbitration proceedings under section 1032(2) German Code of Civil Procedure was submitted in time, it was not admissible. It stated that the ICSID Convention had a closed legal system with its own procedural rules. This, it argued, meant that no other legal remedies were admissible. It stated that an arbitral tribunal seized under the ICSID Convention conclusively decides on its own jurisdiction and whether an arbitration agreement is valid.

10. Nor was this changed by the case law of the Court of Justice of the European Union on intra-EU investment disputes. The CJEU's case law, it found, did not relate to the procedural rules of the German Code of Civil Procedure and their applicability to ICSID arbitration proceedings. It held that it was for the arbitral tribunal to decide whether the applicant's consent pursuant to Article 26 ECT was also valid in an intra-EU investment dispute and, in doing so, to also consider the case law of the Court of Justice of the European Union.

11. It held that it was not a violation of EU law not to apply section 1032(2) German Code of Civil Procedure to ICSID arbitration

proceedings. It is a domestic procedural provision. That constellation, it found, was neither comparable to a subsequent application for setting aside nor to arbitration proceedings under the UNCITRAL Arbitration Rules, which did not contain any exclusive procedural rules comparable to the ICSID Convention.

12. C. The appeal on points of law is admissible (section 574(1) sentence 1 no 1 German Code of Civil Procedure in conjunction with section 1065(1) sentence 1, section 1062(1) no 2 case 1, section 1032(2) German Code of Civil Procedure) and also admissible in other respects (section 574(2) German Code of Civil Procedure). It is also well-founded. Contrary to the view of the Berlin Higher Regional Court, the application for a declaration of inadmissibility of the arbitration proceedings is admissible (see C.I). It is also well-founded (see C.II). A referral to the Court of Justice of the European Union is not necessary (see C.III).

13. I. The application pursuant to section 1032(2) German Code of Civil Procedure is admissible. The question of whether recourse to the ordinary courts is open is not subject to review by the appellate court (see C.I.1). The German courts have international jurisdiction to decide on the application (see C.I.2). The application was filed in time (see C.I.3) and is also permissible (see C.I.4). There is also a need for the protection of a legal interest (*Rechtsschutzbedürfnis*) for the application (see C.I.5).

14. 1. Contrary to the view argued in the response to the appeal, pursuant to section 17a(5) German Court Constitution Act (*Gerichtsverfahrensgesetz*—GVG), the question of whether, for such a request, recourse to the ordinary courts is available, pursuant to section 13 German Court Constitution Act and section 40(2) sentence 1 of the Code of Administrative Court Procedure (*Verwaltungsgerichtsordnung*—VwGO), is not subject to review by the appellate court.

15. a. The Berlin Higher Regional Court assumed that recourse to the ordinary courts was open pursuant to section 13 German Court Constitution Act and section 40(2) sentence 1 VwGO. It held that the claims asserted were essentially claims for compensation arising from the violation of public law obligations, for which legal recourse to the ordinary courts was available under Article 14(3) sentence 4 of the German Constitution (*Grundgesetz*—GG). A preliminary ruling pursuant to section 17a(3) sentence 2 German Court Constitution Act was not necessary because the defendants had only raised the admissibility of the legal recourse taken as an alternative point. Moreover, it stated that an appeal against a preliminary ruling pursuant to section 17a(4) sentence 4 German Court Constitution Act

would not be admissible anyway, because no reasons for admitting the appeal were apparent.

16. b. Pursuant to section 17a(5) German Court Constitution Act, the court that decides on an appeal against a decision on the merits of the matter does not review whether the legal recourse taken is admissible. A decision on the merits includes decisions to dismiss a claim or a request as inadmissible, due to some other conditions for the proceedings not being met, after legal recourse to the civil courts has been affirmed (see Federal Court of Justice, Order of 23 September 1992—I ZB 3/92, BGHZ 119, 246 [juris, para. 14]—*Rechtswegprüfung*). The provision also applies to orders that are capable of formal res judicata (see MünchKomm. ZPO/Pabst, 6th ed., section 17a German Court Constitution Act para. 25). This is the situation in the current case. In its order, the Berlin Higher Regional Court expressly affirmed that recourse to the civil courts was admissible, but considered the application under section 1032(2) German Code of Civil Procedure to be non-permissible and therefore inadmissible.

17. c. The admissibility of the legal recourse taken is also not subject to review by the Senate, even exceptionally. If, contrary to section 17a(3) sentence 2 German Court Constitution Act, the court does not decide by way of a preliminary order on the admissibility of the legal recourse taken following an objection, but only decides on that objection when deciding on the merits, then section 17a(5) German Court Constitution Act is not applicable (see BGHZ 119, 246 [juris, para. 15]—*Rechtswegprüfung*; Federal Court of Justice, Order of 3 November 2021—XII ZB 289/21, NJW-RR 2022, 217 [juris, para. 9], with further references).

However, due to the fact that there was no objection regarding the legal recourse chosen (*Rechtswegrüge*), no such preliminary decision was required from the Berlin Higher Regional Court.

18. aa. If the parties did not make an objection challenging the admissibility of the legal recourse taken and, therefore, the court of first instance could refrain from making a preliminary ruling pursuant to section 17a(3) German Court Constitution Act, then the appellate court is bound by this affirmation of jurisdiction, even if it is only tacit, and even in doubtful cases (see Federal Court of Justice, Order of 18 September 2008—V ZB 40/08, NJW 2008, 3572 [juris para. 13 et seq., 16 et seq.]; Jacobs in Stein/Jonas, ZPO, 23rd ed., section 17a German Court Constitution Act para. 24).

19. bb. The defendants only raised an objection to the admissibility of the legal recourse taken as an alternative point before the Berlin Higher Regional Court. An objection pursuant to section 17a(3)

German Court Constitution Act is a procedural act which can generally be subjected to conditions within the proceedings—as in this case (see Anders in Anders/Gehle, ZPO, 81st ed., preliminary remarks on section 128 para. 62; Zöller/Greger, ZPO, 34th ed., preliminary remarks on section 128 para. 20, with further references). That condition did not arise in the current dispute, because the defendants had already succeeded with their prioritised objection to the admissibility of the application under section 1032(2) German Code of Civil Procedure.

20. 2. Pursuant to section 1025(2) German Code of Civil Procedure, the German courts have international jurisdiction for the application pursuant to section 1032(2) German Code of Civil Procedure.

21. a. The international jurisdiction of the German courts must be reviewed ex officio in appeal proceedings. Such a review is not precluded by section 576(2) German Code of Civil Procedure; the same rules apply to proceedings regarding a complaint on a point of law (*Rechtsbeschwerdeverfahren*) as apply to proceedings for an appeal on a point of law (*Revisionsverfahren*), in respect of which section 545(2) German Code of Civil Procedure does not preclude a review of the international jurisdiction (see Federal Court of Justice, Order of 13 August 2009—I ZB 43/08, WRP 2009, 1559 [juris para. 10]; Order of 22 September 2016—V ZB 125/15, RIW 2017, 138 [juris para. 8]; on section 545(2) German Code of Civil Procedure, see Federal Court of Justice, Judgment of 14 July 2022—I ZR 121/21, GRUR 2022, 1675 [juris para. 29] = WRP 2022, 1519—*Google-Drittauskunft*, with further references).

22. b. In the current case, the international jurisdiction for the application pursuant to section 1032(2) German Code of Civil Procedure arises from the application of section 1025(2) German Code of Civil Procedure by analogy.

23. aa. Pursuant to section 1032(2) German Code of Civil Procedure, an application for a declaration regarding the admissibility or inadmissibility of arbitration proceedings may be filed with the court until such time as the arbitral tribunal has been constituted. Pursuant to section 1025(2) German Code of Civil Procedure, the provisions of sections 1032, 1033 and 1050 German Code of Civil Procedure are also applicable in cases where the place of arbitration is abroad or has not yet been determined.

24. bb. Section 1025(2) German Code of Civil Procedure thus governs the international jurisdiction of the German courts for—inter alia—the proceedings pursuant to section 1032(2) German Code of

Civil Procedure (see Geimer, IZPR, 8th ed, paras. 1258 et seq.;
MünchKomm.ZPO/Münch loc. cit. section 1025 para. 18; Schlosser
in Stein/Jonas loc. cit. section 1062 para. 4, section 1025 para. 6; Voit
in Musielak/Voit, ZPO, 20th ed., section 1062 para. 1, section 1025
para. 5; different opinion in Kröll, IHR 2005, 142, 144). Insofar as the
defendants argue that including section 1032(2) German Code of Civil
Procedure in section 1025(2) German Code of Civil Procedure is a
legislative oversight, this argument fails. It is true that the explanatory
memorandum to the Act only makes reference to an application for a
stay of arbitration proceedings in legal proceedings before the ordinary
courts pursuant to section 1032(1) German Code of Civil Procedure
(see Government Draft of an Act on the Novation of Arbitration Law of
12 July 1996, Bundestag printed paper 13/5274, p. 31). However, if
there was an intention to exclude section 1032(2) and (3) German Code
of Civil Procedure when applying section 1025(2) German Code of
Civil Procedure, then this was not expressed in the Act. However, when
construing a statutory provision, the objectified intention of the legislature expressed therein is decisive, as it results from the wording of the
statutory provision and the context in which it is placed. That interpretation, which must be based primarily on the objective spirit and
purpose of the law, cannot be bound by motives that were set out in the
legislative process, but which have not been expressed in the wording of
the law (see Federal Court of Justice, Judgment of 6 June 2019—I ZR
67/18, GRUR 2019, 970 [juris, para. 66] = WRP 2019, 1304—
Erfolgshonorar für Versicherungsberater, with further references).

25. cc. The wording of section 1025(2) German Code of Civil
Procedure does not in itself give rise to the international jurisdiction of
German courts. The arbitration proceedings initiated by the defendants
neither take place "abroad" within the meaning of this provision (case
1) nor is the place of the arbitration proceedings "not yet determined"
(case 2).

26. (1) The arbitration proceedings were initiated by the defendants
before the Centre. Pursuant to Article 2 sentence 1 ICSID Convention,
the seat of the Centre is where the International Bank for
Reconstruction and Development has its seat, i.e. in Washington,
DC, United States of America (USA). Pursuant to Articles 62 et seq.
in Chapter VII of the ICSID Convention, the arbitration proceedings
take place at the seat of the Centre, which must be distinguished from
the arbitral tribunal (see Schöbener/Markert, ZVgIRWiss 2006, 65,
73), unless something different has been agreed between the parties.

27. (2) Contrary to what is argued in the appeal, it does not follow
from this that the place of arbitration relevant for the purposes of

section 1025(2) German Code of Civil Procedure is in the United States and thus abroad.

28. Contrary to what the title of Chapter VII of the ICSID Convention—"Place of Proceedings"—might suggest, Articles 62 et seq. ICSID Convention only stipulate that the place of the hearing is that place where the arbitral tribunal actually holds its hearings. This venue cannot be equated with the place of arbitration as the legal domicile of the arbitration proceedings, which serves to anchor the arbitration proceedings to a particular jurisdiction (see Bundestag printed paper 13/5274, p. 47; BeckOK.ZPO/ Wilske/Markert, 48th ed. [as of 1 March 2023], section 1043 para. 1; Münch-Komm.ZPO/ Münch loc. cit. section 1043 paras. 3 and 5; Zöller/Geimer loc. cit. section 1043 paras. 1 and 4).

29. This corresponds with the overwhelming view taken in domestic and international literature on the ICSID Convention. According to this, investor–State arbitration proceedings under this Convention take place in a delocalised manner (see Kern, *Schiedsgericht und Generalklausel*, 2017, pp. 62, 78; Bertolini, *Die Durchsetzung von ISDS-Entscheidungen in Deutschland*, 2019, p. 92; Köster, *Investitionsschutz in Europa*, 2022, p. 16 et seq.; Schütze/Thümmel, *Schiedsgericht und Schiedsverfahren*, 7th ed., section 25 para. 6; Happ in Schütze, *Institutionelle Schiedsgerichtsbarkeit*, 3rd ed., XV Chapter, Section II para. 13, Section IV Rule 13 ICSID Arbitration Rules para. 5; Sasson in Fouret/Gerbay/Alvarez, The ICSID Convention, Regulations and Rules, A Practical Commentary, Art. 62 paras. 7.03 et seq.; Schütze in Wieczorek/Schütze, ZPO, 5th ed., section 1025 para. 56b; Gaillard, ICSID Review—Foreign Investment Law Journal 1988, 136, 138 et seq.; Berger, SchiedsVZ 2017, 282, 289; von Marschall, RIW 2021, 785, 787; Nikolov, EuR 2022, 496, 501; Seelmann-Eggebert, SchiedsVZ 2023, 32, 35 et seq.; different opinion in Semler, SchiedsVZ 2003, 97, 101).

30. The arbitral awards rendered by ICSID arbitral tribunals are therefore neither domestic nor foreign arbitral awards within the meaning of sections 1060 et seq. German Code of Civil Procedure, but rather arbitral awards sui generis (see Semler, SchiedsVZ 2003, 97, 99; von Marschall, RIW 2021, 785, 787). Contrary to the principle applicable in commercial arbitration that there are no private arbitration proceedings detached from any national legal system (see Geimer loc. cit. para. 3718, with further references; MünchKomm.ZPO/ Münch loc. cit. section 1025 para. 11; Schütze in Wieczorek/Schütze loc. cit. section 1043 paras. 6 et seq.), an investment dispute before the

Centre exceptionally results in a non-national arbitration (Köster loc. cit. p. 16 et seq.).

31. (3) There is also no case where the "place of arbitration has not yet been determined" (section 1025(2) 2nd case German Code of Civil Procedure). The wording "not yet determined" suggests that this refers only to a temporary situation. Pursuant to section 1043(1), sentence 1 German Code of Civil Procedure, the parties are free to agree on the place of arbitration. In the absence of such an agreement, the place of arbitration is determined by the arbitral tribunal (section 1043(1) sentence 2 German Code of Civil Procedure). Until such a determination is made, there is a state of limbo, without the possibility of a territorial connection. In cases of such a state of limbo, the provision in section 1025(2) case 2 German Code of Civil Procedure applies (see MünchKomm.ZPO/Münch loc. cit. section 1025 para. 24).

32. Such a—temporary—state of limbo is not given in the current dispute. In an ICSID arbitration, no place of arbitration is determined, but only a venue. This means that any later determination of the place of arbitration by the arbitral tribunal is therefore precluded from the outset.

33. dd. However, at least where it refers to section 1032 German Code of Civil Procedure, the provisions set out in section 1025(2) German Code of Civil Procedure must be applied accordingly, if there is no domestic place of arbitration (for a similar opinion see BeckOK.ZPO/Wolf/Eslami, 48th ed. [as of 1 September 2022], section 1032 para. 39; different opinion in BeckOK.ZPO/Wilske/Markert loc. cit. section 1062 para. 2.4, with further references).

34. (1) In order to apply a provision by analogy, there needs to be an unintended regulatory gap in the law and comparable circumstances of interest (longstanding jurisprudence; see for example the German Federal Court of Justice's Judgment of 7 November 2019—I ZR 42/19, GRUR 2020, 429 [juris para. 32] = WRP 2020, 452—*Sportwetten in Gaststätten*, with further references). These conditions are satisfied.

35. (2) Insofar as the delocalised and thus non-national ICSID investment arbitration proceedings are not covered by the wording of the law, this constitutes an unintended regulatory gap in the law. There is no indication that the legislator intended to exclude this special constellation from the 10th Book of the German Code of Civil Procedure.

36. (a) Pursuant to section 1025(1) German Code of Civil Procedure, the provisions of the 10th Book of the German Code of Civil Procedure are applicable if the place of arbitration within the

meaning of section 1043(1) German Code of Civil Procedure is in Germany. Moreover, as already shown, section 1025(2) German Code of Civil Procedure also opens up a scope of application beyond this for some provisions of the 10th Book of the German Code of Civil Procedure, such as the existence of an arbitration agreement pursuant to section 1032(1) German Code of Civil Procedure as well as the declaratory proceedings under section 1032(2) German Code of Civil Procedure, which are relevant here, if the place of arbitration is abroad or has not yet been determined (see Schlosser in Stein/Jonas loc. cit. section 1062 para. 4, section 1025 para. 6; Voit in Musielak/Voit loc. cit. section 1025 paras. 5 to 7).

37. (b) As far as commercial arbitration within the meaning of the UNCITRAL Model Law, which serves as the basis for the reform of arbitration proceedings (see Bundestag printed paper 13/5274, p. 24; for the scope of application of the Model Law, see Melis in Kronke/Melis/Kuhn, *Handbuch Internationales Wirtschaftsrecht*, 2. ed., part P para. 230), was concerned, the three types of cases resulting from section 1025(1) and (2) German Code of Civil Procedure—"place of arbitration in Germany", "place of arbitration abroad" and "place of arbitration not yet determined"—covered all conceivable constellations.

38. (c) The German legislator deliberately chose to extend the 10th Book of the German Code of Civil Procedure beyond the scope of the UNCITRAL Model Law to all arbitration proceedings (see Bundestag printed paper 13/5274, p. 25 and 31). This covers all domestic and international private law arbitration proceedings—and not just the commercial law ones (see Kulick/Scheu in Fouret, Enforcement of Investment Treaty Arbitration Awards, 2. ed., p. 385, 389; Lachmann, *Handbuch für die Schiedsgerichtspraxis*, 3rd ed., para. 190; MünchKomm.ZPO/Münch loc. cit. preliminary remarks on section 1025 paras. 23 et seq., section 1029 para. 93). Although closely related to international law, international investment arbitration between private investors and States also belongs here as a special form (on arbitration proceedings based on a bilateral investment protection treaty, see Federal Court of Justice, Order of 3 March 2016—I ZB 2/15, SchiedsVZ 2016, 328 [juris para. 15]; Order of 31 October 2018—I ZB 2/15, SchiedsVZ 2019, 46 [juris para. 16]; Order of 17 November 2021—I ZB 16/21, IWRZ 2022, 129 [juris paras. 8, 34]; Raeschke-Kessler in Prütting/Gehrlein, ZPO, 14th ed., section 1061 para. 11; Köster loc. cit. p. 30; Schwab/Walter, *Schiedsgerichtsbarkeit*, 7th ed., Chapter 41 para. 22, with further references; see also BeckOK.ZPO/Wolf/Eslami loc. cit. section 1025 para. 9a, with further references; MünchKomm.ZPO/Münch loc. cit.

preliminary remarks on section 1025 paras. 18 to 22), which also includes ICSID investment arbitration proceedings (see Herdegen, *Internationales Wirtschaftsrecht*, 13th ed., section 23 para. 97; Kern loc. cit. p. 66 to 88; Schöbener/Markert, ZVgIRWiss 2006, 65, 68 to 70, with further references; undecided Schwab/Walter loc. cit. chapter 41 para. 5, fn. 42; different opinion in Raeschke-Kessler in *Festschrift Schlick*, 2015, p. 57 et seq., 75; overall in this respect see Pirrung, *Die Schiedsgerichtsbarkeit nach dem Weltbankübereinkommen für Investitionsstreitigkeiten*, 1972, p. 183 to 192, with further references).

39. (d) Insofar as the response to the appeal argues that the legislator intended to make a conclusive provision for ICSID proceedings by amending Article 2(2) of the Act ratifying the ICSID (InvStreitBeilG) in the course of reforming the law on arbitration by way of the Act of 22 December 1997 (Federal Law Gazette I p. 3224), that argument fails.

40. If, prior to the reform of arbitration law, the legal provisions regarding the process for filing a request for a declaration of the admissibility of enforcement of an ICSID arbitral award provided that the legal provisions governing the enforceability of domestic arbitral awards (which, pursuant to section 1044(1) sentence 1 German Code of Civil Procedure, old version, also applied by analogy to foreign arbitral awards) were applicable, the provisions regarding the process for the declaration of enforceability of foreign arbitral awards must now be applied accordingly (section 1025(4), sections 1061 to 1065 German Code of Civil Procedure).

41. This amendment is merely one of many necessary consequential amendments of existing provisions to correspond to the new provisions of the 10th Book of the German Code of Civil Procedure (see Bundestag printed paper 13/5274, p. 68). It does not change the fact that Article 2 InvStreitBeilG still only regulates the post-arbitral phase after an award has been made and that the corresponding application of provisions of the 10th Book of the German Code of Civil Procedure only concerns the enforcement of ICSID awards. It is not possible to infer from this any statement regarding the (non-)applicability of section 1025(2) German Code of Civil Procedure (and section 1032(2) German Code of Civil Procedure) in ICSID arbitration proceedings, especially considering the deliberate extension of the material scope of application of the 10th Book of the German Code of Civil Procedure beyond the UNCITRAL Model Law to all arbitration proceedings (see Bundestag printed paper13/5274, p. 25 and 31).

42. (e) At least for the declaratory proceedings pursuant to section 1032(2) German Code of Civil Procedure, which are at issue here, the

existing regulatory gap in section 1025(2) German Code of Civil Procedure also becomes apparent when looking at the provisions governing local jurisdiction in section 1062(1) and (2) German Code of Civil Procedure, which essentially open up a global scope of application, only by distinguishing a domestic place of arbitration.

43. Section 1062(1) no 2 case 1 German Code of Civil Procedure provides for the jurisdiction of the Higher Regional Court designated in the arbitration agreement or, where no such designation has been made, that Higher Regional Court in whose district the place of arbitration is located, for decisions on applications to declare the admissibility or inadmissibility of arbitration proceedings (section 1032 German Code of Civil Procedure). If there is no German place of arbitration in this case, then the Higher Regional Court in whose district the defendant has its seat or habitual residence or in whose district the assets of the defendants or any other object claimed or affected by the arbitration proceedings are located, shall have jurisdiction for the decisions, alternatively the Berlin Higher Regional Court (section 1062(2) German Code of Civil Procedure).

44. Taking into account the legal concept of the dual function of local jurisdiction, this provision suggests that—like section 1062(2) German Code of Civil Procedure for local jurisdiction—section 1025(2) German Code of Civil Procedure for international jurisdiction is always applicable (accordingly) in cases where there is no German place of arbitration, despite the positive wording ("abroad", "not yet determined").

45. If there are no specific rules on jurisdiction, then international jurisdiction is indirectly derived from the provisions on local jurisdiction (so-called "dual function"; on section 32 German Code of Civil Procedure see Federal Court of Justice, Judgment of 28 June 2007—I ZR 49/04, BGHZ 173, 57 [juris, para. 23]—Cambridge Institute, with further references; generally Roth in Stein/Jonas loc. cit. preliminary remarks on section 12 paras. 32, 32b; Zöller/Schultzky loc. cit. section 1 para. 8). Where a German court has local jurisdiction according to these provisions, then, according to German law, it also has international jurisdiction (see MünchKomm.ZPO/Patzina loc. cit. section 12 para. 90).

46. It is true that section 1025(2) German Code of Civil Procedure contains a special provision regarding international jurisdiction. However, that provision must be interpreted in accordance with section 1062(2) German Code of Civil Procedure. If section 1062(2) German Code of Civil Procedure generally provides that as an alternative the Berlin Higher Regional Court has jurisdiction for the

declaratory proceedings pursuant to section 1032(2) German Code of Civil Procedure in cases where—as in this case—there is "no German place of arbitration", then a lack of international jurisdiction in this case reveals an unintended regulatory gap.

47. (3) The test of comparable circumstances of interest requires the assumption that the legislator, weighing the interests according to the principles that guided it when enacting the laws referred to, would have reached the same conclusion (Federal Court of Justice, GRUR 2020, 429 [juris, para. 34]—*Sportwetten in Gaststätten*). This is the situation in the current case.

48. The legislator's intention, as expressed in the wording of the law, is that it should also be possible to seize the German courts in the cases listed in section 1025(2) German Code of Civil Procedure even where the arbitration proceedings take place abroad (see Bundestag printed paper 13/5274, p. 31). The intention expressed therein, that the German courts should have a global jurisdiction in the cases mentioned, applies equally in delocalised arbitration proceedings under the ICSID Convention and in arbitration proceedings where the place of arbitration is abroad. This is particularly evident in section 1032(1) German Code of Civil Procedure stipulating an objection of an existing arbitration agreement which may be raised in legal proceedings before the ordinary courts, which is explicitly referred to in the explanatory memorandum to the Act. Such an objection, with the possible consequence of the claim being found to be inadmissible, is also only made possible in the case of ICSID arbitration proceedings if section 1025(2) German Code of Civil Procedure applies by analogy. If it was not possible for the objection of an (ICSID) arbitration agreement to lead to the inadmissibility of the claim before the ordinary courts due to section 1032(1) German Code of Civil Procedure (via section 1025(2) German Code of Civil Procedure) not being applicable, then this would contradict the spirit and purpose of arbitration agreements, including those within the scope of application of the ICSID Convention.

49. 3. The application pursuant to section 1032(2) German Code of Civil Procedure was lodged with the Berlin Higher Regional Court in good time.

50. a. The relevant date for deciding whether an application pursuant to section 1032(2) German Code of Civil Procedure has been submitted in time, which can be submitted up until the time that the arbitral tribunal is constituted, is the date on which the application is received by the court, not the date of service of the application on the other party (see Federal Court of Justice, Order of 30 June 2011—III

ZB 59/10, GRUR 2012, 95 [juris para. 10], with further references; MünchKomm.ZPO/Münch loc. cit. section 1032 para. 30; Voit in Musielak/Voit loc. cit. section 1032 para. 10). A non-permanent arbitral tribunal within the meaning of section 1032(2) German Code of Civil Procedure is constituted when all arbitrators have been appointed and the arbitrators have not only been nominated but have also accepted their appointment (see Federal Court of Justice, Order of 9 February 2023—I ZB 62/22, NJOZ 2023, 497 [juris, para. 15], with further references).

51. b. This means that the time limitation has been complied with. The application was received by the Berlin Higher Regional Court on 17 August 2021 and thus before the arbitral tribunal was constituted on 14 September 2021.

52. 4. The application pursuant to section 1032(2) German Code of Civil Procedure is also admissible. In the context of such application, the ordinary court will review whether an effective arbitration agreement exists, whether it is practicable, and whether the subject matter of the arbitration proceedings falls within the scope of the arbitration agreement (Federal Court of Justice, Order of 19 September 2019—I ZB 4/19, SchiedsVZ 2020, 50 [juris, para. 11], with further references). In the present context, the court may carry out this review, also with a view to the ICSID arbitration proceedings already initiated beforehand, which, pursuant to Article 41(1) ICSID Convention, provides for a genuine *Kompetenz-Kompetenz* of the arbitral tribunal. The blocking effect of the ICSID arbitration proceedings with respect to proceedings before the ordinary courts (see C.I.4.b) exceptionally does not apply here, due to the primacy of EU law (see C.I.4.c and d).

53. a. The Berlin Higher Regional Court took the view that section 1032(2) German Code of Civil Procedure did not apply with respect to ICSID arbitration proceedings. It held that the procedural rules of the ICSID Convention were a closed legal system which does not allow for any other procedural rules to be applicable. Pursuant to Article 41(1) ICSID Convention, it was up to the seized arbitral tribunal to conclusively decide on its own competence and the effectiveness of any arbitration clause. It stated that by way of the Investment Disputes Settlement Convention Act (InvStreitBeilG), Germany had recognised this regime and confirmed in Article 2(2) thereof, that it only referred to a corresponding application of the German Code of Civil Procedure for a request for a declaration of the admissibility of enforcement action. This did not allow for either a review of the procedure nor a review on the basis of public policy within the meaning of section 1059(2)

German Code of Civil Procedure. Nor was section 1032(2) German Code of Civil Procedure applicable (by analogy) to ICSID arbitration proceedings. Nor was this changed by the case law of the Court of Justice of the European Union on intra-EU investment disputes. This case law did not relate to the procedural rules of the German Code of Civil Procedure and their applicability to ICSID arbitration proceedings. The arbitration had been duly initiated in accordance with the provisions of Article 26 ECT. The applicant's consent to be a party of the Energy Charter Treaty pursuant to Article 26(3)(a) ECT had been given by being a contracting party to the treaty and had been given without reservation. The defendants had given their consent to the arbitration agreement by submitting the request for arbitration to the Centre. Pursuant to Article 41(1) ICSID Convention, the question of whether the consents were also effective in an intra-EU investment dispute was a matter for the arbitral tribunal to decide, taking into account the case law of the Court of Justice of the European Union. It held that it was not a violation of EU law not to apply section 1032(2) German Code of Civil Procedure to ICSID arbitration proceedings. It was a domestic procedural provision. The dispute, it found, was neither comparable to a subsequent application for annulment nor to arbitration proceedings under the UNCITRAL Arbitration Rules, which did not contain any exclusive procedural rules comparable to the ICSID Convention. This does not stand up to legal scrutiny.

54. b. However, as a rule, proceedings before the ordinary courts are precluded, at least from the point in time that ICSID arbitration proceedings have been initiated, due to the *Kompetenz-Kompetenz* of the arbitral tribunal pursuant to Article 41(1) ICSID Convention, as this provision is more specific and therefore has priority.

55. aa. The international ICSID Convention ranks like a simple federal law in the German legal order due to the fact that it was ratified by the 1969 Act pursuant to Article 59(2) sentence 1 German Constitution. The provisions of the treaty are given domestic effect by an order giving effect to an international treaty at the national level (*Rechtsanwendungsbefehl*) within the meaning of Article 59(2) sentence 1 German Constitution (see BVerfGE 141, 1 [juris, paras. 45 et seq.]; von Arnauld, *Völkerrecht*, 5th ed. para. 509; BeckOK.GG/Pieper, 55th ed. [as at 15 May 2023], Art. 59 para. 41, with further references; Nettesheim in Dürig/Herzog/Scholz, GG, 90th supplementary edition, February 2020, Art. 59 paras. 177 et seq.; on the ICSID Convention see Seelmann-Eggebert, SchiedsVZ 2023, 32, 36). Where domestic laws have the same status, if there is a conflict between

them, the principles of lex posterior and lex specialis apply. The principle of the German Constitution's openness to international law requires that domestic laws should, where possible, be interpreted in such a manner, that they do not cause any conflict with the Federal Republic of Germany's obligations under international law. Therefore, if the relevant methodological principles of interpretation allow for a statute to be interpreted in several possible ways, then the interpretation that is open to international law is generally to be preferred (BVerfGE 141, 1 [juris para. 71], with further references; von Arnauld loc. cit. paras. 517, 525 et seq.; BeckOK.GG/Pieper loc. cit. Art. 59 paras. 38, 44). However, this does not result in a constitutional obligation to comply with every provision of international law without limitation (BVerfGE 141, 1 [juris, para. 69]).

56. bb. The Berlin Higher Regional Court correctly pointed out that the ICSID Convention has a closed legal system with its own procedural rules. Whereas under domestic arbitration law and the UNCITRAL Model Law, both in the pre-arbitral phase up to the formation of the arbitral tribunal, the arbitral phase during the arbitration proceedings and the post-arbitral phase after the award has been made, the ordinary courts can be called upon to review and support the arbitration proceedings (see for example section 1032(2), section 1033, section 1040(3) sentence 2 and sections 1059 to 1061 German Code of Civil Procedure) and have the final decision-making competence (see Federal Court of Justice, GRUR 2012, 95 [juris para. 11]; Schütze in Wieczorek/Schütze loc. cit. section 1032 para. 17, with further references), the ICSID Convention deliberately deviates from involving the ordinary courts in that manner.

57. cc. In order to resolve the question of the jurisdiction of the Centre within the meaning of Article 25 ICSID Convention and, consequently, the question of the jurisdiction of the arbitral tribunal, it is the arbitral tribunal alone that is the competent forum pursuant to Article 41(1) ICSID Convention, at any rate as from the date of the registration of an ICSID arbitration—in this case on 13 May 2021.

58. (1) Pursuant to Art. 25(1) sentence 1 ICSID Convention, the jurisdiction of the Centre extends to all disputes between a contracting state, and a national of another contracting state, which are directly related to an investment, provided that the parties have agreed in writing to submit the disputes to the Centre.

59. Pursuant to Article 36(3) sentence 1 ICSID Convention, the Secretary-General of the Centre is responsible, from the time the request for arbitration is submitted (Article 36(1) ICSID Convention) until the time it is registered, for the preliminary

examination on whether the dispute obviously does not fall within the competence of the Centre pursuant to Article 25 ICSID Convention (so-called "screening power"; see Escher, RIW 2001, 20, 23 et seq.; Escobar in Fouret/Gerbay/Alvarez loc. cit. Article 36 paras. 4.23, 4.35; Kern loc. cit. p. 60, with further references; Schöbener/Markert, ZVgIRWiss 2006, 65, 76 et seq.). The Secretary General's power to refuse registration is defined so narrowly that it does not interfere with the *Kompetenz-Kompetenz* of the arbitral tribunal (see von Wobeser in Fouret/Gerbay/Alvarez loc. cit. Article 41 para. 4.184).

60. This *Kompetenz-Kompetenz* of the arbitral tribunal is justified by Article 41(1) ICSID Convention, according to which the arbitral tribunal itself decides on whether it is competent. Irrespective of a positive preliminary finding by the Secretary General, it can still come to the conclusion that the Centre is not competent (see Pirrung loc. cit. p. 94 et seq., 97; Schöbener/Markert, ZVgIRWiss 2006, 65, 77, with further references; von Wobeser in Fouret/Gerbay/Alvarez loc. cit. Article 41 para. 4.184). In such a case, the arbitral tribunal has nevertheless been formed validly, even if the validity of the parties' consent to ICSID arbitration is in dispute and should prove to be invalid (see Kriebaum in Schreuer's Commentary on the ICSID Convention, 3rd ed., Article 41 paras. 7 et seq.). Therefore, pursuant to Article 41(1) ICSID Convention, the decision as to whether the jurisdictional requirements of Article 25 ICSID Convention have been met, fundamentally rests solely with the arbitral tribunal (see Kern loc. cit. p. 60; von Wobeser in Fouret/Gerbay/Alvarez loc. cit. Article 41 paras. 4.182, 4.184).

61. (2) Accordingly, Article 41(1) ICSID Convention already applies in any event from the point in time that the arbitration proceedings are initiated (see Kriebaum in Schreuer's Commentary on the ICSID Convention loc. cit. Article 41 para. 25 and paras. 83 to 85; Kryvoi, International Centre for Settlement of Investment Disputes (ICSID), 4th ed., para. 208, with further references; Pirrung loc. cit. p. 97; von Wobeser in Fouret/Gerbay/Alvarez loc. cit. Article 41 para. 4.179; (presumably) different opinion in Steinbrück/Krahé, IPRax 2023, 36, 38 et seq.), which deviates from section 1040 German Code of Civil Procedure, which, in conjunction with section 1032(2) German Code of Civil Procedure, provides for the (provisional) *Kompetenz-Kompetenz* of the arbitral tribunal only from the time of the arbitral tribunal having been formed (see BeckOK.ZPO/Wolf/Eslami loc. cit. section 1032 para. 2; Schütze in Wieczorek/Schütze loc. cit. section 1032 para. 8). Pursuant to No 6(2) of the Rules of Procedure for the Institution of Conciliation and

Arbitration Proceedings, an ICSID arbitration is deemed to have been initiated as soon as it is registered. Due to the fact that the proceedings have already been registered, no decision is required in this case on whether Article 41(1) ICSID Convention was already applicable in the period from the request for arbitration being made until the proceedings being registered.

62. (3) From a systematic point of view, the idea that the arbitral tribunal has jurisdiction, at least from the point in time when proceedings have been initiated by registration, is certainly supported by the fact that this ensures a seamless continuation from the preliminary assessment by the Secretary General of the Centre. Pursuant to Article 36(3) sentence 1 ICSID Convention. This covers the period from the request first being made until it is registered, following which the preliminary assessment is concluded. Therefore, the relevant point in time for the Centre and the arbitral court examining whether the conditions of Article 25 ICSID Convention are satisfied is the time of registration; later changes are irrelevant (see Banifatemi/Edson in Fouret/Gerbay/Alvarez loc. cit. Article 25 para. 2.09, with further references; Kriebaum in Schreuer's Commentary on the ICSID Convention loc. cit. Article 41, paras. 83 to 85).

63. The spirit and the purpose of the Convention, which is designed to decouple domestic law and ordinary courts as much as possible (see Pearsall in Fouret loc. cit. p. 117, 118; Sasson in Fouret/Gerbay/Alvarez loc. cit. Article 62, para. 7.04; Happ in Schütze loc. cit. chapter XV, part II para. 13; Kern loc. cit. p. 65; Kröll, NJW 2023, 819, 820), also suggests a comprehensive decision-making power within the ICSID system from the point of a request being submitted or, in any event, from the time proceedings are initiated.

64. In contrast to commercial arbitration, where section 1040(3) sentence 2 German Code of Civil Procedure provides for a mandatory review by the courts in cases of an objection (see Federal Court of Justice, Order of 24 July 2014—III ZB 83/13, BGHZ 202, 168 [juris para. 10], with further references; Schroeter, SchiedsVZ 2004, 288, 290; for the corresponding provision in Article 16(3) sentence 2 UNCITRAL Model Law see Melis in Kronke/Melis/Kuhn loc. cit. part P para. 279), in ICSID arbitration proceedings there generally is no subsequent review of the decision on jurisdiction by the ordinary courts and thus no final decision-making competence for the ordinary courts. Examining the jurisdictional competence must be carried out exclusively within the framework of the arbitration proceedings themselves according to the provisions of the ICSID Convention, which are more specific and therefore generally have priority (see Pirrung loc. cit.

p. 116; Schöbener/Markert, ZVgIRViss 2006, 65, 74; Berger, SchiedsVZ 2017, 282, 290; Raeschke-Kessler, SchiedsVZ 2018, 1, 6; Kröll, NJW 2023, 819, 820 et seq.; Seelmann-Eggebert, SchiedsVZ 2023, 32, 36; Steinbrück/Krahé, IPRax 2023, 36, 38). This also satisfies the priority to be accorded to international treaties, which the legislator considered self-evident when reforming the arbitral procedure (see Bundestag printed paper 13/5274, p. 31).

65. dd. Accordingly, if looking at the provisions of the ICSID Convention in isolation, the *Kompetenz-Kompetenz* of the arbitral tribunal, pursuant to Article 41(1) ICSID Convention, would therefore preclude proceedings pursuant to section 1032(2) German Code of Civil Procedure due to the fact that arbitration proceedings had already been initiated. According to the database available on the ICSID website (icsid.world-bank.org), the arbitration proceedings were registered with the file number ICSID ARB/21/26 on 13 May 2021 and thus commenced, whereas the application pursuant to section 1032(2) German Code of Civil Procedure was only received by the Berlin Higher Regional Court in August 2021.

66. ee. Due to the fact that the arbitration proceedings have already been initiated, it is not of decisive importance what the precise meaning of the provision of Article 26 sentence 1 ICSID Convention is, which stipulates that the consent of the parties to arbitration under the Convention is also deemed to be a waiver of any other remedy, unless a declaration to the contrary is made. This provision only applies directly up until such time as a request has been submitted to the Centre (see Alexandrov in Schreuer's Commentary on the ICSID Convention loc. cit. Article 26 para. 6; Haridi in Fouret/Gerbay/Alvarez loc. cit. Article 26 paras. 2.258 et seq.).

67. c. Intra-EU investor–State arbitration proceedings under the ICSID Convention on the basis of Article 26 ECT are a special scenario, where, exceptionally, the blocking effect of Article 41(1) ICSID Convention does not prevent an application under section 1032(2) German Code of Civil Procedure from being admissible, because of the primacy of EU law—also vis-à-vis public international law.

68. aa. According to the settled case law of the Court of Justice of the European Union, EU law originates from an autonomous source, namely the Treaties, and takes precedence over the law of the Member States. The autonomy of EU law exists both vis-à-vis the law of the Member States and vis-à-vis international law (see CJEU, Opinion of 30 April 2019—Gut 1/17, EuGRZ 2019, 191 [juris para. 109]—CETA Agreement EU–Canada, with further references; on primacy

over public international law, see also CJEU, Judgment of
3 September 2008—C-402/05, C-415/05, [2008] 1-6351 =
EuGRZ 2008, 480 [juris paras. 281 to 285]—*Kadi and Al Barakaat
Foundation* v. *Council and Commission*). The supremacy of EU law
requires that the domestic courts, which have to apply the provisions of
EU law within their jurisdiction, ensure the full effect of these provisions. To that end, they must exercise their own decision-making
power to disapply any conflicting domestic provision, if necessary,
without first requesting or awaiting a change in the national law by
the legislator or some other constitutional process to eliminate such a
conflicting provision (see CJEU, Judgment of 4 December 2018—
C-378/17, NZA 2019, 27 [juris para. 35]—Minister for Justice and
Equality and Commissioner of An Garda Síochána, with further references; Judgment of 2 September 2021—C-741/19, SchiedsVZ 2022,
34 [juris para. 43]—Komstroy; see also BVerfGE 126, 286 [juris
para. 53]; Nettesheim in Grabitz/Hilf/Nettesheim, *Das Recht der EU*,
48th Supplementary Edition, August 2012, Article 288 TFEU
paras. 47 to 53).

69. bb. Also according to settled case law of the Court of Justice of
the European Union, Articles 267 and 355 TFEU must be construed in
such a way that they preclude the application of a provision in an
international agreement entered into between two Member States,
pursuant to which an investor from one of these Member States may
initiate arbitration proceedings against the other Member State where
there is a dispute about investment in that other Member State, and to
initiate such proceedings before an arbitral court whose jurisdiction that
Member State accepts (see CJEU, Judgment of 6 March 2018—C-284/
16, SchiedsVZ 2018, 186 [juris paras. 32, 60]—Achmea; CJEU,
SchiedsVZ 2022, 34 [juris paras. 42 to 46]—Komstroy; CJEU,
Judgment of 26 October 2021—C-109/20, EuZW 2021, 1097 [juris
para. 44]—PL Holdings; Judgment of 25 January 2022—C-638/19,
RIW 2022, 219 [juris para. 138]—European Food; Opinion of
16 June 2022—C-1/20, juris para. 47 with para. 20—Modernised
contract for the Energy Charter; Order of 21 September 2022—
C-333/19, BeckRS 2022, 26460 para. 33—Romatsa).

70. An ICSID award must be considered incompatible with EU law,
in particular with Articles 267 and 344 TFEU, if the arbitration clause
underlying the arbitration proceedings calls into question the respect for
the specific nature of EU law guaranteed by the preliminary ruling
procedure, in breach of the principles of loyal cooperation and the
autonomy of EU law (see CJEU, RIW 2022, 219 [juris para. 142]—
European Food; BeckRS 2022, 26460 paras. 41 et seq.—Romatsa).

An arbitral award that is incompatible with EU law in this way cannot have any effect and thus cannot be enforced. A court of a Member State involved in the compulsory enforcement of such an ICSID award is under an obligation not to apply the award and consequently must not enforce it under any circumstances (see CJEU, BeckRS 2022, 26460, paras. 43 et seq.—Romatsa [in French]; for the translation of the operative part, see OJ C 24 of 2023, p. 14).

71. cc. According to these principles, in the intra-EU context, a review of an ICSID award by an ordinary court is absolutely required in the subsequent enforceability proceedings for reasons of EU law and contrary to the system of the ICSID Convention (see (1) below). In such a case, however, the principle of effectiveness ("effet utile") requires that, when deciding on the admissibility of an upstream remedy such as section 1032(2) German Code of Civil Procedure, Article 41(1) ICSID Convention, which is contrary to this in this respect—and which ranks like a simple federal law in the German legal order due to the fact that it was ratified by the Act of approval—be left unapplied in order to ensure the full effect of EU law as early as possible (see (2) below).

72. (1) According to the case law of the Court of Justice of the European Union, judicial review of an ICSID award in an intra-EU investor–State constellation, such as here, is mandatory in the downstream proceedings regarding a declaration of the admissibility of enforcement action.

73. (a) The decisions in "European Food" and "Romatsa" make it clear that the Court of Justice of the European Union considers its jurisdiction under Articles 267, 344 TFEU for the subsequent enforcement of an arbitral award to be unaffected by the ICSID Convention. Notwithstanding the complete exclusion of a review of an ICSID award by the domestic courts, as provided for in Articles 53, 54 ICSID Convention, the domestic courts must disapply an arbitral award that is incompatible with EU law and, consequently, must not enforce it under any circumstances (see CJEU, BeckRS 2022, 26460 paras. 43 et seq.—Romatsa; see also CJEU, RIW 2022, 219 [juris para. 142]—European Food; on the annulment of an intra-EU ICSID award see Cour de Cassation du Grand-Duché de Luxembourg, Judgment of 14 July 2022—CAS-2021-00061 paras. 26 to 40 and 43, www.italaw.com/sitesidefault/files/case-documents/italaw170526 .pdf—last accessed on 3 June 2023).

74. (b) Such a downstream review of ICSID awards in the intra-EU context, which is required by EU law, is not precluded by the provision of Article 2(4) InvStreitBeilG, according to which the request to declare

the admissibility of enforcement action may only be rejected if the award has been set aside in proceedings pursuant to Article 51 or Article 52 ICSID Convention. The primacy of EU law (para. 68 above) requires that, in the intra-EU context, this domestic provision is not applied as it is a conflicting domestic provision.

75. (2) As a subsequent revision of ICSID arbitral awards by the German courts is therefore mandatory for reasons of EU law, notwithstanding Articles 53, 54 ICSID Convention and Article 2(4) InvStreitBeilG, the principle of effectiveness ("effet utile") requires that the primacy of EU law must also be extended to the preceding declaratory proceedings under section 1032(2) German Code of Civil Procedure and, thus, its admissibility must be affirmed.

76. (a) According to the settled case law of the Court of Justice of the European Union, the principle of effectiveness requires that the applicable national legislation is not such as to render practically impossible or excessively difficult the exercise of the rights conferred by EU law. This must be assessed in the light of the position of the legislation in the proceedings as a whole, the course of the proceedings and the specific features of the proceedings before the various national bodies (CJEU, Judgment of 11 November 2015—C-505/14, EuZW 2016, 57 [juris paras. 40 et seq.]—Klausner Holz; Judgment of 5 March 2019—C-349/17, EuZW 2019, 379 [juris paras. 137 et seq.]—Eesti Pagar; Judgment of 7 April 2022—C-116/20, juris paras. 100 et seq.—Avio Lucos, all with further references). Where a provision of domestic law precludes the application of a domestic remedy, then it must be disapplied if the domestic remedy would otherwise be capable of giving full effect to EU law (see CJEU, Judgment of 19 June 1990—C-213/89, [1990] 1-2433 = NJW 1991, 2271 [juris para. 23]—Factortame and others; Judgment of 13 July 2006—C-295/04 to C-298/04, [2006]1-6619 = EuZW 2006, 529 [juris para. 62]—Manfredi and others; see also Hess, *Europäisches Zivilprozessrecht*, 2nd ed., section 11 para. 11.9).

77. (b) For procedural and economic reasons, with section 1032(2) German Code of Civil Procedure, the domestic legislator has deliberately provided for a special remedy which (at least initially) precedes the arbitration proceedings. These proceedings are a German peculiarity and have no counterpart in the UNCITRAL Model Law (see Bundestag printed paper 13/5274, p. 38; Saenger/Saenger, ZPO, 9th ed., section 1032 para. 13; on the advantages and disadvantages, see Steinbrück, *Die Unterstützung ausländischer Schiedsverfahren durch staatliche Gerichte*, 2009, pp. 347 to 350). A final decision on an application pursuant to section 1032(2) German Code of Civil Procedure is binding on the

(domestic) ordinary courts in subsequent court proceedings, in particular in proceedings for annulment or a declaration of enforceability under sections 1059 to 1061 German Code of Civil Procedure and in other legal proceedings, where the objection of arbitration proceedings may be raised under section 1032(1) German Code of Civil Procedure (see German Federal Court, Order of 6 May 2021—I ZB 71/20, juris para. 16; BeckOK.ZPO/Wolf/Eslami loc. cit. section 1032 para. 42; Voit in Musielak/Voit loc. cit. section 1032 paras. 13 et seq.; Zöller/Geimer loc. cit. section 1032 para. 24, section 1040 para. 4 and section 1059 para. 39). For the parties, the remedy of section 1032(2) German Code of Civil Procedure provides an option to save time and costs, if, for example, the arbitration proceedings are not initiated at all or not pursued further upon determination of the inadmissibility, where the arbitral tribunal is persuaded of the inadmissibility or, in any event, where the subsequent court proceedings are simplified and accelerated by the determined result.

78. (c) Article 41(1) ICSID Convention, which precludes the application of section 1032(2) German Code of Civil Procedure with these effects, must not be applied in intra-EU investor–State arbitration proceedings (see Steinbrück/Krahé, IPRax 2023, 36, 41; critical opinion in Wilske/Markert/Ebert, SchiedsVZ 2022, 111, 130), in order to allow EU law to take full effect at an early stage.

79. In the intra-EU context, the ex-ante control provided for by the German legislator in section 1032(2) German Code of Civil Procedure can bindingly anticipate the ex-post control required in the context of ICSID arbitration proceedings (see CJEU, BeckRS 2022, 26460, paras. 43 et seq.—Romatsa; paras. 72 to 74 above). A finding that the arbitration proceedings are inadmissible pursuant to section 1032(2) German Code of Civil Procedure prevents any (later) declaration of enforceability of an ICSID award in Germany due to the binding effect of this decision.

80. Applying section 1032(2) German Code of Civil Procedure also takes into account the case law of the Court of Justice of the European Union, according to which the Member States, as soon as a dispute is brought before an arbitration tribunal on the basis of an obligation violating EU law, are obliged to object to the validity of the arbitration clause or any ad hoc arbitration agreement on the basis of which that body was seized, either before that arbitration tribunal or before the competent court (see CJEU, EuZW 2021, 1097 [juris para. 52]—PL Holdings).

81. To the extent that the response to the appeal in this context complains that the case law of the Court of Justice of the European

Union does not give rise to an obligation under EU law to create a sui generis domestic remedy for a declaration of inadmissibility of the arbitration proceedings, it overlooks the fact that such a remedy is already provided for in national law in section 1032(2) German Code of Civil Procedure, which is also applicable via section 1025(2) German Code of Civil Procedure.

82. (d) The primacy of EU law is not achieved by an impermissible interpretation of domestic law contra legem (on this limit, see CJEU, EuZW 2016, 57 [juris para. 32]—Klausner Holz; CJEU, Judgment of 11 February 2021—C-760/18, NZA 2021, 333 [juris para. 67]—M. V. and others, with further references; Federal Court of Justice, Order of 29 July 2021—I ZR 135/20, GRUR 2021, 1320 [juris para. 36] = WRP 2021, 1290—Flaschenpfand III, with further references). The admissibility of the application under section 1032(2) German Code of Civil Procedure results from the wording of the provision of section 1032(2) German Code of Civil Procedure, given the inapplicability of Article 41(1) ICSID Convention as required by EU law (on the primacy of EU law see supra para. 68). The provisions in Articles 2 et seq. InvStreitBeilG apply only to the phase after the ICSID arbitral award has been issued; statements on the preceding phase and the applicability of section 1032(2) German Code of Civil Procedure cannot be inferred from these provisions.

83. (e) There are no exceptional circumstances, thus the primacy of EU law over Article 41 ICSID Convention is not excluded pursuant to Article 351(1) TFEU.

84. (aa) Article 1(1) TFEU provides that the rights and obligations arising from agreements concluded prior to 1 January 1958 or, for States that acceded thereafter, before the date of their accession, between one or more Member States on the one hand, and one or more third countries on the other, shall not be affected by the provisions of the Treaties. The purpose of the provision is to protect the Member States from breaches of international law vis-à-vis third countries, which would be caused by the primacy of EU law, and thus takes into account the maxim "pacta sunt servanda" (see Schmalenbach in Calliess/Ruffert, EUV/AEUV, 6th ed., Article 351 TFEU para. 1; Streinz/Kokott, EUV/AEUV, 3rd ed., Article 351 TFEU para. 1).

85. (bb) According to its wording, Article 351(1) TFEU is not directly applicable in the case at issue. For the applicant, as a founding member of the European Economic Community, the relevant date is 1 January 1958. For the defendants, the relevant date is the accession date of Ireland, the State of domicile of defendants 1 to 3, to the European Community in 1973. The ICSID Convention entered into

force for the applicant in 1969 and for Ireland in 1981, the Energy Charter Treaty in 1998 for both parties.

86. (cc) According to the case law of the Court of Justice of the European Union, Article 351(1) TFEU cannot be applied by analogy to cases in which rights and obligations are concerned that have arisen from agreements which—as in the current case—were concluded after the relevant dates specified in the provision, but which concern a subject matter for which the EU only became competent at a later date as a result of an increase in its competence (see CJEU, Judgment of 28 October 2022—C-435/22, NJW 2023, 349, paras. 115 to 127— PPU). Contrary to a widespread opinion in the literature (see Lorenzmeier in Grabitz/Hilf/Nettesheim loc. cit. Article 351 TFEU paras. 24 to 28; Schmalenbach in Calliess/Ruffert loc. cit. Article 351 TFEU paras. 6 to 9; on the Energy Charter Treaty, see Köster loc. cit. p. 176 et seq.), the provision of Article 351(1) TFEU, which, if its requirements are met, permits derogations from EU law, including primary law, must be interpreted narrowly as an exceptional provision. It only covers agreements concluded before 1 January 1958 or, in the case of States that acceded thereafter, agreements concluded before the date of their accession (see CJEU, NJW 2023, 349 paras. 119 et seq. and 126—PPU). The current wording of the provision was adopted in the Treaty of Amsterdam and was not changed since in the Treaties of Nice and Lisbon, even though shifts of competence were known in each case through the developments of the EU's competences. Nevertheless, a transfer of competence to the EU was not determined as another relevant date in time (see CJEU, NJW 2023, 349, paras. 123 to 125—PPU).

87. 5. The requirement under section 1032(2) German Code of Civil Procedure of a need for the protection of a legal interest is met.

88. a. Like any procedural remedy, the application pursuant to section 1032(2) German Code of Civil Procedure requires a need for the protection of a legal interest. In general, this need already arises from a potential party status in the arbitration proceedings (see Federal Court of Justice, Order of 8 November 2018—I ZB 21/18, NJW 2019, 857 [juris para. 15]). The (subsequent) formation of the arbitral tribunal does not mean that the need for the protection of a legal interest for the applicant under section 1032(2) German Code of Civil Procedure has ceased to exist. In section 1032(2) and (3) German Code of Civil Procedure, the law assumes a subsequent coexistence of the state court and arbitration proceedings in the case of an admissible application filed before the formation of the arbitral tribunal (see Federal Court of Justice, GRUR 2012, 95 [juris para. 11], with further

references; on the continuing interest for legal protection in case an arbitral award is issued in the meantime, see Federal Court of Justice, Order of 11 May 2017—I ZB 75/16, NJW 2017, 3723 [juris paras. 10, 14]).

89. However, the need for the protection of a legal interest is missing if the claimant or applicant can achieve their objective by simpler or less expensive means or not at all by the remedy applied for (regarding the application for a court decision see Federal Court of Justice, Order of 10 February 2016—IV AR (VZ) 8/15, NJW-RR 2016, 445 [juris para. 10], with further references; for an application for an injunction under trade mark law see Federal Court of Justice, Judgment of 15 October 2020—I ZR 210/18—GRUR 2020, 1311 [juris para. 27] = WRP 2021, 42—Vorwerk, with further references; on enforcement law, see Federal Court of Justice, Order of 13 October 2022—I ZB 69/21, GRUR 2023, 105 [juris para. 13] with further references.

90. b. Accordingly, there is a need for the protection of a legal interest in the current case. The application relates to concrete arbitration proceedings in which the applicant is the respondent. The declaratory proceedings for a declaration pursuant to section 1032(2) German Code of Civil Procedure are not objectively pointless; above all, they are not merely limited to expressing a legal opinion, but will have legal and factual effects. In particular, a finding of inadmissibility of the arbitration proceedings pursuant to section 1032(2) German Code of Civil Procedure prevents a subsequent declaration of the admissibility of enforcement action of an ICSID award in Germany (see above para. 79).

91. Furthermore, a preceding declaratory decision by one of Germany's highest courts can have a strong signalling effect for other ordinary courts bound by EU law in proceedings for the recognition or declaration of enforceability of arbitration awards (see Scheu/Nikolov, Arbitration International 2020, 253, 267 to 269). Such a decision in proceedings for a declaration of enforceability can have persuasive force through the "doctrine of comity" in third countries, despite the binding effect of an ICSID award provided for in Articles 53, 54 ICSID Convention (also "mutual sovereign respect", see in this regard Gibbons/Myers/Dolzer, RIW 2004, 899; Späth, IPrax 2006, 184 and 185 et seq.) (see US District Court for the District of Columbia, Order of 29 June 2021—Civil Action No 20-817—*Infrared Environmental Infrastructure GP Ltd* v. *Spain*, https://casetext .com/case/infrared-envtl-infrastructure-gp-ltd-v-kingdom-of-spain—last accessed on 3 June 2023, where "considerations of comity" are explicitly

addressed; on the (inconsistent) case law of the US District Court for the District of Columbia, see Hindelang/Naßl/Jena, Achmea goes to Washington, VerfBlog, 2023/4/19; see also Scheu/Nikolov, Arbitration International 2020, 253, 271 et seq.; Steinbrück/Krahé, EuZW 2022, 357, 364 et seq.; van der Beck, *Schiedsgerichtlicher Investitionsschutz innerhalb der Europäischen Union*, 2022, p. 255 et seq.; on the dangers of possible enforcement proceedings in third countries such as the USA under Article 54 ICSID Convention, see COM [2022] 523 final of 5 October 2022, p. 1).

92. Moreover, an at least factual-indirect effect on ICSID arbitration proceedings that already have been initiated cannot be excluded (see Steinbrück/Krahé, IPRax 2023, 36, 38; van der Beck loc. cit. p. 259). An arbitral tribunal is obliged to work towards an effective award (see Federal Court of Justice, Judgment of 5 May 1986—III ZR 233/84, BGHZ 98, 32 [juris para. 15]; Schroeter, SchiedsVZ 2004, 288, 296; Spohnheimer in *Festschrift Käfer*, 2009, p. 357, 371, 373 et seq.). The non-observance of a prior final court decision on the inadmissibility of the arbitration proceedings pursuant to section 1032(2) German Code of Civil Procedure leads—in the case of a domestic arbitral award—to nullity (see Federal Court of Justice, Order of 11 October 2018—I ZB 9/18, SchiedsVZ 2019, 150 [juris para. 6]; Saenger/Saenger loc. cit. section 1032 para. 17; Voit in Musielak/Voit loc. cit. section 1032 paras. 14 et seq.) or at least to a setting aside (see MünchKomm.ZPO/Münch loc. cit. section 1032 para. 40; Schroeter, SchiedsVZ 2004, 288, 295 et seq.). It is true that this does not apply to an (a-national) ICSID award. In such a case, however, a binding declaration must be made to the effect that the award is not enforceable in Germany.

93. Moreover, the arbitral tribunal has to take into account that the European Commission has practical means to implement the case law of the Court of Justice of the European Union against arbitral awards in intra-EU investor–State arbitration proceedings. As the decision in the "European Food" case (CJEU, RIW 2022, 219) shows, compliance with an arbitral award that is contrary to EU law may constitute impermissible state aid within the meaning of Articles 107 et seq. TFEU, which in turn may lead to infringement proceedings against the Respondent Member State under Article 108(2), second subparagraph, TFEU in conjunction with Articles 258 et seq. TFEU (see von Marschall, RIW 2022, 228, 230; van der Beck loc. cit. p. 262 et seq., 266; see also Rösch, *Intraeuropäisches Investitionsrecht*, 2017, p. 162 et seq.).

94. It cannot be argued that there could not be a de facto, indirect impact on intra-EU investor–State arbitration because arbitral tribunals

were per se opposed to finding invalidity of arbitration agreements based on EU law. In the arbitration *Green Power Partners* v. *Spain* a tribunal constituted under the arbitration rules of the arbitration institute of the Stockholm Chamber of Commerce (SCC) unanimously considered the consent of a Member State to the arbitration agreement under Article 26 ECT in an intra-EU dispute as invalid because of the violation of EU law and, therefore, denied its jurisdiction (see Award of 16 June 2022—SCC Case No V [2016/135] paras. 170, 411 et seq., 468 et seq., 476 to 478; in this regard Lavranos/Lath/Varma, SchiedsVZ 2023, 38, 41 et seq.; see also US District Court for the District of Columbia, Order of 29 March 2023—Civil Case No 21-3249, *Blasket Renewable Investments* v. *Spain,* https://jusmundi.com/en/document/pdf/decision/en-aes-solar-and-others-pv-investors-v-the-kingdom-of-spain-memorandum-opinion-of-the-united-states-district-court-for-the-district-of-columbia-wednesday-29th-march-2023—last retrieved on 3 June 2023, according to which an [UNCITRAL] arbitral tribunal in an intra-EU investor–State arbitration is bound by the interpretation of EU law by the Court of Justice of the European Union on the basis of Article 26 ECT).

95. II. The application pursuant to section 1032(2) German Code of Civil Procedure is also well-founded. The arbitral proceedings are inadmissible due to the lack of an effective arbitration agreement. According to the case law of the Court of Justice of the European Union, the arbitration clause contained in Article 26(2)(c) ECT is not applicable to intra-EU investor–State arbitration, precluding the conclusion of a valid arbitration agreement (see C.II.2 and 3). Nor can an arbitration agreement be based on Article 25 ICSID Convention (see C.II.4).

96. 1. The law applicable to an arbitration agreement is decisive to assess the validity of such an arbitration agreement (see Steinbrück, loc. cit. p. 379). The law applicable to the arbitration agreement is determined by applying Article V(1)(a) NYC by analogy (see Federal Court of Justice, Judgment of 26 November 2020—I ZR 245/19, SchiedsVZ 2021, 97 [juris paras. 48, 51]). Pursuant to this provision, the law chosen by the parties prevails. The validity of the arbitration agreement on arbitration proceedings initiated on the basis of the Energy Charter Treaty is therefore determined according to the parties' intentions, in particular according to Article 26(2) to (4) ECT (see Rösch loc. cit. p. 176).

97. 2. According to the now settled case law of the Court of Justice of the European Union, Articles 267 and 344 TFEU must be interpreted as precluding a provision in an international agreement between

Member States under which an investor of one of those Member States may, in the event of a dispute concerning investments in the other Member State, institute proceedings against this Member State before an arbitral tribunal to whose jurisdiction that Member State has agreed, if a such an arbitration provision may result in such investment disputes not being resolved in a manner which guarantees the full effectiveness of EU law (see CJEU, EuZW 2021, 1097 [juris paras. 44 et seq.]—PL Holdings; RIW 2022, 219 [juris paras. 138 et seq.]—European Food; BeckRS 2022, 26460 paras. 33 et seq.—Romatsa; see also Federal Court of Justice, IWRZ 2022, 129 [juris paras. 10, 20 et seq.]).

98. a. The Court of Justice of the European Union has based its case law on the principle that an international agreement must not affect the system of competence laid down by the Treaties and, consequently, the autonomy of the EU's legal system, which the Court of Justice safeguards. This principle is enshrined in particular in Article 344 TFEU, according to which the Member States undertake not to settle disputes concerning the interpretation or application of the Treaties otherwise than as provided therein. On the basis of mutual trust, and in accordance with the principle of sincere cooperation laid down in the first subparagraph of Article 4(3) TEU, it is the responsibility of the Member States to ensure that EU law is applied and observed in their respective territories and, to that end, to take all appropriate measures, whether general or particular, to ensure fulfilment of the obligations arising out of the Treaties or resulting from the acts of the institutions of the EU. The Treaties have established a judicial system under which, in accordance with Article 19 TEU, it is for the domestic courts and the Court of Justice to ensure the full application of EU law in all Member States and the protection of the rights which individuals derive from it. The key element of the court system thus designed is the preliminary ruling procedure provided for in Article 267 TFEU, which is intended to ensure the uniform interpretation of EU law by establishing a court-to-court dialogue between the Court of Justice and the courts of the Member States (see CJEU, SchiedsVZ 2018, 186 [juris paras. 32 to 37]—Achmea; EuGRZ 2019, 191 [juris paras. 109 to 111]—CETA Agreement EU–Canada; SchiedsVZ 2022, 34 [juris paras. 42 to 46]—Komstroy; see also Federal Court of Justice, IWRZ 2022, 129 [juris para. 10]).

99. b. This case law must be taken into account in the current dispute. This is not contradicted by the fact that the provisions in Article 26(2) to (4) ECT (also) constitute provisions of international law. According to the case law of the Court of Justice of the European Union, the Energy Charter Treaty has a dual nature as an agreement

under international law and as a legal act of the EU because the EU itself is a party to the agreement (see CJEU, SchiedsVZ 2022, 34 [juris, paras. 23, 49 et seq.]—Komstroy; in this regard Köster loc. cit. p. 131 to 135).

100. 3. According to these principles, in intra-EU investor–State arbitration such as the present matter, the dispute resolution mechanism in Art. 26 para. 2 lit. c ECT violates EU law. Due to its incompatibility in particular with Articles 267 and 344 TFEU, there is a lack of effective consent, and thus of an offer by the applicant EU Member States to conclude an arbitration agreement (see Federal Court of Justice, SchiedsVZ 2019, 46 [juris para. 28]; Lithuanian Supreme Court, EuZW 2022, 567 para. 79).

101. a. According to the case law of the Court of Justice of the European Union, the answer to the question whether the possibility for an investor to bring an action before an arbitral tribunal opened up by an investment protection agreement between Member States is compatible with EU law depends, first, on whether the disputes on which the arbitral tribunal has to rule possibly relate to the interpretation or application of EU law. If the answer is in the affirmative, it depends secondly on whether the arbitral tribunal can be regarded as a court or tribunal entitled to request a preliminary ruling within the meaning of Article 267 TFEU or, thirdly, whether the award is subject to review by a court or tribunal of a Member State, which ensures that the questions of EU law which the arbitral tribunal might have to deal with could possibly be referred to the Court of Justice of the European Union by way of preliminary ruling proceedings (see CJEU, SchiedsVZ 2018, 186 [juris paras. 39, 43 and 50]—Achmea; RIW 2021, 661 [juris paras. 48, 51 and 54]—Komstroy; Federal Court of Justice, IWRZ 2022, 129 [juris para. 11], with further references; Scheu/Nikolov, Arbitration International 2020, 253, 256 et seq.).

102. This case law also applies to intra-EU investor–State arbitration proceedings under the ICSID Convention. The Court of Justice of the European Union does not differentiate between the individual arbitration rules which Article 26(2)(c) in conjunction with (4)(a) to (c) ECT offers and which also include ICSID arbitration (see CJEU, Opinion of 16 June 2022—C-1/20, juris para. 47 with paras. 20, 25—Modernised Energy Charter Treaty; same opinion taken in Steinbrück/Krahé, IPRax 2023, 36, 40 et seq.; likewise van der Beck loc. cit. p. 270 et seq., 393). It is also clear from the decisions in "European Food" and "Romatsa" that the case law refers precisely to ICSID arbitration proceedings (see CJEU, RIW 2022, 219 [juris paras. 137 to 145]—European Food; BeckRS 2022, 26460 paras. 33 to 43—Romatsa).

Insofar as it was stated in these decisions that the consent of the state was "now irrelevant" (see CJEU, RIW 2022, 219 [juris para. 145]—European Food; BeckRS 2022, 26460 para. 40—Romatsa), this is solely due to the special nature of the case constellation in these cases, namely the later accession of Romania to the European Union; it does not follow from this that there is a restriction of the case law with regard to arbitration proceedings under the ICSID Convention.

103. b. According to these standards, the dispute resolution mechanism pursuant to Article 26(2)(c) ECT violates EU law in the case at issue.

104. aa. In the underlying investment dispute, the ICSID Arbitral Tribunal must (also) interpret and apply EU law to the merits.

105. Pursuant to Article 42(1) sentence 1 ICSID Convention (a conflict of laws rule, see Lörcher, SchiedsVZ 2005, 11, 17), the ICSID Arbitral Tribunal will decide on the merits of the case primarily in accordance with the legal rules agreed upon by the parties. If the state party has declared its consent to the Centre's jurisdiction in a bilateral or multilateral investment protection treaty, the arbitral tribunal will primarily have to take into account the legal norms laid down therein (see Escher, RIW 2001, 20, 24; Schöbener/Markert, ZVgIRWiss 2006, 65, 101 et seq.). According to the findings of the Berlin Higher Regional Court, the defendants based their request for arbitration on breaches of contract under Articles 10 and 13 ECT. According to Article 26(6) ECT, an arbitral tribunal established under Article 26(4) ECT decides on the disputed issues applying the provisions in the Energy Charter Treaty and the applicable rules and principles of international law.

106. According to the case law of the Court of Justice of the European Union, the Energy Charter Treaty has a dual nature as an agreement under international law and as a legal act of the EU, because the EU itself is a party to the agreement. Accordingly, the decision of the arbitral tribunal on the merits is rendered not only according to international law but also according to EU law (see CJEU, SchiedsVZ 2022, 34 [juris paras. 23, 49 et seq.]—Komstroy; also Köster loc. cit. p. 131 to 135).

107. bb. According to the case law of the Court of Justice of the European Union, an ICSID arbitral tribunal does not belong to the court system of the EU because it is not a court entitled to request a preliminary ruling (see CJEU, RIW 2022, 219 [juris paras. 141 et seq.]—European Food; BeckRS 2022, 26460 paras. 36 et seq.—Romatsa; on an UNCITRAL arbitral tribunal under the Energy Charter Treaty see CJEU, SchiedsVZ 2022, 34 [juris paras. 51 to 53]—Komstroy; also Nikolov, EuR 2022, 496, 497).

108. cc. According to the case law of the Court of Justice of the European Union, in view of Articles 53, 54 ICSID Convention, an ICSID award is not subject to a sufficient review by a court of a Member State with regard to its compatibility with EU law (see CJEU, RIW 2022, 219 [juris, paras. 142 to 144]—European Food; BeckRS 2022, 26460 paras. 37 to 39—Romatsa).

109. The (limited) review in the proceedings for the declaration of the enforceability, which according to the CJEU's case law exceptionally also is required for ICSID arbitral awards (see above paras. 72 to 74), does not lead to a different conclusion. This merely achieves consistency with investment arbitral awards under other arbitration rules, for which such a limited review, however, is also not sufficient (on UNCITRAL proceedings under the Energy Charter Treaty, see CJEU, SchiedsVZ 2022, 34 [juris paras. 54 to 59]—Komstroy; in this regard Nikolov, EuR 2022, 496, 497).

110. 4. The arbitration agreement cannot be based on Article 25(1) sentence 1 ICSID Convention. The ICSID Convention itself does not constitute an arbitration agreement of its own and does not contain the required consent (see Banifatemi/Edson in Fouret/Gerbay/Alvarez loc. cit. Article 25 para. 2.76; Escher, RIW 2001, 20, 23; Kryvoi loc. cit. para. 38; Pirrung loc. cit. p. 74). In paragraph 7 of the preamble to the ICSID Convention, the contracting states declared that the mere ratification, acceptance or approval of the Convention by a contracting state does not imply its obligation to submit a particular dispute to conciliation or arbitration without its consent. Accordingly, Article 25(1) sentence 1 ICSID Convention also requires written consent for the competence of the Centre (see also Article 25(4) sentence 3 ICSID Convention, according to which the notification provided for in this Article does not constitute the consent required under (1); Escher, RIW 2001, 20, 23). Accordingly, Article 26(5)(a) case 1 ECT contains the declaratory statement that the consent of the host state under Article 26(3) ECT and the consent of the investor under Article 26(4) ECT shall be deemed to satisfy the requirement of written consent of the parties to the dispute within the meaning of Chapter II (Articles 25 to 27) of the ICSID Convention.

111. III. There is no need to make a request for a preliminary ruling to the Court of Justice of the European Union pursuant to Article 267(3) TFEU (see CJEU, Judgment of 6 October 1982—283/81, [1982] 3415 [juris para. 21] = NJW 1983, 1257—Cilfit and others; Judgment of 1 October 2015—C-452/14, GRUR Int. 2015, 1152 [juris para. 43]—Doc Generici; Judgment of 6 October

2021—C-561/19, NJW 2021, 3303 [juris paras. 32 f.]—Consorzio Italian Management and Catania Multiservizi).

112. 1. In the case in dispute, there is no question relevant to the interpretation of EU law which has not already been clarified by the case law of the Court or which cannot be answered beyond doubt. In particular, the question that an intra-EU investor–State ICSID arbitration is also incompatible with EU law on the basis of Article 26(2)(c), (3)(a) and (4)(a) ECT has been resolved (see CJEU, RIW 2022, 219 [juris paras. 137 to 145]—European Food; BeckRS 2022, 26460 paras. 33 to 43—Romatsa; see also Steinbrück/Krahé, IPRax 2023, 36, 41; different opinion in Wackernagel, EuZW 2022, 574, 576).

113. There is also no doubt that the principle of the effectiveness of EU law, which has been sufficiently clarified in the case law of the Court of Justice of the European Union, as well as the obligation of the Member States under Article 19(1), second subparagraph TEU require a review of the admissibility of intra-EU investor–State arbitration proceedings on the basis of the Energy Charter Treaty to be carried out as early as possible. The related question of whether the Respondent State in a dispute may have the inadmissibility of the ICSID arbitration proceedings determined in the special German proceedings under section 1032(2) German Code of Civil Procedure before the arbitral tribunal is constituted, on the other hand, concerns national procedural law and is not subject to interpretation by the Court of Justice.

114. 2. There are no grounds for a request for a preliminary ruling to the Court of Justice of the European Union on the basis that the Senate thought that the conditions for an ultra vires act had been satisfied (on the necessity of a referral in such a case, see German Constitutional Court, NJW 2023, 425 [juris para. 139]; E. Klein in Benda/Klein, *Verfassungsprozessrecht*, 4th ed., para. 95; O. Klein, DVBl. 2023, p. 779, 780). The Court of Justice of the European Union did not act ultra vires when deciding on the invalidity of arbitration agreements in bilateral and multilateral investment protection treaties.

115. a. In any event, an ultra vires review can only be considered if a violation of competence by the European institutions is sufficiently qualified (see BVerfGE 126, 286 [juris, para. 61]; 154, 17 [juris, para. 110], with further references). The jurisdictional mandate of the Court of Justice of the European Union, which is linked to the allocation of functions under Article 19(1) sentence 2 TEU, ends

where an interpretation of the Treaties is no longer verifiable and therefore objectively arbitrary (BVerfGE 154, 17 [juris, para. 112]; on the present constellation, see Steinbrück/Krahé, EuZW 2022, 357, 360 et seq.). In the allocation of competences, the principle of proportionality must be taken into account as a corrective to protect the competences of the Member States (see in this regard BVerfGE 154, 17 [juris paras. 119, 123]).

116. b. The Senate already rejected an ultra vires act of the Court of Justice of the European Union in the "Achmea" case (see Federal Court of Justice, SchiedsVZ 2019, 46 [juris paras. 60 to 71]). The decisions of the Court of Justice following the "Achmea" decision were not based on an objectively arbitrary interpretation of the Treaties, either.

117. aa. The allegation that the Court of Justice of the European Union, in its decision in the "Komstroy" case, ruled on a legal dispute that was completely external to the EU and declared an international agreement that was binding on the Member States and the EU— namely the Energy Charter Treaty—to be "inapplicable", although its competences pursuant to Article 267(1) TFEU are limited to the "validity" and the "interpretation" of EU law (opinion in Karpenstein/Sangi, NJW 2021, 3228 para. 7), fails.

118. The Court of Justice of the European Union was duly seized in the proceedings by the Cour d'Appel de Paris with a request for a preliminary ruling pursuant to Article 267 TFEU regarding the Energy Charter Treaty. The statement made in an obiter dictum on the non-applicability of Article 26(2)(c) ECT in an intra-EU context can also not be seen as exceeding its competences (see CJEU, SchiedsVZ 2022, 34 [juris paras. 64 to 66]—Komstroy). The Court of Justice of the European Union has the authority to interpret international agreements concluded by the EU (see CJEU, Judgment of 27 February 2018—C-266/16, juris paras. 45 et seq.—Western Sahara Campaign UK, with further references). It has limited itself to interpret Article 26 ECT solely in the intra-EU context and has not ruled on unlimited inapplicability or amended or repealed provisions of the agreement contrary to the mechanism provided for in Articles 34, 36 ECT.

119. bb. The objection that under Article 267 TFEU the Court of Justice of the European Union was not competent to make the statements made only as obiter dictum due to the lack of a request for a preliminary ruling is also unsuccessful (see in this regard Wilske/Markert/Ebert, SchiedsVZ 2022, 111, 128 et seq.; critical opinion in Schwalb/Weiler, SchiedsVZ 2022, 38 et seq.; for the ultra vires act, Lavranos/Lath/Varma, SchiedsVZ 2023, 38, 42 et seq.). In accordance with the questions referred for a preliminary ruling, the operative part

of the decision in the "Komstroy" case only covers the interpretation of the term "investment" in Article 1 number 6 and Article 26(1) TFEU; the binding effect only extends to this interpretation (see Wegener in Calliess/Ruffert, loc. cit., Article 267 TFEU, para. 50). Thus, the Court of Justice of the European Union was not prevented from making further statements in an obiter dictum.

120. Moreover, the Court of Justice of the European Union subsequently referred repeatedly to its statements in the "Komstroy" decision and thus confirmed them irrespective of the specific facts of the "Komstroy" case. In particular, in its Opinion 1/20 on Article 26 ECT, it referred in general terms to the decision in the "Komstroy" case, irrespective of any specific arbitration rules (Opinion of 16 June 2022—C-1/20, juris para. 47 with para. 20—Modernised Energy Charter Treaty).

121. cc. Neither did the Court of Justice of the European Union disregard Article 351(1) TFEU and the legal rationale expressed therein that the Member States and not the Court of Justice must remedy incompatibilities between international agreements and EU law. The Court of Justice has understandably rejected an application of Article 351(1) TFEU by analogy in view of the fact that the exception must be narrowly interpreted (see CJEU, NJW 2023, 349, paras. 115 to 127—PPU; above paras. 83 to 86).

122. dd. The decisions of the Court of Justice of the European Union also do not violate general rules of international law (Article 25 German Constitution) or the Vienna Convention on the Law of Treaties of 23 May 1969 (Federal Law Gazette II 1985 p. 926; hereinafter "Vienna Convention"), in particular Article 27 Vienna Convention. According to this provision, a contracting party cannot invoke its domestic law to justify non-performance of a treaty.

123. According to Article 3(b) Vienna Convention, the provisions of the Vienna Convention, which are an expression of general customary international law, are also applicable to non-parties—such as the European Union (see CJEU, Judgment of 25 February 2010—C-386/08 [2010] 1-1289 = EuZW 2010, 264 [juris paras. 40 bis 42]—Brita, with further references; Judgment of 27 February 2018—C-266/16, juris para. 58—Western Sahara Campaign UK; Judgment of 20 October 2022—C-111/21, NJW 2022, 3701 [juris para. 22]—Laudamotion). Articles 26 et seq. Vienna Convention are also part of customary international law. However, by acceding to the EU, the Member States have limited their power of disposition under international law and have, among themselves, waived the exercise of rights under international treaties that conflict with EU law. Accordingly,

customary international law conflicting with EU law cannot exist between Member States (see Federal Court of Justice, Order of 24 January 2019—I ZB 2/15, juris para. 7; see also Federal Court of Justice, SchiedsVZ 2019, 46 [juris paras. 40 et seq.], with further references; Cour d'Appel de Paris, Judgment of 19 April 2022—No 48/2022, RG-NR 20/13085 para. 90) and the citizens of the participating member states cannot rely on older obligations of the member states under international law that are in conflict with EU law (see Federal Court of Justice, SchiedsVZ 2019, 46 [juris para. 41]).

124. ee. An accusation of arbitrariness cannot be based on the fact that the Court treats investment arbitration differently from commercial arbitration, which is commonly permissible under EU law. This unequal treatment is objectively justified because the obligation of the host state to engage in investment arbitration is based on its standing offer resulting from its prior consent to other contracting states in an international treaty and not—as in commercial arbitration—on the exercise of party autonomy in the individual case vis-à-vis the respective investor (see CJEU, SchiedsVZ 2018, 186 [juris para. 55]—Achmea; SchiedsVZ 2022, 34 [juris para. 59]—Komstroy).

125. This is not contradicted by the decision in the "PL Holdings" case. The ad hoc arbitration agreement challenged there was in fact aimed at circumventing the obligations arising for the Member State from Article 4(3) TEU and Articles 267, 344 TFEU as interpreted in the "Achmea" decision (see CJEU, EuZW 2021, 1097 [juris paras. 47, 56]—PL Holdings).

126. ff. Insofar as it is alleged that there was an encroachment on concluded matters without transitional rules, this is the recognised consequence of the ex tunc interpretation of EU law by the Court of Justice of the European Union (see CJEU, EuZW 2021, 1097 [juris paras. 58 to 61]—PL Holdings, with further references; see also BVerfGE 126, 286 [juris paras. 83], with further references).

127. gg. The objection that the decisions on investment arbitration lack a proportionality test also fails to substantiate the allegation that there was an ultra vires act.

128. (1) The objection does not concern the principle of proportionality as a corrective to protect the Member States' competences, which must also be observed in the allocation of competences of the EU pursuant to Article 5(1) sentence 2 and (4) TEU (BVerfGE 154, 17 [juris, paras. 119, 123]). The decisions of the Court of Justice on intra-EU investment arbitration proceedings concern the delimitation of the competences of ordinary courts on the one hand, and arbitral tribunals on the other, in their interpretation and application of EU law.

129. (2) Irrespective of this, there is no indication that the decisions of the Court of Justice of the European Union, in reviewing acts of the institutions of the EU, do not satisfy the principle of proportionality, which is recognised as an unwritten element of EU law (in this regard, BVerfGE 154, 17 [juris, paras. 124 to 126], with further references), in order to achieve the legitimate objective of ensuring the coherence, full validity and autonomy of EU law.

130. (a) In particular, the fact that the interpretation of the Energy Charter Treaty is only binding on the Member States, and thus on some of the contracting parties, does not stand in the way of its appropriateness. The binding interpretation by the Court of Justice of the European Union can and must refer solely to the context within the EU (see Article 19(1), first subparagraph, sentence 2, (3) TEU). In this area, however, its interpretation is binding on all and in this way can achieve its objective of ensuring the coherence and uniformity of EU law (see in this regard CJEU, EuGRZ 2019, 191 [juris para. 111]— CETA Agreement EU–Canada).

131. (b) As far as the finding of the Court of Justice of the European Union is concerned that arbitral tribunals are not to be classified as courts within the meaning of Article 267 TFEU (see CJEU, SchiedsVZ 2018, 186 [juris paras. 37, 43, 46] Achmea), this does not result in a lack of necessity because gaps can also occur in the submissions of questions for interpretation by the ordinary courts. In this respect, there are possibilities for redress in individual cases. Under EU law, an infringement procedure under Articles 258 et seq. TFEU may be considered (see CJEU, Judgment of 4 October 2018—C-416/17, EuZW 2018, 1038 [juris operative part 2 and paras. 105 to 114]— *Commission* v. *France*; Wegener in Calliess/Ruffert loc. cit. 35 et seq., with further references) and, domestically, a constitutional court review based on Article 101(1) sentence 2 German Constitution (see BVerfG, EuGRZ 2022, 350 [juris paras. 41 to 47], with further references; Wegener in Calliess/Ruffert loc. cit. Article 267 TFEU para. 36, with further references). However, it would not be possible to have a comparable review in the case of arbitral tribunals entitled to file requests for a preliminary ruling.

132. (c) The decisions of the Court of Justice are also not inappropriate because of colliding economic and foreign policy concerns. Article 26(2)(a) ECT expressly provides for the possibility of recourse to domestic courts. The Senate has already explained that the investors are not denied effective legal protection (Article 2(1) in conjunction with Article 20(3) German Constitution; Article 47 EU Charter of Fundamental Rights) (see Federal Court of Justice, SchiedsVZ 2019,

46 [juris, para. 72]), but rather, with a view to the principle of mutual trust, are granted effective legal protection before the courts of the Member States (see CJEU, EuZW 2021, 1097 [juris para. 68]—PL Holdings; Cour d'Appel de Paris, Judgment of 19 April 2022—No 48/2022, RG-NR 20/13085 paras. 92 to 95; see also Federal Court of Justice, IWRZ 2022, 129 [juris para. 41]; Langenfeld, EuR 2022, 399, 404; van der Beck loc. cit. p. 370, 373, with further references). On the international level, there is also the possibility of appealing to the European Court of Human Rights (see Lavranos/Lath/Varma, SchiedsVZ 2023, 38, 46).

133. D. Accordingly, the appealed order must be set aside and, as requested, a declaration of inadmissibility must be given pursuant to section 1032(2) German Code of Civil Procedure. The Senate can itself decide on the merits of the case because the decision is set aside only as a result of a violation of the law when applying the law to the determined facts, and, thus, the case is ready for final adjudication (section 577(5) sentence 1 German Code of Civil Procedure).

134. The decision on costs is based on section 91(1) German Code of Civil Procedure.

135. E. The value of the subject matter of the appeal is set at €30 million.

136. The value of the subject matter of the appeal in proceedings pursuant to section 1032(2) German Code of Civil Procedure must be set at one fifth of the value of the main matter according to the established practice of the Senate (see Federal Court of Justice, SchiedsVZ 2020, 50 [juris, para. 26], with further references; NJOZ 2023, 497 [juris, para. 22]). Based on the value asserted in the request for arbitration in the amount of €(. . .) million, therefore, a sum of €(. . .) million would be set. Pursuant to section 39(2) German Court Cost Act, however, the maximum amount may not exceed €30 million, unless a lower maximum value is determined.

[Report: ECLI:DE:BGH:2023:270723BIZB43.22.0]

State immunity — Employment — Foreign Airforce Base — Employment on United States Airforce Base in United Kingdom — Claims for unlawful discrimination — Whether employees exercising sovereign or governmental functions — Test for determining sovereign or governmental functions in context of employment — Whether Employment Tribunal applying correct test — The law of England

WEBSTER *v.* UNITED STATES OF AMERICA

WRIGHT *v.* UNITED STATES OF AMERICA[1]

([2022] EAT 92)

England, Employment Appeal Tribunal. 24 *June* 2022

(Tayler, *Judge*)

SUMMARY:[2] *The facts*:—Mrs Webster and Miss Wright ("the appellants") were employed by the United States Airforce at bases located within the United Kingdom. Mrs Webster was employed managing military records and was dismissed in October 2017 after a period of absence due to ill health. Miss Wright was employed as a firefighter but was removed from firefighting duties after being diagnosed with epilepsy. The appellants initiated proceedings against their employer in the Employment Tribunal of England and Wales claiming, inter alia, that they were subjected to unlawful discrimination on the basis of sex, race, age or disability. The Employment Tribunal dismissed their claim agreeing with the United States of America ("the respondent State") that the doctrine of State immunity prevented the case from proceeding in English courts.

The appellants appealed the decision of the Employment Tribunal submitting that it had erred in its finding that their roles involved the exercise of public or governmental functions. They argued that the Employment Tribunal had been too focused on the general context of their employment and had failed to give proper consideration to whether they were actually engaged in the exercise of sovereign or governmental functions on behalf of the respondent State. The respondent State argued that the decision of the Employment Tribunal was correct and that the appeal should be dismissed.

---

[1] The appellants were represented by Mr Tristan Jones and Ms Celia Rooney, instructed by Advocate. The respondent State was represented by Professor Dan Sarooshi QC and Mr Andrew Legg, instructed by Lewis Silkin LLP.

[2] Prepared by Mr D. Peterson.

Held:—The appeal was dismissed.

(1) Whether State immunity applied in respect of employment depended on whether the relationship between the Parties had arisen from the State's sovereign act of employing an individual to carry out functions that were sovereign or governmental (para. 19).

(2) Some roles inherently involved sovereign or governmental functions, while others inevitably did not. For other roles, the question of whether they involved sovereign or governmental functions depended on an analysis of the actual functions undertaken by the relevant individual and whether these were sufficiently close to sovereign or governmental functions (para. 21).

(3) The respondent State accepted that to determine whether the functions of an employee were sovereign or governmental it was necessary to consider what the employee actually did, rather than what the employee could be required to do under their contract of employment or how their role was described in their job description or title. It was also accepted that the functions of an employee were not to be assumed because of the entity for whom, or the location at which, their work was performed (para. 22).

(4) The Employment Tribunal had applied the correct test to determine whether State immunity applied. The employment judge understood that the underlying test to determine whether an act was sovereign in the context of employment depended on the nature of the relationship between the Parties, which in turn depended on the functions which the employee was employed to perform. The employment judge had also appreciated that they had to consider the specifics of the roles undertaken by each claimant and could have reached different conclusions in respect of their different roles (paras. 41-2).

The following is the text of the judgment of the Employment Appeal Tribunal:

1. This appeal concerns the circumstances in which the doctrine of state immunity may prevent former civilian employees of the United States of America, who worked for the United States Airforce Europe (USAFE), in the United Kingdom, from bringing claims in the employment tribunal.

2. Anthea Webster commenced work at RAF Lakenheath (a base that is operated entirely by USAFE). She worked managing USAFE military records. Mrs Webster was dismissed on 10 October 2017 after a period of ill health absence. Mrs Webster describes herself as black and of Afro-Caribbean heritage. Mrs Webster contends that she is disabled by reason of Complex Regional Pain Syndrome. On 5 September 2017, before her dismissal, Mrs Webster presented a

claim to the employment tribunal asserting that she had been subjected to unlawful sex, race, age and disability discrimination, that she had suffered an unauthorised deduction from wages and, possibly, that she had been subject to protected disclosure detriment. Following her dismissal, Mrs Webster presented a second claim on 10 November 2017 claiming unfair dismissal, age, sex, race and disability discrimination. A component of Mrs Webster's claim is that she was, or should have been, carrying out the role of Base Records Manager ("BRM"). The respondent contended that the BRM Role at RAF Lakenheath was designated for military personal only.

3. On 19 May 2013 Caroline Wright began working as a firefighter at RAF Croughton (another base that is operated entirely by USAFE). RAF Croughton is an intelligence and communications centre from which flying operations are not conducted. On occasions Miss Wright worked at RAF Fairford where flying operations take place. Miss Wright was diagnosed with epilepsy in early 2017. Thereafter she was taken off firefighting duties because the US National Fire Protection Association ("NFPA") guideline set out periods for which firefighters with conditions such as epilepsy must not have had a seizure before being permitted to return to firefighting duties.

The preliminary hearing

4. The state immunity issue was considered at a preliminary hearing on 7, 8, 9 and 10 October 2019 and in chambers on 11 October 2019. Employment Judge Foxwell held that state immunity applied and dismissed the claims.

The appeal

5. The claimants appealed asserting two grounds of appeal. The first ground of appeal was permitted to proceed, in terms that are the same for both claimants:

The Employment Tribunal erred in deciding that the Claimant's role involved her in the public or governmental functions of the United States of America such as to engage the State Immunity doctrine.

6. The Notices of Appeal included under the heading "Further Information" in respect of the first ground:

Further, insofar as the ET at [115] placed weight on the prospect that the Claimant's claim may involve a judicial investigation into the policies and objectives of the United States, it was wrong to do so. The claim does not involve any challenge to such policies sufficient to engage the State Immunity doctrine; alternatively, the Tribunal should have permitted those parts of the claim which do not involve such a challenge to proceed.

7. Tristan Jones and Celia Rooney, who represent the claimants in their appeals, through the auspices of Advocate, assert at paragraph 5 of their skeleton argument:

5. The Appellants contend that the Employment Judge misapplied the doctrine of sovereign state immunity in two material respects.

5.1. First, the Judge focused too heavily on the general context of the Appellants' employment, which in each case was at a military base, and failed to give proper consideration to whether each of the Appellants was *personally engaged* in the exercise of the public or governmental functions of the Respondent state. Neither of the Appellants was, in fact, so engaged.

5.2. Second, the Judge wrongly concluded that the claims would involve "judicial investigation" into the Respondent's policies and objectives sufficient to engage the doctrine of state immunity. In fact, no such investigation is or would have been required; alternatively, insofar as it is, the correct approach was for the ET to permit those parts of the claim which did not involve any such investigation to proceed.

8. Professor Sarooshi QC and Andrew Legg, who represented the Respondent in the appeal, as they did in the employment tribunal (where the claimants represented themselves), assert that the second matter raised in the claimants' skeleton argument does not form a part of the ground of appeal that has been permitted to proceed. While the point is referred to in the "additional information", it does not form part of the first ground of appeal, but raises a separate point of law.

9. The second ground of appeal, asserting that the application of the state immunity doctrine in these cases was "contrary to Article 47 of the EU Charter of Fundamental Rights" was not permitted to proceed.

The Law

10. State immunity is part of the common law and of customary international law. As a matter of common law the doctrine historically was absolute, unless the state chose to waive the immunity. The position changed as a result of the judgment of the House of Lords in *I Congreso del Partido* [1983] 1 AC 244 which introduced into the

common law the "restrictive theory" of state immunity. Lord Wilberforce held, at 262 C-G:

It is necessary to start from first principle. The basis upon which one state is considered to be immune from the territorial jurisdiction of the courts of another state is that of "par in parem" which effectively means that the *sovereign or governmental acts of one state are not matters upon which the courts of other states will adjudicate.*

The relevant exception, or limitation, which has been engrafted upon the principle of immunity of states, under *the so called "restrictive theory," arises from the willingness of states to enter into commercial, or other private law, transactions with individuals.* It appears to have two main foundations: *(a) It is necessary in the interest of justice to individuals having such transactions with states to allow them to bring such transactions before the courts. (b) To require a state to answer a claim based upon such transactions does not involve a challenge to or inquiry into any act of sovereignty or governmental act of that state.* It is, in accepted phrases, neither a threat to the dignity of that state, nor any interference with its sovereign functions.

When therefore a claim is brought against a state ... and state immunity is claimed, it is necessary to consider what is the relevant act which forms the basis of the claim: is this, under the old terminology, an act "jure gestionis" or is it an act "jure imperii": *is it* (to adopt the translation of these catchwords used in the "Tate letter") *a "private act" or is it a "sovereign or public act,"* a private act meaning in this context an act of a private law character such as a private citizen might have entered into? It is upon this point that the arguments in these appeals is focussed. [*emphasis added*]

11. There was a degree of codification in the State Immunity Act 1978. The 1978 Act is not applicable in this case because section 16(2) excludes "anything done by or in relation to the armed forces of a State while present in the United Kingdom".

12. The common law doctrine of state immunity was considered in *Holland* v. *Lampen-Wolfe* [2000] 1 WLR 1573, in which Lord Clyde held at 1579 F to G:

In relation to the common law as it has now developed the distinction has to be made between claims arising out of *acts done in the exercise of a state's sovereign authority and claims not so arising,* that is *typically claims arising out of commercial transactions such as might be undertaken by private individuals.* Expressed in the traditional Latin labels, which are convenient as words of reference but do not assist significantly in the application of the distinction, the distinction is between matters jure imperii and matters jure gestionis. *The "restrictive" theory* which through the decisions in *The Philippine Admiral* [1977] AC 373 and *I Congreso del Partido* [1983] 1 AC 244 *has been adopted into the laws of the United Kingdom* calls for this distinction to be made, but it is one which in some cases may be subtle and delicate to define ... [*emphasis added*]

13. He went on to state at 1580 E to G

The solution in any particular case where the question of state immunity arises at common law has to be one of the *analysis of the particular facts against the whole context in which they have occurred. There is little if anything to be gained by trying to fit the case into a particular precedent or to devise categories of situations which may or may not fall on the one side of the line or the other. It is the nature and character of the activity on which the claim is based which has to be studied, rather than the motive or purpose of it. The solution will turn upon an assessment of the particular facts.* The line between sovereign and non-sovereign state activities may sometimes be clear, but in other cases may well be difficult to draw. [*emphasis added*]

14. Lord Millett described state immunity as a "subject-matter" immunity, at 1583 D:

The doctrine of state immunity

It is an established rule of customary international law that one state cannot be sued in the courts of another for acts performed jure imperii. The immunity does not derive from the authority or dignity of sovereign states or the need to protect the integrity of their governmental functions. It derives from the sovereign nature of the exercise of the state's adjudicative powers and the basic principle of international law that all states are equal. The rule is "par in parem non habet imperium:" see *I Congreso del Partido* [1983] 1 AC 244, 262, per Lord Wilberforce. As I explained in *Reg. v. Bow Street Metropolitan Stipendiary Magistrate, Ex parte Pinochet Ugarte (No 3)* [2000] 1 AC 147, 269, it is *a subject-matter immunity. It operates to prevent the official and governmental acts of one state from being called into question in proceedings before the courts of another.* [*emphasis added*]

15. The application of state immunity to employment was considered by the Supreme Court in *Benkharbouche v. Embassy of the Republic of Sudan*, [2017] UKSC 62, [2019] AC 777. Lord Sumption held that the underlying test is that established in *I Congreso del Partido*:

Application to contracts of employment

53. As a matter of customary international law, *if an employment claim arises out of an inherently sovereign or governmental act of the foreign state, the latter is immune.* It is not always easy to determine which aspects of the facts giving rise to the claim are decisive of its correct categorisation, and the courts have understandably avoided over-precise prescription. The most satisfactory general statement is that of Lord Wilberforce in *The I Congreso del Partido*, at p 267 ... [*emphasis added*]

16. Lord Sumption described the nature of state immunity:

17. State immunity is a mandatory rule of customary international law which defines the limits of a domestic court's jurisdiction. Unlike diplomatic immunity, which the modern law treats as serving an essentially functional purpose, state immunity does not derive from the need to protect the integrity of a foreign state's governmental functions or the proper conduct of inter-state relations. It derives from the sovereign equality of states. Par in parem non habet imperium. In the modern law the immunity does not extend to acts of a private law character. In respect of these, the state is subject to the territorial jurisdiction of the forum in the same way as any non-state party.

17. The case concerned domestic workers in diplomatic missions to whom state immunity applied by virtue of the State Immunity Act 1978. The Supreme Court held that the relevant provisions of the State Immunity Act 1978 were incompatible with article 47 of the Charter of Fundamental Rights of the European Union and with article 6 of the Convention for the Protection of Human Rights and Fundamental Freedoms, because there was no basis in customary international law for the application of state immunity in an employment context to acts of a private law character such as the employment of purely domestic staff in a diplomatic mission.

18. Lord Sumption considered how to assess whether the employment of a person is subject to state immunity:

54. In the great majority of cases arising from contract, including employment cases, *the categorisation will depend on the nature of the relationship between the parties to which the contract gives rise.* This will *in turn depend on the functions which the employee is employed to perform.*

55. The *Vienna Convention on Diplomatic Relations divides the staff of a diplomatic mission into three broad categories: (i) diplomatic agents, ie the head of mission and the diplomatic staff; (ii) administrative and technical staff; and (iii) staff in the domestic service of the mission.* Diplomatic agents participate in the functions of a diplomatic mission defined in article 3, principally representing the sending state, protecting the interests of the sending state and its nationals, negotiating with the government of the receiving state, ascertaining and reporting on developments in the receiving state and promoting friendly relations with the receiving state. These functions are inherently governmental. They are exercises of sovereign authority. Every aspect of the employment of a diplomatic agent is therefore likely to be an exercise of sovereign authority. *The role of technical and administrative staff is by comparison essentially ancillary and supportive. It may well be that the employment of some of them might also be exercises of sovereign authority if their functions are sufficiently close to the governmental functions of the mission. Cypher clerks might arguably be an example. Certain confidential secretarial staff might be another:* see *Governor of Pitcairn* v. *Sutton* [1995] 1 NZLR 426 (New Zealand Court of Appeal).

However, *I find it difficult to conceive of cases where the employment of purely domestic staff of a diplomatic mission could be anything other than an act jure gestionis. The employment of such staff is not inherently governmental. It is an act of a private law character such as anyone with the necessary resources might do.* [*emphasis added*]

19. Thus, the test for state immunity in respect of the employment of a person depends on whether the relationship between the parties arises from the state's sovereign act in employing the individual, because the functions carried out by the person are sovereign or governmental. In such cases the employment of the individual is inherently sovereign and so covered by state immunity.

20. Lord Sumption held that this was consistent with the approach of the European Court of Human Rights:

56. This approach is supported by the case law of the European Court of Human Rights, which I have already summarised. In *Cudak* v. *Lithuania* 51 EHRR 15, *Sabeh El Leil* v. *France* 54 EHRR 14, *Wallishauser* v. *Austria* CE:ECHR:2012:0717JUD000015604 and *Radunovic* v. *Montenegro* 66 EHRR 19, all cases concerning the administrative and technical staff of diplomatic missions, *the test applied by the Strasbourg court was whether the functions for which the applicant was employed called for a personal involvement in the diplomatic or political operations of the mission, or only in such activities as might be carried on by private persons.* In *Mahamdia* v. *People's Democratic Republic of Algeria* (Case C-154/11) [2013] ICR 1, paras. 55-7 the Court of Justice of the European Union applied the same test, holding that the state is not immune "where *the functions carried out by the employee do not fall within the exercise of public powers*". *The United States decisions are particularly instructive*, because the Foreign State Immunity Act of the United States has no special provisions for contracts of employment. They therefore fall to be dealt with under the general provisions relating to commercial transactions, which have been interpreted as confining state immunity to exercises of sovereign authority: see *Saudi Arabia* v. *Nelson* (1993) 507 US 349, 360. The principle now applied in all circuits that have addressed the question is that *a state is immune as regards proceedings relating to a contract of employment only if the act of employing the plaintiff is to be regarded as an exercise of sovereign authority having regard to his or her participation in the diplomatic functions of the mission*: see *Segni* v. *Commercial Office of Spain* (1987) 835 F 2d 160, 165 and *Holden* v. *Canadian Consulate* (1996) 92 F 3d 918. *Although a foreign state may in practice be more likely to employ its nationals in those functions, nationality is in itself irrelevant to the characterisation*: see *El-Hadad* v. *United Arab Emirates* (2000) 216 F 3d 29, 31-2, paras. 4, 5. In *Park* v. *Shin* (2002) 313 F 3d 1138, 1145, paras. 12-14, it was held that "the act of hiring a domestic servant is not an inherently public act that only a government could perform", even if her functions include serving at diplomatic entertainments. A very similar principle has been consistently applied in recent decisions of the

French Cour de Cassation: see *Barrandon* v. *United States of America* (1998) 116 ILR 622; *Coco* v. *State of Argentina* (1996) 113 ILR 491 and *Saigniev Embassy of Japan* (1997) 113 ILR 492. In the last-named case, at p 493, the court observed that the employee, a caretaker at the premises of the mission, had not had "any special responsibility for the performance of the public service of the embassy". [*emphasis added*]

21. Although the examples given by Lord Sumption were specific to employment in diplomatic missions, the analysis that there will be some roles that inherently involve sovereign or governmental functions, some that inevitably do not (such as domestic workers) and others which may or may not, depending on an analysis of whether the functions that are actually undertaken by the individual are sufficiently close to governmental functions, can assist in other circumstances.

22. Professor Sarooshi, for the respondent, accepted that the authorities establish that:

22.1. in considering whether the functions of an employee are sovereign or governmental it is necessary to consider what the employee actually does, rather than what the employee could be required to do under a contract of employment, or how they are described in their job title or description

22.2. the functions of the employee are not to be assumed because of the entity for whom, or the location at which, the work is performed.

23. In *Benkharbouche*, the fact that domestic staff were employed at diplomatic missions did not mean that they were engaged in sovereign or governmental functions. The opposite was the case because the domestic duties of the employees were incapable of being sovereign or governmental functions.

24. In a somewhat historical case, *Sengupta* v. *Republic of India* [1983] ICR 221, the application of state immunity was considered in the case of a person who was employed in a role described as a "low clerical grade where he enjoyed very limited diplomatic privileges". Browne-Wilkinson J set out what he considered to be the components of the overall test, at 228 D to E:

In our judgment, in seeking to decide whether the claim in this case is excluded by the doctrine of sovereign immunity, we must ask the following questions: (a) Was the contract of a kind which a private individual could enter into? (b) Did the performance of the contract involve the participation of both parties in the public functions of the foreign state, or was it purely collateral to such functions? (c) What was the nature of the breach of contract or other act of the sovereign state giving rise to the proceedings? (d) Will the investigation of the claim by the tribunal involve an investigation into the public or sovereign acts of the foreign state?

25. I do not consider that point b involves a test that significantly differs to the test in *Benkharbouche* for determining whether a person is employed in a role in which their actual functions are sovereign or governmental.

26. However, in applying point b, the Employment Appeal Tribunal analysed the employment of the claimant as necessarily involving sovereign function because he worked at a diplomatic mission:

If we have asked ourselves the right questions, then in our judgment the necessary result must be that there is no jurisdiction to entertain the applicant's claim. It is true that any private individual can employ another, i.e. can enter into a contract of employment. Therefore in that sense the entry into a contract of employment is a private act. But when one looks to see what is involved in the performance of the applicant's contract, it is clear that the performance of the contract is part of the discharge by the foreign state of its sovereign functions in which the applicant himself, at however lowly a level, is under the terms of his contract of employment necessarily engaged. One of the classic forms of sovereign acts by a foreign state is the representation of that state in a receiving state. From the doctrine of sovereign immunity were derived the concepts that the embassy premises were part of the soil of the foreign sovereign state, and that diplomatic staff are personally immune from local jurisdiction. *A contract to work at a diplomatic mission in the work of that mission is a contract to participate in the public acts of the foreign sovereign.* The dismissal of the applicant was an act done in pursuance of that public function, i.e. the running of the mission. As a consequence, the fairness of any dismissal from such employment is very likely to involve an investigation by the industrial tribunal into the internal management of the diplomatic representation in the United Kingdom of the Republic of India, an investigation wholly inconsistent with the dignity of the foreign state and an interference with its sovereign functions. [*emphasis added*]

27. Professor Sarooshi accepted that the analysis that work *at* a diplomatic mission *necessarily* involves participation in public acts of a foreign sovereign, cannot stand, because it is inconsistent with the reasoning of the Supreme Court in *Benkharbouche*, and was expressly disapproved.

28. Matters other than the nature of the functional role that a person is engaged to perform may result in state immunity applying. Take the example of a member of domestic staff at a diplomatic mission. The employment itself will not be subject to state immunity. But, if the domestic worker is dismissed because of accessing state secrets, the dismissal may be subject to state immunity because it is the exercise of a sovereign power and investigating it would involve

consideration of the state's arrangement for security at their diplomatic missions. This alternative basis for state immunity was considered by Lord Sumption in *Benkharbouche*:

57. I would, however, wish to guard against the suggestion that the character of the employment is always and necessarily decisive. Two points should be made, albeit briefly since neither is critical to this appeal.
58. The first is that a state's immunity under the restrictive doctrine may extend to some aspects of its treatment of its employees or potential employees which engage the state's sovereign interests, even if the contract of employment itself was not entered into in the exercise of sovereign authority. Examples include claims arising out of an employee's dismissal for reasons of state security. They may also include claims arising out of a state's recruitment policy for civil servants or diplomatic or military employees, or claims for specific reinstatement after a dismissal, which in the nature of things impinge on the state's recruitment policy.

29. Mr Jones, for the claimants, accepted that the question of whether the employment of staff is a sovereign act because the person undertakes sovereign or governmental duties is separate to the question of whether the termination of such an engagement, or investigations undertaken by the state into the actions of the person, are protected by state immunity.

The facts found and analysis of the employment tribunal

30. The employment tribunal made findings of fact and carried out its analysis for each claimant clearly and concisely, but in a manner that requires that the relevant sections of the judgment be read together.

Mrs Webster

31. The employment tribunal made key findings of fact under the heading "Mrs Webster's role at RAF Lakenheath":

31.1.   Mrs Webster responded to an advertisement for an "Office Automation Assistant" [43].

31.2.   Mrs Webster was initially given the task of sorting historical records going back many years. She showed great aptitude and soon took on further responsibilities for records management [44].

31.3.   The United States Code ("USC") sets out rules for the maintenance, disposal and archiving of state records that are given effect to in the Department of Defence ("DoD") through its

Records Management Program contained in DoD Instruction 5015.02 [46]. These rules applied to the work Mrs Webster undertook. The instruction provided:

> Effective and efficient management of records provides the information foundation for decision making at all levels, mission planning and operations, personnel and veteran services, legal inquiries, business continuity, and preservation of US history.

31.4.   USAF implemented the DoD's Records Management Program through Air Force Instruction ("AFI") 33-322. Mrs Webster knew and understood the terms of the Instruction and provided training on records management, based on it, to service and civilian personnel [47].

31.5.   Records Custodians ("RCs") are given the primary task of compiling records. This was an additional and often unpopular duty for service personnel [48]. RCs were overseen by Functional Area Records Managers ("FARMs") [49]. Mrs Webster was responsible for training RCs and FARMs and overseeing their compliance with relevant standards [50].

31.6.   Mrs Webster was permitted to use base vehicles to attend units to carry out inspections of their record keeping practices [51].

31.7.   Mrs Webster could theoretically access confidential or sensitive information, but in practice this would have been difficult because she was usually in sight of others and there would have been insufficient time to read or look at individual documents. More importantly, Mrs Webster is a person of integrity who would not do such a thing [52].

31.8.   Mrs Webster trained herself on the Air Force Records Information Management System ("AFRIMS") and then trained other people on how to use it correctly and effectively [53].

31.9.   Mrs Webster oversaw basic records management training which was delivered through an online course to all military personnel joining the base [53].

31.10. A further aspect of Mrs Webster's work concerned the destruction or archiving of records. Documents had to be checked and boxed correctly and then were sent to National Archives and Records Administration (NARA) in Washington DC or the Pentagon depending on their classification [54].

31.11. Mrs Webster dealt with Freedom of Information Act and Privacy Act requests made by US citizens under US law [55].

31.12. Appraisals for the financial year beginning April 2012 showed Mrs Webster's job title as "Knowledge Operation Manager".

Her performance was rated outstanding in every year apart from the first when it was rated "very good" [56]. The job title "Knowledge Operations Manager" was repeated in service awards given to Mrs Webster. Personnel records continued to refer to her as an "Office Automation Assistant" until October 2016, when her title was changed to "Assistant Base Records Manager" [57].

31.13. The organisational chart demonstrated that Mrs Webster's role fell under a line of command culminating in the Communications Squadron Leader and involving other military personnel [58].

32. The employment judge set out his analysis under the heading "Did Mrs Webster's role involve her in the public or governmental functions of the United States of America?", concluding:

32.1. Mrs Webster's role involved the maintenance, preservation and where appropriate, destruction of US military records [112].

32.2. The employment judge stated "In my judgment, military record keeping is a function of the state, the importance of which is illustrated in this case by the provisions of the USC, the DoD Instruction and the AFI Instruction concerning record-keeping described above. Additionally, such records may be classified because they contain state secrets" and "Further evidence that records management is a governmental activity of the United States is the fact that records are archived nationally in Washington DC or at the Pentagon" [113].

32.3. "The provision of training on record keeping and inspection to ensure compliance with record keeping procedures, is also, in my judgment, an extension of the same state function" [114].

32.4. "Litigation of claims of discrimination in the Employment Tribunal is likely to involve judicial consideration of the policies and objectives of the United States in its management of record keeping and of the staff who work within it. The United States might be called on to justify objectively treatment which might otherwise be unlawful under the Equality Act 2010 were it to apply. In my judgment this would amount to an investigation by a British tribunal into the sovereign acts of a foreign state" [115].

Miss Wright

33. The employment tribunal's key findings of fact were made under the heading "Miss Wright's role at RAF Croughton":

33.1. Miss Wright began working for USAFE as a firefighter in May 2013 as a local national direct hire Firefighter (Basic Life Support), Grade 7 [62].

33.2. "Miss Wright was based at RAF Croughton, an intelligence gathering centre with no flying operations. The FES at RAF Croughton was part of the Civil Engineering Squadron, which in turn was part of the Mission Support Group" [73].

33.3. Miss Wright sometimes did shifts at RAF Fairford (where operational flying takes place) and occasionally at RAF Welford [63].

33.4. The main purpose of Miss Wright's role was preservation of life and the protection of property. In addition, large airfields operating military flights have specific safety requirements for fire cover because of the possibility of dangerous payloads, damaged planes and, in extremis, an attack on the airfield itself [64].

33.5. DoD Instruction 6055-56 requires military branches to establish a Fire and Emergency Service ("FES") with the aim of protecting DoD personnel and the public, preventing or minimising injury and damage to property or the environment, assisting civil authorities under mutual aid agreements and enhancing "mission capability". Paragraph 4 of the Instruction describes mission capability as being enhanced by protecting US Bases through prevention, education and emergency response [64].

33.6. Paragraph 1 of the Air Force Emergency Management Program states its purpose is "the protection of the American people, their way of life and advancing their influence in the world". Paragraph 3 describes the policy as a means of "sustaining mission assurance, enhancing maintenance operations and restoring combat readiness" [67].

33.7. AFI 32-2001 describes the scope of the FES mission as fire protection and minimisation, dealing with the release of hazardous substances whether chemical, biological, radiological or nuclear and dealing with weapons of mass destruction. Aircraft rescue and firefighting were identified as operational tasks.

33.8. Miss Wright attended two courses at the Goodfellow Air Base in San Angelo, Texas during her time with USAFE [70]. In 2014 she undertook HAZMAT Commander and Weapons of Mass Destruction training [78].

33.9. Miss Wright completed training modules including "Airport Fire Fighter" and "Munitions Fire Fighter" [79].

33.10. All training was done using American equipment [79].

33.11. Miss Wright cascaded training on a new 911 system to her fellow firefighters [79].

33.12. Miss Wright did not have to attend a fire in the five years she worked at RAF Croughton. Nevertheless, firefighters had responsibility for fire prevention and inspections and she had access to many of the buildings on the base for these purposes [74].

33.13. Miss Wright had the necessary security clearance to do her job [77].

33.14. On the occasions Miss Wright was at RAF Fairford she was part of the firefighting cover for flying operations [75].

34. The employment judge set out his analysis under the heading "Did Miss Wright's role involve her in the public or governmental functions of the United States of America?", concluding:

34.1. "The requirement to maintain an independent FES is imposed by US Law, as is the standard which it is required to achieve. The objectives of this policy go beyond those of any domestic fire service: for example, the Air Force Emergency Program says that it is intended to protect the American people, their way of life and to advance their influence in the World. These are all policy objectives of the United States. The same Program refers to FES's contribution to combat readiness, another function of the state" [120].

34.2. "Those in the FES, including firefighters, are an integral part of the mission of the bases where they work: where there is flying, the planes could not fly safely without such emergency protection; in the case of RAF Croughton where confidential information is processed, the information could be lost or compromised without protection. The ability of the Respondent to provide a first response to emergencies, including fire, enables it to retain control over incidents which may involve classified or controversial information. It is notable that the United States has restricted the power to contract out FES (unlike the UK) and this demonstrates to me that the provision of an independent fire service is an integral part of US military policy" [121].

34.3. "Litigation of claims of discrimination and constructive dismissal in the Employment Tribunal would involve judicial consideration of the arrangements the United States makes to protect its military bases and it could be called on to justify objectively treatment which might otherwise be unlawful under the Equality Act 2010 were it to apply. This would constitute an investigation by a British tribunal of the sovereign acts of a foreign state and that is impermissible at common law under the principle of state immunity" [122].

The employment tribunal's direction as to the law

35. The employment judge noted that [88]:

State immunity, where it applies, means that the sovereign acts of a state cannot be adjudicated upon by the courts of another state, which must dismiss the claim without determining its merits. This principle does not affect any right a claimant may have to pursue the claim in the courts of the foreign sovereign state itself, in this case that would be the USA if the Respondent's case is correct.

36. The employment judge stated [87] of *Benkharbouche*:

The concept of state immunity in the context of employment law was considered by the Supreme Court recently in the case of *Benkharbouche* v. *Embassy of Sudan and Others* [2017] ICR 1327. While I consider the claim in *Benkharbouche* to be distinguishable from the instant cases for reasons I shall come to, the judgment of Lord Sumption nevertheless provides an invaluable insight into the relevant law.

37. The judgment is not particularly clear as to the basis upon which the employment judge considered *Benkharbouche* was distinguishable. I consider that on a fair reading of the judgment EJ Foxwell considered that *Benkharbouche* was "invaluable" as an insight into the relevant law, but was predominantly dealing with different factual circumstances, because [97]:

The case of *Benkharbouche* concerned the lawfulness or compatibility of this sub-section having regard to Article 47 of the Charter and Article 6 of the Convention respectively.

38. In considering the common law the employment judge referred extensively to *Holland*, noting that "the essential question is the nature of the act in issue: whether it is a governmental act ('jure imperii'), or a nongovernmental act ('jure gestionis')" [99].

39. EJ Foxwell was referred to *Sengupta*. The employment judge stated [101] that "a 'lowly clerk' in the Indian Embassy was nevertheless held to be participating in the public functions of a foreign state such that immunity applied". The claimants' core argument is that the employment judge misdirected himself as to the law by relying on *Sengupta* and concluded that the claimants were involved in "public or

governmental functions" merely, or predominantly, because they worked for USAFE.

40. As I explained when considering the relevant law above, the determination in *Sengupta* that the employment of the claimant necessarily involved sovereign function because he worked at a diplomatic mission is not good law, having been disapproved of in *Benkharbouche*. However, I do not consider that it was that element of *Sengupta* that the employment judge relied upon. If he had relied upon that reasoning he would have concluded that the mere fact that the claimants were engaged to work at USAF bases meant that they must have been engaged to carry out governmental or sovereign functions. That is clearly not the case because the employment judge considered the roles that the claimants carried out in detail. The employment judge relied on the four elements of state immunity that Browne-Wilkinson J referred to in *Sengupta*, which I do not consider involved any error of law.

41. On a fair reading of the judgment, I consider that it is clear that the employment judge understood that the underlying test is whether an act is private or sovereign/governmental and that in the context of employment this, as Lord Sumption held in *Benkharbouche*, "will depend on the nature of the relationship between the parties to which the contract gives rise", which in turn will "depend on the functions which the employee is employed to perform". I consider this is clear from the headings the employment judge used when setting out the key findings of fact that referred to the "role" of each claimant, and when he asked whether the "role" of the claimant "involve[d] her in the public or governmental functions of the United States of America". I consider it is clear that the employment judge appreciated that this involved considering the functions that they actually carried out, rather than just considering where, and for whom, they worked. This is made clear when the employment judge stated "I have reached the same conclusion in Miss Wright's case, albeit she performed a very different role from Mrs Webster" [119]. This demonstrates that the employment judge appreciated he had to consider the specifics of the roles undertaken by each claimant and could have reached different conclusions in respect of their different roles.

42. I reject the assertion that the employment judge applied an incorrect test to determine whether state immunity applied.

The analysis of the employment tribunal

43. The claimants contend that "the Judge focused too heavily on the general context of the Appellants' employment, which in each case

was at a military base, and failed to give proper consideration to whether each of the Appellants was personally engaged in the exercise of the public or governmental functions". While the analysis section of the judgment focused on the military nature of the roles that the claimants undertook, that has to be read in the context of the specific factual findings of the employment judge about the functions of the claimants. The ground of appeal is, in reality, one of perversity. In *Benkharbouche* Lord Sumption distinguished between three types of employees in diplomatic missions; those who have inherently governmental function at one end and those whose domestic duties are inevitably private. In the middle there are technical and administrative roles that may, or may not, be sovereign or governmental. Determining which side of the line an employee in the middle category falls is inherently a matter of factual assessment that is for the employment tribunal. The roles and functions undertaken by the claimants put them in this middle territory. I do not consider that the claimants are able to establish that the employment judge erred in his analysis of whether state immunity applied. He reached a factual determination that was open to him.

The employment judge's alternative analysis

44. The employment judge also considered that state immunity applied because the claims would involve "judicial investigation" into the respondent's policies and objectives. While the analysis was included in the same sections as where the employment judge considered whether the job functions of the claimants were such as to attract state immunity, it is a distinct point of law. It is not inherently a part of the ground of appeal that was permitted to proceed. It is not live in this appeal.

45. That said, were the ground properly before the Employment Appeal Tribunal, I consider that the employment tribunal's finding in this regard was a factual determination that was open to it. Furthermore, as the ground of appeal as asserted fails, the alternative ground would not have altered the outcome of the appeal.

The position of the claimants

46. It is hard not to feel sympathy for the claimants who were accepted by the respondent to have been exemplary employees, particularly because the employment tribunal found that they were led to believe that they would be subject to the protections of UK

employment law. Key to the determination that state immunity applies was the fact that the claimants were engaged in sovereign activity, the defence of the United States of America and its allies. It is for the United States of America to decide whether to rely on state immunity, the extent to which foreign nationals who work supporting the defence of the United States may litigate in the United States, and what alternative benefits, if any, are provided for foreign staff. Where state immunity applies it is because it is not the business of judges of one sovereign state to adjudicate on the actions of another sovereign state. The appeals are dismissed.

[Report: [2022] IRLR 836]

Arbitration — Arbitration award — International Centre for Settlement of Investment Disputes — International Convention on the Settlement of Investment Disputes between States and Nationals of Other States, 1965 ("ICSID Convention") — Article 54 — Meaning of prior written agreement — Arbitration (International Investment Disputes) Act 1966 — Recognition and enforcement of award — State Immunity Act 1978 — Section 9 — Exceptions to sovereign immunity — Enforcement of international arbitration award — Whether Spain having sovereign immunity for proceedings to enforce international arbitral awards — Whether Spain's accession to the ICSID Convention constituting a submission to jurisdiction of United Kingdom Courts

Relationship of international law and municipal law — Treaties — International Centre for Settlement of Investment Disputes — International Convention on the Settlement of Investment Disputes between States and Nationals of Other States, 1965 — Arbitration (International Investment Disputes) Act 1966 — State Immunity Act 1978 — Whether Spain entitled to plead foreign State immunity — Whether Spain could challenge arbitral award within United Kingdom courts — Jurisdiction of United Kingdom courts with respect to enforcement and recognition of international arbitral awards granted under ICSID Convention — Relationship between European Union law and international law

Treaties — Interpretation — International Centre for Settlement of Investment Disputes — International Convention on the Settlement of Investment Disputes between States and Nationals of Other States, 1965 — Articles 54 and 55 — Meaning of prior written agreement — Meaning of recognition and enforcement of arbitral award — Whether ICSID Convention excluding any claim for foreign State immunity in proceedings for recognition and enforcement of an arbitral award

State immunity — State Immunity Act 1978 — Exceptions to immunity — Exception based on prior written agreement by State — Exception to immunity in matters of enforcement of arbitral awards — International Centre for Settlement of Investment Disputes — International Convention on the Settlement of Investment Disputes between States and Nationals of Other States, 1965 — Relationship between ICSID Convention and enforcement and recognition of arbitral awards by domestic courts

Jurisdiction — Whether Spain could challenge arbitral award within United Kingdom courts — Jurisdiction of United Kingdom courts with respect to enforcement and recognition of international arbitral awards granted under international Convention on the Settlement of Investment Disputes between States and Nationals of Other States, 1965 — Role and powers of United Kingdom courts in recognizing and enforcing arbitral awards — The law of England

INFRASTRUCTURE SERVICES LUXEMBOURG S.à.r.l. AND ENERGIA TERMOSOLAR BV *v.* KINGDOM OF SPAIN[1]

([2023] EWHC 1226 (Comm))

England, High Court, King's Bench Division (Commercial Court). 24 May 2023

(Fraser J)

SUMMARY:[2] *The facts:*—Infrastructure Services Luxembourg S.à.r.l. and Energia Termosolar BV ("the claimants") were investors in energy infrastructure projects, including solar power installations, within the territory of the Kingdom of Spain ("Spain"). At the time when these investments were made, Spain had implemented certain tariff advantages for investments in renewable energy infrastructure. However, these advantages were slowly reduced and then removed as a means of integrating tariff and tax arrangements within the Europe Union ("EU") single market.

The claimants argued that the withdrawal of these tariff advantages by Spain contravened the Energy Charter Treaty, 1994 ("the ECT") and in 2018 obtained an arbitration award for the approximate sum of 120,000,000 Euros pursuant to a claim under the Convention on the Settlement of Investment Disputes between States and Nationals of Other States, 1965 ("the ICSID Convention"). After obtaining the arbitral award,

---

[1] The claimants were represented by Mr Patrick Green KC, Mr Nicholas Cherryman and Mr Richard Clarke, instructed by Kobre & Kim (the United Kingdom) LLP. The defendant was represented by Mr Tariq Baloch and Mr Cameron Miles, instructed by Simmons & Simmons LLP.
The judgment of the Court of Appeal of 22 October 2024, unavailable when this volume went to press, will be reported in a future volume of the *International Law Reports*.
[2] Prepared by Mr D. Peterson.

the claimants successfully sought an order from the Commercial Court of the High Court of England and Wales to register the award under the Arbitration (International Investment Disputes) Act 1966 ("the 1966 Act").

Spain applied to set aside the order, arguing that both the Court and the arbitral panel lacked jurisdiction on the basis of sovereign immunity. Spain further argued that the order should be set aside on the basis of the claimants' non-disclosure in the application for registration that was made to the Commercial Court. In response, the claimants argued that pursuant to Sections 2(2) and 9(1) of the State Immunity Act 1978 ("SIA") an exception to sovereign immunity applied, because the agreement to arbitrate contained in the ICSID Convention and the ECT constituted a prior written agreement waiving immunity.

Held:—The application by Spain was dismissed.

(1) Spain had no ability to deploy defences before the courts of the United Kingdom to the jurisdiction of the arbitral panel convened under the ICSID Convention. The availability of defences to a foreign State faced with an application to register an arbitral award under the ICSID Convention was narrow, and the 1966 Act dealt specifically with such awards. The prior case law of United Kingdom courts was clear that defences available to States could not directly overlap with the grounds of challenge to an award that were specifically allocated to the Convention organs under Articles 50-2 of the ICSID Convention. The jurisdiction of the tribunal, and matters covered in the annulment application, were exclusively allocated under the ICSID Convention to ICSID itself (paras. 67-79).

(2) Spain could not rely on sovereign immunity. Article 54 of the ICSID Convention fell within the meaning of a prior written agreement for the purposes of the SIA, as did Article 26 of the ECT which provided for arbitration under the ICSID Convention. There was no basis to consider a distinction between "commercial" and other types of arbitration within Section 9(1) of the SIA and any doubts about the exception of sovereign immunity applied to matters of enforcement of international arbitration awards were well-settled (paras. 91-7).

(3) Spain's submission that its dispute with the claimant concerned "sovereign acts" relating to the regulation of energy was irrelevant. This argument invited consideration of the substantive, underlying dispute in respect of which the arbitral award had already been made. Once such an award was made, this was the end of the matter unless Spain could demonstrate any "exceptional or extraordinary" defences as required by the 1996 Act (paras. 98-103).

(4) Where an application was made to the High Court for recognition of an award made by a tribunal under the ICSID Convention, the Court was restricted to ascertaining the award's authenticity. It could not re-examine the ICSID tribunal's jurisdiction, the award on the merits, the fairness and propriety of the proceedings before the ICSID tribunal, or any grounds based

on the general doctrine of *ordre public*. Stays were available pursuant to Articles 50-2 of the ICSID Convention. However, if a respondent State had exercised and exhausted its rights to seek annulment of an award under the ICSID Convention and had failed, then the High Court could not grant a stay (para. 107).

(5) While it was arguable that there were additional defences against enforcement, in exceptional or extraordinary circumstances which were not yet defined, such defences must comply with two conditions. First, English law must have recognized the defences in respect of final judgments of English courts. Secondly, the defences must not overlap with the grounds of challenge to an award, specifically allocation to Convention organs under Articles 50-2 of the ICSID Convention. No such exceptional or extraordinary circumstances existed in the present case (paras. 108-9).

(6) The conclusion of the Federal Court of Australia, that Article 54(1) and (2) of the ICSID Convention showed that a Party with an ICSID award might seek recognition without enforcement and that execution could not be construed as including recognition in Article 55, was correct.[3] That analysis with respect to State immunity held good within the United Kingdom and Spain had no immunity under the 1966 Act as it had already submitted to the jurisdiction of the court by reason of its accession to the ICSID Convention, which was a written agreement to arbitrate and thus fell within the exceptions of the SIA (paras. 113-14 and 116).

(7) The main argument of Spain regarding EU law was that, although Spain was a Party to the ICSID Convention and the ECT, its membership of the EU meant that there could be no valid arbitration where an arbitral tribunal might touch upon matters of EU law. The logical consequence of this argument was that a decision of the Court of Justice of the European Union ("CJEU") was binding on all Parties to the ECT and the ICSID Convention, whether or not they were EU members, and took priority over all treaty obligations entered into by any State. This would have meant that the EU and CJEU could unilaterally change all existing treaty obligations of all States Parties to the ICSID Convention. There was no framework of international law in which such a position could be correct (paras. 122-3).

(8) The United Kingdom enacted the 1966 Act in order to comply with its obligations under the ICSID Convention. The arbitral award at issue was valid, and the operation of the 1966 Act meant that the award was properly recognized as set out in the order. There was no basis for setting aside the order, and even if there were, Spain's challenge to jurisdiction was misplaced (para. 124).

(9) There was no material non-disclosure in the case and Spain's challenge on this issue failed. Even if Spain's argument of a breach of procedural

---

[3]   196 ILR 593.

fairness during the making of the order by the Commercial Court was accepted, which it was not, Spain had been given the opportunity to address all of the arguments that it wished in applying to have the *ex parte* order set aside (paras. 126-59).

The following is the text of the judgment of the Court:

1. This judgment is in the following parts:

A. Introduction and overview
B. Background to the Award and Order
C. The issues on the application
D. Issue 1: Jurisdiction
E. Discussion on jurisdiction
F. Issue 2: Non-disclosure
G. Discussion on non-disclosure
H. Conclusions

A. Introduction and overview

2. This is a judgment upon an application by the defendant, the Kingdom of Spain ("Spain"), to set aside an Order of Cockerill J made on 29 June 2021 ("the Order") which registered an arbitration award ("the Award") which the two claimants had obtained following an arbitration against Spain. That arbitration was one conducted under the Convention which established the International Centre for Settlement of Investment Disputes ("the ICSID Convention"). This means, therefore, that the application to the Commercial Court by the claimants for registration, and the Order, were made under the Arbitration (International Investment Disputes) Act 1966 ("the 1966 Act"). Ordinarily, arbitration awards more routinely encountered are sought to be registered and enforced under the New York Convention, and therefore the Arbitration Act 1996 ("the 1996 Act") would usually apply. That is not the case here, and this case is therefore somewhat different. The underlying dispute between the claimants and Spain which was referred to arbitration arose under the Energy Charter Treaty, and the Award is in the sum of approximately €120 million in the claimants' favour.

3. The application to Cockerill J to register the Award, which is what led to her making the Order, was made *ex parte* by the claimants under CPR Part 62.21(2)(b) and CPR 74.3(2)(b). The Order expressly granted Spain liberty to apply to have it set aside, which is the usual term included in any order that is made without notice to any party.

Spain did so apply, seeking to have the Order set aside. Initially Spain sought to set aside the Order on the grounds of alleged defective service. That attempt to set aside the Order was dismissed in a consent order made by Moulder J on 7 March 2022, and in that order she extended time for Spain to seek to set aside the Order on the other grounds now advanced. That order by Moulder J also states in the recitals "upon the Parties having agreed that the date of service of the Order was 21 October 2021". There is therefore no doubt as to the date of service as a result of this.

4. There are two grounds upon which Spain seeks to set aside the Order. In outline terms only, the first is sovereign immunity; the second is non-disclosure by the claimants in the application for registration that was made to the Commercial Court. The claim for sovereign immunity is broadly based upon lack of jurisdiction both on the part of the arbitral panel that made the Award, and also the court to register it. The foundations of these arguments are decisions of the Court of Justice of the European Union which are said by Spain to be authority, both in the law of the European Union ("the EU") and international law, to found the absence of jurisdiction. This case therefore raises questions of sovereign immunity, recognition by the High Court of ICSID Convention awards, and the effect and operation of the 1966 Act, including potentially issues of international law. I shall explain the non-disclosure issues in Section F of this judgment below at [126] and following.

5. That brief summary is sufficient to set the scene for the somewhat more complicated arguments advanced by the parties. The other point that requires some explanation is that the Order was made in the summer of 2021, and this application was heard by me in late March and early April 2023. That long duration was caused by a variety of different issues and steps. That period also included the European Commission applying to the court for permission to appear as an intervener. That application was refused, following a hearing, by Cockerill J and her judgment is at [2023] EWHC 234 (Comm). The application to intervene did not impact the period of the delay, which totals approximately 21 months, and is explained by other procedural steps that took months, rather than weeks, for a wide variety of reasons. Another factor was that the parties asked for a four-day hearing, and the dates when such hearings can be accommodated depend upon judicial availability. I refer to this overall period because those in charge of the component parts of the Business and Property Courts take pride in the efficient dispatch of disputes, including international disputes. The

short point is that it is not because of the court that it has taken so long
for this application to be heard.

6. The claimants were originally represented by Gibson, Dunn &
Crutcher UK LLP, and the initial witness statement which supported
the application to register the Award was made by a partner of that
firm. The claimants are now represented by Kobre & Kim (UK) LLP,
but nothing turns on that change, and I recite it for completeness. The
evidence on the application was in the form of a number of different
witness statements from Douglas Watson, Erika Saluzzo and Kunhee
Cho for the claimants; and Stuart Dutson for Spain.

7. Finally by way of introduction, the parties between them cited in
the hearing before me almost 200 different authorities, primary domestic legislation, international treaties and declarations, practitioner texts,
law journals, extracts from Hansard, Law Reform Commission materials and also numerous press articles. Of the authorities, there were
domestic cases including decisions of the Supreme Court, international
ones from the International Court of Justice, international arbitral
decisions, EU cases, and decisions of foreign courts including but not
limited to those from the US, Australia, France, Luxembourg, British
Virgin Islands, Lithuania, Netherlands and Germany. There were also
European Commission and Council Decisions on the Energy Charter
Treaty itself. Extensive oral submissions were made on many of them.

8. Given that breadth of material, accommodating the hearing
within only four days was a challenge, and all counsel are to be
commended for the way that this was achieved. There were some very
interesting issues of international law debated in the hearing, and the
ultimate decision in this case may attract a degree of academic interest,
if not interest also within other Member States of the EU who are also
parties to the ICSID Convention. However, I will not be specifically
addressing all of this extensive material in this judgment, although it
has all been considered. This is for two reasons. Firstly, to do so would
lead to this judgment evolving into something approaching a doctoral
thesis, rather than a decision on registration of an arbitral award under
the ICSID Convention and the 1966 Act. Secondly, preparing a
comprehensive judgment of such length that deals with the entirety
of the material cited to the court would take many months. The
overriding objective in CPR Part 1 means that the interests of other
court users have to be taken into account, and to produce a judgment
dealing with every single point raised would take so much time that this
would be to the detriment of other users of the court. I will therefore
only specifically refer to authorities or sources necessary to dispose of
the issues.

9. There were also post-hearing submissions received by the court following judgment which was handed down by the Federal Court in Washington DC in the US on Friday 31 March 2023, the penultimate hearing day of the application. This had not come to the attention of either counsel before the hearing had finished on Monday 3 April, and so the claimants' counsel submitted a copy promptly afterwards and, at the request of the solicitors acting for Spain, I permitted further written submissions from both parties on both the cases that were provided, although I imposed a short page limit. This is because there was a risk that otherwise there would be endless further rounds of lengthy submissions, which after the full ventilation of matters during the hearing itself, would be counter-productive. The parties agreed between themselves that they would lodge these supplemental post-hearing submissions sequentially, and did so.

10. Also, Mr Baloch, who appeared as one of the two counsel instructed for Spain along with his junior Mr Miles, did not seek to make any oral submissions on the second of the two areas of challenge to the Order, namely non-disclosure by the claimants. This had been extensively addressed in the skeleton argument submitted by both him and Mr Miles. That second issue still remained a live issue and was not abandoned by Spain; rather Spain decided that Mr Baloch would use all of his time during the hearing for oral submissions to focus on the more complicated of the two grounds, namely jurisdiction.

B. *Background to the Award and Order*

11. ICSID itself is an international institution that was established in 1966 under the Convention from which it took its name. The full title of the latter is the international Convention on the Settlement of Investment Disputes between States and nationals of Other States. It had three original language texts, English, French and Spanish, and the treaty was opened for signature on 18 March 1965. It was registered by the International Bank for Reconstruction and Development on 17 October 1966. The preamble sets out its purpose, which I will only summarise. It established an agreement between states which took account of the need for international cooperation for economic development, and the role that private investment had in that activity. Disputes would potentially arise between individuals or companies who or which had privately invested in other states, and although those disputes would sometimes be subject to national processes, an international settlement of disputes between such parties would sometimes be appropriate. Therefore, facilities for this were established under the

auspices of the International Bank for Reconstruction and Development ("the IBRD"). That is an international institution that is part of the World Bank. Both the IBRD and ICSID are headquartered in Washington, DC in the United States. IBRD is the seat of ICSID (which is called in the Convention "the Centre") and this is made clear in Article 2 of the Convention.

12. Section 2 of the ICSID Convention established the Administrative Council and Section 3 established the Secretariat. Jurisdiction of the Centre (which is given international status and immunities by reason of Section 6) is dealt with in Chapter II of the Convention. At Article 25, the Convention states:

(1) The jurisdiction of the Centre shall extend to any legal dispute arising directly out of an investment, between a Contracting State (or any constituent subdivision or agency of a Contracting State designated to the Centre by that State) and a national of another Contracting State, which the parties to the dispute consent in writing to submit to the Centre. When the parties have given their consent, no party may withdraw its consent unilaterally.

13. "Recognition and Enforcement of the Award" is set out in Section 6 of the ICSID Convention and Articles 53, 54 and 55 state:

Article 53

(1) The award shall be binding on the parties and shall not be subject to any appeal or to any other remedy except those provided for in this Convention. Each party shall abide by and comply with the terms of the award except to the extent that enforcement shall have been stayed pursuant to the relevant provisions of this Convention.

(2) For the purposes of this Section, "award" shall include any decision interpreting, revising or annulling such award pursuant to Articles 50, 51 or 52.

Article 54

(1) Each Contracting State shall recognize an award rendered pursuant to this Convention as binding and enforce the pecuniary obligations imposed by that award within its territories as if it were a final judgment of a court in that State. A Contracting State with a federal constitution may enforce such an award in or through its federal courts and may provide that such courts shall treat the award as if it were a final judgment of the courts of a constituent state.

(2) A party seeking recognition or enforcement in the territories of a Contracting State shall furnish to a competent court or other authority which such State shall have designated for this purpose a copy of the award certified by the Secretary-General. Each Contracting State shall notify the Secretary-General of the designation of the competent court or other authority for this purpose and of any subsequent change in such designation.

(3) Execution of the award shall be governed by the laws concerning the execution of judgments in force in the State in whose territories such execution is sought.

Article 55

Nothing in Article 54 shall be construed as derogating from the law in force in any Contracting State relating to immunity of that State or of any foreign State from execution.

14. The wording of these articles occupied extensive attention during the hearing by both parties.

15. Both the United Kingdom and Spain are signatories to the ICSID Convention. This clearly imposes certain treaty obligations upon all those Contracting States. These are obligations that are contained in the Convention itself, and so far as dispute resolution is concerned, they are clearly set out in the articles that I have recited above. In accordance with its own treaty obligations, the United Kingdom passed the 1966 Act. The full title of that legislation is the Arbitration (International Investment Disputes) Act 1966 (which in this judgment I refer to as "the 1966 Act"). The preamble states that it is "An Act to implement an international Convention on the settlement of investment disputes between States and nationals of other States". It was specifically passed in order that the United Kingdom would comply with the treaty obligations upon it which it had assumed as a result of the specific act of becoming a Contracting State under the ICSID Convention.

16. The wording of the 1966 Act is clear and there is no need to consult Hansard in order to discern its purpose or clarify ambiguities. The well-known dicta in *Pepper (Inspector of Taxes)* v. *Hart* [1993] AC 593 makes it clear that the rule excluding reference to Parliamentary material as an aid to statutory construction is to be relaxed so as to permit such reference where (a) the legislation was ambiguous, obscure or led to absurdity, (b) the material relied upon was or were statements by Ministers or others promoting the bill (together with the other material necessary to understand those statements and their effect) and (c) the statements relied upon were clear. Accordingly, the statements in Hansard are not necessary, and are not admissible, to construe the 1966 Act because condition (a) in that list of three is not satisfied. The statute can be construed perfectly sensibly by the normal canons of statutory construction, including the meaning of the words themselves in the Act, and there is no ambiguity, obscurity or absurdity.

17. However, the debate in the House of Lords of 10 November 1966 on the second reading of the Bill that became

the 1966 Act was referred to by both parties before me. To be fair to Mr Green KC for the claimants, he did not seek to deploy it and clearly relied upon *Pepper* v. *Hart* to exclude it, but in the alternative he took me to the debate too, as Mr Baloch for Spain had done. I do not take the Hansard passages of that debate into account in discerning the meaning of the Act. However, I will quote from one passage from the debate merely as a useful way of explaining the background to the 1966 Act. The passage also, in so doing, makes it crystal clear that the purpose of the 1966 Act fully aligns with the last sentence of [15] of this judgment above. Lord Walston, the Parliamentary Under-Secretary of State for Foreign Affairs, introduced the Bill and said:

There are actually three main aspects of the Convention which require United Kingdom legislation. First of all, we must provide for the enforcement in this country of any arbitral awards made under the Convention. It was not possible to apply the Arbitration Act 1950 to proceedings under the Convention, because that Act subjects the conduct of arbitration proceedings in England and Wales to certain legal rules and to the control of English courts in some respects. Proceedings under the Convention, on the other hand, will be governed by the provisions of the Convention itself and the rules made under it. It would be inconsistent with the Convention to make the 1950 Act apply. The procedure of registration of awards in the High Courts has therefore been adopted; they will then have the same force and effect for the purpose of execution as judgments of the High Court. Secondly, we must give effect to the provisions of Articles 18 to 24 of the Convention (the text of which is set out in the Schedule to the Bill) concerning the status, immunities and privileges of the Centre, of members of its Administrative Council and its secretariat and of persons taking part in conciliation or arbitration proceedings under the Convention.

. . .

May I go briefly through the clauses of the Bill? Clauses 1 and 2 deal with the enforcement of awards given under the Convention. An arbitral award may be registered in the High Court in so far as pecuniary obligations under the award have not already been satisfied, and subject to compliance with rules of court; the award then has the same force and effect for purposes of execution as a judgment of the High Court. There is, however, a provision for the making of rules for the stay of execution of an award in some circumstances in accordance with the Convention. Clause 3 will enable the Lord Chancellor to make the relevant provisions of the Arbitration Act 1950 and the Foreign Tribunals Evidence Act 1856 apply for the securing of evidence for the purpose of conciliation or arbitration proceedings under the Convention.

18. This is a useful explanation of what the 1966 Act therefore does; that is why I have quoted the passages. In simple and summary terms,

by becoming a party to the ICSID Convention, the United Kingdom acquired treaty obligations as set out in the Convention itself, as (only partially) quoted above in this judgment. These obligations expressly included bringing into domestic law a procedure for awards under the ICSID Convention to be recognised in law as binding, and enforceable, as though such awards were judgments of a competent court within the Contracting State. That obligation upon the United Kingdom to align the domestic law with the state's international obligations under the Convention was complied with by Parliament enacting the legislation in the 1966 Act, as can be seen by the sections of the 1966 Act. The relevant terms of the 1966 Act are:

Section 1. Registration of Convention awards

(1) This section has effect as respects awards rendered pursuant to the Convention on the settlement of investment disputes between States and nationals of other States which was opened for signature in Washington on 18th March 1965.

That Convention is in this Act called "the Convention", and its text is set out in the Schedule to this Act.

(2) A person seeking recognition or enforcement of such an award shall be entitled to have the award registered in the High Court subject to proof of the prescribed matters and to the other provisions of this Act.

(3) [this was repealed by the Administration of Justice Act 1977 and is not relevant]

(4) In addition to the pecuniary obligations imposed by the award, the award shall be registered for the reasonable costs of and incidental to registration.

(5) If at the date of the application for registration the pecuniary obligations imposed by the award have been partly satisfied, the award shall be registered only in respect of the balance, and accordingly if those obligations have then been wholly satisfied, the award shall not be registered.

(6) The power to make rules of court under [the relevant statutes are identified] shall include power—

(a) to prescribe the procedure for applying for registration under this section, and to require an applicant to give prior notice of his intention to other parties,

(b) to prescribe the matters to be proved on the application and the manner of proof, and in particular to require the applicant to furnish a copy of the award certified pursuant to the Convention,

(c) to provide for the service of notice of registration of the award by the applicant on other parties,

and in this and the next following section "prescribed" means prescribed by rules of court.

(7) For the purposes of this and the next following section—

(a) "award" shall include any decision interpreting, revising or annulling an award, being a decision pursuant to the Convention, and any decision as to costs which under the Convention is to form part of the award,
(b) an award shall be deemed to have been rendered pursuant to the Convention on the date on which certified copies of the award were pursuant to the Convention dispatched to the parties.

(8) This and the next following section shall bind the Crown (but not so as to make an award enforceable against the Crown in a manner in which a judgment would not be enforceable against the Crown).

Section 2. Effect of registration

(1) Subject to the provisions of this Act, an award registered under section 1 above shall, as respects the pecuniary obligations which it imposes, be of the same force and effect for the purposes of execution as if it had been a judgment of the High Court given when the award was rendered pursuant to the Convention and entered on the date of registration under this Act, and, so far as relates to such pecuniary obligations—

(a) proceedings may be taken on the award,
(b) the sum for which the award is registered shall carry interest,
(c) the High Court shall have the same control over the execution of the award,

as if the award had been such a judgment of the High Court.

(2) Rules of court [the statutes under which such rules are made are specified] may contain provisions requiring the court on proof of the prescribed matters to stay execution of any award registered under this Act so as to take account of cases where enforcement of the award has been stayed (whether provisionally or otherwise) pursuant to the Convention, and may provide for the provisional stay of execution of the award where an application is made pursuant to the Convention which, if granted, might result in a stay of enforcement of the award.

19. The 1966 Act therefore leaves certain detail to be included in subsequent rules of court. That is what the Civil Procedure Rules are. The two relevant ones here are CPR Part 62.21 and Part 74. It is not necessary to set out their full text, but it should be noted that under CPR Part 62.21(3) the Part 8 procedure must be used on an application to register an award under the 1966 Act, and under CPR Part 62.21(4) the written evidence required by CPR Part 74.4 must also exhibit the award itself and say whether "enforcement of the award has been stayed (provisionally or otherwise) under the Convention". That requirement was complied with in this case.

20. There are a great number of other treaties that have been entered into since 1966 that, by reference, incorporate the terms of

the ICSID Convention within them as a dispute-resolution mechanism. Many of them are what is called Bilateral Investment Treaties ("BITs"). As a result of the ICSID Convention, the international investment world has a free-standing arbitration process in existence, which is administered by ICSID from its headquarters in the US and this will, according to its rules, operate or administer both arbitral panels and also conciliation panels (which do not arise here) to assist or accomplish the resolution of international disputes between private parties (private individuals or, more usually, companies) and Contracting States. The benefits of this are obvious, and do not require recitation here. If a private investing party is successful following the reference to ICSID of a dispute it has with a Contracting State, the arbitration will result in an award in that party's favour. The first step to that party in enforcement is to have the award recognised—as though it were a judgment—in the High Court. This requires the court to have adjudicative jurisdiction.

21. The New York Convention, and the Arbitration Act 1996, do not arise in this case as I explained in the introduction. The Award is an ICSID award and the Order was made under the 1966 Act. However, some of the authorities cited to me were decisions on the New York Convention, which may be potentially persuasive but are certainly not directly on point. Also, some of the authorities concern disputes arising under BITs; where these concern ICSID, they would be relevant, but almost all of them are decisions in other jurisdictions. There are only isolated authorities in England and Wales on the issues that arise here, but as will be seen, there are some.

22. The next step in the process of explanation of what led to the Award is the Energy Charter Treaty ("the ECT"). A European Energy Charter Conference was held and its final plenary session was held in Lisbon on 16 and 17 December 1994. Spain had joined the European Community ("the EC") in 1986, the EC being the predecessor to the EU (the former becoming the latter after the Maastricht treaty was agreed in 1993). The final act of the European Energy Charter Conference in 1994 was to agree the terms of the ECT, which was also approved (in its provisional form) on 15 December 1994, and whose terms are annexed at Annex 1 to the EC Council Decision of the same date (this is at 94/998/EC). The final plenary session at Lisbon, and the signatories of the ECT, are numerous, and include a great many countries including many that were *not* members of the EC, including countries that one could confidently predict never will be, such as the United States and the Russian Federation. Both Spain, and the EC itself, signed the ECT, and their accession to the treaty entered into force on 16 April 1998.

23. The ECT expressly incorporated the ICSID Convention. The states that entered into the ECT are referred to within it as "Contracting Parties". It is necessary only to set out limited parts of the ECT.

Article 2—Purpose of the Treaty

This Treaty establishes a legal framework in order to promote long-term co-operation in the energy field, based on complementarities and mutual benefits, in accordance with the objectives and principles of the Charter.

Part II—Commerce

Article 3—International markets

The Contracting Parties shall work to promote access to international markets on commercial terms, and generally to develop an open and competitive market, for Energy Materials and Products.

. . .

Article 16—Relation to other agreements

Where two or more Contracting Parties have entered into a prior international agreement, or enter into a subsequent international agreement, whose terms in either case concern the subject matter of Part III or V of this Treaty,

(1) nothing in Part III or V of this Treaty shall be construed to derogate from any provision of such terms of the other agreement or from any right to dispute resolution with respect thereto under that agreement; and

(2) nothing in *such terms of the other agreement shall be construed to derogate from any provision of Part III or V of this Treaty or from any right to dispute resolution with respect thereto under this Treaty, where any such provision is more favourable to the Investor or Investment.*

. . .

Part V—Dispute settlement

Article 26—Settlement of disputes between an Investor and a Contracting Party

(1) Disputes between a Contracting Party and an Investor of another Contracting Party relating to an Investment of the latter in the Area of the former, which concern an alleged breach of an obligation of the former under Part III shall, if possible, be settled amicably.

(2) If such disputes cannot be settled according to the provisions of paragraph (1) within a period of three months from the date on which either party to the dispute requested amicable settlement, *the Investor party to the dispute may choose to submit it for resolution*:

   (a) to the courts or administrative tribunals of the Contracting Party party to the dispute;
   (b) in accordance with any applicable, previously agreed dispute settlement procedure;
   or
   (c) *in accordance with the following paragraphs of this Article.*

(3) (a) Subject only to subparagraphs (b) and (c), *each Contracting Party hereby gives its unconditional consent to the submission of a dispute to international arbitration or conciliation in accordance with the provisions of this Article.*

   (b) (i) The Contracting Parties listed in Annex ID do not give such unconditional consent where the Investor has previously submitted the dispute under subparagraph (2)(a) or (b).

   (ii) For the sake of transparency, each Contracting Party that is listed in Annex ID shall provide a written statement of its policies, practices and conditions in this regard to the Secretariat no later than the date of the deposit of its instrument of ratification, acceptance or approval in accordance with Article 39 or the deposit of its instrument of accession in accordance with Article 41.

   (c) A Contracting Party listed in Annex IA does not give such unconditional consent with respect to a dispute arising under the last sentence of Article 10(1).

(4) *In the event that an Investor chooses to submit the dispute for resolution under subparagraph (2)(c), the Investor shall further provide its consent in writing for the dispute to be submitted to:*

   (a) (i) *The International Centre for Settlement of Investment Disputes, established pursuant to the Convention on the Settlement of Investment Disputes between States and Nationals of Other States opened for signature at Washington, 18 March 1965 (hereinafter referred to as the "ICSID Convention"), if the Contracting Party of the Investor and the Contracting Party party to the dispute are both parties to the ICSID Convention*; or

   (ii) *The International Centre for Settlement of Investment Disputes, established pursuant to the Convention referred to in subparagraph (a)(i), under the rules governing the Additional Facility for the Administration of Proceedings by the Secretariat of the Centre (hereinafter referred to as the "Additional Facility Rules"), if the Contracting Party of the Investor or the Contracting Party party to the dispute, but not both, is a party to the ICSID Convention*;

(b) a sole arbitrator or ad hoc arbitration tribunal established under the Arbitration Rules of the United Nations Commission on International Trade Law (hereinafter referred to as "UNCITRAL"); or

(c) an arbitral proceeding under the Arbitration Institute of the Stockholm Chamber of Commerce.

(5) (a) The consent given in paragraph (3) together with the written consent of the Investor given pursuant to paragraph (4) shall be considered to satisfy the requirement for:

   (i) written consent of the parties to a dispute for purposes of Chapter II of the ICSID Convention and for purposes of the Additional Facility Rules;

   (ii) an "agreement in writing" for purposes of article II of the United Nations Convention on the Recognition and Enforcement of Foreign Arbitral Awards, done at New York, 10 June 1958 (hereinafter referred to as the "New York Convention"); and

   (iii) "the parties to a contract [to] have agreed in writing" for the purposes of article 1 of the UNCITRAL Arbitration Rules.

(a) Any arbitration under this Article shall at the request of any party to the dispute be held in a state that is a party to the New York Convention. Claims submitted to arbitration hereunder shall be considered to arise out of a commercial relationship or transaction for the purposes of article I of that Convention.

(6) A tribunal established under paragraph (4) shall decide the issues in dispute in accordance with this Treaty and applicable rules and principles of international law.

(7) An Investor other than a natural person which has the nationality of a Contracting Party party to the dispute on the date of the consent in writing referred to in paragraph (4) and which, before a dispute between it and that Contracting Party arises, is controlled by Investors of another Contracting Party, shall for the purpose of article 25(2)(b) of the ICSID Convention be treated as a "national of another Contracting State" and shall for the purpose of article 1(6) of the Additional Facility Rules be treated as a "national of another State".

(8) The awards of arbitration, which may include an award of interest, shall be final and binding upon the parties to the dispute. An award of arbitration concerning a measure of a sub-national government or authority of the disputing Contracting Party shall provide that the Contracting Party may pay monetary damages in lieu of any other remedy granted. Each Contracting Party shall carry out without delay any such award and shall make provision for the effective enforcement in its Area of such awards.

(*emphasis added*)

24. Article 26(3) states, as clearly set out and emphasised in the paragraph above, that the parties to the ECT, the Contracting Parties, thereby gave their unconditional consent to disputes being referred to international arbitration. Some Contracting Parties which were listed in Annex IA did not give such unconditional consent for some disputes, but that does not arise here in respect of Spain, and that exception does not apply in this case. The international arbitration choices for an investor seeking to refer a dispute are ICSID (under Article 26(4)(a)(i) and (ii)); an arbitrator or ad hoc arbitration tribunal under UNCITRAL (under Article 26(4)(b)); or an arbitral proceeding under the Arbitration Institute of the Stockholm Chamber of Commerce (under Article 26(4)(c)).

25. Article 26(4)(a)(i) and (ii) therefore both clearly refer to, and thereby incorporate, arbitration under the ICSID Convention as the dispute resolution mechanism (or one of them) that can be invoked by an investor who finds themselves in a dispute with a Contracting State under the ECT. The only difference between them is whether (under (a)(i)) both the State of the investor and the Contracting State are parties to the ICSID Convention; or (under (a)(ii)) only one of those is.

26. That therefore sets out the international treaty framework within which the factual circumstances of the dispute between the parties, the arbitration, the Award and therefore the Order, arise.

27. Thereafter the claimants in the arbitration that resulted in the Award became investors in certain energy infrastructure projects in Spain. The investments were entered into in 2011 and concerned solar power installations in Spain. There were certain tariff advantages at the time for such renewable power, but that is background only to this application, as the nature of the precise dispute between the claimants and Spain, its scope and the merits on each side, are not relevant to the issues before me.

28. However, what happened in wider European terms must be explained, as it forms the basis of Spain's arguments under Issue I below. The Treaty of Lisbon, which was signed in December 2007 and came into force after ratification on 1 December 2009, amended (also renamed) the two treaties which form the constitutional basis of the European Union. These two treaties have since then been called the Treaty on European Union ("TEU"), and the Treaty on the Functioning of the European Union ("TFEU"). This step created much greater integration within the European Union, which had been created some years earlier by the Treaty of Maastricht (which was the former name of the Treaty on European Union). All members of the

European Community became members of the EU, which was a wider and more complete integration of certain relations between Member States. As the preamble to the Treaty of Lisbon explains, it followed the resolve within the Member States to mark a new stage in the process of European integration that was undertaken with the establishment of the European Communities. One of the declarations that was annexed to the Final Act of the Intergovernmental Conference which adopted the Treaty of Lisbon made clear at Declaration 17 that the Treaties of the EU, and the law adopted by the EU on the basis of the treaties, have primacy over the domestic law of individual Member States. The exact terms of Declaration 17 are:

The Conference recalls that, in accordance with well settled case law of the Court of Justice of the European Union, the Treaties and the law adopted by the Union on the basis of the Treaties have primacy over the law of Member States, under the conditions laid down by the said case law.

29. EU law therefore clearly has primacy within the Member States of the EU, over the different domestic laws of Member States. For historical interest only, the Treaty of Lisbon also included certain provisions which have become increasingly topical over recent years. Article 50 included a provision whereby a Member State could leave the EU; that has only so far been utilised once, namely by the United Kingdom after the referendum held in 2016 leading to what is now widely known as Brexit. Another creation of the EU was the single market, with free movement of goods, labour and capital within the EU and between Member States, which also included a gradual harmonisation of many tariffs.

30. The Treaty of Lisbon set out the EU's institutions in Article 13, which included—for example—the European Commission (also called simply the Commission) and the European Central Bank, but also the Court of Justice of the European Union, or CJEU hereafter. Article 19 of the Treaty explained its function. It has its seat in Luxembourg, and constitutes the judicial authority of the EU. It has supremacy and the EU Treaties make it clear that it is the sole (and highest) authority for resolving matters of EU law.

31. It is convenient here to identify some provisions of the TFEU, namely Articles 267, 344 and 351. These state:

Article 267

The Court of Justice of the European Union shall have jurisdiction to give preliminary rulings concerning:

(a) the interpretation of the Treaties;

(b) the validity and interpretation of acts of the institutions, bodies, offices or agencies of the Union;

Where such a question is raised before any court or tribunal of a Member State, that court or tribunal may, if it considers that a decision on the question is necessary to enable it to give judgment, request the Court to give a ruling thereon.

Where any such question is raised in a case pending before a court or tribunal of a Member State against whose decisions there is no judicial remedy under national law, that court or tribunal shall bring the matter before the Court.

If such a question is raised in a case pending before a court or tribunal of a Member State with regard to a person in custody, the Court of Justice of the European Union shall act with the minimum of delay.

Article 344

Member States undertake not to submit a dispute concerning the interpretation or application of the Treaties to any method of settlement other than those provided for therein.

Article 351

The rights and obligations arising from agreements concluded before 1 January 1958 or, for acceding States, before the date of their accession, between one or more Member States on the one hand, and one or more third countries on the other, shall not be affected by the provisions of the Treaties.

To the extent that such agreements are not compatible with the Treaties, the Member State or States concerned shall take all appropriate steps to eliminate the incompatibilities established. Member States shall, where necessary, assist each other to this end and shall, where appropriate, adopt a common attitude.

In applying the agreements referred to in the first paragraph, Member States shall take into account the fact that the advantages accorded under the Treaties by each Member State form an integral part of the establishment of the Union and are thereby inseparably linked with the creation of common institutions, the conferring of powers upon them and the granting of the same advantages by all the other Member States.

32. Then what happened is as follows. Over a period of time, Spain firstly reduced, and then removed, the tariff advantages that had been available for solar energy (and therefore had been to the benefit of investors in such renewables). This was done as part of the move by Member States within the EU towards the integration of tariffs and

other tax treatments as part of establishing what is called the single market. The claimants found themselves in dispute with Spain as a result. The basis of the dispute was that the claimants alleged that Spain had breached its obligations under the ECT of fair and equal treatment.

33. That dispute could not be settled amicably and on 22 November 2013 the claimants commenced international arbitration by referring this dispute to ICSID. That is the date that the ICSID Secretary-General registered the Request for Arbitration by the claimants. The claimants had different names at that point but nothing turns on that. The first claimant is a private limited liability company incorporated under the laws of the Grand Duchy of Luxembourg. The second claimant is a private limited liability company incorporated under the laws of the Netherlands, and is wholly owned by the first claimant. Luxembourg and the Netherlands are, of course, both Member States of the EU. The President of the arbitral tribunal was Dr Eduardo Zuleta; the claimants' appointee was Professor Francisco Orrego Vicuña; and Spain's appointee was Mr J. Christopher Thomas QC ("the Tribunal"). The arbitration was conducted under the auspices of ICSID and given designation ICSID Case No ARB/13/31. A hearing was conducted in Paris in October 2016.

34. Spain challenged jurisdiction before the arbitral panel, but this challenge was dismissed unanimously by the Tribunal and was therefore not successful. The claimants were also successful in their substantive claim, the unanimous award of the Tribunal being dated 15 June 2018. A rectification process then followed, which was requested by Spain, and is in accordance with Article 49(2) of the ICSID Convention, which requires the tribunal to rectify "any clerical, arithmetical or similar error in the award. Its decision shall become part of the award and shall be notified to the parties in the same manner as the award". Spain sought to have the amount of compensatory damages awarded to the claimants reduced, contending that there was an error in computation, with the amount of costs being correspondingly reduced. Sadly, during the process of rectification, Professor Vicuña died, and he was replaced by Mr Klaus Reichert SC who took his place on the tribunal. The Award was rectified by a decision on rectification which was issued on 29 January 2019. That decision did reduce the amount of compensatory damages by €11 million approximately. It is the amount of the rectified Award that the claimants applied to the court to register under Article 49(2).

35. The sum awarded comprised damages, interest and costs. The Commission had applied to intervene in the arbitration as a

non-disputing party (also sometimes referred to as an *amicus curiae*) on Spain's jurisdictional objections, and the Tribunal granted authority for this, subject to an undertaking from the Commission that, as a non-party, it would comply with any costs order. This the Commission was not prepared to do, and so it did not participate.

36. Spain then applied to challenge the Award under the annulment procedure, which is contained within the ICSID Convention itself. The ICSID Committee that heard this application was appointed by the Chairman of the ICSID Administrative Council and was Mr Cavinder Bull as President, together with Mr José Antonio Moreno Rodríguez and Dr Nayla Comair-Obeid. The broad basis of the annulment application was that Spain alleged that the Tribunal had exceeded its powers by exercising jurisdiction over the arbitration in breach of EU law. The grounds for the alleged breach of EU law are explained below in more detail and arise under what I have called "the EU law question", but essentially the argument is that any intra-EU arbitration under the ECT is precluded by EU law (as would be any international arbitration to which a Member State is a party). There were other limbs to the application, including objections to the calculations of damages and objections to procedure (including imposing the costs undertaking upon the Commission as a condition of the Commission intervening), but for present purposes these other points do not matter. This is because all of the matters raised were considered by the ICSID Committee appointed for that purpose, who conducted a hearing and heard arguments. A stay had been imposed upon the Award by the ICSID Committee when Spain applied to annul the Award, but that was lifted on 21 October 2019. The claimants applied to the Federal Court in Australia for recognition of the Award. The application by Spain for annulment failed and the ICSID Committee issued its decision on this dated 30 July 2021.

37. For completeness, I should also note that Spain announced its intention to withdraw from the ECT on 13 October 2022. However, that does not affect the Award itself, nor does it of itself affect recognition of the Award under the 1966 Act, and I do not understand Spain to contend that it does. The dispute, the Award, and the application that led to the Order all occurred before Spain did this. Again, I include that purely for completeness.

38. Following the lifting of the stay by the ICSID Committee, the claimants applied for recognition of the Award in Australia. Amongst the many decisions cited to me were the Australian Federal Court decisions on that application, and also those of the US District Court

for the District of Columbia in Washington, DC. Recognition in those different foreign jurisdictions was also challenged in each of them by Spain on, more or less, the same grounds as on this application (but not non-disclosure). Obviously, the domestic law regimes that apply to such challenges are different to the law here. Although the judgments in those other cases in those foreign jurisdictions are potentially at least persuasive, they are neither determinative nor are they binding upon the High Court of England and Wales, nor do they involve the interpretation and application of the 1966 Act. In so far as those other foreign decisions deal with international legal principles, again they do not bind the High Court. The High Court is bound to apply the law as it is set down in domestic primary legislation—and in this case that plainly includes the 1966 Act—and as supplemented and interpreted by legal precedent and the doctrine of *stare decisis*. I shall return to this matter later after explaining the issues.

C. The issues on the application

39. These can firstly be identified at a high level, then sub-divided as necessary. They are:

I. Jurisdiction; and
II. Non-disclosure.

40. Issue I has a number of different strands to it. Essentially Spain advances before this court similar arguments that have already been extensively canvassed and deployed before the ICSID arbitral tribunal initially, and then also the ICSID Committee when Spain applied to annul the Award. However, there are other elements to this challenge before this court, including one based upon the terms and operation of the State Immunity Act 1978, that are specific to the legislative regime in this jurisdiction. Spain challenges the Order in particular on the grounds of state immunity; lack of a written agreement on Spain's part to arbitrate disputes under the ECT; and the validity of the Award itself.

41. Issue II requires consideration both of the extent of disclosure by the claimants upon the application that was considered by Cockerill J, which led to the Order, and whether there was material non-disclosure by the claimants.

42. I shall deal with each of these two areas separately. If Spain were to succeed on either of them, then Spain would be entitled to have the Order set aside.

Issue I. Jurisdiction

43. Spain maintains that the Order was made without jurisdiction. Paragraph 3 of Spain's skeleton states that it seeks "to have the Recognition Order set aside on the basis that the Court lacked jurisdiction to grant it under s 1(1) SIA", by which it refers to the State Immunity Act 1978.

44. This issue requires consideration both of state immunity, the State Immunity Act 1978, the existence or otherwise of a written agreement to arbitrate, and whether the Award is valid. In respect of a written agreement to arbitrate between the parties, Spain alleges that there is none. In order to answer this issue or these sub-issues, Spain deploys arguments which arise under what I have decided to term "the EU law question".

45. The background to the EU law question is summarised in paragraphs 72 to 74 of Spain's skeleton argument. The EU law question was refined during the hearing and Spain, at the request of the court, produced a further document sub-dividing the issue into a number of different sub-issues or questions. I invited Mr Baloch to submit these in writing, following his oral exposition of them during his submissions. They are as follows. The case referred to within them as *Achmea* is explained further below at [57].

The EU law question and its sub-issues:

1. *Achmea* arose out of the BIT between the Slovak Republic and the Netherlands. Does *Achmea*'s reasoning also apply to the ECT?

2. Do TFEU Articles 267 and 344, as interpreted by the CJEU, have primacy over Article 26 of the ECT as a matter of international law? This in turn gives rise to a series of questions:

   a. *Achmea* and the subsequent CJEU decisions have identified a conflict or incompatibility between TFEU Articles 267 and 344 on the one hand, and ECT Article 26 on the other. What gives the CJEU the power to articulate such a conflict, and is it binding as a matter of international law?

   b. What rules of conflict as a matter of international law apply to allow TFEU Articles 267 and 344, as interpreted by CJEU, to disapply ECT Article 26 of the ECT in the intra-EU context?

   c. At what point did the conflict arise? Is it retroactive or prospective from the date the conflict is declared?

   d. Can this reasoning apply to a multilateral treaty such as the ECT? Can it be said that the TFEU has primacy over intra-EU disputes under the ECT but not those involving non-EU Member States?

   e. In such a situation, how does the conflict with TFEU Articles 267 and 344 affect ECT Article 26 as it applies in the intra-EU context? What does disapplication of ECT Article 26 in this context mean?

46. On one interpretation of the EU law question, none of the sub-issues at 2(a) to (e) above arise. This is because it is not necessary to address these sub-issues in order to consider and answer the first part of question 2, namely "Do TFEU Articles 267 and 344, as interpreted by the CJEU, have primacy over Article 26 of the ECT as a matter of international law?" The claimants argue that the proper construction of the ECT and in particular the disapplication of Article 26 for which Spain contends has no foundation in the ECT or the applicable principles of international law. The claimants also contend that such an argument is in any event incompatible with the good faith interpretation of the ECT which is required by Article 31 of the Vienna Convention. I consider the Vienna Convention in outline terms at [81] below.

D. *Issue I: Jurisdiction*

47. Spain challenges the jurisdiction of the court to make the recognition order. This is on a number of different grounds.

48. At this point, it is convenient to reproduce three short passages from the written skeleton argument served by Spain for the application before me.

The EU's longstanding concerns on investment treaty arbitration

72. Investment treaties like the ECT have a long history in Europe [footnote omitted]. They were originally concluded after the end of the Cold War in 1989, prior to the Central and Eastern European states joining the EU from 2004 onwards. These intra-EU investment treaties protected Western European investment in Central and Eastern Europe, as the domestic standard of investment protection was then inadequate.

73. The ECT is a multilateral investment treaty designed to facilitate and protect investment in the energy sector—primarily between Western Europe and Central and Eastern Europe, but also including certain former Soviet states. Concluded in 1994, the ECT has over its lifetime seen several states parties join the EU. Like intra-EU BITs, the ECT contains substantive standards of protection for investments and, in Article 26, an investment arbitration clause.

74. The EU has watched these developments with concern. Investment in EU Member States is comprehensively regulated by the EU Treaties and the legal order based upon them. An essential element of this legal order is the CJEU, which is the final arbiter of all questions relating to the interpretation and application of the EU legal order. But an investment treaty creates an arbitral tribunal that is outside the CJEU's jurisdiction. If that tribunal is required to apply or interpret EU law, its conclusions will be unreviewable, undermining the autonomy of EU law.

49. These passages are, in a sense, all well and good when looked at from the internal perspective of the EU, or from the perspective of Spain as a Member State. But in my judgment they are notable for two reasons. Spain considers that the "standards of protections for investments" in the ECT are "substandard"; and also submits that the EU is "concerned" with the way in which international arbitration operates under investment treaties, including—or even particularly—the ICSID Convention. But that is nothing to the point, in my judgment. However, the sentence "But an investment treaty creates an arbitral tribunal that is outside the CJEU's jurisdiction" goes to the heart of the matter. That is rather the whole point. Indeed, it is central to international arbitration that the tribunal that determines whichever dispute is referred to it is outside the jurisdiction of a domestic court (other than for supervision or enforcement), and also—in this case—outside the jurisdiction of the CJEU (which did not even exist in its current form in 1966 when the ICSID Convention was agreed internationally). In principle, by entering into an arbitration agreement, the parties agree that the arbitral tribunal will resolve their disputes, and not domestic courts. The attractions of that are varied, whether international or domestic arbitration. I would go somewhat further and observe that this is the main purpose of the ICSID Convention itself, which was expressly incorporated into the ECT by the signatories to that later treaty, including Spain. The fact that the EU and/or Spain is concerned that international arbitration works in this way, and/or dilutes or undermines the CJEU's role in affairs, is not relevant.

50. There are likely to be all kinds of wider policy considerations of an international nature for countries when it comes to their treaty obligations. There are also going to be a number of different pros and cons within the EU when the CJEU interprets EU law, or makes rulings on matters that affect Member States. None of those, with respect to the way that Spain has argued its case on this application, have primacy on the issues before this court on this application to set aside the Order.

E. Discussion on jurisdiction

51. The challenge by Spain to jurisdiction can be considered in two ways. One is a shorter point on arbitral awards, and statutory interpretation of the 1966 Act. The other is a longer analysis applying international law principles to the treaty obligations of a sovereign state. I intend to address both routes.

52. The correct place to start when a sovereign state such as Spain asserts lack of jurisdiction on the part of a court to immunity is primary legislation. The 1966 Act has already been referred to. The relevant sections are set out at [18] above.

53. The State Immunity Act 1978 is relied upon by Spain in this respect, in particular section 1(1). Immunity must in any event be addressed because of the terms of section 1(2) of the Act. This is consistent with the approach of the court under the New York Convention too. Sections 1 and 2 of the State Immunity Act 1978 state as follows:

1. General immunity from jurisdiction

(1) A State is immune from the jurisdiction of the courts of the United Kingdom except as provided in the following provisions of this Part of this Act.

(2) A court shall give effect to the immunity conferred by this section even though the State does not appear in the proceedings in question.

2. Submission to jurisdiction

(1) A State is not immune as respects proceedings in respect of which it has submitted to the jurisdiction of the courts of the United Kingdom.

(2) A State may submit after the dispute giving rise to the proceedings has arisen or by a prior written agreement; but a provision in any agreement that it is to be governed by the law of the United Kingdom is not to be regarded as a submission.

(3) A State is deemed to have submitted—

(a) if it has instituted the proceedings; or
(b) subject to subsections (4) and (5) below, if it has intervened or taken any step in the proceedings.

(4) Subsection (3)(b) above does not apply to intervention or any step taken for the purpose only of—

(a) claiming immunity; or
(b) asserting an interest in property in circumstances such that the State would have been entitled to immunity if the proceedings had been brought against it.

(5) Subsection (3)(b) above does not apply to any step taken by the State in ignorance of facts entitling it to immunity if those facts could not reasonably have been ascertained and immunity is claimed as soon as reasonably practicable . . .

. . .

54. These sections are then followed by a number of others, dealing with specific situations such as commercial transactions (section 3), contracts of employment (section 4) and so on. At section 9, the following is stated in the Act:

9. Arbitrations

(1) Where a State has agreed in writing to submit a dispute which has arisen, or may arise, to arbitration, the State is not immune as respects proceedings in the courts of the United Kingdom which relate to the arbitration.

(2) This section has effect subject to any contrary provision in the arbitration agreement and does not apply to any arbitration agreement between States.

55. These provisions and their impact upon Spain's claim to immunity are considered further at [91] below.

56. However, there is an important distinction in terms of jurisdiction, and this is one that was clearly appreciated both by Spain and the claimants on this application. This distinction is between adjudicative jurisdiction and enforcement jurisdiction. Recognition of an ICSID Award falls into the former; this application does not entail consideration of any execution upon Spain.

57. In order fully to follow the EU law question, one has to consider in detail the case of the *Slovak Republic* v. *Achmea BV* Case C-284/16; ECLI:EU:C:2018:158 (Judgment, Grand Chamber) which is central to the arguments advanced by Spain (*"Achmea"*). That case concerned a bilateral international treaty, or BIT, which had been concluded in 1991 between the Kingdom of the Netherlands and the Czech and Slovak Federative Republic. The reason this is referred to as a bilateral treaty is the Slovak Republic became an independent nation in recent times on 1 January 1993, the treaty originally being concluded between the Netherlands and its predecessor state, Czechoslovakia (which then became two separate states, the Czech Republic or Czechia; and the Slovak Republic). Article 8 of the BIT provided for arbitration of disputes between one Contracting Party and an investor of the other Contracting Party. The arbitral body was to be appointed by the President of the Arbitration Institute of the Chamber of Commerce of Stockholm, and was to apply the arbitration rules of UNCITRAL, rather than ICSID, but that does not matter for present purposes.

58. The background to the dispute was the distribution of profits from the commercial operation of the private medical insurance market (explained further at [7] to [9] of the judgment) and in an ensuing arbitration under the treaty provisions in the BIT the Slovak Republic

raised an objection of lack of jurisdiction on the part of the arbitral tribunal. It submitted that as a result of its accession to the EU, recourse to an arbitral tribunal as provided for in article 8(2) of the BIT was incompatible with the law of the EU. German law applied to the arbitration proceedings because the seat of the arbitration was Frankfurt am Main in Germany, the well-known international finance centre. This jurisdictional argument was dismissed by the arbitral tribunal and an award of damages was made against the Slovak Republic. In the course of the proceedings undertaken by the Slovak Republic seeking to have that award set aside, the Bundesgerichtshof (the Federal Court of Justice, Germany) requested a preliminary ruling from the CJEU concerning the interpretation of Articles 18, 267 and 344 of the TFEU.

59. In short form, the CJEU decided that Articles 267 and 344 TFEU must be interpreted as precluding a provision in an international agreement concluded between Member States of the EU, such as Article 8 of the BIT in that case. This is because, as demonstrated by the reasoning in that judgment, Article 8 of the BIT was held to have an adverse effect upon the autonomy of EU law (as summarised in [59] of the judgment).

60. This reasoning is explained in a number of places in the judgment, but for convenience I shall quote only two passages. These are lengthy, but in my judgment ought to be reproduced *in extenso* as the reasoning underpins so much of the argument advanced by Spain before me:

31. By its first and second questions, which should be taken together, the referring court essentially asks whether Articles 267 and 344 TFEU must be interpreted as precluding a provision in an international agreement concluded between Member States, such as Article 8 of the BIT, under which an investor from one of those Member States may, in the event of a dispute concerning investments in the other Member State, bring proceedings against the latter Member State before an arbitral tribunal whose jurisdiction that Member State has undertaken to accept.

32. In order to answer those questions, it should be recalled that, according to settled case law of the Court, an international agreement cannot affect the allocation of powers fixed by the Treaties or, consequently, the autonomy of the EU legal system, observance of which is ensured by the Court. That principle is enshrined in particular in Article 344 TFEU, under which the Member States undertake not to submit a dispute concerning the interpretation or application of the Treaties to any method of settlement other than those provided for in the Treaties (Opinion 2/13 (Accession of the EU to the ECHR) of 18 December 2014, EU:C:2014:2454, paragraph 201 and the case law cited).

33. Also according to settled case law of the Court, the autonomy of EU law with respect both to the law of the Member States and to international law is justified by the essential characteristics of the EU and its law, relating in particular to the constitutional structure of the EU and the very nature of that law. EU law is characterised by the fact that it stems from an independent source of law, the Treaties, by its primacy over the laws of the Member States, and by the direct effect of a whole series of provisions which are applicable to their nationals and to the Member States themselves. Those characteristics have given rise to a structured network of principles, rules and mutually interdependent legal relations binding the EU and its Member States reciprocally and binding its Member States to each other (see, to that effect, Opinion 2/13 (Accession of the EU to the ECHR) of 18 December 2014, EU: C:2014:2454, paragraphs 165 to 167 and the case law cited).

34. EU law is thus based on the fundamental premiss that each Member State shares with all the other Member States, and recognises that they share with it, a set of common values on which the EU is founded, as stated in Article 2 TEU. That premise implies and justifies the existence of mutual trust between the Member States that those values will be recognised, and therefore that the law of the EU that implements them will be respected. It is precisely in that context that the Member States are obliged, by reason inter alia of the principle of sincere cooperation set out in the first subparagraph of Article 4(3) TEU, to ensure in their respective territories the application of and respect for EU law, and to take for those purposes any appropriate measure, whether general or particular, to ensure fulfilment of the obligations arising out of the Treaties or resulting from the acts of the institutions of the EU (Opinion 2/13 (Accession of the EU to the ECHR) of 18 December 2014, EU:C:2014:2454, paragraphs 168 and 173 and the case law cited).

35. In order to ensure that the specific characteristics and the autonomy of the EU legal order are preserved, the Treaties have established a judicial system intended to ensure consistency and uniformity in the interpretation of EU law (Opinion 2/13 (Accession of the EU to the ECHR) of 18 December 2014, EU:C:2014:2454, paragraph 174) . . .

49. *It follows that a tribunal such as that referred to in Article 8 of the BIT cannot be regarded as a "court or tribunal of a Member State" within the meaning of Article 267 TFEU, and is not therefore entitled to make a reference to the Court for a preliminary ruling.*

(*emphasis added*)

61. The second series of passages states:

54. It is true that, in relation to commercial arbitration, the Court has held that the requirements of efficient arbitration proceedings justify the review of arbitral awards by the courts of the Member States being limited in scope, provided that the fundamental provisions of EU law can be examined in the course of that review and, if necessary, be the subject of a reference to the Court for a preliminary ruling (see, to that effect, judgments of 1 June 1999,

Eco Swiss, C-126/97, EU:C:1999:269, paragraphs 35, 36 and 40, and of 26 October 2006, *Mostaza Claro*, C-168/05, EU:C:2006:675, paragraphs 34 to 39).

55. However, arbitration proceedings such as those referred to in Article 8 of the BIT are different from commercial arbitration proceedings. While the latter originate in the freely expressed wishes of the parties, the former derive from a treaty by which Member States agree to remove from the jurisdiction of their own courts, and hence from the system of judicial remedies which the second subparagraph of Article 19(1) TEU requires them to establish in the fields covered by EU law (see, to that effect, judgment of 27 February 2018, *Associação Sindical dos Juízes Portugueses*, C-64/16, EU:C:2018:117, paragraph 34), disputes which may concern the application or interpretation of EU law. In those circumstances, the considerations set out in the preceding paragraph relating to commercial arbitration cannot be applied to arbitration proceedings such as those referred to in Article 8 of the BIT.

56. Consequently, having regard to all the characteristics of the arbitral tribunal mentioned in Article 8 of the BIT and set out in paragraphs 39 to 55 above, it must be considered that, by concluding the BIT, the Member States parties to it established a mechanism for settling disputes between an investor and a Member State which could prevent those disputes from being resolved in a manner that ensures the full effectiveness of EU law, even though they might concern the interpretation or application of that law.

57. It is true that, according to settled case law of the Court, an international agreement providing for the establishment of a court responsible for the interpretation of its provisions and whose decisions are binding on the institutions, including the Court of Justice, is not in principle incompatible with EU law. The competence of the EU in the field of international relations and its capacity to conclude international agreements necessarily entail the power to submit to the decisions of a court which is created or designated by such agreements as regards the interpretation and application of their provisions, provided that the autonomy of the EU and its legal order is respected (see, to that effect, Opinion 1/91 (EEA Agreement—I) of 14 December 1991, EU:C:1991:490, paragraphs 40 and 70; Opinion 1/09 (Agreement creating a unified patent litigation system) of 8 March 2011, EU:C:2011:123, paragraphs 74 and 76; and Opinion 2/13 (Accession of the EU to the ECHR) of 18 December 2014, EU:C:2014:2454, paragraphs 182 and 183).

58. In the present case, however, apart from the fact that the disputes falling within the jurisdiction of the arbitral tribunal referred to in Article 8 of the BIT may relate to the interpretation both of that agreement and of EU law, the possibility of submitting those disputes to a body which is not part of the judicial system of the EU is provided for by an agreement which was concluded not by the EU but by Member States. Article 8 of the BIT is such as to call into question not only the principle of mutual trust between the Member States, but also the preservation of the particular nature of the law established by the Treaties, ensured by the preliminary ruling procedure

provided for in Article 267 TFEU, and is not therefore compatible with the principle of sincere cooperation referred to in paragraph 34 above.

59. *In those circumstances, Article 8 of the BIT has an adverse effect on the autonomy of EU law.*

60. Consequently, the answer to Questions 1 and 2 is that Articles 267 and 344 TFEU must be interpreted as precluding a provision in an international agreement concluded between Member States, such as Article 8 of the BIT, under which an investor from one of those Member States may, in the event of a dispute concerning investments in the other Member State, bring proceedings against the latter Member State before an arbitral tribunal whose jurisdiction that Member State has undertaken to accept.

(*emphasis added*)

62. Therefore, the CJEU made two fundamental points (amongst other important points). The first was to draw a distinction between commercial arbitration, and arbitration under an international treaty provision. The second was to find that an arbitral tribunal such as the one in that case would, or could, be called upon to consider or rule on the applicability of EU law, yet was not competent to do that under the EU Treaties or the law of the EU, because it had no jurisdiction to do that. Such a tribunal could not be regarded as a court or tribunal of a Member State, nor could it make a reference to the CJEU for a preliminary ruling (a point made clear at [49] of the judgment in that case). This meant that treaty provisions permitting or establishing international arbitration for disputes involving Member States was contrary to the EU Treaties, and the CJEU therefore held that these were effectively invalid.

63. The case of *Achmea* did, however, involve a BIT, and both of the Contracting Parties were members of the EU, although not at the time that the BIT was concluded. However, even if these were potential points of arguable distinction then, in terms of the law of EU at least, they became of lesser (or no) importance given a subsequent decision of the CJEU on the ECT itself, namely the case of *Republic of Moldova* v. *Komstroy LLC (successor in law to Energoalians)* Case C-741/19; EU: C:2021:655 (Judgment, Grand Chamber); [2021] 4 WLR 132. Spain heavily relies upon this case too.

64. That case specifically concerned the ECT itself. It was a reference by the cour d'appel de Paris (the Court of Appeal, Paris) and the substantive underlying claim which arose from a contract for the sale and supply of electricity to the Republic of Moldova which was assigned to the defendant's predecessor, a Ukrainian company. That company referred a dispute concerning the sale and re-sale of electricity to arbitration under Article 26 of the ECT. This was an ad hoc

arbitration which was established in France, and the tribunal made an award in favour of the company against Moldova. This was challenged by Moldova, and the Court of Appeal in Paris referred a question to the CJEU for a preliminary ruling on the meaning of "investment" within the ECT. The Commission, and several intervening states, raised an associated question concerning whether an arbitral tribunal under the ECT could rule on an intra-EU dispute between an investor of one Member State and another Member State.

65. The CJEU ruled that it had jurisdiction itself to give preliminary rulings on questions concerning the interpretation of the ECT, because the EU and many of its individual Member States were parties to it. This included the interpretation of what constituted an "investment" under the ECT. The court also held that the EU had exclusive competence in relation to foreign direct investment and shared competence in relation to indirect investment. It also held that it was in the interests of the EU that, in order to forestall future differences of interpretation, "investment" should be uniformly interpreted. It also found of note that the parties to the dispute had chosen to submit the dispute to arbitration in a Member State in which the ECT was applicable as a matter of EU law. It then applied its reasoning on the issue of whether the underlying dispute constituted an "investment" for the purposes of the treaty, and found that it did not.

66. It also found, applying the same reasoning as in *Achmea* and applying that case specifically, that since the EU was a contracting party to the ECT, that treaty itself was an act of EU law and an ad hoc tribunal could be required to interpret and apply EU law when deciding a dispute under Article 26 of the ECT. Yet, because (for the same reasons as set out in [49] of *Achmea* and explained above) such an arbitral tribunal was not entitled to make a reference to the court for a preliminary ruling, the arbitration provisions under Article 26 of the ECT could not and did not apply intra-EU. Strictly speaking in English law terms, given the conclusions set out concerning the interpretation of the term "investment", this part of the judgment could be considered *obiter*. However, that concept does not strictly speaking apply to decisions of the CJEU in any event, because this was part of the conclusion to a question that had specifically been referred to it by the French court. This is made clear at [64] to [66] of the judgment, which makes this point following on from the reasoning of *Achmea*, and appears in the judgment under the overall heading "Consideration of the questions referred" and the specific heading "The first question". The law report in the Weekly Law Reports supports this and states this to be *per curiam*. But whether it is *obiter*

or not, the reasoning within the judgment entirely aligns with that of *Achmea*, and there is no reason to doubt that the CJEU would answer any similar question, or even an identical one, in anything other than exactly the same way, even were that to be the only question referred to it for a ruling. It is therefore, within the sphere of EU law, undoubtedly the case that the CJEU has ruled that the provisions of Article 26 of the ECT are in conflict with Member States' obligations arising under the EU Treaties. The case of *Komstroy* makes it crystal clear that the CJEU considers that the provisions of Article 26 in the ECT, and the mechanism for referring a dispute between an investor and a Member State to arbitration, cannot apply within the EU as such an arbitration provision is incompatible with the supremacy of the CJEU as the ultimate arbiter of matters of EU law under the EU Treaties. The decision does, however, somewhat gloss over the difficulties that such an interpretation would cause in terms of Member States' existing international treaty obligations under both the ECT and the ICSID Convention.

67. Spain argued before me the questions of EU law set out above in a manner that elevated the status of these decisions of the CJEU, almost as though they were decisions of an over-arching international court that must bind all nations. For example, Spain referred to what it called "the international law aspects of the EU legal order" and also stated in its supporting documents for the application that "EU law is an inextricable part of international law." There is no doubt that the law of the EU is correctly described as being international law, as self-evidently it governs relations between Member States which have collectively entered into international treaty obligations under the EU Treaties including the TFEU. Those treaty obligations have international effect and the institutions of the EU have primacy over domestic organs in certain important respects. However, as the claimants point out, this argument ignores the other aspects of international law that requires observance of existing express treaty obligations, and it also ignores the effect of Spain having pre-existing treaty obligations under other treaties such as the ICSID Convention and the ECT. The EU treaties do not trump these, nor do they override the relevant domestic law mechanism in the United Kingdom.

68. There is, however, direct and binding Supreme Court authority on the operation both of the ICSID Convention and the 1966 Act, which includes the subject of recognition of an ICSID award in the United Kingdom and how conflicts with the internal law of the EU impact upon the former. This is the case of *Micula & Ors* v. *Romania (European Commission intervening)* [2020] UKSC 5. It is of

considerable interest, and its reasoning is, in my judgment, directly relevant. It is also binding upon this court.

69. Romania acceded to the EU on 1 January 2007. Before that, in April 1999, Romania had adopted an investment incentive scheme for certain regions (the details of which are not directly relevant, but which was called "EGO 24"). On 30 June 1999, Romania incorporated EU state aid rules into domestic law, as a result of which EGO 24 was modified. During the early 2000s, the claimants invested in a large, highly integrated food production operation in the relevant region in reliance on EGO 24. In 2002, Romania and Sweden entered into a BIT providing reciprocal protection of investments and investor–State arbitration under the ICSID Convention. During the accession negotiations between Romania and the EU before Romania's accession on 1 January 2007, the EU informed Romania that certain schemes, including EGO 24, were contrary to EU state aid rules. As a result, Romania repealed the majority of the incentives under EGO 24 and this led to a claim by the claimants, as a result of which the claimants in July 2005 filed a request for ICSID arbitration under the BIT.

70. An arbitration under ICSID took place and on 11 December 2013, the tribunal issued its award, deciding that Romania had breached the BIT and awarding compensation of approximately £70m plus interest to the claimants. Romania unsuccessfully applied to annul the award and also attempted to implement the award by setting off tax debts owed by one of the claimants. This led to the Commission issuing an injunction against Romania in May 2014 ordering it to suspend any action that might lead to execution of the award, until the Commission had taken a final decision on its compatibility with state aid rules. The Commission thereupon formally opened a state aid investigation which led to a decision by the Commission in March 2015 which concluded that the payment of the award by Romania constituted unlawful state aid. The claimants sought annulment of the Commission Decision before the CJEU in 2015. On 18 June 2019, the General Court (the "GCEU") annulled the Commission Decision on the ground that the Commission had purported to apply its powers retroactively to events pre-dating Romania's accession to the EU. The Commission applied to appeal this decision.

71. Proceedings were started in England in 2014 by the claimants applying for registration of the award under the 1966 Act, and this was granted. In 2015, Romania applied for a stay of enforcement and the claimants sought an order for security. In 2017, the High Court granted Romania's application to stay enforcement pending the

GCEU proceedings and refused the claimants' application for security. The claimants appealed, and in 2018, the Court of Appeal continued the stay but ordered that Romania provide security. Romania appealed the order for security and the claimants cross-appealed the grant of a stay, both of these appeals being set down before the Supreme Court. On the morning the hearing was to have taken place in June 2019, the GCEU handed down its judgment, and this caused the stay to lapse, and the hearing to be adjourned in any event until October 2019. After the hearing later took place, the Supreme Court allowed the claimants' cross-appeal and lifted the stay. It did not therefore need to consider Romania's appeal in relation to security. The claimants had appealed against the stay on five grounds. These were: (1) the effect of the GCEU's judgment was that the duty of sincere co-operation (which arises under the EU Treaties) no longer required the English courts to stay enforcement; (2) there was no power to order a stay under the ICSID Convention and the 1966 Act; (3) the stay was incompatible with the ICSID Convention; (4) the European Communities Act 1972 did not require the United Kingdom to breach pre-accession obligations under the ICSID Convention; and (5) Article 351 of TFEU applied, with the result that the obligations of the United Kingdom under the pre-accession ICSID Convention were not subject to the overriding effect of EU law.

72. Each of the grounds numbered (2) to (5) set out at [71] above are directly applicable to the instant case. The unanimous judgment of the Supreme Court was given by Lord Lloyd-Jones JSC and Lord Sales JSC, and the following extract will make it clear to any reader of this judgment what the approach of the High Court should be, when considering challenges of the type mounted by Spain in this case. This is a lengthy quotation but because it incorporates, and indeed anticipates, so much of the argument mounted in this case by Spain, I have concluded that it is best to reproduce it in full.

[68]. *The provisions of the 1966 Act must be interpreted in the context of the ICSID Convention and it should be presumed that Parliament, in enacting that legislation, intended that it should conform with the United Kingdom's treaty obligations. It is a notable feature of the scheme of the ICSID Convention that once the authenticity of an award is established, a domestic court before which recognition is sought may not re-examine the award on its merits. Similarly, a domestic court may not refuse to enforce an authenticated ICSID award on grounds of national or international public policy.* In this respect, the ICSID Convention differs significantly from the New York Convention on the Recognition and Enforcement of Foreign Arbitral Awards 1958. The position is stated in this way by Professor Schreuer in his commentary on article 54(1):

The system of review under the Convention is self-contained and does not permit any external review. This principle also extends to the stage of recognition and enforcement of ICSID awards. *A domestic court or authority before which recognition and enforcement is sought is restricted to ascertaining the award's authenticity. It may not re-examine the ICSID tribunal's jurisdiction. It may not re-examine the award on the merits. Nor may it examine the fairness and propriety of the proceedings before the ICSID tribunal. This is in contrast to non-ICSID awards, including Additional Facility awards, which may be reviewed under domestic law and applicable treaties.* In particular, the New York Convention gives a detailed list of grounds on which recognition and enforcement may be refused ... (Christoph H Schreuer, *The ICSID Convention: A Commentary*, 2nd ed (2009), p 1139, para. 81)

The Convention's drafting history shows that domestic authorities charged with recognition and enforcement have no discretion to review the award once its authenticity has been established. Not even the *ordre public* (public policy) of the forum may furnish a ground for refusal. The finality of awards would also exclude any examination of their compliance with international public policy or international law in general. The observance of international law is the task of the arbitral tribunal in application of article 42 of the Convention subject to a possible control by an ad hoc committee ... Nor would there be any room for the application of the Act of State doctrine in connection with the recognition and enforcement of an ICSID award ... (Schreuer, pp 1140-1, para. 85)

[69]. *Contracting States may not refuse recognition or enforcement of an award on grounds covered by the challenge provisions in the Convention itself (articles 50-2). Nor may they do so on grounds based on any general doctrine of ordre public, since in the drafting process the decision was taken not to follow the model of the New York Convention.* However, although it is recognised that this is the general position under the Convention, it is arguable that article 54(1), by framing the relevant obligation as to enforcement as an obligation to treat an award under the Convention as if it were a final judgment of a local court, allows certain other defences to enforcement which are available in local law in relation to such a final judgment to be raised.

[70]. The principle that arbitration awards under the ICSID Convention should be enforceable in the courts of all Contracting States and with the same status as a final judgment of the local courts in those States, as eventually set out in article 54(1), was a feature from an early stage in the drafting of the Convention. Mr Aron Broches, General Counsel of the World Bank at the time who chaired the regional consultative meetings ("the Regional Consultative Meetings") that occurred as part of the Convention's drafting, explained to delegates that by virtue of this formula Contracting States would be entitled to apply their local law of sovereign or state immunity with regard to the enforcement of awards, and thereby avoid or minimise possible

embarrassment at having to enforce awards against other friendly Contracting States. Accordingly, it was made clear that article 54(1) had the substantive effect of introducing to some degree a principle of equivalence between a Convention award and a local final judgment as regards the possibility of applying defences in respect of enforcement . . .

[71]. In his report on the Regional Consultative Meetings, Mr Broches referred to certain comments that had dealt with the effect of what was then draft section 15 (which became article 54(1)) on existing law with respect to sovereign immunity. Mr Broches "explained that the drafters had no intention to change that law. By providing that the award could be enforced as if it were a final judgment of a local court, section 15 implicitly imported the limitation on enforcement which in most countries existed with respect to enforcement of court decisions against Sovereigns. However, this point might be made explicit in order to allay the fears expressed by several delegations" . . . Mr Broches again indicated that this was the intended effect of what became article 54(1), but that it could be made completely clear to allay concerns).

[72]. Accordingly, the provision which eventually became article 55 was included in what was designated as the First Draft of the Convention and was retained in the final version of the Convention (*History*, vol I, 254; vol II—1, Doc 43 (11 September 1964) "Draft Convention: Working Paper for the Legal Committee", p 636). The official Report of the Executive Directors on the Convention confirmed that this provision was introduced for the avoidance of doubt (as its text indicates) . . . . The law of State immunity varies from State to State, and the Convention made no attempt to harmonise it. As Professor Schreuer points out in his commentary on article 54, persons seeking to enforce arbitration awards made pursuant to the Convention will tend to choose to do so in those jurisdictions which have the least generous rules of State immunity for the protection of the assets of other Contracting States (Schreuer, p 1124, para. 27).

[73]. The fact that the specific qualification of the obligation to enforce an award like a final court judgment relating to state immunity was expressly dealt with in article 55 for the avoidance of doubt indicates that article 54(1) was itself understood to have the effect of allowing the possibility of certain other defences to enforcement if national law recognised them in respect of final judgments of local courts.

[74]. The *travaux préparatoires* also indicate that it was accepted that further defences available in national law in relation to enforcement of court judgments could be available in exceptional circumstances by virtue of the formulation of the obligation in article 54(1) . . . .

(*emphasis added*)

73. The published works of both Professor Schreuer and Mr Broches were cited to me on this application. The former is a highly distinguished international law jurist, and the latter was General Counsel of the World Bank at the time the ICSID Convention was signed. Both were cited to, and approved by, the Supreme Court and

their writings were expressly referred to by Lord Lloyd-Jones JSC and Lord Sales JSC, as can be seen by the extracts above. They are therefore directly considered in the decision in *Micula*. Their Lordships continued:

[77] Articles 50(2), 51(4) and 52(5) make specific provision for staying enforcement of an award in certain specific situations, none of which applies here. Section 2(2) of the 1966 Act and CPR 62.21(5) make corresponding provision in domestic law for the grant of a stay in such situations. These stays pursuant to the Convention are available only in the context of interpretation, revision and annulment of awards addressed by those articles. In the present case, Romania has already exercised and exhausted its right under article 52 of ICSID to seek annulment of the Award. The ICSID ad hoc Committee upheld the Award on 26 February 2016.

[78] However, in light of the wording of articles 54(1) and 55 and the *travaux préparatoires* reviewed above, it is arguable that there is scope for some additional defences against enforcement, *in certain exceptional or extraordinary circumstances which are not defined, if national law recognises them in respect of final judgments of national courts and they do not directly overlap* with those grounds of challenge to an award which are specifically allocated to Convention organs under articles 50 to 52 of the Convention.

(*emphasis added*)

74. When considering the argument mounted by Romania that EU law both conflicted with, and effectively overrode the obligations in the ICSID Convention, their Lordships stated the following:

[84]. The grant of a stay [by the Court of Appeal, per Arden and Leggatt LJJ, Hamblen LJ dissenting (as they all then were)] in these circumstances was not consistent with the ICSID Convention, on their interpretation of it, under which the United Kingdom and its courts had a duty to recognise and enforce the Award. This was not a limited stay of execution on procedural grounds, but a prohibition on enforcement of the Award on substantive grounds until the GCEU had ruled on the apparent conflict between the ICSID Convention and the EU Treaties. Effect was given to the Commission Decision until such time as the GCEU might pronounce upon it. The logic of the position adopted by Arden and Leggatt LJJ was that if the GCEU upheld the Commission Decision, the stay would continue indefinitely (and the same would be true if the CJEU allows the Commission's appeal against the decision of the GCEU). But the grounds of objection raised by the Commission, even if upheld before the EU courts, were not valid grounds of objection to the Award or its enforcement under the ICSID Convention, as interpreted by Arden and Leggatt LJJ. *The principle laid down in article 53(1) that awards are binding on the parties and are not subject to any appeal or other remedy except those provided under the Convention and reflected in article 54 (on their interpretation of it) was disregarded.* In substance, the Court of Appeal

made use of powers to stay execution granted by domestic law in order to thwart enforcement of an award which had become enforceable under the ICSID Convention.

[85]. On the other hand, if article 54(1) incorporates the principle of equivalence, in line with Hamblen LJ's interpretation, it remains the case that Romania's submission in answer to the Claimants' cross-appeal cannot succeed. This is because article 351 TFEU has the effect that any obligation on the UK courts to give effect to a decision such as the Commission Decision pursuant to the duty of sincere co-operation which might arise under the Treaties in other circumstances does not arise in this case. The discussion below of Original Ground 4 of the cross-appeal, explains that the United Kingdom owes relevant obligations to non-EU member states under the ICSID Convention, a treaty to which the United Kingdom was party before it became a member state. By virtue of article 351 TFEU this means that the obligations on the United Kingdom arising from the ICSID Convention are "not . . . affected by the provisions of the Treaties".

[86]. *Leaving aside the Treaties, in the circumstances of the present case the English courts are obliged under article 54(1) of the ICSID Convention to give effect to the Award in favour of the Claimants and this is not a case in which any of the exceptional possible types of defence to enforcement contemplated by Mr Broches and Professor Schreuer arise.* Leaving the Treaties out of the analysis, if the Award were a final judgment of an English court it would be enforced without question. Similarly, on Hamblen LJ's interpretation of article 54(1) involving the principle of equivalence, it must follow that the Award would be enforced in the same way. Article 351 TFEU means that this obligation cannot be affected by anything in the Treaties, which are the foundation for the legal effect of Commission rulings and for the obligation of sincere co-operation on which Romania seeks to rely. Romania's attempt to pray in aid the obligation of sincere co-operation is an attempt to pull itself up by its own bootstraps. It cannot make out the necessary foundation for its argument, since it cannot show that the obligation of sincere co-operation has any application at all.

[87]. Finally, in this regard, we should refer to the submission on behalf of Romania that to the extent that there is any uncertainty as to the meaning of the relevant provisions of the ICSID Convention and the 1966 Act, this court is bound by EU law to interpret them so far as possible in accordance with EU law in order to comply with the EU principle of effectiveness (seeking to gain support from *van Munster* v. *Rijksdienst voor Pensioenen* (Case C-165/91) [1994] ECR I-4661, para. 34; *Budějovický Budvar národní podnik* v. *Rudolf Ammersin GmbH* (Case C-216/01) [2003] ECR I-13617, paras. 168-9). This is another bootstraps argument on behalf of Romania. *The first step in the analysis should be to ask whether the United Kingdom has relevant obligations arising from the ICSID Convention which, by operation of article 351 TFEU, preclude the application of the Treaties.* As explained below in relation to Cross-Appeal Original Ground 3 (paras. 101-8), on a proper interpretation of the

ICSID Convention, the United Kingdom clearly does have such obligations. *Therefore, the Treaties do not have any relevant effect and this court is not bound by EU law to interpret the Convention in the manner for which Romania contends. In any event, the proper interpretation of the Convention is given by principles of international law applicable to all Contracting States and it cannot be affected by EU law.*
(*emphasis added*)

75. This analysis was then reinforced in the underlined passage below, with the surrounding (and explanatory) passages included to put it in context:

[88]. On behalf of the First Claimant, Viorel Micula, Mr Patrick Green QC advances this ground of appeal, which the other Claimants adopt, on the basis that a conflict might be said to arise between the United Kingdom's obligations under the ICSID Convention and EU law. Mr Green submits that the UK Parliament, in enacting section 2(1) of the European Communities Act 1972, could not have intended to empower the EU to put the United Kingdom in breach of pre-accession international obligations, with only EU institutions as arbiters of the lawfulness of doing so. He says this is so for two reasons. First, it undermines the scheme of the Convention and the express terms and purpose of the 1966 Act. Secondly, at the time Parliament enacted the 1972 Act there was before it a treaty which provided, in what has become article 351 TFEU, that it would not affect the pre-accession international obligations of member states . . .

[89]. *The constitutional principles which underlie this submission are clearly correct. Under the UK constitution Parliament is sovereign and EU law has effect within the United Kingdom only to the extent that it has been given such effect by section 2(1) of the European Communities Act 1972 (R (Buckinghamshire County Council)* v. *Secretary of State for Transport ("HS2")* [2014] UKSC 3; [2014] 1 WLR 324, para. 79; *Pham* v. *Secretary of State for the Home Department* [2015] 1 WLR 1591, paras. 80, 90; *R (Miller)* v. *Secretary of State for Exiting the European Union* [2017] UKSC 5; [2018] AC 61, paras. 60, 61). It is for the UK courts to decide on the scope and effect of section 2(1) and, as Lord Reed observed in *HS2* at para. 79, if there is a conflict between a consti-tutional principle and EU law, that conflict has to be resolved by our courts as an issue arising under the constitutional law of the United Kingdom. However, by contrast with *HS2*, which concerned article 9 of the Bill of Rights, the present case concerns obligations arising under the ICSID Convention which are given effect by the 1966 Act, which is not a statute of fundamental constitutional importance. In these circumstances, there is no sound basis for concluding that the effect of section 2(1) of the European Communities Act 1972 was impliedly excluded so far as the 1966 Act is concerned. In any event, successive treaties which have been given effect in the domestic law of the United Kingdom by section 2(1) of the 1972 Act have included a provision equivalent to the current article 351 TFEU. As a result,

the 1972 Act has already made provision for the effect of accession on pre-accession treaties and, accordingly, this ground of appeal collapses into Original Ground 4 to which we now turn . . .

76. After the decision of the Supreme Court in *Micula*, the question of the scope of potential defences available to a state was referred to at first instance in *Unión Fenosa Gas SA* v. *Arab Republic of Egypt* [2020] EWHC 1723 (Comm), a decision of Jacobs J. In that case, the investor had obtained an award in an arbitration conducted pursuant to the ICSID Convention against the state of Egypt. The investor applied without notice under CPR Part 62.21 for registration of it, and CPR Part 62.21(3) provided that such an application for an ICSID Convention award had to be made "in accordance with the Part 8 procedure". Males J (as he then was) made an order granting permission to register the award, but a dispute arose as to whether, in addition to serving the order of Males J, the investor ought also to have served the Part 8 claim form on Egypt. On a without notice application by the investor, Teare J granted a declaration that service of the claim form was not required; Egypt applied to set aside that order, on the grounds that Part 8 applied to the application to register the ICSID Convention award and that the claim form ought to have been, and was required to be, served on the foreign state.

77. Jacobs J held that it did not, and refused the application. He did so for three reasons. Firstly, it was not required on a proper construction of CPR Part 62.21. Secondly, requiring service of a Part 8 claim form would be inconsistent with the regime for registration incorporated in CPR Part 62.21 and CPR Part 74.6, which required service only of the order made on registration. Thirdly, he observed that it would be surprising if this were required, as it was not required under New York Convention awards unless the court so ordered, and the defences against enforcement under the New York Convention were far wider in scope than for ICSID Convention awards. He also found that CPR Part 8, for these purposes, had to be read consistently with CPR Part 62.21, and this latter rule modified or disapplied elements of Part 8 as they applied to applications to have an ICSID award registered, such that such an application could be made without notice.

78. In deciding the application, which is one of the few reported cases on enforcing awards under the ICSID Convention, the judge considered the Supreme Court decision in *Micula*. He stated, having considered Articles 53 and 54 of the ICSID Convention:

[66]. The effect of these provisions, as stated in *Dicey, Morris & Collins: The Conflict of Laws* 15th edition paragraph 16-189, is to take ICSID awards

outside the normal regime for the enforcement of arbitral awards, including
the New York Convention regime, which enables recognition to be refused by
national courts on specified grounds. *Instead, the ICSID Convention has its own
internal procedure for interpretation, revision and annulment of awards. Requests
for annulment are dealt with by an ad hoc committee, and the grounds for
annulment are limited.* However, as Dicey states:

> Unless an ICSID award is annulled pursuant to this procedure, the courts
> of Contract States are bound to recognise and enforce it in accordance with
> Art. 54(1), to which effect is given in England by ss. 1 and 2 of the
> 1966 Act.

[67]. The recent decision of the Supreme Court in *Micula* confirms that
the ICSID Convention differs significantly from the New York Convention:
see paragraph [68]. The Supreme Court considered it arguable, however, that
there is:

> scope for some additional defences against enforcement, in certain excep-
> tional or extraordinary circumstances which are not defined, if national law
> recognises them in respect of final judgments of national courts and they
> do not directly overlap with those grounds of challenge to an award which
> are specifically allocated to Convention organs under articles 50 to 52 of
> the Convention. (paragraph [78]).

[68]. It clearly remains the case, however, that such a defence, even if it
exists at all (a point which is arguable but has not yet been finally determined),
is far narrower in scope than the possible defences under the New York
Convention. The important point for present purposes is that it would be
surprising if a more cumbersome procedure had to be followed for the
registration of ICSID awards under the 1966 Act, when compared to the
procedure for New York Convention awards, in circumstances where the
arguments available to the state (if they exist at all) are significantly more
limited. Apart from the possibility of "exceptional or extraordinary circumstances", the only available argument to the state is that the enforcement of the
award has been or might be stayed. CPR r. 62.18(4) and (5) expressly cater for
this possibility, by requiring (amongst other things) the award creditor to state
whether a stay has been granted or an application made for a stay.

79. I entirely agree with those observations. The availability of
defences to a foreign state faced with an application to register an
arbitral award under the ICSID Convention is far narrower than those
that would be available if an award were being enforced under the New
York Convention. ICSID is a separate and stand-alone international
convention, with signatories far more numerous than the Member
States of the EU. The 1966 Act is separate legislation dealing specifically with such awards. *Micula* makes it clear that for an additional
defence to be available to a state, it must "not directly overlap with

those grounds of challenge to an award which are specifically allocated to Convention organs under articles 50 to 52 of the Convention." Jurisdiction of the tribunal, and matters covered in the annulment application, are plainly within such areas allocated to such organs. They are exclusively allocated under the ICSID Convention to ICSID itself. Therefore Spain has no ability to deploy such defences in this application. This is an—undoubtedly more lengthy than ideal—explanation of the first route to the answer on this issue on this application.

80. The United Kingdom undoubtedly had existing treaty obligations which pre-date its accession to the European Community, which then became the European Union. These include its own international obligations under the ICSID Convention, which are owed to all the other signatories in what is plainly a multilateral treaty. One can well understand that Spain finds itself on the horns of a juridical dilemma, with its obligations under the ECT for dispute resolution (which treaty plainly incorporates the ICSID Convention) now found by the CJEU to conflict with the law of the EU as set out in the EU Treaties. The ultimate court under those EU Treaties, the CJEU, has found that international arbitration of the type established under the ICSID Convention (and incorporated into the ECT) is not compatible with EU law for the reasons it has explained in both the *Achmea* and *Komstroy* cases. However, with the greatest of respect to the CJEU, it is not the ultimate arbiter under the ICSID Convention, nor under the ECT, and the difficulties in which Spain finds itself do not assist it here, given the United Kingdom's own treaty obligations under the ICSID Convention, which are owed to all signatories of the ICSID Convention. The domestic mechanism established under the 1966 Act was enacted specifically in order to comply with these.

81. However, even if I am wrong in that analysis, and the ECT itself (or the EU Treaties) was (or were) directly in conflict with Spain's (or other Member States') obligations to the ICSID Convention, applying conventional analysis to conflicting treaty obligations, one would turn to the Vienna Convention. That too is a multilateral treaty, and its full title is the Vienna Convention on the Law of Treaties ("VCLT"), and it was concluded at Vienna on 23 May 1969 and opened for signature on that date. Its authentic texts are English, French, Chinese, Russian and Spanish. Article 5 states that the Convention applies to any treaty which is the constituent instrument of an international organisation and to any treaty adopted within an international organisation without prejudice to any relevant rules of the organisation.

82. Articles 26 to 30 are as follows. The headings are included in the text of the treaty:

Article 26. *"Pacta sunt servanda"*

Every treaty in force is binding upon the parties to it and must be performed by them in good faith.

Article 27. *Internal law and observance of treaties*

A party may not invoke the provisions of its internal law as justification for its failure to perform a treaty. This rule is without prejudice to article 46.

Article 28. *Non-retroactivity of treaties*

Unless a different intention appears from the treaty or is otherwise established, its provisions do not bind a party in relation to any act or fact which took place or any situation which ceased to exist before the date of the entry into force of the treaty with respect to that party.

Article 29. *Territorial scope of treaties*

Unless a different intention appears from the treaty or is otherwise established, a treaty is binding upon each party in respect of its entire territory.

Article 30. *Application of successive treaties relating to the same subject-matter*

1. Subject to Article 103 of the Charter of the United Nations, the rights and obligations of States parties to successive treaties relating to the same subject-matter shall be determined in accordance with the following paragraphs.

2. When a treaty specifies that it is subject to, or that it is not to be considered as incompatible with, an earlier or later treaty, the provisions of that other treaty prevail.

3. When all the parties to the earlier treaty are parties also to the later treaty but the earlier treaty is not terminated or suspended in operation under article 59, the earlier treaty applies only to the extent that its provisions are compatible with those of the later treaty.

4. When the parties to the later treaty do not include all the parties to the earlier one:

(a) As between States parties to both treaties the same rule applies as in paragraph 3;

(b) As between a State party to both treaties and a State party to only one of the treaties, the treaty to which both States are parties governs their mutual rights and obligations.

5. Paragraph 4 is without prejudice to article 41, or to any question of the termination or suspension of the operation of a treaty under article 60 or to any question of responsibility which may arise for a State from the conclusion or application of a treaty the provisions of which are incompatible with its obligations towards another State under another treaty.

83. Finally, Articles 40 and 41 state:

Article 40. Amendment of multilateral treaties

1. Unless the treaty otherwise provides, the amendment of multilateral treaties shall be governed by the following paragraphs.

2. Any proposal to amend a multilateral treaty as between all the parties must be notified to all the contracting States, each one of which shall have the right to take part in:

(a) The decision as to the action to be taken in regard to such proposal;
(b) The negotiation and conclusion of any agreement for the amendment of the treaty.

3. Every State entitled to become a party to the treaty shall also be entitled to become a party to the treaty as amended.

4. The amending agreement does not bind any State already a party to the treaty which does not become a party to the amending agreement; article 30, paragraph 4(b), applies in relation to such State.

5. Any State which becomes a party to the treaty after the entry into force of the amending agreement shall, failing an expression of a different intention by that State:

(a) be considered as a party to the treaty as amended; and
(b) be considered as a party to the unamended treaty in relation to any party to the treaty not bound by the amending agreement.

Article 41. Agreements to modify multilateral treaties between certain of the parties only

1. Two or more of the parties to a multilateral treaty may conclude an agreement to modify the treaty as between themselves alone if:

(a) The possibility of such a modification is provided for by the treaty; or
(b) The modification in question is not prohibited by the treaty and:

(i) Does not affect the enjoyment by the other parties of their rights under the treaty or the performance of their obligations;
(ii) Does not relate to a provision, derogation from which is incompatible with the effective execution of the object and purpose of the treaty as a whole.

2. Unless in a case falling under paragraph 1(a) the treaty otherwise provides, the parties in question shall notify the other parties of their intention to conclude the agreement and of the modification to the treaty for which it provides.

84. Both the ICSID Convention and the ECT are plainly multilateral treaties. Mr Baloch drew attention to the bilateral nature of the dispute resolution procedures in the ECT, which involve only two parties. He submitted that such a procedure is a bilateral process. That may be, but I do not consider that the fact that only two parties would be in dispute means that the treaties should be construed as though they were bilateral, as they plainly are multilateral. The mechanism within the ECT for resolving disputes does not make it a bilateral treaty, nor does it mean that any part of it should be considered as though it were. Further, there has been no amendment of the ICSID Convention pursuant to Article 40 of the VCLT, nor has there been a modification under Article 41 either.

85. It is common ground between the parties that the ICSID Convention should be interpreted in accordance with Article 31 VCLT, and that the starting point is that any text "*shall be interpreted in good faith in accordance with the ordinary meaning to be given to the terms of the treaty in their context and in the light of its object and purpose.*" Article 32 allows recourse to supplementary means of interpretation, including the preparatory work of the treaty in order "*to confirm the meaning resulting from the application of article 31, or to determine the meaning*" when the determination when the article 31 exercise leaves the meaning ambiguous, obscure or leads to an absurd result. This latter part has some similarities with the approach under *Pepper* v. *Hart*, but in any event permits reference to what, in international law, is usually called by the French term *travaux préparatoires*. Section 3 deals with termination and suspension. Article 54 allows termination or withdrawal from a treaty in accordance with its terms. Article 58 permits two or more parties to a multilateral treaty to conclude an agreement to suspend the operation of the treaty, temporarily and between themselves alone as long as such suspension is permitted by the treaty and not prohibited. Neither of those had been initiated by Spain either alone, or together with (say) the Member States where the claimants are situated (for temporary suspension under Article 58) before the dispute which led to the ICSID Award, for either ICSID or the ECT.

86. In terms of any conflict, this is governed by Article 30. Here, Article 30(4) would apply, because the ICSID Convention has nation parties to it who are not Member States. Therefore, the ICSID

Convention, for as long as Spain is a party to it, should govern the way in which valid ICSID awards against Spain are dealt with in other domestic courts. This includes enforcing those awards, which includes recognition orders. Spain would probably argue that this is a circular argument, because of the need for a "valid ICSID award" and if Spain were right, such an award could not be valid because there is no valid arbitration agreement. But the answer to that is that such reasoning is, itself, entirely circular. If one considers the matter in a chronological and linear fashion, starting with the ICSID Convention itself, Spain acceded to that freely and so did the United Kingdom. Spain—or any other Member State in my judgment—cannot rely upon the *Achmea* and/or the *Komstroy* cases to dilute the United Kingdom's own multilateral international treaty obligations. It certainly cannot rely upon those cases to interpret the 1966 Act differently to what its clear terms require.

87. I consider that there is a clear conflict between the EU Treaties, as their application to international arbitration involving Member States has been decided by the CJEU and explained by Mr Baloch, and each (or more accurately both) of the ECT or the ICSID Convention. If intra-EU arbitration is contrary to EU law principles governing either primacy of the CJEU or EU principles generally, then this must (and can only) arise from the EU Treaties themselves. I cannot see how it can arise in any other way. Therefore, if that is the case, there must be a conflict. That conflict does not mean that the latter EU law principles as enunciated by the CJEU remove Spain from the ambit and scope of the ECT, or from the ICSID Convention. Spain's arguments, as either amplified or further explained in submissions (including a letter to the court after distribution of the draft judgment) was that there was a conflict between articles 267 and 344 of the TFEU on the one hand, and article 26 of the ECT on the other. In those circumstances, Spain maintained that this conflict should be resolved in favour of the articles of the TFEU by what it called "the treaty conflict rule of EU primacy". However, in my judgment that is simply a different way of Spain maintaining that both the ECT and the ICSID Convention—both of which clearly have signatories who are not Member States of the EU—should be interpreted by ignoring their clear terms regarding dispute resolution, in preference to granting the decisions of the CJEU complete primacy over those pre-existing treaty obligations of all states. I do not accept that is the correct approach, and I do not consider that such a result can be achieved by applying international law principles to conflicting treaty provisions.

88. The answers to the EU law sub-issues which I set out at [45] above are therefore as follows:

Question 1. *Achmea* arose out of the BIT between the Slovak Republic and the Netherlands. Does *Achmea*'s reasoning also apply to the ECT?

Answer: The reasoning in *Achmea* probably does also apply to the ECT, in terms of the applicability of EU law, as considered by the CJEU. This means that the CJEU would be most likely to reach the same conclusion on any EU law question referred to it under the ECT as it did under the BIT in the *Achmea* case. However, these are matters of EU law only. The conclusion does not "apply to the ECT" in the sense contended for by Spain. That conclusion is a purely EU law issue.

Question 2. Do TFEU Articles 267 and 344, as interpreted by the CJEU, have primacy over Article 26 of the ECT as a matter of international law?

Answer: No, they do not. Even if they did, this would go to the jurisdiction of the ICSID arbitral tribunal, and the ICSID Convention makes clear that this is a matter that is reserved to, and can only be resolved by, the procedure set down in the Convention, and not domestic law. This is helpfully stated in the commentary by Professor Schreuer on Article 54 which stated that "A domestic court or authority before which recognition and enforcement is sought is restricted to ascertaining the award's authenticity. It may not re-examine the ICSID tribunal's jurisdiction. It may not re-examine the award on the merits. Nor may it examine the fairness and propriety of the proceedings before the ICSID tribunal." This passage was expressly approved by the Supreme Court in *Micula* at [68] which definitively states the approach under English law to this issue.

The answers to the series of questions that followed at sub-issues 2(a) to (e) are therefore of academic interest only and need not be addressed on this application.

89. Having therefore considered what I consider to be the over-arching submissions of Spain on the impact of EU law upon its other, pre-existing treaty obligations under the ICSID Convention and the ECT, I can turn to consider the specifics of the challenges to jurisdiction on this application. One therefore turns to consider whether the grounds deployed by Spain here fall into the category of what the Supreme Court described as "scope for some additional defences against enforcement, in certain exceptional or extraordinary circumstances which are not defined, if national law recognises them in respect of final judgments of national courts" (to quote from the Supreme Court in *Micula*). They must also not "directly overlap with those grounds of challenge to an award" specifically allocated to Convention organs.

90. The only defence that I consider could potentially fall into that category, even arguably, would be one based upon the State Immunity Act 1978, if such a defence were available. Lack of a written agreement to arbitrate, and validity of the award, are both within the grounds of challenge allocated to Convention organs. The Supreme Court could not possibly be referring to defences being "additional", as well as having to arise in both "exceptional or extraordinary circumstances", if they had as their subject matter challenges to jurisdiction raised before and considered (and rejected) by the ICSID arbitral tribunal and the ICSID Committee. In case I am wrong about that, I will address those briefly in any event.

State immunity

91. I have already referred to parts of the State Immunity Act 1978 ("the 1978 Act") set out at [53] above. The 1978 Act expressly has exceptions to state immunity included within it, with section 2(2) being where there is a "prior written agreement" and section 9(1) being where a state has agreed in writing to submit a dispute which may arise to arbitration. There is a specific exception for states which have submitted to the jurisdiction, and the provision within section 9 can either be seen as a specific sub-set of the more general submission to the jurisdiction by way of a written agreement, or as a free-standing exception relating to arbitration. It does not much matter which analysis is adopted, because under section 9 (and to use its exact wording) no state is "immune as respects proceedings in the courts of the United Kingdom which relate to the arbitration".

92. The claimants rely upon both section 2(2) of the 1978 Act (concerning the state's prior agreement to submit to this jurisdiction) and section 9(1) of the 1978 Act (whereby the state's agreement to arbitrate means submitting to proceedings in this jurisdiction for recognition of any resulting award). Spain argues that neither of these apply. Spain cited a number of authorities that are of limited relevance, including those such as *R v. Bow Street Metropolitan Stipendiary Magistrate & Ors; ex parte Pinochet Ugarte (No 3)* [1999] UKHL 17; [2000] 1 AC 147, as well as other far earlier authorities that pre-date the 1978 Act and deal with submission to the jurisdiction in (what used to be called) the face of the court. The *Pinochet* case post-dates the 1978 Act, and concerned attempts by Spain to extradite General Pinochet from the United Kingdom for human rights abuses including torture whilst he was the head of state of Chile, having seized power in 1973 in a military coup. He was arrested in London in the late 1990s,

having travelled here for medical treatment. None of these authorities assists Spain on this application in its assertion that the High Court has no adjudicative jurisdiction to make an order for recognition of an ICSID award under the 1966 Act.

93. Under section 2(2) of the 1978 Act, a state loses its adjudicative immunity if by prior agreement it has submitted to the jurisdiction of the English courts. Spain denies that the claimants are correct when they rely upon Article 54 of the ICSID Convention as constituting this agreement. Spain challenges that Article 54 of the ICSID Convention satisfies the requirements of prior agreement to submit to the jurisdiction of the courts under section 2(2) of the 1978 Act. Spain maintains that (and here I quote again from its skeleton argument): "(a) it is well established both as a matter of English and international law that only an express submission (or, as it is sometimes called, waiver) by the state itself to the jurisdiction will qualify as a submission within the meaning of s 2(2) SIA; and (b) Article 54 of the ICSID Convention does not come close to meeting that requirement (among others), not least because it is not framed as a waiver or submission by Spain to the jurisdiction of any domestic court bar its own, and indeed does not even refer to a state's adjudicative immunity."

94. Spain also maintains that "as a matter of historical record, Article 54 of the ICSID Convention was never understood as containing a waiver by states of their adjudicative immunity in this jurisdiction. Had it been, it would have been discussed by Parliament in those terms when the ICSID Convention was being ratified, together with the legislative changes necessary to give it effect." Spain maintains that this was not done, and therefore this is the "strongest possible indication that the UK did not consider such a waiver to exist in the ICSID Convention, as giving effect to it would have required a seismic change to the common law, given waiver by prior agreement was impossible in the UK at that time."

95. This argument is misplaced, and entirely ignores, in my judgment, both the content and effect of the ICSID Convention, the terms of the 1966 Act and also the ratio of *Micula*. The terms of the 1966 Act are clear, and the ICSID Convention itself is a schedule to the Act. It is not necessary to consider what was, and what was not, discussed in Parliament or in what terms. Further, if Spain were correct, it would mean that section 1(1) of the 1966 Act could only apply to awards in which the United Kingdom was a party. That is not a sensible interpretation of the statute, and would—if correct—be categorised as an absurd result. It is plainly not correct. In my judgment, Article 54 of

the ICSID Convention falls within "prior written agreement" for the purposes of the 1978 Act, as does the relevant article, article 26, of the ECT which incorporates the ICSID Convention.

96. The claimants also rely upon the second exception, namely the one under section 9(1) of the 1978 Act. Under this exception, a state's adjudicative immunity is removed with respect to proceedings related to an arbitration in which it has agreed to arbitrate, including proceedings for the recognition of any resulting award. Spain originally submitted before me that there were two reasons why the section 9(1) exception did not apply in this case to remove its adjudicative immunity. It was initially submitted by Spain that the exception did not "encompass arbitrations involving sovereign acts, which includes the Award. Customary international law, against which the SIA must be interpreted, only recognises an exception for adjudicative immunity for recognition proceedings where the dispute on which the award is premised involves a commercial transaction." However, that submission was expressly, and in my judgment sensibly, withdrawn in reply. In order to assist, should the argument be contemplated in other proceedings in the future, the distinction is a flawed one and Mr Baloch was right to withdraw it. There are at least two fundamental problems with any attempt to make a distinction between commercial transactions and sovereign acts in this way. The first is that section 9(1) does not restrict itself only to commercial arbitration. The wording is where the agreement is "to submit a dispute which has arisen, or may arise, to arbitration"; note the use of the indefinite article, and the absence of a restrictive adjective with the word "arbitration". There is no basis for reading into the section a word that is not there, namely "commercial", to restrict the type of arbitration to which the section applies.

97. Any doubts about the extent of the exception to matters of enforcement of international arbitration awards should in any event be considered to be well settled, and the judgment of the Court of Appeal in *Svenska Petroleum Exploration AB* v. *Government of the Republic of Lithuania & Anor (No 2)* [2006] EWCA Civ 1529, [2007] QB 886 is directly relevant. In that case the arbitration was conducted in Denmark under the auspices of the International Chamber of Commerce or ICC. That case concerned an award and the New York Convention, not ICSID, but what the court had to say concerning *international* arbitration is equally applicable to an ICSID Convention award. At [111] to [120] Moore-Bick LJ considered Hansard and various amendments to the 1978 Act. At [121] he concluded:

Like the judge, we are not persuaded that section 9(1) is ambiguous or obscure in either respect when read in the context of the rest of the Act, but we also agree that, if it is, the two statements of the Lord Chancellor to which we have referred put the matter beyond any doubt. *It is quite clear that it was the intention of Parliament in formulating section 9 of the Act in unrestricted terms that applications for leave to enforce arbitration awards should not attract sovereign immunity, whether the award was domestic or foreign.* (emphasis added)

98. Exactly the same reasoning applies to whether the award relates to "commercial" arbitration or some other type of arbitration that is not commercial. There is no basis for such a distinction and it does not appear in the 1978 Act.

99. The second fundamental problem with the submission is that it invites consideration of the substantive, underlying dispute, in respect of which the Award has been made, as part of the court's consideration of whether it should be recognised. Spain argued originally that the dispute concerned "sovereign acts" since it concerns the way that Spain modified its energy regulations. But, with the greatest respect to Spain, that is neither here nor there, and in my judgment would be a wholly irrelevant point. Such an argument *might* have assisted it before the ICSID arbitral tribunal (although it did not here, and I doubt it ever would, because arbitrations under the ICSID Convention almost always involve a state as a party). But whether it could have assisted Spain before the tribunal leading to the making of the Award or not, once such an award is made, that is the end of the matter so far as the substantive dispute is concerned.

100. Unless Spain were able to demonstrate that it has some "*additional defences against enforcement, in certain exceptional or extra-ordinary circumstances*" (to use the terminology from [78] in *Micula*) then the proper approach to an application to recognise an award made by an arbitral tribunal under the ICSID Convention is to recognise it in accordance with the 1966 Act which is in accordance with the treaty obligations of the United Kingdom under the ICSID Convention, which is a schedule to the Act. Here, none of the defences deployed by Spain are, in my judgment, "exceptional or extraordinary".

101. Finally, Spain contended that its "offer of arbitration in the ECT did not extend to [the claimants], depriving the Tribunal of jurisdiction". The authorities that are said to justify this analysis that the arbitration provisions in the treaty itself are in some way partial, applying only to some investors and not others, are the two cases of the CJEU that I have already considered under the EU law question, namely *Achmea* and *Komstroy*. However, not only have I answered

those issues above already (and in favour of the claimants), but there is no justification for interpreting their effect as, in some way, creating within the ECT itself, only a partial offer of arbitration to some investors, but not others, depending upon whether those investors were resident within Member States or elsewhere. Spain cannot rely upon any particular wording within the treaty itself that could accomplish such an extraordinary result. There is no such wording.

102. In my judgment, and this is consistent with the cases including *Micula*, the ICSID Convention—a schedule to the 1966 Act—satisfies the requirements of section 9(1) of the 1978 Act and is an agreement in writing by all the Contracting States to submit disputes with investors from other states to international arbitration. The same applies to the ECT for that matter, which expressly incorporates ICSID in article 26. The 1966 Act concerns only awards under the ICSID Convention, and therefore the claimants' application to register the Award qualifies as "proceedings in the courts of the United Kingdom which relate to the arbitration" under section 9(1) of the 1978 Act.

103. Spain therefore cannot rely upon immunity; this is the consequence of the express terms of the 1966 Act and the 1978 Act. Its arguments in this respect are not made out and I reject them.

Lack of a written agreement to arbitrate and the validity of the Award itself

104. These two lines of argument can usefully be considered together. In a sense they can be seen as two sides of the same coin. Spain maintains that there was no written agreement, and also that the Award was not valid. The way this is summarised in the skeleton argument is as follows: "This is because the Award was rendered pursuant to an offer by Spain to arbitrate in ECT Article 26 that did not extend to claims against nationals of other EU Member States, including by the [claimants] *vis-à-vis* Spain. That prohibition on what is known as 'intra-EU claims' in the ECT sounds in international law."

105. This argument implicitly requires an elevation of the case law of the CJEU, namely the *Achmea* and *Komstroy* cases, which I have addressed above when considering the EU law question, to a prohibition in international law, and to grant them a precedence higher than the wording of the ICSID Convention and the ECT themselves. I have already explained above why I do not consider that to be the correct analysis.

106. The Award was issued by a validly constituted ICSID tribunal, and challenges to the decisions of that tribunal were brought by Spain

under the ICSID Convention and the validity of the award was confirmed by the ICSID Committee. These very points have been considered and adjudicated upon by both the tribunal and the Committee, and the ICSID Convention gives these organs the exclusive jurisdiction to determine such matters. It is therefore a valid and authentic award, and Spain has no basis for contending otherwise.

107. I therefore remind myself of what Professor Schreuer said in his writings, approved by the Supreme Court in *Micula* at [68], and together with this, one can put the dicta from [69] and [78] in that case together to establish a summary of the principles, which I have synthesised into the following. This is not an exact and direct quotation from either the writings of Professor Schreuer or from the judgment of Lord Lloyd Jones JSC and Lord Sales JSC in the Supreme Court, but takes some of their phraseology, and is my analysis of what they state the law to be. The *italic* is my emphasis:

Where an application is made to the High Court for recognition of an award made by a tribunal under the ICSID Convention, the court is restricted to ascertaining the award's authenticity. It may not re-examine the ICSID tribunal's jurisdiction. It may not re-examine the award on the merits. Nor may it examine the fairness and propriety of the proceedings before the ICSID tribunal. *The High Court may not refuse recognition or enforcement of an award on grounds covered by the challenge provisions in the ICSID Convention itself. Nor may it do so on grounds based on any general doctrine of ordre public.* There is a provision in the 1966 Act for a stay to be imposed in certain situations, that correspond with those available under the Convention in Articles 50, 51 and 52. However, these stays pursuant to the Convention are available only in the context of interpretation, revision and annulment of awards addressed by those articles. If a respondent state has already exercised and exhausted its right under article 52 of the ICSID Convention to seek annulment of the Award, and has failed (such that the award in question has been upheld by the ICSID ad hoc Committee), then the High Court will not grant a stay.

108. Finally, although it is arguable that there is scope for some additional defences against enforcement, in certain exceptional or extraordinary circumstances which are not yet defined, such defences must, in my judgment, (as a minimum) comply with two conditions. Firstly, the law of this jurisdiction must recognise them in respect of final judgments of the English courts; and secondly, they must not overlap with those grounds of challenge to an award which are specifically allocated to Convention organs under articles 50 to 52 of the ICSID Convention.

109. Here, there are no such exceptional or extraordinary circumstances. The EU law question does not qualify as such; and in any

event, the primacy of the law of this jurisdiction and the adherence of the United Kingdom to its own international treaty obligations under the ICSID Convention (as set out in the 1966 Act) would in any event be given priority by the High Court as stated by the Supreme Court in *Micula*.

110. Nor, in my judgment, does this result mean that the United Kingdom's treatment of such issues makes it some sort of outlier in the field of recognition of ICSID awards, or in its interpretation of international legal principle. Similar outcomes have resulted elsewhere on the same, or very similar, international law issues.

111. The claimants rely upon decisions on ICSID award enforcement against Spain and attempts to have these recognised in both Australia and in the United States. Although the domestic law of each of those jurisdictions is different from that of the United Kingdom, there are distinct similarities, and both of them are signatories to the ICSID Convention. The approach of both of those jurisdictions merits attention, and I shall refer to each in turn.

112. In Australia the case of *Kingdom of Spain* v. *Infrastructure Services Luxembourg S.à.r.l.* [2021] FCAFC 3 concerned enforcement attempts by the claimants against Spain in respect of the same Award. In Australia the statute that is the broad equivalent of the State Immunities Act 1978 here, is the Foreign State Immunities Act 1985 (referred to in that judgment as "the Immunities Act"). At first instance, Spain sought to claim foreign state immunity when opposing an application that Spain pay the amount of the award. The judge at first instance, Stewart J (referred to in the judgments of the Federal Court of Appeal as "the primary judge") had rejected the claim of foreign state immunity and on appeal, the principal issue was whether Spain's accession to the ICSID Convention constituted a submission to the jurisdiction of the Federal Court (per [15] in the judgment of Perram J). Spain had also submitted "that Article 26 of the ECT was unlawful under European law", an argument described by Perram J as "an orphan submission".

113. The Federal Court of Appeal unanimously found that the ICSID Convention was an agreement within the meaning of section 10(2) of the Immunities Act, and thereby constituted a submission to the jurisdiction. It found that there was a distinction between recognition and execution, and this was reflected in the proper construction of Article 54(2) of the ICSID Convention. The judgment of Perram J held at [29] that both Articles 54(1) and (2) showed that a party with an ICSID award may seek recognition without enforcement (by which it plainly means without at that stage execution) and that

execution could not be construed as including recognition in Article
55. I agree with that analysis. Allsop CJ, who at the time as Chief
Justice of the Federal Court of Australia was the most senior judge of
that court, agreed with Perram J but also gave additional reasons and
stated at [4] that Article 54 included enforcement because it was
principally considered that this was to give recourse against a defaulting
investor and "it was considered highly unlikely that the State party to
the Convention would not carry out its treaty obligations" (quoting
Professor Schreuer). The orders at first instance made by the primary
judge had gone beyond those rights available to the claimants, but the
claimants were entitled to recognition of the Award and that was the
outcome of the appeal.

114. In my judgment, that analysis in terms of state immunity and
recognition holds good in the United Kingdom, for the same reasons
but applying the logic to the relevant domestic legislation. Spain has no
immunity to these proceedings under the 1966 Act because it has
already submitted to the jurisdiction of the court by reason of its
accession to the ICSID Convention, which is a written agreement to
arbitrate and hence within the exceptions of the State Immunities Act
1978. Spain made a special application for leave to appeal to the High
Court of Australia from the judgment of the Federal Court, and
judgment was handed down after the hearing before me on 12 April
2023, and is at [2023] HCA 11. The claimants drew this to my
attention during the period after the hearing and whilst this judgment
was being prepared, and I gave both parties permission to lodge short
further supplemental submissions on that matter, and they both did so.

115. In summary, the High Court of Australia dismissed Spain's
appeal and found that Spain was the subject of a binding ICSID
arbitral award, the effect of Spain's agreement to Articles 53 to 55 of
the ICSID Convention amounted to a waiver of foreign State immunity from the jurisdiction of the courts of Australia to recognise and
enforce, but not to execute, the award. The court held that "the orders
made by each of the primary judge and the Full Court are properly
characterised as orders for recognition and enforcement. Spain's challenge to the orders of the Full Court should not be accepted. The
orders of the Full Court should not be disturbed."

116. In its supplemental submissions Spain contended that this
decision "carries little or no weight as an authority on the questions
before this court". I disagree with that characterisation, as I find such an
authority persuasive; I do of course accept that one must obviously take
account of the slightly different domestic statutes involved. However,
even without deploying that decision as an authority of weight, the

claimants are entitled to rely upon what is its conventional analysis of legal principle, including international treaty obligations such as Spain being a state that is party both to the ECT and the ICSID Convention, to support its case. Regardless of that, the outcome of that appeal does not, in my judgment, affect or impinge upon the analysis of the correct approach to be applied by this court on the law in this jurisdiction on the application by Spain to set aside the Order. I would characterise it as separate free-standing support, in the highest appellate court of another common law jurisdiction, for the analysis which I have undertaken. Both my analysis and that in Australia are consistent, and reach the same conclusions.

117. Turning to the United States, a number of decisions were cited to me, including *NextEra Energy Global Holdings BV* v. *Kingdom of Spain* No 1:19-cv-1618 (TSC) (DDC 2023) which was handed down on 15 February 2023 and *9Ren Holding S.à.r.l.* v. *Kingdom of Spain* No 1:19-cv-1871 (TSC) (DDC 2023). These were part of what appears to be a battle on a wide international front between these parties, and these two were anti-anti-suit injunctions by which parties to such awards were seeking to overcome Spain's continuing opposition to enforcement by bringing motions to dismiss, with the corresponding petitions to enforce the award. It is unnecessary to analyse these in any great detail, because in any event the statute which the court had to apply was that which applies in the United States, namely the Foreign Sovereign Immunities Act. For what it is worth, however, and perhaps unsurprisingly, the US courts granted the relief sought, in order to protect their own lawful jurisdiction (explained at Section B[4] of the judgment of US District Judge Kutyan) which prevented Spain from continuing with certain acts in Luxembourg that were, in the view of that judge, plainly aimed at usurping the jurisdiction of the US court (explained at Section B[3] of the judgment in the *9Ren* case). These cases support the claimants' approach.

118. Remaining in the United States, on 29 March 2023 (therefore the first day of the hearing before me) the US District Court for the District of Columbia (usually referred to as "DC") handed down its opinion in the case of *Blasket Renewable Investments LLC* v. *Kingdom of Spain* Civil Case No 21-3249 (RJL) (DDC 2023). In that case, the claimant Blasket had inherited (by way of substitution or otherwise) the claims of two Dutch companies which had the benefit of an arbitration award from a tribunal which had been seated in Switzerland. The judge found that there was no valid agreement to arbitrate as a result of the law of the EU and Spain's motion for Blasket's petition to be dismissed was granted. That case did not however concern an ICSID award, but

rather was one convened under UNCITRAL. That is a very important difference. In particular, it does not assist Spain before me. This is because, as explained on page 10, and as the judge stated, "the presumption [as to lack of an agreement to arbitrate] can be overcome in cases where there is clear and unmistakeable evidence that the parties delegated authority to the arbitrator to resolve challenges to the existence of an arbitration agreement; *First Options of Chicago Inc.* v. *Kaplan* 514 US 938, 944 (1995). As relevant here, one way in which parties may show such clear and unmistakeable evidence is to agree to arbitrate under rules that expressly delegate such authority to the arbitrator." That passage correctly states that authority to resolve jurisdiction issues can be delegated to the arbitrator or the arbitral tribunal. In my judgment, that is what the ICSID Convention clearly does.

119. I explained above at [38] that the claimants had sought recognition of the Award in other jurisdictions, including Australia. That jurisdiction is a signatory to the ICSID Convention and it is a matter of the domestic law in other jurisdictions, wherever recognition is sought, whether the claimants are entitled to recognition in those other jurisdictions. The ratio and decisions in other countries are potentially persuasive and of interest, but as I noted, plainly they do not bind this court. It is however heartening, in terms of the integrity of international treaties, and the purpose and applicability of the ICSID Convention and international arbitration under it, that both in Australia and also the District of Columbia, those jurisdictions have adopted broadly the same analysis as I have. The near-identical conclusion of the highest court in Australia, and its findings of the lack of state immunity there, due to the existence of a binding arbitration agreement, demonstrate in my judgment that my conclusion is correct.

120. There is a decision relied upon by Spain which is listed in a footnote in its skeleton, and was amplified orally at the hearing. This is a decision of the Commercial Court in the British Virgin Islands ("the BVI"), namely *Tethyan Copper Company Pty Ltd* v. *Islamic Republic of Pakistan and others* BVIHC (Com) 2020/0196. In that case, the claimant ("TCC") had sought provisional charging orders and interim relief, together with an application for recognition of an ICSID award in the amount of US$ 6.2 billion which it had obtained following a dispute with Pakistan. In the course of deciding that TCC were not entitled to this in the BVI, Wallbank J considered at [50] the submission made by the TCC that by virtue of Pakistan being a party to the ICSID Convention, it was not immune from the jurisdiction of the courts of the BVI under its State Immunity Act (called "the SIA" in the judgment at [27]), because of a similar provision to the 1978 statute in

the UK concerning an arbitration agreement. The judge dismissed that argument in a five-line paragraph in his judgment that included the following: "However, the ICSID Convention is a treaty that can have no effect under domestic law in and of itself. That includes, for present purposes, the United Kingdom position on state immunity, which is set out in the SIA."

121. I respectfully do not agree with that statement, in so far as it is advanced as authority for stating the position of the law of England and Wales where a claimant seeks recognition of an ICSID award in the High Court. Firstly, the point does not appear to have been fully argued before the judge, and was very much a secondary element to the ratio of the judgment on wider and different issues. Secondly, the decision is one of the courts of the BVI. Thirdly, it does not pay any attention to the terms of the 1966 Act; whether there is a similar act governing that territory or not, that statute is a crucial step in enshrining the United Kingdom's international treaty obligations in domestic law and will be applied here by the High Court. Therefore, the statement that a treaty can have no effect under domestic law is, as a general proposition, broadly correct in terms of the lack of direct effect available to private individuals of international obligations generally contained in treaties, but cannot stand unqualified when one considers the terms of the 1966 Act. Additionally, that there are some differences between the law of England and Wales and the law of the BVI is clear from, for example, the passages at [56] to [64] discussing the procedural differences under the two different CPRs in force in each jurisdiction. But regardless of the position under the law of the BVI—and this is not the place for a comparative analysis of the two jurisdictions—I am satisfied that the position of the law to be applied in this jurisdiction is as I have explained it.

122. What Spain's main EU law argument amounts to is this, at its heart. Spain accepts that it is a party to the ICSID Convention; it accepts that it is a party to the ECT. It freely acceded to both of those treaties. There is no doubt that the ECT expressly incorporates the ICSID arbitration provisions within it, adopting international arbitration to resolve disputes between Contracting Parties (which includes Spain) and private international investors, who are resident or domiciled in other countries. Yet Spain relies upon its membership of the EU, the EU Treaties that created that union, and the strictures imposed on those Member States by the CJEU's rulings on the EU Treaties. These rulings have determined—again, outlined here only in summary—that there can be no valid arbitration provision adopted by Member States which grants jurisdiction to any arbitral tribunal that

may touch upon matters of EU law. This is due to the primacy of the CJEU to determine all such EU law matters. Therefore Spain argues that there can be no jurisdiction, even for a properly constituted ICSID arbitral tribunal, to determine any dispute under the ECT between Spain and an investor from any other state. This is the case regardless of whether that investor is within, or without, another Member State, although it runs both lines of argument in the alternative. It also argues that any ICSID award, such as the Award in this case, must therefore have been reached without jurisdiction and so cannot be a valid award; and/or that it has immunity from recognition in the courts of the United Kingdom for what may broadly be described as the same, or similar, reasons.

123. The logical consequence (or extension) of this argument for it to be correct is that these decisions of the CJEU must be taken as binding all the parties to the ECT and to the ICSID Convention— whether Member States of the EU or otherwise—and take priority over all other treaty obligations entered into by any other state, even those obligations assumed by treaty prior to the creation of the EU. What this would mean, were Spain to be correct (and I am confident that it is not correct) is that by reason of the terms of the EU Treaties, and by reason of the rulings of the CJEU and its supremacy over EU law matters, the EU and the CJEU would have unilaterally changed—if not removed—all the existing treaty obligations of all the Contracting Parties to the ICSID Convention. I know of no framework of international law in which such a position could be correct. I would go further and observe that it simply cannot be correct. It would mean that the existing treaty obligations of any Contracting Party to the ICSID Convention would have been changed, without any intention or involvement on the part of that Contracting Party, a sovereign nation, as a result of rulings by the CJEU. That is not a conventional analysis of how international obligations work, and I reject Spain's arguments. This completes my consideration of what I consider is the longer route.

124. It can therefore be seen that whichever route is navigated—the first based on domestic law analysis, and the second considering international legal principles—one arrives at the same destination. The United Kingdom enacted the 1966 Act in order to comply with its own treaty obligations under the ICSID Convention. The Award in this case is a valid one which is authentic and one that was clearly reached with jurisdiction. Jurisdiction was considered and determined by the ICSID Tribunal, and this was confirmed by the ICSID Annulment Committee. The operation of the 1966 Act means that

the Award was properly recognised as set out in the Order, in accordance with the CPR rules that govern such matters. There is no basis for setting aside that Order under Issue I, jurisdiction, as this is a matter that is reserved to the Convention organs. But even if there were, Spain's challenges to jurisdiction are misplaced. The claimants' arguments are to be preferred on this ground.

125. Were Spain's arguments to be accepted by this court this would mean, in my judgment, that the High Court would be giving effect to EU law and finding invalid the express ICSID arbitration provision which is undoubtedly included in the ECT. This would thereby override both the United Kingdom's own domestic statutes precisely on the same point—both the 1966 Act and the State Immunity Act 1978—but would also be ignoring its own separate international treaty obligations contained in the ICSID Convention itself. There is no reason to do this: indeed, there is every reason not to do so. It would, in my judgment, be wrong in law to allow this argument by Spain based on EU law, as explained in *Achmea* and *Komstroy* by the CJEU, to trump the existing treaty obligations of the ICSID Convention, as enacted into domestic law here by the 1966 Act.

F. Issue II: Non-disclosure

126. This is a separate and free-standing ground upon which Spain seeks to set aside the Order, but obviously it only arises in the event that Spain's challenge to jurisdiction fails. It is said by Spain that the claimants failed to comply with their duties of full and frank disclosure and fair presentation in obtaining the Order.

127. This is explained in the skeleton argument lodged for Spain in this way: "there is a significant amount of information that [the claimants] failed to convey to it when the Recognition Order was made, and failed to update the Court on thereafter." There are therefore two aspects to it. Firstly, disclosure (or as alleged, non-disclosure) when obtaining the Order; secondly, similar failures after the Order was made.

128. Mr Green KC for the claimants, at one stage, invited clarification from the court in terms of direction as to what precisely, in a situation such as this one, ought to be disclosed by an applicant in the position of these claimants. He pointed out that the claimants had lodged over 2,000 pages of evidence and exhibits in their application for recognition that led to the Order. He pointed out the logistical difficulties on the part of any such applicant, and the difficulty of knowing how much was sufficient in terms of satisfying the duty of

disclosure. He also, later in the hearing, argued that there was no obligation for any disclosure on the part of a claimant seeking recognition of an ICSID award by the High Court, although he rowed back from that when, upon discussion with the court, it appeared that he came to consider this position potentially extreme.

129. There are two limbs to what used to be called the rules of "natural justice", and now sometimes described as the duty to act fairly. They both have Latin tags. One is the rule against bias, which can be either actual or apparent bias, which used to be called *nemo iudex in sua causa*, or—loosely translated—no man can act as a judge in his own cause. In modern parlance, this means every litigant is entitled to have their case judged by an impartial tribunal. The other limb used to be called *audi alteram partem*, or hear the other side. This equates to a party knowing the case they have to meet, and being given a fair opportunity to meet that case. What that distils down to, in any case where an *ex parte* order is involved, is this. On applying for the order, the applicant must disclose to the court any matters adverse to him or herself which are material, even if they are adverse to the applicant. This is because making an order against a party without giving them the opportunity to be heard is a narrow exception to the second limb as explained above. Additionally, because the duty of disclosure upon such an applicant is a high one (and it is also, incidentally, an exception in an adversarial system such as ours) the court can demonstrate its disapproval of the failure to comply with the duty by discharging the order even if, otherwise, the applicant on the *inter partes* hearing would be entitled to the same relief.

130. The seminal statement on the scope of the duty is per Bingham LJ (as he then was) in *Siporex Trade SA* v. *Comdel Commodities Ltd* [1986] 2 Lloyd's Rep 428, 437 where he stated that an applicant for *ex parte* relief must:

[I]dentify the crucial points for and against the application, and not rely on general statements, and the mere exhibiting of numerous documents [. . .] He must disclose all facts which reasonably could or would be taken into account by the judge in deciding whether to grant the application. It is no excuse for an applicant to say that he was not aware of the importance of matters he has omitted to state. If the duty of full and fair disclosure is not observed the court may discharge the injunction even if after full inquiry the view is taken that the order made was just and convenient and would probably have been made even if there had been full disclosure.

131. That duty remains upon the applicant until the first hearing on notice; per Saville J (as he then was) in *Commercial Bank of the Near*

East plc v. *A and others* [1989] 2 Lloyd's Rep 319, 323. There was some disagreement between the parties before me regarding the point at which that duty is lifted, and whether service of the Order is the point at which it no longer applies. To support its contention that the duty subsists past the date of service, Spain cited a recent decision of Bacon J, namely *Valbonne Estates Limited* v. *Cityvalue Estates Limited* [2021] EWHC 544 (Ch) at [31], who stated that "the duty of full and frank disclosure is not temporally limited to the hearing of the without notice application, but continues while the proceedings remain on that basis".

132. Here, the consent order of Moulder J to which I have referred at [3] is directly relevant because it demonstrates that the Order was agreed by the parties to have been served on 21 October 2021, and Spain made its first application to set the Order aside by way of an application dated 4 November 2021. The date advanced by Spain at [124] of its skeleton argument as the date of 8 November 2021 being the one prior to which breaches of the disclosure obligation are relevant is therefore slightly wrong. However, nothing of note occurred, or did not occur, between 21 October 2021 and either 4 November or 8 November 2021, and so nothing turns on that minor difference in dates for reasons that will become clear.

133. It is trite law that where the court determines that there has been a substantial breach of the duty, "the court strongly inclines to setting its order aside and not renewing it, so as to deprive the default-ing party of any advantage that the order may have given him. This is particularly so in the case of freezing and seizure orders"; per Christopher Clarke J (as he then was) at [104] in *Re OJSC Ank Yugraneft* v. *Sibir Energy Plc* [2008] EWHC 2614 (Ch), [2010] BCC 475. That there is a particularly high duty in such cases is well known, because, self-evidently, orders of those kinds particularly interfere with, and are invasive of, the respondent's rights. Such orders have in a number of other cases been described as "draconian in nature". In the *Yugraneft* case, a provisional liquidator had been appointed. One of the respondents was Mr Roman Abramovich, a well-known international figure who for many years owned Chelsea FC, an associ-ation football club. The non-disclosure was highly material, and just to select here one small element, the court had not been told that Sibir had alleged in other proceedings in the BVI that he was resident in England (which partially founded the jurisdiction to make the order) that he had denied this on oath in other proceedings, and both the Court of Appeal and the court at first instance in those BVI proceed-ings had accepted that Russia was the country of habitual residence and centre of operations of Sibir and of all of the defendants, including

Mr Abramovich. This was not disclosed to the court at all on the *ex parte* application.

134. That judgment continued to explain that whether to continue such an order in those circumstances was always a matter of discretion in any particular case:

[106] As with all discretionary considerations, much depends on the facts. The more serious or culpable the non-disclosure, the more likely the Court is to set its order aside and not renew it, however prejudicial the consequences. The stronger the case for the order sought and the less serious or culpable the non-disclosure, the more likely it is that the Court may be persuaded to continue or re-grant the order originally obtained. In complicated cases it may be just to allow some margin of error. It is often easier to spot what should have been disclosed in retrospect, and after argument from those alleging non-disclosure, than it was at the time when the question of disclosure first arose.

135. Materiality therefore depends in every case upon the nature of the application and the matters relevant to be known by the judge when hearing it; Jacobs J in *Union Fenosa* at [109], quoting Toulson J (as he then was) in *MRG (Japan) Ltd* v. *Engelhard Metals Japan Ltd* [2003] EWHC 3418 (Comm) at [25].

136. The duty of full and frank disclosure also applies in respect of immunity. Spain argues that section 1(2) of the State Immunity Act itself "charges the Court with ensuring the state's right to immunity is upheld even where it does not appear. But more importantly, the SIA purports to reflect the UK's obligations towards other states under customary international law. A state may breach public international law due to the actions of its courts."

137. I accept that state immunity is a highly important feature, and potential arguments in that respect ought to be brought to the attention of the court on an *ex parte* application. I also accept that the court has to consider this of its own motion given the terms of the 1978 Act. I also concur with the description of such immunity as a matter of "the greatest importance", the terms used by Lawrence Collins LJ in *ETI Euro Telecom International NV* v. *Republic of Bolivia & Anor* [2008] EWCA Civ 880, [2009] 1 WLR 665 at [110]. In that case, Bolivia had nationalised certain assets and as a result the claimant commenced arbitration under the provisions in a BIT between Bolivia and the Netherlands, the claimant being a Dutch company. That BIT contained ICSID Convention arbitration provisions and this resulted in an arbitration claim being submitted to ICSID. The claimant also sought

a freezing injunction against Bolivian assets in London. This was discharged on the grounds, inter alia, of state immunity. This case makes clear that "the court must give effect to immunity even if the state does not appear", and therefore I accept that this point must be considered by the court at the point of considering an application. This is consistent with what is stated in that case, because Stanley Burnton LJ stated at [128] (with whom Tuckey LJ agreed at [129]) that "any claimant who wishes to bring proceedings against a state must be in a position to address the issue as to the jurisdiction of the court when he seeks to invoke the jurisdiction of the court". He also added (after observations in respect of seeking an injunction against a state, which do not apply here) that "in a case such as the present, the court must consider and decide the question of state immunity at as early a stage of the proceedings as practicable."

138. The court here could not finally decide the question of state immunity without full argument from Spain. The issues are complex and a decision of this nature is not apt to be made, even (or especially) at first instance, without giving a sovereign state the ability properly to advance its own arguments by its own counsel, properly instructed. However, there is no doubt that the issue of lack of jurisdiction—however it might be arrived at, whether by reason of lack of jurisdiction on the part of the tribunal, state immunity under the State Immunity Act, or otherwise—was or would be a central feature of whether the Award should be recognised.

139. In *Gold Reserve Inc.* v. *Bolivarian Republic of Venezuela* [2016] EWHC 153 (Comm), [2016] 1 WLR 2829 [67]-[91] Teare J considered similar issues in respect of enforcement of an arbitral award following resolution of a dispute between an investor and Venezuela concerning mining rights and concessions there, which were held by a Canadian company. There was a dispute resolution procedure in place under a BIT between Venezuela and Canada, and because Venezuela was not a signatory to the ICSID Convention the arbitration was conducted under the Additional Facility mechanism. Venezuela had been a party to the ICSID Convention but had denunciated it in accordance with Article 71 in July 2012.

140. In that case, the applicant had drawn the court's attention to Venezuela's immunity, but was held to have breached the obligation of full and frank disclosure by failing to draw the court's attention to the arguments that Venezuela would be likely to rely upon in order to maintain that immunity. Teare J said at [71] the following, in a passage upon which Spain relies:

ENGLAND (HIGH COURT)
208 ILR 624

When a judge is faced with an application for permission to enforce an award against a state as if it were a judgment the judge will have to decide whether it is likely that the state will claim state immunity. If that is likely then he would probably not give permission to enforce the award but would instead specify [. . .] that the claim form be served on the state and consider whether it was a proper case for granting permission to serve out of the jurisdiction. He would envisage that there would be an *inter partes* hearing to consider the question of state immunity. For that reason any applicant for permission must draw the court's attention to those matters which would suggest that the state was likely to claim state immunity. Indeed, since the court is required by section 1(2) of the State Immunity Act to give effect to state immunity even though the state does not appear, it is important that the court be informed of the available arguments with regard to state immunity. [. . .] [W]here, as here, it was known that Venezuela was continuing to rely upon those arguments and therefore was likely to rely upon state immunity it was incumbent upon the applicant to summarise those arguments for the benefit of the judge. That was the more necessary where the application was on documents alone and the judge might well be considering the application after a busy day in court dealing with other matters.

141. Spain relies upon this passage in two ways. Firstly, it is said to provide guidance for the court when dealing with state immunity that this subject is sufficiently important to be drawn to the court's attention in its own right. Spain submitted in its skeleton "Put simply, where it appears likely that a state will rely on its immunity before the Court, the Court should make no *ex parte* order, but instead 'envisage that there would be an *inter partes* hearing to consider the question of state immunity'."

142. The nature of the non-disclosure in that case is clear from [68] of the judgment:

[68] With regard to state immunity Mr Dunning submitted that Mr Miller, who made the witness statement in support of the application without notice, did not refer to the fact that the arbitration agreement had been disputed in the arbitration or to the fact that the arbitration agreement was still being disputed by Venezuela in proceedings in Paris and Luxembourg. In the result it was said that the court was not alerted to the fact that there was a substantial and continuing dispute concerning the agreement to arbitrate.

G. Discussion on non-disclosure

143. Dealing with the substance of the complaints raised by Spain in this respect, the following points must be made. This is a very different set of facts to those in *Gold Reserve*.

144. There is nothing of substance in the complaint that the Order was made *ex parte* without the judge convening an *inter partes* hearing to consider and determine Spain's challenges to jurisdiction and/or claim of state immunity. This is because CPR Part 62.21 contains a specific regime for registration of ICSID awards. This is headed "Registration of awards under the Arbitration (International Investment Disputes) Act 1966". Teare J was considering the procedure under CPR 62.18 as made clear at [54] in his judgment where he sets this out. That is a different rule.

145. The Practice Direction to CPR Part 62 does not deal specifically with whether an order recognising an award under the ICSID Convention should, or should not, be determined without a hearing in the first instance, but it does state in the commentary in the White Book on PD62(1) that:

It is not necessary for a party seeking to enforce an award against a state under this provision to issue a claim form; it suffices to issue a without notice application, and the state is then able to apply to set aside any order made against it.

146. That entry in the commentary supports the approach adopted by the claimants in this case. As observed by Jacobs J in *Unión Fenosa v. Egypt* (which has already been referred to at [76] above), there have been very few reported cases on recognition of ICSID awards. At [59] he stated:

Indeed, even though the procedure for registering awards under the 1966 Act has now been in place for over 50 years, there is no reported example of an application for registration coming before the court initially on an ordinary *inter partes* application under Part 8 or its equivalent under the rules of the Supreme Court. If there is to be a contested application, then it would be expected to arise on an application to set aside the without notice order.

147. The Commercial Court Guide states in its 11th edition that such an order "may be made without a hearing" in section O.11. Further, this supports not only the approach in the commentary, but also that suggested by Jacobs J in the *Fenosa* case.

148. Spain therefore, as a matter that amounts to alleging a breach of procedural fairness, maintains that the judge ought not to have made the Order in the way that she did, and ought instead to have set the matter down for a fully contested hearing. The implication is also that had she been aware of the full nature of the objections and arguments which Spain would advance, she would have done so. I disagree with both of those propositions for reasons which will become clear.

149. Further, and in any event, even if the judge was wrong to have made the Order, and even if I am wrong in agreeing that she adopted the correct procedural way forward (and even if my reasons for so agreeing do not withstand scrutiny) this does not matter for two reasons. Firstly, Spain has been given the opportunity to address all of the many arguments that it wished to advance on this subject in any event, under its liberty to apply to have the *ex parte* Order set aside. Secondly, given this was an Order recognising the Award, Spain has suffered no prejudice whatsoever in any event. And thirdly, departing from the consideration of the principles to be applied, and finally— perhaps conclusively—these points raised by Spain have no basis in fact in this case. This is because the claimants expressly *did* draw the jurisdiction issues to the attention of the court in their first witness statement and the extensive evidence lodged in support of the application for recognition. Unlike the *Gold Reserve* case, where these matters were not referred to, the claimants explained in considerable detail the arguments that Spain had deployed to challenge jurisdiction, and the EU law basis of them.

150. Three examples will suffice from the witness statement of Mr Watson:

1. In section "B Background" at (iv) under the heading "The European Commission's Applications for Leave to Intervene in the ICSID Arbitration" he sought to explain this, which included reference to the US and Australian enforcement proceedings, which he explained later in his statement;
2. In the same section at (v) under the heading "The ICSID Annulment Proceedings" he summarised the arguments advanced by Spain, including at 41.1 that it had been contended by Spain that the ICSID tribunal had manifestly exceeded its powers by exercising jurisdiction over the Arbitration in breach of EU law. This included the following passages "On Spain's case, because the dispute is 'intra-EU' in nature, it is contrary to EU law, including the 'principle of primacy', for the Tribunal to have accepted jurisdiction. Spain also argues that the *Achmea* judgment—which was not analysed by the Tribunal as it was not on the Arbitration record—should have been applied and that the effect of *Achmea* is to preclude intra-EU arbitration under the ECT ...";
3. At 43.3, in a section dealing with Spain's contentions that the Tribunal failed to state reasons, these included "in relation to its determination of ... the applicability of EU law. Spain claims that the Tribunal failed to state reasons because it did not explain why EU

law could not deprive the Tribunal of its jurisdiction under the ECT." The statement also explained that Spain had submitted three separate and new expert reports "in support of its EU law arguments ... who opined on two main issues of EU law: the application of the ECT to intra-EU disputes; and EU state aid issues." He also set out the counter-arguments being advanced by the claimants to meet these points. In my judgment, more than enough was provided to explain to the court that Spain was contending that the correct application of EU law meant the arbitral tribunal had no jurisdiction. These issues were perfectly properly and sufficiently brought to the attention of the court by the claimants before the Order was made.

151. Mr Watson also dealt with the application by the Commission to intervene in the Annulment proceedings, as well as the steps taken by the claimants in Australia and the United States to enforce the award, including reference to the decisions of the courts in those two jurisdictions in so far as those were then available. He referred to the assertion by Spain in Australia before Justice Stewart of foreign state immunity under the Foreign State Immunities Act 1985. In a separate section of his statement, headed "E. Full and frank disclosure", he set out in 17 separate paragraphs Spain's "anticipated arguments" and also some other points to put those in context.

152. There are four matters listed in Spain's skeleton argument which it is argued before me were not disclosed. Firstly, it is said that the claimants failed to update the court when the judgment of the CJEU in the *Komstroy* case was handed down on 2 September 2021. Secondly, the claimants failed to inform the court of "various developments which followed the CJEU's judgment in *Achmea* ... including, most egregiously, the fact of Intra-EU Declaration 1 and the UK's signature of the same". It is said that these were, or were likely to be, relevant to Spain's defences. Thirdly, that the claimants "failed to update the court on developments at the European Commission, in the courts of EU Member States and elsewhere, which are clearly relevant to Spain's argument that section 9(1) [of the State Immunity Act 1978] cannot apply to displace its immunity, and which have transpired since the Recognition Order." Finally and fourthly, although the judgment in the *Gold Reserve* case *was* expressly brought to the attention of the court by the claimants on the *ex parte* application, Spain contends that they failed to draw the attention of the court specifically to the "guidance" in [71] of that judgment, which I have quoted at [140] above, to the effect that an *inter partes* hearing would (or on Spain's case, should) be held.

153. Intra-EU Declaration 1 arises as follows. The full title of this is Declaration of the Representatives of the Governments of the Member States of 15 January 2019 on the Legal Consequences of the Judgment of the Court of Justice in *Achmea* and on Investment Protection in the European Union. On 15 January 2019, the EU Member States of the EU, including at that time the UK (as it had not at that stage left the EU) signed a declaration ("Intra-EU Declaration 1") which stated the following:

International agreements concluded by the [EU], including the [ECT], are an integral part of the EU legal order and must therefore be compatible with the [EU] Treaties. Arbitral tribunals have interpreted the [ECT] as also containing an investor–State arbitration clause applicable between Member States. Interpreted in such a manner, the clause would be incompatible with the Treaties and thus would have to be disapplied.

154. However, Intra-EU Declaration 1 does not bind this court, it did not bind the judge who made the Order, and it certainly does not apply in priority above the 1966 Act, or in preference to the ratio of the Supreme Court as set down in *Micula*. In my judgment, it is not relevant to the issues on the application, which can be taken from the *Achmea* case. The sentence "and thus would have to be disapplied" from the Intra-EU Declaration also, as observed above at [81], directly contradicts Article 5 of the Vienna Convention specifically dealing with conflicting treaty obligations. It does not therefore need to be considered further, and I do not consider it to have been material non-disclosure for the claimants not to have drawn the attention of the judge to this on the *ex parte* application pursuant to which she made the Order.

155. The judgment in *Komstroy* was handed down on 2 September 2021, which falls in the period after the Order was made on 29 June 2021, and before the first set-aside application was made by Spain on 4 November 2021, following the Order having been served on 21 October 2021 (the agreed date in the consent order made by Moulder J). There is no doubt therefore that it became known directly in the period covered by the duty of full and frank disclosure upon the claimants. The claimants' response to that complaint is three-fold. They observe that the decision of the CJEU affirmed the Opinion of AG Szpunar, which had been brought to the attention of the court in Mr Watson's witness statement in any event; that as of 2 September 2021, they had by that date "already sought to have the order served via diplomatic channels on Spain"; and finally they proffer an apology if they had misjudged matters in this respect.

156. I do not consider the failure to provide the court with a copy of the judgment in *Komstroy* in September 2021 to be of any particular import, or to constitute non-disclosure. It was handed down about 2½ months after the Order had been made, and after the claimants had initiated the process (which is done via the Foreign, Commonwealth and Development Office) for service of the Order. Its reasoning and conclusion was no surprise, and the judgment is entirely consistent (as is to be expected) with the view of the CJEU as set out in *Achmea*, and also as expounded by the Opinion of AG Szpunar (which was brought to her attention in Mr Watson's statement). The case is entirely aligned with the ratio of *Achmea*. All that the decision in *Komstroy* did was add to the weight of material supporting Spain's arguments on what I have called the EU law question; it did not raise a new argument. Out of an abundance of caution, the claimants' advisers could have provided the court with a copy (as they have done of later international decisions even when the *ex parte* duty clearly no longer applied), but one has to be realistic about this. The court was not likely to be assisted by a steady notification of material relevant to the development of the law in this area within the EU, nor is that required, for months after the Order had been made. The issue was put fairly and squarely by the claimants in the material already lodged with the court supporting the application that led to the Order, and the court had already been put on notice that these were arguments which Spain would be likely to mount. In my judgment that was sufficient.

157. So far as the failure to cite [71] specifically of *Gold Reserve* to the court is concerned, one has to be realistic too, about what that case actually states, its standing and the effect of the contents of that paragraph. Whether to hold an *inter partes* hearing or not prior to recognition is effectively, in the instant or any similar case for recognition of an ICSID award, a matter of procedure. It is true that Teare J was the Judge in Charge of the Commercial Court at the time of his judgment in *Gold Reserve*, and his views on such matters hold weight. However, it is equally true to observe that Cockerill J occupied exactly the same post at the time she made the Order, as she was the Judge in Charge by then. One can safely assume that she would not have needed the dicta of her predecessor citing to her, in order to be aware that the powers of the court include ordering an *inter partes* to be held. The case itself in any event had been specifically drawn to her attention. Further and in any event, an *inter partes* hearing is not the procedure generally adopted for recognition of arbitral awards, ICSID or otherwise, and this is supported by the commentary in the White Book. As the Judge

in Charge, she followed the procedure for recognition and considered the matter *ex parte*. This approach is not only correct procedurally, but is supported by the decision in *Unión Fenosa* that the order is what must be served on a foreign state, not the claim form. If the construction of CPR Part 62.21 by Jacobs J is correct, and I consider that it is, then an order would ordinarily be obtained *ex parte* in the first instance in almost all, if not all, cases. This is also consistent with section 1(6)(c) of the 1966 Act itself. Here, the Order expressly included liberty to Spain to apply to set it aside, as all such orders will. I do not consider the failure to identify [71] of *Gold Reserve* to be a non-disclosure issue at all.

158. The overriding objective requires the court to consider the full list of matters at CPR Part 1 in everything that it does, including saving expense, acting proportionately, dealing with court business expeditiously and fairly, and allotting to any case appropriate resources, including considering resources necessary for other court users. Although Spain had previously deployed certain arguments extensively, both before the arbitral tribunal, the ICSID Annulment Committee and in the courts of Australia and the United States, there was no guarantee that this would necessarily continue, and the making of the Order in the way adopted here (and in other cases) gives any respondent a chance to consider, take advice specific to this jurisdiction, and then reflect upon whether it will challenge the order, and if so, on what grounds. If *inter partes* hearings were to be required as a matter of routine (or irregular routine, given how seldom ICSID awards are brought before the courts), the utility of having an arbitral award recognised by the courts will be undermined, and the efficient dispatch of court business would be damaged. In my judgment (and putting to one side the existing procedural rules), declining to have made the Order on the usual *ex parte* basis and instead listing the matter for an *inter partes* hearing—which as experience of this case shows, would have required four court days, according to the parties, inevitably some way in the future—would not have been in accordance with the overriding objective, still less in accordance with both the terms and ethos of the 1966 Act and the ICSID Convention itself.

159. Taking these matters about which Spain complains, and considering them both separately and also collectively, I do not accept that there was any material non-disclosure in this case. Spain's challenge on this issue also therefore fails, and there are no grounds to set aside the Order on the basis of non-disclosure.

H. Conclusion

160. Spain argued in its skeleton argument regarding ICSID arbitrations that "the approach of these tribunals (and [the claimants]) in second guessing the sovereign prerogative of the treaty parties circumvents the essentially consent-based character of international jurisdiction, and forces those treaty parties to have recourse to the bluntest tool available—treaty termination—to regain control. From the point of view of an orthodox international lawyer, this is bizarre." I understand this submission to mean that Spain considers that it ought not to have to terminate (or withdraw from) earlier treaties in order to "regain control", by which I take it to mean, not to have to submit to arbitration under the ICSID Convention. But this submission is, with respect, to misunderstand the effect of treaty obligations in international law. Any state that becomes a party to any treaty, by definition, becomes subject to the obligations contained in that treaty. That is what acceding to a treaty accomplishes. Those treaty obligations subsist, in broad terms, for as long as that state is a party to the treaty in question. If it wishes to "regain control" over the matters that are the subject of the treaty obligations, then it may do so (depending upon the terms of the treaty) by making reservations (if the treaty permits this) or terminating, or withdrawing from it. This is not the "bluntest tool" as Spain describes it; but even if it were, it is preferable to a particular state insisting that its own international treaty obligations be interpreted differently for itself, rather than for the other treaty nations, or for those who have rights under the ICSID Convention.

161. The law of England and Wales, as set out in the 1966 Act, clearly requires the High Court to recognise the Award, which was the result of the valid ICSID arbitration process between the claimants and Spain concerning their dispute under the ECT. It was this valid procedure which led to the Award, which is a valid and authentic one. Recognition was achieved by the making of the Order, which was done *ex parte* as required by the Civil Procedure Rules. Spain was not heard on that application, and this too is as required by the rules, although Spain was entitled to apply to set that Order aside.

162. However, there are no proper grounds for setting aside the Order or refusing to recognise the Award, and on all the different arguments raised by Spain on its application—those based on lack of jurisdiction or immunity, no arbitration agreement, an invalid award and so on—and also non-disclosure to the judge who made the Award, Spain has failed. I would add only this. I have produced this judgment in order to explain the analysis that I consider both underpins the

domestic enforcement regime for ICSID awards under the 1966 Act, and to address Spain's carefully advanced and argued multiple grounds of opposition to the Order. This should not be taken as encouragement by any state in a similar position to Spain that there is a lengthy and costly legal argument, based on wide-ranging arguments under international law, to be had on all or any attempts to obtain recognition of an ICSID award by an investor under the 1966 Act. There is not.

163. I explained at [38] above that the High Court will apply the law as it is set down in primary legislation together with judicial precedent applied by the doctrine of *stare decisis*. To do so in this case would lead to a very short judgment, and that is what parties must expect on applications of this type, on these types of jurisdictional grounds, in the future. The entire purpose of the ICSID Convention and the 1966 Act would be undermined if lengthy and complex arguments of the type advanced by Spain in this case were routinely advanced. Given the relative lack of authority on enforcement of ICSID awards under the 1966 Act, I hope that I might be forgiven for producing a judgment of this length on an application to which there is such a short answer available. In cases such as this one in the future, if the ICSID Committee have considered and dismissed objections under the Convention procedure and the award is a valid and authentic one, I wish to make it clear that there are no grounds for repetition or rehearing of those in the Commercial Court. Unless a case is truly exceptional, it is difficult to foresee how a hearing of the length required in this case, and a judgment of this length, would occur again. To do so would be contrary to the ICSID Convention and the 1966 Act, and is exactly what international arbitration is designed to avoid.

164. It therefore follows that this application by Spain to set aside the Order fails.

[Reports: [2024] 1 All ER 404; [2024] 1 All ER (Comm) 135;
[2023] 2 Lloyd's Rep 299]

Relationship of international law and municipal law — Treaties —
Washington Convention on the Settlement of Investment Disputes
between States and Nationals of Other States, 1965 — Arbitration
award by International Centre for Settlement of Investment
Disputes tribunal — Application for annulment dismissed by ad
hoc committee — Application for recognition and enforcement in
national court — Whether State immunity engaged — Whether
national court entitled to examine whether tribunal had jurisdiction — Whether there being distinction between recognition,
enforcement and execution

State immunity — Jurisdictional immunity — Immunity from
execution — Proceedings for recognition and enforcement of
International Centre for Settlement of Investment Disputes arbitration award in national court — Whether engaging State immunity — United Kingdom State Immunity Act 1978, Sections 2 and 9

Economics, trade and finance — Investment disputes —
International Centre for Settlement of Investment Disputes —
Enforcement of awards — The law of England

BORDER TIMBERS LTD AND HANGANI DEVELOPMENT CO.
(PRIVATE) LTD *v.* REPUBLIC OF ZIMBABWE[1]

([2024] EWHC 58 (Comm))

*England, High Court, King's Bench Division
(Commercial Court).*   19 *January* 2024

(Dias J)

SUMMARY: *The facts:*—In 2015, Border Timbers Ltd and Hangani
Development Co. (Private) Ltd ("the claimants"), which were incorporated
in Switzerland, obtained an arbitration award in their favour against the
Republic of Zimbabwe ("Zimbabwe") relating to the expropriation of their

---

[1]   The claimants were represented by Christopher Harris KC and Rumen Cholakov, instructed by
Baker Mackenzie LLP. The Republic of Zimbabwe, the respondent State, was represented by Salim
Moollan KC, Benedict Tompkins and Andris Rudzitis, instructed by Gresham Legal.
    The judgment of the Court of Appeal of 22 October 2024, unavailable when this volume went to
press, will be reported in a future volume of the *International Law Reports*.

land in Zimbabwe.[2] The award was made by a tribunal established under the auspices of the International Centre for the Settlement of Investment Disputes ("ICSID") under the terms of the Washington Convention on the Settlement of Investment Disputes between States and Nationals of Other States, 1965 ("the ICSID Convention").[3] The tribunal found that it had jurisdiction because Zimbabwe had agreed to arbitration in Article 10 of the bilateral investment treaty between Switzerland and Zimbabwe ("the BIT"). The tribunal awarded the claimants USD 124 million together with USD 1 million in moral damages and costs. Zimbabwe applied under Article 52 of the ICSID Convention to have the award annulled by an ad hoc committee. In 2018 the ad hoc committee dismissed that application and directed Zimbabwe to pay the claimants' costs.[4] The award and the costs order remained unsatisfied. The claimants applied to the English courts for registration and entry of the judgment on the award pursuant to Section 2 of the Arbitration (International Investment Disputes) Act 1966 ("the 1966 Act").[5] The High Court of England and Wales ("the Court") granted that application and ordered that the award be recognized and entered as a judgment by the Court in the same manner and with the same force and effect as if it were a final judgment of the Court.

Zimbabwe applied to set aside the order on the ground that it was entitled to State immunity under Section 1(1) of the State Immunity Act 1978 ("the 1978 Act"). The claimants maintained that Zimbabwe fell within the exceptions to immunity in Section 2 (submission to the jurisdiction of the United Kingdom courts) and Section 9 (agreement to arbitration) of the 1978 Act.[6] The Court ordered the trial of certain preliminary issues[7] concerning the claim to immunity.

Held:—Zimbabwe's application was dismissed.

A. *The structure and effect of the ICSID Convention*

(1) The ICSID Convention fell to be interpreted in accordance with the principles of treaty interpretation set out in the Vienna Convention on the Law of Treaties, 1969 (the "VCLT"). Article 31(1) of the VCLT required that the terms of a treaty be interpreted in their context and in the light of the object and purpose of the treaty. It was therefore unnecessary and unproductive to try to

---

[2] *Border Timbers Limited, Timber Products International (Private) Limited, Hangani Development Co. (Private) Limited* v. *Republic of Zimbabwe* (ICSID Case No ARB/10/25), Award of 28 July 2015. The award has not been made public.

[3] The relevant provisions of the ICSID Convention appear at paras. 11 and 14 of the judgment.

[4] Decision of 21 November 2018. The decision has not been made public.

[5] The relevant provisions of the 1966 Act appear at para. 16 of the judgment.

[6] The relevant sections of the 1978 Act appear at para. 9 of the judgment.

[7] See para. 4 of the judgment.

disentangle the text from the object and purpose. That did not mean that the treaty was to be interpreted by reference to a deemed intention of the Parties who may have had no common intention beyond what could be discerned from the text and any other expression of intention (paras. 25-9).

(2) The *travaux préparatoires* of a treaty were a subsidiary means of interpretation. The *travaux préparatoires* of the ICSID Convention demonstrated that this Convention imposed an obligation on every Contracting State to be bound by an ICSID award. The same obligation was not imposed on individual investors who were not Party to the Convention. It was for that reason that Articles 53 and 54 of the ICSID Convention prescribed a method of enforcement. The ICSID Convention was not intended to alter the law of State immunity. It provided only that an ICSID award was to be equated with a final judgment of a national court. It was then for the laws of the State concerned to determine whether State immunity barred enforcement (paras. 30-2).

(3) There was a distinction between the recognition of an award and its enforcement in Articles 54(1) and (2) of the ICSID Convention, while the execution of an award was addressed separately in Article 54(3). Every State Party to the ICSID Convention was obliged to recognize an ICSID award as binding for the purposes of *res judicata* and to enforce any pecuniary obligations which the award imposed by giving the award the same status as a final judgment of its own courts. An enforcing court was not entitled to re-examine the award on its merits or refuse enforcement on grounds of public policy, in contrast to the position under the New York Convention, 1958. Questions of execution, however, were left to be determined by each State in accordance with its own laws on State immunity (paras. 33-52).

B. Submission to the jurisdiction: Section 2 of the 1978 Act

(1) Under English law, any waiver of immunity by means of a treaty provision must be express. Article 54 of the ICSID Convention amounted to a waiver of immunity with regard to the recognition and enforcement of an award but not with regard to its execution (paras. 53-64).

(2) The fact that the ICSID Convention was adopted prior to the 1978 Act and at a time when English law still recognized absolute immunity did not prevent the ICSID Convention from amounting to a waiver of immunity or submission to the jurisdiction of the English courts (para. 75).

(3) In considering whether an award had been rendered "pursuant to [the ICSID] Convention" for the purposes of Article 54, it was not open to an English court to reopen the finding of the tribunal and ad hoc committee that the tribunal had had jurisdiction to render the award. An award was rendered pursuant to the ICSID Convention if it was rendered pursuant to the processes set out in the Convention (paras. 76-8).

(4) Article 54 of the ICSID Convention was not, however, a sufficiently clear and unequivocal submission to the jurisdiction of the English courts for the purposes of Section 2 of the 1978 Act. Under Section 1(1) a

foreign State was immune from the jurisdiction of the English courts except to the extent that the proceedings fell within one of the specific exceptions set out in the 1978 Act. Section 2 was drafted with reference to the submission of a State in specific proceedings. A general waiver of immunity was not the same as submission to the jurisdiction in respect of a particular action (paras. 53-73).

C. The arbitration exception: Section 9 of the 1978 Act

(1) Section 9 of the 1978 Act applied where a State had agreed in writing to submit a dispute to arbitration. Before finding that Section 9 was engaged, an English court was therefore required to satisfy itself that the dispute in question fell within the scope of the arbitration agreement, in this case Article 10 of the BIT. That required the Court to satisfy itself that the arbitration tribunal had jurisdiction, irrespective of whether the award had been rendered under the ICSID Convention or under a different arbitral process. Section 9 was, in this respect, different from Section 2 (paras. 80-90).

D. Whether State immunity was engaged

(1) Zimbabwe's application failed, however, because State immunity was not engaged on an application for the registration and enforcement of an ICSID award and was relevant only in relation to an attempt, after registration and enforcement, to execute the award. The decision to register and enforce an ICSID award under Section 2 of the 1966 Act involved no exercise of discretion by the Court and did not require service of process. Accordingly, it did not implead the foreign State (paras. 92-111).

(2) Although the claimants should have addressed the issue of State immunity in applying to have the award registered and enforced, the failure to do so was not a sufficient ground to set aside the order (para. 118).

The following is the text of the judgment of the Court:

Introduction

1. The matter before me arises out of an arbitration award dated 28 July 2015 made under the auspices of the 1965 Washington Convention on the Settlement of Investment Disputes between States and Nationals of Other States (the "ICSID Convention"). The arbitration in question was brought by the Claimants against the Defendant, the Republic of Zimbabwe ("Zimbabwe") and related to the alleged expropriation of the Claimants' land in Zimbabwe. By the award, Zimbabwe was ordered to pay to the Claimants some US$ 124 million plus interest, together with a further US$ 1 million in moral damages and costs.

2. Zimbabwe applied to have the award annulled by means of a process provided for in the ICSID Convention itself. That application was dismissed by the ICSID annulment committee on 21 November 2018 with further costs ordered to be paid by Zimbabwe. The award was not satisfied and on 15 September 2021, the Claimants applied to the English court without notice under CPR Part 62.21 for registration and entry of judgment on the award in England pursuant to section 2 of the Arbitration (International Investment Disputes) Act 1966 (the "1966 Act"). That application was granted by Mrs Justice Cockerill on 8 October 2021, who ordered that the award be recognised and entered as a judgment by the High Court in the same manner and with the same force and effect as if it were a final judgment of this court.

3. Cockerill J's order was served on Zimbabwe on 27 May 2022. On 25 July 2022, Zimbabwe applied to set it aside on the grounds that Zimbabwe was immune from the jurisdiction of the UK courts by virtue of section 1(1) of the State Immunity Act 1978. In response, the Claimants argued that Zimbabwe fell within one or both of the exceptions to immunity set out in sections 2 and 9 of the 1978 Act on the basis that it had submitted to the jurisdiction by virtue of its agreement to the ICSID Convention and/or had agreed to submit the underlying dispute to ICSID arbitration and so was not immune in respect of proceedings in the United Kingdom relating to that arbitration.

4. In these circumstances, it was directed by Jacobs J on 27 January 2023 that the following preliminary issues (in essence) be determined in advance:

(a) Whether Zimbabwe was entitled to claim state immunity in relation to these proceedings;

(b) Whether Zimbabwe had waived such immunity under section 2 of the State Immunity Act by operation of the ICSID Convention;

(c) Whether the English court was bound for the purposes of section 9 of the State Immunity Act by the determination of the ICSID tribunal and the annulment committee as to the jurisdiction of the tribunal;

(d) Whether Cockerill J's order should in any event be set aside for breach of the Claimants' duty of full and frank disclosure in failing to draw the attention of the judge in the without notice application to potential arguments on state immunity and/or in failing to establish any legal basis for an exception to immunity.

5. This is the hearing of those issues.

6. I mention one point at the outset in order to dispose of it. On behalf of the Claimants, Mr Christopher Harris KC made much of the fact that Zimbabwe had participated fully in the ICSID arbitration but had failed in its defence before a vastly experienced tribunal. Its attempt to have the award annulled had likewise failed on all points, yet it was now resisting enforcement of the award on substantially the same grounds as had been advanced and rejected previously (albeit with the addition of one further ground). He observed that it was now 10 years since the original award was issued and the Claimants were still no closer to receiving the damages awarded to them.

7. I have no doubt that this protracted chronology is a source of immense frustration to the Claimants and that in their eyes the present application is no more than a further attempt by Zimbabwe to frustrate and obstruct the enforcement of the award so as to avoid having to meet its obligations. Whether true or not, however, it is irrelevant to the question I have to decide, which is whether Zimbabwe is entitled to have Cockerill J's order set aside on the grounds asserted or not.

The legislative framework

State Immunity Act 1978

8. The starting point is the State Immunity Act 1978. Prior to 1978, England was almost alone in continuing to adopt a pure, absolute doctrine of state immunity in all cases: *I Congreso del Partido*, [1983] AC 244 at 261. Any waiver had to be declared in the face of the court, for example by pleading a defence to a claim: *Mighell* v. *Sultan of Johore*, [1894] 1 QB 149. Moreover, an agreement to arbitrate did not amount to a submission to the jurisdiction: *Duff Development Co. Ltd* v. *Government of Kelantan*, [1924] AC 797.

9. The common law rules were, however, replaced and restated in the 1978 Act which provides in material part as follows:

1. General immunity from jurisdiction

(1) A State is immune from the jurisdiction of the courts of the United Kingdom except as provided in the following provisions of this Part of this Act.

(2) A court shall give effect to the immunity conferred by this section even though the State does not appear in the proceedings in question.

2. Submission to jurisdiction

(1) A State is not immune as respects proceedings in respect of which it has submitted to the jurisdiction of the courts of the United Kingdom.

(2) A State may submit after the dispute giving rise to the proceedings has arisen or by a prior written agreement; but a provision in any agreement that it is to be governed by the law of the United Kingdom is not to be regarded as a submission.

(3) A State is deemed to have submitted—

(a) if it has instituted the proceedings; or
(b) subject to subsections (4) and (5) below, if it has intervened or taken any step in the proceedings.

(4) Subsection (3)(b) above does not apply to intervention or any step taken for the purpose only of:

(a) claiming immunity; or
(b) asserting an interest in property in circumstances such that the State would have been entitled to immunity if the proceedings had been brought against it.

(5) Subsection (3)(b) above does not apply to any step taken by the State in ignorance of facts entitling it to immunity if those facts could not reasonably have been ascertained and immunity is claimed as soon as reasonably practicable.

(6) A submission in respect of any proceedings extends to any appeal but not to any counter-claim unless it arises out of the same legal relationship or facts as the claim.

. . .

9. Arbitrations

(1) Where a State has agreed in writing to submit a dispute which has arisen, or may arise, to arbitration, the State is not immune as respects proceedings in the courts of the United Kingdom which relate to the arbitration.

(2) This section has effect subject to any contrary provision in the arbitration agreement and does not apply to any arbitration agreement between States.

. . .

13. Other procedural privileges

. . .

(2) Subject to subsections (3) and (4) below—

(a) relief shall not be given against a State by way of injunction or order for specific performance or for the recovery of land or other property; and
(b) the property of a State shall not be subject to any process for the enforcement of a judgment or arbitration award or, in an action in rem, for its arrest, detention or sale.

. . .

(3) Subsections (2) and (2A) above do not prevent the giving of any relief or the issue of any process with the written consent of the State concerned; and any such consent (which may be contained in a prior agreement) may be expressed so as to apply to a limited extent or generally; but a provision merely submitting to the jurisdiction of the courts is not to be regarded as a consent for the purposes of this subsection.

. . .

17. Interpretation of Part I

. . .

(2) In sections 2(2) and 13(3) above references to an agreement include references to a treaty, convention or other international agreement.

. . .

10. The following were common ground before me:

(a) The default position under the 1978 Act is that a foreign state is entitled to blanket immunity from the jurisdiction of the UK courts except as provided in Part I of the Act.

(b) The Act is a complete code, and a state is therefore immune unless one of the exceptions applies: *Benkharbouche* v. *Embassy of the Republic of Sudan*, [2017] UKSC 62; [2019] AC 777 at [39].

(c) The applicant bears the burden of proving the application of an exception on the balance of probabilities: *Al Masarir* v. *Saudi Arabia*, [2022] EWHC 2199 (QB); [2022] PIQR P3 at [8].

(d) The court is bound to give effect to any sovereign immunity of its own motion; the point cannot escape scrutiny *sub silentio*.

The ICSID Convention

11. The Preamble to the ICSID Convention provides as follows:

Preamble

The Contracting States

Considering the need for international cooperation for economic development, and the role of private international investment therein;

Bearing in mind the possibility that from time to time disputes may arise in connection with such investment between Contracting States and nationals of other Contracting States;

Recognizing that while such disputes would usually be subject to national legal processes, international methods of settlement may be appropriate in certain cases;

Attaching particular importance to the availability of facilities for international conciliation or arbitration to which Contracting States and nationals of other Contracting States may submit such disputes if they so desire;

Desiring to establish such facilities under the auspices of the International Bank for Reconstruction and Development;

Recognizing that mutual consent by the parties to submit such disputes to conciliation or to arbitration through such facilities constitutes a binding agreement which requires in particular that due consideration be given to any recommendation of conciliators, and that any arbitral award be complied with; and

Declaring that no Contracting State shall by the mere fact of its ratification, acceptance or approval of this Convention and without its consent be deemed to be under any obligation to submit any particular dispute to conciliation or arbitration,

Have agreed as follows . . .

12. Chapter I of the Convention establishes the structures and organs of ICSID, while Chapter II defines its jurisdiction. It is clear from these provisions that the Convention does not itself constitute an agreement to arbitrate but merely provides a framework for the resolution of such disputes as the parties may agree in writing to submit to ICSID. A separate agreement to arbitrate is therefore required, commonly to be found (as in this case) in a Bilateral Investment Treaty between two states.

13. Article 27 of Chapter II provides that no Contracting State shall give diplomatic protection or bring an international claim in respect of a dispute which has been submitted to ICSID arbitration unless the other Contracting State has failed to comply with the award.

14. Chapter III deals with conciliation while Chapter IV covers the processes and procedures for arbitration. The following provisions lie at the heart of this application and I set them out in full:

Article 41

(1) The Tribunal shall be the judge of its own competence.

. . .

Section 5 Interpretation, Revision and Annulment of the Award

. . .

Article 52

(1) Either party may request annulment of the award by an application in writing addressed to the Secretary-General on one or more of the following grounds:

. . .

(b) that the Tribunal has manifestly exceeded its powers;

. . .

(3) On receipt of the request the Chairman shall forthwith appoint from the Panel of Arbitrators an ad hoc Committee of three persons. None of the members of the Committee shall have been a member of the Tribunal which rendered the award, shall be of the same nationality as any such member, shall be a national of the State party to the dispute or of the State whose national is a party to the dispute, shall have been designated to the Panel of Arbitrators by either of those States, or shall have acted as a conciliator in the same dispute. The Committee shall have the authority to annul the award or any part thereof on any of the grounds set forth in paragraph (1).

. . .

(5) The Committee may, if it considers that the circumstances so require, stay enforcement of the award pending its decision . . .

. . .

Section 6 Recognition and enforcement of the Award

Article 53

(1) The award shall be binding on the parties and shall not be subject to any appeal or to any other remedy except those provided for in this Convention. Each party shall abide by and comply with the terms of the award except to the extent that enforcement shall have been stayed pursuant to the relevant provisions of this Convention.

(2) For the purposes of this Section, "award" shall include any decision interpreting, revising or annulling such award pursuant to Articles 50, 51 or 52.

Article 54

(1) Each Contracting State shall recognize an award rendered pursuant to this Convention as binding and enforce the pecuniary obligations imposed by that award within its territories as if it were a final judgment of a court in that State . . .

(2) A party seeking recognition or enforcement in the territories of a Contracting State shall furnish to a competent court or other authority which such State shall have designated for this purpose a copy of the award certified by the Secretary-General. Each Contracting State shall notify the Secretary-General of the designation of the competent court or other authority for this purpose and of any subsequent change in such designation.

(3) Execution of the award shall be governed by the laws concerning the execution of the judgments in force in the State in whose territories such execution is sought.

Article 55

Nothing in Article 54 shall be construed as derogating from the law in force in any Contracting State relating to immunity of that State or of any foreign State from execution.

The Arbitration (International Investment Disputes) Act 1966

15. This is the statute by which the ICSID Convention was implemented in English law. It was therefore common ground before me that it must be interpreted in the context of the ICSID Convention and that the presumed intention of parliament was to comply with the United Kingdom's treaty obligations thereunder. It is nonetheless important to note that although the Convention is scheduled to the Act, that does *not* mean that it is itself a part of English law. On the contrary, it is trite law that international treaties do not have direct effect in English law save to the extent that they are specifically enacted or incorporated.[1] The position is simply that the statute will be construed in a way which is consonant with the Convention and, so far as possible, with the United Kingdom's other international obligations, including those relating to state immunity.

16. The relevant provisions of the 1966 Act are as follows:

1. Registration of Convention awards

(1) This section has effect as respects awards rendered pursuant to the [ICSID Convention] . . .

(2) A person seeking recognition or enforcement of such an award shall be entitled to have the award registered in the High Court subject to proof of the prescribed matters and to the other provisions of this Act.

. . .

---

[1] Specific provisions of the ICSID Convention were in fact directly incorporated into English law by the 1966 Act, but not the Convention as a whole.

(4) In addition to the pecuniary obligations imposed by the award, the award shall be registered for the reasonable costs of and incidental to registration.

. . .

(6) The power to make rules of court under section 84 of the Senior Courts Act 1981 shall include power—

(a) to prescribe the procedure for applying for registration under this section, and to require an applicant to give prior notice of his intention to other parties,
(b) to prescribe the matters to be proved on the application and the manner of proof, and in particular to require the applicant to furnish a copy of the award certified pursuant to the Convention,
(c) to provide for the service of notice of registration of the award by the applicant on other parties,

and in this and the next following section "prescribed" means prescribed by rules of court.

(7) For the purposes of this and the next following section—

(a) "award" shall include any decision interpreting, revising or annulling an award, being a decision pursuant to the Convention, and any decision as to costs which under the Convention is to form part of the award.

. . .

2. Effect of registration

(1) Subject to the provisions of this Act, an award registered under section 1 above shall, as respects the pecuniary obligations which it imposes, be of the same force and effect for the purposes of execution as if it had been a judgment of the High Court given when the award was rendered pursuant to the Convention and entered on the date of registration under this Act, and, so far as relates to such pecuniary obligations—

(a) proceedings may be taken on the award,
(b) the sum for which the award is registered shall carry interest,
(c) the High Court shall have the same control over the execution of the award,

as if the award had been such a judgment of the High Court.

The issues

17. As already indicated, the Claimants rely on either or both of the exceptions to immunity set out in sections 2 and 9 of the State Immunity Act. So far as section 2 is concerned, they submit that the

provisions of the ICSID Convention, in particular Article 54, amount to a prior written agreement submitting to the jurisdiction of the English courts for the purposes of enforcement of any award. Alternatively, the Claimants argue that Zimbabwe agreed to submit the dispute to arbitration within the meaning of section 9 and that although Zimbabwe argued before the tribunal and the annulment committee that the particular dispute did not fall within the scope of the relevant arbitration agreement, the tribunal's decision (upheld by the annulment committee) that it did have jurisdiction is final and binding on the English court.

18. These are deep waters. It is only in the last few years that the relationship between ICSID and state immunity has begun to be explored and I was referred to a number of recent judgments touching on the point, both English and from other common law jurisdictions. The latest contribution is the comprehensive and impressive judgment of Mr Justice Fraser (as he then was) in *Infrastructure Services Luxembourg S.à.r.l.* v. *Spain*, [2023] EWHC 1226 (Comm).

19. All of these cases were subjected to minute scrutiny before me and their reasoning either applauded or disparaged as best suited each party. It is fair to say that the legislative context in which the various foreign judgments were delivered is not the same as that which pertains in the United Kingdom. Nor were the issues which arose in each case necessarily identical to those raised by this application.

20. In particular, none of the English cases to date appears to have considered the ramifications of the Claimants' arguments for awards which fall to be enforced under the 1958 New York Convention. So far as I am aware, it has not hitherto been argued that a state is precluded from claiming sovereign immunity in relation to the recognition and enforcement of an award under the New York Convention. Yet if the Claimants are right that state immunity is lost by virtue of the obligation in Article 54 to recognise an ICSID award as binding and enforce it as if it were a final judgment of a national court, the same consequence must logically flow from the materially identical obligation in Article III of the New York Convention to recognise an award as binding and enforce it in accordance with the rules of procedure of the relevant country. Indeed, this is precisely the consequence which has been held to follow in two recent decisions in Australia and the USA respectively.

21. This would represent a seismic development so far as non-ICSID awards are concerned, and I was not persuaded by Mr Harris' argument that New York Convention awards could be distinguished on the grounds that recognition and enforcement were subjected to the procedural laws of the enforcing state and that state immunity was to

be regarded as a procedural matter. On the contrary, the blanket
immunity provided for in section 1 of the State Immunity Act confirms
that state immunity is very much more than a matter of mere procedure, being a substantive bar to proceedings where it applies. It is
procedural only in the sense that the court must dismiss a claim in
respect of which a state can claim immunity without adjudicating on
the merits: see *Benkharbouche* v. *Embassy of the Republic of Sudan*
(*supra*) at [18]. I cannot therefore accept that the mere reference to
procedural laws has the effect of preserving state immunity for the
purposes of the New York Convention when it would otherwise have
been lost. Nor can I accept that it makes any difference that the New
York Convention permits wider grounds of challenge to an award than
the ICSID Convention. The extent to which an award can be reviewed,
if at all, has nothing whatsoever to do with state immunity.

22. Notwithstanding that this point was not apparently raised
before or considered by Fraser J, I was nonetheless urged by the
Claimants to follow his decision unless I was convinced that it was
wrong. Permission to appeal to the Court of Appeal has in fact been
given in that case and it is therefore clear that others also find this an
area deserving of further consideration. In those circumstances, knowing that the Court of Appeal will soon be examining the matter, I have
allowed myself slightly more latitude in reaching my own conclusions.
As it is, I have listened to all the arguments with the greatest care and
formed my own views where I am not bound by authority. On some
issues, I agree with the reasoning in other judgments; on others, I have
reached different conclusions. In particular, while I have reached the
same ultimate conclusion as Fraser J, I have done so on different
grounds reflecting the considerably fuller argument that took place
before me on the relevant issues.

Discussion and analysis

23. For the purposes of exposition, I address the issues under the
following heads:

(a) The correct interpretation of Articles 53-5 of the ICSID
    Convention;
(b) Section 2 of the 1978 Act;
(c) Section 9 of the 1978 Act;
(d) Whether state immunity is engaged at all in relation to an applica-
    tion for registration of an award under the 1966 Act;
(e) Full and frank disclosure.

(1) Interpretation of Articles 53-5

Principles of treaty interpretation

The Vienna Convention

24. It was not in dispute that the ICSID Convention, as an international treaty, falls to be interpreted in accordance with Articles 31-3 of the Vienna Convention on the Law of Treaties 1969 which provide as follows:

Article 31: General rule of interpretation

1. A treaty shall be interpreted in good faith in accordance with the ordinary meaning to be given to the terms of the treaty in their context and in the light of its object and purpose.

. . .

3. There shall be taken into account, together with the context:

(a) . . .

(b) any subsequent practice in the application of the treaty which establishes the agreement of the parties regarding its interpretation;

(c) any relevant rules of international law applicable in the relations between the parties.

. . .

Article 32: Supplementary means of interpretation

Recourse may be had to supplementary means of interpretation, including the preparatory work of the treaty and the circumstances of its conclusion, in order to confirm the meaning resulting from the application of article 31, or to determine the meaning when the interpretation according to article 31:

(a) leaves the meaning ambiguous or obscure;

(b) leads to a result which is manifestly absurd or unreasonable.

*Article 33: Interpretation of treaties authenticated in two
or more languages*

1. When a treaty has been authenticated in two or more languages, the text is equally authoritative in each language, unless the treaty provides or the parties agree that, in case of divergence, a particular text shall prevail.

. . .

3. The terms of the treaty are presumed to have the same meaning in each authentic text.

4. Except where a particular text prevails in accordance with paragraph 1, when a comparison of the authentic texts discloses a difference of meaning which the application of articles 31 and 32 does not remove, the meaning which best reconciles the texts, having regard to the object and purpose of the treaty, shall be adopted.

Correct approach: Textual versus teleological

25. There was considerable argument before me as to the relative weight to be accorded to the text of the Convention on the one hand and its object and purpose on the other. Mr Moollan KC, who appeared for Zimbabwe, submitted that the Vienna Convention mandated a textual approach to interpretation and that I should not be seduced by the Claimants' submissions into adopting a teleological or purposive approach.

26. Ultimately, however, it seemed to me that this was an arid debate, given that Article 31 expressly requires the terms of any treaty to be interpreted in their context and in the light of its object and purpose. Text and object/purpose thus go hand in hand and in my judgment it is unnecessary and unproductive to try to disentangle them. What is required is a holistic approach and I do not read the International Court of Justice as saying anything different in paragraph 41 of its judgment in *Libya* v. *Chad (3 February 1994)*. The comment by the court in that case that "Interpretation must be based above all upon the text of the treaty" must be understood in the context of an argument by Libya that the court could go beyond the matters set out in Article 31 so as to alter the natural meaning of the text by reference to the intentions of the parties to the treaty. It is hardly surprising that in rejecting this argument, the court emphasised the primacy of the text, but it is clear from the remainder of the judgment (in particular, paragraph 52) that the text was nevertheless to be read in the light of the object and purpose of the treaty.

27. I agree, of course, that it is impermissible, if not impossible, to interpret a treaty by reference to the deemed intention of the parties, not least because they may never have had any common intention. In the context of an international treaty, the parties are therefore deemed to have intended what they have actually said: *Czech Republic* v. *European Media Ventures SA*, [2007] EWHC 2851 (Comm) at [17]; *Brown* v. *Stott*, [2003] 1 AC 681 at 703E. The object and purpose of a treaty are accordingly to be found primarily in the preamble to the treaty or any other common expression of intent and the court should be cautious before going further: *Czech Republic* v. *European Media Ventures SA (supra)* at [19].

28. This latter case also confirms the following principles which I bear in mind:

(a) The task of the court is to interpret the treaty, not the supplementary means of interpretation (paragraph [31]);
(b) It is important to give the treaty an independent interpretation divorced from any distinctive features of a particular legal system (paragraph [34]);
(c) The ordinary meaning of the terms used is to be assessed as at the date of conclusion of the treaty (the principle of contemporaneity) (paragraph [36]);
(d) The court should try to ascribe meaning to each of the words being interpreted (paragraph [37]).

29. A further matter debated before me was the extent to which I could or should be guided by decisions of courts or tribunals in other jurisdictions. Mr Harris referred me to several which he submitted showed a consistent trend, although he did not go so far as to assert that they established a subsequent practice within the meaning of Article 31(3)(b) of the Vienna Convention. However, none of these decisions is binding on me and while they may be more or less illuminating, much will depend on the issues raised and the potentially different legal landscapes in which they were decided. Thus, the Claimants submitted that any differences in the applicable statutory provisions were irrelevant, while Zimbabwe argued that they were significant. I consider this further when I discuss these cases below.

The travaux préparatoires
30. Article 32 of the Vienna Convention permits resort to the *travaux préparatoires* to confirm a meaning, or to determine that meaning but, in the latter case, only where the wording is ambiguous or would lead to manifest absurdity.

31. I was treated to a detailed excursus through the *travaux préparatoires* by both parties who frequently relied on the same passages for diametrically opposed conclusions. The architect of the ICSID Convention was the General Counsel of the World Bank, Mr Aron Broches. Following his preparation of a Preliminary Draft, a series of consultative meetings was held in Addis Ababa (December 1963), Santiago de Chile (February 1964), Geneva (February 1964) and Bangkok (April-May 1964) attended by representatives (predominantly lawyers) from many countries. A Revised Draft was then the subject of intensive deliberation by a special legal committee in Washington in

November/December 1964, following which the Convention was
concluded in March 1965.

32. I do not propose to rehearse the respective arguments of the
parties on the *travaux*; suffice it to say that in my view they demonstrate the following:

(a) The Convention imposed a direct obligation at international level
    on every Contracting State to be bound by an ICSID award;
(b) The firm assumption was that a Contracting State would honour a
    binding award against it. It was therefore sufficient for Article 53 to
    stipulate that an award was binding on the parties and unnecessary
    to provide for any further sanction against a defaulting state
    beyond the revival of diplomatic protection in Article 27 backed
    by the risk of indirect sanctions from the international community
    if the state in fact failed to honour its obligations;
(c) By contrast, individual investors, not themselves being parties to
    the treaty, were not subject to any obligations thereunder,
    whether direct or indirect. It was therefore necessary to provide
    some means whereby a successful state could enforce an award
    against the assets of a defaulting investor, and this was the primary
    objective of the provisions which ultimately became Articles 53
    and 54;
(d) The purpose of requiring Contracting States to recognise an award
    as final and binding was to give effect to its status as *res judicata*;
(e) From the outset, there was never any intention to harmonise or
    change the law of state immunity as applied by each Contracting
    State since this varied from state to state. Instead, the Convention
    adopted the approach of equating an award with a final judgment
    of the national court leaving questions of execution to be governed
    by the domestic laws of the enforcing state under Article 53(3).
    Thus, if an equivalent judgment could be enforced against a state,
    so could an award; if it could not be so enforced, neither could
    an award;
(f) This was not thought to present any problem, because the expect-
    ation and assumption was that Contracting States would honour a
    binding award. The question of enforcement against a state was
    therefore viewed as an academic question such that there was no
    risk of a third party state finding itself in the embarrassing position
    of being asked to enforce an award against another state.
    Nonetheless, Article 55 was inserted at a late stage by way of
    clarification and reassurance to make clear that the Convention
    did not allow for forcible execution against a state;

(g) The procedural processes and requirements for seeking recognition and enforcement were left to the domestic law of the enforcing state;

(h) As emphasised on multiple occasions by Mr Broches during the course of the negotiations, and reiterated in his Memorandum dated 19 January 1965 accompanying the Convention, the word "enforce" in Article 54(1) should be understood as meaning "enforceable" in the sense that an award be given the same status as a final judgment.

Articles 53-5

33. Against this background, I turn to the critical provisions of the ICSID Convention, namely Articles 53-5, starting with the words of the text themselves. One of the major difficulties in this respect is that the terms "recognition", "enforcement" and "execution" are not defined, and the precise scope of each term is not always clear. In particular, there is a question as to whether "enforcement" and "execution" are used synonymously or discretely, or whether they overlap.

34. Article 53(1) encapsulates the agreement of each Contracting State to the fundamental obligation that the parties to a dispute shall abide by and comply with the terms of an award except to the extent that enforcement is stayed. The reference to "enforcement" here can only be to the "enforcement" contemplated by Article 54 since that is where the obligation to enforce is set out.

35. The first sentence of Article 54(1) is a composite provision comprising two distinct obligations. The first is an obligation on each Contracting State to recognise as binding an award rendered pursuant to the Convention. As a matter of language, this applies to the entirety of the award and involves acceptance of both the binding character of the award and its preclusive effects as regards, for example, *res judicata* and issue estoppel. The second is an obligation on Contracting States—limited to pecuniary obligations only—to enforce such pecuniary obligations in the award as if they were contained in a final judgment of a national court.

36. The obligation to recognise and enforce contained in Article 54(1) is not self-executing; some formal step is required. However, the process by which recognition and enforcement is to be achieved is not prescribed in the Convention itself but is left to each Contracting State to determine as a matter of its own internal procedures, subject only to the formal requirements set out in Article 54(2). Thus, in some

countries, the obligation to recognise and enforce an award under Article 54(1) is given effect by entering judgment in the amount of any pecuniary obligations, while in others it may simply be by ordering that the award be recognised or take effect as if it were a judgment of the court.[2]

37. Article 54(3) is directed at the execution of an award and provides that execution is to be governed by the laws concerning the execution of judgments in force in the country in which execution is sought.

38. Article 55 contains the clarificatory saving for immunity from execution referred to in paragraph 32(f) above, although it should be noted that this article is not expressed to be exhaustive of the circumstances in which state immunity can be claimed. Moreover, the *travaux préparatoires* make clear that this was a "belt and braces" insertion which was not thought to be strictly necessary as the drafters of the Convention believed that Article 54(3) in any event sufficiently preserved the effect of each Contracting State's domestic law on state immunity so far as concerned execution against assets.

39. As a matter of language, therefore the wording of Articles 54(1) and 54(2) draws a clear distinction between "recognition" and "enforcement". Each is the subject of a separate obligation in Article 54(1) and the reference to an application for "recognition or enforcement" in Article 54(2) clearly contemplates that an application can be made for one without the other.[3] Mere recognition on its own, however, says nothing about the ability of the successful party to proceed further along the enforcement path.

40. A distinction is likewise drawn between "recognition" on the one hand (Articles 54(1) and (2)) and "execution" (Article 54(3)).

41. However, the relationship between "enforcement" and "execution" is altogether more elusive. On the one hand, it is noteworthy that the French and Spanish texts of the Convention, both of which are also designated as authentic, use the same word (*exécution* and *ejecución* respectively) for both concepts where the English text distinguishes between them.

42. On the other hand, the terms can hardly be regarded as synonymous, since that would give rise to an immediate and obvious tension: either Article 54(1) would have to be read as preserving state immunity also in relation to enforcement in the sense that the word is

---

[2] In the English courts, registration of ICSID awards under the 1966 Act is governed by a bespoke procedure set out in CPR Part 62.21.

[3] Although it is fair to point out that enforcement must necessarily presuppose recognition.

used in Article 54(1), contrary to the obligation to enforce awards contained in that article, or Article 54(1) would have to be read as referring also to execution which would then conflict directly with Articles 54(3) and 55. This possibility can accordingly be rejected as nonsensical and manifestly absurd.

43. I do not derive any assistance in this respect from the preamble to the Convention. This is therefore a situation where the meaning of the terms is ambiguous or obscure such that it is appropriate to have regard to the *travaux préparatoires*. In my judgment, the clue to the correct interpretation is to be found in the repeated comments of Mr Broches that the intention underlying Article 54(1) was that the word "enforce" should be understood as meaning "enforceable" in the sense that the award should be equated to a final judgment.

44. On this basis, the basic scheme contemplated by the Convention is as follows:

(a) Every Contracting State undertakes (i) to recognise an ICSID award as binding for the purposes of *res judicata and* (ii) to enforce any pecuniary obligations it imposes by giving the award the same status as a final judgment of its own courts. An enforcing court cannot re-examine the award on its merits or refuse enforcement (in this sense) on grounds of public policy. This is in stark contrast to the position under the New York Convention where recognition and enforcement of an award can be refused on certain specific grounds, including public policy.

(b) However, "enforcement" in this context means no more than according to an ICSID award the same status as a final judgment of the national court. By contrast, questions of execution are left to individual national courts so that if the enforcing court's law of state immunity prevents any further steps being taken to execute the award, that will be the end of the matter.

45. As to the conundrum of the French and Spanish texts and the fact that they do not distinguish linguistically between the concepts of "enforcement" in the sense of enforceability and "execution", I find the reasoning of the High Court of Australia in *Spain* v. *Infrastructure Services Luxembourg S.à.r.l.*, [2023] HCA 11 to be compelling on this point. The High Court concluded that in truth there was no inconsistency which needed to be reconciled on the basis that:

(a) The French, Spanish and English texts are equally authentic. Article 33(3) of the Vienna Convention therefore presumes the terms of the treaty to have the same meaning in each text.

(b) However, the French and Spanish texts have to be understood in the context of the civilian concept of *exequatur* which combines recognition with a declaration of enforceability. The terms *exécution* and *ejecución* thus encompass both recognition and enforcement in the sense of enforceability (Article 54(1)) on the one hand, and enforcement by way of execution on the other (Article 54(3)).

(c) This is the sense which best reconciles the texts having regard to the object and purpose of the Convention as required by Article 33(4) of the Vienna Convention.

46. Accordingly, even if "execution" can be regarded in a general sense as an aspect of "enforcement", in my judgment the French and Spanish texts provide powerful support for interpreting the word "enforcement" as used specifically in Articles 54(1) and 54(2) as meaning a declaration of enforceability by according an award the same status as a final judgment.

47. As the High Court of Australia pointed out, such an interpretation would also accord with the definitions of "recognition", "enforcement" and "execution" contained in the proposed US Restatement of the Law of International Commercial and Investor–State Arbitration. I accept of course that these definitions have no authoritative status and that the ICSID Convention must be interpreted on its own terms. It is nonetheless instructive to note that according to the proposed Restatement:

(a) "recognition" is defined as the court's determination that an award is "entitled to be treated as binding", which involves "acceptance of the award's binding character and its preclusive effects";

(b) "enforcement" is defined as "the legal process by which an international award is reduced to a judgment of the court that enjoys the same status as any judgment of that court";

(c) "execution" is defined as "the means by which a judgment enforcing an international arbitral award is given effect" commonly by taking measures against the property of the judgment debtor pursuant to a writ of execution.

48. To my mind, such an interpretation makes perfect sense of the Convention in all of its authentic texts. It is also consistent, or at least not inconsistent, with the decision of the Supreme Court in *Micula* v. *Romania*, [2020] UKSC 5; [2020] 1 WLR 1033.

49. In *Micula*, the question was whether an English court had power under the 1966 Act and the ICSID Convention to stay execution of an ICSID award. The Court of Appeal held that a stay could and should be granted although there was a divergence in the reasoning of the court as to the basis on which such a stay could be ordered.

Leggatt LJ (as he then was) took the view that the purpose of equating an award with a final judgment of the enforcing court was to give legal force to an award preparatory to executing it and to provide machinery for that purpose—in other words adopting an interpretation of Article 54(1) along the lines suggested above. He and Arden LJ (as she then was) were of the view that it would be inconsistent with the scheme of the ICSID Convention for a national court to refuse enforcement simply because, if it had been a domestic judgment, giving effect to it would have been contrary to a provision of national law. The only circumstances in which the validity or enforceability of an award could be challenged were those set out in the Convention itself. Thus, a national court could not refuse enforcement on substantive grounds, or stay enforcement on grounds which would justify a stay of a final domestic judgment, or grant a permanent or indefinite stay. That said, Leggatt and Arden LJJ also agreed that the court could nonetheless grant a temporary stay of execution provided always that to do so was just in all the circumstances, *and* consistent with the purposes of the Convention. By contrast, Hamblen LJ (as he then was) held that the effect of the ICSID Convention was to assimilate an award to a final domestic judgment for all purposes such that a stay could be granted where it would be granted in the case of a domestic judgment.

50. In the event, it was unnecessary for the Supreme Court to decide between the two approaches. Lords Lloyd-Jones and Sales, who gave the leading speech with which the other members of the court agreed, recognised that the proper interpretation of Article 54(1) so far as regards the availability of a stay could only ultimately be resolved by the International Court of Justice. Nonetheless, since Romania's argument failed either way, it was not necessary for the English court to grapple further itself with the correct interpretation of Article 54(1) and the distinction, if any, between "enforcement" and "execution".

51. While the actual decision in *Micula* is therefore not directly relevant to the present case, the reasoning of the Supreme Court was heavily relied upon by the Claimants in support of their argument that Zimbabwe had no immunity. As part of that reasoning, the Supreme Court held that:

(a) The 1966 Act implements the ICSID Convention in UK domestic law, and section 1(2) of the Act entitles a person seeking recognition or enforcement of an ICSID award to have it registered (paragraph [63]);

(b) The 1966 Act must be interpreted in the context of the ICSID Convention, and it should be presumed that Parliament intended it to conform to the United Kingdom's treaty obligations (paragraph [68]);

(c) A notable feature of the ICSID scheme is that once the authenticity of an award is established, a domestic court called upon to recognise it may not re-examine the award on its merits or refuse to enforce it on grounds of public policy (paragraph [68]);

(d) Contracting States may not refuse recognition or enforcement of an award on grounds covered by the challenge provisions in the Convention itself or on the basis of any general doctrine of *ordre public* (paragraph [69]);

(e) Article 54(3) is concerned with execution and provides that the available processes of execution will be those of the enforcing court. However, this provision does not limit the obligation of Contracting States to enforce awards (paragraph [76]);

(f) It is arguable that there is scope for some additional defences against enforcement in exceptional or extraordinary circumstances, if national law recognises them in respect of final judgments of national courts and if they do not directly overlap with the grounds of challenge specifically reserved to ICSID under Articles 50-2 of the Convention (paragraph [78]);

(g) Hamblen LJ's view that Article 54(1) operates on the basis of a principle of "equivalence" had some support in the *travaux préparatoires*. However, the contrary view of Arden and Leggatt LJJ was also arguable that the only circumstances in which the validity or enforceability of an ICSID award can be challenged are those set out in the Convention itself (paragraphs [80]-[81]);

(h) If Leggatt LJ's approach to Article 54(1) was right, then Article 54(1) simply provided a basis for execution such that an English court could not refuse to enforce an award just because there were grounds that would justify staying enforcement of a domestic judgment (paragraph [81]).

52. Notwithstanding that the Supreme Court has not decided which approach to the interpretation of Article 54(1) is correct, it has nonetheless accepted that Leggatt LJ's view is arguable. Importantly, it has also held that the fact that Article 54(3) leaves matters of execution to the national courts does not limit the obligation of Contracting States to recognise and enforce awards. This, in my judgment, provides powerful support for the analysis suggested in paragraphs 44-8 above. For good measure, although I accept that the tail cannot be allowed to wag the dog, the distinction between "enforcement" (in the sense of "enforceability") and "execution" is also mirrored in sections 1 and 2 of the 1966 Act.

Waiver of immunity?

53. If this interpretation is correct, the next question is whether Articles 53 and/or 54 amount to a waiver of sovereign immunity by Contracting States and, if so, to what extent.

54. In this connection, I was referred by the Claimants to the decisions of the Federal Court of Australia and the High Court of

Australia in *Spain* v. *Infrastructure Services Luxembourg S.à.r.l.*, [2021] FCAFC 3 and [2023] HCA 11, the decision of the High Court of New Zealand in *Sodexo Pass International SAS* v. *Hungary*, [2021] NZHC 371 and various United States decisions. All of these decisions were made in different statutory contexts. Specifically: the ICSID Convention has been expressly incorporated into both Australian and New Zealand law; the Australian equivalent to the State Immunity Act does not have an arbitration exception equivalent to section 9 of the 1978 Act; New Zealand has no State Immunity Act at all; and the US statutory framework is very different and contains a very broad arbitration exception. While I have found some of the reasoning illuminating and instructive, I do not propose to rehearse them in detail since none of them is directly binding on me.

55. As a matter of English law, the general principle is that any waiver of sovereign immunity by treaty must be express although it need not be in writing: *R* v. *Bow Street Magistrates, ex parte Pinochet (no 3)*, [2000] 1 AC 147 at 215 *per* Lord Goff.[4] Where the alleged waiver is in writing—for example, in a prior treaty provision—it must be express and cannot be implied. Where it is not in writing—for example, actual conduct in submitting to the jurisdiction—it must be expressed in a clear and unequivocal manner. The latter is sometimes referred to as implied waiver but, as Lord Goff pointed out (at 217), this is the only example given of an implied waiver and it is in any event probably better regarded as a form of express waiver.

56. On behalf of the Claimants, Mr Harris relied heavily on the decision of the High Court of Australia in *Spain* v. *Infrastructure Services Luxembourg S.à.r.l.* (*supra*) that Spain's agreement to Articles 53-5 of the ICSID Convention amounted to a waiver of state immunity from the jurisdiction of the Australian court to recognise and enforce (but not to execute) the award. The case thus fell within the exception to state immunity contained in section 10(2) of the Australian Foreign States Immunities Act (which is equivalent to section 2 of the 1978 Act). Mr Moollan urged me to exercise caution in relation to this decision on the basis that the High Court was under particular pressure to find a submission to the jurisdiction within section 10(2) because there was no Australian arbitration exception equivalent to section 9 of the 1978 Act. That may or may not be so but it is in my view irrelevant. The reasoning of the court either withstands scrutiny on its own merits or it does not.

---

[4] Although Lord Goff dissented in the result, his exposition of the law on waiver of immunity was not in issue and is considered as authoritative.

57. As to waiver, the High Court of Australia accepted the principle, which it regarded as having been correctly articulated in *Pinochet*, that waiver of state immunity must be express or unequivocally implied from conduct. It recognised that the distinction between express and implied terms was somewhat elusive because of the inherent imprecision of language, meaning that some form of implication was almost inevitably involved even in the construction of express words. The court therefore concluded that the requirement for an express waiver meant only that the expression of waiver must be derived from the express words used and not, for example, implied from conduct. However, waiver could be implied from the express words of a treaty read in their context and in the light of their purpose, although a high level of clarity and necessity was required before inferring that a state had waived its immunity in a treaty.

58. Adopting that approach, the High Court held that (i) the stipulation in Article 53(1) that awards were binding on Contracting States and (ii) the preservation in Article 55 of immunity in relation only to execution meant that it would distort the terms of Article 54(1) to require separate conduct amounting to a waiver of immunity before an applicant could obtain recognition and enforcement of an award. The express terms of Article 54(1) accordingly amounted to a waiver of immunity in relation to recognition and enforcement and the requirements of section 10(2) were thus satisfied.

59. Mr Moollan submitted that this decision was not binding on me and that I should decline to adopt its reasoning. In his submission, whatever the High Court of Australia may have said, the Claimants could only establish a waiver by a process of implication. He further argued that whereas Article 53 is dealing with the situation of a Contracting State which is party to an award, Article 54 was only directed at non-party Contracting States. I do not accept this distinction. The term "Contracting State" in Article 54 is not qualified in any way and thus applies to all Contracting States, whether parties to an award or not. Furthermore, while the *travaux préparatoires* make clear that the primary objective of Article 54 was to give a Contracting State an effective means of enforcement against an investor (who did not assume any direct obligations under the Convention), the provision is drafted in terms which apply as much to enforcement against a state as they do to enforcement against an investor.

60. I accept that the immediate import of the words in Article 54(1) is to enjoin each Contracting State to recognise and enforce an award in its own territory. However, *Micula* confirms authoritatively at [105] that the duties imposed by Articles 53 and 54 are unqualified and owed

to all other Contracting States and not just to the other parties to an award. The Supreme Court regarded this as confirmed by Article 27(1) which recognises that if a Contracting State fails to abide by an award, it may be subject to an international claim by the Contracting State of the aggrieved investor. Necessarily, therefore, every Contracting State recognises that the duties imposed by Article 54(1) are undertaken by every other Contracting State and that every other Contracting State is accordingly obliged to recognise and enforce an award as if it were a final judgment, including awards against the first state.

61. Does this amount to an express waiver of immunity? I have not found this an easy question to decide. A case on which Mr Moollan placed great reliance was a decision of the BVI court in *Tethyan Copper Company Pty Limited* v. *Pakistan*, (Claim No BVIHC (Com) 2020/0196, 27 April 2021). This was a case in which the applicable statutory framework was identical to that which pertains in the United Kingdom. At paragraph [51] of his judgment, Mr Justice Wallbank held that Article 54(1) imposed an obligation on Pakistan as a Contracting State to allow recognition and enforcement of an award before its own courts but did not impose any obligation on it before the BVI courts. Accordingly, Article 54(1) could not amount to a waiver of immunity.

62. Mr Moollan submitted that this reasoning, albeit concise, was nonetheless compelling and directly applicable to the present situation. However, with great respect to the learned judge, I am unable to agree. Given the scheme of the Convention as set out above and in the light of the *travaux préparatoires*, it is difficult to conclude otherwise than that Article 54(1) was intended to amount to a waiver of state immunity in respect of recognition and enforcement but not in relation to processes of execution against assets, which were expressly carved out in Articles 54(3) and 55.

63. While (like the High Court of Australia) I accept that the line between construction and implication is sometimes a fine one, I do not regard this conclusion as in fact involving any process of implication. In my judgment and in agreement on this point with the High Court of Australia, it is simply a question of elucidating the meaning of the express words used and drawing the inevitable consequences.

64. However, that by no means concludes the argument in favour of the Claimants, since it is still necessary to determine whether a waiver of immunity in general terms such as this is a sufficient submission to the jurisdiction of the English courts for the purposes of section 2 of the State Immunity Act. I therefore now turn to the arguments relating to section 2.

(2) Section 2 of the 1978 Act

65. Mr Harris submitted that by agreeing and accepting that all other Contracting States were obliged to recognise and enforce an award, Zimbabwe was not only waiving immunity generally but was necessarily also agreeing to submit to the jurisdiction of all other Contracting States for that purpose. He found powerful support for this argument in the judgment of Fraser J in *Infrastructure Services Luxembourg S.à.r.l.* v. *Spain* (*supra*) who at paragraphs [95] and [114] held that Article 54 was a prior written agreement for the purposes of the 1978 Act and that Spain had therefore submitted to the jurisdiction of the English court by reason of its accession to the Convention.

66. With no little diffidence and the greatest respect to the learned judge, I have some difficulty with this reasoning. Under the 1978 Act, a state is entitled to blanket immunity from jurisdiction except in so far as one of the stipulated exceptions can be established. It follows that even a general waiver of immunity will not necessarily deprive a state of its immunity for the purposes of the Act unless it can be brought within one of those exceptions.

67. Section 2 of the 1978 Act has been set out above. It was common ground that the Act should be interpreted as far as possible in a way consistent with the 1966 Act and the United Kingdom's international obligations under, for example, the ICSID and New York Conventions. Conversely, however, the Act is of general application and contains no specific mention of ICSID or any qualification differentiating ICSID from other matters. Applications concerning ICSID awards must therefore be approached in the same way and be subject to application of the same principles as proceedings involving any other type of award.

68. In my judgment, section 2 is drafted with reference to specific proceedings before a specific court and accordingly requires any submission to be in respect of the jurisdiction which is actually being exercised in those proceedings. A waiver of immunity unrelated to any identifiable proceedings is therefore not synonymous with a submission to the jurisdiction under section 2, even though the two may overlap, for example when a state waives its immunity by submitting to the jurisdiction in respect of a particular action.

69. Authority for the distinction between a general waiver of immunity and a submission to the jurisdiction can be found in the decision of the Court of Appeal in *Svenska Petroleum Exploration AB* v. *Lithuania* (*supra*) which is the only one of the authorities cited to me

to consider the point. Upholding the decision of Mrs Justice Gloster at first instance, the court held at [128] that:

The judge was unable to accept that a general waiver of immunity of the kind found in article 35.1 amounted to a submission to the jurisdiction of the English courts within the meaning of section 2(1). We agree, not only because we think it is too imprecise, but because we think it must be read in the context of the government's agreement to submit to ICC arbitration (which was in fact the context in which the waiver of immunity is found in the earlier drafts of the agreement).

70. It is true that one of the reasons given by the Court of Appeal for finding that there had been no submission to the jurisdiction of the English courts in that case was the fact that the parties had agreed to submit their disputes to ICC arbitration. Clearly, that reasoning cannot apply here where the relevant submission to the jurisdiction does not concern the underlying dispute but rather the recognition and enforcement of an award which has emerged at the end of the arbitral process.

71. Nonetheless, it remains the case that there is a conceptual distinction between a general waiver and a submission to the jurisdiction which it is necessary to consider with some care. In the present case, Article 54 did not contain any express submission by a Contracting State to the jurisdiction of, for example, "the courts of any other Contracting State called upon to enforce an award against it". Had it done so, the position might have been very different. As it is, however, the waiver of immunity which I have held to be established is entirely general and unrelated to any specific or identifiable proceedings. To the extent that it might be argued that such a submission is implicit, then it falls foul of the requirement in *Pinochet* for any waiver and, *a fortiori*, any submission to the jurisdiction contained in a treaty provision to be express.

72. Ultimately, I have concluded that Article 54 is not a sufficiently clear and unequivocal submission to the jurisdiction of the English courts for the purposes of recognising and enforcing the award against Zimbabwe in these proceedings. I recognise that this conclusion is contrary to that of Fraser J, but it is not apparent that the potential distinction between waiver and submission was argued before him. I also recognise that it could be said to run counter to the object and purpose of the ICSID Convention which was to preserve state immunity only in respect of execution while providing for mandatory recognition and enforcement across the board. However, this is simply the inevitable result of applying what seem to me to be the clear words of section 2 of the 1978 Act. The Convention itself is not part of English

law and I must give primacy to the words of the statute, particularly bearing in mind that it applies generally and so extends far beyond the limited and somewhat niche category of ICSID awards.

73. I therefore hold that the Claimants have failed to establish that Zimbabwe submitted to the jurisdiction of the English courts within the meaning of section 2 for the purposes of obtaining recognition and enforcement of the award.

74. For completeness, I should deal with two further points advanced on behalf of Zimbabwe under this head.

75. First, I was unpersuaded by Mr Moollan's argument that the principle of contemporaneity precludes the argument that Article 54(1) could amount to a waiver or submission to the jurisdiction. He submitted that in 1965, when the ICSID Convention was signed, English law did not permit waiver of state immunity by prior agreement. Accordingly, if Article 54(1) did constitute a waiver or submission the UK delegate would have been agreeing to something which could never have been effective. However:

(a) As noted in paragraph 8 above, English law seems to have been something of an outlier in this respect: *I Congreso del Partido* (*supra*) at 261. But in any event, the Convention has to be interpreted in an autonomous way without regard to the national laws of any particular state, and what the UK delegate may have thought subjectively is irrelevant. Other Contracting States may have thought differently.

(b) In any event, if the Convention on its proper interpretation amounts to a waiver of immunity or submission to the jurisdiction, it must retain that quality even if effect could not have been given to it prior to 1978. This is nothing to do with giving the treaty a different construction from that which it would have received contemporaneously; it is simply that once the State Immunity Act was passed, the waiver/submission which had always been inchoate could finally be given effect.

76. Secondly, I would likewise have rejected Mr Moollan's further submission that even if there was otherwise a submission to the jurisdiction, the award in question was not rendered "pursuant to this Convention" for the purposes of Article 54(1) in circumstances where, irrespective of what the tribunal and the annulment committee had decided, the tribunal in fact had no jurisdiction. In truth, of course, this was a thinly disguised argument that the court could reopen the award on jurisdictional grounds under section 2.

77. The question in this regard is whether the conclusion of ICSID on its own jurisdiction is final and binding on the English court such that the award can properly be regarded as having been rendered "pursuant to this Convention" even if the English court thinks that ICSID may have been wrong. I am quite clear that the award is final and binding for this purpose and that it is not open to the English court to review the merits of the decision or the jurisdiction of the tribunal. In this specific context,[5] I regard it as highly relevant that ICSID is a self-contained regime and that the only permitted avenue of challenge to an award is via the process for annulment within the confines of the Convention.

78. Accordingly, the words "pursuant to this Convention" in my judgment mean no more or less than that the award has been rendered pursuant to the processes set out in the Convention. If the annulment process has been pursued but failed, the award has been rendered pursuant to the Convention because the Convention processes have been followed. That remains the case *even if* the application for annulment should have succeeded because the tribunal did not in fact have jurisdiction. This is not a question of treating the ICSID determination as binding for the purposes of state immunity; it is simply a question of whether the Convention processes have been correctly observed without regard to the content of the decision which emerged at the end of those processes.

79. I would not therefore have rejected the Claimants' arguments on either of these grounds.

(3) *Section 9 of the 1978 Act*

80. The exception in section 9 of the 1978 Act applies where a state has agreed in writing to submit a dispute to arbitration. It was not contentious before me that the ICSID Convention does not itself confer jurisdiction on a tribunal and that independent consent to arbitrate is required. This is clear from, amongst others, Articles 25(1), 25(4) and 36. It was further accepted before me that the relevant arbitration agreement in this case consisted of Article 10 of a bilateral investment treaty (the "BIT") concluded between Switzerland and Zimbabwe on 15 August 1996 which refers to "disputes with respect to investments between a Contracting Party and an investor of the other Contracting Party", coupled with the Claimants' acceptance (or purported acceptance) of the offer to arbitrate contained in that Article.

---

[5] Albeit not in relation to section 9 of the 1978 Act, as to which see paragraph 89 below.

81. Without going into unnecessary detail, it was Zimbabwe's case that the dispute was not in fact covered by Article 10 because the tribunal did not have jurisdiction over the dispute for a variety of reasons. Certain of these arguments were put before the annulment committee and all failed as put. It was nonetheless Zimbabwe's case that it is entitled to raise them again under section 9, together with other arguments going to the tribunal's jurisdiction. Its alternative case was that a waiver of state immunity under section 9 is subject to any contrary provision in the arbitration agreement and that such contrary provision is to be found in Article 10(6) of the BIT which provides that the award "shall be final and binding for the parties involved in the dispute and shall be enforceable in accordance with the laws of the Contracting Party in which the investment in question is located."

82. The substantive merits of these arguments are for another day, if at all. My task is simply to determine whether it is open to Zimbabwe to raise these jurisdictional points in order to argue that the exception to immunity in section 9 cannot apply. Mr Harris argued forcefully that it was not, because the question had been foreclosed by the decision of the annulment committee. He sought to impress on me the glowing credentials and vast experience of both the tribunal members and the annulment committee. I have no doubt that is so, but it is wholly irrelevant to my assessment of whether or not their determination as to the applicability of the arbitration agreement is binding on an English court for this purpose.

83. As it seems to me, section 9 raises two issues: first, whether section 9 requires or permits the English court to re-examine the jurisdiction of the tribunal (whether an ICSID tribunal or any other tribunal) and, secondly, whether ICSID awards fall to be treated differently from other awards in this respect.

84. As to the first of these issues, I have already emphasised the hermetically sealed nature of arbitration under the Convention under which there are no means of challenge other than by annulment and which gives rise to an award which is final and binding with no possibility of further review. Nonetheless, the wording of section 9 is quite clear that the statutory exception only applies if a state has agreed in writing to submit a dispute to arbitration. If it has not so agreed, then there is no loss of immunity. On the plain and ordinary meaning of the statute, therefore, before finding that section 9 is engaged, the English court must satisfy itself that the person accepting the offer of arbitration was entitled to do so and that the dispute in question fell within the scope of the arbitration agreement.

85. The interpretation of section 9 was considered by Mr Justice Butcher in *PAO Tatneft* v. *Ukraine*, [2018] EWHC 1797 (Comm); [2018] 2 CLC 290. This case involved a non-ICSID award under UNCITRAL rules which Tatneft sought to enforce in England. Ukraine argued that it had not in fact agreed to submit any of the relevant disputes to arbitration and that the section 9 exception did not apply. In response, Tatneft argued that these were points which went to the jurisdiction of the tribunal, and that while Ukraine had raised other jurisdictional objections before the tribunal, it had *not* relied on these specific arguments. Accordingly, it submitted that Ukraine should not be permitted to raise new jurisdictional points at this stage but should be confined to the same points as had already been argued.

86. Butcher J held at [35] that Ukraine was not precluded by what had occurred before the tribunal from raising the arguments which it now sought to rely on:

By reason of s.1(1) of the SIA [Ukraine] is immune from the jurisdiction of the court unless an exception provided for in the SIA applies, and indeed the court is obliged to give effect to that immunity even if the state does not appear. What that entails in the present case is that the court would have to give effect to the immunity unless it is satisfied that the state has agreed in writing to submit a dispute to arbitration and the proceedings relate to the arbitration. If there is an issue which is either apparent to the court of its own motion or is raised by the state and which goes to the question of whether there was such an agreement in writing in relation to the relevant dispute, then I consider that the court is obliged to consider it and can only exercise jurisdiction over the state if satisfied that the s.9 exception is nevertheless applicable. There is nothing in the SIA which suggests that there can be a foreclosure of the points which the state may raise as to the applicability of the immunity afforded by the SIA by reason of what may have occurred in front of an arbitral tribunal in a way similar to that provided for by the Arbitration Act. In particular there are no provisions similar to those in s.73 of the Arbitration Act, and I do not consider that such constraints can be read into the SIA.

87. It is true that there was no express consideration of what the position would have been if the relevant points had been taken and conclusively determined against Ukraine, but the thrust of Butcher J's reasoning is that the English court must be independently satisfied that there was an agreement to submit the particular dispute and that this is so whether or not any particular points were argued in the arbitration. I find this reasoning compelling and while the decision of Fraser J in *Infrastructure Services Luxembourg S.à.r.l.* v. *Spain* (*supra*) is to contrary effect, *Tatneft* is not referred to in his judgment.

88. The question then arises, however, as to whether ICSID awards fall to be treated differently for the purposes of section 9. In principle, it is difficult to see why this should be so. Section 9 is of general application and must apply equally to ICSID and non-ICSID awards. In this context, it seems to me irrelevant that ICSID is a self-contained regime under which the ICSID tribunal is the final arbiter of jurisdiction. Unless there was in fact an agreement to submit a particular dispute to ICSID arbitration, the ICSID process should not by rights be engaged at all, and the hermetically sealed nature of the regime is neither here nor there.

89. The position under section 9 is therefore different from that which pertains under section 2 in relation to Article 54. The enquiry which the court has to conduct under section 2 is whether there was a submission to the jurisdiction. On my analysis, the existence of a valid award is a given in that context, and the only question is whether it was rendered pursuant to Convention procedures. Questions of jurisdiction simply do not arise.

90. In my judgment, therefore, the Claimants have likewise failed to establish the applicability of the section 9 exception to immunity. For the avoidance of doubt, I would not have accepted Mr Moollan's submission that article 10(6) of the BIT amounted to a "contrary agreement" for the purposes of section 9. Article 10(6) does not purport to be exhaustive of the right to enforce; it simply confirms the enforceability of an award in Zimbabwe in addition to any other enforcement rights that the Claimants may have.

91. Even so, however, this does not determine the application in Zimbabwe's favour, since I have concluded for other reasons set out below that it is not in any event entitled to assert state immunity in relation to the Cockerill J order.

(4) Whether state immunity is engaged at all on an application for registration under section 2 of the 1966 Act

92. Although the point was not argued in this way before me, reference was made in the various cases cited to the specific regime established under rules of court in relation to the registration of ICSID awards. This is to be found in CPR Part 62 and was comprehensively considered by Mr Justice Jacobs in *Unión Fenosa* v. *Gas SA*, [2020] EWHC 1723 (Comm); [2020] 1 WLR 4732.

93. As there discussed, Part I of CPR Part 62 is concerned with claims under the Arbitration Act 1996. This covers the majority of arbitration-related claims, for example applications to appoint an

arbitrator or to appeal against an award. Such claims are required to be commenced by an arbitration claim form issued in accordance with the Part 8 procedure and the claim form must be served on the defendant within one month of issue unless the court orders otherwise.

94. Part 2 of CPR Part 62 deals with applications under the regime pre-dating the 1996 Act. This also requires service of the arbitration claim form.

95. Part 3 of CPR Part 62 deals with the enforcement of awards. Non-ICSID awards (which may of course also include awards against states) are covered by Part 62.18 while ICSID awards are separately covered by Part 62.21. The default position in relation to a non-ICSID award under Part 62.18 is that the application to enforce may be made without notice and the arbitration claim form does not need to be served unless the court so orders. Part 62.18(4) provides for permission to be given for service out of the jurisdiction where necessary. However, even though it may not be necessary to serve the claim form, service of the registration order giving leave to enforce the award is mandatory under Part 62.18(7) and permission to serve out is not required.

96. By contrast, the regime for ICSID awards under Part 62.21 is different. There is no express reference to any requirement for a claim form or to service out of the jurisdiction notwithstanding that such awards will inevitably involve a foreign state on one side or the other. Part 62.21(3) merely states that an application for registration of an ICSID award must be made in accordance with the Part 8 procedure.

97. Part 62.21(2) applies certain provisions of Part 74 (with necessary modifications) in so far as they apply to the registration of judgments under the Foreign Judgments (Reciprocal Enforcement) Act 1933 but always subject to the provisions of Part 62.21. For the most part these provisions relate to the evidence which needs to be served on an application for registration. Part 74.6, however, provides that the order granting permission to register the judgment (or award) must be served on the judgment debtor. It is also noteworthy that the provisions of Part 74.6(3)(c)-(e) giving the judgment debtor the right to apply to have the registration set aside are expressly *not* applied to ICSID awards.

98. Mr Justice Jacobs considered at [50] that it was no accident that the regime put in place for ICSID awards was different from that applicable to other awards:

It reflects the different and simplified procedure which exists for registration of awards to which CPR r 62.21 applies. This procedure is explained by the important cross-references in CPR r 2.21(2) to particular provisions within

CPR Pt 74, as further discussed below. It also reflects (also as further discussed below) the very limited circumstances in which a state may be able to resist enforcement of an ICSID award. Apart from the possibility of exceptional and extraordinary cases,[6] those circumstances are limited to those contemplated in CPR r 52.21(4) and (5): ie that enforcement has been stayed under the ICSID Convention, or where an application for a stay has been made.

99. On that basis, he concluded that it would be inconsistent with the registration regime incorporated via CPR Part 62.21(2) to require service of a claim form, let alone a fully fledged Part 8 procedure leading to determination of an application for registration at a contested hearing. Indeed, if service were required, permission to serve out would have to be sought under CPR Part 6 as Part 62.21 (unlike Part 62.18) did not address service out of the jurisdiction at all.

100. Jacobs J further drew attention to the requirement incorporated from Part 74.6 that the judgment creditor should draw up the order and serve it on the judgment debtor and that permission to serve out of the jurisdiction was not required. The fact that express provision was made for service of the order out of the jurisdiction indicated to him that this was the only service that was required.

101. In the light of this compelling analysis, it occurred to me while considering my judgment that if the application to register an ICSID award did not have to be served, then there was an argument that the application did not require Zimbabwe to be impleaded with the result that the doctrine of sovereign immunity was not engaged at that stage at all. Since this point had not featured in any of the written or oral arguments, I invited counsel to submit further brief submissions on the question "whether, in the light of the fact that the bespoke procedure for registration of ICSID awards set out in CPR 62.21 does not require service of any originating process on the respondent (see *Unión Fenosa*), the doctrine of sovereign immunity is engaged at all in relation to such an application."

102. The Claimants' response can be summarised as follows:

(a) The decision of the Supreme Court in *General Dynamics United Kingdom* v. *Libya*, [2021] UKSC 22; [2022] AC 318 determines (albeit in the context of an application to enforce a non-ICSID award under CPR Part 62.18) that where service of the claim form is not required it is the order granting permission to enforce the award which is the document which institutes proceedings against the state.

---

[6] A reference to *Micula*.

(b) Service of the order invokes the jurisdiction of the court and triggers Zimbabwe's ability to seek to assert immunity, subject always to any exceptions.

(c) In *AIC Limited* v. *Nigeria*, [2003] EWHC 1357 (QB), Mr Justice Stanley Burnton was faced with an argument that registration of a judgment under the Administration of Justice Act 1920 did not involve any exercise by the court of its adjudicative immunity and that section 1 of the State Immunity Act was accordingly inapplicable. He held that the registration of a judgment under the 1920 Act did involve the exercise by the court of its jurisdiction and that "even if the registration of a judgment were a purely administrative act, I should hold that it is subject to the immunity conferred by section 1 [of the State Immunity Act]." In any event, registration under the 1920 Act was an adjudicative act as the court was not bound to order a judgment to be registered but had a discretion to do so. His decision in relation to applications under the 1920 Act was approved by the Court of Appeal in *Svenska Petroleum Exploration AB* v. *Lithuania* (*supra*) at [135].

103. On behalf of Zimbabwe, Mr Moollan submitted that:

(a) State immunity is a substantive statutory rule which is engaged whenever the jurisdiction of the courts of the United Kingdom is invoked against a sovereign state.

(b) Operation of the State Immunity Act does not depend on whether or not the relevant process involves service on a state or, if so, at which stage of the proceedings the state is served.

(c) *General Dynamics United Kingdom* v. *Libya* (*supra*) establishes that service of an order for registration necessarily entails an exercise of jurisdiction and thereby engages the State Immunity Act.

(d) On its plain meaning, section 1 of the State Immunity Act is engaged by an application for the registration of ICSID awards as this entails an exercise of the court's jurisdiction by the making of, and then service of, a court order.

104. This is a novel question which does not appear to have been considered previously save for Stanley Burnton J's passing comment in the context of the 1920 Act. However, the registration of judgments under the 1920 Act is in a materially different category to the registration of ICSID awards, since the former requires the court to exercise a discretion, while the latter involves no discretion at all. On the contrary, under section 2 of the 1966 Act, the applicant is *entitled* to have the award registered, subject only to proof of authenticity and other

evidential requirements. I have therefore looked at the matter from the specific perspective of ICSID awards.

105. The classic statement of the doctrine of state immunity is that of Lord Atkin in *The Cristina*, [1938] AC 485 at 490:

the courts of a country will not implead a foreign sovereign, that is, they will not by their process make him against his will a party to legal proceedings, whether the proceedings involve process against his person or seek to recover from him specific property or damages.

106. However, in the case of applications to register ICSID awards, I have reached the conclusion that the foreign state is not impleaded unless and until the order granting registration is served on it, and that the doctrine of state immunity has no application at the anterior stage of registration. This is for the following reasons:

(a) In contrast to the position under the 1920 Act, no exercise of the court's adjudicative jurisdiction is required when registering an ICSID award. As previously stated, section 1(2) of the 1966 Act confers an entitlement on the applicant to have the award registered which is unqualified save in respect of purely procedural requirements.

(b) Accordingly, on an application for registration, the court is being asked to perform an essentially ministerial act in compliance with the UK's international obligations under the ICSID Convention. This does not involve the initiation of any substantive steps against the state, since the application is only for recognition and enforcement (in the sense discussed in paragraphs 44-8 above) of an award which is the result of a prior adjudicative process.

(c) It is undoubtedly the case that service of the order granting recognition must be made on the state, but it is only at that stage that the state is formally impleaded and the jurisdiction of the English court formally invoked against the state. It is therefore only at that stage that the doctrine of sovereign immunity becomes engaged.

(d) The distinction between the application for registration, of which it is only necessary to give notice, and the resulting order, which must be formally served, is expressly drawn in section 1(6) of the 1966 Act itself.

(e) Once served with an order, a state may apply (as is the right of any litigant where an order is made without notice) to have the order set aside. However, the only grounds on which it may do so are if the order made has strayed beyond mere recognition and enforcement or if there was a failure to make full and frank disclosure. It is *not* open to it to do so on the grounds that the order should not have been made on the merits because, for example, it was entitled to claim state immunity.

(f) In this respect, it is telling that the provisions of Part 74 which permit an application to set aside the registration are expressly *not* applied to ICSID awards whereas they are preserved in relation to the enforcement of non-ICSID awards under Part 62.18 and in relation to the registration of foreign judgments by Part 74.

(g) The state may, of course, assert immunity in relation to any further steps that the judgment creditor may seek to take to execute the award.

107. This analysis seems to me to be confirmed by the decision of the Supreme Court in *General Dynamics United Kingdom* v. *Libya* (*supra*) at [43]-[44] that (*emphasis added*):

> [43] The exercise of jurisdiction by the courts of one state over another state is an act of sovereignty. The institution of such proceedings necessarily requires that the defendant state should be given notice of the proceedings. *The service of process on a state in itself involves an exercise of sovereignty and gives rise to particular sensibilities* . . .
>
> . . .
>
> [44] In the particular context of enforcement of arbitration awards against a state, an application may be made to the court without notice (with or without issuing an arbitration claim form), in accordance with CPR r 62.18(1), for permission to enforce. Although the court may order service of the arbitration claim form (CPR r 62.18(2)) this is not usually required. However, under CPR r 62.18(7) the resulting order giving permission to enforce must be served on the defendant state which may then apply under CPR r 62.18 (9) to set aside the order. If the order giving permission were not served, the defendant state may well be unaware of the enforcement proceedings *and may not have the opportunity to assert immunity from enforcement before an attempt is made to attach or to seize the state's assets within the jurisdiction* . . .

108. As I read the first passage, the view of the Supreme Court is that it is the *service of process* on a state which involves an exercise of sovereignty. This can be contrasted with the mere notification of the application for registration which is all that is required under section 1(6) of the 1966 Act and CPR Part 62.21. As for the second passage, the concern of the court was that a state should have the opportunity to assert immunity before any attempt is made to execute against its assets. However, that opportunity is adequately secured by requiring service of the order for registration.

109. I therefore respectfully disagree with the view of Fraser J in *Infrastructure Services Luxembourg S.à.r.l.* v. *Spain* (*supra*) at [20] and

[56] that the mere recognition and enforcement of an ICSID award involves the exercise of the court's adjudicative jurisdiction. The court's jurisdiction to make the order derives directly from the 1966 Act and involves no exercise of discretion or adjudication at all but merely gives effect to the applicant's statutory entitlement.

110. It follows in my judgment that the question of sovereign immunity does not arise in relation to an application to register an ICSID award. It is therefore not open to Zimbabwe to apply to set it aside on that basis, although it may of course claim immunity in relation to any further steps towards execution. I should add that if Cockerill J's order had gone beyond mere recognition and enforcement, this might also have been a legitimate ground for an application to set aside *pro tanto*. However, I am satisfied that it does not and that (subject to the question of full and frank disclosure which is considered below), Zimbabwe has no basis for its application.

111. I accept that this is a novel approach for which there is no direct authority. However, to my mind, it has the following positive merits:

(a) It gives full force and effect to the United Kingdom's international obligations under the ICSID Convention to recognise and enforce ICSID awards;

(b) It recognises the self-contained nature of the ICSID regime with its internal appellate review process;

(c) It gives full weight to statements of the highest authority that, provided the enforcing court is satisfied of the authenticity of the award, it is not entitled to review either the substance of the award or the jurisdiction of the tribunal or to refuse recognition or enforcement (save possibly in the exceptional and extraordinary circumstances contemplated in *Micula*);

(d) It does no violence to the principles of state immunity because an order for recognition and enforcement goes no further than recognising the award as binding—something which the state in question has already undertaken to do under the Convention. In particular, it does not involve taking any substantive steps against the state and no adjudicative jurisdiction is asserted over the state or its assets as such;

(e) It also enables a principled distinction to be drawn between applications to enforce ICSID awards, which are not served and where the award cannot be reviewed, and applications to enforce awards under the New York Convention, which not only do potentially require service but, more importantly, expressly require the court to exercise its adjudicative jurisdiction in determining that none of the defences to recognition and enforcement applies. The potentially far-reaching consequences which would otherwise ensue for enforcement of awards under the New York Convention are thus avoided altogether and the well-established case law in this field, such as *Svenska Petroleum Exploration AB* v. *Lithuania, Tatneft* and *General Dynamics,*[7] is left intact.

(5) Full and frank disclosure

112. There remains to consider Zimbabwe's argument that Cockerill J's order must in any event be set aside on the grounds that the Claimants failed to make full and frank disclosure.

113. It was not in dispute that Mr Poulton's first witness statement in support of the application for registration made no mention of state immunity at all. Indeed, it did not even address the question of full and frank disclosure, as it should have done given that this was a without notice application.

114. The explanation given by Mr Poulton in his second witness statement was that there was nothing to disclose because it was patently obvious that Zimbabwe was not immune by virtue of section 2 and/or section 9 of the State Immunity Act 1978. As will be apparent from what has gone before, I do not accept that either section of the Act has deprived Zimbabwe of any immunity, so the premise of the Claimants' argument is flawed. It is true that I have ultimately concluded in favour of the Claimants, but that was not on the basis relied on.

115. It is the overriding duty of the court to give effect to state immunity even if the state does not appear. It is therefore incumbent on anyone making an application which names a state as respondent to address the question in order to allow the court to satisfy itself that immunity is not engaged: see the comments of Stanley Burnton LJ in *ETI Euro Telecom International NV* v. *Bolivia*, [2008] EWCA Civ 880; [1989] 1 WLR 665 at [110], [128] and Butcher J in *General Dynamics United Kingdom Ltd* v. *Libya* [2022] EWHC 501 (Comm) at [25], [30]. It is not for the applicant to assess for itself whether a point is arguable or not. That is the function of the court, and on this point I agree with Mr Justice Wallbank in *Tethyan* at [42].

---

[7] It is for this reason that Mr Harris' argument that *Tatneft* is contrary to the decision of the Supreme Court in *Micula* at [69] (i.e., that a Contracting State cannot refuse recognition or enforcement of an award on grounds covered by the challenge provisions of the ICSID Convention) can never arise.

116. The fact (if such indeed be the case, which was disputed) that Zimbabwe may have given no indication that it would rely on state immunity may be relevant to my exercise of discretion, but it does not absolve the Claimants from raising the point. The comments of Lawrence Collins J in *Konamaneni* v. *Rolls Royce Industrial Power (India) Ltd*, [2002] 1 WLR 1269 at [180] (quoted by Butcher J in *General Dynamics* (*supra*) at [25]) suggesting the contrary are in my judgment directed at failure to make full and frank disclosure in general and did not specifically have in mind cases such as this where the court is obliged to take the point of its own motion.

117. I therefore regard the breach of duty in this case as culpable, albeit not deliberate. This means that I have a discretion to set aside the order without considering the substantive merits, the purpose of doing so being to deprive the wrongdoer of any advantage improperly thereby obtained. Nonetheless, I am not bound to set the order aside and must exercise that discretion taking into account all the relevant circumstances.

118. In the event, I have decided that it would not be appropriate to set aside Cockerill J's order on this ground alone. As I have found, the Claimants have an entitlement to register the award conferred by the ICSID Convention and given effect by the 1966 Act. On the view I have taken of the case, state immunity is irrelevant to applications for registration with the result that the failure to disclose was in fact immaterial. Moreover, since in applying for registration the Claimants were merely exercising a statutory entitlement rather than seeking direct relief against or invading the rights of Zimbabwe, they have not received any benefit which they ought not to have had: *General Dynamics* (*supra*) at [45]. Nor can I discern any tangible prejudice to Zimbabwe. An application for registration and enforcement merely recognises the status of something which has substantively already happened, namely the award, and Zimbabwe can in any event rely on state immunity in order to resist any attempt by the Claimants to proceed beyond mere registration towards execution.

119. I accept that, albeit culpable, the breach was not deliberate or contumelious and in my judgment it would be excessively harsh to deprive the Claimants of their entitlement to register the award. It is sufficient in all the circumstances to penalise them in costs.

120. Zimbabwe's application to set aside accordingly fails and is dismissed. I will hear counsel on any consequential matters.

[Reports: [2024] 1 WLR 3417; [2024] All ER (Comm) 360;
[2024] 1 Lloyd's Rep 427]

INDEX

Abbreviations used in the index
ACHPR (African Charter on Human and Peoples' Rights (1981) (Banjul Charter)
ACHR (American Convention on Human Rights (1969))
AIIDA (Arbitration (International Investment Disputes) Act (1966) (UK))
CCAIL (Code of Crimes against International Law (2002) (Germany))
CCP (Common Commercial Policy (EU))
CEAS (Common European Asylum System)
CFR (EU Charter of Fundamental Rights (2000))
CIL (customary international law)
CLCS (Commission on the Limits of the Continental Shelf)
CPR (Civil Procedure Rules (UK))
EACT (Treaty for the Establishment of the East African Community (1986/2006/2007))
ECHR (European Convention on Human Rights (1950))
ECOWAS (Economic Community of West African States/ECOWAS Treaty (1993))
ECT (Energy Charter Treaty (1994))
GATS (General Agreement on Trade in Services (1995))
IAA (International Arbitration Act (1974) (Australia))
ICCPR (International Covenant on Civil and Political Rights (1966))
ICJ (International Court of Justice)
ICSID (International Centre for Settlement of Investment Disputes)
ICSID Convention (Convention on the Settlement of Investment Disputes between
        States and Nationals of Other States (1965))
ITLOS (International Tribunal on the Law of the Sea)
NYC (New York Convention on the Recognition and Enforcement of Foreign Arbitral
        Awards (1985))
PCIJ (Permanent Court of International Justice)
SIA (State Immunity Act (1978) (UK))
TEC (Treaty establishing the European Community (1957)) (Treaty of Rome as
        updated by the Treaties of Amsterdam and Nice)
TEU (Treaty on European Union)
TFEU (Treaty on the Functioning of the European Union)
UDHR (Universal Declaration of Human Rights (1948))
UNCLOS (UN Convention on the Law of the Sea (1982))
UNGA (United Nations General Assembly)
VCLT (Vienna Convention on the Law of Treaties (1969))
WTO (World Trade Organization)
WTO DSU (World Trade Organization Dispute Settlement Understanding)

INDEX 751